Marilyn

Women in Modern America: A Brief History
Elizabeth Cady Stanton: A Radical for Women's Rights
American Beauty: A Social History . . . Through Two Centuries of
    the American Idea, Ideal, and Image of the Beautiful Woman
Finding Fran: History and Memory in the Lives of Two Women
In Full Flower: Aging Women, Power, and Sexuality
Intertwined Lives: Margaret Mead, Ruth Benedict, and Their Circle
MM—Personal (with Mark Anderson)

Marilyn

The Passion and the Paradox

Lois Banner

BLOOMSBURY

LONDON · NEW DELHI · NEW YORK · SYDNEY

Bloomsbury Publishing Plc
50 Bedford Square
London
WC1B 3DP

www.bloomsbury.com

Bloomsbury Publishing, London, New Delhi, New York and Sydney

A CIP catalogue record for this book is available from the British Library

ISBN 978 1 4088 1410 9

10 9 8 7 6 5 4 3 2 1

Typeset by Westchester Book Group
Printed in Great Britain by Clays Ltd, St Ives plc

To: Stacy Eubank, Mark Anderson, and
Greg Schreiner, with thanks and love.

Contents

Marilyn

Marilyn on subway grate; photo shoot for *The Seven Year Itch*, September 15, 1954. Photo by Sam Shaw.

Prologue

Let Us Now Praise Famous Women[1]

In one of the most famous photos of the twentieth century, Marilyn Monroe stands on a subway grate, trying to hold her skirt down as a gust of wind blows it up, exposing her underpants. The photo was taken in New York on September 15, 1954, in a photo shoot during the filming of *The Seven Year Itch*, which stars Marilyn as a model and dog-faced Tom Ewell as a middled-aged editor of raunchy books who is tired of his seven-year marriage and yearns for an affair with a sexy "girl." In the scene being shot, they leave a movie theater after seeing *The Creature from the Black Lagoon*, a 1954 film about a prehistoric Gil-man on the Amazon River who kills several members of the expedition sent to capture him. It's a hot summer night, and Marilyn stands over the grate to cool off. A subway passing underneath supposedly produces the wind, which was actually caused by a wind machine under the grate.[2]

In her white dress, white underpants, white high-heel sling-backs, and white earrings, Marilyn is a vision in white, suggesting innocence and purity. Yet she exudes sexuality and transcends it; poses for the male gaze and confronts it. Her billowing skirt resembles wings. She might be a guardian angel from the Christian tradition, an Aphrodite from the classical tradition, or a Nike proclaiming victory in poetry or war, like the Winged Victory of Samothrace in the Louvre Museum, with the wind blowing back Victory's wings and chiton. She might be an elegant ballerina on her toes or a working girl standing on the Coney Island fun house ramp, where air gusts blew up the skirts of the women on the ramp. Sam

Shaw, who took the famed photo, derived Marilyn's pose from that setting, though the effect had long been used on the burlesque stage and in pin-up photos to titillate men.[3] Above all, *The Seven Year Itch* photo reveals Marilyn's complexities: her passion and her paradoxical nature, central themes of this book.

The photo shoot was a publicity stunt, one of the greatest in the history of film. Its time and location were published in New York newspapers; it attracted a crowd of over a hundred male photographers and 1,500 male spectators, even though it was held in the middle of the night to avoid daytime crowds. Klieg lights lit the scene; spectators climbed to the roofs of buildings to get a good view; photographers elbowed their way through the crowd to stake out the best locations. Sam Shaw, the stills photographer for the movie, took the famous photo, but the other photographers there shot hundreds of variations. So great was the interest in all things Marilyn that barricades were put up, and police were on hand to contain the crowd.

Billy Wilder, the film's director, did fourteen takes—pausing between them to let the photographers shoot. Every time Marilyn's skirt blew up, the crowd roared, especially those up front, who could see a dark blotch of pubic hair through her underpants, even though she had put on two pairs of pants to conceal it. The draconian 1934 Motion Picture Production Code, enforced by the Production Board, forbade such a display. Any blotch of public hair in photos from the shoot had to be airbrushed out.

Yet the scene in the shoot is naughty, with the phallic subway train, its blast of air, and Marilyn's erotic stance. Yet she is in control. She is the "woman on top," drawing from the metaphor for women's power that runs through Euro-American history. She poses for the male gaze, but she is an unruly woman—the Mere Folle of medieval Carnivale; the white witch with supernatural powers; the burlesque star in "an upside-down world of enormous, powerful women and powerless, victimized men." In the photo Marilyn is so gorgeous, so glamorous, so incandescent—as her third husband, the writer Arthur Miller, described her—that she seems every inch a star, glorying in her success.[4] She can now defy the people who had mistreated her: her father and mother, who abandoned her; foster parents who abused her; Hollywood patriarchs who regarded her as their toy; even Joe DiMaggio, then her husband, who physically abused her. Present at the shoot, he stalked off in a fury when her skirt billowed up and revealed her underpants. She had, indeed, dramatized her child-hood dream of walking naked over a church congregation, lying on their backs, eyes wide open, looking up at her. It's a powerful dream of exposure—and of a Marilyn in control.

But she holds down her skirt in the photo, suggesting modesty. In her only discussion of the shoot—in a 1962 interview—she stated that she wasn't thinking about sex when she posed, only about having a good time. It was the spectators, she claimed, who sexualized her. "At first it was all innocent and fun," Marilyn said, "but when Billy Wilder kept shooting the scene over and over again the crowd of men kept on applauding and shouting, 'More, more Marilyn—let's see more.'" Then Billy bought the camera in close, focusing on her crotch. "What was supposed to be a fun scene turned into a sex scene." "With her wry humor, Marilyn added "I hope all those extra takes are not for your Hollywood friends to enjoy at a private party."[5]

We are not accustomed to seeing Marilyn Monroe as being on top in any but the most superficial way. We view her as irreparably damaged, too victimized to have played much of a role either in launching her career or reinventing herself on the silver screen. Nothing could be farther from the truth. The Marilyn that emerges in *Marilyn: The Passion and the Paradox* is a woman who made herself into a star, conquering numerous disabilities in the process, creating a life more dramatic than any role she played in films. Her disabilities were many. She suffered from dyslexia and from a stutter more severe than anyone has realized. She was plagued through-out her life by dreams of monsters and witches, horrible dreams that contributed to her constant insomnia and that I am the first to describe. She was bipolar and often disassociated from reality. She endured terrible pain during menstruation because she had endometriosis, a hormonal condition that causes tissue like growths throughout the abdominal cavity. She broke out in rashes and hives and eventually came down with chronic colitis, enduring abdominal pain and nausea.

She surmounted all this, in addition to the well-known problems of her childhood—a mother in a mental institution, a father she never knew, and moving between foster homes and an orphanage. Playwright Clif-ford Odets stated that "she always traveled with a dark companion." People who saw "the gorgeous substrata of her life could not even imagine on what subsoil her roots were feeding."[6] Then there were the drugs she took to cope, once she entered Hollywood and had to endure its pressures: she especially took barbiturates to calm her down; amphetamines to give her energy.

Significant among my discoveries about Marilyn are her lesbian inclinations. She had affairs with many eminent men—baseball great Joe DiMaggio, playwright Arthur Miller, director Elia Kazan, actor Marlon Brando, singer Frank Sinatra, the Kennedy brothers—and she married DiMaggio and Miller. Yet she desired women, had affairs with them, and worried that she might be lesbian by nature. How could she be the world's heterosexual sex goddess and desire women? How could she have the world's most perfect body on the outside and have such internal imperfections as endometriosis and colitis? Why was she unable to bear a child? The adult Marilyn was haunted by these questions.

Yet in her career she exhibited a rare genius. Publicists marveled at her ability to generate publicity; makeup artists saluted her skill at their craft; photographers rated her one of the greatest models of their age. She studied with top acting, singing, and movement teachers to create her era's greatest dumb-blonde clown. Voluptuous and soft-voiced, the Marilyn we know exemplified 1950s femininity. Yet she mocked it with her wiggling walk, jiggling breasts, and puckered mouth. She could tone her blonde bombshell image down, project sadness in her eyes, and, like all great clowns, play her figure on the edge between comedy and tragedy.

There were many Marilyns, not just one. Revealing and analyzing her multiple personas is a major contribution of mine to Marilyn scholarship. As a pin-up model early in her career she posed for her era's most famous pin-up photo—a nude that became the centerfold for the first issue of *Playboy* in December 1953. By mid-career she created a new glamour look that combined the allure of the pin-up with the aloof, mature sensuality of a glamour star of the 1930s like Greta Garbo. Another Marilyn had a talent for drama, evident in films like *Clash by Night* (1952) and *Bus Stop* (1956) and in her poses for celebrity photographers like Milton Greene and Eve Arnold. "Marilyn Monroe," her most famous alter ego, was one among many.

Marilyn was nothing if not complicated and in ways that has never been revealed. She was shy and insecure, lacking self-confidence. But she was tough and determined. She had an ironic and sometimes ribald wit, engaging in puns and wordplay. She could swear like a trooper. She loved to play practical jokes. I have discovered that she could be an eccentric who followed her own irrational logic. She sometimes was a party girl who did "crazy, naughty, sexy things," including engaging in promiscuous sex, displaying what we now call "sex addiction."[7] In her paradoxical manner, however, she covered untoward behavior with a mask of good intentions, justifying her promiscuity through advocating a free-love philosophy, which connected friendship to sex. That philosophy circulated sub rosa among the avant-garde throughout the twentieth century. In another guise she was a trickster who assumed aliases, wore disguises, and lived her life as though it was a spy story, with secret friends and a secret apartment in New York. "I'm so many people," she told British journalist W. J. Weatherby, "I used to think I was going crazy, until I discovered some people I admired were like that, too."[8]

A spiritual Marilyn, never before revealed, studied mystical texts. A radical Marilyn pioneered the sexual revolution that erupted in the 1960s, appreciated her roots in the working class, and honored the men who made her a star through their fan mail—"the ordinary people, the working class, those who struggled through wars and the Depression." She opposed McCarthyite oppression and supported racial equality. In a play on the term "black face," Bruno Bernhard wrote that the intellectual, radical Marilyn was hiding under "black lace."[9]

Unlike all Marilyn biographers, except Gloria Steinem, I argue that the sexual abuse she endured as a child was formative in molding her adult character. We now know that such abuse can produce lesbianism, sex addiction, exhibitionism, and an angry, frightened adult. It can fragment a personality, producing, in Marilyn's case, multiple alters, of which she was aware. However dominant, "Marilyn Monroe" was only one persona among many that emerged from and were created by the original Norma Jeane Baker before her name was changed to Marilyn Monroe. That happened when Norma Jeane signed a contract with Twentieth Century–Fox in August 1946 and began her ascent to stardom.

The 1950s was a paradoxical era. Americans were exuberant over victory in World War Two and the booming consumer economy, while they were frightened by the Cold War with the Soviet Union and the threat of nuclear destruction, and paranoid about homosexuality and internal communism in the United States. Marilyn's comic style soothed the nation's fears, while reflecting the 1950s "populuxe" style in design, which spoofed consumption and laughed at fears through a populist version of luxury. When she put on her Betty Boop character, whom I call Lorelei Lee, she was populuxe to the hilt.

Her innocent eroticism and joy made her the ultimate playmate for men in a postwar age worried about male feminization, as warriors became husbands with the end of the war. Beyond feminization lay homosexuality, demonized in the 1950s as a perversion that threatened everyone. In her films Marilyn often plays against an impotent man whom she restores to potency by praising his gentleness as necessary to true masculinity, as she does for Tom Ewell in *The Seven Year Itch*. In real life she often chose powerful older men as partners, overlooking their domineering ways in her quest for a father, falling into sado-masochistic behavior patterns again and again.

As an exemplar of her age, she relates to 1950s rock 'n' roll musicians and beat poets that were forerunners to 1960s rebels, as did actors like Montgomery Clift and Marlon Brando, who were both identified with new, rebellious acting styles. From that perspective, joined with her support for sexual freedom, she was a rebel pointing to the radicalism and sexual rebellion of the 1960s.

I was drawn to writing about Marilyn because no one like me—an academic scholar, feminist biographer, and historian of gender—had studied her. I was also intrigued by similarities between my childhood and hers. I grew up in the 1940s in Inglewood, California, a Los Angeles satellite city only a few miles from Hawthorne, where Marilyn spent her first seven years. Her Hawthorne family was fundamentalist Christian; so was my childhood family. Blonde and blue-eyed, I had her body dimensions and won beauty contests. Like her, I had relatives in the film industry who encouraged me to aim for stardom. But I loved learning. After graduating from UCLA, I moved to New York to achieve a Ph.D. at Columbia University. Becoming a college professor, I remained in and near New York for the next twenty years. I married a Princeton professor and travelled in New York intellectual circle; I spent summers in rural Connecticut, as Marilyn had.

During those years I became a founder of "second wave feminism" and the new women's history. I dismissed Marilyn as a sex object for men. By the 1990s, however, a generation of "third wave feminists" contended that sexualizing women was liberating, not demeaning, for it gave them self-knowledge and power. The students I taught were swayed by this argument. Had I dismissed Marilyn too easily? Was she a precursor of 1960s feminism? Was there power in her stance as a sex object? To answer these questions, I decided to explore her life.

I began by joining Marilyn Remembered, the Los Angeles Marilyn fan club. Members shared their collections with me. Branching out, I interviewed nearly one hundred Marilyn friends and associates. I researched archives in the United States and Europe. I gained access to never-before-seen collections—including Marilyn's personal file cabinets and the papers of Ralph Roberts, Stacy Eubank, Norman Mailer, Greg Schreiner, Antonio Villani, Peter Lawford, James Spada, Lotte Goslar, and many new collections in the Margaret Herrick Library of the Motion Picture Academy of Arts and Sciences and elsewhere. I collected several hundred fan magazines with articles on Marilyn, buying many on eBay. I bought Marilyn items at auctions. In an act of great generosity, Anthony Summers allowed me access to his over three hundred interviews for his biography of Marilyn, published in 1985. I found rich materials in those interviews that he hadn't used.

I salute Marilyn for a major—and unacknowledged—feminist act. Sexually abused as a child, she named that abuse as an adult. She refused to keep quiet in an age that believed such abuse rarely happened and when it did, the victimized girl was responsible. Such self-disclosure would become important to the feminist movement in the 1970s. Neither Ruth Benedict nor Margaret Mead, eminent American anthropologists and public intellectuals, whose lives I chronicled in a dual biography, disclosed the episodes of sexual abuse in their childhoods. I didn't expect to find such episodes in any of these lives, but the rates of such abuse have been high throughout our history. In an act of great bravery, Marilyn named the abuse she endured.

As a biographer, I follow the school of "new biography." I analyze Marilyn in her historical context and in terms of her interactions with the men and women in her life, what I call the "geography of gender." Throughout my book I present a new Marilyn, different from any previous portrayal of her, including my own, in my brief overview of her in *MM-Personal*. I probe her interior self and see her life as a process of self-formation. I have identified all eleven families she lived with in her childhood—providing new information on them. I analyze the gender themes of her films and explore the gendered personas of Hollywood producers and photographers, pointing out the homoeroticism endemic to many of them.

I have done deep readings of unexplored texts, like Arthur Miller's autobiography, *Timebends*, Ralph Greenson's psychiatric writings, and the themes in the poetry and works of literature Marilyn read. I figured out why she extolled Eleanora Duse. I discovered Anna Freud's findings when she analyzed Marilyn during a week in London in 1956. According to Anna, Marilyn was bisexual. Her childhood dream of naked exposure to a church congregation was a product of the sexual abuse she endured as a child.

I follow the chronological format standard in biography as a genre, although I innovate in adding a section I call "entre'acte." I pause there to delve into her psyche and her historical resonance before proceeding on. Like many world historical figures, Marilyn stood astride her age. She reflected its mores and helped to create them. Her glittering position partly explains why she has become an icon for our age. And I am amazed by what she accomplished in her brief lifespan of thirty-six years. When she died she was hardly more than a child by our contemporary lexicon of the stages of life.

When Marilyn posed for *The Seven Year Itch* photo in 1954, she was Hollywood's preeminent star. She was "a national institution as well known as hot dogs, apple pie, or baseball" and "the nation's celluloid H-bomb." Her fan mail, some ten thousand letters a week, surpassed that of any other star. Reporters called her "The Monroe" and referred to the "Monroe Doctrine," defining it as eroticism, shrewdness, lack of materialism—whatever might sell a story and not be too farfetched. Her sexual double-entendres, called "Monroeisms," were famous. "What do you wear to bed?" photographers asked her. Her reply: "Chanel Number Five."[10] *The Seven Year Itch* photo ratified Marilyn's fame. Within days it appeared in newspapers round the globe, from New York to Hong Kong,

Los Angeles to Tokyo. It was called "The Shot Seen Round the World." By the mid-1950s people everywhere could identify "Marilyn" and "MM." She had become an American icon for the world.[11]

This book is about how Marilyn was created, how she lived her life, and how that life ended.

A Note on Sources

Readers familiar with the biographical tradition on Monroe will realize that I have not used memoirs by Hans Jürgen Lembourn, Ted Jordan, Lena Pepitone, Robert Slatzer, or Jeanne Carmen. In "Mimosa," his unpublished memoir of Marilyn, Ralph Roberts, her masseur and best friend, exposed them as frauds. So did articles in *Runnin' Wild*, an early Marilyn fan magazine.

These five individuals knew Marilyn, but they weren't close to her. Danish journalist Lembourn was on a State Department fellowship that sent him nationwide and didn't give him time for the liaison he describes. Ted Jordan, actor, was burlesque star Lili St. Cyr's fifth husband. He claimed to have had a three-way affair with Marilyn and St. Cyr. But both St. Cyr and her biographer dismiss his claim. Lena Pepitone, Marilyn's cook for several years in her New York apartment, didn't speak English and Marilyn didn't speak Italian. Jeanne Carmen was a trick golfer and high-priced call girl who lived in her Doheny Drive apartment complex in 1961. After she held an all-night party, Marilyn wouldn't speak to her. Carmen, Jordan, and Pepitone possess no photos of Marilyn with them, and Slatzer's one photo with Marilyn looks staged. Slatzer's claim that Marilyn married him in Tijuana in the spring of 1952 is unsubstantiated.[12]

Recent Marilyn biographers overlook excellent earlier Marilyn biographies, especially those by Maurice Zolotow (1960), Fred Guiles (1969), Carl Rollyson (1986), and Anthony Summers (1985). They often disregard Marilyn memoirs written by close friends such as Louella Parsons, Susan Strasberg, Norman Rosten, Milton Greene, and Sam Shaw. Realizing their worth, I have used these biographies and memoirs.

My special thanks go to Anthony Summers, who gave me access to his many interviews for *Goddess*, his 1985 biography of Marilyn. He is a gifted interviewer, writer, and interpreter of Marilyn. Although I don't always agree with him, I respect his work. He put many of the puzzles about Marilyn into perspective, enabling me to construct my narrative of her life.[13]

Part I

The Matrix, 1926–1946

Persons of genius with mysterious gifts: in many cases a wound has been inflicted early in life, which impels the person to strive harder or makes him or her extra-sensitive. The talent, the genius, is the scab on the wound, there to protect a weak place, an opening to death. Men and women who come successfully out of misfortune, they have strength that is extraordinary.

Elia Kazan, Elia Kazan: A Life

Chapter 1

Mothers, 1926–1933

Marilyn Monroe was born Norma Jeane Mortenson in the charity ward of Los Angeles County General Hospital on June 1, 1926. Her mother, Gladys Monroe Baker, was a poorly paid film cutter in a Hollywood editing studio. Her father never recognized her, and Gladys placed her in a foster home when she was three months old. In 1933, when Norma Jeane was seven, her mother brought her to live with her in Hollywood. Soon after, Gladys broke down emotionally, leaving Norma Jeane with her best friend, Grace Atchison McKee. When Gladys was declared paranoid schizophrenic and admitted to a state mental hospital, Grace became Norma Jeane's guardian. During the next eight years, until Norma Jeane married in 1942 at the age of sixteen, Grace placed her in eleven foster homes and an orphanage. Why Gladys broke down and why Grace kept moving Norma Jeane are central issues in examining her childhood.

Five women dominated Norma Jeane's childhood. They included Gladys and Grace, plus Della Monroe, Gladys's mother; and two of Norma Jeane's foster mothers, Ida Bolender and Ana Atchinson Lower, Grace McKee's aunt.[1] All five women were working class or lower middle class, with little money or education. All moved to Los Angeles with their families from the Upper South and the Midwest between 1900 and 1920, during the great migration to the city. That movement turned a small provincial city into a major metropolis, with suburbs and cities radiating out from a downtown core.

Della Monroe, Marilyn's grandmother, came from Missouri by way of Mexico in 1902, with her husband, Otis Monroe, and her daughter, Gladys, then two years old; they settled near downtown Los Angeles. Grace came from Montana in the 1910s in her late teens, looking for a film career; she settled in Hollywood. Ida, an Iowa farm girl, arrived with her husband, Wayne, in the early 1920s and settled in Hawthorne, in the South Bay area southwest of downtown. Ana, considerably older than the other four, was born in 1880 in Washington State. She came to Los Angeles by way of Sacramento, eventually settling in the Sawtelle area on Los Angeles's West Side.

Like most participants in the great migration to Los Angeles, these five hoped for better lives in the Southern California paradise of beaches, mountains, exotic vegetation, and a Mediterranean climate. The Hollywood film industry was there, with its ethic of leisure and pleasure. So was a major evangelical movement, among the largest in the nation, with imposing churches and a doctrine that promised individual re-birth through renouncing sin and uniting with Christ. The pulpit and the screen—an uneasy pair—would profoundly influence Norma Jeane.[2]

The story of Marilyn's childhood, like much of her life, contains texts and counter-texts, with hidden episodes beneath surface narratives. Most families have secrets; alcoholism, marital discord, and mental issues are possibilities. The Monroe family had all these, and more. Della and Gladys had up-and-down moods. Both were divorced several times; in divorce petitions both accused husbands of alcoholism and physical abuse. Ida, Norma Jeane's first foster mother, between 1926 and 1933, disciplined her for childhood sexual experimentation, and Grace couldn't prevent her from being sexually abused in several foster homes. Della, Grace, Gladys, Ana, and Ida clashed over religion. Ida was an evangelical Christian; Della was a follower of evangelist maverick Aimee Semple McPherson. Ana, who provided foster care for Norma Jeane between 1938 and 1942, was a Christian Science healer, while Gladys and Grace were flappers who lived sexually free lives and didn't faithfully attend any church during Norma Jeane's early childhood. She got caught in the middle, a pawn for a while in a rivalry among the five of them.

Marilyn's paternal ancestry is obscure because of uncertainty over the identity of her father. The best candidate is Stanley (Stan) Gifford, a supervisor at the Hollywood editing firm where Gladys worked. Stan was Gladys's boyfriend and bed partner, although she had a husband from whom she was separated, not divorced—Edward Mortensen, a meter reader for the gas company. Stan was born and raised in Providence, Rhode Island, the son of a wealthy shipbuilding family whose ancestry went back to the founders of Providence and beyond them to Pilgrims on the Mayflower. If Stan was Marilyn's father, she came from revered American roots.[3]

Gladys Monroe, Marilyn's mother, also claimed distinguished descent. Her heritage came through her father, Otis Monroe, who traced his roots to James Monroe of Virginia, fifth president of the United States. But Otis can't be trusted. Born in Indiana in 1866, he spent much of his adult life as an itinerant painter, traveling through the Midwest and the Upper South, painting buildings to make money and occasionally selling his landscapes and portraits. Wearing fancy clothes, he passed himself off as a gentleman and spun fantasies of moving to Paris and living on the Left Bank. His death certificate lists his mother and father as unknown. Something of an eccentric, he was not the last unusual character in Marilyn's ancestry.[4]

On a swing through Missouri in 1898, Otis met Della Hogan. Born in 1878, she was twenty-two, still living with her mother and siblings. Her childhood had been difficult. Her father, Tilford Hogan, was an itinerant farm laborer who worked long hours for low wages, following the harvests and doing odd jobs. He married Jennie Nance, a Missouri farm girl, in 1870. Living in tenant cabins and farm shacks, they nonetheless had three children in eight years.

Yet Tilford's financial woes weren't unusual in post-Reconstruction Missouri. The building of railroads as well as a dramatic population growth through immigration caused a rise in prosperity in the state— for those able to exploit it. Most Missourians remained tenant farmers or landless laborers employed part-time to harvest crops or do odd jobs. Pro-slavery and secessionist during the Civil War, Missourians remained loyal to the South for decades. Jennie Nance, Marilyn's maternal great-grandmother, was raised in Chariton County, settled by migrants from the Upper South who owned slaves. It was called "Little Dixie." As Tilford's wife, Jennie moved with him as he sought employment, often in Ozark hillbilly country, moving her children from school to school.[5] When

Marilyn played Cherie, the hillbilly singer in *Bus Stop*, she could draw on her family's past to create the character.

Tilford had a quirky independence and a love of learning. He taught himself to read and write so that he could read the classics of Western literature. In an era when ordinary people memorized Shakespeare and distinctions between high and low culture weren't rigid, such learning wasn't that unusual.[6] He suffered from chronic arthritis but remained pleasant and well liked. But it wasn't enough for Jennie. In 1890, after twenty years of a difficult marriage, Jennie and Tilford divorced, violating the strictures against divorce in a region dominated by conservative Baptists. Each moved in with a relative; the children went with Jennie, who showed an independent streak in divorcing Tilford—a streak that would run through the Monroe women.

Nearly nine years after the divorce, in 1898, Otis Monroe appeared in Della's town and swept her off her feet with his rakish, upper-class air, fashionable clothing, and fantasies about moving to Paris. He was ten years older than she. He offered her a way out of Missouri, where she seemed stuck as an old maid at the age of twenty-two. Captivated by him, disregarding the objections of her parents, she overlooked the reality that he was, like her father, an itinerant laborer.[7]

The marriage was disappointing. Instead of moving to Paris, they moved to Mexico, to the town of Porfirio Díaz, now Piedras Negras, on the border with Texas. Otis found a job there painting railroad cars for the Mexican National Railway. The town was dirty, with poor sanitation, and Della didn't like it. Family lore held that, despite her discontent, she served as a midwife for impoverished Mexican women. Once her daughter, Gladys, was born in 1902, she and Otis moved to Los Angeles, where he found a job as a painter with the Pacific Electric Railway. That company operated the "red line" trolleys that ran throughout the Los Angeles region, linking its far-flung, expanding communities. Otis and Della's son, Marion, was born in 1905. Shortly thereafter, Otis was promoted, and they bought a small house near downtown—or Otis built it himself.[8] They seemed to be achieving the American Dream.

Then it fell apart. Otis began to suffer from memory loss, migraines, and bouts of mania. Seizures and paralysis followed. Della thought he was going insane. He was admitted to Patton State Mental Hospital in San Bernardino, a sprawling structure that housed several thousand patients.

It was one of seven such hospitals in the state built in the late nineteenth century to house the insane, chronic alcoholics, aging people with dementia, and individuals with syphilitic paresis, the final stage of syphilis, in which the infection destroys the connective tissues in the brain. Overcrowded, with insufficient doctors or trained staff, the hospitals provided minimal treatment.[9]

Otis was diagnosed with syphilitic paresis, probably of the endemic variety, caused by a bacteria spread by mosquitoes, not through sexual intercourse. He probably picked up the bacteria in Piedras Negras, with its poor sanitation. He died in 1909. To hide two shameful diagnoses—syphilis and psychosis—Della claimed that he had died from breathing paint fumes.[10]

With two children to support, Della cleaned houses and rented rooms in her house to male boarders, while she looked for another husband. In 1913 she married Lyle Graves, one of Otis's co-workers at the trolley company. A year later she divorced him on the grounds of "habitual intemperance" (alcoholism) and failure to provide financial support. The charge may have been true or trumped up to obtain the divorce. Adultery, physical abuse, and alcoholism—these were the only legal grounds for divorce in this era. Spouses wanting a divorce often colluded in making up tales of bad behavior, and wives brought most of the actions because of the belief that men were more likely to be abusers and alcoholics than women. Della won by default, since Graves skipped town. He may have had a nasty streak. According to Gladys he killed her cat by throwing it against a wall. Della then married a man named Chitwood, and she and her children moved with him to a farm in Oregon. Gladys liked Chitwood and the farm. She had happy memories of picking blueberries in Oregon as a child. But Della soon divorced her third husband. The charge was alcoholism, which again may have been true or trumped up, as was the custom, to provide a legal grounds for divorce.[11]

Della, not yet forty, was adventurous. Moving back to Los Angeles, she settled in Venice, a town on the Pacific Ocean twelve miles west of downtown. A fantasy place dreamed up by developer Abbot Kinney, Venice combined the look of Coney Island in New York with Venice in Italy. Neo-Renaissance buildings bordered canals where gondoliers plyed gondolas. There was a St. Mark's Square with jugglers and mimes, a promenade along the beach, and a pier jutting into the ocean, containing a large dance hall as well as concessions: rifle shoots, ring tosses, pretty-girl dunks, and penny arcades. Until the late 1920s, Venice had the largest amusement zone on the West Coast.[12]

It wasn't entirely honky-tonk. Charlie Chaplin and Mary Pickford had second homes on the canals, and film scenes were shot there. Elite groups held dances in the dance hall on the pier, and film stars mingled with ordinary people on the streets. Colored eggs were handed out on Easter and flowers to mothers on Mother's Day. There were bathing-beauty contests, boxing matches, bicycle races, and a Mardi Gras festival each year.

Once in Venice, Della got a job managing a small apartment building. She sent her son, Marion, to live with a relative in San Diego; as a single mother she found raising a son difficult. Such arrangements weren't uncommon in that era. Child-care experts of that time didn't regard bonding with parents as necessary for a child's healthy development; living in an intact family was their only requirement.[13] Della, like her daughter, Gladys, and her granddaughter, Marilyn, was prone to emotional highs and lows. Marion was also moody. Whatever mental issues Gladys and Marion inherited, their tumultuous childhoods didn't help them to cope with emotional ups and downs.

On New Year's Eve 1917, Della met her fourth husband, Charles Grainger, at the dance hall on the pier. Marilyn claimed that Della was the real beauty in the family, and she did, indeed, attract men. Grainger was an oil driller for Shell Oil. A smooth talker, well dressed, he had just returned from drilling jobs in India and Burma. Like Otis Monroe he was adventurous, with a similar air of distinction. Some Marilyn biographers contend that Della and Charles never married, but on a 1925 passport application Della gave the date of their marriage as November 20, 1920.[14]

Angry over her father's death, the two stepfathers, and the moving, Gladys became difficult. Fifteen years old in 1917, she was a full-fledged adolescent. Like her mother, Gladys was small—five feet tall—and she was beautiful, with a voluptuous body, green eyes, and reddish-brown hair. She also had a ladylike quality attractive to men, a quality that Marilyn internalized. Della had been raised in Missouri, a border state influenced by the Southern tradition of tough women with genteel veneers. She passed this gentility to Gladys. In 1946, Emmeline Snively, the head of

Marilyn's first modeling agency, described Gladys as the most ladylike woman she had ever met.[15]

The Venice pier, with its temptations, was not far from their apartment, and Gladys often went there. In the 1910s urban adolescents, especially working-class girls, rebelled against Victorian conventions by going to dance halls and amusement zones to meet men. The 1920s flapper, independent and free, already existed before World War One, and female screen stars shaped her behavior. Gladys was passionate about films, and she avidly read movie fan magazines. Like many girls of her era, she patterned her behavior after the stars.[16]

Then Gladys became pregnant. The father, John Newton Baker, called Jasper, was twenty-six years old and the owner of the apartment building Della managed. They married on May 17, 1917. Why a fifteen-year-old girl would marry a twenty-six-year-old man is puzzling, although Jasper had been an officer in the army cavalry and a trick horseback rider; he had dash. In addition, bearing an illegitimate child was a disgrace in that era. Even in the 1920s, when young people "parked" in cars with their dates and "petted," which could mean more than simply kissing, mainstream society scorned unmarried women who became pregnant. They were considered outside the bounds of respectability.[17]

Della swore in an affidavit attached to the marriage license that Gladys was eighteen. But she lied; Gladys was fifteen. The lie was necessary to get around the law requiring girls to be sixteen to engage in consensual sex. Before then intercourse was classified as rape, and the man involved could be brought to trial and sent to prison.[18] Gladys and Jasper's son, Jackie, was born seven months after their wedding. A daughter, Berniece, was born in 1920.

With Della and Gladys married, the Monroe women seemed stable. But the stability didn't last. Both of them were difficult and moody, hard to live with. Della and Charles began arguing, and Della moved to a house they bought in the newly developed city of Hawthorne, southwest of downtown, not far from the beach and on the trolley line. It was a good investment, although Charles wasn't there that much. Still, the 1925 Hawthorne City Directory lists him as living there with Della.[19]

In 1922 Gladys experienced a mother's worst nightmare. She threw the pieces of a broken drinking class into a trash can, and Jackie rummaged through the trash and embedded a shard of glass in an eye, damaging it. Several months later, Jasper and Gladys drove to Flat Lick, Kentucky, his hometown, for a visit. On the way there they quarreled ferociously, failing to notice that a back door to their car had opened and Jackie had fallen out, injuring his leg. Jasper and Gladys didn't have a good marriage, and they struggled with alcohol, violence, and appropriate parenting.[20]

Once in Flat Lick, Gladys went hiking with Jasper's brother, unaware that she was violating the community's strict moral code. When she returned from the hike, Jasper beat her publicly with a horse bridle, asserting his marital rights. No one stopped him; the Flat Lick residents approved his action. That was enough for Gladys. Once they returned to Venice, she filed for divorce. She charged that Jasper was a drinker who beat her, while he countercharged that she was an unfit mother who left her children with neighbors and went to the pier to have fun. He didn't mention that she often went there to tend a concession that he owned. The judge accepted her version of their issues, giving Gladys custody of the children, with Jasper given visiting rights. (The decree also forbade Jasper from selling his concession on the pier without Gladys's consent.)

But Gladys's problems hadn't ended. During a visit, Jasper kidnapped the children and took them to Kentucky to live with him. From his point of view Gladys wasn't a good mother, and he had had it with the "pleasures" of Venice, which he now regarded as immoral. He wanted his children to be raised with conservative values. He married a Kentucky woman seventeen years his senior, saying he was fed up with child brides.

In an effort to get Berniece and Jackie back, Gladys moved to Kentucky, settled near her children, and found a job as a housekeeper and child tender. Unlike today, the courts didn't track down children kidnapped by a divorced spouse. After a few months Gladys gave up and returned to Los Angeles. She ran out of money; she was afraid of Jasper; and she was only twenty years old. She may have already been involved with Stanley Gifford, and he may have wanted her back. Marilyn often criticized Gladys in later interviews, but in this case she preserved the fantasy that her mother, like Barbara Stanwyck in the movie *Stella Dallas*, gave up her children to their father so that they would have a better life. The truth is that their stepmother was kind to them, but Jasper had difficulty holding down a job. He did drink a lot, and he probably wasn't a good father.[21]

Meantime, the middle-aged Della, involved in another difficult marriage and looking for uplift, became a follower of evangelist Aimee Semple McPherson, who combined Hollywood spectacle with faith healing in her Foursquare Gospel Church. Sister Aimee's Angelus Temple, located in Echo Park on the trolley line near downtown, drew crowds of worshippers. A Christian fundamentalist and millennialist who viewed Christ's second coming as imminent, she used theatrical backdrops and mechanical devices to illustrate her sermons. Actors in costumes played out topics for moral instruction such as the fleshpots of Egypt and the temptations of the jazz age. The divorced McPherson had no use for marriage or for women's traditional roles. Moreover, she ran a home for unwed mothers and a Big Sister League for wayward girls. Women were the majority of her congregation.

This was a transitional era after the women's suffrage amendment had finally passed in 1920. Women's reform groups proliferated, while the sexual revolution of the decade both advanced and impeded women's progress, as it substituted sexual freedom for legal and political gains. Gladys and her friend Grace didn't think of themselves as feminists, a new term for that age, although they were working women, belonging to unions. Nor did Della, despite her woman-centered faith.[22]

Back in Los Angeles from Kentucky, Gladys found work as a cutter and paster of film negatives at Consolidated Film Industries. Directed by a senior editor—always male—the cutters removed unwanted frames from reels and pasted the reels back together again in an approved order. The work was monotonous and poorly paid. When the production schedule was heavy, cutters worked ten hours a day and a half day on Saturdays. The editing labs were dark, without windows, to prevent light from damaging the negatives. The cutters wore white gloves so that perspiration on their hands wouldn't harm the film. The darkness of the labs could cause depression, as could the smell of the glue. Almost all film cutters were women.[23]

In its early days the film industry was composed of independent producers in small studios who hired men and women equally as production assistants, screenwriters, editors, and the like. But in a process of consolidation typical of the growth of monopoly capitalism in many industries, by 1920 smaller companies were being combined into larger ones. By the late 1920s Wall Street money was financing films, and film studios were listed on the stock exchange. By the 1930s the hundreds of studios that had existed in the industry's formative years had been reduced to five major studios—MGM, Twentieth Century–Fox, RKO, Warner Brothers, and Paramount—and three minor ones, Columbia, United Artists, and Universal, with others, such as Republic Studios and Samuel Goldwyn, mainting their ground. The majors had larger production facilities and more employees than the minors, and they owned both the agencies that distributed their films and the theaters that showed them. The minors didn't. They had to use independent theaters or make deals with majors to show their films.

Driven by the profit motive, the studios became like factories, with films their products, and employees, including actors, their workers. Most of the studios were run by East European Jews who had been born to poor families in Poland and Russia and had migrated to New York in the 1890s and 1900s. With little education or money but with immense intelligence and drive, they realized the potential of the nickelodeons that were opening in immigrant enclaves and of the flickering images of the film reels shown on large screens at these places. They raised the money to buy both nickelodeons and film reels. As the images were developed into feature films, these entrepreneurs marketed and distributed them. Finally, they created chains of movie theaters, and they built studios in Hollywood. Thus the movie industry was born. Shrewd and combative, men like Louis B. Mayer at MGM, Joe Schenck at Fox, and Harry Cohn at Columbia consolidated the industry and ruled their studios with iron hands, turning themselves into what film historians call "the moguls."[24]

As often occurs during the process of monopolization, the film business became gendered. Men took over supervisory positions, with women their subordinates—aside from departments like makeup and costume design, associated with female activities. By the early 1920s the negative film cutters were women and the editors who decided on the cuts were men, a division that continued through the 1950s.

Gladys seemed content with her job; she remained a film cutter for the next ten years, shifting to the editing studio at Columbia shortly before Norma Jeane's birth and later to the one at RKO. She was a good worker, but she wasn't ambitious and wasn't promoted. After losing her children to her husband, a shattering experience, she liked routine, the security of repetition. She tolerated the dark editing studios and the smelly glue.

There were compensations. In his 1922 novel *Souls for Sale*, screen-writer Rupert Hughes celebrated Hollywood's female film cutters as models for the "new women" of the age who were entering the work-force and, adopting flapper behavior, were rebelling against Victorian conventions. Watching film fantasy all day on the reels they cut, they saw "battles in Chinese opium dens; Lon Chaney as the monstrous Franken-stein; glamorous women living in luxury." By the mid-1920s they were cutting and pasting the many films being made about "flappers."[25]

According to Hughes, the film cutters lived like men, scorning conven-tion. They participated in what was called the "new paganism," evident in avant-garde communities like Hollywood and Venice. They drank, danced, and wore makeup and the new, daring short skirts that rose above the knees. This was, after all, the "roaring twenties." But there were limits. According to Hughes, the film cutters respected their "health" and "per-sonal reputation." (I read "health" as meaning venereal disease and "per-sonal reputation" as meaning avoiding pregnancy and the reputation of being a "slut." The implication is that they used birth control.)[26]

Gladys was especially drawn to the "new paganism" once she met Grace McKee, one of the few women to hold a supervisor position at Consolidated. Twice divorced, five years older than Gladys, Grace was a leader among a group of Hollywood workers who went out after hours to night spots and dance halls in Hollywood and Venice. In Gladys's eyes Grace was dazzling. She was energetic, birdlike, and tiny, hardly five feet tall, with a high voice and peroxide blonde hair, a daring color in that era. A co-worker at Consolidated called her "a sparkling lady." "Her energy and cheerfulness bubbled at you, and her laugh was contagious, so even if you didn't know what you were laughing about, you were still laugh-ing."[27] Both Gladys and Grace were passionate about films, and both read the movie fan magazines. Two months after Gladys began at Con-solidated, they were sharing an apartment.

Coming to Hollywood from Montana in the 1910s, Grace joined the legions of young women from throughout the nation who moved to the film capital hoping to become stars, following the mythology of the Amer-ican Dream: anyone could make it if they had talent and gumption. Like most of them, Grace didn't succeed in the movies; but she found work in the industry and didn't have to wait on tables or enter the sex trade, which was flourishing in Hollywood. Grace was a take-charge person, and she took Gladys under her wing. During her years in Hollywood Grace had learned how to copy the dress styles and makeup of the stars, and she liked to make over her friends. Gladys welcomed Grace's control, but she sometimes became angry at her domineering ways.

When Gladys first came to Consolidated, she was depressed over her failure to retrieve her children. Her co-workers remembered her as mousy, with straggly brown hair—until Grace persuaded her to dye her hair red and to dress in the latest fashions. Male co-workers charged that she and Grace smoked, drank to excess, and were promiscuous.[28] Women co-workers said they were hardworking and conscientious. But their work was volatile: layoffs were called when film production was slow; the studios closed down during the month of March to avoid California taxes; and the cutters frequently switched from one editing studio to another.

Gladys was ambivalent about the "new paganism" of the 1920s, just as she had been of two minds about the pleasures of the Venice pier when she married Jasper Baker. Once settled in Hollywood, she looked for a husband. Her best bets were Edward Mortensen, a meter reader for the Southern California Gas Company who hung out with the film crowd in Venice, and Stanley Gifford, a supervisor at Consolidated Films, where Grace and Gladys worked. Both became involved with Gladys; on their death beds, each claimed to have sired Marilyn.[29]

In the competition between the two men, Stan won hands down. Mortensen was good-looking, but he was only a meter reader. Tall, dark, and handsome, Stan came from Rhode Island wealth. He owned his home in Culver City and was on the Santa Monica equestrian polo team. Two of his sisters worked in film editing, one of them at Consolidated, with Gladys and Grace. By 1923, however, he was going through a messy divorce. His wife charged that he drank and abused her, neglected their children to party in Venice, and was a heroin addict. Stan denied the charges and filed countercharges, but his wife won and he had to pay her alimony and child support. He was in no position to make a commitment to Gladys.[30]

In October 1924, Gladys married Mortensen. Della, worried about Gladys's up-and-down moods, advised her to do so because he was stable; Grace advised her against the marriage because he was boring. Grace was right. After a few months of marriage, Gladys walked out. An angry

Mortensen filed for divorce in May 1925, charging that she had "willfully and without cause deserted [him]."[31] The final decree wasn't granted until 1928, because Gladys paid no attention to the divorce action and Mortensen let it ride, hoping she would go back to him.

Born on June 1, 1926, Norma Jeane was conceived in late August or early September 1925, three months after Mortensen filed for divorce. Mortensen claimed paternity on his death bed, and so did Stan Gifford, as he lay dying. Gladys maintained that Gifford was Norma Jeane's father. The truth depends on the extent of Gladys's promiscuity after she left Mortensen, and the reports we have on that subject are conflicting. But Marilyn was convinced that Gifford was her father. She was thus "illegitimate," a terrible stigma in that day. Marilyn called herself a "love child" and a "mistake," indicating that if Gladys and her partner had used birth control, it hadn't worked.[32]

The emotional Gladys made a hash of Norma Jeane's birth certificate when filling it out at the hospital after giving birth. She listed Edward Mortensen as Norma Jeane's father—although she spelled his name *Mortenson*, causing confusion in her own day and ever since, because an Edward Mortenson lived in Venice at the time and was no relation to Edward Mortensen. And she listed her children in Kentucky as dead, although they were very much alive. Having relinquished them, this may have been how she dealt with her guilt for failing to retrieve them. She didn't derive Norma Jeane's name from film stars Norma Talmadge and Jean Harlow, as is often assumed. Norma Jeane was the name of the child Gladys had cared for as a nanny in Kentucky and had left behind when she returned to Los Angeles—a child to whom she had been close. Now she had her own Norma Jeane.[33]

According to Stan Gifford's relatives, he loved Gladys, but she didn't give him time to sort out his feelings. During the winter of 1925, he took her to the Gifford home to meet his family. Her pregnancy upset Stan's mother and sister, who were deeply religious. They reminded Stan that he had just gone through a difficult divorce and that Gladys was the mother of two children being raised by someone in another state. Torn between his loyalty to his family and his love for Gladys, Gifford didn't know what to do. In an attempt to keep everyone happy he refused to marry Gladys, but he offered her money. In a moment of anger, he made the mistake of telling her she was fortunate she was still married to Mortensen, so she could use his name on the birth certificate and register the child as legitimate.[34]

That callous statement made Gladys so angry she refused the money and walked out on Stan. Stubborn, sometimes set in her ways, she engaged in a defiant gesture that only hurt her. She bore the child by herself and didn't allow Stan to see the baby. Della missed the birth, since she was in Borneo, chasing Charles Grainger, who had gone there for an oil-drilling job. Grace also was absent, although one of Gladys's co-workers may have been present, since the cutters at Consolidated Films took up a collection for the baby.[35] Stan seems to have been devastated by the situation. He gave up regular work, floated for a while, and drank heavily, until he settled down, married, and bought a dairy farm in Hemet, near Palm Springs, which he operated until he died many years later. Gladys never saw him again, and he refused to see the adult Marilyn when she contacted him. He was sorry not to see her, he stated on his deathbed, but he didn't want his wife to know he had an illegitimate daughter.

The birth shook Gladys, who developed such a severe post-partum depression that she neglected her baby. When Grace chastised her, Gladys became so angry she picked up a knife and tried to stab her. Grace took the knife away from her before anything happened and calmed her down, but the episode was alarming. Della then suggested that Gladys board Norma Jeane with Ida Bolender. Della lived in Hawthorne, forty minutes by the Red Car trolley from Hollywood, and Ida ran a foster home across the street from her. The efficient Ida, Della thought, would be a good caretaker for Norma Jeane. Della could help with her care, and Gladys could visit on the weekends. Placing the child in day care didn't seem a possibility. In 1926 day care centers were few and far between; they were associated with Soviet communism, already feared and despised in the United States. Foster care was the most available option.[36]

For the next seven years, until Gladys took Norma Jeane to Hollywood to live with her, the child lived with the Bolenders. During those years, Gladys never missed paying Ida twenty-five dollars a month for her care. And Gladys clung to the dream that she could save enough money from her salary to buy a house, bring her children together, and establish a family.

In 1926, when the Bolenders began caring for Norma Jeane, Hawthorne had open fields, small farms, unpaved roads, and excellent trolley service. Children roamed at will; I remember that halcyon freedom from my childhood in nearby Inglewood. Marilyn biographers who describe Hawthorne as a slum are mistaken. I was there; I walked its streets. Small frame bungalows sat on large lots. Like my family and many others in the area who had been farmers before they moved to Los Angeles, the Bolenders raised vegetables and chickens to supplement the food they bought in a local store. They weren't wealthy, but they weren't poor. Wayne was a postman; he had a secure civil service job throughout the Great Depression.

Enterprising and hardworking, the Bolenders took in children partly for the money but also because they loved children and Ida seemed unable to conceive. Their house wasn't fancy, but it had six bedrooms, enough to accommodate a number of children if they shared bedrooms, a common practice in that era. During the six years she lived with the Bolenders, Norma Jeane usually shared a bedroom with Lester Bolender, a foster child who had been born the same week as Norma Jeane and who looked like her. The family called them "the twins"; Lester's last name was Bolender because they adopted him. Norma Jeane played with the Bolender brood and with children in the neighborhood. They climbed trees, built forts, and played fantasy games.[37]

"I was a shy little girl," Marilyn stated. "While very young, I developed my make-believe world. Every afternoon when I took my naps, I would pretend things. One day, I would be a beautiful princess in a tower. Or a boy with a dog. Or a grandmother with snowy hair. And at night I would lie and whisper out, ever so softly, the situations that I had heard on the radio before bedtime." She listened to *The Lone Ranger* and *The Green Hornet*. Those programs were about male adventure and bravado. But it wasn't "the chases and the horses" that excited her. It was the drama she liked; she would pretend to feel what she imagined each character in the radio show had felt.[38]

Norma Jeane liked to play house because she could make her own rules. She could be mother, father, or child—whatever she wanted. She had control—unlike in real life, where she had to obey others. Sometimes she pretended to be Alice in Wonderland after she fell down the rabbit hole and wound up in an unreal world. She stood in front of her mirror, wondering if the image in the mirror was really she. "Could it be someone pretending to be me? I would dance around, make faces, just to see if that little girl in the mirror would do the same," she said. She was a leader among the children, because she always thought up interesting games. "Even if the other kids were a little slow on the imagining part," she asserted, "you could say 'Hey, what about if you were so and so and I were such and such—wouldn't that be fun?'"[39]

She felt part of the Bolender family, but she knew that Ida and Wayne weren't her parents. When she called Ida "Mother," she was told not to. The "lady with red hair," she was told, was her mother, but Gladys, sometimes responsive, sometimes not, came and went. Norma Jeane was allowed to call Wayne "Daddy"—because she didn't have a real father, they said—and she and Wayne became close. He was gentle and caring, though not much of a talker, but he loved Norma Jeane, who was bright and inquisitive. She was always asking questions, always wanting to know about everything.

Still, Norma Jeane wanted her own father. She decided that the man in a picture on the wall of her mother's living room was her father. Over the years she developed fantasies about this "father," a male figure who spoiled her and made her feel safe. He wore a jaunty slouch hat. He never took it off, no matter how much Norma Jeane asked him to. When she was in the hospital in 1933 to have her tonsils removed, he was there with her in her daydreams. She gave him dialogue to say: "You'll be well in a few days, Norma Jeane. I'm very proud of the way you're behaving, not crying all the time like other girls." The man in the picture looked like Clark Gable, and Norma Jeane developed the fantasy that Gable was her father.

In 1931, five years after Norma Jeane arrived at the Bolenders', another child, Nancy, became a Bolender foster child. (Her surname is Bolender because, like Lester, they adopted her.) Nancy Bolender contends that Ida and Wayne were model parents and they didn't spank the children. Faithful to the Bolenders, she may overstate her case. Children were spanked in this era, mostly with an open hand on the backside. The enforcement of discipline was especially important to evangelical families, who expected their children to "follow God's rules." More humiliating than painful, discipline was meant to curb rambunctious behavior. On the other hand, Marilyn later alleged in magazine interviews that she was beaten by the Bolenders (without mentioning them by name), and that description may also be an overstatement. Yet Ida told Marilyn biographer Fred Guiles that Norma Jeane was a mischievous child who had to be disciplined.[40]

The Bolenders were evangelist Christians who attended the Hawthorne Community Church, mostly Baptist in orientation. They took the children in their care to Sunday services and Sunday school and to prayer meetings during the week. On special occasions they attended the Church of the Open Door in downtown Los Angeles. Located in a multistory edifice that dominated the skyline, that church was the center of evangelism in the West. Marilyn biographers have incorrectly identified the Bolenders as Pentacostal. On the contrary, they were followers of Dwight Moody, the Chicago evangelist.[41]

Unlike many evangelists, Moody didn't practice faith healing or Pentacostal speaking in tongues, although he held mass revivals and sent missionaries throughout the nation from his Moody Bible Institute in Chicago. Several Moody missionaries traveled to Los Angeles, and in 1920 they founded the Bible Institute of Los Angeles (Biola) as a seminary for preachers. It evolved into Biola University, still in operation, located in Orange County. Nancy Bolender graduated from Biola with a B.A.[42]

Moody was a fundamentalist who attacked Darwinian evolutionism and the "new paganism" of the 1920s. He emphasized the "original sin" of every human—supposedly inherited from Adam and Eve when they took the forbidden fruit from the serpent in the Garden of Eden and ate it to gain knowledge of worldly matters. He anticipated a Final Judgment, when Christ would appear on earth to send believers to heaven and unbelievers to hell. In the words of Reuben Torrey, longtime pastor of the Church of the Open Door, hell was a place of utter agony that lasted for eternity.[43]

"What shall it profit a man if he shall gain the whole world, and lose his own soul?" That verse from the Gospel of Mark was a favorite text of the adult Marilyn, as well as of Biola preachers. Reuben Torrey described individual souls—and the external world—as battlegrounds between good and evil, God and the devil, and described the devil as an invisible demon bent on seducing humans into violating God's rules. The Moody god was unrelenting, but salvation could be gained through faith in Jesus Christ. He was the "good shepherd" who had been crucified on the cross to exonerate the sins of humans. He represented the gentle part of the deity. He showed by his example how humans should live their lives.

The Bolenders quoted scripture. They taught their children Bible passages and held family devotions, reading Bible passages and reflecting on them, every evening. They had their charges kneel by their beds to recite the prayer that generations of Christian children have recited every night over the centuries—before they ask God to bless each member of the family.

Now I lay me down to sleep
I pray the Lord my soul to keep
If I should die before I wake
I pray the Lord my soul to take.

That prayer is soothing, but its allusion to death can be disturbing. Marilyn didn't forget that prayer when as an adult she dealt with her "sins," with nightmares, and with insomnia—the inability to go to sleep and the fear of doing so. That prayer links sleep to death and asks God's grace in keeping the supplicant safe. It also alludes to his possible vengeance in refusing what is asked for—ascent to heaven, not descent to hell.[44]

Marilyn biographers have overlooked the influence of evangelist religion on her, but Arthur Miller considered it a central factor in the creation of her adult self. In his autobiography, *Timebends*, he repeated a tale she often told him about sin and salvation. When she was six, she participated in a children's chorus at an Easter sunrise service at the Hollywood Bowl. The children stood in the shape of a cross, and they wore black capes. As the sun rose, they removed the capes to reveal the white clothes they wore underneath. Changing dark capes to white clothing symbolized that with the dawn—and Christ's resurrection after he had died on the cross—darkness had become light; Christ had risen from the grave; purity had triumphed over sin. But Norma Jeane forgot to remove her black robe. She stood there, humiliated, the only child in black rather than white. Chastened by Ida for her mistake, she felt that God had abandoned her.[45]

When Marilyn told Arthur the story, she laughed with sympathy for the little girl caught in the wrong. Yet he sensed that anger and guilt lay beneath her laughter: guilt at having failed the assignment; anger because she felt unfairly condemned. No matter what she did, Miller stated, she had to deal with her sense that she had sinned and had to defend herself against the "condemnation of religion." "And the stain kept reappearing like a curse," he wrote.[46] In *After the Fall*, Arthur's play about their marriage, he identified Marilyn's sin as refusing to admit her complicity in acceding to men's sexual demands, a complicity that made her as guilty as the men in the dishonorable sex behavior they had engaged in. But Arthur's interpretation was colored by his own puritanism, his sense that honorable men and women had to admit guilt for bad behavior as a way of reattaining the innocence of the original state of grace—the purity accorded all humans at birth. Yet beneath Marilyn's adult promiscuity lay the trauma of her childhood, a trauma that scarred her soul.

What was that trauma? Was it connected to Ida Bolender? In her stories about her childhood, Marilyn remembered the Bolenders as fanatical Christians who chastised her when she forgot to take off her black cape at the Hollywood Bowl Easter celebration. That sounds like a "screen memory"—a term coined by Freud, still in use today, that refers to the brain substituting a false memory for a real one to conceal trauma. Sex can be a difficult issue for evangelical Christians, particularly someone like Ida, raised in the Midwest Bible Belt. Nineteenth-century evangelists condemned masturbation as "the secret sin." They believed it could cause insanity and send those who practiced it to hell. Such beliefs still existed in the mid-twentieth century.[47]

The recently published *Fragments*, containing scraps of Marilyn's writings in the form of fugitive essays and autobiographical musings, provides insight into her Hollywood Bowl memory. In a piece dated 1955, Marilyn states that she had strong sexual feelings as a child. She also relates that she was caught in a sex act and was spanked and threatened with being sent to hell, where she would "burn with dirty bad people." She felt as though she was one of the "dirty bad people." The fragment refers either to masturbation or to childhood sex play. Marilyn wrote about such play in *My Story*, her autobiography, with a boy who may have been Lester Bolender. Such play is normal and innocent, but the evangelistic Ida Bolender may have punished Norma Jeane for it. In another fragment Marilyn wrote that Aunt Ida had whipped her for having touched "the bad part" of her body. She was left, she said, with a lifelong fear of and fascination with her genitals. She expressed such feelings in acts of public exposure in her later life.[48]

When Norma Jeane moved out of the Bolenders' home in 1933, she was a loving child, still happy, still asking questions all the time, as she had with Wayne Bolender. Whatever flaws there were in Ida's child-rearing, it was more positive than negative for Norma Jeane. Ida realized that, given the child's background—the mental instability in her family and her status as illegitimate, stigmas in the 1930s—Norma Jeane might have difficulties as an adult. She attempted to neutralize those difficulties by raising her to be self-reliant.

Ida had other sides. Both she and Wayne were antiracist, even though evangelical Christians often held racist views and the South Bay area in which Hawthorne was located was a center of the Ku Klux Klan. Wayne's postal route was in Watts, which was becoming African-American by the 1920s. He delivered mail mainly to black households. A gentle man and a devout Christian, he became close to the people on his route. They gave him cards and gifts at Christmas, and he helped them when they were in need. Ida and Wayne believed that Christ's love extended to all humans, regardless of skin color. They held no discriminatory attitudes. They were Democrats and enthusiastic supporters of Franklin D. Roosevelt and his New Deal. They were upset for a long time after Roosevelt died.[49]

Gladys didn't desert Norma Jeane when she left her with Ida, as some biographers charge. Once her daughter moved in with Ida in 1926, Gladys moved in too, sharing a bedroom with Norma Jeane for a time. Perhaps she nursed her daughter and needed to be with her. When her workload increased in early 1927, six months after Norma Jeane's birth, Gladys moved back to Hollywood. By then she may have weaned her daughter. Still, she visited Norma Jeane: She went to Hawthorne Saturday afternoons when she was finished with work and stayed overnight, attending church with the Bolenders on Sunday morning. Sometimes she took Norma Jeane on outings—to the beach, to Venice, to Hollywood. Nancy Bolender remembers Gladys often spending the night at their house.[50] By 1927 Gladys and Grace were roommates again, and Grace sometimes went along with Gladys and Norma Jeane on their excursions. But Grace also spent time with two nieces, who functioned as her surrogate daughters until they moved away from the area in 1934.

Some people who knew Gladys during these years described her as cold, with little affect, seeming to exist in her own world. Yet Reginald Carroll, a co-worker at RKO, recalled her as having twinkling green eyes and a lively spirit. Leila Fields, another cutter there, thought she was the most beautiful woman she had ever met. Gladys was delightful, Fields said, smiling and friendly. She always had a joke to tell to cheer you up if you were down.[51] Both Carroll and Fields remembered Gladys bringing Norma Jeane to work with her as soon as the child could walk. She dressed her daughter in the style of Mary Pickford, in black Mary Jane shoes and fluffy dresses, fixing her hair in Pickford's sausage curls. She often stated that Norma Jeane was destined to become a star.

Then the black cloud that stalked the Monroe family descended again, enveloping Della Monroe, Norma Jeane's grandmother. Soon after Norma Jeane's birth, Della exhibited symptoms of mental disturbance. She wasn't present at the birth in June; she was chasing Charles Grainger to Borneo. By October, she was back in Hawthorne alone, angry at her husband, angry at the world. She ousted the family that was renting her house and moved back into it. She was observed muttering to herself, and she frightened the newspaper delivery boy with her rants. Gladys was concerned, and she moved in with her mother.

One day when Gladys wasn't there, Della went to the Bolenders' house, angry because she had seen Ida spank Norma Jeane. There were other issues between them. Gladys and Ida were at odds over the relative merits of Aimee Semple McPherson and Dwight Moody. It may seem a trivial argument, but it was important to these two true believers. Della had won an important round when Norma Jeane was baptized by Sister Aimee instead of by Ida's minister. Della pounded on the Bolenders' door; when they didn't answer her knocking, she broke a glass pane in the door and opened it herself. Entering the house, she went into the room where Norma Jeane was sleeping and tried either to rearrange her blanket or to smother her. The Bolenders called the police, who took Della to Norwalk State Mental Hospital. Norma Jeane was eighteen months old.

As an adult she claimed that she remembered Della trying to smother her. Remembering an experience from the age of one and a half years seems improbable: it may have been a screen memory derived from stories others told her. Perhaps, though, the trauma was severe enough to imprint the memory in her brain. No record exists of Della's thoughts about the "smothering episode."

Della was either hysterical or incoherent, and she was admitted as a patient to Norwalk State Mental Hospital. She was diagnosed as manic-depressive. Two weeks later she died. The cause of death listed on her death certificate is myocarditis. Biographers allege she had heart disease. That diagnosis is debatable, as is the assumption that her up-and-down moods were related to heart issues. No known heart disorder causes bi-polarity. And myocarditis refers to the heart having been attacked by a virus, not to a mental condition.[52] Norma Jeane was later told that Della died from malaria. That is a more probable cause of her death, since she had traveled to Borneo the previous year. Malaria is common to Borneo, especially a rare strain known as falciparum. Della could have been bitten in Borneo by a tropical bug carrying the disease. Resistant to quinine, falciparum usually caused death in the 1930s. Even today, travelers to Borneo are warned to be vaccinated against it. All forms of malaria cause high fevers and hallucinations. Such fevers may have caused any hallucinations Della experienced during the weeks before she died.[53]

Marilyn sometimes claimed that her mother locked her in a closet when she visited her in Hollywood and didn't permit her to make any noise because it made her anxious. In her 1962 interview with photographer George Barris, however, she reversed her narrative of maternal abuse by stating that she loved to visit her mother because Gladys and her friends were carefree. "When I was with my mother and her friends," Marilyn said, "it felt like one big happy family." On Saturdays they went for a walk and to the movies; Sunday mornings they went to church. "It was heaven when we went to church. The singing and services always excited me. I was in a sort of trance." Then they returned to Gladys's apartment. "We always had a chicken lunch with our family—mom and her friends. Then off we would go for a stroll, looking in the fancy store windows at things we couldn't afford." She finished: "We were dreamers."[54]

Was Marilyn fantasizing when she told Barris this story? In fact, she was relating one strain in her mother's behavior. Gladys could be paranoid and controlling, but she could also be carefree. The problem for Norma Jeane was that she saw Gladys in too many negative moods and situations not to be troubled by her.

Yet by 1930, four years after her daughter's birth, Gladys seemed stable. She managed to handle her mother's death in 1928 without falling apart, and she didn't break down the next year, when her brother, Marion, disappeared, after telling his wife he was going to the store to buy a paper and failing to return. Gladys continued on with her life, even taking on a more modern look. She bobbed her hair, began smoking, and resumed dating. She took a boyfriend with her to the Bolenders', and the two of them took Norma Jeane to the beach. Grace and a boyfriend, plus her favorite niece, Geraldine, were along. Gladys showed courage when a fire broke out in Consolidated Film Industry in 1929. Keeping from panicking, she led the women in the editing studio out of the building, saving a lot of lives. The fire, which the *Los Angeles Times* called a "holocaust," gutted the building.[55]

The Bolenders wanted to adopt Norma Jeane but Gladys, who wanted her daughter to live with her eventually, wouldn't permit it. Ida resisted the possibility of Norma Jeane moving in with her mother just as firmly, worried that the unmarried Gladys, with her complicated emotions, demanding work schedule, and search for a husband, wouldn't be a good mother. In the spring of 1933 Gladys took several weeks off from work when Norma Jeane came down with whooping cough. She moved in with the Bolenders and nursed her daughter, displaying a maternal affection that Ida thought had too often been absent in her dealings with the child. Perhaps she could be an effective mother, after all. That same spring an earthquake nearly leveled the nearby city of Long Beach and severely damaged Norma Jeane's school. Then a car ran over and killed Norma Jeane's beloved dog Tippy, a stray that the Bolenders had allowed her to keep.

These events were decisive for Grace, a take-charge person who decided that Norma Jeane's future had to be settled. Grace, a modern woman, liked neither Ida's childrearing methods nor her evangelical religion, and in the end Gladys had the definitive claim. Grace persuaded Gladys that Norma Jeane had to be moved. Given the disappearance of both Norma Jeane's school and her beloved dog, it may not have been the best time to move her from her regular home, but Ida gave up. The bickering among the adult women wasn't good for her. Grace and Gladys drove to the Bolender home and picked up Norma Jeane, taking her to Hollywood to live. As their car approached the Bolender house, Norma Jeane hid in a bedroom with the other children. She looked at them as her family, and she didn't want to leave them.

Once Gladys brought Norma Jeane to Hollywood in June 1933, she placed her with a family of English actors who were friends of Grace and hers. George Atkinson, the father in the family, was a stand-in for the eminent English actor George Arliss. Maude Atkinson, his wife, played bit parts. Their daughter, Nellie, was the stand-in for English actress Madeleine Carroll. Norma Jeane lived with the Atkinsons for the next two years, acquiring overtones of an English accent from them. The family seemed carefree. Former vaudeville performers, they bought Norma Jeane a grass skirt and taught her the hula, as well as how to play cards. After her years with the religious Bolenders, Norma Jeane prayed for the English family and worried that they were going to hell.[56] But she learned secular values from them, which is what Gladys and Grace wanted.

Gladys continued taking Norma Jeane on outings. They spent a weekend on Catalina, an island in the Pacific forty-five minutes by ferry from Long Beach. Catalina had—and still has—a large casino–dance hall, a picturesque town, and a huge nature preserve. Glass-bottom boats moving slowly in the ocean near the island reveal the fishes swimming underneath. It's a child's paradise. Lester Bolender remembered Gladys taking Norma Jeane and him one July Fourth to Catalina on a big white steamship that had a dance floor. Norma Jeane got on the floor by herself and danced until she was dizzy. Everyone on the ship watched her, according to Lester. Norma Jeane returned to live on Catalina in 1944 with her husband Jim Dougherty when he was stationed there with the merchant marine.

Gladys and Norma Jeane also went to Gay's lion farm, a favorite tourist place in El Monte, east of downtown Los Angeles, where lions were bred, raised, and trained for the movies, and lion shows were put on. Reacting to a show, Norma Jeane revealed a confused sense of self. It was worse than being Alice in a Wonderland down a rabbit hole and in a magical world, she said, for the lions were located in a real world, and they were being trained as show animals. She thought that the lions were being trained "in ways that were not natural for them if they'd been left on their own." She said, "That thought scared me because I saw if I wasn't doing what I was supposed to be doing, then I would have no idea what I was supposed to [have been] doing since I was born."[57]

Her favorite activity, though, was watching movies in the palatial movie theaters on Hollywood Boulevard—with her mother, with Grace, and, when she was old enough, by herself. It was not uncommon in those days for working mothers to use movie theaters as babysitters for children old enough to be admitted by themselves. Sometimes Norma Jeane sat there all day and into the night, watching the matinee and evening shows. The two major theaters on Hollywood Boulevard, Sid Grauman's Egyptian Theater and his Chinese Theater, weren't far apart, and they were in the center of the city of Hollywood. They were ornate and fantastical, places for dreaming, palaces for the people. The Egyptian Theater, which opened in 1922, had columns with hieroglyphs in the interior. Its large forecourt contained huge statues of an elephant with bespangled trappings and of a man with a dog's head—the Egyptian god Anubis protecting his temple.[58] Norma Jeane remembered the monkeys in cages in that forecourt.

Grauman's Chinese Theater, which opened in 1927, was built in the shape of a pagoda, with a large sculpted dragon on its exterior. Antique heaven dogs stood at either side of the entrance, guarding it. The interior was painted flame red with gold accents. A large sunburst pendant chandelier hung from the ceiling, and a massive proscenium curtain had red figures on a peacock-blue background. In its courtyard were the famed footprints and handprints of stars imprinted in cement, a tradition initiated by Norma Talmadge in 1927. Following the tourist custom, Norma Jeane compared the size and shape of her hands and feet with those of the stars in cement.

The actresses she saw in the films she watched influenced Norma Jeane—Claudette Colbert in *Cleopatra*; Greta Garbo and Joan Crawford in *Grand Hotel*; Katharine Hepburn in *Little Women*. They were spunky women, "fast-talking dames," meant to appeal to unmarried working women, who constituted the major audience for Hollywood films in this era. Many spoke in clipped tones and moved with precision and pride. Jim Dougherty claimed that Norma Jeane picked up her ladylike quality partly from these stars, not just from Gladys and Della.[59] Take a look at Marilyn's stance, aside from the hip-swinging walk. She stands tall, with her shoulders high and her chest forward, following the day's rule that women should look regal and not slouch.

Norma Jeane loved the films of Clark Gable, her fantasy father, and of Jean Harlow, the day's platinum-blonde sex goddess. As a young child Norma Jeane's hair was nearly white. She hated the color because other children teased her for it, calling her a towhead. But Jean Harlow's hair was that color, and she felt vindicated. At Grauman's Egyptian and Chinese theaters, Norma Jeane saw the extravagant live prologues staged before each movie. A mixture of vaudeville and revue, they were themed to the movie being shown. Scores of showgirls and dancers wore elaborate costumes and moved and danced on spectacular sets. Grace and Gladys took Norma Jeane to the movie premieres held at night, as searchlight beams crisscrossed the sky and the stars arrived in limousines and walked to the theater on a red carpet, lined by thousands of fans. Flashbulbs popped; the crowd roared.

Grace dreamed of being Jean Harlow, and she projected that dream onto Norma Jeane. Grace pointed out to her how she could change her face and hair to more closely resemble Harlow. "Grace would touch the bump on the end of my nose," Marilyn remembered. "'You're perfect except for this little bump, sweetheart,' she'd say to me." Norma Jeane had a receding chin similar to Harlow's that Grace also thought could be fixed. "There's no reason you can't grow up to be just like her, Norma Jeane," Grace said, "with the right hair color and a better nose."[60] Yet in praising Jean Harlow, Grace did Norma Jeane a disservice. Harlow was the nation's major sex symbol, erotic and enticing, hardly an appropriate model for a little girl. Grace was sexualizing Norma Jeane, making her even more vulnerable to unwanted attention from men.

In the summer of 1933, Gladys bought a house. It was an astonishing purchase for a woman in this era, when banks rarely extended them credit. Determined to realize her dream of bringing her children together in her own home, Gladys had saved money from her salary, and she secured a loan from the New Deal Home Owners' Loan Corporation, established in June 1933. She bought furniture at auctions, including a baby grand piano that Fredric March had owned. She told Norma Jeane that she dreamed of sitting in front of the fireplace in their living room, listening to her play the piano.

The location and size of the house are important to understand Gladys and her dreams. It was located off Highland Boulevard, near the Hollywood Bowl, a mile or so up the hill from Hollywood Boulevard. It was easy walking distance from the two Grauman theaters and Norma Jeane's elementary school. It wasn't a small house. It had four bedrooms, a living room with a fireplace, and enough space to hold the baby grand piano. There was a porch on the back of the house and a Georgian portico on the front. Music from the nearby Hollywood Bowl could be heard in the evenings.

It was next to the exclusive Whitley Heights Tract. In the 1910s, H. J. Whitley, who developed much of Hollywood, purchased a huge tract of land in the Hollywood Hills, up from the center of Hollywood. By the 1920s he subdivided it into plots for homeowners. It was luxurious land, with winding roads and breathtaking views of the ocean. Major stars lived there, including Jean Harlow, Carole Lombard, William Powell, Marie Dressler, Charlie Chaplin, and Bette Davis. The homes were in Mediterranean style: stucco painted creamy white, red tile roofs, terraced yards, and arched doorways.[61] It was a short walk from Gladys's home on Arbol Drive. Taking that walk, Gladys and Norma Jeane might catch a glimpse of Jean Harlow in her yard or Carole Lombard welcoming guests. The Arbol Drive home made Norma Jeane's dreams of stardom vivid. She was now living among the stars.

To be certain that she could pay the mortgage and provide after-school care for Norma Jeane, Gladys persuaded the Atkinsons, Norma Jeane's most recent foster family, to move in with them. In fact, she rented much of the house to them, keeping two bedrooms for herself and Norma Jeane.

Then disaster struck, as Gladys went into a tailspin in January 1934, three months after they had moved into the Arbol Drive house. One morning before breakfast she came down the stairs screaming that men were trying to kill her. An ambulance was called, and Gladys was taken to a rest home in Santa Monica for several months before being transferred to Los Angeles County General Hospital, where Norma Jeane had been born. A year after the breakdown, in January 1935, at the recommendation of Gladys's doctors, Grace had the court declare Gladys an "insane incompetent" and commit her to Norwalk State Mental Hospital (sometimes called Metropolitan.) It was where Della Monroe, her mother, had died. Her doctors diagnosed Gladys as paranoid schizophrenic. Grace took over her affairs, becoming her guardian, so that she could sell the house and Gladys's possessions, in order to pay her bills. She also took over managing Norma Jeane.

Was Della manic-depressive? Was Gladys schizophrenic? The relationship between individual behavior and categories of mental illness was as fuzzy in the 1930s as it is today. No physical tests existed to determine the kind and degree of illness, nor do such tests exist today. Diagnosis was—and is—based on the application of categories devised by experts to the symptoms subjects display.

The major text used by psychiatrists in mental hospitals from the early 1930s on was *Modern Clinical Psychiatry* by Arthur P. Noyes. Surprisingly modern in his approach, Noyes warned that it was difficult to distinguish schizophrenia from manic-depressive disorder and from temporary emotional states. Noting correctly that Austrian neurologist Emil Kraepelin had invented the categories in the 1890s, he implied that they were out of date. Noyes concluded that there were many gradations between them. Yet he drew distinctions between the categories in terms of behavior and treatment. A manic-depressive syndrome could be healed by exercise, diet, and removal from stress. But such treatment had no effect on schizophrenics, with their hallucinations and paranoia. Unless they suffered from alcoholism, syphilis, or were elderly people with severe dementia, inhabitants of mental institutions were always diagnosed as either manic-depressive or schizophrenic. The worst form of the latter was the paranoid variety.[62]

Della heard voices, and she sometimes thought that people were following her. Gladys had similar symptoms. Hearing voices, however, is common in the general population. We all hear voices in our heads; the issue is whether they stay in our brain or appear to come from outside of us. The former is ordinary; the latter is not. Indeed, according to Patricia Traviss, the head of the Rockhaven Sanitarium during the years that

Gladys lived there (from 1953 to 1967), Gladys didn't think she had anything wrong with her. Thus she didn't think that the voices she heard came from outside her.[63] Moreover, some paranoia is healthy. It's part of an evolutionary development to keep humans alert to external threats.

Both Della and Gladys had difficult lives, with enough traumas to wreak havoc with their brain chemistry. Until recently, most people drew a sharp distinction between sanity and insanity, believing that individuals with mental issues stood apart from everyone else. Della and Gladys were women who sometimes operated on the borderline between ordinary and antisocial behavior; they were easily singled out as disorderly.

It's possible that Gladys's behavior didn't become psychotic until she entered a state mental institution: that's what she later claimed.[64] She had a point. California mental hospitals were overcrowded, with insufficient doctors and nurses and poorly trained attendants. By the 1930s physical restraints weren't used much anymore, but they were replaced by baths in which patients were strapped into large tubs, with water running over them for as long as eight hours a day. It's not surprising that hysterical individuals calmed down after that treatment—or that Gladys often tried to run away from the hospitals.

By 1939 electroshock therapy was in use. It produced such strong convulsions that bones could break. It was the new utopian treatment for mental illness, as water baths had once been. Gladys told Emmeline Snively, the head of Marilyn's modeling agency, that she had been given electroshock therapy. That's not surprising, since it was applied to most patients in California state mental hospitals from 1939 on. *The Snake Pit*, a fictionalized depiction of California mental institutions, filmed in 1948, includes graphic scenes of treatments including restraints, water baths, and electroshock therapy.[65]

In those hospitals, placement in wards was first by sex and then by docility. If patients followed orders and didn't act out, they could be moved to wards with greater privileges, to walk in the grounds and work in hospital industries. If a patient became especially difficult, he or she could be sent to another state hospital, since individuals committed to state mental hospitals had few rights. Gladys attempted to escape from Norwalk State in the winter of 1935. She was captured and returned to the hospital, and she was moved that spring to Agnews State Hospital near

San Jose, which had better security, but which was far away from Grace and Norma Jeane. The tragedy of the escape was that Gladys had arranged it with Edward Mortensen, who had phoned her. But the authorities confused him with Edward Mortenson, who had died in a motorcycle accident in 1929. Thus when Gladys told the attendants she was meeting Mortensen, they thought she was talking about a dead man and was delusional.

In a letter Grace wrote to a friend, she stated that a doctor took X-rays of Gladys's brain and decided that one third of it had disintegrated. Recovery was impossible, although she might stabilize if she were placed in a home environment under supervision, removed from stress. Metropolitan was so overcrowded, he said, that they would release Gladys to a family member or close friend. In her letter Grace stated that neither she nor anyone she knew could afford to keep Gladys in their home.[66] So she remained in state institutions for the next eight years, all in Northern California, away from Norma Jeane.

Largely abandoned by family and friends, Gladys developed her own world. Her ability to work long hours at negative film editing suggests she had an obsessive side. She now turned that side of herself toward religion. Ana Lower, Grace's aunt and a Christian Science healer, visited her at Agnews State Hospital. Ana gave Gladys a healing and encouraged her to read Mary Baker Eddy's *Science and Health* in order to access God's love. Gladys did so, and she developed the fantasy that she was a Christian Science nurse who could cure illness. She began to wear a nurse's white uniform, and she continued to do so the rest of her life. The figure she created combined Ana Lower, kind and authoritative, with the hospital nurses, who both served and controlled the patients. Gladys thus gained a sense of independence and power over her environment.

She constantly wrote letters—to the Christian Science Mother Church in Boston; to the government; to whoever might listen. I possess letters she wrote when she was in Rockhaven Sanitarium, near Glendale. In those letters she is gentle and concerned about others, but also paranoid and delusional. She thinks that radio waves are destroying her brain and that her nurses are plotting against her.

Once Gladys was sent to Agnews, she didn't hear from Edward Mortensen again. Grace and Norma Jeane rarely visited her. Narcissism can be the product of vanity and insecurity, a soul that can't find itself.

That was Gladys, so hurt by others that she couldn't relate to them, mostly passive, fixated on her fantasies, engaging in occasional outbursts of rage. But questions remain. Why did Gladys break down completely in 1934? What caused her to fall apart after she had bought the house on Arbol Drive and brought Norma Jeane to live with her? Moreover, Grace's treatment of Norma Jeane needs to be evaluated. Eventually she placed her in eleven foster homes and in an orphanage. Why did she do so, repeating Gladys's seeming abandonment of Norma Jeane so many times? The answers to these questions aren't simple. They require a fuller exploration of Gladys's breakdown and its impact on Grace and Norma Jeane's lives.

Chapter 2

Trauma, 1933–1938

As an adult, Marilyn Monroe seemed obsessed with her childhood. She often told friends and reporters stories about it. In those stories the Bolenders were religious fanatics who beat her and most of her other foster families treated her as unwanted—although she never mentioned any by name, except for Grace and Ana, whom she always praised. She said the matrons in the orphanage (the Children's Aid Society orphanage in Hollywood) required her to wash stacks of dishes, clean bathrooms, and scrub floors. Newspapers and magazines worldwide ran those stories. They became so well known that in 1955 *Silver Screen* reported, "Hillbillies who can't tell you who's president right now could probably recite the details of Marilyn's life."[1]

The tales contributed to making her an icon in her own day. She was the Little Orphan Annie who became a star, the Cinderella who, rising from poverty to fame, achieved a female version of the American Dream. No other film star endured a childhood so traumatic—not Joan Crawford, Rita Hayworth, or Lana Turner, all of whom had difficult childhoods. "The life story of almost any Hollywood star reads like a combination of Cinderella and Horatio Alger," wrote a journalist. "But Marilyn has topped them all. Let one critic raise his voice in protest over her habitual tardiness or so-called rudeness and a protesting public looks beyond the present to Marilyn's pathetic drudgery in the dreary place where she washed 'a horrifying pile of soiled dishes for 5 cents a month.'"[2]

Were her stories accurate? Or were they part of an outsized legend she invented? My research suggests she sometimes exaggerated her childhood experiences but her tales were often true. The story of her childhood after Gladys broke down isn't simple. In telling it, I will approach it chronologically, giving the surface story. I will then rework it, excavating the layers that lie underneath, probing the texts and counter-texts that, as so often in her life, defined it. I will evaluate the truth of Marilyn's account. As I progress, keep in mind that once Gladys was committed to state mental hospitals Norma Jeane was especially vulnerable to disapproval. She was illegitimate in an age when it was stigmatized. She was a "charity case" at a time when many Americans regarded taking welfare as a disgrace. Relatives of hers had been diagnosed as mentally ill in an era that regarded such illness as inherited and almost inevitably degenerative.

One night after Gladys broke down in 1934, Norma Jeane, then eight years of age, stayed at Grace's apartment. Lying in bed, she overheard Grace talking to her friends about her in the next room. They were advising Grace not to become Norma Jeane's guardian because of her family "heritage." They said her grandfather, grandmother, brother, and mother were "mental cases," and she would become one, too. "I lay in bed shivering as I listened," Marilyn remembered. "I didn't know what a mental case was but I knew it wasn't anything good."[3] Soon after that she learned about the diagnosis of Gladys's brain as disintegrating. It was a horrible fate for an impressionable girl like Norma Jeane to contemplate. She would be afraid of going crazy for the rest of her life.

After Gladys collapsed, Grace left Norma Jeane living in the Arbol Drive house with the Atkinsons. It seemed the right thing to do, since Gladys might soon recover and return home. Norma Jeane's school was nearby, and so were her friends. The Atkinsons were fond of Norma Jeane, and they seemed to take good care of her. Grace worked full-time and acted in plays; she never lost the love of acting that had brought her to Hollywood in the first place. Some of her time was freed up when her nieces moved away in 1934, but not enough for her to raise a child.[4] The Atkinsons were Grace's friends. She could visit Norma Jeane and see them, too. She lived on Lodi Drive in the center of Hollywood, ten minutes by car from Arbol Drive. As Gladys or she had for years, she took Norma

Jeane to a movie and then to a restaurant on the weekends. She continued to tell her she would be another Jean Harlow.

Grace's apartment was across the street from the Hollywood Studio Club, an inexpensive, chaperoned residence for aspiring actresses. In the 1920s influential Hollywood actresses and wives, fearing that Hollywood apartments were recruiting grounds for prostitutes, raised the money to build it. When Norma Jeane visited Grace, her mother's friend told her about the stars who had lived in the Studio Club. Designed by architect Julia Morgan in the Mediterranean style of Los Angeles architecture, it had cachet. During her early years as a Hollywood actress, Marilyn sometimes lived at the Club.

Yet Grace did nothing to help Norma Jeane become an actress. Acting and singing lessons aren't listed in Grace's record of expenditures for her ward. Stage mothers were everywhere in Hollywood, pushing their children into films, as did the mothers of Shirley Temple, Betty Grable, Ginger Rogers, and Judy Garland. After years in the movie business Grace had connections, but she didn't use them on Norma Jeane's behalf, although she launched the acting career of Ervin (Doc) Goddard, whom she married in 1935. Grace's fantasies about Norma Jeane becoming a film star were just that: fantasies.

Still, once Gladys broke down, Grace took over responsibility for both Gladys and Norma Jeane. She didn't have to do this, but she didn't want both of them committed to state institutions. No Monroe family members lived nearby, except for Olive Monroe, Marion Monroe's wife, who was struggling to support three children after he disappeared in 1929 and left her penniless. She wasn't a good candidate to be a foster mother. Given the difficulty with Ida Bolender, Grace didn't want to return Norma Jeane to her, although Ida later claimed that she visited Norma Jeane and took her to see Gladys at Metropolitan. According to Lester Bolender, the Bolender house was so full of foster children by then that there wouldn't have been room for Norma Jeane.[5]

In late 1934 Grace filed the papers for Gladys to be committed to Metropolitan. Its medical superintendent stated that Gladys wasn't in good enough shape mentally or physically to appear in court then and for "an indefinite time to come."[6] In March 1935 Grace petitioned the court to appoint her Gladys's legal guardian so that she could sell Gladys's house and possessions and pay her expenses. The petition was granted, and she held the sale that spring. Ana Lower, Grace's aunt, purchased the piano that Gladys had bought for Norma Jeane and kept it in her apartment, indicating that she knew the child and was fond of her. The piano, which remained there, became a symbol of past, present, and future for Norma Jeane. As a young adult and a Hollywood starlet living on her own Marilyn painted it white to resemble the white pianos often present in the art moderne sets of 1930s movies. Those pianos were a symbol of elegant sophistication.

Norma Jeane stayed with the Atkinsons until June 1935, when Grace sold the Arbol Drive house. They then moved to a house on Glencoe Way, in the Hollywood Hills close to Arbol Drive—not to England, as some biographers suggest. The 1935 Los Angeles census lists them at that address, but it doesn't list Norma Jeane. George played in the Hollywood movies *Little Lord Fauntleroy* in 1936 and *Raffles* in 1939; and he and his wife attended Marilyn's wedding in June 1942. Maude Atkinson's obituary in the *Los Angeles Times* on March 9, 1944, notes that she had lived in Southern California for the previous twenty-five years.[7]

Once the Atkinsons left, Grace had to find a place for Norma Jeane. She still didn't bring her ward to live with her; instead, she placed her with Harvey and Elsie Giffen, a well-to-do couple who lived near Arbol Drive and whose daughter was Norma Jeane's best friend at school. Harvey Giffen was a sound engineer at RCA, and Elsie stayed at home to keep the house and raise their children. Now nine years of age, Norma Jeane was quiet and disciplined. Sensitive to others, always willing to help out, she seemed an ideal child. Whatever happened in the Bolender home, Ida had raised her well. She moved in with the Giffens, a loving family. When they offered to adopt her, Grace agreed to ask Gladys to allow them to do so.

Norma Jeane liked the Giffens. They had an aviary of tropical birds, including parakeets and other talking parrots. She was fascinated by the birds; she loved to feed them and talk with them. The Giffens were moving to New Orleans and wanted to take her along, but Gladys wouldn't hear of it. Grace next approached Reginald Carroll and his wife to adopt Norma Jeane; he had been Gladys's co-worker and friend at Consolidated Film Industries, and he and his family lived in Los Angeles, so Norma Jeane would remain in the city. Gladys again refused to allow the adoption.[8]

When the Giffens left Los Angeles in July, Grace finally brought Norma Jeane to live with her. She told her she wouldn't have to go to an orphanage, and the child was vastly relieved. She didn't want to go to a place where she didn't know any of the children. Some biographers contend that state law required Grace to put Norma Jeane in an orphanage while her situation was evaluated, but Grace, clever and manipulative, often got around such obstacles. Doc Goddard may now have entered the picture. He and Grace were discussing marriage, and he had children living in Texas with his ex-wife. There was a possibility they might come to live with him, and he didn't want to take on Norma Jeane as well.

Tall and handsome, a courtly "cowboy" from Texas, Doc had come to Hollywood hoping for a career as a film actor. He landed bit parts in the movies and became the stand-in for Joel McCrea, who played tough-guy roles in cowboy films and crime dramas. Doc was ten years younger than Grace and more than a foot taller, but they joked about their differences in age and height. He worked as a part-time inventor, making electrical gadgets in his garage workshop, but he didn't make much money, either from acting or from his inventions, and his children in Texas were still young. In 1935 Eleanor (Bebe) was nine, Fritz seven, and Josephine (Nona) five.

Grace didn't mind Doc's shaky finances. Now in her mid-thirties, she was too old for the Hollywood party scene, and she welcomed marriage to the dashing, handsome Doc. Grace considered her new family her primary responsibility, with Norma Jeane second. It's unclear what financial responsibility Doc had to his ex-wife and children, but he probably sent them something. Grace married Doc in Las Vegas in early August 1935. Ana Lower was at the ceremony, but Norma Jeane wasn't there. A month later, in September 1935, Grace placed her in an orphanage. The way was clear for Doc's children to move in with them, although they didn't do so until 1940. Rather, they remained in Texas.

There is a backstory to the events I have related. It involves Marilyn's claim that she was sexually abused when she was eight years old. She made the claim in interviews with screenwriter Ben Hecht in 1953 and 1954 for an autobiography of her he was to ghostwrite.[9] She also told her tale of childhood sexual abuse to Maurice Zolotow for his 1960 biography of her. Then in 1962, several months before her death, she amplified the story in interviews with photographer George Barris. Barris's interviews were supposed to be published in *Cosmopolitan*, but when Marilyn died the magazine canceled the story. Barris then sold it to newspapers worldwide, and it was widely published. Barris's interviews were thus available to Marilyn's biographers soon after she died, although biographers have mostly overlooked them. When I spoke with Barris in 2010 he told me that, with the exception of Gloria Steinem, who wrote a brief biography of Marilyn to accompany his photos of her, previous Marilyn biographers hadn't contacted him. Thus Marilyn's most detailed account of the episode of sexual abuse has been largely disregarded.[10]

She was eight years old when it happened, she said. She was living with a family that rented a room to a man named Mr. Kimmel. He was elderly, stern and formal, and everybody respected him. One evening he asked her to come into his room, and when she did, he locked the door behind her. He put his arms around her. She kicked and struggled to no avail. He did what he wanted, telling her to be a good girl. (In the Barris interview she stated that the abuse involved fondling.) When he let her out of the room, he handed her a nickel and told her to buy herself an ice cream. She threw the nickel in his face. Then she ran to tell her "aunt" what had happened, but her aunt wouldn't listen. (Marilyn called all her foster mothers "aunt.") "Shame on you," her aunt said, "Mr. Kimmel's my star boarder." Norma Jeane went back to her room. Throwing herself on her bed, she cried all night.[11]

In her interview with Georges Belmont of *Paris Match*, Marilyn explained that the real name of her attacker wasn't Kimmel, and that she always changed the names of the individuals in her childhood stories to conceal their identities. If she was eight when the attack occurred, she was living with the Atkinsons, since she lived with them in the Arbol Drive house for nearly two years, from October 1933 to the spring of 1935, when Grace sold the house. She may have lived with them earlier, from the time Gladys brought her to Hollywood in June 1933. Marilyn made that claim in her interview with Belmont.[12]

Most male biographers of Marilyn dismiss the sex-abuse story as a fabrication because Jim Dougherty, her first husband, stated that she was a virgin when he married her. Thus, they conclude, she couldn't have been sexually abused as a child. They don't seem to know that experts on child sex abuse agree that the act usually involves fondling, not intercourse. The perpetrators, not wanting to leave evidence, don't bruise the victim or penetrate the hymen. Even today, the conviction of an adult for abusing a child is based mainly on the testimony of the child, since physical evidence usually doesn't exist and perpetrators rarely admit guilt. Without total vaginal penetration, Norma Jeane would have been a virgin when she married Jim.[13]

In the 1962 Barris interview, Marilyn described the fondling. "He put his hand under my dress. He touched me in places no one had ever before." And she stated that the "foster mother" who refused to believe her about the abuse slapped her across her face. Marilyn told her cousin Ida Mae Monroe that she felt dirty after the attack and took baths for days after it happened to feel clean. Such repeated attempts to feel clean through showers or baths are typical behavior for a rape victim.[14]

The name Mr. Kimmel, which she used for her attacker in *My Story*, has led some Marilyn biographers to identify English actor Murray Kinnell as the abuser. There is, however, no proof for this charge—except that George Atkinson and Kinnell knew each other. Both worked with the renowned British actor George Arliss, who had control over his films and cast many of the same actors in supporting roles in them. Kinnell was often one of these actors, while Atkinson was Arliss's regular stand-in. Kinnell was a founder of the Screen Actors Guild, and he lived on Beverly Glen Boulevard in Westwood, not far from the Fox Studios, where Arliss made his films. Westwood and Culver City are both distant from the Hollywood Bowl and the Arbol Drive house.[15]

It's possible that the abuser was a boarder in Gladys's house, which had four bedrooms. Norma Jeane occupied one, her mother another, and the English family the third. Thus an extra room remained to rent out.[16] If Kinnell is eliminated, the abuser might have been George Atkinson or Doc Goddard, the two older men close to Norma Jeane during this period of her life. Circumstantial evidence could suggest either of them. In his autobiography, George Arliss described his stand-in (namely, Atkinson) in negative terms.

> The stand-in for the elderly star is a pathetic figure. More often than not he is an old actor who has played everything, but has "never had his chance." And now he is nothing—a shadow. And yet he feels within himself a certain sense of importance. He is dressed

like the star; he believes that he looks like the star; almost unconsciously he takes on the walk, the mannerisms of the star; he poses
like him before the cameraman, and he sees himself as a star.[17]

In Arliss's description Atkinson is a poseur, a shadow man lacking a
sense of self, but with an inflated ego that compels him to assume Arliss's
identity, cloaking himself in the star's fame. In *My Story* Marilyn described the English couple as jolly and carefree, former vaudevillians who
taught her to dance the hula, play cards, and juggle oranges. As Arliss's
stand-in, however, Atkinson must have resembled him. Both men were in
their sixties. Bette Davis, who played in Arliss films, described Arliss as
looking like a combination English gentlemen and uninhibited satyr.
"His small dark eyes held an ancient sadness, his taut triangular mouth
seemed always to be repressing an irrepressible mirth."[18] He often played
English statesmen, representing the Depression taste for calm heroism
and puckish independence in the face of disaster.

In her interview with Maurice Zolotow, Marilyn called the abuser
"Mr. K." She described him as a stern old man who wore dark suits and
a gold watch in his vest pocket, with a gold chain across his vest. That's
what George Arliss wore. She states that "Mr. K." was always called
"Mr.," an honorific always bestowed upon the dignified George Arliss.
Playing the role of a British gentleman in real life as in his films, Arliss
always wore a monocle. We can assume that Atkinson, who copied Arliss's dress and behavior, also dressed this way.[19]

Marilyn told Jean Negulesco, a Hollywood director and friend, that
an elderly actor had raped her when she was eight. She told *Photoplay*
editor Adele Whiteley Fletcher that she had difficulty calling studio executives on their bad treatment of her because they reminded her of her
abuser. Grace Goddard stated that she took Norma Jeane away from the
Atkinsons because she found that they were not treating her well. In
1959 at a party in New York, Marilyn spent the evening discussing the
attack with the husband of Peggy Fleury, a fellow student at the Actors
Studio. Marilyn said she felt lucky that the experience hadn't made her
psychotic, as it did many victims of such attacks.[20]

Could Doc Goddard have been the abuser? When Norma Jeane lived
with Doc and Grace in 1937, he tried to fondle her. He admitted he had
done so to Marilyn biographer Fred Guiles. Jim Dougherty, who respected

Doc, knew about it. It may have been the one-time advance of someone who was drunk and out of control; it may have had precedents.[21]

Interviews and newspaper articles I've found provide new information about Doc. A *Los Angeles Times* article of August 19, 1935, announced that Doc and Grace had eloped to Las Vegas the previous week. It stated that he had come to Los Angeles in 1933, not 1935, the year cited by previous Marilyn biographers. If the *Times* is correct, he was in Hollywood when the first sexual assault on Norma Jeane occurred and Gladys broke down. That same year Grace introduced him to Al Rangell, who directed westerns, and Rangell cast him in a bit part.[22] Doc continued to land small roles, eventually becoming the stand-in for Joel McCrea.

In fact, Doc Goddard was not just a courtly Texas cowboy. He was also a "man's man" who loved going to bars to drink liquor and swap stories with male buddies. He was such an enthusiastic bar man that he was often hours late for dinner. Aside from minor movie work and an occasional sale of one of his gadgets, he was unemployed until Adel Precision Parts, which made equipment for airplanes, hired him in 1938. Given the growth in the 1930s of the aircraft industry, located largely in Southern California, and the preparations by 1938 for a possible war with Germany, there was a shortage of skilled workers in the industry. Doc didn't work for Adel before 1938, as some biographers have claimed, because Adel wasn't founded until that year.[23]

Doc was a "hale-fellow-well-met" kind of man, but his life in Texas before he moved to Hollywood had been filled with tragedy. He was the offspring of a prominent Austin family. His father had been dean of the medical school of the University of Texas in Austin, but he had committed suicide. Doc's mother had broken down emotionally and had been committed to a mental institution. Doc had been a medical student, but he dropped out when he married his first wife in 1925. He was called "Doc" because he had attended medical school. After the birth of Bebe, Fritz, and Nona, Doc and his wife divorced in 1931.[24]

The children lived in Texas, in the custody of their mother. According to Bebe, their mother was so mentally unstable that she placed them in foster homes, where they were mistreated. Nona made similar allegations. Bebe even contended that Marilyn derived her stories of bad treatment as a child from Bebe's experiences in Texas.[25] That may be partly true, but Marilyn had her own issues in foster homes. Deeply attached to Doc and Grace, Bebe didn't want them accused of wrongdoing. She had her own reasons for challenging the truth of Marilyn's stories about her childhood.

Under the terms of his divorce Doc had visitation rights with the children. Yet he didn't try to gain custody of them or to prevent his disturbed ex-wife from putting them in abusive foster homes. In fact, the divorce decree issued to Doc and his wife notes that Doc didn't show up for the final hearing. But he could be charming. By late adolescence, Norma Jeane forgave him for whatever had happened between them, and she became close to him. In a 1942 letter to Grace she called him Daddy.[26] In the early 1950s, when Grace managed Marilyn's business matters, Doc helped her.

The episode of sexual abuse raises another possibility. My evidence suggests that it occurred toward the end of 1933 and that it may have caused Gladys's breakdown in January 1934. Some writers claim that Gladys was upset by the suicide of her grandfather Tilford Hogan the previous spring at the age of eighty-two, by the death of her son Jackie that fall, and by a strike in the film editing studio where she was working. But she had survived the death of her mother in 1928 and the disappearance of her brother, Marion, the next year. She had weathered strikes and crises in the film editing studios over the years. Buying the house in 1933 suggests that she felt better about herself. Renting most of it to the Atkinsons gave her a way to pay for it. In another indication of confidence, she bought a new car. Gladys seemed ready to handle potential problems—until the attack on her daughter occurred.

Marilyn states in the Barris interview that when she told her foster mother about the attack, she slapped her across the face for having accused her "star boarder" of a crime. In other words, her foster mother thought Norma Jeane made up the charge of abuse. That belief rested on the assumption in this era that only lower-class men molested girls and that the girls involved provoked the abuse by arousing sexual desire in the men.[27] A distinguished-looking man, whom everyone called "Mr.," couldn't have committed such an act. Norma Jeane had to be lying. Or she had invited the attack.

In line with her practice in interviews of using pseudonyms for the actual individuals in her life situations, Marilyn referred to a foster mother, not her actual mother. George Atkinson was Gladys's "star boarder," since the rent the Atkinsons paid her covered most of the monthly mortgage payment on the Arbol Drive house. Once she broke down, Gladys didn't live there again. In later years she was angry with her daughter for being a sexual icon. As she aged, Gladys turned against the free sexuality of her twenties. She wanted her daughter to be on the cover of *Ladies' Home Journal*, not raunchy men's magazines. It appears that she tended to connect her daughter to inappropriate sex.

Marilyn told George Barris that she began to stutter after she was sexually abused. She also informed him that stuttering is sex-linked, appearing more frequently in men than in women. She was correct. And when women stutter, a severe trauma has often caused it. Although Marilyn controlled her stuttering, she never overcame it. She especially reverted to it in moments of stress. When she told Adele Whiteley Fletcher of *Photoplay* about the sexual abuse inflicted on her, she began stuttering. It could be a problem for her when speaking her lines in films. Speech therapists today suggest that Marilyn's soft voice and her facial mannerisms may have been strategies to disguise the stuttering.

She told Maurice Zolotow that as a child she mostly stopped talking to adults because of her fear that she would stutter. The talkative, inquisitive Norma Jeane of Wayne Bolender's experience became a "mouse" in front of adults. She didn't talk in school because she feared that if a teacher called on her she would stutter in replying. "Naturally shy to begin with, my stuttering made me withdraw into myself altogether. I would start to say something and my lips would get fixed into an 'O' shape. A lost feeling would come over me, and I would stand there frozen for a long period of time." It took many years for Marilyn to control the stuttering and to open herself up to others.[28]

The sexual abuse inflicted on Norma Jeane shouldn't seem surprising. From the mid-nineteenth century to the present, the rate of sexual abuse of girls has remained constant at twenty percent. In other words, one in five girls is molested today, as in the past. The perpetrators are usually the male heads of the households in which the girls live, and they come from all social classes and ethnic groups. Like rape in general, sexual abuse of girls is not a crime perpetrated only by strangers or by violent lower-class men.

The impact of sexual abuse on girls can be profound. The victim can experience the assault as a penetration of the self that causes shame, self-hatred, and guilt. In other words, abused girls may blame themselves for the crime committed against them. They may regard themselves and other women with contempt, and they may develop an aversion to sex. Or they may degrade themselves through prostitution or "sex addiction," the drive for continual sex and the inability to resist seduction. They may develop an irresistible urge to expose their naked bodies and even their genitalia. They may become obsessed with being perfect or develop a sadomasochism in which they identify with powerful individuals and then try to destroy them. A low self-image can exist alongside megalomania. Such symptoms can appear immediately after the attack, later in life, or episodically.[29] Many seem present in the adult Marilyn.

Abused girls may develop what psychologists call "dissociation," in which the self fragments and generates multiple identities. Thus Norma Jeane Baker produced Marilyn Monroe, her major alter ego, who was sexual and self-confident. Such dissociation can occur in the process of personality fragmentation, as the shy persona located in childhood remains present into adulthood, while a self-confident adult emerges, possessing knowledge initially triggered by the loss of innocence resulting from sexual assault. On the other hand, the personality fragmentation can be multiple, producing fully developed personas, which psychologists call alters. Or it can be partial. In that situation the boundaries between parts of the self aren't rigid, and the personas produced are intermixed. By this definition, any personality can become a series of shifting entities.[30] We all dissociate to a certain degree, while actors, creating characters out of their internal selves to play on stage, become expert in accessing their interior dimensions and bringing what is inside to the surface.

Taking the point farther, some psychiatrists argue that mental disorders can exist between standard diagnostic categories, such as bipolar disorder, schizophrenia, and multiple personality disorder. Or "spectrum" conditions exist that draw from several categories. Some psychiatrists posit that each individual's mental makeup is different and no one can be slotted into one category.[31]

The original classifications devised by Emil Kraepelin in the 1890s still dominate definitions of emotional disorder today, although even

Arthur Noyes, in his 1934 work, maintained that individual situations could combine categories or be located between them. Jim Dougherty's portrayal of the fifteen-year-old Norma Jeane as more physically and emotionally mature than other girls her age, while still acting like a child—playing with dolls and young children—sounds like a description of dissociation. Marilyn herself described personality as shifting and her own as multifaceted. "I can be anything they want me to be," she told Susan Strasberg. "If they expect me to be innocent, I'm innocent. There are lots of cards in my deck, so to speak."[32]

But Marilyn wasn't always able to control her personas. Her first acting coach, Natasha Lytess, with whom she lived on and off, described her insecurities as making her seem as though she was "under water," a "moon walker," oblivious to her surroundings, not part of the real world. "She was accustomed to hiding everything," Natasha stated. "She had learned this behavior from her childhood." Many of her directors spoke of her as moving into her own world to create a role; friends described the "strange nobody's-home look she could get into her eyes."[33]

Some experts on abuse find that a frightening episode can be embedded in the brain, producing long-term trauma, akin to post-traumatic stress disorder. A sudden attack can trigger the human "self-preservation" response. High levels of adrenaline and other stress hormones circulate through the blood, imprinting the experience in the brain. It may be replayed over and over, as the individual tries to blunt the horror through familiarity. This process may partly explain Marilyn's adult fixation with her childhood, her replaying of episodes from that childhood so often.

Recent research on trauma and memory suggests that she wouldn't retain a precise memory of a trauma that happened before the age of six because the memory region of the brain isn't mature at that age. By the age of eight, however, that region is more developed, able to record more accurate memories. Thus she didn't have a precise memory of the episode of sexual repression connected to Ida Bolender, but she remembered the sexual abuse visited on her by "Mr. Kimmel" when she was eight. In a diary fragment she wrote in 1955 she stated that she had accessed a memory of Aunt Ida punishing her for touching her genitals.[34]

According to experts on sexual abuse, abused girls may have nightmares about witches and demons. For much of her life Marilyn saw such figures in her dreams and daydreams. In 1952, on a visit to New York,

Sam Shaw took her to an exhibition of Goya's drawings of figures in the Napoleonic Wars in Spain at the Metropolitan Museum of Art. Shaw remembered, "When she saw Goya's black horrors of war and violence, witches on a broomstick flying through the night, she grabbed my arm and said, 'I know the man [Goya] very well; I had those dreams since I was a kid." She told Ralph Roberts, her personal masseur from 1958 until her death, that the demonic figures in her nightmares looked like the illustrations in Rossell Hope Robbins's 1959 *Encyclopedia of Witchcraft and Demonology*, which contains seventeenth-century drawings of witches and demons.[35]

Marilyn told *New York Post* entertainment columnist and friend Earl Wilson that she thought her chronic insomnia was caused by her dread of her nightmares. Wilson remembered her describing them as "horrendous dreams . . . of guilt. Frightening ghosts accusing her of the wrongs she'd done." Susan Strasberg wrote that the figures in Marilyn's dreams resembled figures from the paintings of Brueghel and Bosch—demons, orgies, the underworld. In a diary fragment written in 1956, when she was in London with Arthur Miller making *The Prince and the Showgirl*, she writes about lying in bed, unable to sleep. "On the screen of pitch blackness reappears the shape of monsters, my most steadfast companions."[36]

Some psychologists conclude that the "demons" in these dreams represent the attacker. They may also represent death, which can be threatening or alluring, promising a return to the preconscious state in the mother's womb. Marilyn told Ralph Greenson, her last psychiatrist, that the calm haze produced by the drugs she took—barbiturates like Seconal and Nembutal—made her feel "womby and tomby," a reference to a mother's womb and to a tomb holding a dead body.[37]

Marilyn's dreams of witches and demons suggest that the episode of abuse was traumatic and that she connected it to Christian beliefs about the devil and dark angels. Arthur Miller thought that she had a Puritan sense of sin. Louella Parsons, who was close to her, described her concept of "sin" as like that of the revivalist preachers of her childhood: hard and unrelenting. According to Earl Wilson, Marilyn's rape as a child left her with a stammer and the belief that all men wanted to bed her. Maurice Zolotow wrote, "She was obsessed by her guilt. She had committed the unpardonable sin. If she died she would go to hell. The terrors of her childhood return in twisted shapes, and as long as possible she resists sleep by reading or talking."[38] Her insomnia worsened as she grew older, and she took ever more pills to go to sleep.

In *My Story* Marilyn connected the assault to Christianity when she described a revival meeting her "aunt" forced her to attend after the attack. In her memory Mr. Kimmel was present at the meeting. When the revival preacher called on sinners to go to the altar and repent, Norma Jeane rushed up to tell the preacher about the episode of sexual abuse, which she called her "sin." But the other "sinners" around the altar wailed so loudly that they drowned her out. Then she saw Mr. Kimmel standing among the "non-sinners." He wasn't repenting for what he had done. He was praying for God to forgive the sins of others.

I interpret this story as a reflection on sin and guilt. The abuser blended into the congregation, while the victim was blocked from repentance and absolution. Her "aunt" made Norma Jeane attend the revival meeting, which suggests that the aunt considered her responsible for the attack. Yet Marilyn's recollection that she threw the nickel her abuser gave her in his face is important. It shows toughness under her fractured self, a place where she preserved a sense of self-worth. It is connected to the human "self-care system," an evolutionary mechanism designed for the survival of the species. The self can be sadistic, like the id in Freud's theory, but it can also be supportive. As humans we are capable of "mothering" ourselves.[39]

Fantasy is basic to the self-care system, where the ability to create a cocoon of dreams can nurture the individual, blunting a traumatic past and projecting a positive future. Marilyn often created fantasy worlds in which dissociation was curative. She moved through her childhood as the princess being wooed by the prince, the famous actress beloved by the world, the adored daughter of a father who looked like Clark Gable and was protective and caring. She often daydreamed about colors—red and crimson, gold and green—the colors of kings and queens in the fantasy world of children's fairy stories. In her bedroom she acted out all the parts in the movies she saw, creating another fantasy world for herself.

When she lived in the orphanage she could see the flashing sign on the RKO building, a radio tower atop a globe of the world, from her bedroom window. That sign, which was the studio's trademark, promoted RKO as a communicator of information to the world. Her mother had worked at RKO. Watching the sign, Norma Jeane thought of the smelly dark lab where Gladys cut and pasted films. Smell is the most primitive of the senses; remembering a smell brings into the mind a vivid snapshot of episodes connected to the smell. Norma Jeane rejected her negative image of the cutting lab by an act of will. Having done that, she saw the sign as the beacon to a promised land, a Hollywood inhabited, she said, by stars like Joan Crawford and Bette Davis. They were powerful women, called by film historians "fast-talking dames," similar to the perfect ladies of Gladys's imagination.[40]

Marilyn had a fantasy, she said, about wearing a hoop skirt and being naked in a church, walking over the bodies of the congregation as they lay on their backs and looked up at her with open eyes. That fantasy, with its sexual overtones, is another powerful dream of conquering the world. It seems the product of the Norma Jeane who threw the nickel back at her abuser and then cried all night when her foster mother wouldn't believe her. It also seems related to later episodes of exposing her genitals in public, another strategy to deal with the abuse by enacting it on a grand scale.

According to Arthur Miller, she regarded her body as possessed by men and as something that she had to bestow on them when they wanted it. She told screenwriter Nunnally Johnson that she gave sex to men as a "thank you" for favors. "I sometimes felt I was hooked on sex," she told W. J. Weatherby, "the way an alcoholic is hooked on liquor or a junkie on dope."[41] Despite her ladylike demeanor, what is now called sex addiction became an issue for her, although, as I will presently discuss, her belief in "free love" doctrines placed it in an acceptable context in her mind.

Norma Jeane's placement in so many foster homes and in an orphanage may have been excessive, but it wasn't necessarily exceptional among people with limited means in the 1930s, when unemployment was high and public welfare was limited. Most children in orphanages nationwide, like Norma Jeane, were "half orphans," with a father absent from their home and a mother without means. Their impoverished families intended to retrieve them when their financial situation improved. Most of the children in Marilyn's orphanage were half orphans.[42]

Contrary to Marilyn's belief, orphans weren't shunned by most

Americans. But children can be cruel to one another, sometimes stigmatizing any sign of difference. When Norma Jeane reported that other children in her schools taunted her as an "orphan," she was referring to children's meanness, not to social realities. Had her schoolmates known that her mother was in a mental institution, the taunting would probably have been even worse. Thus Norma Jeane claimed that her mother and father were dead and that she was an orphan, rather than divulging the true state of affairs. It was also in line with her feelings about her situation, with both a mother and a father absent from her life.

The fictionalized orphan Horatio Alger, who sold newspapers on New York streets, was a central character in the mythology of the American Dream. He was a symbol of the pluck and resilience of young Americans in the face of difficult odds. During the Great Depression, abandoned children on the streets and in orphanages were emblematic of the nation's suffering, of innocence threatened yet surviving. Orphan Annie, depicted in the hugely popular comic strip, became a national heroine. Child film star Shirley Temple, often motherless in her films, had a preternatural wisdom and an ability to solve problems that baffled adults.[43]

In September 1935, Grace placed Norma Jeane, then nine years old, in one of the best private orphanages in Los Angeles, the Children's Aid Society orphanage (later renamed Hollygrove). It was located in the center of Hollywood, only a few blocks from Grace's apartment on Lodi Drive. It had been founded in 1883 by a group of well-to-do Los Angeles women, following the example of many such groups of women throughout the nation. Located on a residential street close to RKO and Paramount, it housed about fifty children. It had an auditorium, a library, and—with five acres of land—playing fields, a swimming pool, and an organized sports program. Residents of the orphanage who lived there with Norma Jeane were unanimous in praising it. When Maurice Zolotow visited the orphanage in the late 1950s, he found it a model institution, with a large staff and a dorm mother for every ten children. The staff did the dishes and cleaned the bathrooms. The residents were required only to keep the dorms tidy and to set the tables for meals.[44]

According to orphanage records, Norma Jeane was docile and well mannered. Another resident who lived there at the same time remembered her as so generous that she gave other children anything of hers they wanted. There was a piano in the living room, and Norma Jeane sometimes played it. She had a well-coordinated, athletic body, and she was taller than most children her age. She became a star of the girls' softball team. But she was also withdrawn and sometimes frightened. Tall and gawky, she often reminded her friend of a doe caught in the lights of an oncoming automobile. Individuals close to the adult Marilyn often used that metaphor to describe her.[45]

Grace visited most weekends, taking Norma Jeane to the movies and then to a restaurant, as she or Gladys had for years. On one occasion she took Norma Jeane to a beauty parlor and had her hair curled into smooth ringlets. She put makeup on her face, although wearing makeup was against orphanage rules. Several weeks before that another girl in the orphanage had been disciplined for doing so. But the matron was kind to Norma Jeane. When she returned to the orphanage with the makeup still on, the matron patted her head, washed her face, and told her not to do it again. The matron knew about her background and her relationship with the redoubtable Grace.

Yet the orphanage represented betrayal and abandonment to Norma Jeane. She had been in too many foster homes and had adjusted to too many families. "When I came to the orphanage," she told George Barris, "it seemed that no one wanted me, not even my mother's best friend." She never forgot the evening Grace took her there. Her description of it never varied. When the car pulled up in front of the building and she saw the sign for the orphanage, she had an anxiety attack. "My heart began beating fast, then faster. I broke out in a cold sweat. I began to panic. I couldn't catch my breath."[46] As the incident of sexual abuse had the previous year, it triggered her survival syndrome—a rush of adrenaline and stress hormones in her blood—that imprinted it on her brain.

Then Norma Jeane, usually well behaved, threw a tantrum. When Grace asked her to get out of the car, she clutched the door handle. The orphanage attendants had to pry her hands off the handle and half-carry her into the building. "I'm not an orphan! I'm not an orphan!" she cried. Her next memory was of being in a dining room where a lot of children were eating dinner. Startled and humiliated, she stopped crying—and began stuttering.[47]

The orphanage became a Dickensian horror in Norma Jeane's memory. No matter how caring the orphanage staff was and how extensive the programs for the residents were, she didn't like it. She knew she had a mother, even though she claimed that her mother was dead. She wanted to live in a family, not in an institution like the mental hospital in which her mother lived. She had visited her mother at Norwalk State. She had seen her bed in a ward, with attendants watching her. She saw people listless in hallways, muttering to themselves; she knew about straitjackets and continuous water baths. When children see their parents in hospitals, they often become frightened.

Underneath her docility at the orphanage Norma Jeane had difficulty coping. "The world around me was kind of grim. I had to learn to pretend in order to block the grimness. The world seemed sort of closed to me. I felt on the outside of everything." Retreating from reality, she wrote a postcard to herself and signed it with the names of fictitious parents. She made a feeble attempt to escape but was soon found and taken back. She began to respond to the instability in her life by closing down her emotions. "I had learned not to bother anyone by talking or crying. I also learned that the best way to keep out of trouble was by never complaining or asking for anything." She cried herself to sleep at night.[48]

By the beginning of 1936 the orphanage staff was worried about her. She was anxious and withdrawn; she was stuttering; she came down with colds; she cried a lot. The orphanage didn't have the resources to give her the in-depth care she needed. The matron told Grace that Norma Jeane needed to be placed with a family. Grace realized that she had to do something. On February 26, 1936, she petitioned the Los Angeles Superior Court to become Norma Jeane's official guardian. Her petition was granted a month later. Grace made the last payment to the orphan home for Norma Jeane's care on June 21 and her first payment to herself in October 1936. She took Norma Jeane to live with her sometime that summer.[49] None of Doc's children was living with them; Bebe, Fritz, and Nona didn't move in with Doc and Grace until 1940.

In November 1937, a little over a year after the first payment of Norma Jeane's stipend to herself, Grace moved Norma Jeane again, this time to the home of Olive Monroe, the wife of Marion Monroe, Gladys's brother. Grace and Doc were living in the Hollywood Hills, while the Martin-Monroes lived in North Hollywood, over the Cahuenga Pass, not that far from the Goddards. Ida Martin, Olive's mother, owned the house they lived in. The situation in the Monroe family hadn't improved since Gladys broke down in 1934 and Grace rejected them as caregivers for

Norma Jeane. But Grace was at her wits' end. Olive's daughter, Ida Mae, was close to Norma Jeane in age, and the two girls might like being together. (Ida Mae told me that she found Grace controlling and mean. She didn't like her.)

Once Norma Jeane moved into their house, she and Ida Mae played together, slept in the same bed, and became confidantes for a while. They attempted to make wine in a barrel by stamping on grapes, producing only a mess; they spent days planning a trip to San Francisco to find Ida Mae's father, a trip they never took. In these adventures, they were pre-adolescent girls inventing fantasies together. But the Monroe-Martin family wasn't functioning well. Olive and Ida were angry with Marion for deserting them, and they were also angry at the court rule that the children couldn't go on relief stipends until ten years after his disappearance, when he could be officially declared dead. That year would be 1939. Grace was able to manipulate them into taking Norma Jeane, using the stipend as her tool.[50]

With two adults and Olive's three children—Ida Mae, Jack, and Olive—already living in Ida's house, it was overcrowded. The sullen Norma Jeane was another burden—although they received her half-orphan stipend. Norma Jeane didn't like living with them; they treated her as though she was unwanted. Ida Martin, who was in her seventies, told stories of having known Buffalo Bill and Wild Bill Hickok. Norma Jeane liked those stories, but she didn't seem able to please either Ida or Olive. In later years, the experience in the Monroe home became a major example of mistreatment in her stories, although she never mentioned them by name.

Why did Grace suddenly place Norma Jeane in this situation? It seems that she felt she had little choice. Shortly before the sudden move, Doc returned home drunk one night and attempted to fondle Norma Jeane as she lay sleeping in her bed. Norma Jeane awakened, and she ran to Grace to tell her what had happened. Grace's response was immediate: she moved Norma Jeane. She was committed to Doc; he and his family came first. Norma Jeane had to go. The Martin-Monroes, who needed money, didn't live far away. Grace could still oversee Norma Jeane. But by this point Norma Jeane had lived with five foster families: the Bolenders, Atkinsons, Giffens, Goddards, and now the Martin-Monroes, with the orphanage between the two periods she lived with Grace and Doc Goddard.

Yet Norma Jeane's saga didn't end once she moved in with the Martin-Monroes. In March 1938 the Los Angeles River overflowed its banks, severely damaging many houses in North Hollywood, including the Martin-Monroe home. (The river wasn't yet encased in concrete, as it is today, to prevent flooding.) All family members had to be relocated after the flood. Grace moved Norma Jeane on a temporary basis to the home of her friends Ruth and Alan Mills, who also lived in the San Fernando Valley, so that she could continue attending her North Hollywood school.[51]

When the school year ended, Grace moved her to another temporary location—the home of her brother, Bryan Atchinson, and his wife, Lottie, in the industrial city of Compton, on the east side of downtown Los Angeles, far from Hollywood and the San Fernando Valley. Norma Jeane hadn't liked living with the Martin-Monroe family, and she didn't like living with the Atchinsons. Lottie drove around Los Angeles County delivering the furniture polish her husband made to hardware stores, and she took Norma Jeane along with her, even though the child didn't want to go. Norma Jeane had motion sickness, but Lottie didn't pay any attention to her nausea. Norma Jeane's stay with Bryan and Lottie lasted from late June to September 1938. As she began junior high, she moved to the home of Ana Lower, Grace's aunt, where she lived on and off for the next four years.[52]

By the time she went to live with Ana Lower, Norma Jeane had lived with seven foster families: the Bolenders, the Atkinsons, the Giffens, Grace and Doc, the Martin-Monroes, the Millses, and the Atchinsons. Ana Lower would constitute an eighth foster mother. There was also the family of Reginald Carroll, Gladys's co-worker at Consolidated, who had wanted to adopt Norma Jean. Moreover, she stayed with several families for short periods of time between more permanent arrangements. These included the families of Sam and Enid Knebelkamp, Grace's sister and brother-in law, and Doris and Chester Howell, friends of Ana's. Both the Knebelkamps and the Howells lived in Westwood, not far from Ana. Both seemed like foster parents to Norma Jeane. She called Enid and Doris "Aunt," as though they were foster mothers.

In her early teenage years Norma Jeane often babysat the Howells' twin daughters, Loralee and Doralee. She went on excursions with the Howells, and she stayed overnight at their house, which was large, befit-

ting Chef Howell's position as a lawyer. Marilyn documentaries sometimes contain home-movie footage of her as a young teenager frolicking
on the beach with several younger children: that footage is of a Howell
family outing. Actor Howard Keel—then Harry Keel—was the son of
the Howells' housekeeper. He met Norma Jeane when she was thirteen
years old and dated her when she was living with the Howells. It was his
impression that she was staying there between foster homes.[53]

The total number of foster homes in which Norma Jeane lived now
stands at eleven. Marilyn often cited that number in interviews.[54] But she
never revealed that all her foster parents were either relatives or friends
of Grace Goddard—in fact, in her interviews she rarely mentions the
names of any foster parents. Rather, she implies that they were anonymous families to which the county welfare board assigned her. Marilyn
didn't want the real families bothered by the press, and she wanted her
childhood story to be as dramatic as possible. In fact, she knew every
foster family she lived with before she moved in with them. The county
welfare board allowed Grace to find foster families for Norma Jeane,
and she turned to her network of kin and friends to do so.

Possessing a strong survival drive, children often avoid displeasing
parents or adults on whom they depend. Thus some children aren't honest about their feelings—or they repress them. Moving from foster home
to foster home, having to adjust to new situations and family dynamics
so many times, was hard on Norma Jeane. Changing schools when she
moved was also difficult, as she entered new classrooms, dealt with new
teachers, and had to make new friends. Grace tried to keep her in the
same school when she moved her, but it wasn't always possible. Moving
schools increased her fears of abandonment and catastrophic destruction. She never lost those fears.

But the moving also made her shrewd and manipulative. In describing Marilyn to a reporter, Nona Goddard drew on her own experience
of having lived in foster homes. "Once you've been in a couple, you've
had it. You become cagey, cynical, and you know how to get the most out
of people." Louella Parsons wrote that Marilyn's youth "had taught her
to be self-contained, self-assertive, and always self-protective, but it had
brought with it a brashness that was too often taken for hardness."
"When you're an orphan," Marilyn told Susan Strasberg, "you kind of

have to learn how to get what you need to survive."[55] The adult Marilyn was a mix of people, and one of them was the manipulative child from the foster homes.

Throughout her childhood, Norma Jeane refused to criticize Grace. She knew that she was a "charity case" and the daughter of a "paranoid schizophrenic," and she considered herself lucky that Grace paid attention to her. Besides, Grace was fun. Norma Jeane was cheered up experiencing her optimism, bubbling energy, friendliness to everyone, and contagious laugh. Grace lived a complex life, filled with dreams and schemes, and Norma Jeane easily got caught up in them. According to Bebe Goddard, Grace was nonjudgmental. You could tell her anything, Bebe said, and she would be sympathetic. She was affectionate and jokey, with a smile on her face and a kind word for everyone. In *My Story* Marilyn called Grace her "best friend."[56]

Marilyn claimed that if Doc hadn't appeared in Grace's life, Grace wouldn't have placed her in the orphanage and the later foster homes. Grace, out of work, couldn't afford to support Doc, herself, and Norma Jeane plus whatever child-support payments Doc made. Yet that claim is questionable. In 1935, the *Los Angeles Times* reported that Grace was the film librarian at Columbia. The 1936 *Los Angeles City Directory* listed her as still holding that position. The 1937 directory listed only her address, with no notation about employment.[57] Grace's income was stable in 1935 and 1936, but she lost her job in 1937. She then had to scramble to make ends meet. Marilyn's stories of standing in bread lines with Grace and having to skimp on food and clothing happened in 1937, not earlier.

In Ben Hecht's notes from his interviews with Marilyn for her proposed autobiography, she states that she accepted Grace's explanation for her actions: because of her stepchildren she could do more for Norma Jeane. Besides, without Grace's intervention she might have been placed in a dreadful public orphanage, worse than the private one Grace found for her. "I always knew she loved me," Marilyn told Hecht. "I could trust anything she'd say. I called her up whenever I was depressed. She was my confidante."[58] When Hecht wrote down these comments, Grace had died only several months prior. A grieving Marilyn may have overstated her reliability.

On Grace's 1953 death certificate, the official cause of death is suicide.

Indeed, she took an overdose of Nembutal because she had terminal liver cancer. Her years of heavy drinking as a flapper and her marriage to a man who drank caught up with her. Marilyn paid for Grace's burial in the Westwood Memorial Cemetery and Mortuary where Marilyn and other Goddard family members are buried. In unpublished comments to Hecht, Marilyn described in loving detail Grace's appearance as her dead body lay in a coffin in the mortuary viewing room. It was dark in the room, with light coming only from candles placed around the coffin. The flowers that Marilyn had sent were there, in the purples, oranges, and browns that were Grace's favorite colors. At first the corpse frightened Marilyn and she couldn't look at it, but she remembered how Grace had loved her and that gave her courage. Reaching down, she adjusted the white scarf around Grace's neck and fluffed up her hair, caressing her skin.

It's quite a testimony to a woman who was a puppet master pulling the strings that moved the child Norma Jeane all over Los Angeles, living in eleven foster homes and an orphanage. Grace was kind and loving, but she was also controlling, as she had been throughout her relationships with Gladys and Norma Jeane, determining their lives, deciding what to do with them. Until she reached the heights of Hollywood stardom, Norma Jeane/Marilyn didn't like to criticize anyone, and Grace was the closest version to a mother she had in much of her childhood. Yet Jim Dougherty, like Ida Mae Monroe, didn't like Grace. He thought she never did anything that wasn't in her own best interests.

Families are never simple. They can enter new phases, welcoming new people into their circle—and they can just as easily fall apart. A family chronicler can discover new material that revises existing narratives. Like many individuals in Norma Jeane's life, Grace's sister Enid Knebelkamp, whom Norma Jeane and Grace often visited, suffered from bouts of depression. She feared dying in childbirth, as a sister of hers had, and she continually talked about it, imprinting her own death narrative in Norma Jeane's memory. She converted to Catholicism. In a family drawn to Christian Science, that action amounted to a declaration of independence.[59] In contrast to Enid, her husband, Sam, was a trickster who told jokes all the time. Norma Jeane loved his jokes, the way he could bring joy into dark situations.

Then in the mid-1940s, Doc's ex-wife appeared in Los Angeles from

Austin, Texas, apparently cured of her mental issues. She was now the wife of the chief of staff of an army engineering unit stationed near Los Angeles. Nona Goddard lived with her and, after a year at Beverly Hills High School, attended the prestigious Hollywood Professional School, anticipating an acting career. In the early 1950s Nona became a featured player at Columbia under the name Jody Lawrance.[60]

But she and Marilyn, friendly as adolescents, grew distant as adults, as Jody (born Josephine and called Nona) rejected the entire Goddard family. According to Bebe, Nona was perpetually angry. She decided that Doc and Grace preferred Norma Jeane to her, and she wrote Grace a nasty letter in 1953 about feeling rejected by them. That letter, according to Bebe, was the reason that Grace committed suicide that year. I've read the letter, and it is nasty, although Grace was already dying from cancer when she took the overdose of Nembutal that killed her. In harsh language in the letter, Nona blames Grace and Doc for the repossession of her house by the bank because the two of them refused to lend her money for mortgage payments. She claims that they always preferred Norma Jeane to her and concludes by saying that she never wants to see them again.[61]

Marilyn is feminine in her films, with strong elements of parody and independence in many of her characterizations, but Nona/Jody Lawrance is a spitfire, sometimes engaging in physical battles with lovers, even disguising herself as a man in *The Mask of the Avenger* (1951), her first film. She has talent, but she looks like the other dark-haired featured players of the day. Unlike Marilyn, Jody was unable to carve out a distinctive look for herself. As she aged, she faded from the screen.

A home movie of Norma Jeane with Grace, Doc, and other family members was made in the early 1940s. The film begins on a moving train and then cuts to a group of people clowning in front of a house. Three adolescent girls in the movie are modeling fur coats. Bob Herre, Nona's son, told me that they are Bebe, Norma Jeane, and Nona and that Grace and Doc are in the film, which celebrated Fritz Goddard's return home by train after having served in the military during World War Two. The home movie further confuses the story of the Goddard family. Bob told me that his grandmother, Eleanor Goddard, owned the furs featured in the film. She was the presumably demented ex-wife of Doc who had put their children in abusive homes. It's surprising that she, Doc, and their children would become friendly, clowning for the camera in a home movie. Nonetheless, it's possible.

Between the ages of nine and twelve—from the time she entered the orphanage until she moved in with Ana Lower—Norma Jeane was far from a beauty. That lack of beauty influenced her perception of herself, even as an adult. As with many preadolescents, Norma Jeane's body prepared for the hormonal rush and physiological rearrangements of adolescence by becoming gawky and out of proportion. By the age of ten she shot up to her adult height of five feet six inches, making her much taller than other children her age. She had a straight body and was flat-chested, with short and scraggly hair. She looked like a boy.[62] Previous Marilyn biographers have overlooked this development, which is evident in photographs taken of her during these years. Moreover, she rarely smiles in those photos; she looks depressed.

The years between nine and twelve were unhappy ones for Norma Jeane. Her elementary school classmates made fun of her, calling her "Norma Jeane, string bean" or "Norma Jeane, human bean." The girls made remarks about her clothing, which wasn't of the best quality. When she told the other students she intended to be an actress, they laughed. Ida Mae Monroe remembered Norma Jeane telling her over and over again that she wasn't going to get married when she grew up; she was going to be a schoolteacher and raise dogs. Like many tall and gawky preteen girls, she took up athletics as a way of gaining distinction. She had excellent hand-eye coordination, a relatively large frame, and long legs for a girl her age—in other words, she was a natural athlete. "I was an excellent athlete," she told Georges Belmont. At the orphanage, she was an outstanding player on the girls' softball team, and at the North Hollywood school she attended, she ran long-distance races.[63]

Defining Marilyn as an athlete may seem startling, given her later aversion to sports, but her athletic ability, in addition to the exercise regimens she pursued for years, stood her in good stead when she became a film actress. If you look closely at her body in films like *Gentlemen Prefer Blondes* you can see her muscles. Her leg muscles are evident in the photo with her skirt blowing up from *The Seven Year Itch*.

Until she was elected the "Oomph Girl" at Emerson Junior High in 1941, Norma Jeane didn't think that she was beautiful. Even then, she still felt that her appearance was imperfect. She retained that point of view even when she was celebrated as the most beautiful woman in the world. There was always the bump on her nose (cosmetic surgery didn't eliminate it entirely); legs too short for the fashion ideal; and a heavy chin. She spent hours in rituals of self-adornment, but she disliked her body at the same time.[64]

After Norma Jeane's unhappy stay with the Martin-Monroe family, and her obvious depression, Grace had to do something special to figure out the puzzle of what to do with her. She had developed over the years from a joyful, loving child to a sullen, depressed preadolescent. The solution in the form of her aunt, Ana Lower, had been there for a long time. A special bond already existed between Norma Jeane and Ana, and the child had spent an occasional Sunday with her. But Ana had a heart condition, and she felt she couldn't handle raising a child. Still, Grace had run out of friends and relatives willing to take in Norma Jeane. Given the child's depression and the issues with Doc, Ana felt duty bound to do it. She was a healer in the Christian Science Church who helped people cope with physical illness and emotional depression. And Norma Jeane badly needed healing.

So in September 1938, at the beginning of the school year, Norma Jeane went to live with Ana Lower. The experience would change her life, this time much for the better.

Chapter 3

Transcendence: Ana and Jim, 1938–1944

In Ana Lower, Grace finally found an effective foster mother for Norma Jeane. The matriarch of Grace's extended family, Ana was fifty-eight years old when Grace's ward went to live with her. Ana was dignified and loving. Bebe Goddard described her as a "picture-perfect white-haired grandmother," even though she was only fifty-eight—an age then considered old. She was also shrewd and practical. The initials "C.S.," she said, meant Christian Science, but they also meant common sense. Like Grace, she was nonjudgmental, but she wasn't controlling and manipulative, as Grace was. She radiated what could be called spirituality, a sense of being in tune with nature and herself, a state of contentment apparent to anyone who met her.[1]

She didn't wear jewelry or fashionable clothing; material possessions didn't interest her. By 1925 the *Christian Science Journal* listed her as a practitioner (healer), certified to counsel people who needed emotional or physical help, using the Bible and Mary Baker Eddy's *Science and Health*, the church's major texts, as guides. She would eventually convert Grace and Gladys, as well as other Atchinsons and Goddards, to Christian Science. Ana was dedicated to helping others. Once a week she went to the Los Angeles jail to give Christian Science healings to the inmates.

Married and divorced twice, Ana had no children of her own. She lived in the second-floor apartment of a duplex she owned in the Sawtelle area of West Los Angeles, not far from the Knebelkamps and the Howells, who were relatives and friends of Grace and Ana with whom

Norma Jeane had occasionally stayed. In her second divorce Ana had been awarded the duplex and several small houses, although she wasn't wealthy. The rents on her properties were low, and her healings were often free. Sawtelle was solidly working class. It was known for its many Japanese residents, who had nurseries and truck farms and tended the lawns and gardens in the nearby wealthy communities of Bel Air and Brentwood. Mexican families who worked for the Japanese gardeners also lived in the area.[2] Even today Sawtelle Boulevard in West Los Angeles has a number of Japanese restaurants and nurseries on it.

The Sawtelle population—whether Anglo-American, Japanese, or Mexican—was hardworking and family-centered. Dorothy Muir, the mother of Bob Muir, Norma Jeane's first boyfriend, lived in Sawtelle. She bridled when Marilyn biographers described it as a slum. The homes there were modest, she said, but they were owner-occupied and well cared for. In the class-conscious society of Los Angeles's West Side, however, Sawtelle was considered lower class. Because Norma Jeane lived there, she wasn't accepted at first at the school she attended, Emerson Junior High School, located in an upscale area of Westwood, with students from Bel Air and Brentwood. Those students set the school's tone. "I came from the poor part of the district," Marilyn stated in *My Story*, "where all the Mexicans and Japanese lived."[3]

That fall, Gladys Baker suddenly reentered her life. Gladys's condition had improved. She was still a patient in Agnews State Hospital near San Jose, after having lived in a group home in San Francisco for a time, but she was hoping to leave the state mental system and return to regular life. Gladys wrote Grace in the fall of 1938, asking her to tell Norma Jeane about her half-sister, Berniece, now nineteen and recently married. Norma Jeane hadn't known she existed. Gladys had visions of reconstituting her family, as she had in 1933, when she and Norma Jeane moved into the Arbol Drive house. Norma Jeane was hopeful; she hadn't given up on her mother. Wanting a family of her own, she was happy to learn about Berniece. They began to correspond. Now that she was living with Ana Lower and was in touch with her half-sister, Norma Jeane's life seemed to have stabilized.

During her first year with Ana, Norma Jeane was still gawky and tall. Former Emerson students remembered her early on as "neat but plain" and "shy and withdrawn." She didn't talk much in classes, and her grades were mediocre. When she spoke, she sometimes stuttered. Some students made fun of her clothes. Grace bought her two blue suits before she entered Emerson, and she alternated them during the year. Her classmates concluded that she owned only one piece of clothing—a cardinal sin in this upper-class school. She wore tennis shoes to save money, and that was also unacceptable.[4]

Like many Los Angeles middle schools, Emerson was large, with five hundred students per grade. Given the size, it was difficult for a student to know many classmates. And it took time until the popularity system characteristic of middle and high schools was in place. Student government leaders, class beauties, and athletes had to emerge. During her first year at Emerson, many students shunned Norma Jeane, as they had in elementary school. Yet William Moynier, who was in several classes with her, remembered her as "giggly" and "friendly"; she was beginning to open up in some situations.[5]

Norma Jeane wasn't a loner. She made friends with Gladys Wilson, another Sawtelle student at Emerson, and she became friends with a group of older Emerson students. As an adult, Marilyn had separate groups of friends that she kept apart from one another. Such separation gave her a sense of control and allowed her to be secretive, conducting different lives at the same time. The beginning of this behavior, like other behaviors of hers, emerged in junior high. It's not uncharacteristic of children who have been institutionalized.

Soon after entering Emerson, Norma Jeane became friends with Bob Muir, a student who was a grade ahead of her. In 1973 Dorothy Muir, Bob's mother, published an account of their friendship, unknown to previous Marilyn biographers.[6] Bob had a circle of male friends at Emerson drawn from boys he had known in elementary school. Now in junior high, they were interested in girls. Wanting to maintain their group while dating, each boy identified a girl he considered special and brought her along with him when the group got together. Bob Muir brought Norma Jeane.

Over the next several years she was often at the Muir house. Bob's group played Monopoly or danced in the living room, with the rug pulled back and a record on the phonograph. Norma Jeane was the youngest person in the group, but she was the best dancer. They went on hikes in the nearby Santa Monica Mountains and to the more distant San

Bernardino Mountains in the winter to play in the snow. In the spring they went to the desert to see wildflowers in bloom. Norma Jeane was bubbly, telling jokes about herself. Dorothy Muir remembered her as a "sweet girl we all grew to love." She was unusually mature and sympathetic to others, although she avoided discussing anything personal. Dorothy knew only that she lived with her aunt in Sawtelle. Eventually she stopped going to the Muir house. Dorothy heard she was dating an "older guy," probably Jim Dougherty.

During her first year at Emerson, when she was twelve years old, Norma Jeane began to menstruate. By the summer that followed, her breasts and hips had grown in size, and she attracted boys. Realizing her appeal, she devised a strategy to become popular—or at least noticed. In a version of her later campaign for screen popularity, she mocked current fashions by wearing them in an unique way. The "sweater girl" look, launched by Lana Turner when she wore a tight sweater in the 1937 film *They Won't Forget*, was coming into vogue. But it hadn't yet reached Emerson.

Norma Jeane devised a way to copy the new style. Teenage girls in this era often wore a front-buttoned cardigan sweater over a white blouse with a Peter Pan (round) collar. Norma Jeane eliminated the blouse as well as the bra and camisole worn under it. She then took a cardigan, turned it around, and buttoned it in the back. The sweater clung to her breasts, achieving the "sweater girl" style. She called that sweater, which was red, her "magic sweater." She had outfoxed her female classmates, showing a cleverness at dress that would remain characteristic of her. Then she put on a pair of tight blue jeans. When the principal warned her they were immodest, she substituted a tight skirt for the pants. Shocking the girls and intriguing the boys, she put on a lot of makeup, following the methods Grace had taught her.[7]

Her primping paid off. Emerson boys began walking her home and vying for her attention. When her name was mentioned in a class, the boys in the class sometimes breathed a collective sigh, "Mmmm." Even the girls noticed her, since she was winning the competition among them for boys—an important part of their culture. As graduation approached, she was elected the school's "Oomph Girl." "Norma Jeane the human bean" had become an acclaimed beauty.[8] If Aunt Ana had known what she was doing, she probably would have put a stop to it, but her foster child had learned during her years in foster homes and the orphanage how to be secretive. She arrived at school early, taking her makeup with her and putting it on in the girls' bathroom before classes began and taking it off before she went home.

Norma Jeane displayed other skills. She began to show an appealing wit, often directed at herself. Her humor was "cute," Bebe Goddard remembered, and it "popped out" unexpectedly. Despite her poor grades, she was a good writer and she contributed articles to the school newspaper, including one on the ideal dream girl for men. She claimed she had sent out five hundred questionnaires on the subject. The results proved that men preferred blondes. "Gentlemen prefer blondes!" she exclaimed, copying the title of the 1925 Anita Loos novella. (In 1953 she would star in the movie *Gentlemen Prefer Blondes*, based on the Loos work.) Referring to herself, Norma Jeane described the dream girl as having honey-blonde hair, blue eyes, a molded figure, classic features, a good personality, and athletic ability—while retaining her femininity. She was also a loyal friend.[9]

By her last year at Emerson, when she was fifteen, her reputation and her grades had improved. She developed a passion for Abraham Lincoln when she studied his life in a class. She identified with his impoverished upbringing in rural Kentucky and the death of his mother when he was young; she liked his democratic attitudes and his identification with ordinary people. His physical appearance—dark and rugged—appealed to her. He became another father figure for her.

Yet she nearly failed her class in rhetoric and spoken arts because she couldn't get her words out. Despite her growing confidence, she still stuttered. When she was chosen secretary of her English class her last year at Emerson and had to read the minutes of the previous meeting aloud, she stumbled. She got stuck on the letter "m," finally blurting out "M-m-m-minutes of the last m-m-m-meeting." In the graduation yearbook she was one of twenty-six students representing the letters of the alphabet. She chose the letter "M" for herself, and she wrote her own caption—"Norma Jeane, the 'mmm girl.'" It was a wry comment on both her stuttering and her increasing appeal to boys.[10]

During her years at Emerson, she wasn't involved in athletics. She sang in the glee club and was cast in several plays, mostly in boys' parts—as a prince in one—because she was so tall. But she wasn't successful at acting because she stuttered when speaking on stage. That failure didn't end her aspirations to become an actress. She continued to go to the movies and to act out the roles in them in her bedroom at home, paying attention to body movements and facial expressions. Establishing a habit she later followed, she practiced in front of a mirror until she got every gesture right. Figuring out that the mind can control facial expressions as well as body movements, she had stumbled on a Hollywood acting technique. According to her close friend, photographer Sam Shaw, in later years she often practiced leg, arm, and facial movements in front of mirrors.[11]

She pored over the stars' images in the movie fan magazines passed on to her by a neighbor, becoming familiar with "every gesture, every plucked eyebrow, every dewy eye." She clipped pictures of Ginger Rogers from those magazines and tacked them on her bedroom walls. At one point she had twenty-four Gingers tacked up. Gladys Wilson thought she lived in a dream world, but she was also calculating her future. She noticed that many film actresses had been models before they entered films. She put together a plan; she would first model and then act in films. But she was too shy to do anything more than dream about it at this point in her life.[12]

In addition to Ginger Rogers films, she saw films starring Joan Crawford and Bette Davis. Crawford and Davis had headed the list of actresses in the fantasy land of her imagination at the orphanage.[13] Even in her early fantasies about stardom, Norma Jeane saw herself as a serious actress, not just a pinup girl.

Beyond schoolwork, dating, and going to the movies, Norma Jeane had a life with Ana Lower, who was with her before and after school and on the weekends. Ana was able to lift her spirits. She encouraged her foster child to read aloud to improve her diction, and she praised her singing and even her whistling. (Norma Jeane had a loud whistle.) She listened while Norma Jeane played the piano. Deciding that she needed a life goal, Ana encouraged her aspirations to become a film star. When she came home one day crying because the girls at school had made fun of her clothes, Ana soothed her by telling her that what the girls said about her didn't matter, what mattered was how she felt about herself.[14]

Above all, Ana introduced Norma Jeane to Christian Science, taking her to Science Sunday services and sometimes Wednesday evening meetings. The services included singing hymns and listening to readings from the Bible and Mary Baker Eddy's *Science and Health*. They were restrained, without a minister, a sermon, or the emotionalism of evangelical church services. At Wednesday evening meetings members testified about healing experiences. Norma Jeane and Ana read *Science and Health* aloud together in the evenings. The church became an important part of Norma Jeane's life; meditating on *Science and Health* helped her to find purpose and meaning.[15]

Mary Baker Eddy founded the Church of Christ, Scientist in 1879. For many years she had been an invalid who suffered from mood swings and indeterminate pain; she was a nineteenth-century "hysterical woman." By reading the Bible and asserting her will, she managed to take control over her illness, forging a powerful personality in the process. She wrote *Science and Health* and turned herself into a charismatic healer and leader, the founder of a major religion. She was a role model for women, and that would matter in Norma Jeane's life.

Eddy was a voracious reader, without much formal education. As a result, *Science and Health* is a sprawling text. Filled with Eddy's passion, however, it is inspirational. Its looseness encourages meditating on it to understand it, reading passages slowly until they make sense. In writing *Science and Health*, Eddy relied on the Bible, riffing on its meaning. She was also influenced by nineteenth-century mystical thinkers like the transcendentalists, who drew from Hindu and Sufi thinkers to posit that a spiritual connection existed between nature, the universe, and the individual. Norma Jeane, schooled in evangelical spirituality, was attracted to the mysticism implicit in Christian Science, as Eddy concluded that spirit is so powerful that the material world doesn't exist. Spirit, emanating from God, is the only reality and God is defined by love. Flowing through the cosmos, God's love is available to everyone. To become a whole person, one has only to access that force and apply it in one's life.

In Eddy's universe, death and the devil, heaven and hell don't exist; they are illusions. There is no such thing as "original sin," passed down to all humans because of Adam and Eve's violation of God's command not to eat the apple on the Tree of Knowledge in the Garden of Eden. Guilt is a futile human emotion. Christ didn't die on the cross to vindicate human sins; rather, his life is a model for humans to follow. And if reality is illusion, then illness doesn't exist, and doctors and drugs are unnecessary. Mind can overcome the material world, and anything is possible. To confound her detractors and link her ideas to modernity, Eddy used the word "science" in the name of her religion.

Christian Science doctrines propose that individuals can attain the grace of God's love through reading and meditating on *Science and Health* and Eddy's other texts. Reading is so important that separate reading rooms, with chairs, tables, and bookshelves containing those books, are built, usually close to Christian Science churches. Norma Jeane recommended the reading rooms to her half-sister, Berniece Miracle, calling them "little libraries."[16]

Members become practitioners by taking a brief course with a successful healer and documenting three successful healings to the church board in Boston. The board then lists their names and addresses in the *Christian Science Journal.* Healers recruit people to the church and counsel individuals in physical and emotional crisis. But they aren't psychiatrists: they help individuals align mind, body, and spirit with God's love through prayer and reading *Science and Health*.

By the 1920s, Christian Science was a major religion in Los Angeles. It had large congregations and church buildings that rivaled in size those of the evangelical churches. Many still stand. Then, as now, the church's membership was largely female. It had many features that appealed to female worshippers. Mary Baker Eddy's god is both female and male. The central church in Boston is called the "mother church." The majority of its practitioners have always been women. In his study of Los Angeles religion in the early twentieth century, Gregory Singleton found that the transfers from evangelical Christianity to Christian Science were mostly women, many of them divorced.[17] Grace Goddard, Gladys Baker, and Ana Lower each had been divorced twice. Like Della Monroe, who joined Aimee Semple McPherson's church, they turned to a religion of women after men disappointed them.

After a year with Ana, Norma Jeane's mood improved considerably. Her humor emerged; she had learned from Sam Knebelkamp, Grace Goddard's brother-in-law, how to joke as a way of coping with life and pleasing others. She developed a winning laugh, joy and playfulness, and the same sense of curiosity that Wayne Bolender had seen in her as a child. A natural mimic, she was influenced by Grace Goddard's "sparkling characteristics."[18] Grace covered over discontent with laughter. Norma Jeane did the same.

She also internalized Ana Lower's dignity and spirituality, generating her own ability to charm. She later stated that Ana had been the most positive influence on her in her childhood. "She changed my whole life. She was a wonderful human being. She showed me the path to the higher things of life and she gave me more confidence in myself. She never hurt me, not once. She couldn't. She was all kindness and love." She and Ana became like a mother and daughter. "I can't help calling [you] cousin," a relative of Ana's later wrote Marilyn, "because dear aunt Ana—my favorite aunt, considered you her girl."[19]

Nonetheless, Norma Jeane's underlying issues didn't go away—the demons in her dreams, her shyness and insecurity, her deep sensitivity. She would later maintain that her sweet, giggly personality was a facade she developed to hide the terror inside her. She made fun of herself, she said, before others could make fun of her. Both Grace and Ana had experienced difficulties: alcoholic husbands, the lack of children, financial setbacks. Ana had turned to Christian Science to put her life together, and it had worked. Her serenity was achieved through struggle and asserting her will. She was an example to Norma Jeane. In 1939 Grace Goddard joined the church, a commitment that acknowledged its importance to her. In 1944, at age eighteen, Norma Jeane followed their example and joined the church.

She didn't have temper tantrums during the years with Ana. Focused on healing, meditating daily with Ana, she wasn't plagued by anger, which would slowly emerge as she delved deeply inside herself to become an actress and a mature human being. She had shut down her emotions as a child and now, with Ana, she was beginning to open them up. Under the impetus of Christian Science, the positive parts of her split self emerged first. Her air of innocence remained a part of her self, as well as a maturity beyond her years. She developed the ability to look people in the eye—a remarkable achievement, since many shy individuals can't do that. Eyes are a major means of human communication. We express emotions through our eyes, exert control over others through them, hide ourselves behind them. Norma Jeane had beautiful, large blue eyes; when she focused them intently on others she could mesmerize them. She transmitted an extreme vulnerability through her eyes, a vulnerability that made people want to help her. She was the child that is in everyone, expressing the hurt and longing we all feel, needing to be loved and nurtured.

To a Christian Scientist anything is possible through God's love; the "power of positive thinking" connects to divinity. Without Christian Science, Norma Jeane wouldn't have had the nerve to try for stardom. With the positive attitude Ana taught her and the power transmitted through Ana's healing, Norma Jeane was able to access the tough and determined part of her self. Her antimaterialist attitudes, her dislike of jewelry, her love of nature, her lack of concern about money, wanting only to be "wonderful"—these ideas came from Ana Lower.

Christian Scientists consider themselves rational, not mystical. That stance is apparent in a letter Ana wrote to Norma Jeane in 1944. Norma Jeane had gone to Detroit to meet her half-sister, Berniece Miracle, and to Chicago to see Grace, who was living there for a time. On the train ride she suffered from motion sickness, and she wrote Ana asking for help. In the letter Ana sent in reply, she called the motion sickness "nonsense." You do not cease to be God's perfect child because you take a train ride, Ana wrote. Norma Jeane's self-control was out of alignment and it needed fixing. God's love was always present. "I'll pray God to so fill your consciousness with his presence that there will be no room for error." In Ana's Christian Science view, Norma Jeane's anxiety didn't exist. "The divine understanding reigns, is all, and there is no other consciousness."[20]

Christian Science had other impacts on Norma Jeane. Despite its claims to rationality, there is a mysticism inherent in connecting to the "divine understanding," a state that can produce emotional highs. At peak moments in life, the brain can produce a feeling of oneness with the universe. Freud called it the "oceanic feeling"; Jung called it "the numinous." It's not surprising that Norma Jeane, raised in an evangelical religion and then in Christian Science, experienced transcendent highs.

It first happened in 1940 when she was fourteen and in her second year at Emerson. Her body had developed; she had made new friends. She went to the beach with a boyfriend, wearing a skimpy bathing suit for the first time. It was a sunny day, and the beach was crowded. She felt as though she were in a dream. She stared at the ocean. It was full of gold and lavender colors, blue and foaming white. Everybody on the beach seemed to be smiling at the sky. Then she walked down to the water's edge. Young men followed her, and they whistled at her. But she paid no attention. In fact, she didn't hear them. "I was full of a strange feeling, as if I were two people. One of them was Norma Jeane from the orphanage, who belonged to nobody. The other was someone whose name I didn't know. But I knew where she belonged. She belonged to the ocean and the sky and the whole world."[21] It was out of that passion and sense of empowerment that the actress we know as Marilyn Monroe would be born.

There were downsides in Christian Science for Norma Jeane, especially its ban on taking medicine for illness. After she began menstruating in the fall of 1938, she suffered severe menstrual cramps and irregular periods. As a Christian Scientist, she wasn't supposed to take even aspirin for pain. In fact, she suffered from endometriosis, a condition where the uterine lining grows outside the uterus, resulting in great pain during menstruation. Exactly when she was diagnosed with the condition is unclear. Endometriosis can't be diagnosed vaginally and often worsens over time; in the 1950s it would have only been diagnosed by abdominal surgery. The scar above her pubic hair in the drawing of her body at the time of her autopsy indicates that at some point the abdominal surgery was performed, probably not before her mid-twenties. (Jim Dougherty contended that her menstrual pains weren't that bad during their marriage.) The abdominal incision could subsequently be reopened to access the interior of the abdomen and cut out endometriosis.[22]

Endometriosis often causes pain during intercourse. Opening the incision to remove the endometriosis can cause the formation of scar tissue, which can also cause pain. Marilyn was often hospitalized over the years for operations; the first one occurred on November 4, 1953. The newspapers usually described these operations as gynecological procedures, and sometimes as "cleaning out the fallopian tubes." That is a misleading term that can mean many things, including removing detritus left from a miscarriage or an abortion. It can also mean surgical treatment for an infection produced by gonorrhea or chlamydia.[23]

Marilyn told actor Robert Mitchum, who had been Jim Dougherty's workmate at Lockheed Aircraft and became a friend of hers in Hollywood, that whenever she was in crisis, her period began. She made the same statement to Henry Rosenfeld, a New York manufacturer of clothing who was a close friend. On the other hand, she told both Mitchum and Rosenfeld she could go for months without a period. In later years she had false pregnancies, when her body assumed the physical symptoms of pregnancy, without the existence of a fetus.[24] Such a condition is unusual, but not unknown. Thus even Marilyn's magical body, the body of the world's great sex queen, was riddled with paradox. Externally flawless, it was flawed in its internal anatomy, requiring surgical procedures to make her whole.

Like her mother she was proud, and she thought of herself as a lady. Aside from close friends, she kept her menstrual and reproductive issues to herself. Ralph Roberts claimed that she had a clause in her contract stating that she didn't have to perform if she had her period, but it may have been a separate agreement, since such a clause isn't in her Twentieth Century-Fox contract.[25] Her later vomiting and tendency to nervous disorders like hives and skin rashes, in addition to false pregnancies, seems to indicate that Marilyn's body was especially sensitive to her emotional state.

By the age of eighteen, Norma Jeane was taking drugs for pain—often codeine with aspirin, sometimes stronger medications. Barbiturates had been prescribed to Grace Goddard, who had a heart condition as well as cancer of the liver and needed to be calmed down. Grace gave some to Norma Jeanne, although they aren't a medication for pain. They eventually caused a serious addiction problem for her, as she took them for insomnia and general anxiety once she encountered the rigors of film shooting schedules.

It was hard for Norma Jeane to remain faithful to Christian Science, given its strictures on taking medicine. And its negative views on sexual intercourse created other issues for her. Sex outside of marriage is wrong, according to *Science and Health*, and physical passion within marriage should be controlled. Mary Baker Eddy was a Victorian woman, influenced by the Victorian spiritualization of sex and by the belief that the male sex drive needed to be constrained. "The senses confer no real enjoyment," she wrote in *Science and Health*. "The harmony between man and woman is in spiritual oneness. The broadcast powers of evil so conspicuous today show themselves in the materialism and sensualism of the age. Spirit will ultimately claim its own, all that really is, and the voices of physical sense will be forever hushed."[26] Ana Lower and her

Christian Science doctrines liberated Norma Jeane while constraining her. Her mind was freed by its discourse about spirituality, which brought her transcendent experiences. But her adolescent body was restrained from sex.

Yet Christian Science neither barred Hollywood film people from its churches nor attacked the industry's liberal sexual behavior. Many film people were attracted to the church because of its validation of ambition and its focus on practical measures to achieve personal serenity, which was appealing to individuals in an industry prone to anxiety, where failure was common. Mary Pickford, Ginger Rogers, Jean Harlow, Joan Crawford, Doris Day, and others attended Christian Science churches. Joan Crawford and Marilyn first met at a Christian Science church. But its restraints on sexual expression ratified Norma Jeane's guilt over the sexual abuse she had undergone, no matter how Ana tried to teach her how to neutralize that guilt. Those constraints gave her pause about the sexual practices standard in the day's dating scene and pointed her toward marrying the first appropriate man. It was a complex mixture to absorb as she moved toward adulthood.

By her last year at Emerson, Norma Jeane was dating a number of boys, not just Bob Muir. Like Bob, they were mostly older than she. She went dancing and to the movies with them. She roughhoused with them on the beach, but she didn't permit them liberties with her body. "The boys knew better than to get fresh with me," she stated. Even after a date, "the most they could expect was a good-night kiss." Because of her sexy clothing, the students at Emerson called her "racy," but they considered her a "good girl." She followed the precepts of Christian Science, but even at fourteen, she pushed the bounds of what might be considered appropriate. She started dating Harry Keel after meeting him at the Howells'. Already attracted to older men, she developed a crush on him. Twenty-three years old in 1940 and an aspiring Hollywood actor, he was attracted to her, but he rejected her because she wasn't yet sixteen, the legal age of sexual consent. At fourteen she was, in his eyes, "jail bait." His rejection hurt; she cried for several weeks after he stopped seeing her.[27] Keel was tall, dark, and imposing. With a booming voice, he later became a musical comedy star.

Later, when she and Jim Dougherty were engaged to be married in the spring of 1942, they parked their car and "necked" on Mulholland Drive, which is high in the Santa Monica Mountains and was a favorite place for "parking" in that era. Thus they engaged in the long kissing bouts that were standard for dating couples in the 1940s. According to Jim, however, Norma Jeane "expertly managed his sexual advances." Grace and Ana had raised her to be a good girl, according to Jim's sister.[28] And the "double standard" was still in force: good girls were supposed to keep their male partners in check.

Norma Jeane's actions reflected the transitional sexual behavior of the 1940s, in which a resurgent sexuality during World War Two provoked a conservative reaction. America's entry into the war, after the Japanese attacked Pearl Harbor on December 7, 1941, produced social dislocations. Young men joined the military, and young women took over their jobs. Servicemen were sent to coastal bases to be deployed overseas, and young women became available for a sexual fling or for marriage. Prostitution was contained at the bases, but teenage girls out for a good time got by. They were called "Victory Girls" or "V-Girls."[29] Resembling the flappers of the 1920s, they were the vanguard of a new teenage culture whose participants danced the jitterbug to the music of big bands, while its female members swooned over Frank Sinatra—a thin young man with a big voice whom they wanted to both love and mother.

As they had for decades, respectable families tried to restrain their adolescent children, and conservatives in churches and women's clubs joined them. Traditionalism in the form of "plain folk Americanism" also appeared by the mid-1930s, as the nation turned inward to regenerate a national spirit in the face of the ongoing Depression and the advancing totalitarian regimes abroad—Hitler in Germany; Mussolini in Italy; Franco in Spain. American democracy and its small towns became the ideal. In his famed realistic paintings, Norman Rockwell idealized simple values; composers like Aaron Copland incorporated folk tunes into their work. The new traditionalism appeared on the screen in the "girl next door" and the "all-American girl." MGM's Louis B. Mayer created these types, and they swept the industry. Actresses like Jane Powell played women who lived in houses surrounded by white picket fences in picture-postcard towns, embodying a storybook life.[30] In her early photographs and films, Norma Jeane/Marilyn often posed as a "girl next door."

Norma Jeane, like many "good girls" of the era, tried to be respectable by engaging in sex play without intercourse. Yet in *My Story*, Marilyn recounted a different version of her teenage sexuality. She stated there that sex hadn't interested her. She didn't think of her voluptuous body that appeared with puberty as connected to sex but rather as a "friend" who had mysteriously appeared. She envied the boys she knew because they liked sex so much that she worried she might be missing out on something important. But she didn't respond to them; they might as well have desired "a bear in a log." She wondered if she was "frigid" or "lesbian," although in sources other than *My Story* she reported being attracted to older men, like Hary Keel.[31] These issues bothered her even more as she became older and achieved success as the world's great heterosexual sex queen, and yet was attracted to women. How could she hold this position and desire women? Why had she been given a stunning body and an interior filled with abnormalities and pain? No previous biographer has addressed her bisexuality, which was a major issue in her life, as was her inability to find a cure for her menstrual issues or to bear a child.

America of the 1950s demonized homosexuality. During the war servicemen lived with each other for long periods of time in barracks and on battlefields, which raised the specter of same-sex behavior among them. The end of the war produced a backlash against homosexuality as strong as that against Communism. Alfred Kinsey's two best-selling reports on human sexuality, *Sexual Behavior in the Human Male* (1948) and *Sexual Behavior in the Human Female* (1953), were considered definitive on their subjects. Kinsey, whose researchers interviewed ten thousand individuals, found high rates of homosexual encounters among both men and women. His findings prompted psychologists, many of whom were schooled in Freud in this period, to emphasize Freud's belief that everyone is bisexual at birth, while they enter a stage of latent sexuality in later childhood, in which they suppress their early sexual desires. About the age of twelve, they begin to desire the opposite sex. But same-sex desire remains present, beneath the surface. It can resurface at any point.

The fear was that individuals might not give up their homosexual inclinations. Thus heterosexuality needed reinforcement. Federal and state governments passed laws identifying homosexuals and lesbians as dangerous perverts. California passed a law sentencing those convicted of homosexual behavior to state mental institutions, with electroshock therapy administered to change sexual orientation.[32]

Given such attitudes, Norma Jeane sometimes felt like an "anomaly" because she didn't respond to men. At times she didn't feel human; sometimes, she said, she wanted to die because of her same-sex desire. She described these feelings in *My Story*. But her moods were contradictory. A crush on Howard Keel? That involvement didn't go beyond a few kisses, but he had an impact on her. He was the kind of man from Clark Gable on that attracted her. Moreover, Marilyn liked athletic male bodies; that's one reason she married Jim Dougherty, a high school athlete. She also liked Joe DiMaggio's athletic body: he looked like a Michelangelo statue to her. But female bodies also attracted her. "There was also the sinister fact that a well-made woman had always thrilled me to look at."[33] Note her use of the word "sinister." It indicates her recognition of the power of an uncontrollable desire, which frightened her.

During her last semester at Emerson Junior High, in the spring of 1941, Norma Jeane moved in with Grace and Doc, who could now accommodate her. Their finances were finally stable. With a possible war looming ahead, the Los Angeles aircraft industry boomed, and Adel Precision Products hired Doc at a full-time job. He and Grace bought one of Ana's houses in Van Nuys. It was large enough to house Doc's three children and Norma Jeane. She and Bebe Goddard slept together in an enclosed front porch.

That fall, along with Bebe, Norma Jeane entered Van Nuys High School in the tenth grade. She began crafting an image. Her makeup and clothes were noticed; Jim Dougherty's girlfriend called her a "little sexpot." She tried out for a school play because, she said, she had a crush on Warren Peck, who played the lead in the play. But her audition was embarrassing: she froze when she had to speak lines she had memorized perfectly. When the teacher gave her the cue, "I opened my mouth—and nothing! There was a long silence and then curtain!"[34] Once again, as at Emerson, Norma Jeane seemed unable to act. Van Nuys High had an extensive acting program, and Norma Jeane might have taken advantage of it. Four years previously, Jim Dougherty had been a star of that program, along with Jane Russell, who later became a Hollywood star.

Norma Jeane didn't take acting courses at Van Nuys, and in fact she stayed at the school for only one semester.

She still dreamed of film stardom. She became friendly at the school with a Mexican boy who was one of sixteen children and who was scorned by the other students because of his ethnicity. The school was in a well-to-do area; Norma Jeane and the Mexican boy came from less well-to-do areas. Hurt by the racial prejudice at the school, he felt like a misfit. Norma Jeane reached out to him. She told him that she felt out of place because she was an orphan. They spent time together during breaks from classes and after school. Despite her negative feelings about herself, she told him that she was going to be a movie star.[35]

Grace, however, found another possible future for her, this one in the form of marriage. In the fall of 1941 Adel Precision Parts offered Doc a job in West Virginia as manager of their East Coast sales division. But Grace and Doc couldn't take Norma Jeane with them: neither Gladys nor the state of California would permit it. Ana Lower's health had slipped again, so moving in with her on a long-term basis wasn't an option. Norma Jeane was only fifteen; she couldn't live on her own. Grace asked the Howells if they would adopt her, but with three children of their own—the twins plus another child—they didn't want to take on an additional child.

The only option for Norma Jeane was to return to the orphanage until she reached the legal adult age of eighteen. But Grace knew she wouldn't stand for this solution; she had detested the place. So Grace offered her an alternative. Ethel Dougherty and her family lived in a house across the alley from the Goddards, and Grace had become friendly with her. In their conversations they came up with a solution to Norma Jeane's plight. She could marry Ethel's son Jim, whose girlfriend had broken up with him. Ethel liked Norma Jeane, and Grace liked Jim.

The scheme wasn't as absurd as it sounds at first. Norma Jeane hadn't received good grades in school—in fact, she hadn't seemed that interested in her classes. Since she was wooden in her movements on stage and stuttered in speaking, it was hard to see how she could become an actress, much less a film star. Marriage to Jim would solve her problems. He was a catch. He had been a star at Van Nuys High, where he'd been a halfback on the football team, student body president, and a leading actor in school plays. It was Jim, not Norma Jeane, who seemed to have the talent to succeed as an actor. After all, he had played the lead in a school play opposite Jane Russell. According to Jim's sister, it was Jim, not Jane, who had received the acting plaudits. Jim played the guitar, and he'd formed a band with three Mexican classmates. He was still renowned when Norma Jeane entered the high school. Five years older than she, he was masculine and athletic, but he was also kind. He could take care of her, which was what Grace wanted.

By Christmas 1941, Norma Jeane's sex appeal became an issue, as the numbers of servicemen in Los Angeles soared with the attack on Pearl Harbor on December 7. Fearful that the Japanese would bomb Los Angeles, the government rushed troops to the city. San Pedro became an embarkation point for sailors bound for the Pacific; the racetracks—Hollywood Park and Santa Anita—were turned into military bases; even Van Nuys was home to an army base. On December 10 the streetlights throughout Los Angeles were turned off—and the city remained dark until the end of the war. Antiaircraft guns were placed throughout the city. Jim Dougherty remembered, "Pearl Harbor turned the country upside down. We were all afraid."[36]

Fears of prostitution and venereal disease were widespread. In February 1941, the *Los Angeles Times* proposed that young women join the "crusade" against venereal disease by marrying the men who were going to war and with whom they were having sex. "You cannot stifle the instincts of a man," the paper warned, as it pointed to "the health problems created by concentrations of large numbers of our male population removed from home environments."[37]

Ana and Grace worried about Norma Jeane's sex appeal and her dating. In fact, Grace was surprised when Norma Jeane told her she didn't know anything about sex, given the many men she dated. Grace had been a promiscuous "party girl" as a young woman, but as she grew older she became critical of such behavior and enforced a strict moral code on Norma Jeane. Harry Keel was an issue: Marilyn later stated that she married Jim Dougherty partly because her feelings about Keel frightened her.[38] In addition, Mary Baker Eddy glorified marriage, and even Ana Lower supported the scheme to marry Norma Jeane to Jim. Perhaps they feared that Norma Jeane, like her mother, might become promiscuous and then get caught in the trap of illegitimacy that had destroyed Gladys.

But Norma Jeane wasn't opposed to marrying Jim. Although she dreamed about stardom, she was also an adolescent girl who fantasized about marriage. In those days few working-class girls went to college, and most married soon after high school. Football players, models for the tough warrior masculinity the nation prized in wartime, held top position in the popularity system. School communities expected that their star athlete would marry the high school beauty, bringing the prince and the princess of the fairy tales together. This model of heterosexual marriage was a national fantasy by the 1940s, as the high school years assumed the position they still hold in the United States today as the central period in everyone's life. They were enshrined in the figures of the "all-American girl" and "all-American boy."

Norma Jeane said she had a crush on Warren Peck, but Jim's picture hung on the wall outside the drama classroom, honoring his success as an actor at the school. When Norma Jeane met him, he worked on the night shift at Lockheed Aircraft, helping to support his large family. But his past glory, not his present status, impressed her. Like the Doughertys, many of the families who had raised Norma Jeane were working class. She had no illusions about marrying a doctor or a lawyer. Nor was she encouraged to continue her education. The fact that she had become something of a leader at Emerson Junior High was forgotten. For a girl with a background like hers marrying a high school star was a signal achievement.

Norma Jeane seduced Jim into marriage. Grace was manipulating her at this point, but Norma Jeane honestly believed that's what she wanted. Grace maneuvered him into driving Bebe and her to school, and she sat close to him in the car. Scheming with Ethel Dougherty, Grace persuaded him to take her ward to the Adel Precision Parts Christmas dance. As they danced with bodies pressed together, Norma Jeane's sensuality was in full force. She was feminine and sweet, deferring to Jim, asking him about himself—a technique guaranteed to please. She represented the security of commitment. Several days after the Christmas dance, a Japanese submarine torpedoed an American carrier in Catalina Channel. It was a frightening experience for a city already on the edge.[39]

They courted all spring, going to movies, to dinner, on family picnics, on hikes in the mountains. Because Grace, Doc, and Bebe left for West Virginia in the middle of the spring of 1942, Norma Jeane moved back to Ana's house, attending University High School in West Los

Angeles for the second semester of her tenth-grade year. A dutiful suitor, Jim made the drive over the Santa Monica Mountains from Van Nuys to West Los Angeles to see Norma Jeane. At a Dougherty family picnic she brought three homemade lemon pies she said she'd made from her mother's recipe: by "mother" she probably meant Ana Lower. Jim played his guitar at that picnic and Norma Jeane sang, following his accompaniment in a high, sweet voice.

Before Grace left for West Virginia, she told Norma Jeane that she was illegitimate, which Norma Jeane hadn't known. She had been told that her father had died soon after her birth (which wasn't true), but she hadn't been told that her mother, Gladys, hadn't been married to him; and Grace assumed Stanley Gifford was Norma Jeane's father. Jim was also told this family secret, since he might consider it serious enough to break off their engagement. But he didn't. He was a kind man, and he took it in stride. He hadn't been put off by the presumed insanity in Norma Jeane's family or by her position as a charity case. He had come to relish the role of being her savior, of taking this sweet "love child" under his protection. He was not the last man to cast himself in the role of Norma Jeane's protector—a standard role for men in relationships with girlfriends and wives in the 1950s. He honestly loved her for her loving spirit, her beauty, her kindness and grace.

The wedding occurred on June 19, 1942, three weeks after Norma Jeane's sixteenth birthday, when she attained the legal age of sexual consent. It was an eerie repetition of Gladys's situation at her marriage, which had also been arranged with the age of sexual consent in mind. Norma Jeane and Jim were married at the home of the Howells, people of means whose impressive house in Westwood had an elegant curving staircase, like the ones in movies Norma Jeane had seen. She walked down the staircase in white bridal splendor. Ana Lower had made Norma Jeane's wedding dress—a traditional one of white satin and lace—and she gave her foster daughter away. The ceremony was held in front of the fireplace in the Howells' living room.

Loralee and Doralee Howell were flower girls. Grace was in West Virginia with Doc and Bebe, but six of Norma Jeane's foster mothers were there. By my calculation they included Ida Bolender, Ana Lower, Maude Atkinson, Olive Monroe, Doris Howell, and Enid Knebelkamp. Lester Bolender and his wife were also there. (Bryan and Lottie Atchinson,

Grace's brother and sister-in-law, with whom Norma Jeane had lived for several months, were out of town.) Gladys wasn't present; she was still in Agnews State Hospital in Northern California. After years of living in other people's homes, Norma Jeane finally had a family of her own.[40]

Jim had saved enough money to pay for a wedding reception and dinner at the Florentine Gardens, a local nightclub. The floor show went on during the wedding banquet. Called "Red, White, and Beautiful," it featured showgirls playing famous film stars, in a recapitulation of the history of Hollywood glamour. Showgirls impersonated Greta Garbo, Marlene Dietrich, Dorothy Lamour, Katharine Hepburn, and Hedy Lamarr. Norma Jeane could hardly have missed it when one of the showgirls pulled Jim on stage and had him dance with her. The world of entertainment was all around her in Los Angeles, and even at her marriage she was experiencing it firsthand.[41]

In a previously unknown letter from Norma Jeane to Grace that I discovered, Norma Jeane describes how excited she is to set up her new home. The letter is dated September 1942, nearly three months after she married Jim Dougherty. She and Jim had rented a one-room apartment with a Murphy bed that they pulled down to sleep at night. Although the place was small and compact, she was spending all her time keeping it spotless, shopping for food, and cooking their meals. A friend, she said, had told her that being a housewife was time-consuming, and her friend was right. But, she added, "it really is a lot of fun." She described her love for her husband. "Jimmie is so swell to me; in fact, I know that if I had waited 5 or 10 years I couldn't have found anyone who would have treated me better. I just think the world of him and we get along so nice. He is just so sweet about every little thing." Was Norma Jeane telling Grace the truth? Or had she retreated into a fantasy world? Jim once characterized her in their early marriage as seeming like a child playing a game of house. After all, she was only sixteen.

She described her wedding gifts with enthusiasm. They were items typically given at showers and weddings in the 1940s—an age of chips and dips, casseroles, glass candy dishes, and glass salad sets. Aunt Ana gave her starting sets of basic household items like towels and kitchen utensils. Mr. and Mrs. George Yeager (he worked with Jim at Lockheed) gave them a set of liquor glasses, although Norma Jeane hastened to add that they would use them for something other than liquor. Hazel and Chester Patterson gave them "the cutest little electric clock" shaped like a teapot. Aunt Doris and Uncle Chet (Howell) gave them a "very beautiful" picture that his mother had painted. They were given glass Pyrex dishes for baking and a number of glass salad bowls with glass plates. Sterling silver pitchers, serving pieces, and crystal glassware were typically given at weddings of the well-to-do in this era. They are notably absent from Norma Jeane's wedding gifts.[42]

Once married, they spent a lot of time with his family. It was large and tightly knit, since the Doughertys had survived years of poverty during the early 1930s, when they lived in tents in public parks and ate at soup kitchens. They had once lived in a tent they pitched in the backyard of a Mexican family who took pity on them. With wartime prosperity their finances improved, but they were far from well-to-do. With her sweet ways and her desire to please, Norma Jeane fit into their family. She seemed like a daughter to Jim's mother, Ethel, and a sister to his brothers and sisters. She loved to take care of Jim's young nieces and nephews. Such behavior would become standard for her, as she entered families and left them, testing her ability to charm again and again. She adjusted herself to Jim's needs, but that's what she had done with her foster families.

Sometimes Norma Jeane and Jim went dancing or to the movies. They also hunted and fished, pursuing Jim's interests; they socialized mostly with his friends. On weekends they went to Muscle Beach in Venice, a famed hangout for bodybuilders, so that Jim could participate in the contests there. Norma Jeane liked going there because the young men on the beach flirted with her, until she held up her hand with her wedding ring on it and they moved away. She liked to show off her body and experience her attractiveness to men.

In ghostwritten articles and books, Jim later described his marriage to Norma Jeane as perfect. He stated that she willingly went hunting and fishing with him, and she kept the house spotless. She was also a good cook—she made delicious lamb and venison dishes—and she loved going to prizefights. In essence, she did anything that Jim wanted her to do. She was also extraordinary in bed, he maintained, and they had sex all the time.

Was any of it true, or did Jim make it up? Norma Jeane was undoubtedly a good housekeeper. Throughout her life she liked to do housework and to cook, but as a Hollywood star—even an aspiring starlet—she didn't have time for it. She told reporter Lisa Wilson that when married to Jim she clipped recipes from magazines, listened to cooking experts on the radio, and asked neighbors for advice. That's how she learned to cook.[43] Her emerging drive for perfection led her to construct herself as a perfect partner for Jim. And she was beginning to develop the ability to play a role in a life situation. She tried to please, to make herself into the person others wanted her to be.

With Grace gone and Ana Lower living at a distance, she became dependent on Jim. She exhibited a fear of abandonment when she was with him, clinging to him and calling him Daddy. Such behavior is typical of victims of childhood sexual abuse, as they cope with adult life. In a 1953 *Photoplay* article, Jim said she easily became hysterical; in a 1976 article in *McCall's*, he said her moods were sometimes scary and it took a lot of reassurance to get her over them. The infantile part of her self would suddenly appear, and she would become like a baby. She would then do a speedy turnaround and become a mature woman. His statements are the first indication that Norma Jeane's fragmented self was showing through.[44]

Other incidents contradict the rosy picture Jim painted of their time together, events indicating that Norma Jeane sometimes behaved strangely. Late one night she ran outside in a nightgown after they quarreled and came back sobbing that a man had been following her. (This episode has been cited as evidence of mental illness, but it's possible that a man was following her.) Moreover, she tried to pull a cow into their apartment in the middle of pouring rain to stop it from being soaked. She put too much sugar in coffee and poured a large amount of bourbon into drinks she was making. She was too insecure to tell Jim she didn't like hunting and fishing.

What about Jim's claims that they had wonderful sex? When his former wife became the world's sex icon, his masculine self-esteem demanded that he claim they both had performed superbly at sex. But Marilyn stated that she hadn't liked their sex. "The first effect marriage had on me was to increase my lack of interest in sex." And "my husband either didn't mind this or wasn't aware of it." But, she continued, they were too young to discuss such an embarrassing topic. According to Elia Kazan, Marilyn told him that she hadn't enjoyed sex with Jim, except when he had kissed her breasts. He had made no effort to satisfy her. After he was satisfied, he'd fall asleep. It sounds as though Jim didn't understand female sexual response, which wasn't uncommon among young men and women in the 1950s.[45]

Jim often was fixated on himself and his male activities. When reporter Jane Wilkie interviewed him for *Photoplay*, she found him macho and not overly bright. Robert Mitchum, Jim's workmate at Lockheed who later became a Hollywood star, described him as decent and good-humored. "He looked like a large brick," Mitchum said, "red-haired, square-shouldered and solid all the way down." Jim admitted to Wilkie that he stayed out late at night shooting pool with his buddies, even though this upset Norma Jeane. When she talked about her dreams of becoming a film star, he replied that there were plenty of girls seeking stardom in Hollywood, all of whom could sing, dance, and act. What makes you think you're better than they are? he had asked. A traditional man, he didn't want her to work outside the home. He noticed that she spent a lot of time on her appearance, washing her face many times a day, fixing her makeup, eating wholesome food, and exercising; but he thought she did it for him.[46]

Yet he could be kind and considerate. He didn't complain when she told him she didn't want to become pregnant because childbearing might cause her body to sag. (She told others she thought of bearing a child as in the distant future. "Women in her family," she said, "had always made such a mess of mothering.")[47] Jim also worried about the mental illness in her family; he thought they should wait until she was older to place the stress of childbearing on her. Norma Jeane also feared she might go insane; her emerging emotionalism allowed her to feel more in touch with herself, but she was concerned that it also might indicate some abnormality in her brain. The diagnosis of a disintegrating brain given to Gladys at Norwalk State Mental Hospital would always haunt Norma Jeane, as would the demons and monsters of her dreams. Pressured by Jim, she got a diaphragm.

Jim signed up for the military in the spring of 1944. Given his immersion in male culture, he responded to the pressure on young men to serve their country in wartime. All his friends were enlisting in the services or being drafted into them, and he didn't want to be shamed for staying behind. Norma Jeane became hysterical when he brought up the subject. He was her major support, the one person who hadn't abandoned her. To soothe her, he joined the merchant marine, in which shore duty was more likely than in the other services. Indeed, he was sent to Catalina Island, which had been turned into a merchant marine base. Promoted to physical education instructor and given officer status, he was permitted to rent a house on the island and to move Norma Jeane there to live with him. They remained on Catalina Island for nine months, until he was assigned to duty in the South Pacific.

Those months on Catalina brought Jim and Norma Jeane closer together, but they also strained their marriage—while they became important to the genesis of the sexualized Marilyn Monroe. The economy of Catalina depended on the tourist trade, which was suspended during the war. With the ferry to the island taken over by the military, much of the island's population, especially its women, moved to the mainland, leaving the island to the thousands of men stationed there. "You never saw so many sailors, so many men," Marilyn remembered.[48] Norma Jeane was one of the few women on the base. Other officers brought wives along, and she became friendly with them. She went to the beach with them, exchanged recipes, and helped them care for their babies. Yet her fame as a sensual woman spread. When she walked into town or on the beach, men watched her.

Jim was her protector; no one would take on the tough athletic instructor. Norma Jeane often wore tight sweaters and shorts, or a bathing suit, displaying her body, which infuriated Jim. He accused her of dressing that way to stimulate male desire. "Don't you realize," he said to her, "that the men are raping you in their minds?"[49] His admonitions made her angry, since she didn't think she was dressing differently from the other women on the island. This was in many ways her first exertion of independence in a marriage in which her husband felt he should be in control.

Substitute the camera eye for the eyes of those men. Norma Jeane was at the center of attention. She was seductive, posing, a model in the making. She welcomed the male gaze. Norman Rosten, later a close friend who wrote a memoir of her, described her as enjoying the idea of men desiring her. "It aroused, flattered, and excited her. Such attention, constantly directed toward her, denied her inner and overwhelming dread of not being wanted."[50] Perhaps she saw power in it, a means of controlling men. Perhaps she couldn't stop herself from doing so. Perhaps she was angry at Jim Dougherty for his sexual demands and was getting back at him.

As a professional model she later faced the camera boldly, confronting the male gaze. Photographer Philippe Halsman stated that Marilyn "knew that the camera lens was not a glass eye but a symbol for the eyes of millions of men." His remark was a metaphor for her performance. She was able to direct "the entire impact of her personality" on Catalina Island, engaging the eyes of the men there. She could look people in the eye in personal encounters; she could do the same in front of a camera.[51]

Life magazine first brought the pinup into mainstream culture in 1939. That figure combined the big-breasted babe with the sweet all-American girl.[52] She must have seen the pinups the men collected, the photos of young women—usually starlets in bathing suits and negligees—that movie studios distributed by the hundreds of thousands and that were featured in the military publications such as *Stars and Stripes* newspaper and *Yank* magazine. Moreover, the government subsidized an edition of *Esquire*, the day's major upscale men's magazine, that was sent to the troops. In every issue *Esquire* published an illustration by Alberto Vargas of an airbrushed, perfect woman, known as a Varga girl, lush, voluptuous, and long-limbed. His perfect woman was a smash hit. The policy of distributing these magazines and pinups to the troops was intended to create "morale," to inspire soldiers to remember they were fighting to preserve American ideals, represented by their girlfriends and wives. That goal seems preposterous until one realizes that the faces of the pinups were modeled after the sweet, innocent face of the "girl next door."

Norma Jeane could be clingy and dependent, shy and insecure. But she could also tap into the independence she'd developed at Emerson Junior High, when she designed an unusual wardrobe to attract attention from the boys, and on Catalina, when she had defied Jim Dougherty by wearing sexy clothes. She also became friends with Howard Corrington, a former Olympic weight lifting champion who was in her husband's unit, and she studied weight lifting with him. It was a rebellious act. In the 1950s, women were permitted to engage in sports like tennis and swimming, but weight lifting was out-of-bounds. It was designed to develop muscles, which women weren't supposed to have. Norma Jeane said that she lifted weights to keep her breasts firm and to hold her weight down. She also must have realized its benefits for modeling and acting: she needed to be strong, with a flexible body, to stand the rigors of those careers.

Meantime, Jim had become annoyed with Norma Jeane's emotionalism and her flirtatious behavior. He needed a break from her. He asked for duty overseas, and he was assigned to the South Pacific. It suddenly seemed to Norma Jeane that she was being abandoned. Reverting to the devoted wife, she begged him to allow her to become pregnant, so that she would have a baby to care for. He didn't do that, and Norma Jeane moved in with his parents on the mainland. Even more than on Catalina, men on the streets must have stopped her and told her that she could be a model, even a movie star. That was a typical male come-on to beautiful women in an era when the film industry dominated the city. But Norma Jeane didn't act on these comments. It wasn't until photographer David Conover found her working on an aircraft factory assembly line and pointed her toward modeling as a career that her life was transformed.

Chapter 4

Photographers and Producers, 1944–1946

In April 1944, Jim Dougherty left for the South Pacific, and Norma Jeane moved in with his parents. Ethel Dougherty, coconspirator with Grace Goddard in marrying Norma Jeane to her son, was now watching over her, in what amounted to a reprise of the foster families of her childhood. Norma Jeane was still doing what she was told to do, dependent on others to make her decisions for her. When she became restless, starting to want a life of her own, Ethel found her a job on the assembly line of Radioplane, a munitions factory in Burbank where Ethel worked in the infirmary. Norma Jeane was now a Rosie the Riveter. Still a perfect wife, she wrote Jim every day.

Radioplane made remote-controlled drones that served as practice targets for fighter planes and antiaircraft artillery. After an initial assignment inspecting the parachutes that were attached to the drones to bring them back to earth, Norma Jeane was transferred to the "dope room," where she painted varnish on the drones' canvas fuselages and sanded the finish smooth. She worked long hours, mostly standing.[1] The varnish was smelly, and the work exhausting. The conditions were reminiscent of the long hours and smelly glue in her mother's film editing labs that she had rejected when she saw the RKO sign from her bedroom window at the orphanage and decided to become a star. Yet Norma Jeane tried to be outstanding in her work and, indeed, she was so good at it that Radioplane awarded her a gold medal.

Disliking the work in the "dope room," she found a desk job at the local Van Nuys army base. She quickly returned to Radioplane, however, when she realized that her co-workers at the base would all be men. That raised the specter of Catalina, where Jim had become angry at her for causing the men to ogle her. She now had to deal with her mother-in-law, her husband's stand-in. "There are enough of those wolves at Radioplane," she wrote Grace, "without a whole army full of them."[2]

Despite living with the Doughertys, Norma Jeane remained loyal to Ana Lower and Christian Science. In August 1944 she took the ultimate pledge of fidelity by becoming a church member, signing a document affirming her support of the church. Such signing parallels the rite of confirmation in other Christian churches. Norma Jeane's membership document was witnessed by Ana Lower and Emma Easton Newman, a renowned healer who had been trained by Mary Baker Eddy. Such a link to the founder conferred great prestige, validating Ana's importance in the church and her hopes for her foster child.

In October Norma Jeane traveled to Chicago and Detroit for two months to visit Grace and to meet Berniece Miracle, her half-sister from Gladys's first marriage, with whom she had been corresponding. Grace was living temporarily in Chicago; Berniece lived in Detroit. Ana sent Norma Jeane the letter that chided her for having car sickness—only an illusion to a healer—and counseled her to seek God's love. In her memoir of Marilyn, Berniece describes their good times together in Detroit shopping and reminiscing about their childhoods, but she notes that Norma Jeane stammered throughout her visit.[3]

In December, soon after she returned to Radioplane, Norma Jeane's fortunes drastically changed when a group of army air corps filmmakers arrived at the plant to make a training film for new recruits. Pinup photographer David Conover was among them. He was on the lookout for young women to photograph for *Yank* and *Stars and Stripes*. When he saw Norma Jeane on the assembly line he was immediately attracted to her and he asked if he could photograph her. She agreed. He then asked her to put on a sweater, since he was taking "morale" photos and the shape of her body needed to show. She put on a red sweater she had with her. It was, Conover stated, "a flashy red cashmere that enhanced her astonishing figure delightfully." Once again a red sweater was her "magic sweater." She would often wear it in subsequent pinup photos, since the models had to provide their own clothes for photographs.[4]

The Conover photos showed that Norma Jeane was very photogenic: she possessed that rare quality of skin tone and vitality that radiates on film. And she had a look of knowing innocence. In those photos, as in all her early pinup photos, she is a child-woman enjoying her body and seeking attention, sometimes coyly, sometimes boldly, although she never looks vulgar. Conover was so impressed that he told Norma Jeane that she should be on magazine covers, not on an assembly line.

It was a transformative moment. The click of the camera flashed with clarity, like the moment at a revival meeting when the participant realizes God's grace and is "born again" as a new person with new goals. Mary Baker Eddy had taken charge of her chronic pain in a moment of inspiration when she read the Bible passage about Christ healing a crippled man by telling him to throw away his crutches and walk. As a Christian Scientist, Norma Jeane was steeped in Eddy's life story, and so her success seemed like a sign from God. She too could transform herself into a new person. Aside from her sweet nature and a maturity beyond her years, Norma Jeane hadn't displayed any special abilities so far, except her drive for perfection, apparent in her perfect behavior as a wife and as a factory worker. Not much else, aside from her dreams about stardom, suggested she would turn into a dynamo of ambition when her goal seemed possible. Conover's photos released a genie inside of her.

The most recent writers on genius, creativity's greatest manifestation, agree that it can appear at any point in the life cycle, not just in childhood. They reject the nineteenth-century romantic belief that it exists only in a small set of heroic people. They find three factors key to what they see as a more general phenomenon. First is a grandiose and mystical sense of the world, what Einstein called "cosmic religiosity." Such an elevated mood can appear in the hypomanic phase of the up-down cycle of someone with a bipolar disorder, as depression lifts and elation appears. The second element of genius is an ability to concentrate obsessively on a goal and to strive for perfection in reaching it. The third element is a resonance to one's historical era, being in sync with current ideals, living when one's gift or invention can be appreciated.[5]

By luck of the draw these three factors lined up in Norma Jeane's life in late 1944. Both the evangelical religion of her early childhood and the Christian Science of her adolescence and early adulthood fostered a sense of connection to a deep spiritual force. Her drive for perfection would become central to her work as a model and actress. Through luck Norma Jeane's look matched her day's prevailing definition of ideal beauty: innocent face, large breasts, long-looking legs.

Although Norma Jeane's emotions continued to swing up and down, as they had during her marriage, she possessed considerable energy, which the Conover shoot released. "When nothing in her life was happening to distract her, she'd get restless, hyper," said her friend Susan Strasberg. "She had tremendous energy, which came out in Herculean bursts of activity, followed by total depletion and depressions." Arthur Miller experienced her manic-depressive cycles as extreme: "She meant to live at the peak always; in the permanent rush of a crescendo." When the wave receded, she would turn against herself as worthless and then she couldn't sleep. Through it all she could summon up hope "like a fish swimming up through black seas to fly at the sun before falling back again." Norman Rosten described her mood swings in gentler terms. "When she's high, a sweet chime of music surrounds her; when she's low she moves to another plain, withdrawn, private."[6]

When she pursued modeling, she did so in this hyper state, with great energy followed by occasional crashes, combined with up-and-down moods that could fluctuate over the course of a day. What would become her characteristic emotional pattern was emerging. Her genius was swift to appear: she was a leading West Coast model within two years of the Conover shoot and a contract player at Twentieth Century–Fox by 1946. It took her six more years to achieve stardom, but she demonstrated creativity, guts, and a major ability at manipulation in achieving it. The passivity of her childhood slowly ended, but her compulsions began to appear in its place.

The secular language of the movies resembles religious hagiography, with charismatic stars spoken of as gods and goddesses and with mythologies attached to their lives. Once Conover photographed her, Norma Jeane drew from that discourse by stating that she had been "discovered." That was movie language, used everywhere in star texts. Those were the narratives created by publicists from the lives of actors that were threaded through their publicity and even their films. The word "discovery" was used to describe the moment when a movie industry representative, usually a male talent scout, suddenly recognized a young hopeful's "star quality"—the indefinable look on the screen, akin to photogeneity, that mesmerized audiences. Gifted talent scouts presumably saw it immediately.

Like movie scouts, photographers "discovered" models, who sometimes went on to careers in Hollywood—as did Ava Gardner, Lauren Bacall, and Shelley Winters. David Conover found Norma Jeane by accident in December 1944, and pinup photographer Bruno Bernard (Bernard of Hollywood) independently stumbled upon her when she was walking on Sunset Boulevard near his studio. Struck by her look, he stopped her and persuaded her to model for him. By the 1940s modeling was becoming glamorous, shedding the last vestiges of its old association with prostitution. It received a boost from the 1944 smash-hit movie *Cover Girl*. In that film Rita Hayworth wins a beauty contest that leads to modeling for eminent photographers and a role in a Broadway show.[7]

Not long after the Conover shoot, Jim Dougherty arrived in Los Angeles on his first leave in nine months. He and Norma Jeane went horseback riding, dancing at the Coconut Grove, to movies and the beach, and for a week in the snow in the San Bernardino Mountains. Jim noticed that Norma Jeane was drinking mixed drinks, not just ginger ale, as she previously had. She was still sensitive and shy, with emotional ups and downs, but she seemed more confident. She told him about her modeling. He didn't oppose it, since the work at Radioplane was exhausting and modeling was better paid. But he was bothered by her new opposition to becoming pregnant; she didn't want to have a child in the immediate future. Troubled by her independence, he began to see the birth of a child as a way of cementing their relationship.

After this leave ended, Jim was stationed on vessels that protected shipping up and down the West Coast, allowing him to visit Los Angeles on weekend passes. For the next year and a half, until his stint with the merchant marine ended, he was alternately sent to the Far East and then stationed on vessels along the West Coast. Norma Jeane continued to change. She talked more about modeling and less about their future. She modeled for Conover's photographer friends, and she made the rounds of photographers' studios, looking for assignments. When Jim arrived at his parents' home on weekend passes she was sometimes on a shoot, and she didn't hurry home. A gulf grew between Norma Jeane and Jim.[8]

In April 1945 Jim was assigned to the Far East. At this point Ethel

Dougherty intervened. She was fed up with Norma Jeane's modeling, fed up with phone calls from strange men and mysterious trips with them. She wrote to Jim, complaining about her daughter-in-law. Jim became upset. He wrote Norma Jeane sternly, reprimanding her. Like most Americans in the 1940s he believed that men should be the family breadwinners and women should stay at home. Besides, for a family like the Doughertys, working poor for many years, a stay-at-home wife signified a greater degree of affluence. In his letter Jim wrote that the situation during the war, with women working, was temporary. When it ended, she had to give up modeling, go back home, and have a baby. "You can have only one career," he wrote.

Jim's letter angered Norma Jeane, finally annoyed at being ordered around. Success at modeling had increased her independence. Taking a bold step, she moved out of the Dougherty house and into the bottom apartment of Ana Lower's duplex. Ana supported her decision to focus on her modeling career, although Norma Jeane didn't end her marriage to Jim.

In July Norma Jeane went to the Mojave Desert and Death Valley with Conover, so that he could photograph her in natural settings. Linking models to nature, standard in pinup photos, was meant to tone down salaciousness by connecting erotic female images to the generativity and purity of nature and the out-of-doors. Some Marilyn biographers doubt the trip happened, since Conover published only a few photos from it and he could have taken them locally. Challenged about this while he was alive, he claimed the army suddenly ordered him overseas and he had hurriedly mailed the photos of Norma Jeane to a photographer friend, Potter Hueth, who never received them. They were presumably lost in the mail.[9]

Before he left, Conover asked Hueth to help Norma Jeane, and he did. He took his own photos of her and recommended her to Emmeline Snively, head of the Blue Book Model Agency, who interviewed Norma Jeane on August 2, 1945.[10] That same day one of Conover's Radioplane photos of her appeared on the cover of *Stars and Stripes*. It was a considerable achievement. Sent to soldiers worldwide, the magazine had a huge circulation.

Snively found Norma Jeane irresistible in the interview. She wore a white dress, and Snively thought she looked like a cherub in a church choir. Entering the room, she stared at a bulletin board with magazine covers featuring Blue Book models tacked on it. "All the girls are so beautiful," she said plaintively to Snively. "Can I be a cover girl, too?" Snively melted and said, "Yes, you're a natural." She offered her a contract.

Snively remembered that meeting: "She had a high, little-girl voice and an astonishing bust which made her size-twelve dress look too small, although she knew nothing about carriage, posture, walking, sitting, or posing."[11] Snively's statement sounds self-serving, since photographers had already responded positively to Norma Jeane. But Snively would not be the last individual to enlarge her role in the creation of Marilyn Monroe. Snively ran a modeling school attached to her agency, and Norma Jeane signed up for three months of classes. It was a moneymaking enterprise, one of many such schools in the city designed to teach young women poise through teaching them how to model. Norma Jeane was, according to Snively, the best student in the class. She attended every session, and she was always on time. Her habitual lateness didn't take over until later in her life, when she faced the challenge of making movies.

Norma Jeane defied her husband and mother-in-law and signed with the Blue Book Model Agency during the summer of 1945, when the end of World War Two was energizing Americans. The troops were coming home, and rationing was over. People could buy new cars, appliances, clothing. Women no longer had to paint the seams of stockings on the backs of their legs, as they had during the war; they could buy nylons again. Parades and festivals were held. On V-J Day in August, when Japan surrendered, people poured into the streets, dancing with strangers. After four years of blackouts, the lights of the city—and of its movie marquees—were turned on. "The city was adazzle with blazing bulbs," Lana Turner remembered, "brilliant and glittering and fun."[12]

Norma Jeane liked earning her own income. As the daughter of Gladys and the ward of Grace, both working women, she honored their values. They upheld the ideal of marriage and motherhood, but they valued their independence. Norma Jeane was raised to expect to marry, but also to be able to support herself if necessary. Even when she later slept with producers to advance her career, these wealthy men didn't support her. Taking money for sex meant that she was a prostitute, and she tried to avoid that designation. During her marriages to Joe DiMaggio and Arthur Miller she supported herself, and she supported Miller during their marriage. She took pride in her financial independence.

As her modeling career began to take off, Norma Jeane chose a new name she thought more appropriate for a model: Jean Norman. It was more sophisticated than Norma Jeane Dougherty, which suggested midwestern provincialism. She also changed her handwriting. The script she had used during her childhood and marriage, with round and deliberate letters, looks like a child's careful printing. She now adopted a sprawling cursive, hasty in look, as though she were dashing through life.

She was witty and zany with the photographers, an adolescent Marilyn filled with joy. She posed for hours in their studios, joking and laughing. When they shot her on the beach she eagerly ran over the sand and climbed up sand dunes and rock cliffs. When she became melancholy on a Zuma Beach shoot with photographer Joseph Jasgur, he had her stick out her tongue. That silly gesture triggered her playful side: it was as though a switch had clicked on. "She raced across the sand to the water's edge and back like a demented wind-up toy, exulting in the sea air on her bare skin and the feeling of powdery sand between her toes." She had boundless energy. "Her enthusiasm and tenacity are infectious," Bruno Bernard stated. "After hours of continuous shooting, she still remains fresh."[13]

Her body had a flexibility that allowed her to assume almost any pose the photographer wanted. She continued her Catalina exercise regimen—bending, lifting weights, bicycling, fast walking. Moreover, she had a natural rapport with the camera. "When she moved into position," photographer William Carroll remembered, "it was so rapidly as though she was reading my mind. Then, after hearing the camera click, she would modify the pose to give me something fresh and brightly new to photograph." Describing their interaction fifty years after it happened, Carroll may have exaggerated her early ability, yet he caught her when she was in the process of shaping it. To do so, she examined every print taken of her, posing shrewd questions to the photographers. What were her best angles? How could she minimize her hips? How could she improve her hair and her smile? Marilyn remembered, "I wouldn't settle for second best. I would take home photographs of myself to study how I looked and if I could improve myself posing in front of a mirror."[14]

Despite such determination and success, her emotionalism continued. In November 1945, after three months of modeling training and numerous sessions with photographers, Norma Jeane still seemed to Snively a "scared, pretty lonely little kid who wore mostly fresh white cotton dresses." In March 1946, photographer Joseph Jasgur found her shy and anxious. She was an hour late for their appointment. She had been worried about her appearance, and she had repeatedly redone her makeup and hair. When photographer Bob Shannon shot her that year, he found her up-and-down moods disconcerting. He was worried when she took five aspirins for menstrual cramps: it seemed too many pills to him. But she rarely took barbiturates, or strong pain medications like Percodan or Demerol; at this point, her endometriosis and her anxiety weren't yet that severe.[15]

The Doughertys sometimes experienced Norma Jeane as being in another world, dissociated from her surroundings. She was sometimes very late to family gatherings without any explanation. "She sometimes had a vacuous expression on her face," David Conover remembered, "as though she lacked an identity." Her visions and nightmares of demons and witches periodically reappeared. She remained afraid of going insane, like her mother. She recounted a dream to Conover in which men in hospital garb forced her into a straitjacket and took her into a building that looked like the orphanage where she had lived. They marched her through one black door after another, until they put her, still in a straitjacket, into a bleak room, and left.

By 1945 the profession of modeling had many faces, from projecting upper-class elegance for fashion magazines like *Vogue* and *Harper's Bazaar* to embodying raunchy sensuality for men's magazines. Illustrators in the tradition of George Petty and Alberto Vargas used live models to paint idealized airbrushed women, sexy and elegant, often to adorn the calendars that Americans bought in the millions of copies. Wholesale clothing manufacturers and retail department stores employed models to display clothing, while businessmen exhibiting products at expositions hired models to show off their wares. Photographers shot advertising spreads and illustrations for middlebrow magazines like *Collier's* and *Redbook*, as well as photos of movie players for the movie fan magazines, which had sizable readerships.[16]

During the war, the demand for models grew with the launch of "girlie" magazines—like *Twitter, Eye,* and *Bang,* loosely modeled after *Life* and *Look*—in which photos of semiclothed women appeared alongside stories about current events—and crude humor. The style of the magazines ranged from peek-a-boo to raunchy. At the end of the war *Esquire* dropped its pinup photos when its editors became tired of fighting the censors in the post office, who were enforcing the 1873 Comstock Act, which prohibited sending obscene material through the mail. As a result of *Esquire*'s action, the "girlie" magazines took off. They were logical places for Jean Norman photos.

From the start of their relationship, Emmeline Snively pegged Norma Jeane as a pinup model. Fashion models were mostly tall and skinny, with small breasts, because those bodies didn't draw attention away from the clothing being modeled. But Norma Jeane's large breasts and hips drew attention to her. And her bust was too large for her to fit into the standard size twelve that clothing models wore. When Snively sent her to model clothing for a Montgomery Ward catalog, she was let go after two days because she was too voluptuous. She was also hopeless at the slinky model walk. She had double-jointed knees that threw her hips off center so they swayed as she walked. She later used the sway as the basis of her signature walk.

Moreover, Snively didn't find Norma Jeane that sexy, except for her large breasts. Bruno Bernard sometimes found her attempts to look sexy ridiculous. When she affected hooded eyes and a round mouth, he called it her "French baby whore" look and told her to stay with her "child-woman" expression. Other photographers disagreed. They liked her "over-the-top" sexy persona. Norma Jeane overheard their comments: "That Norma Jeane—she's built like a sex machine. She can turn it on and off."[17] She later refined her hooded eyes and round mouth into a characteristic expression of hers.

Norma Jeane had expressive eyes and a large head, which photographed well. But Snively and the photographers found other problems with her face and figure. Some were the same as those Grace Goddard had noted years before. She had a bump on her nose and a chin so weak that from some angles she looked double-chinned. Her nose photographed as too long.[18] She had a bad bite. Her hips were broad and her legs weren't that long; the idealized long legs of the Petty and Varga girls remained in vogue.

Makeup, lighting, and camera angles hid some of these deficiencies. By shooting from low angles, Jasgur gave her chin definition and made her appear taller. He made her broad nose look thinner by carefully adjusting the light he directed on her face and the angle of the camera. Bruno Bernard, who still considered women's legs their most erotic body part, shot Norma Jeane from an angle that extended her short legs, to the point that Norma Jeane asked him if he was making her into a Varga girl. "What's wrong with Vargas?" he responded.[19] In later years, photographers continued using these techniques to cover over Marilyn's bad features; in 1950 she had cosmetic surgery to correct what were seen as the deficiencies in her chin and nose.

Then Snively and Jasgur decided that her gum lines were too high, and they had her lower her upper lip when she smiled. Norma Jeane practiced lowering it in front of a mirror until she got it right, but she never managed to eliminate the quivering upper lip that is apparent in her films. They also didn't like her curly hair, since Lana Turner's smooth-hair look was in vogue. Snively and the photographers also wanted Norma Jeane to dye her hair blonde, because they thought it would suit her pale skin better than her natural brown. But she wanted to remain natural, and she worried about the expense of having her hair straightened and dyed. In February 1946, a shampoo company considering her for an ad demanded that she dye her hair blonde and straighten it. When the photographer shooting the ad offered to pay for the process, Norma Jeane acquiesced.

The process was time-consuming and complicated. First her hair was straightened, using chemicals. Then blonde dye was applied. The hair was then permed to get some of the curl back. Finally, it was fixed in curls close to her head with bobby pins and dried under a floor-standing dryer. It was arduous, but Norma Jeane was willing to do whatever it took to succeed as a model.

At this stage in her career, she cooperated with photographers, mostly showing up on time. She was willing to work for them on "spec," which meant that she posed for free, using her own clothes and doing her own makeup. When they sold a photograph, she received a percentage of the fee. But photographers were notorious for not paying under such an arrangement and many models refused to work on spec. "She was a go-getter," stated photographer Andre de Dienes. "Her success wouldn't have happened if she hadn't cooperated so whole-heartedly with so many photographers." Her cooperation led her to sign releases that gave photographers control over their photographs of her. Enthused by success, Norma Jeane didn't realize that granting such rights would later cause problems—namely that she might be oversold, resulting in fewer requests to photograph her in the future, since advertisers could use existing photos. At the beginning of her career, she felt she had to be accommodating to get assignments.[20]

Norma Jeane's waiflike persona brought out Snively's maternal feelings. Unlike many of her models, Norma Jeane didn't have a mother to watch out for her. Neither Grace nor Ana showed up to help her, although she was only nineteen years old. Marilyn claimed in *My Story* that they were working hard to support themselves and she didn't mind managing her career herself. Generous to a fault, Norma Jeane gave them money when she had it, and she talked to Grace frequently on the phone. "She started out with less than any girl I ever knew," Snively stated, "but she worked the hardest . . . she wanted to learn, wanted to be somebody, more than anybody I ever saw before in my life." The photographers were charmed by her interest in them. "When I introduced her to a photographer," Snively stated, "she would look him straight in the eye and cling to his every word. She made everyone she talked to feel as if he were the only one in the world." Added to her personal charm was her compelling photogeneity; sometimes she seemed to glow.[21]

In another indication of her chameleonlike abilities, she modified her manner to suit each photographer. With William Carroll she was a confidante. They discussed her failing marriage, and she suggested that if he intended to display her photo in camera shops, she should wear shorts or a playsuit, not a bathing suit, so that mom-and-pop customers wouldn't be offended. She approached Bruno Bernard—a courtly European—as a paternal figure. But he photographed her in a yellow bikini swimsuit that she had made out of several scarves, tied at the sides with string. She attached a brief skirt to it, which she removed for some photographers. The bikini was so abbreviated that it showed off her midriff and most of her breasts. In 1945 the bikini swimsuit had only recently been invented by a French swimsuit designer, who named it after the South Pacific atoll where the hydrogen bomb had first been tested. Only a few women were wearing it, and certainly no Americans.

In 1950 photographer Anthony Beauchamp called her bikini costume "explosive" and "a parody of a bikini." Pinup photographer Laszlo Willinger liked it so much when Norma Jeane put it on for him that he not only photographed her in it but also had other models he photographed wear a copy of it.[22]

The most insightful description of Norma Jeane during this period is in Andre de Dienes's memoir of their month-long trip to Death Valley, Yosemite, and Oregon in December 1945. They went to those places to shoot photos of her in natural settings. Posing for de Dienes was a coup, since he was known internationally for his work. Born in Transylvania, he was raised by an elderly relative after his mother committed suicide and his father moved to Budapest. At the age of eighteen, he moved to Paris. Self-trained as a photographer, he met the prominent fashion photographer George Hoyningen-Huene one day when he was photographing Parisian street scenes. The older photographer, impressed with his work, became de Dienes's mentor.[23]

De Dienes had a volatile personality, talked nonstop, and was considered to be an eccentric. He was also ten years older than Norma Jeane. The year before he met her, he had photographed Shirley Temple and Ingrid Bergman for *Look* magazine. He'd lived in New York, but at the end of 1945 he'd moved to Los Angeles to find a model to pose for him nude in natural settings as they toured unsettled areas of the West.

Photographing the naked female body had become his passion. He loved the female body, loved to look at it, loved to make love to it. As a photographer he saw it as a landscape of lights and shadows, hills and valleys, and he aimed to glorify it in his photographs. A pioneer in what came to be known as aesthetic nude photography, he shot naked women in terms of the high-art tradition that had entered photography with the nudes of Clarence White and Edward Steichen in the 1900s.[24]

He asked Emmeline Snively to find him a model. Although posing nude was considered scandalous, Snively thought Norma Jeane might do it, perhaps because she was married and thus accustomed to being naked in front of a man. She sent Norma Jeane to de Dienes's room in the fashionable Chateau Marmont on Sunset Boulevard, an upscale hotel that was bound to impress her. Norma Jeane was also impressed by his portfolio, which was filled with his photos of celebrities and stars.

She turned on her charm, and de Dienes fell for her. A replica of a beloved peasant girl from his childhood in Transylvania, she also resembled his favored Shirley Temple. She had Temple's innocent look, curly hair, and enchanting laugh. She also seemed to appreciate his jokes and stories, which he told endlessly. De Dienes often fell in love with his models—he'd fallen in love with Temple—and he fell for Norma Jeane. She kept him at arm's length. She flirted with him, refusing to say whether or not she would pose for him nude, although she went into the bathroom in his hotel room and put on a two-piece bathing suit she had along with her so that he could evaluate her body. She asked him many questions, showing interest in his life and work, flattering him. She said little about herself.

She refused to go with him on his trip without Ana Lower's permission, and so she invited him to dinner at the Sawtelle apartment to meet Ana. Norma Jeane told Ana about his fame as a photographer, while making certain that Andre saw the religious pictures on the wall and heard them say grace before the meal. It was her way of putting up boundaries, of showing him that she was a "good girl." After all, she was still married to Jim Dougherty.

While Norma Jeane was dealing with de Dienes, Jim returned on leave after many months overseas, and he moved in with her in Ana Lower's downstairs apartment. Pleading their need for money, Norma Jeane refused to cancel her trip with de Dienes. Once on the road, she sent Jim a postcard stating how much she missed him. She addressed the card to "My Dearest Daddy," and she signed it "Your baby."[25] She was doing her best to maintain the seductive wifely voice that would convince Jim of her loyalty. She was still afraid of losing him.

Norma Jeane's trip with de Dienes turned into a madcap adventure. They drove through uninhabited land, encountered hoodlums, had flat tires, and lost a wallet. When Norma Jeane telephoned Grace, now back from her eastern adventures and living in Van Nuys, Grace told her that Gladys had been released from Agnews and was living in a hotel in Portland. Norma Jeane hadn't seen her mother for six years. De Dienes agreed to take her to see Gladys, since they were planning on being near there anyway. It was a miserable visit. Gladys was mostly silent and morose. Then she told Norma Jeane that she wanted to live with her—a startling statement after six years of absence, although Gladys would show up that spring (1946), and Norma Jeane would take her in.

Norma Jeane was quiet on the trip, but de Dienes talked continually. She read from a Christian Science prayer book and slept a lot, keeping calm to prevent an attack of motion sickness. He read to her from a book of quotations he had, philosophical thoughts of great men about spirituality, and she read to him from her prayer book.[26]

They exchanged nicknames: she called him W. W., for worry wart, and he called her Turkey Foot because when they reached Mount Hood in Oregon her hands turned purple from the cold, resembling the feet of a turkey. It doesn't seem especially affectionate, but it amused Norma Jeane, who loved nicknames. The attempts at affection turned more serious when he pressed her for sex: she refused, telling him once again she was married. But the night after they visited her mother, he said she gave in. De Dienes claimed the sex was superb (of course he would say that). On Christmas Day she failed to lock the car door, and some of his photography equipment was stolen. She called Aunt Ana from a pay phone, interrupting her as she was eating Christmas dinner with Jim Dougherty. She said she was miserable and wanted to come home. It's not surprising that the visit to Gladys, followed by an ambivalent sex episode and the loss of de Dienes's equipment, plunged her into a funk. From an adventurer she turned into a little girl who wanted to come home.

De Dienes persuaded her to continue the trip. After all, he was a famous photographer. He decided they were engaged, and Norma Jeane went along with the fantasy. He talked about moving to the desert, growing their own food, and having many children. Or they would settle in New York, and she would be his muse. When he asked her what she would do there, she surprised him by replying that she would go to Columbia Law School and then help the poor. But she didn't really intend to marry him. She told a friend that she liked de Dienes a lot, but after the years with Jim she wasn't interested in marriage.[27]

De Dienes found Norma Jeane extraordinary. Everywhere they went she discovered something in nature to admire: the mist on the distant mountains, tiny bugs she held in her hand. She seemed on a transcendent high. When their car got stuck in a snowbank in the mountains, she became spellbound by the silence of the woods around them, covered by a blanket of snow. She filled the backseat of the car with pine branches because she wanted to take the scent with them. That touching gesture overwhelmed him.[28]

They cut their trip short when de Dienes learned that a close friend of his in New York had died. They hurried to Los Angeles so that he could catch a nonstop train to New York. When he returned several months later, Norma Jeane was with another man, although they remained friends. She went with him on a tour of Spanish missions near San Diego—San Gabriel and San Juan Capistrano—and to the beach, where he read lines of poetry to her and she memorized them. In January 1947, she sent him a copy of *Science and Health*. In the frontispiece she noted a passage. "Divine Love always has met and always will meet every human need": in other words, she didn't want a physical relationship with him.

De Dienes's photos were important to Norma Jeane's success. On their trip in December 1945, he photographed her in a variety of settings. She was a woodland sprite, a girl frolicking in the snow in a snowsuit; a peasant girl wearing a pinafore and holding a lamb. The lamb photo was the first photo of her to appear on a nonmilitary magazine cover—*Family Circle*, a magazine for housewives. De Dienes shot three of the first five mainstream cover photos in which Norma Jeane appeared: *Family Circle*, in April 1946; *U.S. Camera* in May 1946; and *Pageant* magazine in June 1946.[29] He sold her photographs to European publications as well as American ones, initiating her transatlantic reputation. But she never agreed to pose for de Dienes in the nude. The famous 1949 nude photo of her was taken by Tom Kelley, a photographer with a modest reputation as a photographer of nudes.

Jim Dougherty was there when Norma Jeane returned from the trip with de Dienes; he had moved into Ana's downstairs apartment, where Norma Jeane had been living. He couldn't do anything about his wife's behavior, so he stoically retreated emotionally, even though he discovered that not only had she used up the stipend from his salary she was sent during the months they had been apart but she also had cleaned out their savings and pawned their jewelry to pay for her modeling expenses. She was able to charm Jim into forgiving her. And she was on a roll. In February 1946, Snively sent her to sit for famed illustrator Earl Moran. During the next two years, she modeled for him once a month. He took photos of her, sketched a charcoal outline of the photos, and went over them with colored chalk, producing an idealized image of her. Yet, in the many illustrations by Moran for which she posed, she looks like just another blonde, nothing special. Sometimes she violated the day's conservative morality by posing topless for him, but her look was so unexceptional that even when she was a star no one identified her as the model for those illustrations.[30]

Well-known Hollywood photographers shot her: Lazlo Willinger, Earl Leaf, David Miller, Earl Theisen, and others. (Theisen had worked at Consolidated Industries years before and had known her mother.) Jim Dougherty was amazed at the number of magazines and ads featuring her—on covers, on inside pages, in advertisements for makeup, shampoos, clothing, shoes, cars. Bruno Bernard even photographed her with his dog and sold the photograph for a dog food ad.[31]

Did Marilyn have sex with any of these photographers? In 1956 she told Colin Clark she did. Clark was an elite Brit, the son of art critic Kenneth Clark, and Laurence Olivier's assistant on *The Prince and the Showgirl*. He became friendly with Marilyn when she starred in that film opposite Olivier in 1956. In 1960 she also told Jaik Rosenstein she had slept with photographers. Rosenstein was a maverick journalist who published a mimeographed newsletter, *Hollywood Close-up*, in which he exposed Hollywood's hidden sexual side: prostitution, call-girl rings, extortion schemes. Once a legman for Walter Winchell and then for Hedda Hopper, he became disgusted with their reporting, which he found biased and sometimes made up. In 1960 he was one of the few journalists to support Marilyn's version of her affair with Yves Montand, in which Montand was the seducer as much as she. Grateful to Rosenstein, she gave him a candid interview, including telling him about her past behavior.[32]

Marilyn told Colin Clark she slept with photographers as a way of thanking them; she told Jaik Rosenstein she slept with them because of the competition for modeling jobs. We should also remember that morality was freer during World War Two than before. With Jim often absent and men coming on to her, Norma Jeane may have become a "V-Girl," one of the young women who slept with servicemen. As for the photographers who shot her, Conover and de Dienes claimed to have had brief affairs with her. Joseph Jasgur stated that he and Norma Jeane "respected" her marriage and only cuddled in the back seats of movie theaters.

On the other hand, photographer William Carroll told me that the Blue Book Model Agency was connected to a call-girl ring. The models weren't required to participate in it, he said, but they made a lot more money if they did. The agency had its offices in the Ambassador Hotel, a Hollywood landmark, where call girls hung out. The hotel was on Wilshire Boulevard, not far from the studios; it occupied twenty-two acres and included a large swimming pool, a golf course, many fashionable shops, and the Coconut Grove nightclub, a center of Hollywood nightlife.[33]

Visiting dignitaries and businessmen stayed there, and call girls were available to them. Malcolm Boyd was a junior executive in a Hollywood advertising agency and then a producer at Republic Pictures. In both jobs he arranged for visitors to have an expensive dinner, a Cuban cigar, and the services of a call girl. Hollywood had a reputation as being sexually unfettered, and male visitors without wives along sometimes expected their fantasies to be fulfilled. Emmeline Snively seemed to keep her distance from the call-girl rings. She called her agency Blue Book, using the title given to the books in many cities listing the members of high society. She always wore a hat and gloves, signaling her respectability. In 1951 Charles Stocker, head of the Vice Squad of the Los Angeles Police Department (LAPD), called her Blue Book Model Agency the most elite agency on the West Coast.[34] It's possible, of course, that she offered her models a chance to make money on the side through prostitution and that her public respectability was a cover.

As a model Norma Jeane had entered a world of beautiful young females and randy male photographers, a sensual, sexual world. Living as a teen with Ana Lower, she had kept her virtue intact, but at some point after her disillusionment with Jim Dougherty and her signing with Twentieth Century–Fox in August 1946, she became fascinated with her body, began to go nude in her private life, and engaged in extramarital sex. Her demons probably drove her to it, but she justified what amounted to sin in the eyes of the Christians who had raised her through a "free-love philosophy." Such a point of view circulated sub rosa throughout the twentieth century, especially in artistic and bohemian circles. It promoted nudity as the ultimate in healthy activity and regarded sex as a natural outgrowth of friendship. Columnist Earl Wilson, her close friend, said "nakedness, nudity, sex, child of nature" had always been her platform. New York clothing manufacturer Henry Rosenfeld, another close friend, said she regarded sex as an act that brought friends closer together. That attitude was also a way of justifying what amounted to promiscuous behavior.[35]

She probably derived some of these free-love ideas from the photographers, especially de Dienes, Willinger, and Bernard. They were sophisticated Europeans who photographed nudes and justified the practice as aesthetic, not pornographic. Bernard came from Germany, and Willinger had studied in Berlin; Germany had a large nudist movement. Bernard wrote, "The artist's fascination with the female figure is rooted not in simple allure but in the aesthetic satisfaction he gets during the quest for beauty." She followed both their ideas and free-love doctrines when she stated that sex was the key to life and that all aesthetic endeavors came from it—literature, art, music, poetry.[36]

Aside from her dream of walking nude over a church congregation, Norma Jeane hadn't shown any interest in going nude as a child, even though such behavior isn't unusual among young children. Living with Norma Jeane in the early spring of 1945 and again in early 1946, while she was modeling, Jim Dougherty noticed that she wasn't wearing underwear for a modeling assignment. When he asked her why, she replied that she wore her clothing tight to show off her body, and underwear might cause ridges. She made the same statement repeatedly in later years when she wore no underclothes; although other behaviors of hers and comments she made indicate that her drive toward nudity had deep roots in her internal self.

Staking her success on showing off her body, she became attached to it, as though it was her most precious possession. So much else had failed during her childhood. During her preteen years it had seemed as though her body would also be ordinary, but she had gone through an "ugly duckling" phase to turn into a beautiful swan. Like her "magic" red sweater, her body, which women envied and men desired, had also become magical. Yet it must be remembered that Norma Jeane also possessed a streak of prudery, a legacy of her religious upbringing and the influence of her mother. It's not unusual for complicated individuals to demonstrate opposing behaviors at the same time; Marilyn had to fight against that prudery to turn herself into the greatest sex symbol of her age.

In March 1946, after disreputable talent scouts had approached Norma Jeane for films, Emmeline Snively persuaded talent agent (and Christian

Scientist) Helen Ainsworth of the National Concert Artists Corporation to represent Norma Jeane, who signed a contract to represent her. She got Norma Jeane an interview at Paramount, but the executives turned her down. Ainsworth decided to wait until the magazine covers came out to push her again. In the meantime, she assigned Marilyn to Harry Lipton, her assistant.

In April 1946 Jim was sent overseas again, and Gladys acted on the statement she had made when her daughter had visited her with Andre de Dienes the previous December: leaving Portland, she traveled by bus to Los Angeles and moved in with Norma Jeane in Ana Lower's ground-floor apartment. She seemed better, less agitated and morose, although she still wore her white nurse's uniform and was obsessed with Christian Science. She helped Norma Jeane, doing her shopping and making her modeling appointments for her. She visited Emmeline Snively and thanked her for her kindness to her daughter, impressing Snively with her ladylike behavior. Apparently Gladys thought Norma Jeane's modeling was respectable. There was the *Family Circle* cover, in which Norma Jeane cradled a lamb; the next step, she hoped, was *Ladies' Home Journal*. When Jim came home on leave in May, he found Gladys ensconced in the bedroom with Norma Jeane, pushing him out of the marital bed and making it necessary for him to stay at his parents' home. For the first time he realized that the sweet Norma Jeane could be calculating. Still, he thought they could work things out. It appears that, as usual, she used sex to soothe him.

The magazine covers featuring her were appearing, indicating great success as a model: *Family Circle* in April; *U.S. Camera* in May; and *Pageant* in June. In early July, she filed for divorce in Las Vegas, where another of Grace's aunts, Minnie Willette, lived. Norma Jeane moved in with Minnie during the six-week residence required for the Nevada divorce. Afraid of Jim's reaction, she had her lawyer send him a letter informing him of the divorce. It came as a surprise; he was on a riverboat on the Yangtze buying her a camphor chest when he received the letter. He immediately cut off the stipend from his salary she had been sent and waited until he returned in September to confront her.

By July, if not earlier, Norma Jeane was dating other men. They included Bill Pursel, a college student she met in Las Vegas, and Ken Du-Main, an actor she met through another Blue Book model. She read poetry and discussed it with Pursel, as she had with Andre de Dienes. DuMain, who was just a friend, took her to a nightclub in Hollywood featuring impersonator Ray Bourbon. Playing female roles, Bourbon wore elegant women's clothes, while delivering lines so risqué that the *Los Angeles Times* reporter who covered him was nonplussed. Norma Jeane liked Bourbon's humor; she saw how comedy could be created by exaggerating gender roles, playing with femininity as though it were a masquerade.[37] It was a lesson she would never forget.

With Norma Jeane on magazine covers, agent Helen Ainsworth contacted the studios again on her behalf. She persuaded Ben Lyon, talent director at Twentieth Century–Fox, to interview her. He met Norma Jeane on July 17 and was impressed. He thought her photogeneity would translate into star power on the screen. She reminded him of Jean Harlow, whom he had discovered twenty years earlier. Ever since Harlow's death in 1937, Hollywood had hoped to find a replacement for the woman considered to be the screen's greatest sex goddess. In Lyon's opinion no one had measured up to her—not Lana Turner, Rita Hayworth, or Betty Grable. Lyon decided that Norma Jeane should be given a screen test, which was a necessity before any studio offered an aspiring performer a contract.[38]

Darryl Zanuck, head of the studio, authorized all screen tests, but since he was out of town Lyon went ahead on his own, testing Norma Jeane at five thirty in the morning on the deserted set of *Mother Wore Tights*, a Betty Grable movie in production. It was a gamble: Norma Jeane was a successful model, but she had no acting experience. Realizing that lack, Lyon had her do a silent scene, without any dialogue. To ensure quality results, he assembled a group of veteran filmmakers to do the test, including Leon Shamroy, a cameraman who had won several Oscars for cinematography.

Wearing a tight, long, sequined dress, Norma Jeane walked back and forth on the set, sat on a high stool, lit a cigarette, stubbed it out, and walked toward a window. Lyon encouraged her: "I want you to project sex the way you do in the still pictures." Makeup artist Whitey Snyder agreed with Lyon, although Norma Jeane spoke harshly to him at first. The docile Norma Jeane was becoming more forceful. She demanded that he replicate the makeup she applied to herself as a model, even though he told her it was too heavy for films. But he did what she demanded—and Shamroy chastised him for a bad makeup job.

Norma Jeane heard the reprimand, and it set off her nervousness. She began to stutter, and her face broke out in red splotches. Whitey calmed her, telling her she wouldn't have to speak in the scene, that it would be just like modeling. He had her wash off the makeup, and he made her up properly. She never forgot his kindness: several years later she recruited him as her personal makeup man, one of a group of loyal assistants she assembled. In control of herself after Whitey's intervention, she performed the scene, thrilling the men who were present. Shamroy saw Norma Jeane's potential. "She had a kind of fantastic beauty like Gloria Swanson," he enthused, "and she got sex on a piece of film like Jean Harlow." But she "didn't have that wriggle in the ass and the mouth open that she later had," Shamroy said.[39]

Lyon screened the test for Darryl Zanuck, but Zanuck wasn't that impressed. He was also put off by her lack of acting experience. It was an iffy proposition to sign a pinup model to a contract, since the Motion Picture Production Code board might object. He hesitated to sign her up. Then Ainsworth exploited a lucky break. While recuperating from a plane crash, Howard Hughes spent time reading men's magazines, including the August issue of *Laff*, with Norma Jeane in the Bruno Bernard yellow bikini on the cover. Hughes had a breast fetish, and he couldn't miss Norma Jeane's figure in that bikini. He was a Hollywood maverick who used his considerable fortune to finance his films, and he used film contracts as a ploy to seduce women. He instructed his assistant to sign Norma Jeane.

Hearing of Hughes's interest, Ainsworth gave the story to Hedda Hopper, who printed a squib in her column stating that Hughes was going to sign Norma Jeane Dougherty. The competition increased Fox's interest. Norma Jeane signed a contract with Fox on August 24.

The rite of name changing happened next. That was standard after new actors signed a contract. It signaled their rebirth into the world of Hollywood and acknowledged studio control over them. The name Norma Jeane Dougherty wouldn't do: it wasn't catchy; it was too long for a marquee. Lyon chose the name Marilyn because he thought Norma Jeane resembled Marilyn Miller, a star of the Ziegfeld Follies to whom he had once been engaged. Norma Jeane chose Monroe because it was a family name.[40]

Marion Marshall signed a contract the same day. She told me that the studio liked the MM combination because it had a sexy lilt. Thus her name was changed from Marion Tanner to Marion Marshall and the original Norma Jeane Dougherty to Marilyn Monroe. But Norma Jeane didn't like the name, and she didn't assume it immediately. On October 22, 1946, she wrote a friend that she thought her name would be Clare Norman. Fellow Fox starlet Jean Peters suggested that she use the name Meredith, while Carol Lind was the choice for a while. Norma Jeane's screen name wasn't finalized until early December. For a number of years she stated in interviews that she didn't like the name Marilyn Monroe. She said that she had wanted to use her modeling name, Jean Norman.[41]

Once she had a contract, Norma Jeane faced the next hurdle: she had to learn how to act. Could she translate a skill at posing before a still camera into a skill at acting? It also meant dealing with her stuttering and her anxiety. Encomiums from Ben Lyon, Leon Shamroy, and Whitey Snyder helped cheer her on. There was also Helen Ainsworth's artful statement to her when she signed with National Concert Artists Corporation in March 1946, which Harry Lipton, present at the interview, remembered. Ainsworth told Norma Jeane that she had possibilities for film. " 'I can tell by your eyes,' Ainsworth said. Marilyn seemed surprised." Lipton surmised that many people had told her that her voluptuous body was her ticket to success, not her eyes. But, Lipton concluded, Helen was right. "There was something warm and gentle in Marilyn's eyes that had nothing to do with sex."[42]

Like Ainsworth, Ben Lyon also saw something special in Norma Jeane's eyes during her screen test. "I want you to see," he told Louella Parsons, a close friend. So Parsons viewed the test. There it was: fright, sheer fright. "It came out of her eyes and created a feeling of compassion in me that I have never lost." Patricia Cox, a member of the MGM contract pool under the name Carol Eden, recognized that fear. She had been sexually abused as a child, and her grandmother had been committed to a state mental hospital. That's what came out of Norma Jeane's eyes, Patricia said, sadness and fear over the terrible experiences she had undergone as a child that she could never forget.[43]

Meantime, Norma Jeane had become close to Harry Lipton, who took over from Helen Ainsworth as her agent and remained her agent until 1949. He helped her arrange her divorce from Jim Dougherty; he negotiated contracts for her. Soon after he took over, he was startled to receive a phone call from her in the middle of the night. She couldn't go to sleep, she said, and she wanted to talk with him about her fears. He talked to her for a while, calming her down. It was the first of many such phone calls he would receive from her. It is also the first example we have of behavior that would become characteristic of Marilyn, as she would call close friends in the middle of the night when she couldn't sleep and was lonely or frightened of life and wanted reassurance.[44]

When Norma Jeane signed a contract with Twentieth Century–Fox, the studio system was much the same as it had been in the 1930s, when Gladys and Grace worked as film cutters. There were still five major studios: Twentieth-Century Fox, MGM, Paramount, Warner Brothers, and RKO; and three minor ones: Columbia, Universal, and United Artists, with smaller enterprises like Republic Studios still existing and independent production companies formed by actors and agents. (In 1935 Fox Pictures had been combined with Twentieth Century Pictures to form Twentieth Century–Fox.) The men who had founded these major studios—the immigrants, largely Jewish, called "the moguls"—were still their chief executives. They were now in their late fifties and their sixties.

The moguls retained control over the industry against the competing forces of television, foreign films, and independent production companies. By 1970 these forces would bring down the studio system, but for several decades the moguls fought them off. Darryl Zanuck at Fox, Harry Cohn at Columbia, and Louis B. Mayer at MGM, the three most powerful studio heads, involved themselves in all aspects of production, including project creation, hiring and firing, writing and editing, casting and costume design, and publicity. Excellent businessmen, they watched over production costs. Sometimes acting as artists, they made A movies with major stars and competed to win Oscars at the Academy Awards ceremony each year, a showcase for their artistic intentions.

Their operations were split between production facilities in Hollywood and business offices in New York close to the Wall Street banks that often financed their films. At Twentieth Century–Fox, for example, Darryl Zanuck was head of production in Hollywood and Joe Schenck ran the business operations there. Both Zanuck and Schenck reported to

Spyros Skouras, an immigrant from Greece who had risen to the top, and a board of directors in New York. Joe Schenck's brother, Nicholas, ran the business office in New York for MGM.

Anthropologist Hortense Powdermaker published a study of the film industry in 1950, basing it on interviews with three hundred individuals, at all ranks of production. She found the industry filled with tension, with a "constant jockeying for position and power" and an atmosphere like "a gambler's den."[45] The moguls, legendary in their own right, stood above it. Connected by their Jewishness, they fraternized with each other in country clubs and synagogues. Darryl Zanuck wasn't Jewish, although he was as driven as the others. They went to the same restaurants and parties, played poker, tennis, and golf with each other, and served on the boards of the racetracks they founded, Santa Anita in Arcadia and Hollywood Park in Inglewood.

They were both competitive and collegial. They exchanged information and sometimes formed a united front. Powdermaker found their power so great that she depicts them as akin to the plantation owners of the antebellum South, with the actors their slaves. They had created one of the most powerful patriarchies in the history of the United States.

In signing a contract, Norma Jeane came up against their power. Decades before, during the consolidation of the late 1920s, the studio heads had gained control over actors and had written that control into the actors' contracts. Norma Jeane signed a standard beginner's seven-year contract that stipulated her salary at seventy-five dollars a week, guaranteed for forty-two weeks of each year, with regular raises. Beyond that the studio had complete power. The contract provided for reviews every six months, but the actor had no input into the review, and the studio could fire the actor without cause.

In addition, an actor had no control over the roles he or she was assigned. If an actor refused a role, the estimated time that person would have spent playing the role could be added to the stipulated seven years of the contract. In 1944 Actress Olivia De Havilland successfully challenged this provision in the courts as a violation of the legal limit of seven years in indentured-servitude contracts in the California farm industry, but the studios still applied it. Moreover, the studio received any money that an actor under contract made outside the studio, in television or posing for advertisments, for example. And the studio could "lend out" a player to another studio for a large sum and then pocket the difference between that amount and the actor's contractual salary.

Softening the rigors of such contracts and further manipulating their actors, the moguls often adopted a fatherly attitude toward their young contract players, sometimes in their teens. They advised them on their careers, soothed them when they were upset, lent them money, and even arranged for abortions. Shirley MacLaine described how they operated. "The moguls," she wrote, "were hard-fisted authoritarians who had created a system of linked dictatorship. We were the children, to be led, guided, manipulated, bought, sold, packaged, and coddled." Elia Kazan called them "marvelous monsters."[46]

Despite the Motion Picture Production Code, with its restrictions on the open display of sex in movies, Hortense Powdermaker found sex omnipresent in Hollywood. "Sex relations are constantly used by those ambitious to succeed and by the successful in demonstrating their power. There is an obsession on sex in conversation and in print. The whole industry revolves around sex. Despite the Production Code, sexuality is omnipresent on the movie screen, and no one becomes a star without having sex appeal." Its major manifestation, according to Powdermaker, was the large number of young girls who went to Hollywood hoping to become stars and who used sex as a means of getting ahead.[47]

Studio executives also manipulated the system to fulfill their sexual desires. Louis B. Mayer was an "old goat" who liked "party girls." Harry Cohn, called "White Fang," was reputed to like kinky sex. The story with regard to Darryl Zanuck was that he had closed down the Fox executive offices every afternoon before World War Two to have sex with a different starlet each day. According to his major biographer, he believed that he needed to bed as many women as possible to maintain his virility.[48]

Some of these men were short—between five feet and five feet five inches tall, including Zanuck at Fox and Mayer at MGM. They seemed driven by a "Napoleonic complex" that impelled them to boost their egos by having sex with beautiful women who otherwise would have rejected them.[49] When Marilyn wore three-inch heels, she was five feet nine inches tall. She must have towered over Zanuck and the others.

Zanuck hadn't liked Marilyn when he saw her test, and his opinion of her didn't change over the years. He grudgingly acknowledged that she had a talent similar to Betty Grable's, but he refused to cast her in dramatic roles. Yet Zanuck had his own issues with blonde women. In the 1930s he mentored blonde actresses Alice Faye, Sonja Henie, and Betty Grable to stardom. Then he became an army officer during World War Two, stationed in Europe. His taste in women changed from blondes to dark-haired Europeans. No less than Marilyn, his childhood may have influenced his choices. He both adored and detested his beautiful blonde mother, who was sexually promiscuous and drawn to rough sex. As a child he heard his stepfather beat her, followed by passionate lovemaking. He grew up a pugilist and a polo player, tough and muscular.

Before the war blonde actress Carole Landis had been a favorite of his. Evidence suggests that she may have rejected him, angering him in the process. Whatever happened, she became known as the "studio slut" and was demoted to "grade B" movies.[50] It was after that episode and his experiences in Europe that Zanuck turned to dark-haired women.

Zanuck was a major Hollywood producer. He returned to the film business after serving in Europe during World War Two, and he then made movies about social issues, including *Gentleman's Agreement*, about anti-Semitism, and *Pinky*, about racial discrimination. Yet he realized that Fox, with its major market in rural areas, needed to make lightweight entertainment. Instead of casting Marilyn in serious films, he designated her as the next Betty Grable, whose musicals had brought in millions of dollars of revenue to the studio. From the beginning of Marilyn's career in films, he would be her antagonist, engaging in an epic struggle with her.

In mid-August, while Norma Jeane, still modeling, was waiting for her Fox contract, her half-sister Berniece and her daughter, Mona Rae, arrived from Florida for a long visit. They displaced Norma Jeane, moving in with Gladys in the bottom apartment in Ana Lower's duplex. Norma Jeane moved into the Hollywood Studio Club for a time, before returning to Ana's duplex to share the upper apartment with Ana. Once again Norma Jeane was involved in a scheme to re-create Gladys's family. Berniece talked of moving permanently to Los Angeles so that all of them could live together. Norma Jeane seemed enthusiastic over this prospect. In September, when Jim returned from his last tour of duty, he went to see Norma Jeane in her apartment about the divorce papers. There are differing stories of what happened at that meeting. According to Jim, Norma Jeane told him that she wanted to stay married to him while she pursued her acting career, and he refused. Marilyn told Arthur Miller that Jim wanted to have sex with her before he would sign the divorce papers.[51] Perhaps he thought that such intimacy would change her mind. Both stories sound plausible; divorce is never easy. Nonetheless, Jim signed, and the divorce was final. When Norma Jeane received her divorce papers, she celebrated with Ana, Grace, Gladys, Berniece, Mona, and other female Goddard family members at a local restaurant. They seemed like a united family of women, toasting one of their members now free of a husband.

But the arrangement ended after several months. After years of institutionalization, Gladys had difficulty living with other people. Wearing her white nurse's uniform, continually reading *Science and Health*, she had become fixated on geographic freedom and escape, and she frequently moved her residence. One day she moved out, stating that she wanted to be on her own. Then Berniece's husband decided he didn't want to move to Los Angeles, and he asked her to come home. Berniece, a dutiful wife, returned to him sooner than she had planned. Their community of women fell apart. Norma Jeane remained living with Ana until the spring of 1947. Then, at the age of twenty-one, she finally left the foster families of her childhood, while continuing to re-create them in various forms for much of the rest of her life.

Part II

Hollywood, 1946–1955

I knew how third-rate I was. I could actually feel my lack of talent, as if it were cheap clothes I was wearing inside. But, my god, how I wanted to learn, to change, to improve.

Marilyn Monroe, My Story

Chapter 5

Storming the Citadel, 1946–1951

By 1946 Twentieth Century–Fox was the top Hollywood studio, with four thousand employees, sixteen soundstages, and seventy-five films in production. Central buildings housed makeup, publicity, wardrobe, photography, and administration. The architecture was utilitarian, softened by lawns and palm trees, but the three-hundred-acre back lot—the site of Century City today—contained a fantasyland, where the sets of Fox's legendary films, looking like "oases" in a "heavenly" landscape, along with ghost towns, mountains, and a large lake, stood. It was a place for walking and for dreaming, of other times and places, of the past and future of Hollywood.[1]

Despite rivalries and tensions, endemic to the studios, Fox had a family feeling. Everyone ate lunch in the commissary; the guards at the gate knew everyone's name. Workers played in a baseball league and put on amateur theatricals; the older film cutters and grips knew Gladys and Grace, and some had met Marilyn as a child. They considered her one of their own. They gave her their support; sometimes they gave her acting tips they had learned from long experience on film sets. Marilyn was close to Hilda, the Fox wardrobe mistress, and she would visit the wardrobe department to daydream among the silks and satins there, exploring the Hollywood history they contained. Marilyn knew the contents of every closet and who had worn what in what movie. Even as a star she borrowed clothes from the Fox wardrobe department, especially fancy dresses to wear to premieres and parties.[2]

* * *

After Marilyn signed the Fox contract in August 1946, she was assigned to the contract pool, composed of eighty young women and men who had also signed contracts. They took acting, singing, and movement classes; did walk-on roles; posed for publicity photos and attended public events on behalf of the studio. Yet there was room at the top for only a few. Contract pools, existing at most studios, were an inexpensive way to have beautiful young people on call. Most contract players were let go after a year or so.

During her first year at Fox, Marilyn was a dynamo. She hounded producers, watched films being shot, observed makeup artists at work. She hung out at the publicity department, joking with the publicists, always willing to pose for cheesecake photos. When the studio gate was locked, she whistled loudly, and the publicists let her in. In appreciation for her hard work, they gave her their "eight ball" award, named after the title of their newsletter. She never missed an acting class and was never late. Ben Lyon called her "the most conscientious youngster on the lot."[3] She was cast in several scenes in *Scudda Hoo! Scudda Hay!*, about a family and several mules, but her scenes were cut. Still, her contract was renewed after six months, in February 1947.

In publicity materials issued about her, Fox publicists claimed she had been discovered while babysitting the children of a studio executive. The story was absurd, but she may have been under consideration for the ingenue role in *Sitting Pretty*, a comedy starring the amusing and avuncular Clifton Webb as an aging babysitter. She wasn't cast in the role, but she visited Webb on the set of the film, in production that summer, and they became friends. They liked each other's humor; both had a dry, self-deprecating wit. Homosexual in orientation, Webb didn't come on to her—a welcome relief. A major Fox star, he did what he could to promote her career.[4]

Then she had a lucky break. In June she was sent to study acting at the Actors' Laboratory in Hollywood, one of the nation's best acting schools, with an acclaimed theater attached to it that functioned as a showcase for professional actors. A group of Broadway actors lured into films by high salaries founded the Actors' Lab in 1941 to practice their craft away from studio commercialism. A number of them, like Phoebe Brand and Morris Carnovsky, came from New York from the Group

Theatre, established by leftist theater people during the 1930s to produce plays about the working class. Their major playwright was Clifford Odets.[5]

The Group Theatre members also explored the techniques of Konstantin Stanislavsky of the Moscow Art Theatre, considered the founder of modern acting. Classic acting—as performed by Sarah Bernhardt, for example—was based on fixed gestures and expressions, codified in manuals and performed dramatically. Today, we would call it "overacting." Stanislavsky favored a more subtle, realistic style that allowed for individual interpretation. He encouraged actors to create their own version of the characters they played by probing their psyches and their memories of past events that related to the experiences of those characters.

The great twentieth-century acting teachers—including Michael Chekhov and Lee Strasberg—based their approaches on Stanislavsky's ideas. (Marilyn eventually studied with both Chekhov and Strasberg.) Chekhov, the nephew of playwright Anton Chekhov, studied with Stanislavsky in Moscow, but he rejected his mentor's memory technique to stress intuition, imagination, and a mystical approach in which actors tried to develop a spirituality through which they would project radiance on stage. After founding acting schools in England and New England, he established one in Hollywood in 1942. Strasberg, a member of the Group Theatre, continued to act and teach in New York before he became the head of the Actors Studio in New York in 1951. He adopted and refined Stanislavsky's memory system, although he rejected Chekhov's mysticism.[6]

The Actors' Lab took an eclectic approach to acting. Following standard practice, its teachers taught students exercises for relaxation, body control, and proper breathing. Students also did improvisations. Phoebe Brand had her students act out the meaning of a word, for example, or what they did after getting up in the morning. They read texts and performed scenes from plays. They were introduced to Stanislavsky and Chekhov, although lab teachers were critical of them. Many of the teachers were social realists from the Group Theatre, and they didn't like Chekhov's mysticism. They also downplayed Stanislavsky's memory exploration as a way of creating a character because Lab students included World War Two veterans funded by the G.I. Bill, who suffered from post-traumatic stress disorder (PTSD, then called shell shock) because of terrible battle experiences. If they fully unlocked their memories, they might break down. The Lab teachers wanted to avoid that possibility.

Marilyn learned about acting at the Lab, while at the Lab theater she saw exciting productions of plays like Odets's *Awake and Sing.* "It was my first taste of what real acting in real drama could be, and I was hooked. It was as far from *Scudda-Hoo* as you could get." With ties to Broadway, the Lab teachers had luminaries like Elia Kazan lecture when they were in Hollywood. Marilyn began to regard Broadway as a mecca for actors. She thought a lot about the "far, far-away place called New York, where actors and directors did very different things than stand around all day arguing about a close-up or a camera angle."[7]

She also met African-American actors at the Lab, which was boldly progressive in that racist era in admitting students of color. She became friends with Dorothy Dandridge, later a star dubbed the "black Marilyn Monroe" because she looked like Marilyn. Through Dandridge she met other black performers, like Sammy Davis Jr., and she began studying voice with Phil Moore, Dandridge's coach and lover, a well-known jazz artist and voice coach. During this time Marilyn had an affair with a black man. They didn't meet in public, Marilyn said, because they were too scared. "I used to sort of sidle into his room when nobody was looking. We liked each other. But it couldn't last in those conditions. It was like trying to love someone in jail."[8]

While studying at the Actors' Lab, she met influential columnist Sidney Skolsky—either on the Fox lot or at Schwab's Pharmacy, located in front of the Lab on Sunset Boulevard. Skolsky spent a lot of time at Schwab's, plugging the drugstore in his column in return for being given an office there. Lab students and aspiring film actors also hung out at Schwab's, since the food was cheap and regulars could run a tab and read the trade sheets for free. A dyed-in-the-wool New Yorker, Skolsky didn't drive a car. In return for a line in his column, young actors who owned cars chauffeured him. In the 1930s he had written up unknown players like Carole Lombard and Betty Grable, who became stars. Marilyn owned a car and loved to drive; she joined Sidney's pool of drivers.[9]

Lab students also discussed acting and politics at Schwab's. Marilyn learned about the Lab's leftist views and about the anticommunist movement that was sweeping the nation. By 1947 Hollywood was the major target of the House Un-American Activities Committee (HUAC), and studio leftists were being called to Washington to testify before the committee about Communism in their industry. To avoid being jailed they had to "name names" of Communists they knew to the committee. Even being summoned by HUAC to testify could ruin a career. Focused on her acting, Marilyn wasn't much interested in politics at that point. But she had a strong sense of justice and fair play, and she identified with the working class and the underdog.

In August 1947 Darryl Zanuck didn't renew her contract after the first-year review, even though early that month she had done well in a bit part as a waitress in *The Dangerous Years*, a film about juvenile delinquents. Unfortunately for her, it was a B movie without much cachet. Zanuck still didn't think much of her acting, and there were plenty of blondes in the contract pool. Besides, the teachers at the Actors' Lab weren't impressed by her. Phoebe Brand found her shy and insecure, without much promise. But Marilyn didn't give up. After she was dismissed from Fox, she took to her bed for a week, deeply depressed, but she rallied, following her characteristic pattern of energetic recovery after deep depression. She continued at the Lab, paying for the classes herself. She explored the local small theater scene. In the fall of 1947 she played the blonde vamp in *Glamour Preferred*, a hackneyed comedy at the Bliss-Hayden Theater. Lela Bliss-Hayden, who managed the theater, remembered Marilyn as "a nice little girl" with modest talent, although she cast her in several plays in succeeding years.[10]

Marilyn supported herself through modeling, found wealthy men to pay for clothes and meals, haunted producers' offices, and was employed as a studio "floater." Roddy McDowall met her when she was a "pacer" at Columbia, doing his dancing steps on the sidelines to keep him on target. She never spoke to him. When he asked someone why she didn't talk to him, he was told that Marilyn didn't like men because everyone tried to "lay" her.[11] To further her career, however, she had sex with influential men. She resorted to the legendary casting couch, which actually exited in the 1950s.

During her year at Fox as a contract player and even after Zanuck dropped her in August 1947, Marilyn entertained important out-of-town visitors, serving as a "party girl." Not all contract players did this. Marion Marshall and Felice Ingersoll Early told me they had nothing to do with this part of the business, although Felice also said that she was no-where near as ambitious as Marilyn. Marilyn was an easy mark. She had appeared nearly nude in men's magazines. A divorced woman, she was regarded as sexually awakened and eager for sex, and she couldn't claim that she was saving her virginity for a husband—a common goal for young unmarried women in the 1950s. The sexual abuse she had endured as a child had programmed her to please men. And she didn't have an assertive mother to protect her, or an upper-class background or Broadway acting experience to impress studio executives. According to Fox star actress Gene Tierney, these three attributes, which she herself possessed, kept her off the "casting couch."[12]

Actress Jean Peters was in the Fox contract pool with Marilyn. She remembered Marilyn wearing a baby blue angora sweater, a straight white skirt, and white pumps. She looked adorable in the outfit, Peters said. That was the innocent Marilyn. Peters described the studio pool as like a college dormitory, filled with respectable young women. She failed to mention that Hollywood men called it "the stable." Designer Oleg Cassini, one of a group of rakes known as the Wolf Pack, found his major source of "horseflesh" (women) at studio commissaries. Starlets, Marilyn included, paraded informally at the commissaries at lunchtime, showing off their bodies and hoping to catch a producer's eye. One day at lunch, Ben Lyon chided Marilyn for wearing a pink angora sweater without a bra. "Marilyn," he said, "I tell you all the time, there are some very important people in this commissary. Why don't you dress better?" Marilyn delivered a typical double entendre to a companion: "I guess Ben doesn't like pink."[13]

Sidney Skolsky called the contract pools "harems" for studio executives and out-of-town visitors. Marilyn told Lee Strasberg that she had served as a "call girl" for visiting executives, and she told Colin Clark and Jaik Rosenstein that she had slept with producers to get ahead. She told W. J. Weatherby, "I was never kept; I kept myself. But there was a period when I responded too much to flattery and slept around too much, thinking it would help my career, though I always liked the guy at the time." In *My Story* she called Hollywood "an over-crowded brothel, a merry-go-round with beds for horses." John Springer, head of magazine publicity at Fox, was appalled by how the executives treated her. "She was just their nutsy little blonde that they would fix up with the visiting bigwigs." Mike Cowles, *Look*'s publisher, visited the Fox studio in 1946. A studio executive said to him, "We have a new girl on the lot with something unusual. Instead of sticking straight out, her tits tilt up." (That, in fact, was true of Marilyn.) The executive sent for Marilyn, who came in smiling. He lifted her sweater to show what he meant. "She never stopped smiling."[14]

Pat DiCicco, a leader of the Wolf Pack, now entered Marilyn's life. Tall, dark, and handsome, with a sophomoric wit and a cool demeanor, DiCicco resembled Dean Martin. Hollywood men liked him: he was good at gin rummy and poker and always ready for a game. He charmed Gloria Vanderbilt into marriage, but she divorced him after he physically abused her. The source of his money was obscure; he was rumored to be a Mafia plant, a talent agent, or Howard Hughes's procurer for the "harem" of women he kept in apartments after signing them to contracts. He bought RKO in the spring of 1948. DiCicco kept an address book with the telephone numbers of "available" starlets, including Marilyn, which he shared with other Hollywood men. Along with the rest of the Wolf Pack, his name often appeared in the gossip columns as the date of a starlet.[15]

DiCicco was a regular at Sam Spiegel's mansion in Beverly Hills, where Marilyn sometimes went. A refugee from Hitler's Austria, Spiegel was a talented salesman, a gifted poseur, and a stellar poker player. He held a weekly salon at his mansion and a famed New Year's Eve party that in 1947 drew seven hundred guests, including call girls. Backed by his wealthy friends, Spiegel became a producer, most notably of *The African Queen*.[16]

He also set up a "boys' club" in his mansion, where Hollywood men could play poker and gin rummy nonstop—obsessions among some—and where liquor and "party girls" were available. Spiegel modeled his enterprise after Polly Adler's upscale New York City bordello, where the sex workers were intelligent and educated. Writer Budd Schulberg called Spiegel "an inspired pimp. He could create those very high-class mush pits. Women were looking for acting jobs and it was a knee up the ladder."[17] Spiegel knew the studio publicists. Harry Brand, head of publicity at Fox, was a link to Marilyn.

Prominent Hollywood men frequented Spiegel's "boys' club," including directors John Huston, Billy Wilder, Otto Preminger, and Orson

Welles and agents Charles Feldman and Johnny Hyde, eventually agents for Marilyn. (Huston, Wilder, and Preminger later directed her in films.) Evelyn Keyes, Huston's wife at the time, remembered Marilyn as "one more little blonde with the preferred size tits and a funny walk." But "party girls" weren't powerless. They could choose their partners and specify the sex acts they were willing to perform.[18]

And being a party girl could be fun. Actress Mamie Van Doren stated, "The casting couch did exist, and I did occasionally find myself on it. Many of us who made a career out of the movies did—many, many more than want to admit it. If you are young, healthy, and with the normal set of biological urges, the casting couch can also be fun with the right person." Columnist Earl Wilson wrote, "She did crazy, naughty, sexy things she probably shouldn't have." Director Elia Kazan, later Marilyn's lover, cautioned her against going to parties with DiCicco. "You'll never find anyone there except people you despise. In your heart, which is both honest and very perceptive, you despise those jerks."[19]

In this milieu, Marilyn became skilled at sex, especially at performing fellatio, which was often the preferred form of sex in Hollywood, since it obviated the need for birth control. It also got around any problem Marilyn had with painful intercourse due to endometriosis. In steam rooms and bars—private male spaces—Hollywood men discussed the performances of the women they bedded. In such male bonding rituals they indulged in a vicarious homoeroticism. In *My Story*, Marilyn stated that she was suspicious of men she dated who asked her about the sex behavior of her other male companions. She thought their curiosity revealed homosexual inclinations.[20]

Party girls occupied an ambiguous position. Sexual behavior usually wasn't questioned in Hollywood, but to be labeled a slut could damage a career. According to Evelyn Keyes, expressing a sentiment Gene Tierney seconded, "Studio men liked it when actresses responded to their sexual overtures. They thought that if they found you fuckable, so would the audience. But they also had to be kept at bay. If they thought you slept around, they wouldn't give you a job."[21]

There were other dangers in playing the sex game. At one party three men as a group tried to rape Marilyn. Moreover, participating in the sex scene could damage a sensitive psyche. There was always the danger of pregnancy and then abortion. (Amy Greene and Paula Strasberg both maintained that Marilyn had as many as twelve abortions.) David Brown, a producer who ran Fox's story department, stated that party girls often experienced "a certain loss of self-esteem, a feeling of being victimized, and always the desire to please in order to advance a career." Brown knew Marilyn; his comment might apply to her.[22] He might have added that such victimization could also produce anger. Such anger became a constant in Marilyn's behavior once she became a star.

Marilyn's work as a party girl was episodic. She compartmentalized her life as she did her friends, living different lives at the same time. She visited Ana Lower and Grace Goddard and occasionally saw foster parents of hers she had liked—the Knebelkamps and the Howells, in particular. She rarely saw Bebe and Nona, whose lives diverged from hers. Bebe got married, had a child, became a housewife, and worked as a waitress. Nona, a contract player at Columbia, was angry with the Goddard family. She turned herself into the film actress Jody Lawrance, a dark-haired tough-girl type. She achieved a measure of fame, but nothing on the order of what Marilyn attained.

Marilyn also had regular dates. In late November 1946, she rode as a Fox starlet on a float in the annual Hollywood Boulevard Christmas Parade. Comic actor Alan Young saw her and asked her out on a date. He picked her up at Ana Lower's apartment, where she was living. He saw the photo of the Christian Science Mother Church on the living room wall and mentioned that he was a Christian Scientist. Marilyn was overjoyed; for the rest of the evening she talked about how much she liked the religion. They made a connection, but they didn't go out again. Marilyn also dated Charles Chaplin Jr., a son of the great Chaplin and a fellow student at the Actors' Lab. Unprepossessing in appearance, emotionally damaged by a rejecting father, Charlie drank too much, but he didn't take drugs, as has been alleged. Marilyn's relationship with him was mostly platonic, cuddly more than sexual, which wasn't unusual for Marilyn, who sometimes craved affection more than sex.

Charlie arrived home one day to find her in bed with his brother Sydney, a Hollywood rake, good-looking and witty, a sometime romantic hero in films. Even after this betrayal she and Charlie remained close friends; she boosted his ego and gave him good advice. Shelley Winters claimed that the four of them (Sydney, Charlie, Marilyn, and she) sometimes double-dated, exploring the Hollywood scene.[23]

Marilyn also dated Tommy Zahn, a member of the Fox contract pool. An orphan raised in a foster home, he was a Christian Scientist and a world-class surfer—an attractive combination to Marilyn. She went tandem surfing with him at the Santa Monica beach, holding acrobatic poses as he lifted her to his shoulders, performing for the crowd of girls who clustered on the beach and tried to snag surfers (who had become, like bodybuilders, models of masculinity for the nation). Marilyn had once stood on the sidelines to watch the bodybuilders; she was now a performer with the surfers. Peter Lawford, later important in Marilyn's life, was passionate about surfing. When he appeared on the beach one day, Tommy Zahn introduced him to Marilyn.[24]

Photographer Bill Burnside, another Marilyn boyfriend, represented the British J. Arthur Rank Company in Hollywood. He met Marilyn at Bruno Bernard's studio. She liked his learning, and they read Keats and Shelley together and walked on the beach. He was fascinated by her off-beat ways. Scattered in her thinking, she jumped from one subject to another. With sudden mood shifts from "grave" to "gay," she was sometimes hard to follow. And she wouldn't talk about her private life. She was wary of men, but she wasn't sexually frigid. She could be underhanded and sly: she was "dumb like a fox."[25]

Marilyn never lost her innocent look and manner, but she developed a cynical side, as she came to feel exploited by the industry and by men. Still, she was always sweet and generous, as she had long been. She easily assumed this persona. Many people who knew her during her early Hollywood years described her as looking like a waif or a kitten, a curious description, since she was five feet eight inches tall in her platform shoes. This estimation of her probably reflected the sweet docility and sometimes tough, tomboy manner that she projected, not her height. MGM costume designer Edith Head said that she looked like a fluffy Persian kitten. Tom Prideaux, entertainment editor of *Life*, described her as looking like a "street urchin."[26] This was Marilyn the trickster, appealing to people's sympathy, a Little Orphan Annie doing a Shirley Temple turn. An astute observer of human behavior, Marilyn knew men liked the little-girl look, while it stirred women's maternal feelings. Femininity and its variations were her stock in trade.

But Marilyn could drop the childlike persona in a heartbeat to become the sexy Marilyn of the pinups or the mature person that Dorothy Muir had known. Billy Travilla, who designed her costumes for eight of her films, said she liked to shock people and her "dirty little bum pose" was one way she did it. She still mesmerized people—especially men—by looking them directly in the eyes. According to Travilla, "She was one woman I knew who could make a man feel tall, handsome, fascinating, with that unblinking look of hers, dead in the eye." Columnist Sheilah Graham called her look a way of making all men she met feel she was in love with them. Joan Greenson, the daughter of Ralph Greenson, Marilyn's last psychiatrist, said that Marilyn often couldn't do ordinary things that most everyone could do, but she could undertake bold actions most people wouldn't even contemplate doing.[27]

The part of her that had internalized her mother's gentility and the evangelical and Christian Science strictures against sin didn't like the direction she was taking, but it was clear that her path to success lay in creating an outrageously sexualized persona. Trying to become a "girl next door" at Fox hadn't worked; and the fan magazines were calling for a more extreme sex symbol to compete with sexy Italian actresses, like Gina Lollobrigida, who were invading Hollywood, and the buxom blonde beauties on the TV screen. Thus she created the synthetic Marilyn Monroe, whom she played most often in her personal appearances at parties and premieres. In her movies, however, she varied that persona considerably.[28]

Even before Zanuck fired Marilyn from Fox in August 1947, she had met other individuals who could promote her career. These individuals especially included Lucille Ryman, head of new talent at MGM, and her husband, John Carroll, a B player who resembled Clark Gable and did a lot of action movies. This power couple became her new champions. Ben Lyon was still promoting her, and he was close friends with Lucille, who held the same job at MGM that he held at Fox. Marilyn met John at Ben Lyon's Santa Monica beach house in the early summer of 1947. They began an affair. He seems to have been attracted to blonde starlets, since

Lila Leeds, another young blonde contract player, had lived with them the previous year.[29]

Given Lucille's clout at MGM, John had no intention of leaving her. In fact, Lucille at first liked Marilyn, describing her as a "stray waif" and a "sex kitten" with considerable charm. When Marilyn told them that fall she had nearly been raped in her apartment by an off-duty policeman, they invited her to live with them. (The Black Dahlia murder, involving the rape and mutilation of a young woman trying to make it in Hollywood, had occurred the previous January, sending shock waves through the industry.) When Marilyn confessed she was broke, John agreed to pay her a hundred dollars a week while he promoted her career. For her part, Lucille let Marilyn borrow clothes from her wardrobe.

In the contract Marilyn signed with Carroll, she called herself Journey Evers, an ironic reference to her "stray kitten" behavior, as she moved around Hollywood, without a permanent home, often thinking of herself as a foster child roaming from place to place, unable to release herself from the emotional hold of her childhood. Like many contract players, Marilyn had trouble getting by financially. She paid for acting and voice lessons, clothes, and a car. She splurged on gifts for friends. At one point she was so much in debt that Harry Lipton, still her agent, put her on an allowance, using the rest of her salary to pay off the credit agencies dunning her.[30]

Hollywood columnists called Lucille Ryman Marilyn's "best friend," although years later Ryman was vicious in describing her, claiming that Marilyn had used her waiflike persona and her tales of being abused to gain emotional control over John and her. Lucille claimed she went nude in their house and disappeared on the weekends with no explanation. Lucille denied that Marilyn and John had an affair, and she accused Marilyn of inventing the attempted rape. Yet Harry Lipton verified the affair, and gossip columnists pegged Marilyn and John as a couple. Lipton also verified the attempted rape, since she called him in a panic after it occurred and he rushed to her apartment to help her.[31]

Lucille also claimed that Marilyn prostituted herself on Hollywood Boulevard in return for meals. It's hard to take those claims seriously. After all, Lucille was an older woman whose husband had an eye for young blondes. Lila Leeds, who had lived with them the previous year, was a known drug offender. She may have been the streetwalker, not Marilyn.

It's possible, however, that Marilyn's compulsions led her to offer herself sexually—for food, not for money. She may have felt compelled to punish herself for the sexual abuse visited on her as a child, but she didn't want to consider herself to be a prostitute.

In early 1948, if not before, Marilyn met Joe Schenck, a founder of Fox and its business manager in Hollywood, by then nearly seventy and in semiretirement. A legendary womanizer, he kept an eye on the Fox starlets, and Marilyn seemed fair game. Lucille wanted Marilyn out of her house and out of John's life. Schenck, friends with Lucille and John, could take over. Marilyn moved into the Studio Club in the spring of 1948, but she often stayed in the guesthouse on Joe's estate in Beverly Hills over the next several years. It was a place to retreat to if there were tensions elsewhere in her life.

Clarice Evans roomed with Marilyn at the Studio Club. Her account of Marilyn's behavior differs markedly from Lucille Ryman's. The Marilyn Clarice knew was organized and owned many books. She was devoted to Christian Science, attended services, and consulted a healer. She meditated on Mary Baker Eddy's *Science and Health* every day, using it as her "medicine" for discontent. "She never complained," Clarice stated. "She reacted to adversity by refusing to dwell on it and by taking immediate positive action." Her motto was "Make yourself the best in the field and you will reach the top. That's why I'm spending my last penny on lessons." She told Clarice, "If one hundred percent of the movie bigshots in Hollywood told me I couldn't make it to the top, I wouldn't believe them."[32]

In March 1948 Ana Lower succumbed to her heart condition. She was buried in Westwood Memorial Cemetery and Mortuary, in the middle of Westwood, with Grace and Marilyn present at her funeral. Marilyn was bereft; she contended she threw herself in Ana's grave as it was being dug, despairing Ana's fate, but it sounds like an imagined dramatic gesture more than a real one, since Ana had been ill for a long time and Marilyn had met other middle-aged mentors, Lucille Ryman and Joe Schenck, in particular. Some weekends she went with Whitey Snyder and his family to the Ocean Park Pier, where they rode the rides and played arcade games. Once Ana was interred, Marilyn sometimes went to the Westwood cemetery, where she would sit on a bench and read a book in the calm of its green lawn and trees in the middle of urban sprawl, remembering Ana. At the Studio Club she was often on the phone in the hall, talking to agents, producers, and the men she dated. She dated a lot of men, according to Clarice, although Clarice never met any of them and Marilyn didn't talk about them.[33]

Joe Schenck was one of those men. An immigrant from Russia who came to New York at the turn of the century, he opened a drugstore in Brooklyn, where he made a lot of money selling illegal drugs. He and his brother Nicholas, who eventually became the New York head of MGM, built an amusement park on the New Jersey Palisades. By 1910 Joe managed a national vaudeville chain and one of movie theaters. He married Norma Talmadge in 1916 and promoted her to stardom. In 1926 he became president of United Artists; and in 1935, along with Darryl Zanuck, he created Twentieth Century–Fox by merging Twentieth Century Studios with Fox Pictures.

Joe had been a leader in raunchy Hollywood circles. Earlier in his life he had embodied "almost every Hollywood cliché of decadence and debauchery." The gambling crowd revolved around him; his yacht trips to Catalina, accompanied by starlets, were legendary. He had been a founder of Agua Caliente, the Mexican gambling resort that preceded Las Vegas as a place of uninhibited entertainment for Hollywood people. Several years before Marilyn met him he had taken the rap for the studio moguls in a tax evasion scheme connected to the mob and had spent several months in prison.[34]

Bald, with ice-blue eyes and thin lips, Schenck looked like an inscrutable Buddha. Still, he was a good listener and he gave good advice. These qualities attracted young women to him as friends and companions. On Saturday nights he held a formal dinner party at his Beverly Hills mansion and sent a limousine to pick up the starlets he invited. Marilyn was often among them. But they weren't the only guests. Noreen Nash attended the parties with her husband, Lee Siegel, who was the Fox studio physician. Gloria Romanoff also went to them, along with her husband, Michael Romanoff, the owner of Romanoff's restaurant, a favorite place for film people to dine and to hold parties. Columnist Louella Parsons also attended Joe's Saturday night parties. Marilyn charmed her by calling her Miss Parsons and telling her that Gladys and Grace had taught her to read by using her columns as their primer. According to Gloria Romanoff, Marilyn arrived at her first Schenck party wearing white gloves and a hat, to look like a lady; she developed a taste for expensive champagne at those parties, and she always drank it in later years. "Each popping cork proclaimed: Look at me, this is no abandoned child, no orphan!"[35]

Marilyn also attended Joe Schenck's poker parties. The rumor was that "party girls" dressed in scanty costumes served liquor at them and were available for sex, although Marion Marshall dismissed those rumors. She and Marilyn poured drinks at those parties, she said, but they wore regular clothing and didn't engage in sex. "Schenck was a lonely old man," Marion said. "He was a father confessor to me." In Marilyn's version of the poker games, she sat in a corner and kept to herself, annoyed at the men for showing off by betting huge sums of money.[36]

Marilyn charmed Joe. He liked her offbeat ways and her stories about her childhood. He soon seated her next to him at his dinner parties, in the place of honor. Albert "Cubby" Broccoli, who was Pat DiCicco's cousin as well as a movie producer and a poker player, was often at Joe's mansion when Marilyn was there. Cubby thought Joe adored her. "He just wanted to have this sweet and giving creature as a friend. Many times I'd see his face light up when she walked into the room. We'd all sit together by the pool, and just to hear her laughter was a tonic to him."[37]

Marilyn asked Schenck to persuade Zanuck to reinstate her, but Schenck and Zanuck were at odds. Marilyn stated in *My Story*, "Mr. Schenck looked at me and I saw a thousand stories in his face—stories of the girls he had known who had lost jobs, of all the actresses he had heard boasting and giggling with success and then moaning and sobbing with defeat. He didn't try to console me. He didn't take my hand or make any promises. The history of Hollywood looked out of his tired eyes at me and he said, 'Keep going.'" Marilyn sometimes stayed in his guesthouse and aided him sexually when he had issues with potency. But they were also friends. She consulted him on studio matters, getting advice on her career. "He described to me the workings of the 'inner circle' and how to deal with them. He pointed the signpost to me many times."[38]

Schenck, who was wealthy, offered to marry her to give her financial security, but she turned him down. She didn't love him, and she told him that, after a loveless marriage to Jim Dougherty, she wouldn't do it again. She didn't want money; she wanted stardom. Schenck got her a bit part in a Fox film, *You Were Meant for Me*, but her scenes were cut. She performed in a Fox employee production called "Strictly for Kicks." But Schenck couldn't budge Zanuck in his decision not to reinstate her. So he persuaded Harry Cohn, a poker buddy, to give her a six-month contract at Columbia.

When Marilyn started working at Columbia in March 1948, it seemed a windfall. Cohn had his makeup and hair stylists turn her into a glamour girl. He was looking for a backup for Rita Hayworth, his reigning female star, and he briefly thought Marilyn might be the one. Her hairline was lifted through electrolysis to emphasize her widow's peak, then thought sexy, and to square off her face, giving her a more sophisticated look. Her hair was styled into a smooth pageboy. In photos of her taken during the Columbia period, she looks like a young Lana Turner.

Cohn cast her in a B musical, *Ladies of the Chorus*, about a mother and daughter burlesque team. These "ladies" are proper; they don't do the bumps and grinds of burlesque, which the Production Code restricted in films. Striving for perfection even in a small-budget B movie, Marilyn did a stint in a downtown burlesque theater, under the name Mona Monroe. She also went with Bruno Bernard to watch Lili St. Cyr perform. St. Cyr was Bernard's signature model and a striptease star, who was headlining at the Florentine Gardens. Tall and buxom, with a long statuesque body, St. Cyr brought a new elegance and glamour into striptease, as she did slow movements of her own devising, in contrast to the rowdy striptease performances that predominated in burlesque.[39]

Marilyn was on time for shooting for *Ladies of the Chorus*, and she knew her lines.[40] She sings effectively and moves gracefully in the production numbers, although she looks more like a "girl next door" than a glamour queen. In one number she leads the chorus in singing, "Every baby needs a da-da-daddy." With her baby face and her innocent look, it was an eerie tribute to the infantilization of women that was a subtheme of 1950s gender attitudes.

While at Columbia, Marilyn became romantically involved with Fred Karger, her voice coach. Suave and well educated, he composed music, led his own band, and dated stars. He liked her introspective side and her mystical bent, which he thought was the product of her Christian Science faith. When in a deep mood, she would talk for hours about the meaning of life. She told him that she hadn't used sex to advance her career and that she was faithful to one man at a time. It was an effective, although debatable, statement. Marilyn wanted to marry him, but he refused. He berated her for illogical thinking and excessive ambition, and he didn't think she would be a good mother for his daughter, Terry. When I interviewed Terry, however, she told me his stance was a rationalization for his preference for domineering women. He never would have married the soft, gentle Marilyn, Terry said, even though Terry adored her. By the end of 1948, Fred broke up with Marilyn. Some authors maintain she was so upset that she attempted suicide, although she claimed in *My Story* he eventually wanted her back.[41]

Marilyn had fallen deeply for Fred, in what amounted to her first serious love relationship since her infatuations with Howard Keel and Jim Dougherty. In *My Story* she contended her sexual response to Fred made her realize she wasn't a lesbian. She told Elia Kazan their sex life was superb and her sex drive became so strong that the vaginal fluid it produced sometimes stained her dress. She consulted a doctor, who gave her shots to control it.[42] Whether she told Kazan the truth or was trying to arouse his interest, her statement disputes the charge that she was frigid. It does not, however, address the issue of her various internal problems with pain.

Fred introduced Marilyn to his family, who adored her and hoped he would marry her. Fred and Terry, along with his sister Mary Short and her two children, lived with Anne Karger, Fred and Mary's widowed mother. She was a Hollywood grande dame with great sensitivity to others. She had left a career in vaudeville in the 1910s to marry Max Karger, a Hollywood producer, who died several years after their marriage, leaving her with two young children to raise. She was beloved in Hollywood.

The Kargers held Sunday night songfests, at which Fred played the piano and Marilyn sang. They held Thanksgiving and Christmas parties, which Marilyn attended. Marilyn and Anne became close: Marilyn gave her presents on Mother's Day and birthdays and called her Nana. The family, helping Marilyn with her career, pooled their resources to pay to have a dentist adjust her bite by fitting her with a retainer. She was close to the children, attending their birthday parties and playing games of tag with them. She dubbed Mary Short "Buddynuts," and she and Patti Karger, Fred's first wife, played practical jokes together: when Fred married actress Jane Wyman, they put a full-size cutout of the *Seven Year Itch* Marilyn photo on their lawn. Marilyn was also close to Terry, Fred's daughter, and she took her to Christian Science services for many years.[43]

In addition to the Kargers, Marilyn became close to Natasha Lytess, head drama teacher at Columbia, who became her personal acting coach. Natasha had been a member of Max Reinhardt's acting troupe in Berlin and Vienna. Like many German Jewish actors, including others from the Reinhardt troupe, she immigrated to Hollywood when Hitler rose to power. Natasha claimed to be the widow of German novelist Bruno Frank, another Jewish refugee in Hollywood. Yet most records list Liesl Frank, not Natasha, as Bruno Frank's widow, and they identify her as working with refugee organizations. No source on Natasha connects her to such work. Donald Wolfe, who studied with Lytess, told me that she was Liesl Frank, living under a different name. But sources on the Hollywood German Jewish refugee community identify Liesl Frank as living at an address different from Natasha's. Perhaps Natasha was Frank's mistress, not his wife.

Yet if Natasha was Liesl Frank, her influence on Marilyn would be breathtaking. For Liesl Frank was the daughter of Fritzi Massary, a star of the Berlin and Vienna music hall stages. Liesl Frank's father was Max Pallenberg, a German actor well known for his portrayal of clowns. Such a background, passed to Marilyn through Natasha, would link her to major European stage traditions.[44]

When Natasha met Marilyn in 1948, she thought she was hopeless. "She was more than inhibited, more than cramped. She didn't say a word freely." It was as though she were disconnected from reality. She wore a low-cut, tight-fitting knitted red dress to their first interview. Her nose had a lump on it, which she attempted to conceal with heavy makeup. "Her voice, a piping sort of whimper, got so on my nerves that I asked her not to speak unnecessarily until we had progressed." Marilyn speaks in a normal voice in *Ladies of the Chorus*, filmed soon after she met Natasha; it's probable that Natasha, who could be harsh, frightened her. But Marilyn persevered; she realized that she needed someone like Natasha to turn her into an actress, someone tough who would devote hours of attention to her.

Natasha taught Marilyn for six years and coached her on twenty-two movies. With a demanding manner, she put people off, but she was crucial to Marilyn's development as an actress. She also taught Marilyn about literature and art, took her to museums, and introduced her to antiquing as a way to learn the history of design, initiating Marilyn's lifelong love of the hobby. She gave her a list of two hundred books to read, and Marilyn read them. Marilyn told photographer Anthony Beauchamp, "Miss Lytess made me free. She gave me inner balance and made me understand life. I owe everything to her." According to syndicated columnist Arnold Arburo, Marilyn and Natasha were inseparable. "They study every free moment between scenes and at night, too."[45]

Lytess gave Maurice Zolotow a revealing interview in the form of a memoir, but it was never published. A draft of it, however, is in his papers at the University of Texas. The Marilyn Natasha describes in the memoir, as well as in subsequent interviews with Zolotow and his assistant, Jane Wilkie, is darkly complex. She relates to men through sex, but she feels guilty about it. Suffering from a "bad-girl" complex, she has little self-respect. She is secretive. "Even an inquiry as to where she might be going on a certain evening would be regarded as unpardonable prying." She can dissociate from reality, seeming "under water," impossible to reach. "Only a wild inner faith in herself keeps her going."[46]

Marilyn had hugely complicated her life. By the spring of 1948 she was involved with Fred Karger and his family, Joe Schenck, Natasha Lytess, Pat DiCicco, John Carroll, Lucille Ryman, and probably others. Milton Berle contended that he had an affair with her during the filming of *Ladies of the Chorus*, and Howard Keel maintained that he became re-involved with her that year. According to designer Oleg Cassini she consulted him about a dress he had designed for Gene Tierney, his wife. They had sex, and he invited her to a large party that he and Gene were hosting. Gene was furious. "How could you!" she exclaimed. "How could you invite that little tramp! She's a nothing!"[47]

It's difficult to visualize how Marilyn had time for so many involvements, if, in fact, some aren't fabrications by others. The descriptions of many were crafted years after they supposedly occurred. Yet her kindness and joy, plus her sexual aura and her lilting laugh, could be irresistible. Milton Berle related that, when he took her to nightclubs, she'd sit at the table, wide-eyed, and ask question after question, which she'd follow with comments like " 'Oh! I didn't know about that!' There wasn't anything cheap about her. She was a lady." According to him, their affair was casual and short-lived.[48]

When Marilyn's contract with Columbia came up for renewal in September 1948, Harry Cohn let her go. He didn't think much of her acting—and she refused to accompany him on his yacht to Catalina unless his wife went along. Marilyn could sometimes be naive; she had mentioned his wife, which Cohn considered insulting, since he kept his philandering separate from her while placing her on a pedestal. Cohn flew into a rage and called Marilyn a "goddamn cunt," telling her he never wanted to see her again. He had lived up to his reputation for being uncouth. But Marilyn's refusal to go to Catalina was perhaps wise; Rita Hayworth called him a "monster," and actress Corinne Calvet had had to fight him off several years earlier when she had made the Catalina trip with him. Max Arnow, Cohn's assistant, thought Cohn had made a mistake. Marilyn was tested for the lead role in *Born Yesterday*, the dumb-blonde role of the decade, which went to Judy Holliday. But Cohn refused to even look at Marilyn's test.[49]

Soon after Marilyn left Columbia, independent producer Lester Cowan cast her in a cameo role as a sexy blonde in *Love Happy*, a Marx Brothers film. In a brief scene with Groucho, who plays a private detective, Marilyn says that someone is following her. She walks away, hips swaying. Leering at her backside, Groucho replies, "I can see why." Marilyn is both sexy and funny in the scene, both a blonde bombshell and a parody of the figure. Her part is small, not much more than a cameo, but you can see the glamorous and sexy Marilyn Monroe emerging in this film.

Letters in the Lester Cowan Papers reveal an unknown side to *Love Happy*. After testing her, Cowan was so impressed with her that he decided to launch a national campaign featuring her, with cover stories in *Life* and *Look*. "I have just signed a young girl who is a real find," he wrote in early November. "She has the Lana Turner–Ava Gardner type of appeal. She sings and dances better than Betty Grable." The campaign was to begin in January, with visits to New York and other cities. But nothing happened then. In March Cowan received a telegram from *Look*. "We have shot final color shots for the cover of the *Look* article.

Entire piece is completed and will be sent east probably tomorrow." Neither a *Look* nor a *Life* cover story on Marilyn appeared. What happened to stop the magazine articles is unknown, although Cowan ran out of funds and didn't distribute the film for another year.[50] In June and July, however, Marilyn toured New York and several midwestern cities, plugging the film.

Did Cowan plan the publicity campaign himself? It's probable that Marilyn had already met agent Johnny Hyde, a vice president at William Morris, then Hollywood's premier talent agency. Hyde had the clout to arrange the national tour. An immigrant from Russia as a boy, he'd come to the United States in 1898 with eight members of his Haidabura family. Small and wiry, they formed a renowned vaudeville acrobatic team. Hyde left them in the mid-1920s to work in vaudeville management, before joining the William Morris agency and moving to Hollywood to promote actors there. He was considered one of the best agents in the business, and he had mentored Rita Hayworth and Lana Turner to stardom. David Miller, the director of *Love Happy*, stated that Hyde brought Marilyn to Lester Cowan's attention.[51]

Marilyn and Johnny were first identified as a couple at Sam Spiegel's 1948 New Year's Eve party. Spiegel and Hyde were friends. Hyde, in his fifties and with a heart condition, was looking for a purpose to his life—and he fixed on Marilyn. He saw "star power" in her, the possibility of creating another Rita Hayworth or Lana Turner who would adulate him as her mentor. He had, in Hollywood parlance, "discovered" her. He was more than thirty years older than Marilyn, who was twenty-two in 1948.

In the spring of 1949 Hyde left his wife and children. He rented a house in Beverly Hills; Marilyn lived there sometimes, but she kept her own apartment, paying for it out of her own earnings. Johnny became her mentor. As she waited for the *Love Happy* tour to happen, he took her to industry "in" places, like Romanoff's, Ciro's, and the Brown Derby. Important studio people stopped by their table, exchanging confidences. Marilyn rarely spoke, but she learned a lot. Johnny often counseled her. He told her that to become a star she had to become a presence, to dominate the gossip columns as well as the screen. He told her to watch silent films, especially Charlie Chaplin's. The most expressive acting ever done was in silent films, he said, when actors had to use their bodies and their eyes to express emotion and couldn't retreat behind a screen of words.[52]

Career-wise, Marilyn floated that spring, living mostly on fees from modeling. In March Johnny bought her contract from Harry Lipton and had her sign with William Morris. He took her to meet Nunnally Johnson, a major writer at Twentieth Century–Fox, especially close to Zanuck, but Johnson wasn't impressed by her. He thought she was a call girl passing as a starlet. In April she had more success when the eminent photographer Philippe Halsman chose her as one of seven starlets featured in a *Life* story about starlets and their acting skills. He shot the reaction of each in several situations: meeting a monster, hearing an inaudible joke, kissing an irresistible man. Except for the kissing photo, Marilyn wasn't effective. She was painfully shy and wooden in movement. Halsman thought that her desire to be provocative and her fear of exposing too much of her body were waging a tug of war.[53]

Perhaps Marilyn sensed his reaction. In May she decided to pose in the nude—a startling action. The Production Code—and middle-class opinion—condemned nudity as immoral. But Marilyn was already indulging in it in private, even as she was creating her sexualized persona for the screen. Women were flaunting half-clothed bodies in burlesque and on TV screens. The TV star Dagmar, who led a dance band, became a household name when bumps on the front fenders of the day's flashy cars became known as Dagmars, in a subtle reference to her large breasts. In 1948 the publication of the Alfred Kinsey study on male sexuality, based on ten thousand respondents, caused a national sensation, since it suggested that the actual sex practices of people behind closed doors weren't Puritan at all.

Marilyn had confidence in her body, but that confidence could conflict with her prudery, a legacy of her upbringing. Tony Curtis, a contract player whom Marilyn dated a few times, remembered that she wore see-through blouses that caused men to stop and stare. She continued to parade herself at the studio commissaries at lunch, now distinguishing herself by wearing no underwear under her tight skirts. When journalists Jim Henaghan and Sheilah Graham separately interviewed her that spring, each noticed her sluttish clothing—tight skirts, no bra, breasts hanging out—which contrasted with her affect: she seemed a scared rabbit. Confident before the still camera, indulging in free love in private, with a mesmeric appeal when she summoned it up, she had a long way to

Figures Marilyn saw in her dreams, from Rossell Hope Robbins, *The Encyclopedia of Witchcraft and Demonology*, entitled "Witches; Sabbat." Marilyn told Ralph Roberts the figures in this book replicated figures in her dreams.

Autopsy sketch: this shows the scar above the pubic area from surgery to remove endometriosis.

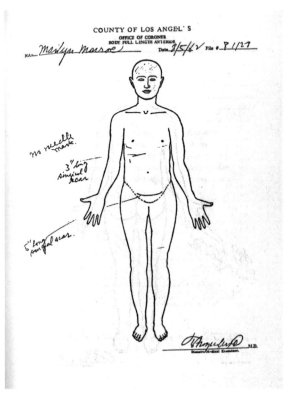

Della Monroe's passport photo.
(Courtesy of the Roy Turner Collection)

House of Ida and Wayne Bolender in
Hawthorne, California. (Collection of the
author)

Grace (left) with Norma Jeane in
front of her and Gladys (right)
with her niece Geraldine and
friends on the beach. (Courtesy of
the David Wills Collection)

Grace (left) and Gladys (right) with a young Norma Jeane (right) and Gladys's niece Geraldine (left). (Courtesy of the David Wills Collection)

Dinner at the Children's Aid Society Orphanage at about the time Norma Jeane lived there. (Courtesy of Stacy Eubank)

Tall, skinny "ugly duckling" Norma Jeane at age ten. (Courtesy of the David Wills Collection)

Norma Jeane with a double chin.

Norma Jeane and Jim
Dougherty's wedding photo.
(Collection of the author)

Norma Jeane with a friend on Catalina Beach. (Collection of the author)

Norma Jeane at a party for surfers in Malibu.
(Courtesy of the Los Angeles County Lifeguard Association)

Marilyn as an assistant for trick golfer Joe Kirkwood Jr. (Collection of the author)

Marilyn in an employee show, *Strictly for Kicks*, at Fox, in her guise as a street waif starlet.
(Collection of the author)

Marilyn dancing with Johnny Hyde. (Photographed by Bruno Bernard © Renaissance Road, Inc. Bernard of Hollywood is a trademark of Renaissance Road, Inc.)

Marilyn as the marshal for the Miss America parade.

Marilyn with Natasha Lytess on the set of *Gentlemen Prefer Blondes*.

Marilyn and Jane Russell at Grauman's Chinese Theatre, fixing handprints in cement.

go in charming these movie columnists. She baffled Graham by carrying a large book containing Freud's works to her interview with her.

In early May she learned that her mother had married John Stewart Eley, an electrician. That must have stunned her, sparking her toward rebellion, leading her to further displays of her body that her mother wouldn't like. She tried to be generous to Gladys, but they had a love-hate relationship made more complex by Marilyn's periodic attempts to meet Stanley Gifford, who she thought was her father, and his refusals to see her.

Marilyn claimed that she posed in the nude because she needed money—to get her repossessed car back, to stop credit agencies from hounding her. Marilyn was usually in debt during these years. The fee for posing nude—fifty dollars—was much higher than for posing in a bathing suit. She might have asked Johnny Hyde for money, but he was in Europe, attending Rita Hayworth's wedding to Prince Aly Khan. Besides, Marilyn took pride in supporting herself.

Marilyn had posed topless for Earl Moran, and she had posed for Bruno Bernard and Laszlo Willinger in her yellow bikini. Photographer Andre de Dienes, famous for his nudes, had asked her to pose in the nude, but she had refused. Now she agreed to pose nude for Tom Kelley, a photographer with a modest reputation for his work with nudes. Marilyn sometimes made decisions impulsively, on the spur of the moment. But once her mind was made up, she usually didn't retreat.

The backstory to the nude photo begins in the early spring of 1949, when Marilyn went by Kelley's studio to solicit modeling work, while she was waiting for the *Love Happy* tour to begin. She didn't impress him at first: her makeup was overdone, her skirt was too tight, and her blouse was too low-cut. Kelley thought she looked like a trollop. But she used a low, sexy voice to plead poverty, and he relented. Once he'd photographed her in a bathing suit for a beer ad, his opinion of her changed. She was highly professional as a model. Her body was voluptuous; she parted her lips; she assumed a mocking smile. She was on the way to developing her complete sexy Marilyn Monroe look.

Shortly after the session, John Baumgarth, head of one of the nation's largest calendar publishing companies, happened to stop by Kelley's

studio to see if he had any nude photos to sell. Nude calendars constituted only ten percent of Baumgarth's sales, but that amounted to two
million calendars a year. Kelley had hung one of his photos of Marilyn
on his wall. Baumgarth remarked on her beautiful body and told Kelley
that he should photograph her nude.[54]

Kelley asked her if she would pose nude, but she refused. Then she
remembered she'd met him by accident in the fall of 1947. Marilyn had
been driving to an audition, when her car broke down opposite where he
was shooting pinup photos. Kelley had given her ten dollars to help her
out. She hadn't had the money to repay him. In keeping with Ana Lower's creed, Marilyn always tried to repay her debts, and so she accepted
Kelley's request. When she hesitated, worried that such a photo might
damage her career, Kelley promised her his female partner would be in
the room and by the time he finished retouching the photo, she wouldn't
be recognizable as the model.

Kelley arranged the setting. He positioned Marilyn on a red velvet
theater curtain on the floor, invoking the tradition linking red velvet to
female sexuality. With Marilyn lying on the curtain, he shot her from a
ladder ten feet above. He played rhumbas on a phonograph during the
shoot. Marilyn directed the two-hour shoot with her sensuous body movements. She seemed to know exactly what she was doing. Kelley kept quiet.

Two versions of the nude Marilyn became famous. In the first one,
titled "Golden Dreams," her body is bent into an S-curve, following the
feminine "line of beauty" established by the painter William Hogarth in
the eighteenth century, based on the curves of a woman's body. In the
second one, called "A New Wrinkle," her body is stretched out. "Golden
Dreams" suggests ancient tales of Zeus impregnating Danae in a shower
of gold and modern references to raunchy sexuality. "A New Wrinkle"
refers to the wrinkling in the velvet curtain—and to Marilyn's ingenuity
both as a model and as a fresh new face on the scene. In both of them the
red nipple on her breast and her red lips match the red in the velvet curtain, although the makeup she wears is discrete, not extreme.

Her mouth is open, inviting sex, although she has neither glossy lips
nor a lascivious look. In "A New Wrinkle" she looks both triumphant
and afraid. With one arm extended and a hand in her hair, she looks as
though she might be climbing up a wall—to achieve an exciting future or
to escape a threat. Her curly sprawling reddish-gold hair forms a cloud

around her face, giving it a dreamlike quality. Resembling Rita Hayworth (a skilled Latin dancer), she blends into the background while dominating it. She invites the viewer to look at her, but she is in control of the sight lines, with a relaxed tension in her body that suggests motion. She is poised for the male gaze, but she gazes back at the same time. She doesn't look vulgar in these photos. In neither of them does her pubic hair show—or Kelley airbrushed it out. Her breasts don't look large and her body looks as much exercised as voluptuous.

Given Marilyn's perfectionism, she studied famous nude photos for the session. As Sheilah Graham noted, her poses reflect famed reclining nudes of the Western high art tradition: Manet's "Olympia" and Goya's "Naked Maja," in particular. Marilyn's favorite among the two nudes was "A New Wrinkle." It is, in fact, the more aesthetically complex of the two. She looks like an Art Deco woman in it, one of those long, elegant female bodies in 1920s sculptures. Those figures led the way to the Varga girl that Bruno Bernard wanted her to be—with long legs stretching into infinity.[55]

The major influence on her, however, was burlesque star Lili St. Cyr. St. Cyr often posed lying down, sometimes on a bed on stage, with her long body stretched out, beckoning and eluding the viewer. That's what striptease is about: fulfilling and resisting the male gaze. In "A New Wrinkle" Marilyn's body looks tall, even Amazonian. Lili St. Cyr often looked that way. When Marilyn had done a stint at a downtown burlesque house, she called herself Mona Monroe. When she signed the release for the nude photograph for Tom Kelley, she also signed her name as Mona Monroe. The parallels between the two experiences weren't lost on her.[56]

Yet when John Baumgarth received the nude photos of Marilyn, he wasn't impressed. Perhaps they weren't bawdy enough for him. He filed them away, and he put one on a calendar only after Marilyn created a stir in *The Asphalt Jungle* in the summer of 1950, more than a year after the original photographs were taken. He used "Golden Dreams," the sexier of the two. Even then sales were low. They were better in 1951, after Marilyn appeared in *All About Eve*. But they didn't soar until the spring of 1952, after Marilyn was identified publicly as the model.[57]

Paradoxically, the nude photo would make her into a major star, as the public became fascinated by her daring behavior. But she would be identified with her nude body ever after, making it difficult for her to land dramatic roles. She had violated a fundamental rule: stars could wear sexy clothes, but posing nude wasn't acceptable.

This wasn't a still photo from a movie, so the Production Code didn't apply. But the post office censors didn't like it. To get around them, Kelley produced an alternate version of the photo, with a skimpy black nightgown covering Marilyn's body. Kelley also assembled a board of artists to judge the photographs. They rated them aesthetic and in the high-art tradition. Those nude photos of Marilyn, with no pubic hair showing, became the standard for acceptability in nude photographs.

In June Marilyn finally embarked on her promotional tour for *Love Happy*. She made appearances in New York and several midwestern cities. While in New York, she went by train to Warrensberg, near Albany, with Adele Whiteley Fletcher, editor of *Photoplay*, to honor the winner of a *Photoplay* contest who lived there. Fletcher had promised to bring a starlet along, and she found Marilyn. At first Marilyn annoyed her. She went into the ladies' room at Grand Central Station at the last minute to redo her makeup, and she almost missed the train. Fletcher's assistant, who followed Marilyn, reported that she was painfully insecure about her appearance; thus the makeup redo. Fletcher didn't like Marilyn's dress—a shirred sundress, cut low front and back, which she feared would offend provincial New Yorkers. When they arrived at Warrensberg, Marilyn asked Fletcher to go to the ladies' room with her. She had spilled coffee on her dress during the train ride, and she wanted to wash it out. She was stuttering badly.[58]

In the bathroom she took off all her clothes. Standing nude, she rinsed out her dress, slip, and skimpy panties. A townswoman barged in, looked at Marilyn, and, horrified, backed out. "What's she so cross about?" Marilyn asked, in a bewildered voice, with no stutter. Fletcher was amazed Marilyn didn't realize that the woman's reaction would set off a scandalized buzz in the town. It seems that Marilyn was playing a joke on Fletcher, experimenting with nudity, or caught by her compulsions. Raised by religious people, she knew about provincial morality.

The *Love Happy* tour generated some publicity. Cowan's publicists dubbed Marilyn the "Mmm girl," and some newspapers picked up the title. Earl Wilson interviewed her in New York but, like Sheilah Graham and Jim Henaghan, he wasn't impressed by her. He thought she was a pretty girl being oversold. Yet, he compared her in print to the "It Girl" (Clara Bow) and the "Sweater Girl" (Lana Turner). Given his stature, those comparisons were invaluable. He also noted that she didn't wear underpants. She was using a new publicity gimmick.[59] In New York she met Henry Rosenfeld, a women's clothing manufacturer. Called the "Christian Dior of the Bronx," he made stylish clothing at reasonable prices for a middle-class market. When she went with Earl Wilson to El Morocco, a fashionable New York nightclub, they were seated at an ordinary table. Intrigued by her, Rosenfeld invited them to join him in the upscale section. He and Marilyn were drawn to each other. She would remain close to Rosenfeld for the rest of her life.

During the tour Marilyn revealed another side of herself. With a humanitarian conscience, she insisted on visiting an orphanage and a medical clinic. In Oak Park, Illinois, she met every child in a state orphanage, and in Newark, New Jersey, she met every patient at a clinic for the disabled poor. She was garnering a reputation for generosity, but the impulse was genuine, a result of Ana Lower's teachings and her Christian Science faith. She still attended Christian Science services, although she would soon leave the church, as other spiritual paths began to attract her.

Disappointed with the tour, Marilyn left early and returned home. Cowan was angry with her, but Johnny Hyde persuaded Zanuck to cast her as a saloon girl in *Ticket to Tomahawk*, a musical spoof of westerns. Hyde also arranged an audition for her with Ken Murray to take the place of Marie Wilson, the comic dumb blonde in his revue *Blackouts*, on a national tour at the time. Murray thought Marilyn resembled a fluttering bird, but she spoke in a low, sultry voice. She hadn't yet settled on the soft, childlike intonations of the full-developed Marilyn. He regretfully rejected her, because her breasts were too small to fit into Wilson's costumes. Marilyn was a size thirty-six; Wilson a size forty.[60]

In October, at Johnny Hyde's insistence, Lucille Ryman pressured John Huston to cast Marilyn in MGM's *The Asphalt Jungle*. The movie, shot in black and white, fits into the genre of film noir, a postwar category generated by Cold War fears and influenced by German expressionism that highlights social corruption and often features an evil, seductive vamp. In film noir, menacing shadings highlight a corrupt urban scene, which in *The Asphalt Jungle* forms the background to a story about a jewel heist. Marilyn, playing Angela Phinlay, the "niece" of a crooked lawyer, is brilliant. Working with Natasha Lytess, she grafted a lush sexuality and a dumb-blonde innocence to her sweetness, making her a victim as well as a predator. Hints of Marilyn Monroe are there. Huston, known as an actor's director, helped her with her role. After her success in the movie, Johnny Hyde expected Louis B. Mayer to give her a contract at MGM, but he didn't. He was close to Zanuck and shared his opinion of Marilyn. Besides, he was grooming other players to succeed Lana Turner, his blonde star. He didn't need Marilyn.

Johnny pressured Dore Schary, Mayer's assistant, to do something for her. Schary was considering producing a film version of *The Brothers Karamazov*, and Johnny convinced him that Marilyn could play Grushenka, the prostitute in the novel whom no man can resist. Schary gave Hyde a script for Natasha and Marilyn to work on. Schary didn't like Marilyn's reputation for promiscuity, but *The Asphalt Jungle* was being played in the screening rooms of Beverly Hills mansions of film executives and major directors, and everyone was saying that Marilyn had stolen the film.[61]

While Johnny waited to hear from Schary, he landed Marilyn supporting roles in Mickey Rooney's *Fireball* as the tough girlfriend of a gangster and in MGM's *Right Cross* as a nightclub singer. Even in her early career, she didn't always play a "dumb blonde." He had a print made of her scenes in *The Asphalt Jungle*, and he showed them to anyone he could pin down at the studios. Then he got lucky. Director Joseph Mankiewicz, a William Morris client, was about to film *All About Eve*. Johnny persuaded him to cast Marilyn as showgirl Claudia Caswell. When Lew Schreiber, Zanuck's assistant, vetoed the idea, Johnny called in a favor that Zanuck owed him. Marilyn got the part.

All About Eve is the story of Margo Channing, a forty-year-old Broadway star, and a younger actress, Eve Harrington, who lies and cheats to take over her starring role in a Broadway play. It's a fable about aging women in the glittery world of Broadway, about the perfidy of female—and male—friendships and love, about jealousy in a volatile profession based on public favor. Claudia Caswell is a party girl, using her body to advance her interests, who has latched onto Addison DeWitt, a famous newspaper critic. Claudia is a trophy companion who relies on her beauty and her body; she is the reverse of the hardworking Eve. "A graduate of the Copacabana School of Acting," she fails in an audition because she can't act. (The Copacabana was a well-known New York nightclub.) She is expendable but, like Angela Phinlay in *The Asphalt Jungle*, she is indomitable. As long as she is young and beautiful, she will find another man. And she speaks "dumb-blonde" lines, as when Addison sends her to vamp a middle-aged producer and she comments, "Why do they always look like scared rabbits?" It's a silly line, but it contains the ironic truth often displayed by the dumb blonde, a resonant female clown.

With Marilyn's triumph in *All About Eve*, Johnny Hyde persuaded Zanuck to give her a six-month contract and to consider her for roles in *As Young As You Feel* and *Don't Bother to Knock*.[62] Marilyn was featured that year in *Photoplay* in an article on rising Hollywood stars; Johnny had persuaded *Life* magazine to include her in a story on "Hollywood's Apprentice Goddesses" to appear in the January 1951 issue. Toward the end of 1950, Hyde paid for cosmetic surgery for Marilyn. The surgeon removed the bump on the end of her nose and inserted a plate in her chin to give it more definition. Johnny wanted her to be perfect.

But he could be harsh. Like some of the moguls, he was short, not much more than five feet tall. He looked like a gnome. He was sensitive about the size of his sex organs. He had a misogynist side, calling all women, including Marilyn, "tramps" and "chumps." He frequented Sam Spiegel's "boys' club." After Marilyn told Elia Kazan that Fred Karger and Johnny Hyde had abused her, Kazan asked her if she was attracted to men who belittled her because that judgment coincided with her own view of herself. She replied, "I don't know."[63]

Just before Christmas 1950 Johnny died of a heart attack. Marilyn was bereft. He had begged her to marry him during his last months, but she had refused. His family held her responsible for his death because she had imposed her youthful energy on him despite his heart condition, demanding sex and a good time. In their eyes she was a tramp. They prohibited her from attending his funeral. Marilyn went anyway, weeping copiously over his grave. The family refused to give her any money from his large estate.

Soon after Johnny died, Natasha found Marilyn unconscious in the apartment she shared with her at that point, with sleeping pills dissolving in her mouth. Did she try to commit suicide? Biographers have accused her of shamming, but suicide can be an ambivalent act, a cry for help as much as the attempt to end one's life. This time Natasha saved her, and Marilyn pulled herself together, although she soon moved out of Natasha's apartment, while giving her mentor the money for a down payment on a house by selling an expensive fur jacket that Johnny had given her. She was rearranging her life.

Soon after the New Year, Marilyn took Natasha to Hemet, near Palm Springs, where Stanley Gifford had his farm. Having lost Johnny, she wanted to find her father, and she was convince that Gifford, not Mortensen, had sired her. They stopped before reaching the farm, and Marilyn telephoned him from a pay phone. A woman answered the phone and screamed at her when she identified herself. She didn't have the nerve to go to the house and confront Stan. Several years later she took Sidney Skolsky on the same mission and met the same resistance. But she kept trying: she desperately wanted a father. Her desire may seem excessive, until we remember the sexual abuse of her as a child by older men and realize that after World War Two, as Freud's theories about the oedipal complex became popular and men returned from the war, a girl's relationship with her father was seen as the most important part of her development into a woman. Marilyn was driven by the tenor of the times, as well as by her own desires.[64] It was only during the last two years of her life, when her father tried to contact her, that she gave up the quest.

A week after the Hemet trip, she met Arthur Miller on the set of *As Young as You Feel*. That meeting launched a romance that would occupy her thoughts for the next nine years. She also began an affair with Elia Kazan. And on December 31, 1950, *Stars and Stripes* crowned her "Miss Cheesecake" of the year. That honor, which celebrated her popularity among the servicemen in Korea, would have a major impact on her career.

Did Marilyn have an affair with Natasha Lytess? Previous biographers have dismissed the possibility. The evidence for their affair, however, is substantial, and it needs to be seriously considered. Bruno Frank died in 1945. By 1948, when Natasha and Marilyn met, all sources identify Natasha as lesbian, without naming a partner. When Natasha met her, Marilyn was a failure. Fox had rejected her; she was hanging by a thread at Columbia; and Louis B. Mayer wasn't interested. Natasha was head of Columbia's acting program. She had previously taught at the Samuel

Goldwyn studio, where she coached several leading actors, including most of the cast of *The Best Years of Our Lives*. A large photo of Max Reinhardt hung on the wall of her office at Columbia, and bookshelves contained classics of Western drama and literature.

Why would Natasha give up her career to coach Marilyn? The tight red dress Marilyn wore in her first interview with Natasha was a vamp outfit. Natasha was smitten. Susan Strasberg and Peter Lawford confirmed their affair. Several of Marilyn's friends told me she was "experimental" in sex, while Steffi Skolsky, Sidney Skolsky's daughter, said that her father knew about Marilyn's lesbian affairs but concealed them. In his autobiography, however, he stated that noted lesbian actresses visited Marilyn when she was on the sets of her movies. One, famed for her masculine wardrobe, sent flowers to Marilyn. (It sounds like Marlene Dietrich.) Donna Hamilton, a Fox contract player, stated that Hollywood men "passed Marilyn around" so much that she turned to women for relief, although she was not a habitual lesbian. Elia Kazan told her to stay away from Natasha; "I know those types," he wrote. Natasha told reporter Ezra Goodman, "I have letters in my drawer saying that she needs me more than life itself."[65]

The Hollywood lesbian and bisexual culture of the 1950s was hidden from public view because of the era's homophobia. The Production Code forbade any reference to homosexuality in films. Lesbian and gay stars contracted heterosexual "white" romances and marriages to hide their orientation. It was an open secret that Lana Turner and Ava Gardner were lovers. When Boze Hadleigh interviewed Barbara Stanwyck, known to be bisexual, she denied the charge, stating that only European actors crossed sex lines. Joan Crawford is also widely identified as bisexual—in *My Story* Marilyn charged that Crawford had made a pass at her. Evidence places Marilyn near the group of lesbians, called "The Sewing Circle," which formed around Greta Garbo and Marlene Dietrich. Both were close to Salka Viertel, a refugee actress from Berlin whose Hollywood home was a center for German and Austrian refugees. Bruno and Liesl Frank often attended Viertel's gatherings.[66]

Both Marlene and Salka had acted in Max Reinhardt's productions in Berlin in the early 1920s, placing them close to Natasha Lytess, who was also a member of the troupe. The Hollywood refugee community wasn't that large. Nor were the lesbian groups connected to it. It's reasonable to assume that Natasha knew Salka, Marlene, and Greta, all of whom had begun their careers in the Berlin theater at a time when Berlin had a reputation for sexual experimentation and residents who were "connoisseurs of sexuality in all its forms and manifestations." As John Baxter wrote, "It was common knowledge in the industry that Salka, Greta, and Marlene, plus Gloria Swanson, Janet Gaynor, and Barbara Starr, were part of a huge underground lesbian and bisexual element in Hollywood."[67]

Marilyn acknowledged her bisexual impulse and rumors about it circulated throughout her career. When W. J. Weatherby asked her about it, she replied obliquely, "No sex is wrong if there's love in it." Women were attracted to Marilyn, and Greta Garbo and Marlene Dietrich were open about her attractiveness to them. Marlene stated that she found Marilyn so fresh "that she'd like to bite her." Greta stated that she wanted to do a film version of Oscar Wilde's *The Picture of Dorian Gray* in which she would play Dorian Gray and Marilyn would play one of the young women he seduces. When Marilyn traveled to New York in 1954, she told a reporter that Marlene was a close friend; she made the same statement to W. J. Weatherby, although Marlene denied it.[68]

An interview with Natasha Lytess was published in the British tabloid *The People* and other European tabloids in the summer of 1962, shortly before Marilyn's death. When I first read it, I thought it was a hoax. Then I found letters about it in the Guido Orlando Papers in the Academy of Motion Picture Arts and Sciences' Margaret Herrick Library. Letters between Orlando and Lytess discuss his negotiations to set up the interview, and there are letters from him to various European tabloid editors and their replies to him as he negotiated with them to publish the interview. An internal memo in the Arthur Jacobs Papers at Loyola Marymount University warns about the imminent Natasha Lytess story, which it validates as accurate. Lytess, living in Rome, was broke, and Orlando, finding her by accident, convinced her that he could make her a lot of money if she did it. In the end, she realized $25,000.[69]

Orlando was a failure as a press agent in the United States, but he was a success in Europe. He was, however, known for perpetrating hoaxes. Thus he kept a low profile in marketing Lytess's story. His friend, journalist Bernard Valery, the Paris correspondent for the *New York Daily*

News, taped the interview with Lytess during twelve hours and then had it transcribed, producing a manuscript of five hundred pages. Unfortunately, the manuscript isn't in Orlando's papers.[70]

In the interview in *The People*, Natasha describes an affair between Marilyn and Howard Hughes. Marilyn was living with her, and Hughes sent dozens of yellow roses to both of them. He also had a limousine take them to fine restaurants, after which he came to their apartment and spent the night with Marilyn. Natasha contended that she taught Marilyn everything she knew about sex, especially after she found a pile of books on sex techniques by Marilyn's bed, including an Asian one, probably the Kama Sutra. Natasha taught her the French ways of making love, especially the intricacies of oral sex. Natasha and Marilyn lived together as husband and wife, although Marilyn often simply wanted to be held. She was like a child in her need for physical affection.[71]

Marilyn often went naked in their apartment. Being naked seemed to soothe her. She went naked in the studio among female employees— wardrobe women, hairdressers, and makeup artists. Natasha thought her body was the one part of Marilyn's self that had become what she wanted it to be. Natasha encouraged her to copy Mae West's way of walking, a strut that was witty as well as sensual. What does sensual mean? Marilyn asked. "It means being able to enjoy things with your body," Natasha answered. "Like you eat a luscious fruit, you taste the colors with your eyes, and the perfume with your nose, and the sweetness with your tongue. You revel in it—like being made love to by a wonderful man."

In evaluating this source, it is important to realize that Natasha essentially directed Marilyn on every picture she made from *Clash by Night* through *The Seven Year Itch*, including *Don't Bother to Knock*, *Gentlemen Prefer Blondes*, *How to Marry a Millionaire*, *There's No Business Like Show Business*, and *River of No Return*. It was Natasha who decided what Marilyn would do with her body, face, and voice. Having figured it out, she had Marilyn mimic her. "I worked with her on every gesture, every breath, every movement of the eyes," Natasha said. Natasha didn't like theories of acting; she wanted to be in control. Despite Marilyn's assertion that Natasha wasn't her Svengali, the older woman stood behind the directors on Marilyn's films and relayed what Marilyn should do through hand and eye signals.

From *Clash by Night* on, Natasha Lytess was on the set with her, directing her from the sidelines. Natasha defended herself against attacks by stating that she didn't like doing it, because she made enemies of powerful studio directors, and their animosity damaged her career. But Marilyn insisted on it, because she needed a tough woman to challenge the tough male directors. Sidney Skolsky was on Natasha's side. Marilyn can be standing still on a set, Sidney wrote, "and at the same time going off in all directions. She needs someone on the set showing special interest."[72]

Ultimately, Marilyn came to resent Natasha's controlling personality and her dictatorial ways. She had become Natasha's puppet, and she realized it. She went to other acting teachers—first Michael Chekhov and then Lee Strasberg—to figure out how to do it on her own. Natasha was responsible for her early acting success in films, but Marilyn knew that she needed to find a way toward self-motivation. Chekhov and Strasberg gave her that way.

Chapter 6

Marilyn Ascending, 1951–1954

In early January 1951, Elia Kazan and Arthur Miller traveled from New York to Los Angeles by train, bound for Hollywood to pitch Miller's screenplay "The Hook," about Brooklyn dockworkers, to studio heads. They'd become close when Kazan directed the Broadway productions of Miller's *All My Sons* in 1947 and *Death of a Salesman* in 1949. Both were the sons of immigrants; both were college graduates who had become leftist social critics committed to the theater. They shared a fascination with the working class; both often wore blue jeans, T-shirts, and lumberjack jackets. They considered themselves soul mates, brothers under the skin.

Yet Kazan had another reason for the trip. He wanted to introduce his best friend to the Hollywood sex scene, which he knew from previous visits to Hollywood to direct films for Darryl Zanuck, including *Gentleman's Agreement* (1947) and *Panic in the Streets* (1950). He knew about Sam Spiegel's mansion and Pat DiCicco, with his book containing the names and phone numbers of starlet party girls. His taste veered to beautiful blondes—a fixation that began in high school, when they rejected him because he was scrawny and ethnic looking. All was changed once he had the charisma of fame. His infidelities strained his marriage, but his wife put up with them. Miller, by contrast, remained faithful to his wife, although Kazan suspected that he was tired of his marriage and had fantasies about bedding beautiful women.[1]

In this frame of mind they encountered Marilyn, who had reentered

the party scene after Johnny Hyde died. They met her when they visited the set of *As Young as You Feel*, being directed by Harmon Jones, a
Kazan protégé. Upset about Hyde's death, she was crying softly in a corner of the set. Miller went over to console her. When he shook her hand,
a jolt went through him. Marilyn's magic was working. A week later
they met again at a party at the home of Charles Feldman, a top agent
and player in both elite Hollywood and its sexual side, who was a longtime Wolf Pack denizen. Pat DiCicco and Raymond Hakim, another
playboy, were guests at the party, as were a number of Hollywood starlets, including Marilyn, and several Hollywood power brokers. This party
was about sex, not just having a good time.[2]

In Miller's memoir, *Timebend*s, Marilyn symbolizes Hollywood to
him as a place of pleasure and danger, with a sexuality both freeing and
cloying. Using vaginal metaphors, he characterized it—and Marilyn—as
"a contradictory mixture of certain scents. A sexual damp, I have called
it, the moisture in the clean creases of a woman's flesh, combined with a
challenging sea-salt smell, the exciting sea air surrounding a voyage on
water and the dead ozone inside a sound stage."[3] Miller can be ambiguous
in his autobiography, particularly when he uses these sorts of literary
flourishes. But he combines his memory of the past with his critical intelligence in the present, "bending time," in a manner that is both masterful
and self-indulgent.

That Marilyn fell for Miller isn't surprising. He was an esteemed
intellectual and a key player on Broadway, which was already a mecca to
her. On top of this, he didn't seem to mind her checkered past—whatever
version she told him. Kazan, chasing another woman, had Miller deal
with Marilyn the evening of Feldman's party. As a "party girl," she drove
her car to parties and back home the next day, or took cabs, placing no
burden on the men. But Arthur insisted on driving her. He respected her,
sometimes rare among the Hollywood men she knew. And he looked like
Abraham Lincoln, an idol of hers. They danced at the party, and they
talked for much of the night. They may have gone for a drive on Mulholland Drive, stopping to look at the lights of the city. They didn't have
sex, she told Natasha. Marilyn sensed that Miller was different from the
Hollywood men she knew.

After they met, Miller, Kazan, and Marilyn formed a threesome.
They went to bookstores and walked on the beach, laughing and joking.

Over dinner at an Italian restaurant, Miller and Kazan argued over the relative merits of Botticelli and Leonardo. Marilyn had never heard of these Renaissance artists. Intimidated by the conversation, she enrolled that month in a course on art and literature at UCLA's extension branch, open to all comers.[4] The three of them also played a prank on Harry Cohn, head of Columbia. When Miller and Kazan met with him to pitch "The Hook," Marilyn went along. They called her Miss Bauer and passed her off as their secretary. Cohn did a double take when he saw Marilyn, but he kept quiet. He didn't buy "The Hook"; no producer did. It was too leftist for that era. In 1953 Cohn would produce *On the Waterfront*, an anticommunist version of "The Hook," in which the labor unions are corrupt and an informant is the hero. Kazan, anticommunist by then, would direct it.

Arthur was getting in too deep with Marilyn. He wasn't willing to compromise his marriage; he had to leave. He abruptly took a plane back to New York. Arthur was Jewish, with a large puritan streak and a lot of free-flowing guilt. He was also introspective and romantic enough to store Marilyn in his dreams and work out his fixation on her in his writing—which he did in subsequent plays. They didn't have sex, although he deeply desired her. When he left, he wrote that he had "the smell of her on his hands."[5]

Marilyn and Elia began an affair even before Miller left, whether because of simple desire or an erotic triangle between Miller, Kazan, and Marilyn, with Marilyn in the middle, putting sex into the relationship between Elia and Arthur—which obviously was homoerotic to begin with. Marilyn said that her affair with Kazan lasted for several years. She contended that he fell in love with her and wanted to marry her. Kazan implies in his autobiography that for him it was simply an extramarital fling. According to him, he and Marilyn mostly talked about Miller, whose photo was on her nightstand.

Yet in a 1951 letter to Marilyn, Kazan expresses deep affection. No matter where they are, he says, she will always be with him and he will always try to see her. He gives her advice: stop feeling worthless and don't settle for second best in a man. Stay away from abusive men. (The reference is to Johnny Hyde and Fred Karger.) Don't moon over Art or me. Find a worthy man to marry. Stop taking taxis to parties. Drop Pat DiCicco and Natasha Lytess. Read Ralph Waldo Emerson on self-reliance. The letter suggests that Kazan valued Marilyn and wanted her to become independent and strong.

Once Johnny Hyde died in December 1950, the pressure was off Zanuck to cast Marilyn in a film. The William Morris agents, now her official representatives, didn't press her case because they agreed with the Hyde family that she had been responsible for Johnny's death by overtaxing his weak heart. She turned to Charles Feldman, who was head of the Famous Artists Agency. He was friends with Zanuck, and she knew him through Kazan and DiCicco. Perhaps he could pressure Zanuck into drawing up the contract. So long as the Morris agents got their commission, they didn't mind Feldman's involvement. Then in January 1951 Zanuck honored a promise to Johnny Hyde by casting Marilyn in the small role of a sexy secretary in *As Young as You Feel*. She met Arthur Miller on the set of that movie. Then Zanuck hesitated, stalling on her contract, not casting her.

During the spring of 1951, while waiting for Zanuck to make up his mind, Marilyn drove to the Fox ranch in the San Fernando Valley to visit Kazan, who was directing *Viva Zapata!* there. Photographer Sam Shaw, the stills photographer on the movie, a New Yorker who didn't drive, sometimes went with her. They became close friends; he would play a major role in her life. He found Marilyn's sense of joy, as well as her "tremendously sincere desire for the arts," irresistible. She never complained or spoke negatively about anyone. Her humor was hilarious and spontaneous. One could never predict what she was going to say: she could be at the same time smiling, reflective, sad, and bursting with fun, until her sadness suddenly took over, and she became melancholy for a time. But she always bounded back.[6]

Born to a Jewish family on New York's Lower East Side, Sam was a populist who photographed dockworkers, jazz musicians, and ordinary people, as well as film stars. He also took documentary photographs, compiling photographic essays on the harshness of working-class life.[7] An autodidact with knowledge of literature, music, and art, he liked to teach others. Marilyn was an apt pupil, eager to learn. She liked to listen to informed people talk; she learned a lot that way. She liked Sam's politics and his identification with ordinary people.

Sam was gregarious, with an eclectic taste in people: he was close to avante-garde filmmakers as well as to Joe DiMaggio, soon to become a major figure in Marilyn's life. Sam liked to help others; he introduced Marilyn to photographers Eve Arnold and Richard Avedon and talked her up at *Life*. She became close to Sam's wife, Anne, and their daughters, Meta and Edith. When in New York, Marilyn visited them. They became another of her families, the series of good foster families she chose to become part of both representing her childhood experience and trying to erase her negative memories.[8]

Marilyn shared an apartment briefly with Shelley Winters that spring. Actress Diane Ladd, close to Shelley, told me that spirituality and politics brought them together. Shelley had a spiritual side, and she found Marilyn intuitive to the point of being psychic. Like Shelley, Marilyn believed in justice and fair play. The insecure and domineering Shelley, a leftist since she joined a union as a teenager working at a dime store, compelled her friends to attend political events with her, especially rallies protesting anticommunist violations of civil liberties. In line with their populist views, Marilyn and she went to a Henry Wallace rally together. Wallace, a leftist and Franklin D. Roosevelt's vice president, was the Progressive Party candidate in the election of 1948.[9]

Shelley was a "dumb-blonde bombshell" at Universal, as Marilyn was at Fox. According to Ladd, "tits and ass" girls like them had to hide their politics and their spiritual beliefs, otherwise they would be laughed out of town. Shelley was aware of Marilyn's shyness: she didn't have the nerve to attend Shelley's acting class with the formidable British actor Charles Laughton. But she exhibited more self-assurance than the outspoken Shelley when she negotiated a rock-bottom price on a fur coat they both wanted. That was Marilyn: unable to do the simplest things and then able to do things that even bold people like Shelley couldn't do. Shelley, who identified with Marilyn to the point that she claimed Marilyn patterned herself after her, tells of Marilyn meeting Laurence Olivier at her apartment and of their cooking dinner for Dylan Thomas when each was in Hollywood.[10]

There is also Shelley's story that, listening to music one Sunday, they each made a list of men they desired. It began when Marilyn said, "Wouldn't it be nice to be like men and just get notches in your belt and sleep with the most attractive men and not get emotionally involved?"[11] Going through the Actor's Directory, each compiled a list of men. Shelley's was composed of young actors, but Marilyn's was of older men—Arthur Miller, directors Nick Ray and John Huston, scientist Albert Einstein—in line with her tendency to date and marry older men. ("Men, like wine, improve with age," she once said.) According to Ralph Greenson, Marilyn's last psychiatrist, she was proud of her older male conquests: Joe Schenck, Johnny Hyde, Joe DiMaggio, Arthur Miller.[12]

As always, Marilyn led a busy life. She continued her singing lessons with Phil Moore, maintained her daily exercise routine, attended her evening course at UCLA, and worked on her acting with Natasha Lytess.[13] In mid-March she presented the Oscar for Best Sound Recording to the sound recorder for *All About Eve*, but she was never again a presenter at the awards celebration, nor did she ever win an Oscar. In a year, a story identifying her as a model in a nude photo would break and the industry would became ambivalent about Marilyn, suspicious of her intentions.

She had also begun studying acting with Michael Chekhov after the Actors' Lab closed down in 1949, a victim of the anticommunist Tenney Committee of the California state legislature, which accused it of being a Communist front organization. The charges were never proven, but the Lab lost its funding and most of its students. Marilyn had to find an alternative arrangement. She turned to Chekhov, who had a spiritual bent that attracted her. Chekhov had been a student of Stanislavsky's in Moscow and had adopted his teacher's memory technique. But it brought painful repressed memories to the surface of his mind, and he broke down.

To heal himself, he turned to quietest religions, especially to Anthroposophy, the spiritual path devised by Austrian philosopher Rudolph Steiner. Grounded in Christianity, Steiner's Anthroposophy proposed that a spiritual force permeated the universe, linking nature and man. It had similarities to Mary Baker Eddy's Christian Science: both were outgrowths of the antimodern, mystical movement at the turn of the century that was a reaction against the age's secularism and scientism. Unlike Christian Science, however, Anthroposophy doesn't prohibit its followers from consulting doctors and taking drugs. That was attractive to Marilyn, who felt guilty violating Christian Science strictures as she took drugs for menstrual pain, insomnia, anxiety, weight control, and to counteract the grogginess during the day that was caused by the pills she took at night to sleep. Chekhov and his Anthroposophy gave her a reason to leave Christian Science.[14]

She also liked the Steiner approach because it included dancing. Many leaders of early-twentieth-century spiritual paths devised dances based on ancient Sufi and Hindu dances. Steiner created slow movements designed to tap into the colors of the universe—what the Hindus call chakras. Steiner called his dance system eurythmy. Chekhov advised his acting students to study dancers as they danced to learn how to control their bodies and to express emotions through them. Exploring external stimuli was also important to him. He respected what he called "atmospheres," which were feelings that he contended emanate from natural objects, in a kind of elemental animism. In other words, living things possess a vitality that sensitive individuals can access. He called the actor's projection of spiritual vitality "radiation" and contended that most great actors possessed it.

Imagination and intuition, in Chekhov's view, are the actor's real tools, and they can lead the actor in many directions. One is to the written text, as actors intuit and imagine characters' motivations from the lines the author has given the actor to speak. Another was what Chekhov called the "psychological gesture," the one movement of a character that encompassed all the rest and would serve to remind the actor of all of them before he went on the stage, like a flower opening in his or her mind.

Like most of Marilyn's acting teachers, Chekhov regarded Italian actress Eleonora Duse, whose career took form in the 1900s, to be unsurpassed among actors in the modern theater. Marilyn kept a photo of Duse in her bedroom, and there are fascinating parallels between them. Duse projected sadness and vulnerability. She had little formal education, and she read constantly to compensate for this lack of knowledge. As Marilyn later did, she became versed in mystical writings in order to find a spiritual source for her acting. Some claimed a nimbus surrounded her on stage. "Duse knew how to give to her body and her presence a radiance that emanated out to the audience," wrote actress Eva Le Gallienne.[15] Marilyn would also project an aura, both on stage and in photographs.

On Chekhov's recommendation Marilyn read Mabel Todd's *The Thinking Body*, and it influenced her. Todd was a professor of physiotherapy at the Teachers College at Columbia University and an innovator in therapeutic dance. In *The Thinking Body*, published in 1937, Todd discusses the relationships between muscles and bones and suggests exercises and visualizations to promote relaxation. Todd's system parallels that of present-day movement systems like Pilates. As in this system, Todd's approach is geared toward reorienting breathing and control of movement to the diaphragm and the pelvis and away from the spine.[16]

Marilyn also liked Todd's work because it resonated to that of Andreas Vesalius, the sixteenth-century physician who is considered to be the founder of modern anatomy. Marilyn found a reprint of Vesalius's work *De Humani Corporis Fabrica* (1543) in a bookstore. With its artistic engravings of medical school professors dissecting the corpse of a prostitute in a sixteenth-century medical school, it offered a unique way to learn human anatomy, one that appealed to Marilyn, with her idiosyncratic mind. Marilyn studied it. From Todd and Vesalius she concluded that movement should be generated from inside the body's frame, not from outside it. In 1961 she talked about Vesalius with Joan Greenson, the daughter of psychiatrist Ralph Greenson, who was fascinated by the way Marilyn moved from the inside of her skeleton rather than from outside it. "It was as if her inner movement would start and then her body would go along with it." Joan described the movement as feline, catlike.[17]

Ballerina Margot Fonteyn met Marilyn in the early 1950s and was also impressed by her undulating movement when she walked. "Whereas people normally move their arms and head in conversation," Fonteyn wrote, "those gestures, in Marilyn Monroe, were reflected throughout her body, producing a delicately undulating effect like the movement of an almost calm sea. It was in no way an affected 'wiggle,' as some writers have suggested." Fonteyn must not have seen Marilyn's movies in which the wiggle is featured, although her comment indicates that Marilyn moved differently in different situations. Bruno Bernard contended that Lili St. Cyr also had an undulating walk.[18]

Chekhov sent Marilyn to study mime with Lotte Goslar, another German immigrant from the European theater in Hollywood. Famed as a clown, Goslar had electrified audiences in Europe and the United States with hilarious and pathetic portrayals of such figures as a young ballerina refusing to obey her teacher and a talent show contestant playing a violin with her feet. She thought that Marilyn was a gifted comic, especially in the small and telling human touches that she brought to her characters in her films. In Goslar's class Marilyn did brilliantly in an exercise in which the students portrayed the aging process from infancy to old age. They became friends, and Marilyn often had Goslar go to her sets when she was filming to help her with her performance. Every year she called Goslar on Christmas Eve, the night when Goslar's beloved husband had died, to express her devotion to her mime teacher. That considerate gesture was typical of Marilyn.[19]

Chekhov told Marilyn that she could make a fortune by performing sexually for the camera; he'd picked up her sexual vibes. When he asked her why she was studying with him, since he specialized in dramatic roles and mostly taught from the classic plays of the Western theatrical tradition, she responded, "I want to be an actress, not an erotic freak. I don't want to be sold to the public as a celluloid aphrodisical [*sic*]. It was all right for the first years. But now it's different." Chekhov had inspired her to regard acting as a sacred calling performed by transformed beings who electrified audiences and changed their lives, rather than simply performing for them.

That point of view marked a significant shift in her attitude toward acting. She often told the story of playing Cordelia to Chekhov's Lear in one of their sessions, in which he suddenly became Lear, transfoming himself. That experience enabled her to bring a transcendent sense to her interpretation of Cordelia, Lear's daughter. She was becoming convinced that practicing Chekhov's mysticism in her acting was the way to find her true self, the calm, transcendent center that she, like all human beings, possessed. Finding that center—the goal of most mystical spiritualities— had become Marilyn's goal. Putting Chekhov's technique together with Lee Strasberg's Method technique eventually became her method of acting.

Chekhov told actor Jack Larson that she was the most gifted young actress in Hollywood. She made friends with him and his wife, Xenia, and she often visited them. Marilyn told Ralph Roberts, later her personal masseur, that she listened to conversations at dinner parties at the Chekhov home between Kazan, Clifford Odets, Ben Hecht, and other New Yorkers. In retrospect those conversations seemed to her as though they had happened in a fairy tale: it's possible, of course, they never occurred. Her relationship with the Chekhovs also had a practical side: Marilyn found a secretary for a time in their neighbor Betty Rosenthal. Marilyn's career was growing to the point that she couldn't handle the practical demands on her, even with the help of Grace and Doc Goddard, who by 1951 were doing her taxes and overseeing her business affairs.[20]

During the early 1950s, besides working on her acting and her interior self, Marilyn also promoted her career, becoming masterful at publicity. She went to Hollywood cocktail parties because journalists attended them and a clever self-presentation might get a line in a gossip column. George Sanders, who played the cynical Broadway columnist in *All About Eve*, approached her at a party when he was drunk and made a pass at her. Sanders's wife, Zsa Zsa Gabor, publicly raked Marilyn over the coals for bad behavior. Her display of anger resulted in several lines for Marilyn in fan magazine columns, which was to her benefit. But she found the parties boring, and she didn't make small talk easily. She felt she had to do it. "Going out socially," she wrote, "was the hardest part of my campaign to make good."[21]

Photographer Philippe Halsman watched her force herself to overcome her lack of confidence. "I sensed the fear and tension inside her every time she came face to face with a man she did not know. She was deathly afraid of not being liked, and she had to win over everyone in a room." Halsman concluded, "Her very weakness is her strength." Part of her strategy was to arrive late and make an entrance. She wore a black or a bright red dress, molded to her body, cut very low, nearly exposing her nipples. "As soon as I could afford an evening gown, I bought the loudest one I could find. It was a bright red low cut gown and it infuriated half of the women in the room because it was so immodest. I was sorry in a way to do this, but I had a long way to go, and I needed a lot of advertising to get there."[22]

Marilyn worked on her publicity with the Fox publicity department, but she kept control over it. In her early career she always cultivated the publicists, whom she called "the boys" and her "buddies." "They howl and growl at you ninety percent of the time," she said, but "if you try to understand their jobs and their problems they will devote a lot of attention to you." She could be a pal to men, as she had been with Miller, Kazan, and Shaw. She often quarreled with Harry Brand, head of publicity at Fox. One of Brand's assistants who heard those disagreements concluded that Marilyn "understood the American public better than did Harry Brand, who was one of the great figures of Hollywood publicity."[23]

Brand assigned the sympathetic Roy Craft to her as a personal publicist. Craft had worked for both *Life* and *Look*, and he had connections
to those magazines, which he used on Marilyn's behalf. Craft accompanied her to parties and on publicity tours, often consulting with her. He
stated that Marilyn was a superb publicist. Her quips and "newsmaking
frivolities," he said, were often her own ideas. "They just happened to her.
She was a literate, perceptive gal, and she didn't need anyone to dream up
her stunts. She was vivacious, funny, with a rich sense of humor." His
major complaint was that when they traveled together she sometimes stayed
in women's bathrooms redoing her makeup and hair for so long that he had
to send waitresses to bring her out. "She is a beauty with brains," wrote
Peer Oppenheimer. "She calculates her actions carefully. She is responsible
for her own success." In 1952 Aline Mosby concluded that at the beginning
of her movie career she looked too much like a "girl-next-door" type,
before she found a sexy look. Most of her publicity, Mosby contended,
she had done herself.[24]

She was also friendly with journalists. "She knew all the newspaper
men and photographers," Sidney Skolsky said, "and she always made
herself available to them." Marilyn had enchanted Louella Parsons at
Joe Schenck's dinner parties, and Louella always remained loyal to her.
Columnist Sheilah Graham hadn't liked Marilyn when she interviewed
her in 1949, but within two years her attitude changed. Considerably
more relaxed, Marilyn was now fey and funny. Her terrible childhood was
always present in interviews, according to Graham, but she didn't talk a
lot about herself, as most stars did. "She asked about your problems and
your interests," Graham stated. She was "extremely appealing."[25]

Marilyn used her body to attract reporters. According to Joe Hyams,
"She would knock your knees under the table; vamp you from time to
time." To charm journalist Jim Henaghan, she went beyond a sexual approach. When he first interviewed her in the spring of 1949, he thought she
was too naive to make it to the top. By 1950 she had changed. She now
used a sexual approach. She stood up and turned around so that her buttocks faced him. She asked him if her skirt was tight enough. Henaghan
thought, "This little animal is learning." A year later, she showed up at
his Malibu house. She talked about her terrible childhood, gaining his
sympathy. Then they went to a bar and played skee-ball: that was the
Marilyn who liked being a "buddy" to men. Henaghan gave her his BB

gun and told her that it was the most precious possession a boy could give to a girl. Marilyn treasured it; he became a friend. He taught her, she said, how to broil a steak "to a man's taste" and how to make a salad of ice-cold lettuce with a vinaigrette dressing.[26]

She gave journalist Mike Connolly a photo of herself and signed it: "To Mike—I'd like to have you on my team." Connolly, who wrote a column for the *Hollywood Reporter*, admired her wit. At a party he overheard someone telling her a risqué story. Marilyn moved away, and Connolly asked if she was annoyed. Innocent-eyed, Marilyn replied, " 'No, I'm angry with myself because I didn't get the point.' Then she gave it away. She winked at me!" Connolly was indeed won over to her team.[27]

Her greatest success among the journalists was becoming close to Sidney Skolsky, who had been a Broadway publicist before becoming a columnist and whose columns were as important as those of Hedda Hopper and Louella Parsons. Even before Johnny Hyde died, Marilyn had brought Sidney into her camp. The two of them met frequently and dreamed up publicity stunts. Like Marilyn, he was an insomniac, so he didn't mind if she phoned him late at night, which was her practice with close friends. She drove him to appointments. When her mood was bleak, she drove with him in her convertible along the Pacific Coast Highway toward Santa Barbara. With the sun on her face and the wind blowing her hair, in control of a masculine machine, she felt free.

When she telephoned Sidney, she called herself Miss Caswell, the name of the character she played in *All About Eve*. According to Steffi Skolsky, Sidney's daughter, her father and Marilyn were drawn to each other because their personalities were similar. Both were dramatic and secretive, neurotic and paranoid.[28] A recently discovered letter from Sidney to Marilyn dated April 1952 suggests they were more than friends, as Sidney writes of "the intensity and fierceness" of his love for her and calls her "sweet sunshine" and "an infinitely beautiful being." As she did with so many others, Marilyn had swept Sidney away.

Sidney was short, hardly five feet tall. He was another Marilyn friend raised in a poor New York Jewish family who was a political liberal. He had been converted to that stance by playwright Clifford Odets, now in Hollywood after his years with the Group Theatre in New York.[29] In his columns Skolsky presented himself as a man of the people, who was closer to young actors and Schwab's drugstore than to nightclubs and stars. A graduate of New York University, he wrote columns for the *New York Post* and the *Hollywood Citizen News*, which were syndicated nationwide. He ended every interview he did with a female star by revealing what she wore to bed. Like Marilyn, Sidney was fascinated by Jean Harlow. A producer of biopics as well as a reporter, he spent years trying to do one on Harlow, with Marilyn playing Harlow. He often discussed it with Marilyn, but it was never made.

Determined to end the hiatus in her career in the spring of 1951, as Zanuck hesitated to cast her in any films, Marilyn engaged in several sexy stunts. She became the talk of the Fox lot when, assigned to do a promotional photo, she slowly walked the six blocks from the Fox wardrobe department to the still department, barefoot and wearing a see-through negligee. She caused a near-stampede on the lot, as phones rang in every office to announce her progress and the men in those offices rushed to the windows and the sidewalks to watch her, sometimes following her. So startling was the walk and the response to it that fan magazines featured stories about it.

In late March she vamped Spyros Skouras, the head of the New York office, when he visted the Fox studio in Hollywood for a conclave to introduce movie theater owners nationwide to forthcoming Fox films. A banquet was held at the studio commissary, fancied up as the Café de Paris, with all the Fox stars and starlets present. Marilyn was the hit of the evening. She arrived late, wearing a tight, strapless black cocktail dress, making the grand entrance she had perfected at Hollywood parties. Out-of-towners clustered around her to ask her what new films of hers they could order. (Aside from *As Young as You Feel*, there weren't any.) Cameras clicked; flashbulbs popped. Skouras took Marilyn's arm and escorted her to the head table, where she sat next to him for the rest of the evening. He ordered Zanuck to stop hesitating over her contract and cast her in sexy-blonde parts. But he brushed off her request for dramatic roles. He is supposed to have said to her, "You make money only with your tits and ass. Your talent is located above your waist and below your navel."[30]

Zanuck had only to look at Marilyn's fan mail to realize her value. After *Stars and Stripes* named her Miss Cheesecake of 1951, she was inundated by fan mail from servicemen, especially from the troops stationed in

South Korea to enforce the truce between the Communist army in North Korea and the international force in the south. Pinup photos were popular among these men, and Marilyn, with a large number in circulation, was their favorite. Marilyn's drive in 1945 to make herself into a top West Coast model was paying off. By March 1951 she was receiving more fan mail than many Fox stars.

Zanuck may have hesitated in signing Marilyn to a contract because she demanded that Natasha Lytess be put on the Fox payroll, but he finally capitulated. It was obvious that Natasha had been central to Marilyn's superb performances in *The Asphalt Jungle* and *All About Eve*. Marilyn signed the Fox contract on May 17. It was a duplicate of her original contract, with her salary raised to $750 a week and with a raise every six months to a total of $3,250 per week. It may seem like a large amount, but she had many expenses—acting, singing, and dancing lessons; agents and lawyers; clothes and makeup; the money she sent her mother; and the $250 a week she paid Natasha.[31] (Given Natasha's salary from Fox and the amount Marilyn paid her, her income was sometimes larger than Marilyn's.)

When Johnny Hyde died, Dore Schary of MGM shelved the idea to cast Marilyn as Grushenka in *The Brothers Karamazov*, which was unfortunate for her. Had she played Grushenka at this point in her career she might have been recognized as a dramatic actress before she was typecast as a sexy blonde. Grushenka was identified with the high-art tradition of Dostoyevsky, not the burlesque tradition of the dumb blonde. And Dostoyevsky's description of Grushenka uncannily replicates Marilyn. Grushenka is voluptuous and her movements catlike. She is proud and insolent, with an innocent look in her eyes and a childlike good nature. It would have been fascinating to see Marilyn, with similar characteristics, in the role. Milton Greene later optioned it for her, to be produced by MMP, the production company they established. But that plan to film the novel didn't work out.[32]

Once Marilyn signed with Fox, Zanuck cast her in two more fluffy comedies in the spring and summer of 1951, *Love Nest* and *Let's Make It Legal*. In *Love Nest*, she is an ex-Wac who rents an apartment in the building owned by her male army buddy, which causes complications in his marriage. In *Let's Make It Legal*, she is a beauty queen–party girl who is elected Miss Cucamonga; the beauty title is a takeoff on Miss Cheesecake of *Stars and Stripes* and Miss Caswell's "Copacabana School of Dramatic Arts" in *All About Eve*. Playing the companion of a divorced husband, Marilyn mostly stands around, looking fetching in tight clothes and a bathing suit. In a scene that flirts with reality, she serves drinks to men who are playing poker, as she had at Joe Schenck's poker parties.

In these films, Marilyn is mostly sexual decoration. She speaks only a few lines in a few scenes. Her acting has little flair, although male critics, like her male fans, found her interesting to watch. Natasha wasn't on the sets during the filming of these movies, which may explain Marilyn's weak performances in them. In addition, she is sexually objectified in each, as the camera lingers on her breasts and hips, while other characters make fun of her body.

As a result, she ran the risk of being typecast as a "blonde bomb-shell." Such typecasting was common in Hollywood, because producers felt safe repeating successful formulas. No less than Marilyn, producers identified a need to hire voluptuous blondes to compete with such figures in burlesque, on TV, and in the foreign films that were invading the American market. Moreover, voluptuous, glamorous women were popular among the general public. They served as an emblem of American prosperity and its pleasure ethic to challenge the Soviet ideal of women as tough and stolid, workers in men's jobs who didn't pursue glamour—which was considered a capitalist vice.[33] Finding sexy women was a Hollywood strategy to win back audiences, as were large-screen Cinemascope, religious films like *The Robe* for conservatives, and realist dramas like *On the Waterfront* for the literati.

By this time Marilyn was attracting a male audience important to the studios. In the 1930s and '40s the majority of moviegoers had been young working women, who were the fan base for the "fast-talking dames" that dominated movie screens in these decades. By 1951, however, due to Marilyn's exposure in men's magazines, military magazines, and pinup photos, she had captured a male market—a market that Hollywood had been trying to reach for some time through westerns and action films. Zanuck now thought of Marilyn as the next Betty Grable, a star who mostly made musicals and played a blonde working-class "girl-next-door" type with elements of a tough-talking dame to her persona. Grable appealed to both male and female moviegoers.

Marilyn was indomitable in promoting her career. In August 1951, after finishing *Let's Make It Legal*, she went to New York to see Carol Channing as Lorelei Lee in the Broadway version of *Gentlemen Prefer Blondes*. Zanuck was considering casting Marilyn as Lorelei in the screen version, although Betty Grable and other stars wanted the role and Channing had received rave reviews for her Broadway performance. Sam Shaw was Marilyn's guide in New York. He took her to Brooklyn to see Walt Whitman's haunts; to a party for John Huston at the "21" Club where she met photographer Eve Arnold; and to the Metropolitan Museum of Art to see a show of Goya's drawings of the Spanish Civil War. Sam also took her to the Actors Studio and introduced her to Lee Strasberg and Marlon Brando. He took her to the Theosophical Society headquarters in Manhattan because of her interest in mystical religions. She also met Joe DiMaggio on this trip and was seen at El Morocco with Pat DiCicco.[34]

She was already considering changing her image. She wanted to expand beyond the sexy blonde bombshell image that she already felt was limiting her opportunities. She spoke about the possibility of a new approach to photographer Eve Arnold, extolling Arnold for her photographs in *Esquire* of Marlene Dietrich on a bare soundstage, without the glamour makeup and clothing that Dietrich usually wore. "If you were able to do that with Dietrich," Marilyn said, "think what you could do with me!" She remained friendly with Arnold after this meeting, but it wasn't until the fall of 1955 that Arnold photographed her in ways that varied her dumb-blonde image—in a park reading James Joyce's *Ulysses* and as a primeval Eve slithering through tall grass and mud in a marsh.[35]

Once Marilyn returned from New York, Zanuck considered casting her as the disturbed babysitter in *Don't Bother to Knock*. When he hesitated, Sidney Skolsky persuaded Jerry Wald to cast her as a young cannery worker in *Clash by Night*, an adaptation of a Clifford Odets play about love and betrayal among dockworkers and roustabouts set in Monterey, California. Wanting to see if Marilyn could be effective in a complicated dramatic role, Zanuck lent her out to Wald for a modest fee.

To prepare for *Clash by Night*, Marilyn took an all-night bus to Monterey to observe cannery workers and to practice being working class. In fact, she was so successful in that guise that a cannery boss offered her a job cutting off the heads of fish. She was also a girl alone in a strange town, getting wolf whistles, violating the prohibition against respectable girls traveling alone. That was all part of the adventure she had undertaken; Marilyn liked wolf whistles and admiration from men on the streets. Returning home, she was the only girl in a bus of Italian men. Their admiration for her beauty made her feel like a queen. She wrote a free-verse poem about the experience.

> *Such charming gentlemen—they were wonderful*
> *Not only do I love Greeks, I love Italians.*
> *They're so warm, lusty*
> *And friendly as hell—*
> *I'd love to go to Italy someday.*[36]

Marilyn scored a triumph in *Clash by Night*. She is tough and feisty, a working-class girl to the hilt. She stands up to her overbearing boyfriend when he tells her that men have the right to discipline women; in fact, she punches him in the nose. With short, curly hair, dressed in baggy jeans, walking jauntily, she looks like a boy—or the street urchin she sometimes played in real life. At the end of *Clash by Night*, however, she displays an underlying insecurity and gives in to her lover. Her reviews and the box office on the film were excellent.

In September *Collier's* featured an article on her, written by Robert Cahn. It was the first story about her to appear in a national magazine. In October Rupert Allan wrote a story for *Look* about her titled "A Serious Blonde Who Can Act." An American who had been raised in St. Louis and educated at Oxford, Allan was an elegant homosexual. Marilyn, who could be persuasive, talked him into becoming her press agent. In November she won the Henrietta Award of the Hollywood Foreign Press Association as the year's best newcomer.[37] Zanuck was impressed. That month he put *Don't Bother to Knock* into production, with Marilyn in the lead as a psychotic babysitter. The title isn't related to the film, but that's standard for Marilyn's films, which often have sexually suggestive titles that relate only vaguely to the film involved. Those titles include *Love Nest, Let's Make It Legal, We're Not Married, Some Like It Hot*, and *Let's Make Love*. ("It" was then a euphemism for sex.) Given Marilyn's fear that she might go insane like her mother, she was brave to play the disturbed babysitter in *Don't Bother to Knock*. It's also possible she used her mother as a model for the character she and Natasha created.

In the film she is hired to babysit the child of a couple staying in a hotel when they go out to dinner. She vamps Richard Widmark, who is staying in the next room. As her attempt at seduction goes awry and the child she is watching begins to cry, Marilyn gags the child and ties her up. The police are called, and Marilyn is apprehended. Actress Anne Bancroft plays a nightclub singer in the film. In her one scene with Marilyn, toward the end of the film, they encounter each other in the hotel's lobby, as a policeman escorts Marilyn to a waiting police car. Their eyes connect. Bancroft was so moved by the look in Marilyn's eyes, she said, that her own eyes filled with tears. "It was one of my few times in Hollywood," Bancroft stated, "that I felt the give and take that can only come from fine acting [on Marilyn's part]."[38]

Critics were mixed on Marilyn's acting in *Don't Bother to Knock*, and Zanuck wasn't impressed by it. However, her box office draw was still strong, and so he cast her in two sexy-blonde roles. She plays a prostitute in a brief episode in *O. Henry's Full House*, which was drawn from O. Henry's short story "The Cop and the Anthem." Charles Laughton plays opposite her as a friendly bum. She next played in a sequence in *We're Not Married*, about five couples who discover their marriage licenses are invalid. A beauty contest winner, she is suddenly disqualified from the Mrs. America contest because she isn't legally married. The role she plays allows her to wear a bathing suit, thus appealing to her male fans.

Monkey Business was her next film. It began production in February 1952. A research chemist, played by Cary Grant, invents a formula to restore youth to aging people, which he intends to try out on research chimps in his lab. Before he does so, however, a chimp gets out of the cage in the lab and pours the formula into the lab's bottled drinking water. The humans drink it by mistake, resulting in madcap mayhem. Marilyn plays a sexy secretary whose main attributes are her large breasts and hips. Ginger Rogers, playing Grant's wife, calls her "a little pinup girl, half an infant," an apt description of her character. Once again, as in her previous sexy-blonde roles, the camera lingers on her breasts and buttocks, fetishizing them.

Marilyn participates in her sexual objectification more fully in this film than ever before. Wearing a dress with a full skirt that obfuscates her lower body, she pushes the back of the dress's skirt between her buttocks, drawing attention to them. Billy Travilla had designed the dress so that she could move easily in a scene in which she roller skates with Grant. But Marilyn wanted to attract her male fans with tight-fitting clothes.[39] She battled Travilla over the design of the dress and when she lost the battle, she cleverly devised a way to achieve what she wanted.

Filming *Monkey Business* wasn't easy for her. She was suffering from attacks of appendicitis, although she didn't have her appendix removed until May. She had issues with Howard Hawks, the overbearing director of the film, and she began to date Joe DiMaggio. Meanwhile, the rumor was spreading that she had posed nude for a calendar photo—a shocking act for a rising star. It was enough to destroy her career, especially given the "morals clause" in film contracts, which forbade actors from doing anything that might embarrass a studio. She had to deal carefully with the issue of the photo.

By this point in her career, reporters and paparazzi began to follow her every move. She now had to be particularly discreet about her private life. Trying to avoid press scrutiny, she changed her residence every six months or so. She now had fans who were obsessed with her. Even when she lived at the Beverly Hills Hotel or the Hotel Bel-Air, both with tight security, the press managed to find her. She regularly changed her phone number to elude crank callers. She wore disguises to go out in public: Hal Schaefer, her voice coach and later her lover, said she wasn't recognized when she wore a black wig, no makeup, and shapeless dresses. Other individuals who knew her well made similar observations. Sometimes she wore a red wig and sometimes a scarf. According to friends, when she wore no makeup and hadn't psyched herself into becoming Marilyn Monroe, she wasn't recognized.[40]

In 1951 and '52 she dated director Nicholas Ray, a protégé of Elia Kazan and a former lover of Shelley Winters. Fan magazines published photos of them together at parties and nightclubs. Yul Brynner, who studied with Michael Chekhov, was another brief lover; both Susan Strasberg and Rock Brynner, Yul's son, confirmed the relationship. Marilyn also dated Peter Lawford once or twice, but their relationship didn't work. Some say that he pursued her and she rejected him, but a more convincing argument is that the fastidious Peter found Marilyn too messy. Joe Naar, Peter's close friend, double-dated with Peter and Marilyn on their first date. By the end of the evening Peter had persuaded Joe to switch dates with him, and Joe took Marilyn home. When she got busy or seriously depressed, she could be lax about hygiene, not bathing and wearing the same clothes for days on end. Sometimes she didn't walk her dog, Josefa, so there were piles of excrement on the carpet of her apartment—or stains when she cleaned them up.[41]

Marilyn had a sexual fling and a long friendship with Hollywood designer Billy Travilla, who designed her clothes in eight of her thirty films, beginning with *Monkey Business*. They went to jazz clubs on Central Avenue to hear singers like Billie Holiday. But their intimacy mostly involved his calming her down. He was one of the individuals she called late at night when she couldn't sleep, and he soothed her over the phone. If she was especially upset, he went to her apartment and cuddled her, telling her that everything was going to be all right. "It was like helping Shirley Temple get through a Mae West nightmare," Travilla said with regard to those sessions.[42]

Actor Nico Minardos also claimed to have been involved with her that year. By late February 1952, she was dating Joe DiMaggio, but he was frequently out of town doing baseball interviews. Minardos was Greek, tall, dark, and handsome, and he had a small role in *Monkey Business*. Marilyn met him on the set of that movie. According to Minardos, they discussed the theories of P. D. Ouspensky about how to attain serenity. Ouspensky was a turn-of-the-century mystic who mixed Western mathematical theory about a fourth dimension with Sufi ideas about self-realization. Only Marilyn's close friends knew about her spiritual interests, which gives reliability to Minardos's claims. Sidney Skolsky, for one, called her mystic, serious, religious, and superstitious all at once.[43]

The list of friends and lovers goes on. It probably included Sidney Skolsky. Marilyn was still promiscuous, still believed that men posessed her body. She still believed in free love, that true friendship should expand to include sex. David March, a Broadway agent who wanted to become her business manager, became friendly with her after he called her in June 1951 and she mischievously told him she was a housewife named Ethel Hapgood.[44] (Marilyn loved to make up pseudonyms.) She was devil-may-care with him. They bought pizzas and drove around Beverly Hills eating them. They discussed their philosophies of life. March, who arranged Marilyn's first Hollywood date with DiMaggio, was a friend, not a lover;

Marilyn had the unique capacity to be friends with men, even some heterosexual men. March was one of those friends, and so were Sam Shaw and eventually Norman Rosten, Eli Wallach, and others.

As she moved toward stardom, Marilyn faced a number of potential minefields. The first was her use of sex to advance her career. The second was the nude photo. Every Hollywood contract had a clause stating the actor would do nothing to embarrass the studio, and Marilyn could be humiliated and fired under this clause. The women's clubs and the Catholic Church, emboldened by post–World War Two conservatism, were once again attacking Hollywood in the early 1950s for immorality. On the other hand, to retain their audiences, the studios were increasing sex in films and exposing female bodies more than ever before. Conflicts between the studios and the Motion Picture Production Board increased.

The studios had the upper hand, since the moguls appointed the members of the Production Board, who represented their interests while trying to mollify the moralists. The studios also controlled the Hollywood journalists, whom they kept in line through kickbacks, invitations to parties and trips, and access to the stars. Studio publicists had to approve stories written about their stars before they could be published. One industry insider divulged that "all hanky-panky indulged in by the stars was to be blanketed immediately and completely." Star marriages, divorces, and dating were staples of Hollywood journalism, but the physical side of sex was blanked out. Sidney Skolsky and Earl Wilson wrote, "The Hollywood of the fan magazines was a gauzy, oddly sexless place. The dark Hollywood was never recorded in their pages."[45] No one wrote about Sam Spiegel's "boys' club" or Pat DiCicco's activities, except for his dates with starlets. Too many important individuals were involved.

Still, Jane Russell's career was stymied when in 1941 the Production Board vetoed Howard Hughes's emphasis on her breasts in *The Outlaw*. Hughes didn't release the film until 1943. In 1949, Ingrid Bergman's career was destroyed when she had an out-of-wedlock child with Italian director Roberto Rossellini. She didn't return to Hollywood films until 1956. Marilyn's nude calendar photograph could raise a public outcry. As her popularity increased, so did the sales of the calendar.

By 1950, Sidney Skolsky and Marilyn, working with Fox publicists, began to construct a protective star text around her. The "star text," standard for all prominent film actors and actresses, was the narrative of their lives that appeared in newspaper articles about them and that often was threaded through their films as another way to satisfy their fans. In the first instance, Marilyn's text praised her beauty and sexuality. She was a "blonde bombshell," "Miss Cheesecake," and "Miss Flamethrower." Sidney and Marilyn also created a counter-text to the mythos of her titillating self. The narrative of her miserable childhood dominated that text. The counter-text also presented her as simple and shy, getting by on a small income, foregoing the luxurious life of a Hollywood star. In July 1951, an article on her in *Movieland* explained that she had overspent on clothes and nonessentials because she was too young to know how to manage money. After credit agencies started dunning her, she had to learn how to budget.[46]

The articles by Robert Cahn in *Collier's* and by Rupert Allan in *Look* in the fall of 1951 contain the basics of her star text. Both begin by praising her as a sex icon. Yet both writers describe her as shy off camera, with a large inferiority complex. She didn't like nightclubs, and she spent many evenings at home reading great books. Or she went to voice, acting, or body movement classes. Cahn noted that she was taking a course at UCLA. According to her teacher, whom Cahn interviewed, she was so modest that she seemed like a girl from a convent.

Marilyn's star text also emphasized her difference from other starlets: she was independent and sometimes eccentric. Photos in Allan's article show her working out with weights, an activity frowned on for women. Another picture in the Allan article shows her studying with black voice coach Phil Moore, wearing capri pants and a shirt tied in a knot under her bust, exposing her midriff. In a racist age, such a photo was shocking.

In her star text, Marilyn was often compared to Greta Garbo. Like Garbo, Marilyn is described as private, even mysterious. Marilyn increasingly did avoid nightclubs and parties. She had already made her mark through her electric entrances at them. Now she spent time at home, where she studied scripts or read books. In August 1951 she was called "a bachelor girl in the crispest modern tradition and a career woman who doesn't have the time to date."[47]

Before too long, the assertion that she was a hermit who avoided Hollywood social life was expanded by publicists into the claim that she was deeply moral. She was an "unusually straight-laced and moral young lady for any community, let alone Hollywood," according to *Modern Screen. Movie Fan* was more ambivalent. "Rumors started circulating around the studio that the new queen of sex was mistress to a prominent film executive [Joe Schenck]. She is certainly not one of Hollywood's wild set, but the evil whispers and lurid tales continue. So far La Monroe has shrugged off all the gossip." The article concluded: "*Movie Fan* is in her corner." Fan magazines sometimes noted that she shaved several years off her age; by the time she made *Clash by Night* in 1951, for example, she was twenty-five, considered old by Hollywood standards. She got away with it because she looked much younger than her actual years.[48]

The claim that Marilyn was moral was bolstered by the consensus among journalists that she was honest in interviews. "Even seasoned reporters come away from her swearing by her candor and honesty," wrote Ezra Goodman. "She can transfix with the wide eyes of a lost, very appealing little girl." She often seemed to journalists to act like an ordinary young woman, not a star, and they liked that humility. "She looks you in the eye and gives you an honest answer," wrote Bob Ruark. "Here is one of the few honest ones I have ever met in the studio. She is willing to play it straight and not go grand dame." Pro-Marilyn journalists focused on how hard she worked, documented her long hours at the studio, and concluded that her apartment was messy because she had no time to clean it.[49]

She developed a superb interview style. When she wasn't being sincere, she entertained reporters with her Monroeisms, her sexual double entendres directed against herself. When the scandal over the nude calendar broke in March 1952, she had an effective response in place. She fixed her innocent, large eyes on reporters, playing a combination of Shirley Temple and Little Orphan Annie, and they were transfixed. Gazing wide-eyed at reporters, talking almost in a whisper, she sounded as though she were in a confessional. She told them what she wanted them to hear, about her shy self, about her past, about how hard she worked, about how moral she was, cutting them off with a sexual quip. According to historian Daniel Boorstin, she gave the best celebrity interview of the twentieth century.[50]

Yet as hard as she tried, she couldn't entirely counter jokes about her that circulated coast to coast. She was the ultimate blonde in a nation both fascinated by sexuality and uneasy about it, involved both in an ongoing sexual revolution and a conservative reaction against it. Marilyn once said that she joked about herself to get the humor of her character out before someone applied it against her. The "Copacabana" acting school in *All About Eve* became a catch phrase used by comedians and impersonators ad nauseum; the story about "Apprentice Stars" in *Life* magazine in January 1951 referred to her as a "busty Bernhardt," and that phrase inspired many jokes. The nude calendar photo became so famous that comedian Red Skelton brought down the house when he simply pointed to a calendar off stage.[51] "Please don't make me into a joke," she pleaded with the press and the public. She walked a tightrope between sexiness and a parody of it that could be misunderstood. But she created that subtle self-parody as part of her acting style and because she was always ambivalent about her femininity, even when she praised it the most.

Working with Marilyn wasn't easy for the directors and actors in her films. She was often late to filming, and she often flubbed her lines, requiring many takes. The lateness began slowly and wasn't a real issue until *All About Eve* (1950). During the filming of the 1951 comedies she did—*As Young as You Feel*, *Love Nest*, and *Let's Make It Legal*—some of her fellow actors complained about her lateness to the producers, but nothing was done. Joe Schenck, they were told, had given her permission to be late. Jack Paar, who played opposite her in *Love Nest*, stated that she was always late, but everyone knew that her status at the studio had little to do with her ability as an actress. He often felt sorry for her, because she was the object of constant sexual remarks. Richard Sale, who directed *Let's Make It Legal*, became so angry with her that he dressed her down in front of the cast and crew. At first she was furious, threatening to have him fired by "a major Fox executive" (Joe Schenck), but she soon calmed down and apologized.[52]

Marilyn had no difficulty posing for the still camera. But films required speaking lines, which was a problem for her. She was probably dyslexic (she couldn't spell). When she flubbed a single sentence twenty-two times on the set of *How to Marry a Millionaire*, Lee Siegel, the studio doctor, told the producer, "She has a problem with word perception, not memory." Some writers maintain that she developed Meniere's disease in the early 1950s, an ailment that caused dizziness and partial loss of hearing in her right ear.[53] Her stuttering still challenged her speech, and that problem made her anxious. Acting with Marilyn in *Love Nest*, June Haver noted that she had difficulty getting her first words out. Once she got past the first line, according to Haver, she was fine.[54]

Movie acting wasn't easy. Actors were supposed to know how to act before facing a movie camera and to understand the mechanics of film production: how to place their feet in their "marks"—chalk marks on the floor—to keep them in range of the lights and the camera, and to keep their heads in line with their "key light," a light in the ceiling that illuminated only them. Most directors didn't give much help with acting or with toeing the marks; they focused on the technical elements of filming, such as lighting and camera angles. Marilyn was often contemptuous of her directors; many, she felt, didn't know as much as she did about filmmaking. As Arthur Miller pointed out, Marilyn was one of the few Hollywood stars without her own cameraman and lighting man. In her book about the film industry, Hortense Powdermaker concluded that many actors felt that directors were a hindrance to their acting, not a help. Marilyn wasn't alone in criticizing her directors.[55]

Moreover, since movies were expected to make large profits, the studio heads regarded them as akin to factory products. To save money, scenes weren't shot in the same sequence as in the script; they were grouped together in terms of location, the actors involved, and technical issues. Endings could be shot before beginnings, and middle scenes could be mixed up. Production schedules and budgets were established before shooting began, and assistants were on sets to keep films "within budget." Rehearsal time was brief, and films were shot as quickly as possible. Even stars had to be ready to shoot as early as seven A.M., which meant that they had to be at the studio at five thirty to have their hair and makeup done and their costumes put on. Shooting could go into the evening and take place six days a week. According to Maurice Zolotow, Marilyn learned slowly and required a lot of rehearsing, with which directors often dispensed.[56]

Hollywood directors, all male, were often tyrants. Like the studio moguls, they were often hypermasculine. According to Patrick McGilligan, they "made a big show of being swaggering, cigar-chewing, and polo-playing manly men." Many suffered from status anxiety. Because directors as well as actors signed contracts with studios, studio heads wielded control over them, and producers could overrule them. They vented their frustrations on actors. Aware of Marilyn's work as a "party girl" and her status as a dumb blonde, many didn't respect her. Marilyn complained about their rigidity. "They tell you to cry one tear, and if you feel two and cry two, it's no good. If you change 'the' to 'a' in your lines, they correct you. An actress is not a machine, but they treat you like one."[57]

When she posed for photographers, Marilyn had control over the poses she assumed. Connected to the feminized world of fashion, fashion photographers were gentle with their models. Film acting was different. Directors, cameramen, even producers had a say in what Marilyn did, while she often wasn't permitted to watch the daily rushes, the raw film shot during a day's shooting, which was usually reviewed each evening.[58]

Marilyn was most comfortable filming when she was friendly with the director. Henry Koster, who directed her in the "Cop and the Anthem" sequence in *O. Henry's Full House*, found her wonderful to work with, kind and accommodating. Earl Moran was his father-in-law, and he and Marilyn discussed Moran's many kindnesses to her when she had modeled for him.[59] In doing a film Marilyn's concern was with her performance, not the entire film, and she was a perfectionist. She wasn't an ensemble player; it was hard enough for her to achieve perfection in her own performance, much less to think about the other actors.

Marilyn's difficulties in the early 1950s were especially apparent during the filming of *Clash by Night*. Costars Barbara Stanwyck and Paul Douglas, old hands at doing films, intimidated her. Both were furious when reporters wanted to interview "the girl with the big tits," not them, and when they learned that Marilyn was getting star billing because of her large fan base. For the first time since Marilyn's screen test at Fox, her skin broke out in blotches and she vomited before going into a scene. She had problems with Fritz Lang, the film's director, renowned for the expressionist films he had directed in Germany in the 1920s. Lang expected actors to show deference to him, and he spoke harshly to them when they didn't. He dressed formally, and he wore a monocle, reminiscent of the elderly actor in Marilyn's childhood.

Clash by Night was the first film since *The Asphalt Jungle* in which Natasha was allowed on the set to coach Marilyn. Lang tried to throw her off the set when he realized that she was standing behind him, directing Marilyn, but Marilyn got her back. When Marilyn missed her lines, Lang erupted, and she broke down in tears. She seemed unable to handle him. Reporter James Bacon had a different interpretation. After he watched her spoil twenty-seven takes in a single scene, he asked her why she did it. She replied, "I just didn't like the way the scene was going. When I liked it I said the lines in the scene perfectly." Then she continued, "I never intentionally meant to hurt anyone, but you can't be too nice to people you work with, else they will trample you to death."[60]

It wasn't easy to control Marilyn. If she didn't get her way, she might retreat into her dressing room and lock the door. She sobbed; she got headaches and spells of vomiting. According to Maurice Zolotow, "Nobody was sure whether those attacks were genuine or deliberately staged." But she defended herself against the many public attacks on her. Often accused of narcissism because she spent so much time looking at herself in mirrors, she retorted that she wasn't admiring herself. Instead, she was practicing facial expressions, redoing her makeup, or so anxious that she felt frozen in time. Assistants and friends of hers, like Sam Shaw and Rupert Allan, agreed with her. No one had seen such perfectionism before.[61]

As Marilyn's star status increased, her punctuality declined. She always had an excuse for being late: she was ill; she had lost her keys; her car had broken down. People hesitated to criticize her for it, because she might start crying. She told several individuals that deep inside she was punishing her antagonists in the studios for the bad treatment she had experienced in childhood—and later at the hands of producers. Louella Parsons stated that Marilyn never forgave Fox executives for having laid her off in 1947 and not hired her back until 1951. By 1951, Marilyn also said, she had finally broken through the shell she put up as a child. She had been passive for many years, ignoring her own nature. That statement was true, but the "nature" that was surfacing was filled with resentment and anger.[62]

Marilyn was unprofessional, but she wasn't entirely to blame for the problems on her films. Many of her directors were tyrants. Roy Ward Baker, the director of *Don't Bother to Knock*, filmed in December 1961, was a curt Englishman who terrified her. Howard Hawks, her director in *Monkey Business* in February and March 1952, was "a formidable and imperious man," tall and craggy, an American bald eagle, with penetrating ice-blue eyes. He could be ferocious. At their first meeting, he treated her as a "goddamn dumb blonde," terrifying her. Henry Hathaway, who directed her in *Niagara* in the summer of 1952, was called "screaming Henry" because of his bullying behavior on sets, especially toward actresses.[63]

While filming *The Prince and the Showgirl* in the summer of 1956, Laurence Olivier acted like an aristocrat and treated Marilyn like a commoner. According to Jack Lemmon, Billy Wilder, who directed her in *The Seven Year Itch* (October 1954) and *Some Like It Hot* (summer 1958), was a taskmaster. "He permits no ad-libbing. It sounds spontaneous on his films but it isn't." He had a sardonic personality, was always blowing up, and made nasty, cutting remarks about Marilyn to the press that he usually retracted later. Fritz Lang, who directed her in *Clash by Night*, and Otto Preminger, her director for *River of No Return*, were émigrés from Germany who acted like Prussian autocrats.[64]

On the other hand, Henry Hathaway came to respect Marilyn. Once he closed the *Niagara* set to reporters, she calmed down. He realized that Fox executives treated her badly. She had no clothes to speak of and when he asked her why she didn't have an extensive wardrobe, as most stars did, she said that she spent all her money on acting and singing lessons because the studio wouldn't pay for them. He exploded at Zanuck: "This girl's got great talent, why the hell don't you treat her like a human being? Not somebody you put under the desk to suck your cock while you're having story conferences." He found her to be "a very smart girl, but she liked playing dumb. Her dumbness was all acting." He wanted to cast Marilyn opposite James Dean or Montgomery Clift in *Of Human Bondage*, but Zanuck wouldn't allow it. Hathaway spent weeks arguing that Marilyn should be cast as Grushenka in *The Brothers Karamazov*, but the studio executives laughed at him. None of them had read the novel, Hawathay said; they didn't realize that Marilyn was a double of the Russian girl.[65]

Hathaway and Marilyn became friends. He saw that her schedule was extremely demanding, and he worried about her. That perception was confirmed by a journalist who covered her in 1952 and concluded that she did the work of ten women. Up at five thirty, she was on the set by six. Finishing at seven thirty at night, she then studied her lines for the next day with Natasha. Everyone pulled her in different directions. Whenever she had a break, she did interviews. One day she gave an interview to a Tokyo reporter on the transcontinental telephone during a morning break, then tape-recorded an interview with Sheilah Graham during an afternoon break, and then rushed after filming was finished that day for another interview with another reporter.[66]

Joseph Cotten, who played her husband in *Niagara*, defended her. "There's hardly a director alive who doesn't consider any lapse in discipline on his ship a direct insult to the bridge." Cotten didn't think she was seriously rebellious, although she enjoyed challenging authority. But the reasons for her behavior went deeper than that, he thought, into realms of her psyche that Cotten couldn't fathom. At times she glowed with the joy of discovery and then, suddenly, her focus moved into outer space, thrusting her into a cloud of blankness. It could happen to her in the middle of a scene, and recovery wasn't easy for her. On the other hand, she had a healthy sense of humor about herself, and she used it to rescue herself from her fogs.[67]

Jean Negulesco, who directed her in *How to Marry a Millionaire* in February 1953, had minimal difficulties with her. He took the time to get to know her, and paying attention to her personally helped. Sensing that she wanted to be taken seriously, he talked to her about art. Her comments were intelligent, and they became friends. After all, he wrote in his autobiography, she was a great star, with the prerogatives of coming to the set when she wanted to and regarding inflexible schedules as infringements on her civil rights. That was, in fact, the attitude in the French cinema industry, where filming was considered to be an art, not a business. Over the years Negulesco was often assigned to do retakes of scenes in films she had made with other directors. They developed a rapport. She was quick-witted and cooperative in these situations, and her costars and crews loved her.[68]

Over the course of her career, Marilyn was never late for dancing rehearsals or singing lessons. Lionel Newman, head of the Fox music department, reported that she was often early to recording sessions. He found her much less temperamental than most stars, although she was plagued by insecurity and a perfectionism that drove her to demand many takes on her films. In explaining her punctuality for singing lessons and recording sessions, it is important to note that she was in all probability free from anxiety in them. People who stutter don't stutter when they sing.[69]

By mid-February 1952 entertainment columnists were alluding to the "calendar of Marilyn in her birthday suit." It was probable that she would soon be openly identified as the model in the nude photo. That identification might destroy her career. A lucky break came in the form of a date with Joe DiMaggio, the famous baseball player. The date was arranged by David March, who knew DiMaggio from his days as a Broadway agent frequenting Toots Shor's, a restaurant and bar that catered to male sports aficionados and lionized Joe DiMaggio. But this date wasn't the first time that Joe and Marilyn had met. In 1950 Johnny Hyde's nephew, Norman Brokaw, a fledging William Morris agent, had introduced them at the Brown Derby. Joe had asked for her phone number, but she wasn't interested, since she didn't know anything about baseball. When she went to New York in August 1951, she met Joe at Roosevelt Raceway on Long Island. He took her out to dinner, but again she wasn't impressed.[70]

Yet DiMaggio occupied a unique position as a national hero and a model of masculinity. An outfielder for the New York Yankees, he was the most famous sports figure in the nation, beloved by men and women alike. No less than Marilyn, he embodied the American Dream. He was the eighth of nine children of a San Francisco fisherman from Sicily who struggled to support his family. He had made it from sandlot baseball to a position with the Yankees, the nation's most revered baseball team, in 1936, at the age of twenty-one, after four years in the Pacific Coast League. Quiet and dignified, he never argued with umpires or other players. Tall and athletic, he had a majestic grace as a player, especially manifested in 1941, as World War Two thundered abroad, when he batted successfully in fifty-six consecutive games, breaking the record established in 1922, and inspiring national pride. He was called the Yankee Clipper, after the new Pan American airplane, for his unequaled power, range, and style; Marilyn thought his naked body looked like a Michelangelo statue.[71]

His bearing on and off the field was regal. In private life he wore elegant conservative dress (a dark suit, white shirt, and narrow tie). He embodied the aristocratic Italian concept of bella figura, dating from the Renaissance. He shattered ethnic stereotypes. Essayist Roger Rosenblatt eulogized him as having "a sense of civilization, hierarchy, and order that went beyond decorum to the center of middle-class values." In 1951, suffering from numerous physical ailments, he retired from the game at the age of thirty-six. He was twelve years older than Marilyn.[72]

Yet he had no interests outside of baseball and a few other sports, like boxing and golfing. He didn't read books or go to plays or art museums. He spent his leisure hours in the male world of bars, drinking with male friends and talking about his career. Why Marilyn chose him as a partner is a mystery, although he was, like her, very shy, and he had a kind and gentle side. She loved his large family and became close to his sisters. He was a good businessman, versed in how to deal with management, and he helped her stand up to Twentieth Century–Fox executives in crafting her career. He also offered her the security of his moral reputation as she faced a potential firestorm when she was identified as the model for the nude calendar photo.[73]

Joe dated showgirls and starlets. Although his first wife, a Broadway showgirl, had divorced him, he doted on his son, Joe DiMaggio Jr., and he supposedly didn't engage in affairs. Joe's purity was as much mythology as was the puffery about Marilyn being highly moral. Joe had sex with many women, including showgirls and high-class call girls. His gofer and part father, part confidant, Broadway ticket agent George Solotaire, often pimped for him. Joe had friends in the Mafia. He was, after all, Sicilian in background, and he frequented places like Toots Shor's that were financed by the Mafia.

The magic that Marilyn beamed on Joe in 1952 worked. Unlike many beautiful women, he said, she wasn't self-centered. She was kind and generous, and she listened to what he had to say. She didn't mind that he was often quiet. The day after their first Hollywood date, Sidney Skolsky announced in his column that they were a new item, and Marilyn persuaded Joe to visit her on the set of *Monkey Business*. A photo was taken of the two of them together, along with Cary Grant. It was easy to cut Grant out of the photo and put it on the wire services as a photo of Marilyn and Joe as a new romantic couple.

With Joe in Marilyn's life, Roy Craft finalized a deal with *Life* magazine for a photographic essay on Marilyn, shot by Philippe Halsman. An essay in such a respectable magazine, with a tiny reproduction of "A Nude Wrinkle" in it, would take the photo out of the category of "dirty French postcard," as Craft put it, and legitimize it as aesthetic art. Then Sidney Skolsky had her leak the information that she had posed for the photo to Aline Mosby of United Press, who was sympathetic to Marilyn. Mosby's story, as planned, focused on Marilyn's poverty, honesty, and hard work, elements of her star text. Sidney thought up a quip about the radio being on when the photo was taken. When a reporter asked Marilyn what she had on in the nude photo, she replied, "The radio." The nation laughed at her comic skill and was captivated. Public outrage at the photo evaporated.

Her clever handling of the photo enabled her to weather the storm not only over the nude photo but also over the fuss that resulted when in April 1952 a journalist found her mother working in a rest home in Eagle Rock. Marilyn had always said that Gladys was dead. Apologizing publicly for the lie, Marilyn stated that she had done it because she didn't want journalists bothering her mother, whom she rarely saw anyway. The journalists mentioned Gladys's 1949 marriage to John Eley just before Marilyn posed for the nude photo, but they didn't make much of it. In any event, that marriage had broken down. According to Gladys, in a letter to the Mother Church in Boston, a Mrs. Louella Atterberry had forced her into the marriage, and Eley had been alcoholic and abusive, once attempting to kill her with a knife and on another occasion trying to strangle her.[74] In addition, he had another wife.

Gladys filed for divorce in February 1952, although Eley wrote a will that month leaving her ten percent of his property, which wasn't inconsiderable. He called her his legal wife, even though another woman claimed to be married to him and she had a marriage certificate predating Gladys's by several years.[75] Eley died suddenly on April 23. Extant documents indicate that his first wife was awarded all of his estate. Gladys withdrew her divorce action two days later. He was buried in the Westwood Memorial Cemetery and Mortuary, joining the Goddard family members who were buried there. The Goddards seem to have accepted him; they called him Colonel Eley. Following the 1950s practice regarding women's last names, Gladys called herself Mrs. Eley ever after. In June she went to Florida to stay with Berniece Miracle. Marilyn was happy to have her out of town.

At the end of May 1952, capitalizing on the furor over the nude calendar, Zanuck released a number of Marilyn films: *Clash by Night*, *Don't Bother to Knock*, and *We're Not Married*. On June 1, her birthday, he told her she had won the role of Lorelei Lee in *Gentlemen Prefer Blondes*. Meanwhile he put the movie *Niagara* into production.

Niagara, a considerable departure for Marilyn, made her into a superstar. Far from her usual innocent, sexy self, in this film she schemes with a young lover to murder her husband. Her sexual glow is fiery; the comic Marilyn is evident only insofar as she overplays her sexy self in some scenes. Playing Rose Loomis, a showgirl with a murky past, married to a man who has suffered a breakdown during World War Two, she is a film noir villainess—one of those evil women in 1950s films who destroy the men who can't resist them. The genre was an outgrowth of post–World War Two anxiety over the Cold War. Like other films in the genre, *Niagara* reflected the nation's fears about women having left the home for work during the war, while drawing from transhistorical male fears about female sexual insatiability. Like *The Asphalt Jungle*, her 1950 film noir movie, it was a crime melodrama. In *The Asphalt Jungle*, she was a victim as much as a predator. This time Marilyn was the villain.

Marilyn's film noir temptress in *Niagara* is different from those of other actresses who played noir vamps, such as Barbara Stanwyck and Lauren Bacall. Marilyn is as tough as any of them on the exterior, but she projects a softness that is at variance with her evil nature, which makes her hard and human at the same time. The film was shot in Technicolor, unusual for film noir. The light and dark shadings that suggest menace and danger in black-and-white noir films are absent from *Niagara*, and that lack of menace dampens its effectiveness. The scenery and the Niagara waterfall are spectacular in the film, but it doesn't have a compelling noir sense of mystery.

The camera often focuses on Marilyn's body. She is shown in bed lying under sheets, obviously naked, and coming out of a shower with only a towel over her body—shocking scenes for the 1950s. In the film she often wears a tight red dress, which caused a sensation. In a renowned scene, the camera focuses on her backside as she walks down a cobblestone street with her hips swaying in an exaggerated manner. It was after this walk, which doesn't seem like much today, that publicists dubbed her "the girl with the horizontal walk."

The publicity on the film was over the top. She was plugged as a force of nature that couldn't be stopped, as a woman who could inspire men to great deeds while destroying them: she was Aphrodite crossed with Vampira. In an advertisement for the film she is draped across the top of Niagara Falls, with the water from the falls flowing over the cliff beneath her—a wet dream extraordinaire. Advertising copy, alluding to the mythical siren on the rock in the Rhine River who tempts sailors to their doom, describes Marilyn as "a Lorelei flaunting her charms as she lured men to eternal destruction." (Those ads appeared as Marilyn was filming *Gentlemen Prefer Blondes*, in which she played the showgirl Lorelei Lee, a comic Lorelei who collected men as potential husbands.)

In September Fox sent her to New York on a publicity tour for *Monkey Business*. While there she went to Atlantic City to serve as the honorary marshal in the parade that opened the Miss America pageant. After all, she had played a beauty contest winner in several films. Riding in the back of an open convertible, wearing a tight red dress cut almost to the navel, she carried a bouquet of roses and threw them, one by one, to the crowd. She was the hit of the parade. Roy Craft, who was with her, stated that "she murdered those poor little Miss Americas."[76]

But Marilyn didn't see it that way. "Surrounded by all those fresh, young, incredibly beautiful girls," she told Ralph Roberts, "I was terribly nervous, very unsure of myself." After the parade the contestants waited in line to be photographed with her, one by one, for their hometown papers. None of them, she said, would have anything to do with her. But the previous year's Miss America, Yolande Betbeze, took pity on her, exchanging small talk with her. "She took it on herself to make that time bearable to me."[77]

Once again the assertive Marilyn hid the shy person at her core. Then she was photographed with a group of women officers in the female branches of the armed services, the Wacs and Waves. The photo had been printed in newspapers throughout the nation when an army officer suddenly noticed that Marilyn's breasts were improperly exposed.

By then it was too late to do anything. Playing the innocent vixen, Marilyn responded that the photographer had shot her from above her head, exposing her cleavage; she'd had nothing to do with it. Again she denied the obvious, putting on her "dumb-blonde" persona.

She went back to New York to appear with singer Mel Tormé in his nightclub act to publicize *Monkey Business*. Her behavior was unpredictable. At first, according to Tormé, she was wonderful in rehearsals. When she laughed, Tormé said, she raised bumps on your arms with the joyous abandon of her giggles. But fifteen minutes before the performance was to begin, she froze. Tormé joked her back to her normal self, and she went on with the show.[78]

During the New York visit, Earl Wilson interviewed her. He was stunned by the change in her behavior from the interview he'd done with her three years before, when she had been in New York promoting *Love Happy*. In the earlier interview she had been wooden and uninteresting, a young girl being oversold. She was now fire and ice, a brilliant interview subject and photographic model. She even instructed the photographer that Wilson took along with him how to shoot her.

Is it true that you don't wear underwear? Wilson asked her. Certainly, she said. She was wearing a dress she'd bought at designer Ceil Chapman's boutique, and she told him to call up the salesladies there, who would tell him that she didn't wear underwear when she tried on clothes. Then she invited him to frisk her. Her exhibitionism was becoming extreme. Yet as if to exonerate her sexy behavior in Atlantic City and New York, Marilyn exhibited her humanitarian impulse. In Longport, New Jersey, she visited the Betty Bacharach home. It was a convalescent center for children recovering from serious illness, especially polio, which was then epidemic.[79] This was the Marilyn who loved children and identified with the disadvantaged.

From *As Young as You Feel* to *Niagara*, Marilyn had moved from being a sexpot to being a star. She had created her blonde sex goddess character, and it had worked. Now she would modify it, adding comic dimensions, becoming the greatest dumb blonde in the American comic tradition, until she felt trapped by the role and had to flee it. She was already lobbying Zanuck for dramatic roles, but not even directors Henry Hathaway and Jean Negulesco, major Marilyn admirers, could talk him into casting her in them. Blondes had become his bugaboo, and Marilyn had come to represent the dark side of Hollywood to him. In his eyes and the eyes of many Hollywood men, she had slept with too many men on her way to the top, thus stepping outside the bounds of their definitions of respectability. Now she was forcing them to promote her as a star, and she had done it by posing for a nude calendar and becoming involved with Joe DiMaggio. They would continue resisting her, even as she fought back.

Chapter 7

Breakaway, 1954–1955

Filming on *Gentlemen Prefer Blondes* began in November 1952, after Marilyn had returned from her promotional tour for *Monkey Business*. Zanuck had been ambivalent about casting her, but he wasn't happy with the alternatives: Betty Grable was getting on in years and Carol Channing had played Lorelei on Broadway with a bowlegged walk, baby-doll eyes, and a foghorn lisp. Zanuck didn't want his Lorelei to be a complete caricature. He asked Howard Hawks, Marilyn's director on *Monkey Business*, if she could do it. Hawks assured him she could. In fact, he chastised Zanuck for casting Marilyn in dramas like *Don't Bother to Knock*. Her métier, he said, was comedy. "You're making realism with a very unreal girl. She's a completely storybook character."[1]

Hawks's comment was one-sided. She had played a "dumb blonde" in *Monkey Business* and, terrified of Hawks, she had also played that role with him offscreen. He hadn't drawn out her serious side. Both Zanuck and Hawks forgot Marilyn's complex acting in *The Asphalt Jungle* and *Clash by Night* and her effective singing in *Ladies of the Chorus*. Jule Styne, who wrote the music for *Gentlemen*, praised her voice. She'd been a smash hit at Camp Pendleton marine base the previous spring, where she'd brought down the house with her sultry rendition of Cole Porter's "Let's Do It Again." Her voice lessons with Phil Moore were paying off.

Hawks was known for directing male adventure films, but he also specialized in comedies like *Monkey Business* that upended conventional gender roles. Zanuck asked him to direct *Gentlemen*, filled with subtle references to gender crossing and the complexities of femininity and masculinity. Hawks accepted the offer, but only if a strong actress played Dorothy, Lorelei's showgirl sidekick, to offset Marilyn's softness. Hawks suggested Jane Russell, whom he had directed in *The Outlaw*, and Zanuck agreed. She was under contract to Howard Hughes, who demanded $200,000 to lend her out for *Gentlemen*, plus salaries for her cameraman, hairdresser, and makeup artist. The exorbitant sum made Marilyn more attractive to Zanuck, since Betty Grable wanted $100,000 to play Lorelei and Marilyn, still on a weekly salary, would make about $20,000 for the anticipated twelve weeks of filming. She was only on the second year of her May 1951 contract and her salary was at $1,700 a week.

Marilyn realized that she probably could have gotten a larger salary, but she wanted creative input into her films more than money. Most major stars had clauses in their contracts giving them a voice in selecting directors, cameraman, and scripts for their films, but Zanuck refused to grant such concessions to Marilyn. Summoning her courage, she demanded that Zanuck at least give her a dressing room suite, which was standard for stars. That would be a concession. "This is a movie about a blonde," she said, "and I'm the blonde." Zanuck gave in, assigning her the suite that Marlene Dietrich and Alice Faye had once used. The dispute suggests the contempt in which Fox executives held her. Lew Shreiber, Zanuck's assistant, a "a pint-sized Fox executive" hadn't given her a suite, according to actor Robert Stack, because he didn't want her to develop "a swelled head."[2]

As Lorelei Lee, Marilyn is funny and fey, the quintessential blonde of the 1950s. *Gentlemen* is the first film in which she fully displays the Marilyn Monroe persona that she had been constructing since the walk-on role in *Love Happy*. In the movie Lorelei and Dorothy travel on an ocean liner to Paris so that Lorelei can marry her wealthy lover there. His father, who controls his money and doesn't trust Lorelei, hires a private detective to follow her. The film adds additional characters to the novel, including an elderly fake millionaire and another fake one who turns out to be a ten-year-old boy with a foghorn voice. The many plot complications involve a lost diamond tiara, a courtroom scene in which Dorothy pretends to be Lorelei, and a wedding in which Lorelei marries her millionaire and Dorothy the private detective. *Gentlemen* focuses on

Lorelei and Dorothy as they scheme together to confuse the private detective and the millionaires and periodically perform song-and-dance
numbers. "I can be smart when it's important, but most men don't like it,"
Lorelei says, indicating that she hides her intelligence behind her dumb-
blonde persona. Marilyn insisted that the line be added to the film.

In the film Russell wears dresses with squared shoulders and straight
lines that accentuate her large, earthy body, making Dorothy look like a
butch partner for Lorelei. She becomes involved in Lorelei's zany schemes
to elude the detective and catch another millionaire. Wearing a blonde
wig and affecting a soft, seductive voice, Dorothy mimics Lorelei so effectively in the courtroom scene that the judge can't tell which of them is
actually Lorelei. In his confusion femininity seems an unstable position.
It also seems unstable when the father of Lorelei's millionaire boyfriend,
present in the courtroom, describes Lorelei as a shape-shifting monster.
He fears that he may encounter an engulfing swarm of such monstruous
women. "How do you think I feel with thousands of Loreleis coming at
me from everywhere?" In the wedding that ends the film, with Dorothy
and Lorelei wearing the same dress and standing next to each other, it
appears that they are marrying each other, not the men.

But masculinity may also be relative, as *Gentlemen* also suggests. The
Olympic athletes at the beginning of the film exercise their bodies, strike
self-involved poses, and aren't interested in Dorothy, as Russell sings, "Is
there anyone here for love?" They resemble the athletic, semiclothed men
in the day's physique magazines marketed to homosexuals. In the rest of
the film Dorothy and Lorelei easily outfox the male characters. In *My
Story* Marilyn states that most male actors are "pansies" because acting
is a feminine art. "When a man has to paint his face and pose and strut
and pretend emotions, he isn't doing what is normally masculine. He's
acting, just as women do in life."[3] That's the important phrase: "just as
women do in life." Femininity, Marilyn implies, is a masquerade that
women put on to conform to society's expectation.

Jack Cole, Broadway's most innovative choreographer, created and
directed the dance sequences in *Gentlemen*. He was known for an eclectic jazz dance style that drew from ballet, African-American rhythms,
Eastern dance, and burlesque bumps and grinds. Homosexual in orientation, he liked to slip gay themes by the censors.[4] Cole was a superb
dance teacher for movie actresses like Monroe and Russell, who weren't

trained dancers. He broke down his dances into individual movements, and he or his assistant, Gwen Verdon, practiced the movements for hours with them until they knew them by rote. Cole had a hair-trigger temper, but he was gentle with Marilyn. When she performed her dances during shooting, he would do them along with her off camera, to "pump her up" and keep her on target. The technique worked. George Chakiris, a dancer in the "Diamonds Are a Girl's Best Friend" number, told me that Marilyn had more energy than any dancer he had ever known, on a par with the legendary Jerome Robbins.[5]

Marilyn insisted that Cole choreograph the dance numbers in her later musicals: *There's No Business Like Show Business*, *River of No Return*, and *Let's Make Love*. He worked with Hal Schaefer, a jazz pianist and vocal coach, who helped him with musical arrangements and coached Monroe and Russell on their singing numbers in *Gentlemen*. Schaefer had coached both Judy Garland and Peggy Lee. He was a gentle man with a special gift for clarifying phrasing and increasing breath control. Marilyn later had an affair with him when he coached her on *There's No Business Like Show Business*.

During the filming of *Gentlemen* the anger she'd repressed for years began to show. When she first arrived in Hollywood she didn't contradict the power brokers; she was a supplicant. It was easier to withdraw into a dissociative dream world where she couldn't be reached—or to be late to the set and then break into tears when challenged. But she had displayed anger to Jim Dougherty, and once she was a star she raged against Hollywood men. According to Adele Balkan, assistant to costume designer Billy Travilla, when Marilyn fought with Travilla over her costumes, "you could hear the commotions up and down the hall." She fought with Cole over the number of takes on the "Diamonds Are a Girl's Best Friend" scene. She demanded that they do it over and over again. When they decided to go with an early take, she apologized to the cast and crew. Frank Radcliffe danced with Marilyn in "Diamonds" and in numbers in her later musicals. He recalled, "A lot of her so-called temperament was the fact that she knew what she wanted and threatened to pull out of the picture unless she got her way."[6] What she wanted was perfection.

Anger is the reverse side of depression; it can release emotions that might otherwise be internalized and cause self-recrimination and self-doubt. When Marilyn's anger surfaced, it was huge: she called it her "monster" and averred that she couldn't control it. It could be volcanic and slashing, but she could forget it the next day. Billy Wilder, who directed her in *The Seven Year Itch* in 1954 and in *Some Like It Hot* in 1958, described her "moodiness." "She had days bubbling with joy and days of sadness," Wilder said. "She was very unpredictable. She could be uncooperative, obstructionist, explosive. Or she could let things go smoothly."[7]

Marilyn still was shy and insecure. Trivial slights could hurt her deeply; Sammy Davis Jr. said that it sometimes seemed as though she had no skin. She was often late to the set of *Gentlemen*, hiding out in her suite. Whitey Snyder told Jane Russell, occupying the suite next to hers, that Marilyn was scared of Howard Hawks and intimidated by Russell's retinue, a group demanded by Howard Hughes that Russell found amusing. Russell had met Marilyn years before, at a nightclub, when Marilyn was Norma Jeane and with Jim Dougherty. He knew Russell from their acting days at Van Nuys High. She had seemed to Russell then "a little thing, with ash-brown hair and a very sweet smile,"[8] and she still seemed the same. Practical and motherly, Jane cajoled Marilyn onto the set. "Come on, blondie," or "Let's go, baby doll," she would say. Russell was married to football star Bob Waterfield, and she felt a bond with Marilyn because their partners were both famous athletes.

In addition, they both were deeply spiritual. Russell persuaded Marilyn to attend her Christian group, but Marilyn was studying Steiner's Anthroposophy and Freud's theories, and she soon dropped out. Using an excuse she'd repeat in the coming years, she told Russell, "Freud is my religion."[9] That was both true and an exaggeration of the truth. Marilyn studied Freud and underwent Freudian therapy, but she also studied mystical religions like Anthroposophy and practiced them in her life.

Russell was impressed by Marilyn's intelligence. She often quoted poetry or talked about ideas, and she constantly asked questions. One day she was reading *The Rubaiyat of Omar Khayyám* on the set of *Gentlemen*. Khayyám was a Sufi poet who wrote about the love between God and man as though it were love between two humans, bringing the divine and the human together. Marilyn read Jane a passage about the need for personal independence in relationships, even between lovers.

> Do not put your hearts into each other's keeping. For only the hand of life can contain your hearts. And stand together yet not too near

together. For the pillars of the temple stand apart, and the oak tree
and the cypress grow not in each other's shadow.[10]

Marilyn was trying to follow Khayyám's advice in forming a relationship
with Joe DiMaggio based on independence, not on his controlling her,
which was what he wanted. She wasn't succeeding. They conflicted over
her career, especially over her sexy public persona. "Didn't he realize,"
Marilyn said, "who I was? He didn't like actors kissing me and he didn't
like my skimpy costumes. When I told him I had to dress that way for my
job, he told me to quit the job." But Marilyn was finally achieving stardom, and she wasn't going to give it up. Nor was she faithful to Joe.
There was the relationship with Nico Minardos. Moreover, when Elia
Kazan arrived in Hollywood in March 1952 for the Academy Awards
ceremony, she had sex with him, appearing in his hotel room in the
middle of the night. As they made love she told Kazan that she was going
to marry Joe DiMaggio. It is unclear whether this was true at the time or
simply a ploy to attract Kazan.[11]

A pamphlet on Marilyn written in Russell's voice and widely distributed, discusses her relationship with Joe and praises her femininity and
intelligence. A publicist probably wrote it, but Hollywood was surprised
that these two "sex queens" didn't compete with each other, which movie
divas were supposed to do. The pamphlet explored their friendship, promoting both of them. In the pamphlet Russell advised Marilyn on how
to combine marriage and a career. Get a housekeeper, Russell said; get
tough with the studios. Joe DiMaggio is tough; he will give you strength.

When Marilyn married Joe two years later, in January 1954, Russell
was delighted. But several months into the marriage, Russell realized
that it was a disaster. Marilyn hadn't been able to infuse Khayyám's
philosophy about independence into her life with Joe. "Part of Marilyn
was dying in the marriage," Russell told Anthony Summers, "because
Marilyn couldn't express herself."[12] Joe was simply too controlling at
this point.

Filming *Gentlemen* was grueling, and Marilyn's mother was acting up.
After the spring 1952 episode with the press followed by John Eley's
death, Gladys went to Florida to live with Berniece. In September, however, she appeared at Grace's house in Van Nuys. She wasn't in good

shape. The problems with Eley, plus Marilyn's nude photo, had sent her over the edge. From reading *Science and Health*, she had decided that sex was evil, but her daughter was an international sex icon. She was outraged. Ranting on Grace's front porch that demons were out to get her, she seemed out of her mind, so Grace called the police to take her to Norwalk State Mental Hospital. That solution, however, was temporary. Once the press found Gladys in a public mental institution, they would probably excoriate Marilyn, who was supposed to be wealthy, even though, given her expenses, she hardly made enough money to get by. For publicity purposes and for her own good, Gladys had to be placed in a private institution.

The ever resourceful Grace Goddard found a sanitarium for Gladys in a valley in the Glendale hills, close to the center of La Crescenta, on the main road. Named Rockhaven, it had cabins arranged around a central building—all in Mediterranean style—with a lot of trees and shrubbery. It was expensive, but its residents, all women, were well cared for and had private rooms. Psychotherapy wasn't offered, nor was Gladys given shock treatments, since her condition was now considered permanent. Patricia Traviss, whose grandmother had founded Rockhaven in 1923, owned and ran the sanitarium during the fourteen years that Gladys lived there. Traviss told me that from 1953, when Gladys entered Rockhaven, until 1962, when Marilyn died, Marilyn didn't visit her. Marilyn became anxious even thinking of going there. All her demons came out, she told Ralph Roberts. She simply couldn't see Gladys. In her absence, Grace visited Gladys and took care of her for Marilyn. After Grace died in the fall of 1953, Inez Melson, whom Marilyn hired as her business manager and Gladys's guardian, would provide the same service for Marilyn.[13]

On February 8, 1953, Grace moved Gladys to Rockhaven from Norwalk State Mental Hospital. At a ceremony in the Crystal Room of the Beverly Hills Hotel that evening, Marilyn received *Photoplay*'s award as the year's best newcomer. *Photoplay* was the nation's most widely read movie fan magazine, and its awards were as important as the Oscars. But *Niagara* had opened several weeks earlier, and women's clubs throughout the nation were protesting the immorality of Marilyn's character in the movie and especially the red dress she wore in it. Despite the backlash, Marilyn was outrageous in dress and manner at the *Photoplay* ceremony. Was she testing the moralists? Was she feeling guilty about her mother? Did her drive to expose herself take over?

She borrowed a dress from the Fox wardrobe department to wear to the ceremony. It was made of gold lamé with a deep V-neck; Billy Travilla had designed it for a scene in *Gentlemen* that was cut from the movie. Travilla didn't want her to wear it, because it was too small for her. Giving herself enemas, she lost ten pounds in two days. (Film actresses used colonic cleansing to lose weight in a hurry.) Even after the weight loss, the dress was still so tight that it hugged her body, accentuating her hip-swaying walk and the absence of underwear under the dress. She was sewn into it because it hadn't been finished and had no zipper. Reporter James Bacon's description of her as she walked in the dress makes her seem like a soft-porn fantasy. "Her breasts undulated, and her derriere looked like two puppies fighting under a silk sheet."[14]

Dean Martin and Jerry Lewis, a famed comedy team, were masters of ceremony at the event. As Marilyn walked with mincing steps to the podium to receive her award, Jerry leaped on the table and hooted like a chimpanzee, while Dean broke into a hip-swinging dance. The audience howled with laughter.

The reaction was swift in the following days. Columnist Florabel Muir applauded Marilyn for stealing the show from stars like Joan Crawford. Crawford replied by accusing Marilyn of offending the nation by wearing the gold lamé dress—and the red dress in *Niagara*. Marilyn replied to Crawford in an interview with Louella Parsons. She didn't understand why Crawford picked on her: she was a beginner, and Crawford was a star. She wore sexy clothes to publicize herself. Besides, her character in *Niagara* was a slut. In wearing the red dress she was true to the role. She didn't mention the gold dress.[15]

Now that she was a star, she continued, her erotic days were over. Her focus would be on serious acting. Then she delivered a low blow by stating that Crawford's criticism especially hurt because she admired her as a mother. It was a subtle put-down, since it was widely known that Crawford physically abused her adopted children and that she had made an underground nude movie early in her career. Neither Crawford nor Marilyn mentioned the lesbian episode of the previous year, which Marilyn would describe in *My Story* as a pass on the part of Crawford.

Marilyn also replied to Crawford in an article written under her own name in the June issue of *Motion Picture*. It's one of the most revealing articles written about her. She described herself as independent, and she made a brief for the relativity of morality. She cited Abraham Lincoln: "If you call a tail a leg, how many legs has a dog? Five? No. Calling a tail a leg doesn't make it a leg." That comment sounds like the fey Marilyn, using her own bizarre logic. Then she became more rational, as she pointed out that the Supreme Court is often split on decisions, with four judges on one side and five on the other. "Each of us is entitled to a point of view and the right of decision," she said to Crawford. "Name calling won't alter the facts, and it is unlikely to change me. I live as I please, and I like it."[16]

The fan magazines had a field day. *Photoplay* ran an article titled "Hollywood vs. Marilyn Monroe," asserting that "all the town's heavy artillery was hauled out to assail her with a walloping barrage of criticism." During the next year the magazines continued to debate her behavior. Her protective star text was invoked to defend her: she was moral, shy, and a homebody. Her supporters introduced a new theme as they praised her for influencing many Hollywood stars to become more sexy. It was a change, they contended, that would bring the television audience back to films. According to Sheilah Graham, even "girl-next-door" stars like Janet Leigh and Jeanne Crain were wearing tight dresses. The dignified Anne Baxter had dyed her hair blonde and had done a belly dance in her latest film.[17]

In Marilyn's next movie, *How to Marry a Millionaire*, filmed in the spring of 1953, she was more a naïf than a vamp, although she still wore tight, sexy clothing. The movie was shot in Cinemascope, only the second movie shot in the new big-screen technique, which had been introduced recently to appeal to the public's attraction to spectacle, especially given the small size of TV screens. Fox had bought the process from its French inventor and was shooting many of its films in the new process, while leasing its use for a hefty sum to other studios.

Fox capitalized on Marilyn's body in *How to Marry a Millionaire* by making it even more of a spectacle in the large-screen process than in *Niagara*, although Marilyn spoofed her sexuality in this film. Playing the nearsighted Pola Debevoise, she bumps into walls when she takes off her glasses. She does a brilliant comic turn, as a dumb blonde with an idiosyncratic view of the world. Nunnally Johnson, who wrote the screenplay, stated that he based Pola on the real-life Marilyn. *How to Marry a*

Millionaire costarred Betty Grable and Lauren Bacall as Marilyn's chums in another female buddy film, with three women friends rather than two (which had been the case in *Gentlemen*). The three friends rent an elegant New York apartment as part of a scheme to trap three millionaires into marriage, although in the end they settle for ordinary men.

The actresses were friendly on screen and off. Grable, as down-to-earth as Jane Russell, knew that her glory days were over. At thirty she was old by industry standards (Marilyn was then twenty-six). On the first day of shooting a lot of journalists appeared on the set looking for Marilyn, not for her. She publicly welcomed Marilyn and was touched when Marilyn was the only person on the set to express concern when Grable's daughter was injured in a horse-riding incident. She made several more films and then retired.

Lauren Bacall, highly professional, was annoyed by Marilyn's lateness, her need for retakes, and her habit of looking at Bacall's forehead rather than her eyes. (Looking up at foreheads made Marilyn's eyes seem larger. She already knew all the tricks.) Marilyn wasn't bitchy, and Bacall liked her. Both of them were, she said, rebels against an exploitative industry. "I said to her: don't let them push you around. She was just a commodity to them. There were so few she could really trust." Like many individuals, however, Bacall sometimes found Marilyn difficult to understand. She used a logic of her own that didn't always make sense to Bacall. Many people made similar comments about Marilyn.[18]

Nunnally Johnson rehearsed the actors before every scene. Johnson was low-key and courteous, but he was hard on the cast. He threw Marilyn off base; she retreated into her own world. He described her to others as under water, off in space. Jean Negulesco, who directed the film, made an effort to become friends with Marilyn, but he sometimes experienced her as in another world. "She walks right by you with glassy eyes, as though she is hypnotized."[19]

In June, shortly before *Gentlemen Prefer Blondes* was released, Jane and Marilyn, wearing similar sundresses, participated in the major rite of Hollywood stardom by placing their handprints and footprints in cement in the courtyard of Grauman's Chinese Theater. At the ceremony Marilyn quipped that the imprints should have been of Jane's breasts and her butt. The statement wasn't that farfetched. Betty Grable, famed for her legs, had immortalized them in cement in Grauman's courtyard. Above all, Marilyn had survived her insecurity and her difficulty with powerful Hollywood males to be immortalized as a Hollywood icon.

In 1953 Marilyn remained involved with Joe, even though he hated her sexy self-presentation and refused to go to Hollywood events that featured her as a sex symbol. Sidney Skolsky, her close friend, filled in for him. Joe spent a lot of time in New York as a TV interviewer for Yankee baseball games. He was often angry at Marilyn because she would agree to something and then do the opposite. She played along with the idea of developing their relationship by visiting his family in San Francisco some weekends, but she continued to date other men.

As Marilyn came to know Joe better, she found out he was tight with money and often self-absorbed. He could be moody and depressed. He was compulsively neat and obsessively punctual, and his favorite activities were watching television and playing poker with his male friends, drinking with them in bars, and discussing his baseball exploits. He chain-smoked, drank coffee constantly, and had a bad temper. He helped her to be tough in dealing with the moguls, but he didn't trust anyone in Hollywood except for Frank Sinatra, a fellow Italian with roots in Sicily.

Yet he was generous. On Christmas Eve 1952, when Marilyn didn't go with him to San Francisco because she had to attend the studio Christmas party, he was in her hotel room when she returned, and he'd set up a small decorated Christmas tree. He gave her gifts all the time, including a full-length black mink coat at Christmas 1953, which she treasured. Furs were a symbol of luxury in the 1950s, and Marilyn, who usually paid no attention to such things, adored hers. Joe became close to some of her friends, especially the Shaws and the Kargers. She liked George Solotaire, the aging Broadway ticket broker who, as Joe's gofer, was often with him. Solotaire treated her like a daughter. Loving children, she became close to Joe DiMaggio Jr., who returned her affection.

Marilyn always said that Joe was a wonderful lover. She called him her slugger and said that he could hit the ball out of the park. If sex was all there was to a marriage, she said, she and Joe would be married forever. When I asked Tom Sobeck, a friend of Joe's, to explain what she meant by "slugger," he said that Joe was so "well hung" that even prostitutes retreated when they saw him naked. It seems that Marilyn was referring to the mythology that penis size matters to women and that large is always better than small.[20]

Joe's friends in the Mafia both frightened and fascinated Marilyn. Many of his favorite male hangouts and nightclubs had mob backers. In New York, he went to Toots Shor's, a restaurant for male sports aficionados that Sinatra also frequented. He traveled to Atlantic City to the 500 Club, owned by his friend Pasquale (Skinny) D'Amato, whom he had met when he was stationed near Atlantic City during World War Two. Joe first met Sinatra at Skinny's, where Sinatra often performed. Skinny had done jail time under the White-Slave Traffic Act for transporting women across state lines for the purpose of prostitution, but he also was elegant and suave, an Italian bella figura who was a model for Sinatra and his Rat Pack.[21]

The death of Joe's brother Mike in May 1953 brought Marilyn and Joe closer together, as Joe turned to her for solace. Three months later, she began shooting *River of No Return*, a film about homesteading in the American West in the 1890s, in Banff, Alberta, Canada, which had scenery like that of the film's setting. She had agreed to do it because she owed Fox a film, and she liked the songs she was to sing in it. But once filming began, difficulties emerged between Marilyn and Otto Preminger, the film's director. Like Marilyn, he had been ordered by Zanuck to direct it because he owed Fox a film. Like Marilyn, he didn't like the film, but he also didn't like her acting. The combination of Preminger and Marilyn was lethal. Joe flew there to help her.

Among Hollywood's dictatorial directors, Otto Preminger was the worst. Shelley Winters, who was making a movie nearby, went to watch the filming. She observed Preminger terrorize Marilyn "into total immobility." Stanley Rubin, the film's producer, called him a "bully" and became Marilyn's protector. Robert Mitchum found him vicious and crude, especially to women. Preminger and Marilyn stopped speaking after the first day of shooting, and Mitchum became their go-between. Marilyn became increasingly difficult, showing up late and flubbing lines. Mitchum noted, however, that she was having difficult menstrual periods. Many times, Mitchum stated, when people on the set cursed her selfishness at closing down the production, she was in her dressing room immobilized by cramps, suffering and embarrassed.[22]

Preminger predictably clashed with Natasha Lytess, who was there to coach Marilyn. He fired her, but Marilyn got her reinstated. Then Preminger, who frequented Sam Spiegel's "boys' club," barked at Marilyn that she should go back to her "original profession." That statement infuriated her, and she got back at him after she twisted her ankle on a wet rock and returned to the set with her ankle taped. Preminger was kinder to her after her accident. Shelley Winters contended that Marilyn had her ankle taped to make him feel guilty. Winters commented: "Dumb? Like a fox, was my friend Marilyn."[23]

River of No Return is a confused movie about Indians, a shyster gambler, and homesteading beside a river. Marilyn is a dance hall singer who takes care of Mitchum's son while he is in jail on a trumped-up charge and who winds up on Mitchum's ranch. Throughout the film she wears either an abbreviated dance hall costume or tight blue jeans. In one scene, she is drenched with water when she and Mitchum, escaping from Indians, run river rapids on a raft. Her wet clothes cling to her, revealing the contours of her body.

Marilyn detested the movie, calling it her "Z" western (a wordplay on B movies) in which the actors came in third after the scenery and the horses. She saw it with Sidney Skolsky at Grauman's Chinese Theater. Afterward, she walked around the corner out of sight and vomited. Noreen Nash was with Darryl Zanuck when he watched a preview of the movie. He was vocal about disliking Marilyn in it.[24] But Marilyn isn't a dumb blonde in the film. Her character is strong and resilient, as Marilyn had been in *Don't Bother to Knock* and *Clash by Night*. She shows potential as a dramatic actress and only rarely turns on her sexy Marilyn Monroe voltage.

According to Shelley Winters, after turning her ankle Marilyn took a Percodan for pain, washing it down with several shots of vodka. Percodan, an opiate, had been developed in the early 1950s. It soon became the major drug prescribed for severe pain. In addition to lessening pain, it can produce euphoria. It is also highly addictive.

By 1952 Marilyn was using prescription drugs, especially the barbiturates Nembutal and Seconal for anxiety and insomnia, and amphetamines for energy. Developed years earlier, those drugs had been given to soldiers during World War Two and then had been heavily marketed to civilians once the war ended. They were considered miracle drugs that countered the anxiety and depression from which many Americans suffered. Their side effects and addictive potential were poorly understood. By 1947 some 1,500 variants of barbiturates had been developed, and Nembutal, Seconal, and Amytal were among the best known. Doctors freely prescribed them.[25] They were popular in Hollywood, where movie making produced tension among everyone involved. So were amphetamines, which were used to counter the grogginess that barbiturates produced. Actors, in particular, had to get up early in the morning and look fresh through a long day's shooting. Amphetamines were also used as an aide to dieting.

According to Sheree North, who was hired by Fox in 1954 to keep Marilyn in line, most Fox actors were on prescription drugs. "We'd all be working so hard that we couldn't sleep. We had to take sleeping pills to look at all rested in the morning." Amphetamines and barbiturates were handed out at parties, given as house presents, and used as chips in poker games. They were advertised in magazines and distributed at studio conferences in the form of little pills in all colors, sizes, and shapes, to keep one calm, according to writer Terence Rattigan.[26]

Bunny Gardel, who did Marilyn's body makeup on her movies, remembered that by the early 1950s she carried a plastic bag filled with pills, including uppers and downers. By 1955 her prescription drug use was heavy. Typical of addicts, she had an encyclopedic knowledge of drugs. "If I haven't tried it," Marilyn said to Susan Strasberg, "it doesn't exist. I'm a war veteran of the night." Marilyn's friend Delos Smith stated that she was playing Russian roulette with her life. "It took her five pills to get to sleep," he stated. "Seven would kill her. For many years she lived two pills away from dying." She often suggested that they commit suicide together, although she also made pacts with other close friends to call one another if either seriously considered suicide. It was hard to deal with the demons inside of her, what Clifford Odets called the dark subsoil on which her roots were feeding; sometimes she looked on death as a welcome relief. It was, Susan Strasberg said, her "ace in the hole."[27]

Sammy Davis Jr., who knew Marilyn well, maintained that her drug use was no greater than that of many Hollywood actors, although he may have downplayed her problem.[28] The danger with barbiturates is that the body adjusts to them, requiring increasing numbers of pills to provide relief. One can recover from that tolerance only by abstaining for a time or by switching to another class of drugs—from barbiturates to opiates, for example. In the beginning the addiction itself isn't that heavy and withdrawal symptoms are minor. Yet over time withdrawal symptoms can be severe, while the addiction can result in insomnia, panic attacks, bad moods, absentmindedness, and hallucinations. Amphetamines are also dangerous. After long use they reduce the ability of the centers in the body that store serotonin, the body's natural mood elevator, to release the neurotransmitter. Depression can result. Marilyn's depressive episodes became more frequent over the years.

Marilyn also used alcohol to calm herself and elevate her mood, although she kept her drinking under control for many years. It began, she said, when a gynecologist recommended that she take an occasional sip of vodka for menstrual cramps. When Sammy Davis Jr. visited her on the set of *Gentlemen* he concluded she wasn't drinking heavily, although John Strasberg stated that she used Listerine to mask the smell of liquor on her breath. With a natural tendency to gain weight, she worried about the caloric content of liquor. When she lived with Milton and Amy Greene in Connecticut early in 1955, she drank only one glass of wine a day at dinner. Other friends stated that she didn't drink because she was allergic to liquor, although she may have sometimes avoided it because she was taking barbiturates or amphetamines.[29]

Before she began filming *How to Marry a Millionaire* in the spring of 1953, Marilyn hadn't been seriously ill, except for her menstrual issues and the removal of her appendix in May 1952. Her health began to deteriorate. She came down with headaches, hives, and bronchial complications. She sometimes vomited before going on the set, although Nembutal, her major drug of choice, can produce headaches, nausea, and constipation.

She sometimes fabricated illness because she was exhausted or as a bargaining chip with producers. According to Jack Cole, if she saw a single line on her face she called in sick. Cole overstates the case, but the Marilyn who was a perfectionist and the Marilyn who had no self-confidence worked together to impel her to call in sick. Doctors often diagnosed her with anemia and gave her vitamin B12 shots, which can produce a sense of well-being.[30]

She also developed allergies. Drinking and drug taking can overload the liver, the body's detoxification center. Allergies including sensitivity to food or pollen can then develop, causing nasal stuffiness, and the effects can be increased by smoking—in which Marilyn, like most of her generation, indulged. If the nasal passages become consistently clogged, bacteria and viruses easily lodge in them, causing colds and bronchitis. What about the many abortions she had? That was enough to cause a serious issue with scar tissue. When I asked Steffi Skolsky about them, she answered me obliquely, stating that they were a popular form of birth control in Hollywood. Indeed, despite her statements about wanting to have a child, the paradoxical Marilyn, according to Susan Strasberg, was afraid that pregnancy would cause her body to sag, while she feared the pain of childbirth. On the other hand, her miscarriages and abortions produced depression, the sense that she would never have a child again.[31]

Nonetheless, Marilyn tapped into her great energy as she moved between films, sometimes with only a brief rest. The studio was determined to get their money's worth from their stars, and they rushed them into film after film. Marilyn had depressive episodes, but she hid them, as she hid her menstrual pains. Insomnia still plagued her as did her monsters, but she often seemed hypomanic in this period, in an emotional balance that enabled her to finish her films.

At the end of September 1953, Grace Goddard died. It was a blow to Marilyn. Grace had been a major support in her childhood; along with Doc, Grace had served as her business manager for several years, keeping her accounts, figuring her taxes, and answering fan mail. Grace had also overseen Gladys's care and regularly visited her. Marilyn paid for Grace to be interred at the Westwood Memorial Cemetery and Mortuary, where Ana Lower was buried. Joe DiMaggio now stepped in to help Marilyn with her career. He thought she needed a professional business manager to manage her affairs, not another family member. After all, she was a major star. Through his lawyer Loyd Wright, he had met Inez Melson, a tough and maternal older woman who had her own small Hollywood management firm. Joe recommended Inez to Marilyn, and Marilyn hired her. Inez was also a loyalist for Joe among the growing number of Marilyn's assistants.[32]

Marilyn liked Inez, another older woman to depend on for advice. Inez raised parakeets, multicolored talking birds that Marilyn adored.

She had played with parakeets in the Giffens' aviary when she lived with them as a child; she liked to go to Inez's house in the Hollywood Hills and play with her birds. Inez had swings, perches, and birdbaths in their cages. It seemed that Inez might take Grace's place in Marilyn's life, and Inez did become friendly with some of Marilyn's family members, such as Enid Knebelkamp; but she didn't become another Grace to Marilyn. She already had Anne Karger, Xenia Chekhov, and Lotte Goslar to serve as older female mentors and sometime mothers to her.[33]

Inez took over supervising Gladys Eley. She visited her every week or so and made certain she was taken to the local Christian Science church on Sundays. She bought Gladys birthday and Christmas cards, signing them with Marilyn's name. Gladys still wore a nurse's uniform, deep in her fantasy that she was a Christian Science nurse. She spent her time reading *Science and Health* and writing letters to officials in the government or in the Christian Science Church in Boston. Inez never posted them.[34] Inez served Marilyn faithfully for many years, although she was angry when Marilyn didn't leave her anything in her will. Appointed executrix of Marilyn's California estate after she died, Inez kept the file cabinets that were in Marilyn's Brentwood house, which contained many of Marilyn's personal documents.

In September 1953, *Look* magazine sent photographer Milton Greene to Hollywood to do a story on Marilyn. They may have met four years previously, when he went to Hollywood, but this was Greene's first photographic session with her. He was now famous: *Look* had just hired him away from *Life* with a $100,000 yearly salary, a huge sum in the 1950s. He lived a chic bohemian high life in New York, with a studio on the top floor of an old office building on Lexington Avenue. Cavernous and flooded with light, it was a gathering place for celebrities: jazz musicians, theater people, film stars. He was one of the first New Yorkers to remodel a barn in Connecticut as a second home, to combine a marble Noguchi table with Baccarat crystal, to line a coat with mink.[35] He always dressed in black. He looked much younger than his thirty years. When Marilyn met him, she said to him, "You look like a boy!" He replied, "You look like a girl!"

Born Milton Greengold in Brooklyn to a family of modest means, he began his career as an apprentice to a *Life* photographer and soon made his mark by developing a style in which his photos suggested a story. He posed his models as though they were characters in a play he was producing. Marilyn was dissatisfied by the way others were photographing her. She wanted to look distinctive, with less emphasis on sex. Greene promised to photograph her as though she were Garbo, dramatic but mysterious. During the next four years he followed through on this promise many times.

In their sessions together in the fall of 1953 she nestled in a gnarled tree, wearing an ordinary dress; in another photo she wears a long black sweater covering her naked body; in another she cradles a balalaika. That last photo tells a complex story. A woman playing a stringed instrument such as a lute is a standard theme in Western art, denoting a domestic woman soothing a household, a muse for a male artist, or a woman artist herself. Dressed in a long satin shift but with bare feet, Marilyn looks like a goddess of art. The balalaika is the major instrument of Russian folk music. The photograph suggested that Marilyn could play Grushenka in *The Brothers Karamazov*. The movie was still on the drawing board in 1953; it hadn't been cast yet.

Milton, like Marilyn, was shy and introspective. He was also a stutterer who sometimes spoke in non sequiturs. Always agreeable, he could be a little boy lost. He charmed his models, and they adored him: he had a soft, seductive voice. He liked everyone, had a knack at solving problems, and avoided controversy. After posing for him, Gloria Vanderbilt said, "He communicated his vision so subtly that I absorbed it zen-like." Marilyn would become his muse, like Dorian Leigh with Richard Avedon. Marilyn commented: "I've never really liked the way I was photographed until I saw Milton's pictures. He's an artist. Even when he does fashions which are boring he can make something so beautiful."[36]

Marilyn told Milton about her career issues—her low salary, Darryl Zanuck's refusal to cast her in serious films, how producers and directors ordered her around. Greene told her he wanted to form a film production company. They were attracted to each other, but he was due to return to New York to marry Amy Franco, a former model for Richard Avedon. Amy was a determined woman with great organizational skills, and she inspired confidence and brought order to disordered lives. She performed that service for Milton. She later did the same for Marilyn for a time.

Once married to Amy, Milton returned to Hollywood with her to do another shoot for *Look*, and they socialized with Marilyn, taking her to Hollywood parties and ending her "Greta Garbo" period. Amy loved to go to Gene Kelly's Saturday night charades parties, since she was a whiz at the game. Milton and Marilyn were hopeless, and they sat in a corner and talked. When Amy and Joe DiMaggio were both out of town one week, Milton and Marilyn may have had an affair, although Amy always denied it had happened.[37] But Milton wouldn't leave Amy, and Marilyn had decided to marry Joe after his kindness to her in Canada.

She was now a great star. Jean Negulesco described the extraordinary premiere of *How to Marry a Millionaire*, held at the Wilshire Theater in late November. The theater was packed and a large crowd stood outside when suddenly there was a growing roar, "like an approaching earthquake." "Marilyn! Marilyn!" was the cry. She was wearing a dress with platinum and white beads shimmering on white silk, emphasizing every curve of her body. Four policemen carried her over the heads of the crowd and into the theater, where the audience was standing to see her. Some people climbed on their seats to see better—even the legendary Cecil B. DeMille did so. Negulesco concluded, "I witnessed beyond any expectation the luxury of her fame."[38]

But her life was in a muddle. In December her nude photo "Golden Dreams" appeared as the first centerfold in the new *Playboy* magazine. It was an unexpected return of the smutty Marilyn. The fan magazines were now hinting that she and Natasha were lovers.[39] Marilyn needed to stop those speculations, even though in her paradoxical way at the end of December she began including her sexual adventures in an autobiography she was dictating to Ben Hecht, who was to ghostwrite it. Then, despite all her lobbying—and that of Charles Feldman, still her agent— Zanuck refused to cast her in a serious role. It's rumored that he offered her *The Girl in the Red Velvet Swing* and *The Revolt of Mamie Stover*, but she turned down the former because the role she was to play was insipid and the latter because Mamie Stover was an obvious prostitute, and Marilyn didn't want to play such a role.[40] In late 1953 he enraged her further by casting her as a showgirl in a remake of Betty Grable's *Pink Tights*.

Throughout her problems with Zanuck, Marilyn overlooked the memo he issued in March 1953 in which he canceled all serious films, even those already in production. Fox would make only entertainment films, mostly shot in Cinemascope—which Fox owned. A number of Fox dramas had failed at the box office, including *Viva Zapata!*—even though it starred Marlon Brando and Anthony Quinn. He even canceled production of *On the Waterfront*, which Harry Cohn took over. Spyros Skouras had dictated that Zanuck needed to make money for Fox. Letters in the Spyros Skouras Papers suggest that Zanuck didn't want to give up making serious films; he was acting under Skouras's orders. Marilyn was regarded as a great moneymaker, so long as she played a blonde sexpot. Zanuck could make a lot of money casting her in Fox musicals.[41]

Marilyn had to do something to gain the upper hand. Cutting her Gordian knot with one blow, she married Joe DiMaggio. Partnered with the reigning king of America's most popular sport, she now became American royalty: she was the homecoming queen married to the star athlete, the dream of all Americans writ large. She had captured a local athlete when she married Jim Dougherty, but this combination with Joe DiMaggio was epic, a national romance, not a small-town liaison. She increased her large fan base by absorbing Joe's, which included not only male sports fans but also women attracted by his heroic stature.[42] Whatever sins Marilyn had committed, Joe's reputation for virtue canceled them. Marilyn had checkmated Zanuck. He suspended her when she didn't show up for *Pink Tights*, but it was inevitable that he would reinstate her after she married Joe.

The wedding took place in San Francisco on January 14, 1954, in a judge's chambers in the San Francisco city hall, a last-minute affair. Acceding to Joe's wishes, Marilyn dressed in a tailored dark suit with a white collar. Her body was covered; the suit didn't even have a plunging neckline. Nearly five hundred reporters, photographers, and fans jammed the area but they weren't there by accident. When she and Joe decided to go ahead, Marilyn called Fox publicity director Harry Brand and gave him the details, generating the publicity that was never far from her mind.

Yet Zanuck wouldn't compromise on Marilyn's new contract; he still refused to give her creative input into her films. Instead, he offered her the lead in the film version of *The Seven Year Itch*, a hit on Broadway, to be directed by Billy Wilder. Marilyn very much wanted to do the film, although Zanuck demanded as a precondition that she make *There's No Business Like Show Business*. Marilyn gave in, although she didn't like the musical's plot or songs. She was frightened at being cast with some of Broadway's best dancers and singers : Ethel Merman, Dan Dailey, Donald O'Connor, and Mitzi Gaynor. Yet she agreed to do it, hoping it would work out. Under her contract the studio still had control over what films she made.

In early February Joe and Marilyn went on a honeymoon to Japan, where Joe was to hold baseball clinics and coach local teams. Baseball was popular in Japan; Joe had been on such a mission before. During their plane trip to Honolulu, a stop on the way to Tokyo, Joe broke Marilyn's finger when she touched him on the back. Not liking to be touched in public, he spun around, startled, and caught her finger in his huge hand, fracturing a bone. It may have been an accident, but it was a portent of the future. When journalists noted her taped finger and asked what had happened, she replied, "I bumped it against a door."[43]

Joe was supposed to be the star in Japan, but crowds screamed for Marilyn. They called her "monchan," which meant little girl. Or they screamed the Japanese phrase for "swinging buttocks." If he hadn't known before, Joe now realized that people wanted to see Marilyn, not him. A week after they arrived in Japan, Marilyn went to Korea to entertain the troops. An American general issued the invitation, but she had wanted to go there for some time to thank the men whose fan letters had made her a star. In the fall of 1953, when William Holden had toured military bases in Korea, he had seen her nude photo everywhere.[44] Zanuck had refused her request to go there, but she now had the upper hand and she defied him. Joe may have tried to stop her from going, but she didn't listen to him. Her career was uppermost in her mind.

The tour was a triumph. Wearing a plum-colored sequined dress, she performed "Let's Do It Again!" in a typically suggestive Marilyn manner. The ten thousand men at each of the ten military bases she visited went wild. At one stop the crowd surged over the stage, "like bobby-soxers in Times Square," according to the *Los Angeles Times*. At another, the army brass became drunk at a party and made inappropriate remarks. There was talk of a congressional investigation. The *Stars and Stripes* reporter covering it stated that "the week progressed from one form of riot to another." Marilyn brushed it off and always stated that it had been a high point in her career.[45]

The performances she did in Korea that Joe saw on Japanese television enraged him. After she returned to Japan, he threatened to divorce her if she didn't clean up her act.[46] He did that frequently—"crying wolf" in an impossible situation. He should have realized that under her sweetness, Marilyn was stubborn. She had no intention of changing her behavior. For her part, Marilyn had once again violated Elia Kazan's advice in his 1951 letter to her that she should avoid domineering men. Her attraction to male power, which was strong, always carried with it the risk of male domination.

When she finished her tour of Japan, Marilyn went with Joe to San Francisco, to be with his family. He now hoped she would stay put and become a dutiful wife. But she turned her attention to Hollywood. On March 9, she returned there to receive the *Photoplay* award as the year's best actress for her roles in *Gentlemen Prefer Blondes* and *How to Marry a Millionaire*; Sidney Skolsky was her escort to the ceremony. On March 21 she fired the William Morris agency, which had done nothing for her for some time, and signed with Charles Feldman's Famous Artists Agency. Feldman had been representing her since 1951 in her contract negotiations with Darryl Zanuck.

On May 2 she moved to Hollywood to begin filming *There's No Business Like Show Business*. Joe went along. She had to fulfill her contract with Fox, she told him. He hoped they might have a marriage like that of baseball manager Leo Durocher and film actress Laraine Day, in which she focused on their marriage and did only a few films. This vision was no more than a pipe dream; Marilyn would not be held back.

Marilyn's ambivalence about Joe became evident in the spring of 1954 when she told Sidney Skolsky that she intended to marry Arthur Miller. Was she teasing Skolsky or expressing her real desire? She wrote about her admiration for Miller in an article in *Pageant* magazine in April and revealed that she had read most of his works. In any event Marilyn didn't remain faithful to Joe for long after she married him. That spring she began an affair with Hal Schaefer, the jazz musician who had been her singing coach for *Gentlemen Prefer Blondes* and who was coaching her again for *There's No Business Like Show Business*. He was, she said, the gentlest man she had ever known. Joe continued traveling to New York, doing his TV shows and following the Yankees on the road.

His years of traveling as a baseball player had made him into a nomad, in many ways happiest on the road.[47]

Her affair with Schaefer had overtones of her earlier affair with Fred Karger, her voice coach at Columbia in 1948, but unlike Karger, Schaefer wanted her to divorce Joe and marry him. Marilyn agreed to it, but she sometimes agreed to contradictory propositions at the same time. She told Schaefer she would convert to Judaism for him, and she disguised herself with a wig and a shapeless dress to go out with him incognito. She met his parents and spent hours listening to him play the piano. "She liked the company of musicians," Jean Negulesco wrote. "She liked their talk, their jokes. They adored her. I always thought that a music man would have been her right marriage."[48] For a long time Joe overlooked the involvement with Hal, who was said to be gay.

Now that they were married Joe expected Marilyn to obey him, but she didn't. She had been living for a year in an apartment on Doheny Drive, in Beverly Hills. It was centrally located, close to Inez Melson's office, and not far from Hollywood. Many stars had lived there at one time or another; a tall cinderblock wall surrounded it, effectively keeping journalists and fans out. Marilyn loved that apartment, but Joe wanted a place that could also accommodate his son, and the Doheny Drive apartment had only one bedroom. Inez found them a house in the elite section of Beverly Hills to lease for six months. They moved in, but Joe spent much of his time there playing poker and watching television. There were quarrels, and he became physically violent. She may have been afraid of him, but it didn't stop her from doing what she wanted, including continuing the affair with Hal Schaefer.

Obsessed with Marilyn now that he faced losing her, Joe had private detectives follow her. In early July, overwhelmed by threats from Joe's henchmen, Hal attempted suicide. He recovered, and Marilyn nursed him for weeks. One assumes that she and Joe were estranged, although he showed up on the set of *There's No Business Like Show Business* when the "Tropical Heat Wave" number was being filmed. Why Marilyn invited him to the set that day is perplexing, since the number is highly sexual. Dressed in an abbreviated top and a full split skirt, with a Carmen Miranda headdress on her head, she sashays through a sexy rendition of one of Jack Cole's over-the-top numbers. DiMaggio must have realized

full force that he was losing his battle to persuade her to be more discreet. He stormed off the set.

There's No Business Like Show Business went considerably over
schedule, since Marilyn frequently called in sick. She felt outclassed by the
dancers she was cast with, and she felt ridiculous playing opposite Donald
O'Connor, who was much shorter than she. Aside from the musical numbers, which she delivers with verve, she seems bored in her role as a
showgirl—although she doesn't play her character as a dumb blonde. She
is a working woman trying to make it as an entertainer. It was rumored
that she was drinking heavily and taking drugs throughout the filming, but
Hal Schaefer, who spent a lot of time with her, told me that she did neither
when she was with him. He had to encourage her to drink a glass of wine.
She probably suffered from menstrual pain caused by endometriosis that
spring; she had a major gynecological operation in November, one in
which the endometriosis inside her was probably removed.

In the spring of 1954, as was not unusual for her, Marilyn was leading a
number of lives. She was married to Joe DiMaggio, involved with Hal
Schaefer, and struggling to complete *There's No Business Like Show
Business*. She continued dictating her autobiography to Ben Hecht, although by this point Joe DiMaggio, now her husband, demanded that she
take her sexual adventures out of it, while a draft of it suddenly appeared
in a tabloid in Manchester, England, without her permission. Milton
Greene was still in her life, and they were discussing forming a production company.

Milton visited Hollywood that spring and photographed her on the
Fox back lot. In the wardrobe department they found Jennifer Jones's
costumes from *The Song of Bernadette*, a movie about a peasant girl
who becomes a saint, and Milton photographed Marilyn in Bernadette's
peasant clothes on the original set of the film. It was, according to Amy
Greene, the "ultimate in-joke, to put the world's leading sex symbol in
Saint Bernadette's clothes." Marilyn knew about the financial problems
of Hilda, the wardrobe mistress, and after they finished shooting Marilyn slipped a hundred-dollar bill into her pocket. It was a typical Marilyn gesture.[49]

By 1954, elegance was becoming a mantra for Marilyn. Influenced
by Amy Greene, that's what she now wanted. She talked about Amy all

the time with Gloria Romanoff: how Amy dressed, how she acted, what her friends were like. Sam Shaw stated that she was now ambitious to appear in *Vogue* and *Harper's Bazaar*. She wanted to be sleek and fashionable, like the high-fashion models, like Amy. Movie magazines were suggesting that Audrey Hepburn, tall, thin, and small-breasted, the epitome of a high-fashion model, was replacing the voluptuous Marilyn as the female beauty ideal. Marilyn was doubly worried about continuing as a "blonde bombshell."[50]

She was already thinking about moving to New York, where Milton had his studio. Marilyn had dreamed of New York since her days at the Actors' Lab, when her teachers had glorified Broadway. Arthur Miller and Elia Kazan were both New Yorkers. To a naive girl from Los Angeles, a provincial place in the 1950s, New York was the glittering, sophisticated center of book publishing, finance, and fashion, set apart from the rest of the nation.

In 1950 she had picked up a copy of a new magazine, *Flair*, in a bookstore. It had mesmerized her. A combination of *Vanity Fair* and the *Atlantic Monthly*, it was geared to postwar sophisticates and avant garde intellectuals, and it glorified their doings in New York. It was designed and edited by Fleur Cowles, then an editor at *Look*. Expensive to produce, it lasted only a year, with a "yearbook" issued for several years after.

The articles in *Flair* covered subjects as varied as Norbert Wiener and cybernetics, Rudolph Bing and the Metropolitan Opera, Walker Evans and Salvador Dalí, and the new "cool" that was spreading to the broader culture from beboopers, hipsters, and Parisian students in existentialist cafes. Cowles included articles on roses, which Marilyn loved, and on Shelley Winters as the new Jean Harlow. One wonders what Marilyn thought of that comparison. *Flair* seemed like an Aladdin's lamp to Marilyn, a touchstone to a fantasy world.[51]

She may have dreamed about New York, but in June and July 1954 she was still filming *There's No Business Like Show Business*. She finished the movie in mid-August. The next day, with no time off, she began filming *The Seven Year Itch*. Three weeks later, on September 9, she flew to New York to shoot location scenes for the film. She was greeted like royalty. Fans clogged the streets on which she was shooting, while the New York newspapers continually carried photos of her and stories about her. Sam Shaw introduced her to Richard Avedon, who shot her for

Harper's Bazaar. Amy and Milton Greene were there, and Amy took her shopping at Bergdorf Goodman, New York's swankiest clothing store. But she attracted such crowds that Amy persuaded Norman Norell, New York's leading dress designer, to go to Marilyn's hotel suite to discuss designing clothes for her. Amy knew Norell from her modeling days.[52]

During the week in New York, Marilyn had dinner with Amy and Milton to discuss her production company. Many stars were forming such companies to gain control over their careers. Why not Marilyn? Joe DiMaggio, who had come to New York, was at the dinner. He was suspicious of Milton, who seemed to be taking over his wife, but he didn't object to the company. Amy, a baseball fan, adored Joe: he was one of her "gods." With her knowledge of the sport, she may have charmed Joe enough to keep him quiet.

Joe also attended the famed photo shoot on September 15, when Marilyn stood over the subway grate and attracted a host of photographers and fans. As Joe entered the street, the crowd roared for him: he was a national hero, beloved by all. Then as he saw Marilyn's skirt flying up, he became incensed and stalked off. Several hundred men were looking at her crotch, and he felt cuckolded by them. Back in their hotel room after the shoot, Marilyn and he had a ferocious quarrel, and he hit her. Whitey Snyder covered up the bruises with makeup. After Marilyn returned to Hollywood she was seen walking the streets of Beverly Hills, crying.[53]

Once again, as before, she used her relationship with Joe for maximum press exposure. She called Harry Brand to tell him she was leaving Joe, and she hired a well-known Hollywood lawyer, Jerry Geisler, to represent her. Geisler held a press conference outside her house before he filed the separation papers in court on October 5. Reporters and photographers were camped out in front of her house. Geisler had prepped Marilyn for the conference the previous evening. Sidney Skolsky was present. Geisler told Marilyn how to act, and he included Skolsky in the staged drama. It was to look as though Marilyn, holding onto Geisler's arm as they walked to his car, was faltering; then Sidney was to race over to her to give her support. The press conference was held as planned, and Marilyn was brilliant. She looks devastated in the photos taken of her. A cynical AP reporter wrote that she should receive an Oscar for her performance.[54]

On October 27 the divorce hearing occurred. Marilyn charged Joe only with emotional desertion by refusing to speak to her for days on end. She said nothing about his physical cruelty. Inez Melson was her sole witness; her only criticism of Joe was that he once had refused to take Marilyn to the racetrack with him because she attracted such crowds that he couldn't get through them to place bets. Joe didn't contest the divorce, and he didn't attend the hearing. Marilyn was granted an interlocutory divorce; the final divorce would be granted in a year.[55]

Coincidentally, the six-month lease on the house in Beverly Hills was running out, and Marilyn moved into the Hotel Bel-Air. Even in its secluded location, however, the crowds were too great to allow her privacy. She then stayed in her studio dressing room suite for a time before moving into the home of Anne Karger, who remained her close friend. Finally, she leased a new apartment, which suggests she wasn't entirely certain about leaving Hollywood. Throughout her saga, she kept lines of communication open to Joe. He stayed with her physician Leon Krohn, and Marilyn called Joe every night. In typical Marilyn fashion, she worried about him, even though she was divorcing him.

Some have incorrectly speculated she had an affair with Sinatra during this period and moved into his house. She certainly knew him; they had been at parties together. But Frank and Joe were close friends. As Amy Greene maintained, Sinatra would not have romanced Marilyn until the divorce from Joe was final. Both these men respected Sicilian codes of honor, under which a friend's spouse was off-limits. Reporters observed her dining with Joe; the speculation was they would reconcile.[56]

On the night of November 5, Frank joined Joe in an attempt to catch Marilyn with Hal Schaefer. The motive was probably to assert Joe's masculinity by roughing up Hal, who thought Joe intended to break his fingers so that he couldn't play the piano again. Bernard (Bernie) Spindel, a private detective employed by Joe, traced Marilyn to the apartment of Sheila Stewart, a friend of Schaefer's. (Spindel, like others, suspected that Marilyn was involved with Sheila, not Hal.) Joe and Frank had been drinking together and, enlivened by alcohol, they decided to break in. Spindel and several associates went with them—and they broke into the wrong apartment. Spindel, worried about what Joe might do, sent them to the wrong apartment on purpose. The noise of the break-in was deafening; Hal and Marilyn, hearing it from Stewart's apartment, were terrified. They climbed through a back window and ran to their cars. Tearful and disheveled, Marilyn went home.[57] The episode was hushed up; the full story didn't reach the newspapers until it surfaced in an investigation of private detective firms by the California state legisture several years later. It has gone down in history as the "wrong-door raid."

As usual, Marilyn recovered quickly from what must have been a difficult experience. The next night, November 6, she appeared at a party in her honor at Romanoff's to celebrate the completion of *The Seven Year Itch*. She was ebullient as she received the encomiums of members of Hollywood's elite circle, people who had often shunned her. She met Clark Gable, her make-believe father. *Life* magazine published an article on the party, calling Gable the king of Hollywood and Marilyn its princess.[58] Reporters, never daunted, even manufactured a romance between them. Two days after the party she entered the hospital for another gynecological operation. She remained there for five days, the hospital time then allotted to recover from major surgery. She probably had her abdomen opened and her endometriosis cleaned out. Joe was present as she recovered. Throughout the years Joe often visited her in hospitals.

After she and Joe were officially separated, Marilyn spent time with other men. Sex was often not involved. Deciding that she was lonely, Dean Martin and Jerry Lewis took her out to dinner. They had made friends with her after the *Photoplay* awards celebration, and they loved her sense of humor, what Lewis called her "delicious" ability to see the absurdity of life. She also went out on the town with Milton Greene and Sammy Davis Jr., who had become close through a mutual interest in photography. Sammy considered Marilyn to be like a sister.[59] Milton had traveled to Hollywood to make certain that she would follow through on the production company.

Through Sammy Marilyn reconnected with singer Mel Tormé, whom she had met during her *Monkey Business* tour. Milton, Sammy, and Marilyn went to a Tormé show in Los Angeles. The next day she phoned him, calling herself Sadie. They went for hamburgers to Dolores Drive-in, a favorite hangout of hers when she was a teenager. He cheered her up. He found her opinionated and bright, and he enjoyed her boldness; like Ava Gardner and Elizabeth Taylor, she swore like a trooper.[60]

In early December Sidney Skolsky took her to hear Ella Fitzgerald at a small club where she was singing. Marilyn was enthusiastic; she had long studied Fitzgerald's singing. She decided to boost Ella's career. She contacted the owners of the Mocambo, a top Sunset Strip nightclub, and persuaded them to hire Fitzgerald for a week. Marilyn promised to be in the front row every night and to take friends with her. According to Dorothy Dandridge, however, the real problem with Fitzgerald at that time was not that she was African-American but that she was overweight, without much sex appeal. Singing at the Mocambo was a turning point in Fitzgerald's career. With a major nightclub on her resumé, she was no longer relegated to small clubs. She was grateful to Marilyn, although she held back from close friendship because of Marilyn's drug habit.[61]

Then several blows struck Marilyn at once, reigniting her desire to move to New York. The reviews of *There's No Business Like Show Business* were negative. Critics disparaged her for sluttish behavior in the production numbers, especially in "Tropical Heat Wave." Then Zanuck turned her down for dramatic roles at Fox and also refused to lend her out to the Samuel Goldwyn studio to play Adelaide in *Guys and Dolls* with Marlon Brando. Zanuck considered her too valuable to Fox as a blonde bombshell to allow another studio to feature her, no matter what Fox was paid.

Ginger Rogers, Shelley Winters, and Doris Day had begun their careers as flighty blondes and moved on to dramatic roles, but Zanuck had drawn a line in the sand with regard to Marilyn. He told her to report for *How to Be Very, Very Popular*, a film about a showgirl fleeing the police who hides out in a college dormitory and is hypnotized so that she acts as though she is "under water." Marilyn refused to do it. Nunnally Johnson, who wrote the film, had based the character on Marilyn. Sheree North, who replaced her in it, was appalled by the way Fox executives treated Marilyn, constantly belittling her behind her back, calling her a dumb blonde and worse. Watching the insulting way they handled Marilyn, Sheree said, was "an eye-opener that dissolved any illusions [I had] about the nature of stardom. She had her own ideas. She was going against the formula that the studio people had. There would be all this terrible talk about her, which frightened me. I thought, if I have any individual ideas, they'll treat me like that, too." Marilyn was kind to Sheree, and she took her to her Christian Science church, which she still occasionally attended.[62]

Marilyn got wind that *Confidential* magazine was planning a story on her affair with Hal Schaefer. Launched in 1951, *Confidential* had a yearly circulation of over a million by 1954, making it the magazine with the highest circulation in the nation. Its editor paid no attention to the studio embargo on writing about Hollywood sex; he got his material by paying reporters under the table. By 1953 Marilyn, along with Lana Turner and Ava Gardner, was the favorite subject of the magazine, which presented the three of them as an "unholy trinity" of bold and free women, who did whatever they wanted.[63] Marilyn disliked that image of herself as well as the revelations that went along with it. So far she had managed them, but that was soon to change, as *Confidential* published details about her affair with director Nicholas Ray and her supposed affair with Robert Slatzer, a story that Slatzer, a Hollywood hanger-on, made up. She feared that the autobiography she had dictated to Ben Hecht, which had been published in a bootleg version in a Manchester tabloid, might be published in the United States—or might appear in *Confidential*. The *National Police Gazette*, a U.S. tabloid in circulation since 1845, published a story on the bootleg autobiography, contending that Fox executives had excoriated her for it. There was also the problem that *Confidential* specialized in outing homosexual Hollywood actors.[64]

She'd had enough: she erupted in fury against the studio executives for typecasting her in sexy-blonde roles. She vented to a reporter, "I was put into these movies [*River of No Return* and *There's No Business Like Show Business*] without being consulted at all, much against my wishes. I had no choice in the matter. Is that fair? I work hard, I take pride in my work, and I'm a human being like the rest of them. If I keep on with parts like the ones Fox has been giving me, the public will soon tire of me." Stanley Rubin, the producer of *River of No Return*, remembered walking past the Fox executive building with Marilyn, as she stopped and shook her fists. "I'm not just a face in a body. Listen to me, you bastards. I want you to watch me. I'm going to get better and better." She told another reporter, "I'm really eager to do something else. Squeezing yourself to ooze out the last ounce of sex allure is terribly hard. I'd like to do roles like Julia in *Bury the Dead*, Gretchen in *Faust*, and Teresa in *The Cradle Song*."[65]

She was fed up with playing Marilyn Monroe, the sexy glamour queen. For the past three years she had repeatedly stated she wanted dramatic roles, and no one seemed to listen. In early December 1954, she fired Charles Feldman as her agent and signed up with Lew Wasserman of the Music Corporation of America. *How to Be Very, Very Popular* was the last straw. She decided to form the production company with Milton Greene and, defying Zanuck and Twentieth Century–Fox, move to New York. It was a bold and daring action, as she defied Zanuck and waited to see what he would do.

Marilyn's autobiography, which she dictated to Ben Hecht in December 1953 and during the early spring of 1954, deserves special attention, because some Marilyn biographers have dismissed it as a fraud. My reading of the documents about the project in the Hecht Papers at the Newberry Library in Chicago has convinced me it is valid.[66]

Marilyn began considering doing an autobiography when Joe Schenck, who had repeatedly heard her stories about her childhood, suggested that she put them into published form. A well-written memoir, especially if she wrote some of it herself, could help to end the belief that she was a dumb blonde. Schenck contacted Ben Hecht. Able to produce scripts in eight weeks, with a long career as a journalist and writer, Hecht was considered the best screenwriter in the business.[67] Marilyn knew him from *Monkey Business*, for which he had written much of the script.

Hecht was excited about ghostwriting Marilyn's autobiography, since she was Hollywood's biggest star. Marilyn suggested she write some of the book herself, and Hecht liked that idea. "The book under her name," he wrote to Loyd Wright, Marilyn's attorney, "would receive serious literary attention from the entire magazine world. It would bring her a high and widespread type of publicity superior to any she has received." Even before he had final approval from Marilyn, he negotiated deals with *Ladies' Home Journal* and several newspapers to publish portions of the finished memoir.[68]

Hecht met Marilyn in San Francisco in December 1953 to begin the interviews. She was visiting Joe. But Joe had no input into the interviews, at least not then. Before she left Hollywood for San Francisco, Marilyn had called Lucille Ryman and told her she was going to tell Hecht everything. Ryman was taken aback, because she knew about Marilyn's promiscuity. "How can you reveal everything that you have done?" she asked. Marilyn replied, "Perhaps the public should know everything about

me." The interviews in San Francisco lasted five days, and Marilyn's celebrity was such that *People Today* announced that they were happening.
"The deal will shock Hollywood and the rest of the nation."[69]

Marilyn married Joe in early January. By February, as Hecht put it,
she had "vanished in a honeymoon." Joe hadn't intervened in their project in San Francisco but now that he and Marilyn were married, he did.
A traditional Italian man, he felt that his wife should do what he said, and
he didn't want her revealing any of her sexual adventures. "When I first
saw her for five days," Hecht wrote his editor at Doubleday, "she was 100
percent clinging and cooperative. She got married and the picture
changed . . . My next session with her may have to be in a ball park."
Hecht eliminated about thirty percent of a version he had written that
might be seen as "damaging," and he interviewed her again for a few days
in Hollywood. He completed about two hundred pages of a new version.
He read the manuscript aloud to her. She found it so compelling that she
cried. He also gave it to her to edit, and she made only minor changes. In
early June she told Hedda Hopper that she still had the copy she had
corrected.[70]

But by then the project had unraveled. Both Hecht and Marilyn were
outraged when, without either's permission, the memoir began appearing in a tabloid called the *Empire News* in Manchester, England. It turned
out that Jacques Chambrun, Hecht's agent, had sold it to the tabloid.
Twentieth Century–Fox executives were appalled by what they read in
the tabloid, since it exposed the "casting couch," even though Marilyn
stated that she had never experienced it. She also obliquely mentioned
her participation in Joe Schenck's poker parties and her work as an escort to visiting studio dignitaries, although she gave no names. The
studios had kept the lid on sexuality since sex scandals involving film
stars in the early 1920s had exposed its sexual underside, and had begun
the process of self-censorship that resulted in the Production Code of
1934.

According to the *National Police Gazette*, in its story about the Hecht
interviews, "Marilyn Monroe ripped the mask off Hollywood like it had
never been ripped off before. Many big names were deleted from the
manuscript before it was published." Erskine Johnson, writing in *Motion Picture*, stated that the studio bosses were so outraged by it that
they had stopped the *Empire News* articles from being published in the

United States. They called Marilyn into their offices and admonished her harshly, but she contended she had done nothing wrong. The publication didn't arouse any outcry in the United States, although, according to *Movieland*, Marilyn was worried about the *Empire News* episode for a long time.[71]

Furious at the situation, Hecht never completed the memoir's final chapters, although his papers at the Newberry Library contain an outline of them. They were to include Marilyn's reaction to Grace's death, the backstory to the making of *Gentlemen Prefer Blondes* and *How to Marry a Millionaire*, and why Marilyn's career would be stalled if she remained a "dumb blonde" and didn't do dramatic roles. The version published in 1974 ends with Marilyn's marriage to DiMaggio and her joy during her visit to Korea. But the planned version was to end on a different note: she would discuss her intention to end her bitterness about her childhood by bringing a new "Norma Jeane" into the world— her child, whom she would raise like a princess in a fairy tale, and who would mature into a wise, happy adult. Having a child as a way of overcoming emotional distress was probably a recipe for disaster, as was her intention to indulge the child. But Marilyn never gave up the dream of creating a perfect Marilyn through the child she would have.[72]

Neither Hecht nor Marilyn prosecuted the larcenous Jacques Chambrun. A brilliant fabulist, Chambrun posed as a member of the French nobility when he was actually a poor boy from the Bronx. He was the agent for Sherwood Anderson, H. G. Wells, and Somerset Maugham— from whom he also embezzled money. He had represented Hecht for more than twenty years. Angered by the situation with *My Story*, Hecht investigated his financial records to find that Chambrun had negotiated deals for his writing and then pocketed the payments. This was, however, his most outrageous scam.

Despite the disaster, *My Story* is a brilliant piece. In writing it, Hecht said that he had tried to "marry [Marilyn's] point of view with his vocabulary and style," and he succeeded. It is Hecht's most powerful prose writing, superior to his own autobiography, *A Child of the Century,* published in 1954, the same year as the *Empire News* story. Hecht captured the cadences of her speech, the depth of her perceptions, and the fissures in her self.

Hecht began his career in Chicago in the late nineteenth century as a journalist for an urban newspaper, roaming the city in pursuit of the human interest stories that were front-page news in that day. He began writing fiction, especially short stories, and was a founder of the school of writers who formed the "Chicago Renaissance." His work combined urban realism with a lyricism that is both hard-boiled and sentimental. He admired working-class people—and so did Marilyn. In spare, sometimes riveting prose, *My Story* captures the narrative of a girl from the streets. Irony and paradox, central to modernist writing, permeate the text, as Marilyn is positioned as a character both experiencing life and observing it. Like many Hollywood novels, it's a picaresque tale, as Marilyn wanders the streets of Hollywood, a cold unwelcoming city, meeting such characters as a raconteur from Texas who tells her about Abraham Lincoln, a soapbox preacher who wants to marry her, and producers who try to bed her. One suspects that Hecht—or Marilyn—made up the Texas talker and the soapbox preacher, but perhaps they were real. It's also possible, as Lucille Ryman contended, that she walked Hollywood Boulevard to pick up men.

Milton Greene published the Hecht manuscript in 1974 as *My Story*. How did he come to possess it? The answer is simple. Marilyn took her corrected copy with her when she moved in with the Greenes in Connecticut in late 1954, since she and Greene were talking about assembling a book of his photographs of her combined with a text about her life that she would write. They never did so, and Marilyn left her copy of the autobiography in Connecticut with Greene. Once he and Marilyn split up over the production company, she didn't see him again. She may have forgotten that he had the manuscript; perhaps she had another copy of it. When asked why he didn't publish it until 1974 Milton replied that he couldn't find a publisher until Norman Mailer's *Marilyn* biography appeared, in 1973.[73] The passages in it that have been criticized as inauthentic, such as the one about her being a Hollywood starlet who was a potential suicide, may have been added by Marilyn herself, when she lived with the Greenes.

Married to Joe DiMaggio, a man about whom she was ambivalent, and involved in a struggle with Darryl Zanuck, who regarded her as a "dumb blonde," Marilyn showed courage in moving to New York. Until the last minute she wasn't certain she would do it. But there was the lure of Manhattan, the presence of Arthur Miller, and the production company with Milton Greene. She put off telling Hal Schaefer their affair was over until she had gone east; it must have been hard for her to do it. But her determination to conquer the world was too strong for her to settle down with a musician, no matter how gentle and appealing he was. New York beckoned, and that's where she chose to go.

Part III

Entr'acte: A Woman for All Seasons

Monroe was an infinity of character and mystery that was impossible for me, or anyone else, to explore, because it was so vast. There is always more and more and more.

Maurice Zolotow, Marilyn Monroe

Chapter 8

The Meaning of Marilyn

As an avatar of her age, Marilyn both reflected and created trends in beauty, sensuality, femininity, and fashion. Her life needs to be explored in terms of those trends, not just in terms of its chronology, which has been my focus thus far. Marilyn's life constantly spills over a central narrative path into byways with their own chronologies and meanings, as she takes on pseudonyms, wears disguises, pursues many interests, and lives separate lives at the same time. The standard chronological framework of biography doesn't encompass Marilyn's life. Thus in this chapter I pause in my central narrative to examine structures of experience and meaning that provide insight into the paradoxical character of Marilyn Monroe.

To avoid confusing the reader, I focus on the events of the time frame I have covered in Part Two—from her 1946 entry into the Hollywood studio system to her 1954 flight from it to New York—although I occasionally go beyond it. During these years Norma Jeane concentrated on creating Marilyn Monroe, her sexualized self-confident alter ego. But other "alters" also emerged: the first was the "sex kitten" Marilyn, the pinup girl who roamed the streets of Hollywood and ingratiated herself with producers. That Marilyn segued into the comic Marilyn, whom I call Lorelei Lee, the persona who joked with ease and was joyous and playful. There was also a glamorous Marilyn, who combined the sculptured quality of the glamour queens of the 1930s like Marlene Dietrich with the more open eroticism of 1940s beauty queens like Rita Hayworth and their sisters on the burlesque and striptease stage.

By the 1950s, however, the word "glamour" was taking on additional meanings, as photographers of partially clothed and nude women hijacked the word to apply to their photographs. At the same time it retained its original meaning as connected to the mystery of elite status or foreign intrigue. Sensitive to nuances, Marilyn created herself in terms of both definitions, to become the "glamour girl" for her age.[1]

Sometimes Marilyn spiced the characters she played with the open sexuality of Jean Harlow, who electrified the nation in 1929 by wearing no underwear, flaunting her body, and bleaching her hair white blonde, a color that indicated perverse desire.[2] Harlow's antics (plus those of Mae West) brought the strict Production Code of 1934 into being, and its prohibition of open sexuality in films resulted in the appearance of the "fast-talking dames," who radiated desire and mocked it by engaging in flirtatious and swift repartee with men, rather than in open sex. The Production Board monitored their behavior. Marilyn saw their films in her moviegoing as a child; they were the actresses in the "Promised Land" of her childhood; they helped to enable her to challenge the Production Board. When fan magazine writers said they hadn't seen anyone quite like Marilyn since Jean Harlow, they were speaking truth.

With these statements as guidelines for what follows, I turn to discrete areas of Marilyn's life. These areas include her relationship to her times, her varying looks, her concepts of gender, the books she read, and her compulsive sexuality. Throughout, I point to the ways in which Marilyn mixed elements from high culture and low, from the legitimate stage, for example, as well as from burlesque and striptease, which were very popular forms of theater in the 1940s and '50s. The complexities of Marilyn, her paradoxical nature, are important in understanding her great popularity in her own day—and ever since. I end my entr'acte by analyzing some famous photographs taken of her in which her dramatic, trickster side is in evidence.

As a historian, I have been impressed throughout my work on Marilyn by her deep historical imagination. She knew the history of Hollywood, and it fascinated her. She had lived it; she had been part of it. She had spent her childhood reading the movie magazines, going to movies, visiting the studios, and imaging herself as a Hollywood star. When she came to create herself as Marilyn Monroe, those images were in her mind. It's not surprising that, in later years, she often said that the photos Richard Avedon took of her in 1958 as the great sirens of Hollywood—Lillian Russell, Theda Bara, Clara Bow, and Marlene Dietrich—were her favorite photographs. When Simone Signore was friendly with her during the filming of *Let's Make Love*, Marilyn told Simone that she preferred these photographs to any of the films she had made. That was undoubtedly an overstatement, but it pointed to Marilyn's love of history and her creation of herself in history's terms.

Post–World War Two prosperity in the United States produced a new well-to-do class in cities and suburbs, whose members flocked to elite forms of dance and theater such as ballet and opera. They validated the elegant ballerina and the high-fashion model as beauty ideals. They formed a fan base for Audrey Hepburn and Jackie Kennedy, the major exemplars of this look. Hepburn was a ballerina turned actress, tall and thin, with a straight body, who often modeled high-fashion clothing in her films. Jackie Kennedy was another elegant type. She was dressed by some of the world's most famous designers; she brought an aristocratic elegance to her White House world. Her stepcousin and friend, Gore Vidal, said she would have made a wonderful actress.[3]

At the same time, a populuxe style, based on a populist version of luxury, swept the nation, and Marilyn was its symbol. "Americans reveled in a kind of innocent hedonism," wrote Thomas Hine. That innocence was reflected in the decoration of household items—from refrigerators to automobiles—in garish colors, often with a curved shape coming to a point. The colors reflected postwar joy and the popularity of Technicolor and Walt Disney's animated films, shot in glowing colors. The curved shape coming to a point derived from the design of the jet fighter airplane, the new symbol of American power. The most representative product of populuxe was the automobile, which grew ever larger in size. The typical brightly colored model, sometimes in two tones, was trimmed in shiny chrome, with fins on its back sides adapted from airplane wings and shark fins, and bumps on the fenders that served no purpose. They were called Dagmars, after the big-breasted TV performer.[4]

By elite standards populuxe was vulgar, but it captured the nation's fancy. Through its version of reality as an amusing fairy tale, it helped the nation cope with its paranoia in the 1950s about the Cold War, the atom bomb, and the totalitarian Communist Soviet Union. When Marilyn radiated glamour and joy, as in the *Seven Year Itch* photo, she was a symbol of frivolity and fun to the world.

In-demand architect Morris Lapidus created an architecture of joy, based on Coney Island buildings and futurist designs in Hollywood films. Lapidus designed hotels, like the Fontainebleau in Miami Beach, with undulating lines. His free-form decorations, looking like squiggles or space ships, were called "woggles." Architect Wayne McAllister used the "googie" kidney bean shape of Southern California drive-in restaurants in his Las Vegas Sands Hotel, home to Frank Sinatra and the Rat Pack. Woogles, googies, and lines coming to points drew on the female body in this era when women emphasized their curves, wore pointy spike heels, and corseted their breasts so that they would jut out in torpedo points.[5]

This was parody architecture. It incorporated the comic extravagance beloved by Americans, who have often dealt with racial, ethnic, and sexual fears through the mirth of the comedian, while validating themselves and their nation through monumental size: ergo Cinemascope, the huge automobiles of the 1950s, the return of skyscrapers, and the fixation with large breasts. Pop artists like Andy Warhol and Jasper Johns picked up populuxe in their work, which resonated to the forms and features in comic strips, a classic American art that validated and extended the populuxe style. Marilyn became a favorite subject of pop artists, as in Andy Warhol's famous lithograph of multiple Marilyns. In the spring of 1956, *Time* magazine described her as "an adolescent daydream, like the ones served up in the comic strips. The cut of the face is Betty Boop, but the shape and the expressions are Daisy Mae."[6] Betty Boop, who looked like Clara Bow, drew from the 1920s flapper, a sexualized adolescent. Daisy Mae, hopelessly in love with L'il Abner, dated from the 1930s and was more mature and voluptuous, wearing a polkadot peasant blouse that fulsomely displayed her cleavage.

Marilyn's comic Lorelei Lee expressed these American themes and figures, but she also had roots in Western theatrical traditions. The female comic figure dated from the Italian Commedia dell'Arte, from Columbina, the female companion to Harlequin, Pierrot, and the other *zanni* (clowns) of the Commedia. Playful, shrewd servants, they mocked their superiors. Over time, Columbina became the soubrette, the saucy servant girl of the nineteenth-century stage. All these figures were tricksters, mocking their betters, indulging in childish jokes, deflating conventions.

Marilyn was trained in acting by theater people from Germany, in many cases Jewish, who had fled Hitler for Hollywood. Natasha Lytess came from the German stage, where Commedia dell'Arte clowns appeared in expressionist drama, including that of Max Reinhardt, in whose troupe she performed. Absurd characters, they mocked the horrors of World War One and the dictators that followed, with their brutal fascist and Nazi worlds. The clowns upheld the naivete and wisdom of the fool, existing in an innocent, make-believe world, the land of fairy tales and of the circus, the special habitat of the clown. Max Pallenberg, who perhaps was Natasha's father, was famed as a clown; Fritzi Massary, who perhaps was her mother, played soubrette roles before becoming a diva. She was famed for her sexy and ironic delivery, which influenced Marlene Dietrich.[7]

Even if Pallenberg and Massary weren't Natasha's parents, she would have known them from her years with Reinhardt's troupe. Natasha had played clowns in Reinhardt's theater; she was expert in their techniques when she coached Marilyn in "dumb-blonde" roles like Lorelei Lee in *Gentlemen Perfer Blondes*. Moreover, Michael Chekhov, Marilyn's drama teacher in Hollywood, was known for his portrayal of clowns, as well as of dramatic characters. And he sent Marilyn to study with famed mime Lotte Goslar, who mostly played clowns in her solo stage performances. These actors and teachers passed the European comic tradition on to Marilyn.

In creating her comic character, Marilyn also drew from traditions of the American musical hall and comedy theater, which both incorporated European traditions and expanded on them. Thus she can't be understood without examining the women of burlesque and striptease, as well as the "dumb blondes" of stage and screen and the "fast-talking dames" of 1930s films. To begin with, burlesque was an old English stage tradition. It was brought to the United States in the 1860s by the British Blondes, a group of female performers who displayed their legs in tights, did topical reviews, and had women play many of the male roles in their productions. Bawdy, powerful women were typical of burlesque, playing opposite comic men they overshadowed—or in early burlesque, playing the male roles themselves. (Vaudeville, dating from the 1880s, was a cleaned-up version of burlesque.)

By 1929 the audiences for burlesque (and vaudeville) began to decline, due to the popularity of Hollywood films. Striptease was then invented to reinvigorate burlesque by adding nudity to its bawdy sexuality. The stripping women—uniquely American—exhibited curvy bodies, bringing big breasts into vogue, but they also parodied themselves and their inept male partners, as had been typical of the burlesque women. Think of the zany Marx brothers and the other inept grotesque men of the American comic tradition—Laurel and Hardy, the Keystone Kops, Lou Costello of Abbott and Costello, the Three Stooges. These comic men were often partnered with beautiful women who ran circles around them. The impotent man, like the unintelligent female beauty, was a comic type in American entertainment. But stripteasers, in particular, could also be soubrettes, descendants of the saucy servant girls of the nineteenth-century stage. As such, they turned cartwheels and talked baby talk. They were as much comic as erotic.[8]

Moralists closed down many burlesque houses in the 1930s, but the striptease artists moved upscale to Broadway revues and nightclubs like Ciro's in Hollywood, as elite audiences took a fancy to them. Yet, whether performed in dives or nightclubs, the strip was always a tease, the nudity was mostly a "flash," and the bumps, grinds, and shimmies of the stripping women mocked the sex act while mimicking it. Total nudity was rare on the early striptease stage.

Gypsy Rose Lee, who some say invented striptease, called her act a "burlesque of burlesque." She invented the "literary stripper," who read passages from high-culture texts and parodied them. Captivating audiences with her wit, Gypsy took off few clothes, while she challenged the myth that sexy women can't be rational or well read. Lili St. Cyr, whose popularity dated from the 1950s, was as important as Gypsy in the development of striptease, but she was different. She took off her clothes and did much more than a flash; her naked body, which she displayed on stage with impunity, looked like a Greek statue, representing high-class glamour as well as low-class comedy. She didn't speak on stage. She survived a complaint lodged against her as obscene; brought to trial, her act was ruled aesthetic, not pornographic. Other strippers had animals in their acts to parody male "animality": Blaze Starr used a panther. Sally Rand invented the fan dance, in which she manipulated large fans to conceal her nude body and make her "flash" dramatic. Marilyn realized the innovative nature of striptease women in drawing from them to create her alter egos Marilyn Monroe and Lorelei Lee.[9]

Striptease and burlesque also influenced Marilyn's movements and costumes directly. Choreographer Jack Cole haunted burlesque houses to find interesting material. He put modified bumps and grinds into Marilyn's production numbers—dampening them down for the Production Board. Billy Travilla found inspiration in the elaborate costumes that stripteasers often wore when they came on stage, before they removed their costumes piece by piece. As a child growing up in Glendale, not far from downtown Los Angeles, on the way to school he had walked by burlesque houses where striptease artists were performing. Becoming friendly with the artists, he had designed costumes for them.[10]

Female "dumb-blonde" comics also influenced Marilyn. They can be traced to the 1900s vaudeville theater, when male-female duos were introduced—as comedy teams, as trapeze artists, as dancers—dominated by the men. The women in the pairs didn't talk; they were "dumb." In 1910 Harriette Lee of Ryan and Lee modified the formula by talking baby talk and serving as the butt of her partner Ben Ryan's jokes. Called a female dumbbell, she was a smash hit and was widely imitated. By the 1920s the dumbbell of the 1910s had transitioned into a dark-haired flapper, called a "Dumb Dora."[11]

Anita Loos combined "Dumb Dora" with the blonde to create the classic "dumb blonde" in her 1925 novella *Gentlemen Prefer Blondes*. Dark-haired and witty, Loos participated in intellectual New York circles, but she also was friends with Broadway chorus girls. She knew they bedded wealthy men, expecting expensive presents or even marriage in return. In *Gentlemen Prefer Blondes* Loos positioned her chorus girls—Lorelei Lee and Dorothy—in the guise of the traditional fool, a historical character to be found in Shakespeare's plays, who was wise under a mask of stupidity. Loos also made fun of the myth that the chorus girls were "gold diggers" who used their bodies to fleece men. In fact, that's what they did, but Loos implicitly emphasized that the men deserved what they got.[12]

The "fast-talking dames," fictive cousins to the "dumb blondes," first appeared in the early 1930s. They were the product of Production Code prohibitions joined with the popularity of 1920s urban gangsters, who trafficked in illegal liquor and partnered with tough "gun molls." With open sexuality forbidden in films, a comic style based on sexy wordplay between hesitant men and forceful women appeared. It was called "screwball comedy." Even sex symbol Jean Harlow moved from steamy sexuality into the "screwball" mode, in which women talked fast, displaying power in their voices and gestures. In movies like *How to Marry a Millionaire* and *Some Like It Hot*, Marilyn played a soft-voiced variation on screwball, using her double-entendre comic lines to confound the men who longed for her body.

Mae West, who dominated Hollywood in the early 1930s with her Diamond Lil character, modeled on female impersonators Julian Eltinge and Bert Savoy, both represented the "fast-talking dames" and parodied them. She wore six-inch platform shoes, had a staccato voice that oozed sex, and presented a masklike face, marcelled hair that looked like a helmet, and swaying hips. Marilyn was often compared to her, although Mae never varied her character in her films and Marilyn did.[13]

Mae West and the fast-talking dames dominated female style in films in the 1930s, but the dumb blonde still existed, represented especially by Marie Wilson. Wilson isn't well known today, but she was very popular from the 1930s through the 1950s. She had a childlike look, a fey personality, and a zany intellectualism, as she quoted from books and got them mixed up. She was a hit as the dumb blonde in Ken Murray's *Blackouts*, a variety revue, in the 1940s. Monroe borrowed directly from Wilson. The difference lies in three features. Wilson had a typical tinny "dumb-blonde voice—high-pitched, nasal, slightly harsh." Marilyn talked softly, with childlike inflections. Marilyn was deeply sensual and often vulnerable. Marie was much more wooden. And Marie walked normally, while Marilyn sometimes swayed her hips as she walked, as Mae West had.[14]

When Marilyn turned herself into an outré dumb blonde, with hip-swinging walk, puckered mouth, half-lidded eyes, childlike voice, and skin-tight dresses, she parodied herself. None of Marilyn's imitators—neither Jayne Mansfield, Mamie Van Doren, nor Sheree North—matched the subtlety of her parody of sensuous femininity. Eve Arnold called her "a practitioner of camp." Camp is associated with gender crossing, especially with transvestite men who exaggerate femininity. But women who exaggerate femininity can also be included. Marilyn often did so. She sometimes played herself straight; as a feisty young woman in *Clash by Night*, for example. Yet she was a trickster who liked masquerades. After her hip-swinging cameo in *Love Happy* in 1949, Groucho Marx described her as combining Theda Bara, Mae West, and Little Bo-Peep. Marilyn liked that description. She told W. J. Weatherby, "I learned a few tricks from [Mae West]—that impression of laughing at, or mocking, her own sexuality."[15]

Yet Marilyn often went beyond camp when she played her blonde clown. Joshua Logan, who directed her in *Bus Stop* (1956), compared her to Chaplin in being able to portray comedy on the edge between laughter and sadness, which was characteristic of great clowns. Indeed, by 1956 Marilyn could register happiness and sadness in her eyes almost simultaneously. She drew deep into her interior self to do so, but as Johnny Hyde had recommended, she had studied the silent film stars, especially Chaplin, who used their faces, eyes, and bodies to express emotion. John Strasberg, who knew Marilyn from her days with his family and the Actors Studio, told me that Marilyn had consciously incorporated Chaplin's Little Tramp in the "clown" she created.[16]

In all of her personas—the comic Marilyn, the dramatic Marilyn, the glamorous Marilyn—Marilyn combined the "high arts" of photography, drama, and literature with the "low arts" of burlesque, striptease, and the pinup. She moved among them, dividing and uniting them to create varying looks, personas, and meanings.

Whatever persona Marilyn took on, her look wasn't easy to achieve. She had to deal with problems in her body and face that Emmeline Snively had noted in 1946. Even cinematographer Leon Shamroy, who enthused over her screen impact when he shot her first screen test for Fox, was critical of her appearance in later interviews. "When you analyze Marilyn," he told reporter Ezra Goodman, "she is not good looking. She has a bad posture, bad nose, and her figure is too obvious. She has a bad profile." Early pinup photographers of her had covered up the deficiencies with lighting, positioning, and camera angles, and later photographers did the same. Indeed, Marilyn rarely allowed herself to be photographed in profile, and she kept control over all proof sheets produced of her. If she didn't like a proof, she would cross it out.[17]

The perfectionist Marilyn, who lacked self-confidence and wanted to be flawless, spent hours at the makeup table striving to attain perfect beauty. The plastic surgery done on her in 1950 to remove the bump on her nose and to give her chin more definition hadn't completely worked. Part of the bump remained, and she covered it with makeup that took a long time to get right. Whitey Snyder, her personal makeup artist, spent a long time giving her weak chin definition and trying to correct her lack of facial symmetry, which can be seen in her photos. She had freckles on her skin and hair on the sides of her face that she also concealed with makeup. She had dark hair on her arms, which she often concealed with body makeup. She put on fake fingernails to cover up the ragged edges of the ones she had bitten.[18]

In the 1950s women wore heavy makeup—a result of the return to femininity after World War Two and the power of advertising to create a demand for cosmetics. Marilyn led the trend. To make her lips larger and more lustrous, she applied four layers of lipstick and drew her lip line outside its natural shape. She put Vaseline on her lips to make them look wet. It was part of what Billy Travilla called her "fuck-me" look, especially when she held her lips in an O, as she sometimes did. She darkened the mole on the right side of her face near her lips to draw attention to them. She used eyebrow pencil to darken her eyebrows and make them heavy and straight, although she sometimes plucked them into a peak. She often wore false eyelashes. Whitey Snyder said that she knew makeup techniques that she kept secret even from him; one was to put white makeup on her eyelids to make her eyes seem larger. It could take as long as three hours to get her makeup right. Finding a flaw, she might take off the makeup and start over again.[19]

Marilyn had white skin, and she didn't tan. In an era that extolled tans as a symbol of leisure and sports, Marilyn went against the grain by adopting a pale look and warning against the dangers of exposure to the damaging rays of the sun, which can cause wrinkles and premature aging. She used special creams and often went for facials to Elizabeth Arden's in New York and Madame Renna's in Beverly Hills. To intrigue her fans, in her early movie career Marilyn changed her shade of blonde for each film. "Some girls prefer to change hats," she said. "I just prefer to change my hair color." She was ash blonde in *The Asphalt Jungle*, golden blonde in *All About Eve*, silver blonde in *As Young as You Feel*, amber blonde in

Let's Make It Legal, and smoky blonde in *Love Nest*. Fox hair stylist Sydney Guilaroff, who created many star coiffeurs, stated that he redesigned Marilyn's hair for each of her films. Gladys Rasmussen, her personal hairdresser, said that Marilyn asked her for a different hairstyle every time she went on the town.[20]

Her hair remained difficult. She had its kinkiness straightened and then she had it re-permed into soft curls. The color had to be touched up every five days or so. Her widow's peak gave her problems, because its roots didn't take dye well. The lock of hair that often falls casually over her eye in photos was teased into place to hide those roots. Even the tousled hairdo she sometimes wears began with a styling before she messed it up.[21] After about 1949 there are no photos of her with her natural kinky brown hair. Sometimes her dark roots show, but not often. Being blonde had become central to who she was. In the spring of 1955 she changed her name legally to Marilyn Monroe.

Marilyn usually looked glamorous at public events. In Fox wardrobe closets she found satin and sequined dresses designed by studio designers like Jean Louis and Oleg Cassini. She liked dresses that were strapless or with a low V-neckline, and she wore them with dangling diamond earrings to draw attention to her bust and face. Rita Hayworth had originated this look, but Marilyn made it her own. She often stated that she didn't wear jewelry, but she mostly meant necklaces. Even then she wore pearls, a standard fashion accessory, because they have a luster that softens the face.[22] As she moved into her elegant phase in the mid-1950s, she often wore black. In 1954 she said that she loved to wear clinging black dresses and black gloves up to her shoulder. It was a look that combined elegance with eroticism. The long gloves, sometimes worn in the 1890s and adopted by striptease artists in the 1930s, could take time to get off. With typical Marilyn aplomb she told the press, "I like to be really dressed up or really undressed. I don't bother with anything in between."[23]

A trend toward voluptuousness appeared in fashionable women's dress in 1947 with Dior's "New Look," which was based on the bell shape of women's fashions in the Victorian era. With its nipped-in waist, large bust, and full skirt, it was also meant to be sexy. Eroticism in high fashion increased a year later when a pencil-thin skirt was joined to the full skirt as an acceptable alternative silhouette for women. Marilyn seized on the tight skirt. When *How to Marry a Millionaire* was in preproduction,

Billy Travilla put all three actresses in the film—Betty Grable, Lauren Bacall, and Marilyn—into full skirts, but Marilyn complained so loudly that he re-dressed her in tight skirts. Well-known designers like Ceil Chapman made tight dresses with low-cut V-necklines for her.

She also wore strapless dresses—popular in the 1950s—and halter-top dresses. Often used in sundress design, the halter top suggested Southern California leisure while enlarging the look of the breasts. The Production Board, which often fixated on regulating cleavage in this era, didn't mind halter tops. Billy Travilla used the design for Marilyn's white dress in the 1954 *Seven Year Itch* photo shoot. The halter top was usually attached to a full skirt. When worn without stockings or a slip, such a style was titillating to a culture whose dress code for women included a girdle, bra, slip, and nylon stockings. Marilyn was upending those conventions. Moreover, in an era in which the well-dressed woman always wore a hat, Marilyn overturned that convention as well. At most, she wore a beret on her head or a small cap.

But she also sexualized fashions when she played showgirls who wore hourglass corsets, silk stockings, and high-heeled shoes, all sexual fetishes that got by the censors, who didn't seem aware of their meaning. They harked back to the showgirls of the 1890s, when such features were in style. Mae West had reintroduced them into films in the 1930s and Betty Grable, in particular, had continued the tradition. Marilyn wore such clothing, for example, in *Gentlemen Prefer Blondes*, *There's No Business Like Show Business*, and *River of No Return*. Once again the Production Board didn't seem to realize what was going on.

She chose even her shoes for maximum sexual effect. She and Shelley Winters both wore platform shoes in the early 1940s with a bow tied around their ankles: they called them their "fuck-me" shoes. After 1951, when spike heels were invented, Marilyn wore them as often as possible. She made them part of her signature style because men found spike heels sexy (shades of sadomasochism), and they made her legs look longer.[24] Marilyn respected Bruno Bernard's dictate about appearing to have long legs.

Marilyn surprised MGM designer Edith Head with her knowledge of fabrics and fit. Ana Lower, an expert seamstress, had taught her the basics of sewing, and she paid attention to the construction of the clothes in the Fox wardrobe department and consulted with the designers who dressed her for her films. Head found Marilyn a free spirit and thought she should have been dressed like a blithe bohemian, not a raunchy glamour girl. In other words, Head, who never designed for Marilyn, didn't like Marilyn's tight clothing. Such clothing, of course, was meant to transform Marilyn from an ordinary girl into a sex icon. Adele Balkan, Billy Travilla's assistant, stated that Marilyn went into Travilla's studio looking like a ragamuffin and came out looking like "the sexiest, most elegant lady."[25]

As she had as early as junior high, when she created her own style in dress by wearing tight sweaters to attract boys, Marilyn continued to strive for striking effects in her dress. Some Hollywood columnists in her early career accused her of knowing nothing about fashion, but that wasn't the case. She read the Hollywood fan magazines and fashion magazines like *Vogue*. In 1952 she answered the attacks on her as badly dressed. She was too buxom, she said, to wear Parisian fashions. Like most women, she didn't have a boys' figure, as the Parisian models had. Nor did she have the money to buy expensive clothes, because she spent her salary on acting and singing lessons. But when she bought clothes, she bought good clothes, such as an evening gown designed by Oleg Cassini in red velvet that fit snugly to the knees and then flared out. She owned a similar dress in red silk taffeta with black lace over it that she bought at I. Magnin, a premier department store in Los Angeles. She also owned a black cocktail dress by Ceil Chapman and one by Christian Dior and two tailored suits with cleavage. To give the suits flair, she wore a full-blown red or yellow rose in the cleavage.[26]

In the summer of 1952, she wore the red dress from *Niagara* in many of her publicity photos: Dorothy Jeakins had designed it. Henry Hathaway gave it to her when he learned about her small wardrobe. That fall, carrying a wad of money Joe DiMaggio had given her, she bought a number of dresses at Ceil Chapman's New York boutique. As she entered her elegant phase in late 1954, she turned to Norman Norell and John Moore as her major designers.

Like many young Hollywood actresses, in regular life Marilyn dressed in casual clothing: T-shirts, capri pants, pedal pushers. In her younger years, when she was broke, she bought blue jeans at army surplus stores, wore them into the ocean, and then let them dry to the shape of her body, producing a tight fit. She was a leader in creating this fashion, a Southern California innovation. She shopped at Jax, the chic Beverly Hills store that specialized in beautifully tailored cotton leisure clothing designed by Jack Hansen, and whose prices weren't outrageous. In typical Marilyn fashion, she came in to the store to see saleswomen Yuki and Korby, working-class women she identified with.[27]

Marilyn's image percolated into both high and low culture, influencing styles in dress and appearance in obvious and subtle ways. The famed 1952 Revlon Fire and Ice advertisement for blood-red lipstick and fingernail polish, a new sexy trend that the company heavily marketed, drew on Marilyn's style. The dark-haired high-fashion model Dorian Leigh, whose likeness dominates the ad, wears Marilyn's trademark sequined dress and long dangling earrings. The written copy under the photo might as well be referring to Marilyn when it describes the fire-and-ice woman as with pouty lips, large breasts, and smoldering, sad eyes. Marilyn's name is placed at the beginning and end of a list of "typical" fire-and-ice women. All are dark-haired: Rossana Podestà, Silvana Mangano, and Linda Darnell. Podestà and Mangano were Italian film stars being featured in American films. Only Marilyn, the ad implies, can hold her own against them.[28]

Elaine Rounds, beauty editor of *Motion Picture*, wrote in 1954 that the Marilyn lip line, extending beyond the natural line, had come into vogue for all women. Eve Arnold joked about Marilyn's influence on high-fashion models. Her pouty mouth so influenced them, according to Arnold, that "going through fashion pictures of the fifties, you find yourself looking at so many open-mouthed models who seem gasping for breath that you wonder whether you've wandered into an aquarium." "The impact of Marilyn has been felt around the world," wrote Lydia Lane, *Los Angeles Times* fashion editor. "The color of her hair, her skin-tight clothes, her slightly parted lips. Almost every country has a native version of her. Last year in Turkey, I met Istanbul's Marilyn Monroe, a singer who confessed she wasn't too happy about the changes her manager had demanded, but she admitted it had paid off financially."[29]

In real life, Marilyn usually chose tall, dark, and powerful men as partners—all father figures. But in her films from *Gentlemen Prefer Blondes* on, she was often cast against small, unprepossessing men, whose confidence she shores up by praising their gentleness as central to real masculinity. Such redemptive women were everywhere in 1950s films, according to Brandon French, in her classic study of women in 1950s films. In *The Seven Year Itch*, Marilyn describes the Black Lagoon creature in the film she saw with Tom Ewell as only needing "a sense of being loved and needed and wanted" to end his destructive behavior. She tells Tom Ewell's character that "women prefer gentle men, not great big hulks who strut around like a tiger—giving you that 'I'm so handsome, you can't resist me' look."[30]

Many of Monroe's films contain a tall, dark, and handsome man, but these men are usually partnered with other female characters, not with Marilyn. In *Gentlemen* Dorothy snags the tall, dark, and handsome private detective who is investigating Lorelei Lee; Marilyn winds up with the effeminate millionaire. The same partnering occurs in *How to Marry a Millionaire*, in which Betty Grable snags the ranger with matinee idol looks, while Marilyn is left with David Wayne, looking like a schlemiel. In *There's No Business Like Show Business* Mitzi Gaynor gets the handsome guy and Marilyn winds up with pallid Donald O'Connor, much shorter than she.

The Marilyn who taught men to be tender was a figure that assuaged male anxieties in the 1950s. Soldiers returning from the war were plagued with stress disorders, and men in general felt confined by the cult of domesticity and the pressure to conform to corporate life. Fears of impotence and homosexuality were rife, especially after Alfred Kinsey concluded in his 1948 *Sexual Behavior in the Human Male* that forty percent of men had had a homosexual experience and that homosexual latency threatened many more. "In an era of a prevailing fear of male homosexual 'perversion,'" Jessamyn Neuhaus wrote, "strong erections in the marital bed were very important." The tender and sexual Marilyn, often partnered with ordinary men in her films, allowed all men to feel masculine and able to respond sexually to women.[31]

In one guise Marilyn glorified heterosexuality. She was renowned for saying "I love living in a man's world, so long as I am a woman in it." By 1953 Hugh Hefner chose her as his first Playmate in the first issue of *Playboy*; in 1956 *Time* magazine called her "an adolescent daydream." Norman Mailer's description of her sexuality in his biography of her focused on male problems with sexual performance.

Marilyn was deliverance, a very Stradivarius of sex, so gorgeous, forgiving, humorous, compliant, and tender that even the most mediocre musician would relax his lack of art in the dissolving magic of her violin. Marilyn suggested that sex might be difficult and dangerous with others, but ice cream with her. Take me, said her smile. "I'm easy. I'm happy. I'm an angel of sex, you bet."[32]

Marilyn was savvy about men. "Sometimes I watch adult men," Marilyn told George Barris. "They act like little boys who have never grown up." In a conversation with Susan Strasberg about men, Susan said, "I had thought all creative, artistic men were more sensitive, different, until I'd once heard Clifford Odets say, 'I loved Fay Wray, but God forgive me, I left her because she had no tits.'" Marilyn replied, "Men, they're all the same . . . they can't help it." She knew; she had the world's most beautiful tits. Norman Rosten commented, "Marilyn understood the carnal male syndrome," the power of their penis over them, the sexual response to women they sometimes can't control and their desire for an ever-ready woman who seems responsive to every touch, immediately orgasmic.[33]

Marilyn could also be an avenging angel, like the burlesque stars in their "upside-down world of powerful women and powerless men." That theme is evident in the *Seven Year Itch* photo. It's an undertone in *How to Marry a Millionaire*. It's there full force in the production numbers in *There's No Business Like Show Business*. These numbers were choreographed by Jack Cole, with his camp sensitivity. More than any of her films, however, *Gentlemen Prefer Blondes* displays Marilyn's power, as Lorelei and Dorothy triumph over a host of men.

Marilyn most fully illuminates the complex relations between gender, class, and sexuality in her "Diamond's Are a Girl's Best Friend" number from *Gentlemen Prefer Blondes*. The lyrics of the song Marilyn sings in that number are cynical about love. The reason to have affairs with wealthy men, the lyrics state, is so that the women involved can get the money from them to pay their rent, buy food, and become secure as they age. But the lyrics caution that such men often drop women once they have sex with them, having sampled their wares. Thus women should be cynical and get diamonds from these men, since their money can suddenly be lost in stock market crashes.

Early in the "Diamonds" number, Marilyn playfully opens and closes a fan, using it to tap the shoulders of the male dancers dressed in upper-class ties and tails who dance around her. They add to the riffs on sex and class in the number. The fan invokes the fan dancers of burlesque, but when Marilyn sings an operatic trill, her fan also references eighteenth-century aristocratic women who used fans to flirt. The female ballet dancers wear light pink tutus, with dark veils over their faces, and they swirl around Marilyn, waltzing with the men. Dressed in shocking pink, Marilyn stands out from the ballerinas. She has a narrower skirt and a pouf of fabric on her backside. She is both elegant and sexual, an object of desire and a woman who controls men.

Yet, the scene takes place against a vivid red background, lighted by chandeliers with women tied to them, implying that the action is happening in a brothel, with the bound women suggesting an orgy. Wearing sadomasochistic black leather, they evoke Bettie Page, the innocent girl with black hair and white skin who starred in the day's underground sadomasochist films. (Page's biographer calls her the "Dark Angel in the world of bondage and leather" and "the teasing girl-next-door, who is the kitten with a whip.")[34] The reference to Page was an ironic, hidden commentary on the part of Jack Cole, who intended it to add another level to the complexities of gender, sex, and class in the musical number and in the film.

Some may find it surprising to think of Marilyn as a rebel, since she is often identified as quintessentially feminine and not very smart, qualities not usually associated with rebellion. Yet she held radical views on sex, class, and race. She identified with Lorelei Lee's statement in the lyrics of a song from *Gentlemen* that she was "the little girl from Little Rock" who "came from the wrong side of the tracks." She often declared her solidarity with working-class people, the nation's dispossessed. She made friends with the salesladies at Jax; with Amy and Milton Greene's housekeeper, Kitty Owens; and with the makeup artists, hairstylists, and grips on her films. In *How to Marry a Millionaire* Monroe is one of three "gold-digging" women trying to snag a wealthy man, but the moral of the film is that ordinary men, who work at construction jobs and eat in diners, are preferable to wealthy men and their upper-class ways. In that film Betty Grable ends up with a forest ranger and Monroe with a man being pursued by IRS agents for tax evasion. Lauren Bacall's construction worker boyfriend, whom she rejects as too poor, turns out to be a millionaire, although he prefers to live like a laborer.

In *The Seven Year Itch*, Marilyn is hilarious as a television model selling a toothpaste promoted by ridiculous copy and called Dazzledent, a product of a Madison Avenue that has gone mad. In this guise she implicitly critiques the materialist fantasies that underpin capitalist consumption. Marilyn's statement "I don't want to be wealthy; I just want to be wonderful" reverberates through her star text. In her films she is a working-class working woman, usually a showgirl or a model. She sometimes gets the millionaires in her films, but sometimes she doesn't. She allowed Hollywood to commercialize her body, selling her "as one might sell a refrigerator or a car," but she rebelled against it in the end. Her nude calendar photos sold in the millions of copies and the image was affixed to everything from playing cards to serving trays and sold in souvenir shops, but she made no money from it because she had signed the rights away to Tom Kelley. "I don't look at myself as a commodity," she stated, "but I'm sure a lot of people have."[35] She was caught in a bind of her own making. She had done what was required of her to become a superstar, but she had also become an object, ratifying capitalism's connection between sexuality and sales.

Marilyn has also been interpreted as a symbol of whiteness, especially in the work of Richard Dyer. In this interpretation she represents the White Goddess of the Western imagination, a transhistorical figure posed against the presumed animal nature of black people. That theme, made epic in the 1933 film *King Kong*, resonates in *The Creature from the Black Lagoon*. As in *King Kong*, the dark creature abducts a white woman and takes her to his lair before he is tracked down and captured.[36]

Little hard evidence supports the racist interpretation of Marilyn, although it might have originated in a racist dynamic powerful in the movie business—an industry based on the profit motive, which catered to the nation's prejudices. The parade of blonde Marilyn clones that followed her as dumb-blonde bombshells in 1950s films as the Civil Rights movement expanded gives it some credence. On the other hand, producers copied each other, and they may have been trying to replicate Fox's success with the sexy Marilyn at a time that the industry thought it could reenergize itself through emphasizing sexy women. Racism was strong in the film business, but it was declining by the mid-1950s as the Civil Rights movement gained the moral high ground.[37]

Marilyn didn't participate in the Civil Rights protest, but she supported it. The egalitarian attitudes of the Bolenders toward race, her first foster parents, influenced her. She dated a black man during her early years in Hollywood, and she identified with the hero of Joyce Cary's novel *Mister Johnson*, a young Nigerian man who is destroyed by British colonialism. To her he represented innocence killed by the "bad guys." She stated that it was " 'them' against 'us' everywhere." She also had a fan base among blacks. Black newspapers advertised her movies and chronicled her career, comparing her to Lena Horne and Dorothy Dandridge. They wrote about her friendships with Sammy Davis Jr. and Ella Fitzgerald.

When I interviewed Larry Grant, an African-American man who had been one of her guards during her performances at military bases in Korea in 1954, I asked him if Marilyn represented a racist white woman to blacks. My question confused him, as if it were irrelevant to him. She was a beautiful woman, he said, and she was kind to me when I served as her guard. There were men of color everywhere she performed in Korea, he said, and they all loved her.[38]

In June 1955, escorted by Joe DiMaggio, she attended a benefit for Sammy Davis Jr. at the Apollo Theater in Harlem. The audience was composed primarily of African-Americans. Joe and Marilyn entered the auditorium separately, at different times. The audience went wild, giving each of them a standing ovation. James Baldwin was a fan of Marilyn. He recognized the childhood abuse visited on her and called her a "slave" of the Hollywood system. Many blacks responded to her version of her childhood and saw her as a victim of the system as much as they.[39]

In her book on whiteness in Hollywood films, British scholar Diane Negra identifies a category of actors and movie characters she calls "white ethnics." She includes poor whites in that category. Given Marilyn's background, she fits in this grouping. By the 1950s Eastern Europeans, Jews, and Mediterranean peoples were moving into the middle class, and older definitions of them as nonwhite were breaking down. From this perspective Marilyn could be viewed as an emblem of ethnic cohesion, a bridge between minorities, especially given her marriages to Joe DiMaggio, a symbol of Italian-American social mobility, and to Arthur Miller, who was Jewish. When she married him in 1956, she converted to Judaism. She identified with Jews as a dispossessed group.[40]

Marilyn's politics were to the left, in keeping with the politics of many of her foster parents and her identification with the working class. In *My Story* Marilyn states that she read Lincoln Steffens's autobiography on the set of *All About Eve* and liked his discussion of oppression and resistance. When Joe Mankiewicz heard she was reading Steffens, he told her she could get into trouble if studio executives found out. Harry Brand cautioned her: "We don't want anyone investigating our Marilyn." She hid the book under the bed in her apartment and read it at night by the light of a flashlight. She was observed reading other radical literature on the sets of her films.[41]

In 1949 writer Norma Barzman and her husband, screenwriter Ben Barzman, both members of the Communist Party, had scheduled a meeting of Communist sympathizers at their house in the Hollywood Hills to discuss how to respond to the House Un-American Activities Committee's attack on freedom of speech. As they waited for their guests, a young blonde woman in a convertible drove up their driveway and waved them over to speak to her.

The woman, they realized, was Marilyn Monroe. She told them that two policemen at the end of the street were watching their house. They were stopping everyone driving onto the street and questioning them. She had been driving up the road to a friend's house, and she had been stopped. She spoke to Norma and Ben in her blend of metaphor and reality. "I'm glad I stopped in on you guys. I'm real glad there's people like you trying to figure out ways of not getting pushed around. I don't care what you are. I'm glad that somebody's minding the store."[42]

As usual she identified with the exploited. Within a few years, she would become a dedicated leftist, supporting even the Communist struggle against capitalist imperialism. In the spring of 1960 she wrote to Lester Markel, a friend of hers who was a *New York Times* editor, supporting Castro in Cuba. By the year she died, she had subscriptions to *The Nation* and *I.F. Stone's Weekly*, both radical publications. In February 1962, she visited the members of the "Hollywood Twenty" who were living in Mexico City. She talked about her support for the Civil Rights struggle, while praising the Communist leaders of China for bringing equality to a hierarchical society.[43]

Marilyn strove to develop the intellectual skills that would enable her to understand the world around her. She'd missed early chances to develop them, since she'd spent a lot of her time in school fantasizing about being a star. Everyone who knew her well verified her intelligence and her ability to understand the books she read. Paradoxically, the classic "dumb-blonde" figure always read ponderous books—and got them mixed up. That was a characteristic of the type from Lorelei Lee in Anita Loos's *Gentlemen Prefer Blondes* on. The perfectionist Marilyn strove for accuracy in portraying her blonde figure, but her drive for knowledge was real. "Did you know you were born under the same sign as Rosalind Russell, Judy Garland, and Rosemary Clooney?" she was asked. She replied, "I know nothing of these people. I was born under the same sign as Ralph Waldo Emerson, Queen Victoria, and Walt Whitman."[44]

In her 1947 *Photoplay* article "How to Be a Star," which featured Marilyn, author Fredda Dudley stated that learning was essential to Hollywood success, since all good acting was based on intelligence and knowledge. She advised aspiring actors to read important plays and biographies of great actors and to attend college for a year or two. Marilyn met literate people in Hollywood, including Natasha Lytess, Johnny Hyde, Elia Kazan, Sam Shaw, and Michael Chekhov. They taught her about art and literature and suggested books to read. Photographers such as Andre de Dienes and Bruno Bernard, who had a Ph.D. in criminal psychology from the University of Kiel in Germany, had done the same.[45]

As early as 1948 Clarice Evans, Marilyn's Studio Club roommate, was impressed by the number of books she owned. When Philippe Halsman photographed her at her apartment in 1952, he counted two hundred books on her bookshelves. Walt Whitman's *Leaves of Grass* was on the nightstand by her bed. Sidney Skolsky, who went to bookstores with her, noted that she bought books on self-improvement and psychology, the latest plays, books of poetry, and everything on Abraham Lincoln. In conversation she referred to the books she had read: she talked to Jane Russell for hours about philosophers. Russell reported that Plato, Saint

Paul, and the Book of Revelations were among her favorites. Marilyn had a large collection of art books given to her by a writer named Bob Russell, a secret friend of hers.[46]

She wasn't always a diligent reader, but she got the gist of a book. When she browsed the shelves in Pickwick's bookstore, she'd find an interesting paragraph in a book, memorize it, and then go on to find another book. Elia Kazan recommended Emerson to her, and Michael Chekhov recommended Rudolph Steiner. When she met Edith Sitwell in Hollywood in 1954, they discussed Steiner and his eurythymic dancing. Sitwell had attended a Steiner dance group in London, and she described those dances to Marilyn as attempts to connect with Mother Earth.[47]

After she became a star, Marilyn consulted experts in fields that interested her, including religion, literature, and, interestingly, the stock market. Meeting her early in her Hollywood years, actor Cameron Mitchell had assumed she was an airhead who carried large volumes around with her without knowing what was in them. Then they engaged in a discussion of Freud, and she demonstrated an in-depth knowledge of his theories. Mitchell's opinion of her changed. In later years, when Lee Strasberg wanted an opinion of a new movie or play, Marilyn was someone he consulted.[48]

In her reading Marilyn liked romantic writers who dealt with ethical and spiritual issues and had a broad sweep. The German expatriates in Hollywood read Dostoyevsky and Rainer Maria Rilke. Following their lead, Marilyn didn't read fluffy fiction; she read the heavyweights—Dostoyevsky, Tolstoy, Balzac. Poets were her favorites: Whitman, Keats, Shelley, Yeats. They appealed to her poetic imagination, as she aestheticized reality. She liked the poetic novelist Thomas Wolfe. When reporter William Bruce interviewed her, he mentioned that he had heard she was a fan of Wolfe. In response, she plied him with questions about Wolfe's work, even his obscure novels. "I am a great fan of Thomas Wolfe," she told Hedda Hopper. She said to journalist Dorothy Kilgallen, "If you want your ear talked off, mention novelist Thomas Wolfe to me. I've practically memorized his books." She even read his collected letters to his mother.[49]

Many of the authors she liked—Wolfe, Whitman, and Dostoyevsky—created sweeping landscapes and had broad imaginations. Her favorite

book was Rilke's *Letters to a Young Poet*, which young intellectuals in
Hollywood and New York were reading. Like Dostoyevsky, Rilke adored
Russia, with its vast reaches of unpopulated territory. He felt that "alone-
ness" was important to artistic production and personal satisfaction.
His central theme was the need for the artist to examine the interior self
in order to find an aesthetic vision to provide motivation. He'd given up
on Christianity and although he hadn't found a system to replace it, he
counseled young writers to regard the process of writing as akin to sex,
replete with passion and daring. Such internal exploration was similar to
what Stanislavsky was recommending to actors. In his way Rilke was a
rebel who advised his readers to disregard convention and live free lives.
Influenced by Swedish feminist Ellen Key, he wanted women and men to
become more like each other.[50]

Whitman and Wolfe also penned their work on broad canvases. Whitman wrote about the "Body Electric" in his famed poem "I Sing the Body
Electric" from *Leaves of Grass*. It's sensual and lusty, with a love for the
physicality and spirituality of both men and women. In Whitman's imagination, they leap over gender boundaries as they do a dizzying dance in his
poem, although in the end the male is active and the woman exudes a "divine nimbus." Wolfe's work encompassed the history of the United States,
as his heroes moved from the South to New York, leaving a decaying agri-
cultural society for a decadent urban environment.

Wolfe, Whitman, and Rilke all criticized the prevailing materialism
of capitalist societies and sympathized with workers and peasants, but
none was a political radical. Rather, they were vitalists, advising individuals to cultivate an electric energy to empower themselves and their
nations. Wolfe and Rilke were influenced by Nietzsche, who called for
supermen to rejuvenate the world and hoped for a new ecstatic Diony-
sianism for both individuals and for the theater, which he viewed as a
place of transformation for both actors and audiences.

In addition to poets and writers like Rilke and Wolfe, Marilyn was
also attracted to Sigmund Freud, whose theories dominated intellectual
and popular thought after World War Two. His belief that a primitive id,
seething with base urges, underlay human personality and was controlled only with difficulty by a rational ego made sense after the brutality of the war. His ideas drew from the pessimism about mankind that

was a strain in the thinking of Dostoyevsky, Rilke, and Wolfe, although he put forth a specific plan for individuals to come to terms with their neuroses through the process of psychoanalysis. By the time of World War Two, psychoanalysts dominated the psychiatric services offered by the military, and they emerged from the war to fill a majority of posts in clinics and hospitals as well as in the profession of social work.[51]

Articles in newspapers and magazines praised Freudian psychoanalysts as potential saviors of individuals and the nation, while many Hollywood people underwent psychoanalysis. Prominent European psychoanalysts, fleeing Hitler, had arrived in the United States. Terms such as "libido," "ego," and the "unconscious," taken from Freud's work, entered the vocabulary. *Time* celebrated Freud's discovery of the unconscious as comparable in importance to the Enlightenment's discounting of religion in favor of rationality, which had formed a cornerstone of the modern worldview.[52]

For Marilyn, always worried about going insane like her mother, Freud's ideas offered a way to achieve a balanced mind that might keep her from the incarcerations, continuous baths, and electric shock treatments her mother had endured. There was a messianic quality to Freud, who seemed like a secular prophet. Although she continued to explore mystical alternatives and converted to Arthur Miller's Judaism, she called Freudianism "her religion."

Psychoanalysis became a way of life for her, as she consulted therapists even before she left Hollywood for New York. In New York and after she returned to Hollywood in 1961 she entered into a voyage of discovery with them, exploring childhood memories, trying to figure out who she was. As was her way, she went to the top of the Freudian networks, choosing therapists who were close to Sigmund Freud's daughter, Anna, whom Freud had analyzed himself. She finally consulted Anna Freud herself when she was in London, filming *The Prince and the Showgirl*. She saw Anna for daily sessions over the course of a week.

She told Anna that she had read Sigmund Freud's "dream of nudity" in his *Interpretation of Dreams* in 1947, when she was twenty-one, and that it had impressed her. Freud interpreted the dream of being nude in a public situation, as well as the drive toward nudity itself, as the product of some sort of sexual exposure in early childhood.[53] In Marilyn's case, playing sex games with a young boy, being subjected to Ida Bolender's attack on masturbation, or being molested by an elderly actor fit this pattern. When Anna and Marilyn played a game of marbles, Marilyn launched the balls one by one toward Anna. Anna concluded from that action and other statements by Marilyn that she desired to have sex with her and that she was afraid of men. The analysis seems overblown, but we don't know what else happened in their interactions.[54]

Marilyn's free-love attitudes, her belief in the beauty of the naked body, and her attitude toward sex as part of friendship continued through her years in Hollywood—and beyond. She continued to justify her displays of her body in reformist terms, claiming that they were a protest against the resurgent Puritanism of the 1950s and its repressive attitudes about sex. Susan Strasberg called Marilyn a hippie, and to Eunice Murray, her companion and housekeeper in 1962, she seemed like a "flower child," a forerunner of the movement for free relationships and living close to nature that would soon appear.

She was incensed when a number of states banned a book of nude photographs by Bruno Bernard as pornographic. She detested the Production Board and its rulings and continued to challenge it directly and subtly, as she did in the photo shoot for *The Seven Year Itch.* "She has a genius for falling into poses which flirt with the Johnston office regulations," Jack Wade wrote in *Modern Screen,* referring to Eric Johnston, head of the Motion Picture Association of America, which ran the Production Board. "I love to do things the censors won't pass," Marilyn stated. She parodied her desires and drives. At a party in New York people played a game in which they composed epitaphs for their tombstones. Marilyn punned the word "lay" to describe both sex and a minstrel song: "Here lies Marilyn. No lies. Only lays."[55]

As she constructed her sexy persona, she dispensed with wearing underwear. She told many people, as she had told Jim Dougherty, that she had stopped wearing it to avoid bulges in her skin-tight clothing. It's probable that she copied the behavior from Jean Harlow, who was known for not wearing underwear.

Marilyn had a drive to expose her body. She told her psychiatrist Marianne Kris that the drive was sometimes overwhelming when she was in public. In 1956 Sidney Skolsky stated that Marilyn wore panties and bras—mostly black in color—much more frequently than she admitted. But when she took her clothes off to try on clothing in dressing rooms, she usually was wearing no undergarments. On a visit to Atlantic City with Joe DiMaggio to see Skinny D'Amato, Joe's friend who ran the 500 Club, she went shopping for clothes with Skinny's wife, Bettyjane, who hardly knew her. When she took off her clothing in the dressing room to try on clothing she'd selected, she wasn't wearing underwear. When the salesladies objected, she bought all the clothes she'd tried on. Bettyjane was shocked.[56]

Roy Craft, the Fox publicity agent assigned to Marilyn, tried to never let her out of his sight because of her "striptease" inclinations. "She wears no panties," he said, and "when she sees a photographer on the lot, she lifts her skirt and falls into a cheesecake pose." He worried about "bottomless" photos. When Joe Schenck heard about this, he gave Marilyn two dozen panties monogrammed with the initials MM.

Sometimes prudish and sometimes outrageous, Marilyn rationalized her sexual behavior through free-love ideas. She shocked the nation, according to journalists, with statements like "Sex is part of life, it's part of nature—and I'd rather go along with nature." She told her friend Henry Rosenfeld she believed that sex brought people together and enhanced friendships. When she and Joe DiMaggio reconnected after she separated from Arthur Miller in 1960, she was thrilled that Joe finally agreed to an open relationship, in which they would be special friends to each other but would have sexual liaisons with other people with impunity. She had been wanting that concession from him for a long time.[57]

Marilyn considered fidelity and children essential elements of a loving marriage, one that was working. She never nested with DiMaggio, but she did so for a number of years with Arthur Miller. He was persuaded by her views on nudity and nature that she was in the vanguard of a new sexual rebellion that would undermine the Puritanism he now viewed as a central part of the anticommunist movement. Liberating people from conservative views on sex might inspire them to become more liberated in their political views in general.

When she lived alone, Marilyn often went naked in her home or threw a white terry-cloth robe over her nude body. Her bare skin pleased

Marilyn with a broken thumb at the Honolulu airport on the way to Japan. (Collection of the author)

Marilyn performing for American troops in Korea.

Marilyn gives a press conference when she separates from Joe DiMaggio, in front of their Beverly Hills house. To her right is her lawyer, Jerry Geisler.

Marilyn with her white piano.

Marilyn in disguise.

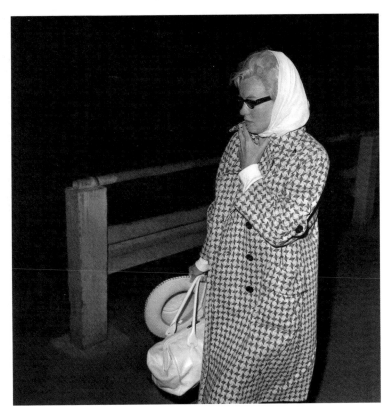

Marilyn with Joe DiMaggio in
New York, wearing the black
mink coat he gave her.

Marilyn judging a beard-growing contest. (Collection of the author)

Marilyn with Arthur Miller.

The cast of *The Misfits*. (Elliott Erwitt/
Magnum Photos)

Marilyn with Anne Karger.
(Courtesy of Terry Wasdyke)

Marilyn with Marjorie Plecher, her
longtime movie wardrobe person and
friend, and wife of Whitey Snyder.
(Collection of the author)

A costume test for *Something's Got to Give*.

Marilyn with Ella Fitzgerald.

The Rat Pack.

Marilyn with Pat Newcomb, the night of
John F. Kennedy's birthday celebration.

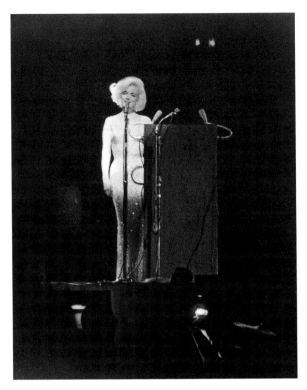

Singing happy birthday to JFK in Madison Square Garden.

A party at Arthur Krim's house after the JFK birthday celebration.

her. She said, "If you have a beautiful body, why not show it?" According to James Bacon, she lost all her insecurities when "she was flaunting that magnificent body." Photographer Anthony Beauchamp noticed her transformation after she put on her skimpy yellow bikini for their photo shoot in 1950. Being uncovered seemed to release her "sparkling personality." As soon as she discarded her clothes, she became animated; she talked with a delightfully unconscious sense of humor, and with almost flamboyant self-assurance. Both Lucille Ryman and Natasha Lytess remarked on her love of going nude. Jean Negulesco maintained that the only way Marilyn felt truly comfortable was nude.[58]

She sometimes exposed herself when posing for male photographers or in costume fittings with male designers—but this action could work against her. Milton Greene and Billy Travilla were both nonplussed when she showed off a breast to greet them on first meeting them. "Wait a minute!" Milton said.[59] In the early 1950s she sat for George Hurrell, who had created the glamour look of the 1930s. Unlike most photographers who shot Marilyn, he wasn't impressed by her. When she came out of the dressing room, she let the robe she was wearing fall "all of a sudden," he said, revealing her nude body beneath it. It was exactly what Harlow had done when he had photographed her in the early 1930s. He wondered if Marilyn had copied Harlow or had thought the action up herself. He implied that she was a bad copy of the original.[60]

One day she and Susan Strasberg came across a copy of the Kama Sutra on the bookshelves in the Strasbergs' apartment in New York. Marilyn exclaimed, "Oh! My goodness! This is the classic dirty book!" Then she added, "Only it's not dirty because it's oriental and they're very classy about this sort of thing, not puritanical, like Americans. It's got hundreds of drawings of all the positions of how to do it, make love, that is." Like children playing a game, Marilyn and Susan acted out the positions, fully clothed. Finding it difficult to twist into the more complicated ones, Marilyn joked, "The highest number I ever got to is sixty-nine." Susan asked her what she meant, and Marilyn replied, "Never mind." Susan was only seventeen years old. She commented, "Marilyn acted as if sex were natural, nothing to be ashamed of, as if it was actually fun."[61]

But there is an ugliness to some of Marilyn's behavior with nudity—a way in which it seems compulsive, not rebellious or free. There was the episode in Warrensburg, New York, when she went there in July 1949 with Adele Whiteley Fletcher of *Photoplay* and took off her clothes in front of a Warrensburg resident in the public bathroom. The first time she visited Robert Mitchum at his home in Hollywood she walked to the fireplace and lifted up her skirt to warm herself. Even the rebellious Mitchum was shocked, since she wasn't wearing underpants.[62] Such exhibitionism may have been meant to seduce or simply show off, but as she grew older its compulsive edge showed. Marilyn gave nude interviews to journalists, and in public she wore the black mink coat Joe had given her for Christmas in 1953 with nothing on underneath it. Holding it closed to cover herself, she would suddenly flash it open to give a glimpse of her body to friends and sometimes strangers. Dan St. Jacques, a New York policeman, often encountered her in 1955 at Rikers coffee shop, on Fifty-seventh Street, near Times Square, as she took a break on one of her nighttime walks in Midtown. One night she asked him to escort her home. Then she leaned over him, and he realized that she had nothing on under the coat.[63]

When she posed for photographers, she sometimes exposed her genitals. In the fall of 1955, photographer Eve Arnold arrived at Marilyn's apartment in New York to show her the proof sheets from photos that Arnold had taken of her. A reporter was waiting in the living room to interview Marilyn. Marilyn asked the reporter if she could comb her hair. The reporter said yes, and Marilyn began combing her pubic hair. The reporter fled.[64] Marilyn the prankster may have done this to play a crude joke. Yet it reflects the schisms in her persona. She was an abused child whose early sexualization led her to inappropriate behavior as an adult.

Reporter Julia Paul chastised Marilyn publicly for that behavior. "She is giving photographers whim wham poses. Asked to raise her skirt a little higher for cheesecake art, time and time again she has embarrassed the lensmen by forgetting that she doesn't have any lingerie on," Paul stated. "Marilyn is simply going too far."[65] These incidents of exposing herself were episodic. Reporters normally didn't mention them. Indeed, when Marilyn pulled her dress high in an interview with Jon Whitcomb for *Cosmopolitan* magazine, the paragraphs he wrote about her exposure of her genitals were excised from the published article. This behavior reflected only a part of a complex individual who was in the public eye, and interviewers and photographers tried to overlook it. Her innocent look offset it, as did the comic character she created who spoofed femininity and sex.

Once she married Arthur Miller, the news media became fixated on her relationship with his children and on her struggle to have children of her own. Her miscarriages became national news. Once again the nation was focusing on her body, this time in a new way. In an article in *Photoplay*, Dorothy Manning articulated an attitude toward Marilyn that influenced her: "The final step on this road to becoming known as a woman and an actress first and a sex symbol second, will be when she becomes a mother."[66] She had articulated her desire for a child in the unpublished ending to her autobiography. It was slowly becoming a fixation for her by 1956, when she married Miller.

Three photographs taken of Marilyn between her move to New York in December 1954 and her journey to Hollywood to do *Bus Stop* in the spring of 1956 illuminate her complexities. The first photograph is from the "ballerina sitting," taken in December 1954 by Milton Greene. Eve Arnold took the second photo in September 1955. Marilyn sat for the third photo in February 1956 for the British photographer Cecil Beaton. I call it the "Japanese photo" because she is posed against a wall hanging with a Japanese figure on it. All these photos tell dramatic stories. They relate to Marilyn's drive for elegance, her desire during her New York years to become a denizen of high culture. But steeped in irony and satire, they also parody that drive, showing Marilyn as a paradoxical being, not someone to be slotted into one category.

Most fashion photographers—including eminent photographers like Greene and Beaton—were gentle, unlike tough Hollywood producers and directors. Often involved with the feminized world of fashion, they weren't macho. Some were homosexual, but many weren't. Marilyn didn't have to remember lines for them or watch for key lights or marks on the floor. Producers weren't there enforcing time constraints. Marilyn had a lot of control in these situations. She was so good at posing that she often set the pace, and the photographer followed her lead. She influenced them in other ways. As Marilyn told W. J. Weatherby, "I've sometimes tried to charm critics, give the impression that I'm really attracted to them, and it works. With journalists and photographers generally. Experienced as they are, they're not beyond being wooed."[67]

Her energy as a model was huge. Richard Avedon, who photographed her for *Harper's Bazaar* in 1954 and on a number of occasions in later years, stated that "she gave more to the still camera than any actress—any woman—I've ever photographed." Sometimes their sittings would go on all night, Avedon said. He would be exhausted and Marilyn, with endless energy, would say, "Let's try one more time." Obsessed with looking perfect, she would pore over the contact photos, looking for an "honest picture."[68]

Greene took the ballerina photo in his spacious Lexington Avenue studio, which contained the many props he had collected over the years. In the photo, Marilyn perches on a chair in front of what appears to be a barre—the dancer's practice rod—holding what appears to be a long tutu (the classic ballerina dress) in front of her. Her breasts are popping out of a strapless top, her feet are bare, her fingernails and toenails are red, and her hair is tousled.

Her appearance burlesques the hauteur of the ballerina, a 1950s icon of sleek female elegance who had become the ideal of young girls throughout the nation, who flocked to ballet classes. Dating from the nineteenth-century Romantic movement, the ballerina still slicked back her hair, usually dark in color; stuffed her feet into toe shoes; had little body fat; held her body straight as a rod; and rarely smiled. In the photos Marilyn seems to humanize and mock the ballerina, looking like the sensual woman that a ballerina could never be. Looking sad in several of the ballerina photos, Marilyn draws on the classic clown, combining comedy with tragedy to resemble Charlie Chaplin's Little Tramp. The white garment that Marilyn holds in front of her wasn't actually a tutu; it was a petticoat removed from an Anne Klein dress that Amy Greene had given her. When the dress turned out to be too small for Marilyn, Milton Greene had her hold the petticoat over her body. Thus another interesting incongruity was added to the photo.[69]

The second photo I have chosen to show Marilyn as a trickster was taken in September 1955, by Eve Arnold. Marilyn is slithering through the tall grass and mud of a marsh, wearing a leopard-skin bathing suit.

One immediately thinks of Moses in the bulrushes, the abandoned child found by the pharaoh's daughter in the biblical tale. Arnold shot the photo on a deserted playground near her house on Long Island. She and Marilyn arrived there just at five o'clock, a time photographers call the "magic hour," when the light turns golden as the sun begins to set. In the photo Marilyn seems to be a primeval creature, an Eve for the ages, hardly a comic woman or a "fast-talking" blonde. Yet Arnold remembered that the idea of a "leopard in the bulrushes" appealed to Marilyn's tremendous sense of fun.

Arnold did, indeed, give Marilyn a different look, as she had requested when they met at the party for John Huston in New York in 1952. It's not the same as Marlene Dietrich without makeup on a deserted soundstage—Arnold's photo that initially impressed Marilyn—but it does show her in a new light. As Arnold described it, Marilyn was in control, setting the style and pace. Arnold followed, "just praying that my reflexes would be fast enough to accommodate to Marilyn's antics." The result was a brilliant photograph.[70]

The third photograph I have chosen to illustrate Marilyn as a trickster was taken in early February 1956 by British photographer Cecil Beaton in his suite at the Ambassador Hotel. Beaton had created the concept of glamour photography in the 1920s, and he had worked for *Vogue* and then for *Harper's Bazaar* ever since. The official photographer for the British royal family, he was a legend in his own time.

He took a number of photos of Marilyn, all focusing on her natural look. They are effective, although not extraordinary. One is different. What I call the "Japanese photo" shows her lying on a bed on which a Japanese wall hanging has been draped. That photo, among the best taken of her, has multiple meanings. *Vogue* editor Diana Vreeland interpreted the figure in the wall hanging as linking Marilyn to the geisha girl. "Marilyn Monroe!" Vreeland exclaimed. "She was a geisha. She was born to pleasure, spent her whole life giving it."[71]

The figure in the hanging may be a geisha. More important, it is an *onnagata*, the actor in Japanese Kabuki theater. In that theater, which dates to the sixteenth century, men play all the roles, female as well as male. Thousands of wall hangings of onnagata were made and sold during the nineteenth and twentieth centuries. This is one of them, identifiable by the costume and the hairstyle. First appearing in Kyoto, which was known for its aesthetic culture and its places of pleasure, the onnagata became models for feminine beauty in Japan: their manner-isms, hairstyles, and makeup set the mode. In turning themselves into women, the Kabuki players were perfectionists. Putting on Kabuki makeup took several hours; it was a ritual through which an onnagata trans-formed his inner self into a woman.[72] Marilyn also used the process of applying makeup to transform herself from an ordinary woman into Marilyn Monroe.

There's an optical illusion at play in the photo that also connects her to the Kabuki performer. When the photo is turned on its right side, her arm seems to extend from the body of the actor, so that the arm and hand of the onnagata seems to be placed on her breast, not her own arm and hand. Thus in the photo Marilyn and the Kabuki actor become one indi-vidual, both masculine and feminine, with the Japanese figure asserting dominance over Marilyn.

Beaton, who dressed like a gentleman and spoke with an upper-class accent, was homosexual. A trickster at heart, he often introduced homo-sexual themes into his photos. Sometimes his subjects knew what he was doing, and sometimes they didn't. In his photos men sometimes look like women, and women like men. Sometimes he put himself into his photos, often as a figure reflected in a mirror. The wall hanging with the onnagata on it was a perfect prop to use in photographing Marilyn, with her hidden bisexuality. Truman Capote and Beaton were close friends, and Capote was a gossip. Beaton knew a lot about Marilyn. The onna-gata figure represents Beaton himself.[73]

Beaton included the photo in his book *The Face of the World*, with a description of Marilyn alongside it. The description captures Marilyn's complexities. She is "narcissistic," "unkempt," and a "hypnotized nym-phomaniac," Beaton writes. She is also "as spectacular as the silvery shower of a Vesuvius fountain" and "an undulating basilisk." "Her per-formance is pure charade, a little girl's caricature of Mae West." She is quintessentially American. She conjures up "two straws in a single soda, juke boxes, running nylons, and drive-in movies for necking. She is a composite of Alice in Wonderland, Trilby, and a Minsky [burlesque] artist."[74]

The ballerina photo, the Eve photo, and the Japanese photo—these three portraits show Marilyn as a beautiful blonde, both aesthetic and dramatic; as a clown satirizing cultural icons; as a resonant and joyous symbol of the nation; and as a cross-gendered individual mocking her position as the world's heterosexual sex queen.

Part IV

New York, 1955–1960

I saw the amazing phenomenon of Hollywood being out-smarted by a girl whom it itself characterized as a dumb blonde.

Philippe Halsman

She was endlessly fascinating, full of original observations and there wasn't a conventional bone in her body.

Arthur Miller, quoted by James Kaplan in "Miller's Crossing," Vanity Fair, *November 1991*

Chapter 9

New York, 1955–1956

In December 1954 Marilyn left Hollywood for New York with Milton Greene, telling only close associates where she was going. News about her sudden departure and the mystery of her destination soon hit the front pages of newspapers nationwide. According to *Screen Life*, Holly-woodites couldn't believe that someone they considered to be a dumb blonde had been so bold, or that she would desert Hollywood for New York, especially after the dinner at Romanoff's in November 1954 honoring her for her brilliant success in *The Seven Year Itch*, with elite Hollywood attending the dinner.[1]

Marilyn's ability to steep her life in drama and mystery and stoke the public's interest had worked again. Using the pseudonym Zelda Zonk on her ticket, she and Milton took a night flight to New York. Amy Greene picked them up at LaGuardia Airport. No reporters were there: the deception had worked so far. They drove to the Greenes' converted barn in Weston, Connecticut. Learning that journalists and photographers were camping outside the house, Marilyn opted to hide out until the press went away. She stayed at the nearby home of Fleur Cowles, Milton's editor at *Look* and the founder of *Flair*.

Fleur had another houseguest: Bertha Spafford Vester, who ran a hospital for abandoned Arab children in Jerusalem. She was in the United States soliciting funds for her project. Marilyn was impressed by her, and Vester was enthralled by Marilyn, the great movie star, who wore a baggy pullover, wrinkled slacks, and sneakers and was happy and relaxed.

Vester was surprised that a movie star could be so approachable. Fleur Cowles spoke about Vester's courage in the midst of the gunfire of the Arab-Israeli conflict. Marilyn vowed, "I must do good for the world in some way. I promise you I will never waste my life again!" Writing about the episode long after it occurred, Cowles wondered if Marilyn ever remembered it in the years ahead.[2]

During her early years in New York, Marilyn would reshape her life. Studying at the Actors Studio with Lee Strasberg, dating Marlon Brando and Arthur Miller, and making many friends, she was in the mecca of her dreams. Sometimes she felt like a character out of the pages of *Flair* magazine. She formed her own production company with Milton Greene; and in the culmination of her dreams, she married Arthur Miller. She was, as Eli Wallach put it, reborn in New York.[3] It was a halcyon period for her, although she continued to take prescription drugs, a portent of problems that lay ahead.

By Christmas, Marilyn was back at the Greenes' home, after her stay with Fleur Cowles. She had sent all her California possessions, including the white piano, there: she expected to stay with them for some time. At Christmas the three of them went to New York for a party at Clifton Webb's apartment in honor of Noël Coward, who wanted to meet Marilyn.[4] Returning to the Greenes', she took long baths, walked in the woods, went antiquing with Amy, and gardened when the weather permitted. She played with the Greenes' son and met their friends at their weekend dinner parties. Prominent New York artists who had second homes in Connecticut near Weston attended these parties: Leonard Bernstein, symphony conductor and composer, and his wife, Felicia; Richard Rodgers, the composer of musicals like *Oklahoma!*, along with his wife, Dorothy; and Mike Todd, the flamboyant theater impresario.

Marilyn helped out in the kitchen. She peeled potatoes, snapped green beans, and washed dishes. She became friendly with Kitty Owens, the Greenes' housekeeper and cook, an African-American daughter of sharecroppers in the South. She told Kitty that she wanted three or four children of her own, but she intended to adopt children from a number of ethnic backgrounds. She was upset, she told Kitty, when she heard that Indian children were difficult to raise. Kitty told her to pay no attention to such nonsense.[5]

On Sundays, Norman Norell, the designer, and John Moore, his protégé, would visit. They sat in the Greenes' living room in front of a roaring fire, and Norell told stories about designing costumes for Broadway stars in the 1930s, an age of elegance on the stage. Norell looked like an aristocrat, but he was born Norman Levinson in Indiana, the son of the owner of a men's clothing store. He used earthy talk, with a swift slangy rhythm. Marilyn liked talking that way. He and Moore were homosexual, and Marilyn felt safe with them.

Norell and Moore dressed Marilyn during her New York years. They had her wear simple clothes for the day—plain skirts and blouses; suits, often beige or black, with white gloves and pearls; for her daytime clothes, they designed simple black silk sheath dresses with spaghetti straps and short jackets. Nighttime was for the glamour of satins and sequins. Norell was famous for his sequined mermaid evening dresses, which Marilyn wore. She also wore casual clothes from Jax and cotton dresses with full skirts from Anne Klein. When the bright, simple silk sheath dresses designed by Pucci came into vogue, she wore that style. Fashion critics accused her of dressing badly, but she created an elegant look with the help of major designers.[6]

During her stay with the Greenes, she read books from their library and from a list that Michael Chekhov had drawn up for her. She read biographies of turn-of-the-century actresses Ellen Terry and Mrs. Patrick Campbell, as well as of consorts of conquerors and kings, such as Marie Antoinette and Napoleon's Josephine. She read one of dancer Isadora Duncan—the epitome of the "new woman" of the early 1900s. When reading these books, she may have been thinking of Arthur Miller as her prince and Broadway as a kingdom, but Fleur Cowles had approached her about marrying Prince Rainier of Monaco, who was looking for a movie-star wife to boost the popularity of his principality as a tourist resort. Before Marilyn replied, Grace Kelly was chosen.[7]

During the Christmas holidays Milton photographed Marilyn in his Lexington Avenue studio in the "ballerina sitting." On January 7, he held a cocktail party–press conference in the New York townhouse of Frank Delaney, his lawyer, to announce the formation of Marilyn Monroe Productions (MMP). Delaney announced that Marilyn's contract with Fox was no longer valid because the studio had missed several deadlines. Fox didn't agree, and the studio lawyers contested the issue with

MMP's lawyers during the next year, negotiating over a new contract for Marilyn. For the press conference, Amy asked Norell to design a white spaghetti-strap dress, which Marilyn wore with dangling diamond ear-rings, white shoes, white stockings, and a white ermine coat. Amy liked an integrated color look, and Milton chose white. The reporters covering the event were sarcastic in writing about it. Diamonds and furs seemed appro-priate for the old Marilyn, not the new one, who was a company presi-dent. She was also an hour late, which annoyed them. And she didn't seem to know much about MMP.

When asked what movie role she wanted to play, she answered Grush-enka in *The Brothers Karamazov*. The reporters laughed. How could a dumb blonde appear in a work by Dostoyevsky? (They didn't know that Dore Schary had considered casting her in this role or that the descrip-tions of Grushenka in the novel fit Marilyn perfectly.) Even Billy Wilder was sarcastic, saying he would direct a sequel to any *Brothers Karam-azov* film she made and title it "Abbott and Costello Meet the Brothers Karamazov." (Comedy team Bud Abbott and Lou Costello had made *Abbott and Costello Meet Frankenstein*.) Hedda Hopper and Dorothy Kilgallen were especially vicious, but Louella Parsons and Earl Wilson were on Marilyn's side. Along with other journalists, they contended that she was more focused and mature since she had moved to New York.[8]

In mid-January, Marilyn went with Milton and Amy to Hollywood for a week to do final scenes on *The Seven Year Itch*. Fox executives tried to sign her for *How to Be Very, Very Popular*, but she eluded them. Gos-sip columns reported her as saying that she loved New York and didn't know how she'd ever stood Hollywood. Back in New York, she moved part-time into the Gladstone Hotel, near Milton's studio. With a lot of appointments in New York, she needed a place to stay there. She also needed a place to meet Arthur Miller. Biographers trace their reintroduc-tion to a cocktail party later that spring, but Amy Greene indicated that they reconnected soon after Marilyn moved to Connecticut. They began an affair. This earlier date suggests that they had had some contact in the years since their original meeting in January 1951, but all we know for certain is that on one occasion Marilyn flew to New York, expecting to meet Arthur in her hotel room, but he never showed up.

In fact, two plays he began writing soon after he left Marilyn in Holly-wood in 1951 indicate that he didn't see much future for them as a couple. The first play had the working title "The Third Play." It concerns a sexually free woman and her love affairs with two men. (He named the woman Lorraine—echoing the name Marilyn.) Both affairs end miserably for the men, as Lorraine leaves the first man, hurting him deeply, and the second man stays with his wife and is equally miserable. This play, existing only in unfinished drafts, eventually evolved into *After the Fall*.

The second play, *The Crucible*, set during the Salem witch trials of 1692, deals with broad issues of guilt, innocence, and individual and legal responsibility—in an analogy to the HUAC investigations. But its plot also concerns a farmer who has an affair with a young woman. When his wife learns about the affair, she is unforgiving. Then the young woman tries to seduce him a second time. When he refuses, she denounces him as a witch, and he is hanged. The resemblances to Arthur, his wife Mary, and Marilyn are uncanny in this play. Again, it appears that there is no future for his relationship with Marilyn, although he seemed to overlook the conclusions of these plays when he met Marilyn in New York and immediately fell for her again.[9]

Amy didn't approve of Marilyn and Arthur's affair because, she said, she didn't approve of married people having affairs. She wouldn't let them meet at her home. She may have known about Marilyn's affair with Milton, although she always denied that it had happened. She may also have not wanted to spend time with Arthur, nor he with her. So Marilyn used the Gladstone Hotel.[10]

Neither Amy nor Milton liked Arthur. Amy was a naturalized citizen from Cuba who adored the United States, and she didn't like it when Arthur criticized her new country. She thought he was stingy—which was true. The Miller family had been wealthy during the 1920s, had gone broke during the 1929 stock market crash, and had barely gotten by during the Depression. As a result, he feared poverty to the point that he was very frugal. Both Greenes found him egocentric, holding court, telling uninteresting stories. (Others found him a gifted storyteller.)[11] He lectured Marilyn, and Amy didn't like it when Marilyn repeated his ideas as though they were her own. Amy and Milton were leaders in creating high style for the elites, and Arthur wasn't interested in fashion. That was another point of contention. As might be expected, Arthur wasn't taken with the Greenes. Milton was too interested in making money, too "show business." Milton saw Arthur's dedication to high art as "dreariness" and "long hairiness." "I write and believe in 'gloomy things,' not 'pink tights,'" Arthur wrote to Marilyn, who was doing a balancing act among these powerful people.

Meanwhile, Amy took over the easily disorganized Marilyn. She encouraged her to go to movies and plays, because Arthur, who was living with his wife and children, saw her only two afternoons a week. She went to museums, and she went antiquing in the many antique shops on Second Avenue. Amy stated that Marilyn didn't like to be alone at night, and she often drove to Connecticut to be with them.[12]

In early February, Marilyn began studying the role of Hamlet's Ophelia with drama coach Constance Collier, who had been a renowned actress on the London Edwardian stage. Collier belonged to a lesbian circle that included Greta Garbo and Marlene Dietrich; she was herself involved with Katharine Hepburn. She held lunches that Marilyn attended, placing her again at the fringes of a lesbian group. Amy remembered that Marilyn, Milton, and she went to a dance at which Collier tried to seduce Marilyn. Collier, age seventy-seven, had a hawk nose and one of those masculine faces that Edwardians found attractive but that were considered witchlike in the 1950s. Marilyn was probably frightened of her. When Collier compared Marilyn's acting talent to a fluttering butterfly, she may have picked up Marilyn's unease in her presence. Marilyn's studies with her ended abruptly when Collier died at the end of April.[13]

Reporters saw Marilyn with Joe DiMaggio, especially at Toots Shor's. He helped her move into the Gladstone, and in late January she went to Boston with him for several days, to raise money for MMP and to visit his brother Dom, a former outfielder with the Boston Red Sox. She also went to New Jersey with Joe to visit Mary Short, Anne Karger's daughter, who had moved there to rejoin her husband, an army officer stationed there. Mary was an excellent golfer, and Joe liked playing the game with her. Did Marilyn use Joe as a screen to hide her affair with Arthur? It's possible.

To counter the negative publicity that Fox was generating about her in the newspapers, Marilyn appeared at several benefits. On March 20 she rode an elephant painted pink in a Madison Square Garden gala to benefit the Arthritis and Rheumatism Foundation. She dressed in an abbreviated showgirl outfit, with spangles and feathers. The production was themed around holidays: a troupe of comics dressed in green uniforms personified St. Patrick's Day; ice-skating star Sonja Henie rode on a Christmas float; and Marilyn represented the day after New Year's Eve, or "a pleasant hangover." The elephant behaved impeccably, bowing before celebrities and before the Short children, who were there with Joe DiMaggio. Milton had dreamed up the pink elephant stunt. Yet reporters pointed out that the showgirl outfit Marilyn wore seemed counterproductive to her attempt to redefine herself as a company president.[14]

The sense of accomplishment that Marilyn and Milton felt from the pink elephant event, which was a smash hit, was damaged by their weak performance with Amy on the popular Edward R. Murrow television show *Person to Person* a month later. The fifteen-minute episode with Murrow was filmed at the Greenes' home in Connecticut. Marilyn and Milton had arranged it as a treat for Amy, who was a huge fan of Murrow. When both of them became quiet on the set, Amy took over. She became a dynamo, feeding lines to Marilyn, whose voice went soft and who stumbled in replying to Murrow. Critics excoriated her, and producers offered Amy leading roles in several movies, which angered Marilyn. Darryl Zanuck probably had a hand in these offers, in an attempt to drive a wedge between Milton and Marilyn. Amy turned everything down, but damage was done to the relationship between Amy and the overly sensitive Marilyn.

On June 1, 1955, Joe and Marilyn attended the premiere of *The Seven Year Itch* at Loew's State Theater in Times Square. Playing a model who has sublet the top-floor apartment of Tom Ewell's brownstone, Marilyn is funny and fey, at the peak of her comic form. She is a fairy godmother who has come to earth to cure Ewell of his fear of women. Sexual double-entendres abound in the movie, as when Marilyn gets her toe caught in a drain spout when taking a bubble bath and a plumber has to get it out, while trying to avoid seeing her naked body under the bubbles. It's a wonder that Billy Wilder got the movie past the censors. In addition to the scene in which her skirt billows upward as she stands over the subway grate, in others Ewell's character fantasizes himself as the masterful men who have sex with beautiful women in famous film scenes, as in the scene with Burt Lancaster and Deborah Kerr passionately embracing on the beach in *From Here to Eternity*. In one fantasy sequence in *The Seven Year Itch* Marilyn spoofed Mae West, but Wilder cut the scene from the movie.

In the film Marilyn cures Ewell of his feeling of impotence by convincing him that women like gentle men—a sentiment she often voices in her movies. "No girl really likes a great big hunk in a fancy striped vest, strutting around like a tiger—giving you that 'I'm so handsome you can't resist me' look. It's the nervous, shy guy in the corner who is really exciting. He'll be tender and nice and sweet—and that's what's really exciting."

The *Seven Year Itch* premiere was the first public event with Marilyn in full Monroe sexy regalia that Joe attended, and it would be the last. After the premiere, which fell on her birthday, he hosted a party honoring her at Toots Shor's. During the evening they had an argument, and Sam Shaw took her home. After that dispute, Marilyn and Joe weren't seen together during the rest of her years in New York, until after she separated from Arthur in the fall of 1960. It appears that she told him firmly that she didn't want to be married to him.

Marilyn's rejection hurt, but Joe wasn't destroyed; rather, he started working on himself, trying to learn to curb his anger. He underwent therapy; he went to Sicily, to visit his ancestral home, taking Sam Shaw along. He accepted a job promoting the Monette Corporation, which supplied army PX stores throughout the world. He played baseball with the soldiers and talked about the sport with them, resuming the peripatetic life he liked. He dated women who looked like Marilyn and hoped to get her back. But he was now out of Marilyn's life for a considerable period of time.

Marilyn began studying at the Actors Studio in the spring of 1955. Elia Kazan, not yet estranged from Lee Strasberg, took her there. In contrast to the Actors' Lab in Hollywood, the Actors Studio had neither a formal school nor a theater associated with it. It was a workshop at which performing actors endeavored to improve their technique. Along with several other theater people, Elia Kazan had founded it in 1947, but when he became overcommitted directing plays and movies, which he preferred to teaching acting, he brought in Strasberg to head it. Kazan and Strasberg had known each other in the Group Theatre. Since then Strasberg had managed to stay afloat as an actor and teacher, although he hadn't had much success. The charisma he had within him would burst forth once he took over as head of the Actors Studio.[15]

Indeed, the Studio's prestige soared as Kazan sent actors to it and Strasberg, newly energized, recruited others. Before long, he had applicants for Studio membership undergo a rigorous audition, which he judged. When several well-known actors didn't make it, the Studio gained even more prestige. Members met twice a week to perform soliloquies or scenes from plays, after which Strasberg criticized their performances. Another group of actors, many of whom worked in Hollywood, were admitted as observers. They could attend the biweekly sessions, but they usually didn't perform. In addition, Strasberg held private classes, separate from the workshop. Marilyn never auditioned for the central group. She didn't trust her acting ability, and she feared failure. She attended the workshop as an observer and joined group classes with Strasberg, although she eventually did soliloquies and scenes from plays in both. She also had individual sessions with Strasberg, a departure from his usual procedure of teaching only in groups. Once she began studying with Strasberg, Marilyn fell under his spell.

Strasberg's approach to acting originated with Stanislavsky, as did that of Michael Chekhov and the teachers at the Actors' Lab in Hollywood. In contrast to both Chekhov and the Hollywood teachers, however, Strasberg emphasized affective memory. He devised exercises for students to enable them to access memories that related to the character they were playing. Believing that using recent experiences might be too traumatic, he established a dividing line of seven years; probing should go on only before those years.

To prevent the kind of breakdown that Michael Chekhov had experienced while using the affective memory technique, Strasberg had students with fragile egos, like Marilyn, undergo psychoanalysis, working with specialists on traumatic memories. By the spring of 1955 Marilyn was spending a lot of time probing into her past, either with Lee Strasberg or with her psychiatrist, Margaret Hohenberg, who had been Milton Greene's psychiatrist. Such probing into her past only increased her obsession with her childhood. Given the sexual abuse she had experienced, psychoanalysis may not have been the best technique for her. Many practitioners of Freudian psychoanalysis emphasized the Oedipus complex, defined as the inevitable sexual feelings that boys feel for their mothers and girls for their fathers. Thus many Freudians either downplayed the reality of sexual abuse or viewed it as not especially negative for the child.[16]

Strasberg was small, stern, controlled, and devoted to his work. His technique differed from Michael Chekhov's. Stressing willpower and discipline, he viewed acting as a controlled enterprise and affective memory as a systematic technique. But he was fascinated by neurosis, which he sought to channel into creativity. Raised in an orthodox Jewish family on New York's Lower East Side, with little formal education, his technique nonetheless resembled that of a Talmudic scholar, vested in the details of interpretation. His critics charged that he "quibbled over interpretations." His supporters, such as Eli Wallach, called him "a superb diagnostician who can detect your weaknesses."[17]

Like most acting teachers, he devised exercises for relaxation and concentration, as well as improvisations to promote spontaneity. Marilyn was given an exercise in which she had to be a cat, and she spent a week observing a cat before imitating it on the stage. She was superb, according to Studio observers. (That's not surprising, given the many descriptions of her movements as catlike.) In filming later Hollywood movies, she perplexed other actors by vigorously shaking her hands before beginning a scene. That was a Strasberg exercise to promote relaxation.

Strasberg was a guru to many Broadway actors, but others found him domineering. Don Murray, Marilyn's costar in *Bus Stop*, left the Studio because he didn't like Strasberg's approach; Murray found his inspiration in interacting with other actors. Farley Granger preferred a text-based approach, in which an interpretation of the text of a play or a screenplay provides inspiration. Strasberg could be a vicious critic, and some actors—Anthony Quinn and Jack Palance, for example—left the Studio because they found him too harsh. Both transferred to Michael Chekhov's acting classes in Hollywood. James Dean attended the Actors Studio only once; Strasberg's grilling incensed him. Marlon Brando called Strasberg ambitious and untalented and stated that he had learned nothing from Strasberg and had gone to the Studio only to meet women, although Strasberg continued to claim him as a student. Elia Kazan, breaking with Strasberg, called Marilyn a "perfect victim/devotee" for Strasberg. Others said that he used Marilyn to bring money and fame to the Studio, or to get back at Twentieth Century–Fox executives who had hired him for a time in the 1940s to direct screen tests and then had let him go.[18]

African-American actor Louis Gossett Jr., who studied at the Studio along with Marilyn, didn't like Strasberg's Method approach, although he rated Marilyn the most gifted actor in his group. He was deeply impressed when she asked him to do a love scene with her from *The Rose Tattoo*. "Do you realize that you would be crossing racial barriers and entering forbidden territory?" he asked her. She replied that such barriers meant nothing to her. In the end they didn't do the scene, but he never forgot her generosity.[19]

After his initial interview with Marilyn, Strasberg decided she had great talent, although he realized her lack of self-confidence. He was gentle with her. He taught her privately at first, until she had the nerve to enter his group classes and then the biweekly sessions of the entire membership. Strasberg realized that Marilyn's sweetness masked a deep rage, and he worked with her to bring it to the surface in order to deal with it. Her rage was so great that she used scatological language with him to express it. (Susan Strasberg heard them yelling at each other in private sessions.) Marilyn soon came to idolize Strasberg as a guru and father figure. She offered herself sexually to him, but he refused her, realizing that a sexual relationship might contaminate their work.[20]

By this point Marilyn had given up trying to find her father, but she still felt bitter over his rejection. In a fantasy game played one night at a party, Marilyn said she wanted to disguise herself, meet her father, and seduce him. It was a powerful fantasy of revenge and punishment, one that may have contributed to the sadomasochist elements in her relationships with men, as she alternately played the victim and the persecutor. Elia Kazan had warned her years earlier about involvements with powerful men. But Kazan hadn't recognized that Marilyn might herself play the sadist, not simply the masochist. That's what she did in her marriages to Arthur Miller and Joe DiMaggio.

The Studio was always in debt, and salaries were often in arrears. Marilyn donated money to the Studio; paid Paula Strasberg, Lee's wife and a former actress, a huge sum to coach her; and gave Lee ten thousand dollars for a trip to Japan to study Kabuki and Noh theater. She gave Paula the pearls the emperor of Japan had given her when she had visited Japan with Joe in 1954. She gave Susan an expensive Chagall print and John a Thunderbird car. Although Marilyn was generous to many people throughout her life, the generosity she displayed toward the Strasbergs indicates how much she felt they'd improved her skills.

From the time she was a child, giving her possessions to other children at the orphanage, her generosity was boundless—from giving money to crew members on her films to pay doctors' bills, to gifts to friends. She gave Natasha Lytess a fur coat, an automobile, and a down-payment on a house; Patricia Newcomb, her publicity agent during the last two years of her life, received a fur coat, an automobile, and the emerald earrings that Sinatra had given Marilyn. She was so generous that her assistants, such as Whitey Snyder, didn't praise items she possessed for fear the items would arrive at their houses the next day. After a shopping spree, she often gave many of the clothes she had bought to others along with her.

Marilyn captivated everyone she met in New York. Her spirits were high and her charm irresistible. Her presence created a stir in the New York arts scene. Actress Elaine Dundy remembered Marilyn's impact at the tea that Tennessee Williams held for his mother at the St. Regis Hotel in March 1955, after the opening of *Cat on a Hot Tin Roof*. Everyone important in the arts scene was there. Marilyn was late. When she made her entrance, a buzz rippled through the crowd, and everyone stopped what they were doing, "freeze-framed with their drinks, hors d'oeuvres, or cigarettes halfway to their mouths." A path cleared, and Marilyn walked through. She wore a simple black silk slip dress with thin shoulder straps and nothing on underneath it. (It was a Norell-Moore design that she owned in multiple copies and often wore.) Her skin was a luminous alabaster with pearly blue and rose tints. Dundy had never seen such skin tones outside of paintings by Old Masters. Marilyn was more beautiful in the flesh than on film.[21]

Marilyn had many friends in New York; the portrayal of her as a loner with few friends is inaccurate. She had met Tennessee Williams and Truman Capote when they were in Hollywood writing screenplays, and she saw Capote in New York that spring. He liked to make friends with iconic women: Elizabeth Taylor and Jackie Kennedy were among his friends. He gave them advice. Homosexual in orientation, he didn't try to seduce them. Marilyn and Truman spoke a private language, filled with sexual gossip. He was witty, campy, and bawdy. He based Holly Golightly in *Breakfast at Tiffany's* partly on Marilyn. Monroe and Capote went dancing at the Copacabana. Standing five feet eight inches tall in heels, she towered above him, as he was only five feet three inches in height. She danced with him barefoot. Marilyn was also seen in nightclubs with Jack Cole and composer Harold Arlen.[22]

She became close to actors at the Actors Studio, and she went with them to neighborhood bars and cafes after class. Eli Wallach became like a brother; she called him Teacake, since he was playing on Broadway in *The Teahouse of the August Moon*. She was also friends with his wife, actress Anne Jackson. She babysat their children, and she sometimes went dancing with Wallach. He was sexually attracted to her, but he hid his feelings, because he didn't want to drive her away. After Broadway shows were over for the night, actors would gather at Downey's on Broadway to drink and talk, and Marilyn sometimes went with them. The walls of Downey's were lined with photos of Broadway actors, and Marilyn wanted her photo to be among them. In order to qualify, though, she needed to appear in a Broadway play. One night Wallach snuck her on stage as a Japanese woman in a crowd scene in *Teahouse*. That participation was considered sufficient. Her photo soon hung on the wall at Downey's.[23]

Marilyn saw Marlon Brando. They went to dinner and sometimes wound up in bed. According to Susan Strasberg, Marilyn had a small apartment on the East Side that she kept a secret. She practiced her lines, read scripts and books, and entertained secret friends there. One of them was Warren Fisher, a publicist with the Arthur Jacobs agency, who she often met for drinks on Fridays at the St. Regis Hotel. She also became friendly with Leonard Lyons, an influential New York columnist who took Sidney Skolsky's place in her life. He introduced her to novelists and dramatists, all the right people.[24]

When she lived at the Gladstone, she became friends with other celebrities who lived there, including novelist Carson McCullers, who chronicled the dark Gothic behaviors in the South. Marilyn was also friendly with Gloria Vanderbilt, who was living there while divorcing symphony conductor Leopold Stokowski. She and Gloria had much in common: Hollywood, modeling and acting, and a previous relationship with Pat DiCicco. Once Gloria left the Gladstone, she married film director Sidney Lumet. They lived in an upscale East Side apartment and threw parties Marilyn attended. To remain incognito, she wore slacks, a baggy sweater, and no makeup when she went out. She told Gloria that Joe DiMaggio frightened her. She may have felt close to Gloria, who had been physically abused by Pat DiCicco after she married him. Joe had similarly abused Marilyn.[25]

As always, Sam Shaw introduced her to new people. He took her to Brooklyn to meet Norman and Hedda Rosten, who had been friends of Arthur Miller and his first wife, Mary, ever since they all attended the University of Michigan. Marilyn was attracted by the Rostens' nurturing natures and their casual lifestyle. She attended the poetry readings they held in their Brooklyn Heights apartment and went with them to neighborhood restaurants and movie theaters. The similarity in the names Norma and Norman intrigued her.[26] She called Norman Rosten, Sam Shaw, and Eli Wallach her brothers. She gave them nicknames: Norman was Claude, for the actor Claude Raines, whom she thought he resembled; Sam Shaw was Sam Spade, a popular detective in crime stories; and Eli Wallach was Teacake.

Marilyn and Norman bonded over their love of poetry. She read and wrote poetry, and she memorized verses from poets she liked. She especially liked poems about the promise and perils of love, as well as elegies about the omnipresence of death: Eros and Thanatos, love and death, were two sides of the same coin to her, as they often are in European literature. Norman wrote: "She understood, with the instinct of a poet, that [poetry leads] directly to the heart of experience. She knew the interior floating world of the poem with its secrets, phantoms, and surprises. And somewhere within her she sensed a primary truth: that poetry is allied with death. Its intoxication and joy are the other face of elegy. Love and death, opposite and one, are its boundary—and were hers."[27]

A poem by William Butler Yeats that she read at one of the Rostens' gatherings was especially meaningful to her: it articulated how dangerous love could be. Like the lines from the *Rubaiyat of Omar Khayyám* that she had recited to Jane Russell during the filming of *Gentlemen Prefer Blondes*, it advised an individual in love to stay independent. According to Rosten, Marilyn was always afraid of love. The Yeats poem is titled "Never Give All the Heart."

Never give all the heart, for love
Will hardly seem worth thinking of
To passionate women if it seem
Certain, and they never dream
That it fades out from kiss to kiss;
For everything that's lovely is
But a brief, dreamy, kind delight.
O never give the heart outright,
For they, for all smooth lips can say,
Have given their hearts up to the play.
And who could play it well enough
If deaf and dumb and blind with love?
He that made this knows all the cost,
For he gave all his heart and lost.

Rosten found the poetry Marilyn wrote dark and menacing, like many of her favorite poems by others. In her poems she was being abandoned. She was a doll in a carriage pushed by a stranger. She was frightened by life and attracted to death. Something so terrible was going to happen that it was better to die and avoid it. She wrote a poem about her own up-and-down nature that expressed her dual self, happy and sad, rational and irrational, strong and weak, calling herself strong as a cobweb, although more often slanting downward, heavy with the cold frosts, cheated by life.[28]

Friends in Hollywood complained that she didn't contact them; Jane Russell, for one, was hurt that Marilyn didn't keep in touch. That inattention gave rise to the myth that she dropped people with ease and made new friends when it suited her. But she was overwhelmed by the time needed to keep up with the many people she knew. Dropping some was a matter of busyness, not meanness, on her part. The only person she dropped without a word was Natasha Lytess. That's understandable. She didn't want rumors of lesbianism to reappear.

Once in New York, Marilyn again established a number of power centers in her life. There were the Greenes, who were supporting her financially until she signed a new contract with Fox. The salary she had received from Twentieth Century–Fox had never been enough for her to save much money. The cost of maintaining her was high: she needed to look glamorous so that Fox executives wouldn't realize that her finances were shaky and hold out longer. Arthur Miller was another power center for her, although they were keeping their relationship secret. She also saw Marlon Brando and Henry Rosenfeld, the clothing magnate she'd met in New York on the *Love Happy* tour in 1948. He sometimes gave her money. Patricia Rosten, Hedda and Sam's daughter, remembered Marilyn and her mother coming back from Rosenfeld's factory carrying piles of clothing.[29]

The Strasbergs and their children, Susan and John, constituted a third power center in Marilyn's life in New York. Marilyn became so dependent on Lee and Paula that Susan and John felt usurped by her. She was often at their apartment. Lee was obsessed with his work, but Paula was a quintessential Jewish mother who provided food and counseling to actors down on their luck. Sunday brunch at the Strasbergs' was de rigueur for Broadway actors, as was their New Year's Eve party, to which everyone from famous artists to struggling actors was invited. Paula had been a member of the Group Theatre and a Broadway actress when she was called before the House Un-American Activities Committee. She named names; as a result, Broadway producers wouldn't hire her. She acted out her unhappiness through her body, becoming very overweight. To hide her weight, she wore expensive black silk muumuus, with gold chains around her neck, and sometime a peaked black hat on her head to protect her skin from the sun. Many actors adored her. Her defenders thought she looked dramatic; her detractors found her ridiculous. Marilyn coined the nickname Black Bart for her, taking it from a character that actor Basil Rathbone, tall and easily menacing-looking, had played.[30]

Paula was devoted to Lee, while he was cool toward her, had affairs, and threw rages. Dramatic and emotional, she sometimes threatened suicide. When the eighteen-year-old Susan became a Broadway star with her performance as Anne Frank in *The Diary of Anne Frank* in 1956, Paula commandeered Susan's salary to support the family and to fund Lee's obsession with buying books on the theater. As Lee's fame spread and he became in demand, Paula took over classes of his and cut back on her domestic activities. Like Lee, she became close to Marilyn, and she praised her to the skies for her acting, her beauty, her sweetness—whatever she could think of.

Marilyn now had the Strasbergs, Greenes, Shaws, and Rostens—in addition to Arthur—to lean on. Most received calls in the middle of the night. A chronic insomniac, Marilyn often said that her telephone was her best friend. She tried to control her pill intake, and sometimes she could; but she was hooked. Amy Greene said that when Marilyn lived with them, she would give Amy the sleeping pills and ask her to dole them out to her, but she would invariably demand them back. Susan Strasberg said that after Marilyn became close to her parents, she sometimes took a taxi to their apartment in the middle of the night and Lee would hold her and rock her gently until she went to sleep and then carry her into John's bedroom and put her into his bed. When Marilyn was there, John slept on the living room couch. John remembered a night when he was sixteen when Marilyn crept into the living room where he was sleeping and started to stroke him. In a haze of drugs, she seemed unconscious of what she was doing. He was both terrified and appalled at what seemed like a sexual approach, but he managed to get her back to her bed before anything happened.[31]

In June Marilyn moved from the Gladstone Hotel to a penthouse suite at the Waldorf Astoria, which Norman sublet at a bargain price from a friend. She remained there through the fall, when she moved to an apartment on Sutton Place that Milton owned. While at the Waldorf, she scrawled diary fragments on the hotel's stationery—thoughts and memories that, in Ralph Roberts's words, "seemed to be constantly swirling like sea-drift and wind-drift inside her head." She wrote of her fear that any praise for her acting was meant for someone else. She had darker fantasies. One was that Lee was a surgeon who was going to cut her open. She didn't mind since Dr. Margaret Hohenberg, her psychiatrist, had diagnosed the case and given her an anesthetic. The operation was to cure her of the disease from which she suffered—"whatever the hell it is." When Lee made the incision, however, he found nothing but sawdust inside—like the stuffing of a Raggedy Ann doll.[32]

She wrote in a fragment that she had to remember that her body was her own; no one else possessed it. Then she had a dream of a repulsive man who was crowding her in an elevator and panicking her. Does that mean I'm attached to him, she wondered? She wrote that she was afraid of Peter. She probably meant Peter Leonardi, who had been her hairdresser the previous year. She had become close to him, but he sued her because, he said, she had promised to buy him a beauty salon and had reneged. The fear, she thought, reflected her belief that he was a homosexual who wanted to become a woman and take her over. Why did she always feel subhuman, she asked? The statement repeats the one in *My Story* in which she connected her fear of being subhuman to her fear that she was lesbian. Being engulfed by someone, taken over by them—her fears had a paranoid edge. She told Ralph Roberts about a recurrent dream she had of drowning in quicksand, slowly being sucked down into its morass. And she still dreamed about monsters. On the surface Marilyn seemed joyful, but her deep fears were still there.[33]

During the summer of 1955 she spent weekends with the Strasbergs in their cottage on Fire Island, a barrier island off Long Island where New York artists and writers vacationed. As always, fans approached Marilyn, creating attention that she both welcomed and feared. "They can get scary, almost like they want to take home a part of you as a souvenir," Marilyn said to Susan Strasberg. When Susan, who shared a bedroom with Marilyn on Fire Island, was in Hollywood filming the movie *Picnic*, actress Eileen Atkins shared the room with Marilyn. Lee hoped that Atkins's self-confidence might rub off on Marilyn. Indeed, the two actresses walked the beach together and stayed up late talking.[34]

One weekend Marilyn drew two portraits. One was of a sad child in a raggedy dress, with a black face. The second was of a sexy woman with a catlike face. Who was the girl with the black face? "Maybe it's a self-portrait." Marilyn said. Who was the woman with the cat face? Marilyn said this figure illustrated her motto: "Life is wonderful, so what the hell!"[35] That cynical attitude reflected Marilyn's fear of going insane, leading her to both contemplate suicide and do whatever she wanted before the black cloud of irrationality might descend on her.

In August Marilyn spent a day in Bement, Illinois. One of the famed debates between Abraham Lincoln and Stephen A. Douglas had been held in Bement, and the town put on a Land of Lincoln festival every August. Tom Chaltham of Bement had studied with Marilyn at the Actors Studio, and Carlton Smith, director of the National Arts Foundation, lived there: they persuaded her to attend the festival because of her love for Lincoln.[36] Smith also invited her to join a delegation to Russia to promote intercultural exchange under the auspices of the foundation. She applied for a visa to travel to the Soviet Union, but she never went. The visa application, in addition to her connection to Arthur Miller, initiated FBI surveillance of her that would continue for the rest of her life.

In Bement she gave a short speech on Lincoln and judged a beard-growing contest among men who hadn't shaved for six months. Eve Arnold went along to photograph her. Arnold was concerned about her, since she was suffering from a kidney infection. But Marilyn was so conditioned by years of doing "cheesecake" photos that she reacted automatically when a camera appeared. She thrust her breasts forward, swiveled her bottom, and assumed her smile. Marilyn Monroe was "on."[37]

In late August 1955 Michael Chekhov died. She went to Hollywood for his funeral, held in a tiny Russian Orthodox chapel. In September Eve Arnold did her first major shoot of Marilyn in a deserted playground near her home on Long Island, as Marilyn posed on the playground equipment, reading James Joyce's *Ulysses* in one of the photos and slithering through tall reeds in a muddy marsh in another, wearing a leopard-skin bathing suit and looking like a newly created Eve. Arnold's photos were an example of the drama that could emerge when Marilyn was photographed by a brilliant photographer.

In October Marilyn asked Elia Kazan to cast her in the title role in Tennessee Williams's *Baby Doll*, which Kazan was to direct. He rejected her as too old (she was twenty-nine); but that was only part of his reason. He didn't want to deal with her neuroses; he never directed her. He stated in his autobiography that he considered her to be a good comedienne, but not much more. Kazan was as tough as the other Hollywood directors.[38] That same month, *Will Success Spoil Rock Hunter?* opened on Broadway. It was a spoof on Marilyn, starring Jayne Mansfield. Despite her deep sensitivity, Marilyn didn't seem to mind it. Its author, George Axelrod, had written both the play on which *The Seven Year Itch* was based and the screenplay for the Hollywood version. He also wrote the screenplay for William Inge's *Bus Stop*. The film version of *Bus Stop* would be one of Marilyn's greatest successes.

From the spring through the fall of 1955, Marilyn spent time with Arthur in her penthouse suite in the Waldorf Towers, high above the noise and confusion of the city. They avoided being seen in public

together, although they went bicycle riding in Brooklyn, away from reporters. Arthur had always loved bicycling for the sense of freedom it
gave, and Marilyn had similar feelings. It became a favorite activity of
theirs.

Having put off their love for four years, it was infused with intensity.
"She was a whirling light to me then, all paradox and enticing mystery,
street-tough one moment, then lifted by a lyrical and poetic sensitivity
that few retain past early adolescence." And "she was endlessly fascinating, without a conventional bone in her body." Arthur was being swept
away by a current he couldn't control. Before she moved to New York, he
was often dour, which was reflected in his stern Abraham Lincoln look,
partly a product of his unhappiness in his marriage. But Marilyn liked
the way he looked—like a perfect father figure.

Just as Lincoln had freed the slaves, Marilyn decided, Arthur could
free her from Hollywood and from Marilyn Monroe, her creation that
had become an albatross. And Marilyn decided that because of his genius, Arthur was an ideal candidate for fatherhood. His genes would
counteract whatever was defective in hers. Feeling embattled, guilty about
breaking up his marriage, they indulged the fantasy that they would create
a perfect marriage, a model for the ages.[39]

In a diary fragment, Marilyn wrote about Arthur: "He is the only
person that I have ever known that I could love not only as a man to
which I am attracted to practically out of my senses about—but he is the
only other human being that I trust as much as myself." In plainer language, she told Susan Strasberg, "He's so gorgeous. I love to cuddle with
him. And he's so brilliant." Fleur Cowles answered attacks on him as
unattractive: "Many sophisticated New York women coveted him. That
crag of a man had a strange appeal to women."[40]

During that summer Arthur spent time with the members of a juvenile gang in Brooklyn, collecting background for a play he was writing
about such gangs. He spent evenings with Marilyn in her penthouse. Yet
he wondered if Marilyn and the gang members were that different. The
gang members were trying to gain respect from a world that scorned
them; Marilyn was trying to win a similar respect in Hollywood.

Perhaps Arthur felt some connection to Marilyn because of Hollywood's low estimation of her dramatic abilities. His reputation as a play-

wright was slipping. The critics had panned *The Crucible* as well as his most recent works, an adaptation of Ibsen's *An Enemy of the People* and his one-act version of *A View from the Bridge*. *The Crucible* had especially angered the anticommunist forces because it implicitly attacked the House Un-American Activities Committee, one of its power centers, for its practice of requiring individuals to name names of Communists they knew before they would have any hope of being let off—exactly the same practice that had been used at the witch trials. The anticommunist forces, which had so far left Miller alone, were now considering investigating him. They stopped his funding from New York City for his play on New York gangs, and he never finished it.

Marilyn's divorce from Joe DiMaggio was granted in October, and Arthur separated from his wife that month. Marilyn attended the opening of *A View from the Bridge*, and she met his mother, Augusta (Gussie), there. She and Arthur seemed more comfortable being linked together publicly. Meanwhile, Frank Delaney was negotiating a new Fox contract for her that would recognize MMP and guarantee her a measure of creative input into her films. Such production companies weren't unusual. What was unique about Marilyn's was that she insisted her name be used in its title, even though the IRS might suspect that the corporation was a front for her to avoid taxes and investigate her tax returns. (In fact, that did happen.) But Marilyn was adamant. She wanted everyone to realize that she had created a company, that she wasn't a "dumb blonde." She was the president of the company, with fifty-one shares—she insisted on that—and Milton had forty-nine.

Reporters who interviewed her in the spring of 1955 were impressed by her knowledge of incorporation, investments, and contracts. She had done her homework in the months since she had seemed like a dunce in the January press conference at the Delaney apartment. Earl Wilson found her serene, confident, and highly professional when he interviewed her in April. She engaged in a detailed discussion of business matters with him. Then he asked to take a photo of her. She sighed, took off her glasses, and became the sexy Marilyn.[41]

Even during these halcyon days of MMP, Marilyn and Milton didn't always agree. NBC offered them three million dollars to do six dramas of their choosing; Marilyn was to star in two. Milton turned the offer down on the grounds that television wasn't right for her. Marilyn was furious—until Milton persuaded Laurence Olivier to play opposite her in *The Sleeping Prince*, an adaptation of a play in which Olivier had starred along with his wife, Vivien Leigh. The film version was renamed *The Prince and the Showgirl*. Marilyn was thrilled; Olivier was the world's greatest actor. Acting opposite him would surely demonstrate her ability to do drama. She acceded to his demand that he direct the film as well as star in it. Unfortunately, she didn't listen to Lee Strasberg's qualms about him; Olivier was opposed to the Method approach. That disagreement would cause many problems during filming.

The negotiations with Fox weren't easy, since the studio contended that Marilyn was bound by the seven-year contract she had signed in 1951, which, they maintained, would apply until 1958. They challenged the argument that it had been voided by their failure to observe some of its clauses, and they fought over every clause in the new contract. Milton's money wasn't endless, and Marilyn had no money of her own, aside from the salary from Fox, which she was returning to the studio. If she cashed any of the Fox checks, she would be implicitly giving in to them. Then in June *The Seven Year Itch* opened. It was a smash hit, and money poured into the studio coffers. It appeared that Marilyn was going to win her struggle. The negotiations, however, continued for the next six months. Zanuck was unwilling to capitulate until Spyros Skouras and the Fox board of directors in New York told him he had to. With the success of *The Seven Year Itch*, Marilyn had become very valuable financially to Fox. She had to be given what she wanted.

The contract was signed on the last day of the year, to take advantage of tax laws. Marilyn won almost completely. She had achieved legitimacy for MMP, as well as approval over director and cameraman: she was to give the studio a list of those she approved, from which the studio would make the final choice. She would keep stipends paid to her for work outside Twentieth Century–Fox; her salary would be $100,000 per picture; and she was to make one film for Fox for every film she made for her production company during the seven years of the contract, up to four films. She didn't receive script approval, but it didn't seem that important at the time. Its absence would later return to haunt her.

Milton also landed her the starring role in *Bus Stop*, to be produced under MMP, working with Fox. It had been a hit on Broadway, with Kim

Stanley in the star role of Cherie, the tawdry dance hall singer pursued by Bo, an unsophisticated cowboy. It was a coup for Marilyn to be chosen over Stanley for the movie part. But there was a problem with the conception of MMP, which would later surface. Milton thought of it as his corporation, with Marilyn his major star. He wanted other performers, such as Marlon Brando, to join them. Marilyn liked that idea, as long as she remained in control. And worried about money, Milton wanted her to continue in her blonde-showgirl roles, which were guaranteed moneymakers. On the other hand, Joshua Greene told me that Milton had secured an option on *The Brothers Karamazov*, and he planned to make it Marilyn's next film.[42]

By the beginning of 1956 Marilyn's spirits were soaring. She had done well in the first scene she presented in her class at the Actors Studio in the fall of 1955, playing the prostitute Lorna Moone, in *Golden Boy*, who is transformed when she falls in love. She had won her fight with Fox, and MMP was functioning. Milton had persuaded Fox to cast her in *Bus Stop*, and Laurence Olivier had signed to do *The Prince and the Showgirl*. Her romance with Arthur seemed solid.

Laurence Olivier traveled to New York in January for the final negotiations for *The Prince and the Showgirl*. When he met the effervescent, sexy Marilyn, he fell in love with her on the spot. He wrote in his autobiography, "She was so adorable, so witty, such incredible fun."[43] He was considering leaving his wife, actress Vivien Leigh, who suffered from mood swings so severe that she was given electroshock therapy. Charmed by Marilyn, Olivier briefly thought she might be a replacement for Vivien.

He didn't realize how powerful Marilyn could be, even though she easily upstaged him at a large press conference at the Plaza Hotel to announce the casting of *The Prince and the Showgirl*. Olivier took center stage, answering all the questions, even those addressed to Marilyn. She became tired of his manner, and she seized control in typical Marilyn fashion. She'd foreseen what he might do, and so she'd loosened a strap on her dress so that she could easily pop it. As her strap fell off her dress, all eyes were riveted on her. She borrowed a safety pin from a woman journalist, pinned the strap to her dress, and the conference went on. But she'd stolen the show. Newspaper headlines the next day featured her rather than Olivier.

In February she posed for Cecil Beaton. That month she also

performed the opening scene in Eugene O'Neill's *Anna Christie* for the membership of the Actors Studio. It must have been difficult for her to play the role. Anna's mother is dead, her father has abandoned her, an older brother has raped her, and she's turned to prostitution. "Men, I hate 'em," Anna says, "all of 'em! It was men on the farm ordering me and beating me—and giving me the wrong start."[44] In playing Anna Christie Marilyn captured the lyricism, earthy sexiness, and sadness of the character, without resorting to her Hollywood mannerisms—the sexy walk, the breathy voice. After her performance, the audience clapped. This recognition was unheard of in the Studio, which was housed in a former Greek Orthodox Church called "the temple" by studio participants, who regarded performances to be like religious rites. They never clapped. But Marilyn overwhelmed them. When she first appeared at the Studio, acclaimed actress Kim Stanley confessed, a lot of the students didn't think she belonged there. "But then she was amazing in *Anna Christie*. So some of us went privately to her and apologized—even if some of us only had the [negative] attitude privately and never put her down in talking to others. She won us all—not just the Studio, but what she went out to win: the intelligentsia, all those people, she won everybody." Marilyn thought she had failed in the performance, but that resulted from her curse, her lack of self-confidence.

Meanwhile, Darryl Zanuck had resigned as production head of Twentieth Century–Fox. He launched his own production company and moved to Europe, where he made a series of movies, mostly art films, under a special contract with Fox. Letters in the Spyros Skouras Papers suggest that he had never wanted to make only entertainment films, but Skouras had insisted on it. Buddy Adler was hired as Fox production head, although Zanuck retained a lot of Fox stock. But he no longer had any direct control over Marilyn.[45]

Magazines and newspapers now praised Marilyn for what she had done. *Look* magazine delivered an extraordinary encomium. "History was made by Marilyn Monroe in the year 1956," *Look* stated. This history will stand as "an example of the individual versus the herd in years to come." It is "the victory of one woman's honest intent to improve and progress against all odds. And with all possible odds against her, she made it. Imitations will come and go," but Marilyn Monroe, the writer concluded, "stands secure as an actress and an example of success in the eyes of the nation and the world."[46]

Bus Stop began production in Hollywood at the end of March. Joshua Logan, a renowned Broadway director, was to direct it. He was aware that difficulties might lie ahead in dealing with Marilyn, but Lee Strasberg had told him that, along with Marlon Brando, she was the most gifted actor in the United States. He accepted the assignment. He met her at a dinner at the Greenes' home in Connecticut, and she deeply impressed him. It was the first time he realized that intelligence might have nothing to do with education. He was enchanted by her wit and her quicksilver laugh. "Perhaps someday," she said, "someone would let me play Grushenka in *The Brothers Karamazov*."[47]

Once on the set of *Bus Stop*, they became confederates: they vetoed the elegant costumes Fox designers had designed and found tatty saloon-girl getups in the Fox wardrobe department, since Cherie was a hillbilly singer without much of a voice who sang in saloons. Milton decided that her makeup should be white, since Cherie stayed up all night and slept all day, but Whitey Snyder put a hint of color in it, so that she wouldn't look like a clown. The studio executives didn't like it, but Milton and Logan prevailed.

She engaged in difficult, but not extreme, behavior. She was sometimes late, irritating the other actors, and she spent a week in the hospital with bronchitis, though it may have been a simple case of exhaustion. From May 1 for the next six weeks Arthur was in Reno getting a divorce, and he secretly spent weekends at the Chateau Marmont in Hollywood with Marilyn. After a weekend with Arthur, she was worn out and depressed by his absence.[48] At one point she slipped into her trance behavior in her dressing room and Logan had to drag her out of it. As president of MMP, she was technically in charge of filming, and she sometimes asserted herself in blocking scenes and deciding on camera angles. Logan didn't mind; he found, as others did, that she had become an expert on filmmaking during her years in Hollywood. Before she made *Bus Stop*, she had done twenty-four films.

But she had a lot to remember, especially given her new Method technique. She had to "take a minute" to get into character. As an actress she had a feverish concentration, and if the action was stopped before she was ready she had difficulty getting back into character. So Logan ran the camera continuously, never cutting in the middle of a scene. If she faltered he would have someone off camera give her a cue. Thus he shot a lot of film that couldn't be used. He later edited what he had into a final cut. He suspected that she was inherently a stage actress, no matter how much she loved the camera. One day, Logan remembered, she danced around like a child, overwhelmed with glee when she found out she was going to have "as big a head closeup as Garbo had had."[49]

Don Murray, playing opposite Marilyn, found her difficult to work with, given her continual lateness and her short concentration spans. Logan had Murray place his hands on her hips to keep her on her marks, which she often missed. In a scene in which Cherie is in bed, Marilyn was nude under the covers, and Murray kept tucking in the sheets because she kept exposing herself. Murray found these assignments perplexing, since she was a star and he had never before acted in films. Moreover, she broke out in a rash in front of the camera so often that they continually had to stop filming to put makeup on her to cover the rash.[50]

When I interviewed Murray, I asked him if he thought Marilyn was on drugs during the filming, as some have speculated; but he said no. On the other hand, Murray was involved with Hope Lange, a blonde actress who played a supporting role, and Marilyn felt threatened by their relationship. She told Milton Greene that Murray didn't give her sufficiently strong reactions for her to work with in creating her character. Logan stated he didn't allow Paula Strasberg on the set, but Murray contended she was there and she masterminded Marilyn's excellent performance. She and Paula practiced after hours every day and talked to Lee Strasberg for several hours every evening on the phone.

Did Marilyn need a coach? Biographer Fred Guiles, who interviewed Lee Strasberg extensively, thinks she did. According to Guiles, she often spoke poetically, in metaphors that someone had to interpret because they were incomprehensible to the ordinary person. That comment sounds like what others described as her illogical thinking. Lee described to Marilyn how to play her roles, and Paula helped her fill in the details. According to Logan, "Strasberg opened a locked part of her head, gave her confidence in herself, in her ability to think out and create character." Susan Strasberg maintained Marilyn and her mother had developed a special language to communicate with each other.[51]

Logan was one of the few theater people in the United States who had studied with Stanislavsky, and Marilyn plied him with questions about the Russian teacher. Logan knew Stanislavsky had rejected the affective memory technique a long time earlier, but Marilyn was too dedicated to it to give it up. Logan remained firm in his judgment that Marilyn was a great actress—a combination of Greta Garbo and Charlie Chaplin. "She was the most constantly exciting actress I had ever worked with, and that excitement was not related to her celebrity but to her humanness, to the way she saw life around her." Criticized for his stance, Logan replied that the problem was not Marilyn but rather that most people didn't think that beautiful women had any brains.[52]

During the filming, the fans and the press wouldn't let Marilyn alone, so Milton Greene barred them from the set and from nearby locations. Shooting took place in Hollywood; Phoenix; and Sun Valley, Idaho. Traveling between these locations was hard enough on the cast and crew without fans and the press in pursuit. No matter the difficulties, Marilyn was superb in *Bus Stop* as the Ozark hillbilly "chanteuse" traveling from Missouri to Hollywood to seek fame who is pursued by Don Murray as a naive rancher looking for an "angel" as a wife. Murray respected Marilyn's acting, but he found her to be more an adolescent than an adult. Still, when I interviewed him fifty years after the film was made, he was mellow about it, filled with praise for everyone involved.

During the making of *Bus Stop*, the Arthur Jacobs agency, Marilyn's publicity firm, assigned Patricia Newcomb to handle her publicity. She and Marilyn had a dispute during the filming, and Pat was dismissed. The official story was that Pat, an attractive blonde, passed herself off as Marilyn to a man interested in dating the star. Given Marilyn's involvement with Arthur and the difficulties of filming *Bus Stop*, it seems unlikely that she had time for other men. Some say she was too affectionate toward Marilyn. Whatever the truth, Pat reentered Marilyn's life four years later, during the filming of *The Misfits*, and she played a crucial role in her last two years.[53]

Meantime, Arthur wrote Marilyn about his disapproval of Milton, about his huckster mentality. He praised Marilyn's progress toward independence and high art. But he worried that Milton acted as though he had control over her, that he was taking her over. Arthur was upset by the expensive diamond bracelet Henry Rosenfeld gave her. Arthur had competitors for Marilyn, and he didn't like it.

By the time Marilyn returned to New York in late May, Arthur was back from Reno with his divorce, but he was involved in his own difficulties. The House Un-American Activities Committee had subpoened him to appear for questioning. He had been named as a Communist years earlier, but the committee knew the charge was inaccurate. He had never belonged to the Communist Party, although he had signed leftist petitions. The committee's interest was aroused when he applied for a passport to go to London for the opening of A View from the Bridge. By 1954 the power of the congressional committees investigating internal Communism was declining. Concluding they needed to prosecute someone important to shore up their power, the committee decided to go after Arthur. They hoped to frighten him into naming names of friends who had been members of the Communist Party, thus acknowledging their power. The tactic had worked many times before.

Marilyn's name became tangled in the matter. At his hearing on June 21, the committee asked Miller why he wanted to go to England. He mentioned A View from the Bridge and also stated he wanted to go there with his wife. At a recess in the hearings, reporters asked him who he meant by "his wife." He answer was bold: he told them that at some point before Marilyn left for England to begin production on The Prince and the Showgirl, he and she would marry. Marilyn was watching the news on television when she heard Arthur's statement, and she was surprised, since he hadn't proposed to her. Ralph Roberts and Rupert Allan thought Arthur had used her, hoping that the committee wouldn't jail someone married to the world's preeminent film star. In one fell swoop he had turned himself from a dangerous subversive into a man in love. When he refused to name names to the committee, he became the darling of the left, even though he was firm in his statement to the committee that he considered communism to be dangerous and subversive.

Arthur's refusal to name names may have moved Marilyn to admire him even more; she wasn't angry at him for announcing their engagement without asking her. There was also her sense of justice; she felt the attack on him was unmerited. "She was like Saint Joan urging the dauphin to fight," wrote Susan Strasberg. "She was a warrior goddess, awakened and full of piss and vinegar."[54] In news footage of them together after his announcement, they look very much in love.

Throughout Arthur's difficulties, Marilyn stayed true to her sense of right and wrong. When a committee member offered to have the charges dropped if Marilyn would pose with him in a photo for his next election campaign, she refused. When Spyros Skouras put pressure on her to persuade Arthur to name some names and get off the hook, she refused, even though Skouras threatened to destroy her film career. She told him if he did that she and Arthur would move to Denmark.[55] That was the country where the king had worn a yellow star in protest against Hitler's discriminatory policies against the Jews. Checking the studio grosses, Skouras backed down. He couldn't stop the hearing, but he arranged for a passport for Arthur to go to England.

With the marriage proposal—perhaps even sooner—Marilyn decided to convert to Judaism. She studied with Rabbi Robert Goldburg, a leftist involved with the civil rights movement. It wasn't important to Arthur that she convert, but Arthur's mother had been estranged from his first wife because she hadn't converted. Marilyn wanted to make the Millers into a real family. This family, unlike others she had joined, would be her own. Gussie told the *Jewish Daily Forward* they hadn't attended their son's first wedding because it wasn't Jewish and they had never been able to be real in-laws to their son's first wife. But Marilyn was more loving to them than their own children. She told Gussie stories of her terrible childhood, and Gussie became a staunch ally.

Goldburg's papers, recently opened, show that Marilyn was sincere, not calculating, in converting. In an unpublished memoir about the conversion, Goldburg wrote that Marilyn had rejected the Protestant fundamentalism of her childhood years earlier. She was impressed by the many Jewish people she knew, and one of her heroes was Albert Einstein, whom she thought of as the great scientist-humanist-Jew-Socialist dissenter. She liked the ethical and prophetic sides of Judaism and its devotion to close family life. Marilyn often met with Rabbi Goldburg to discuss the books he assigned her to read. They became friends; he went to the Millers' Hanukkah and Passover celebrations. She liked his civil rights credentials. He supported the movement, and he led marches and demonstrations.[56]

Once Marilyn and Arthur announced their wedding, they tried to hold the press at bay, but it was impossible. They agreed to hold a press conference on June 29, at Miller's house in Roxbury. On the way there, a female reporter chased their car on the narrow Connecticut roads. Her driver swerved on a sharp turn and crashed into a tree, badly injuring her. She died in the hospital several hours later. Marilyn was shaken; it was a terrible omen for their marriage. They held a brief press conference in Roxbury, with four hundred reporters present. Then, driving to the Westchester County Courthouse in White Plains, New York, they were married that evening.

They followed this civil ceremony with a religious one two days later, held at the home of Arthur's agent, Kay Brown, in nearby Katonah, New York. (Rabbi Goldburg stated that they held the civil ceremony before the religious one to conceal the private ceremony from the press.) Amy Greene planned the second wedding. It seems that Milton and Arthur had reconciled their differences for a time. Marilyn wore Amy's wedding veil, dyed in tea so that it matched the wedding's beige color scheme. Norman Norell and John Moore designed the wedding dress. Amy got special beige panty hose made. Wearing beige shoes, Marilyn achieved Amy's "fashion line": one color, carried throughout the wedding. The beige orchids she carried came from the hothouse of musical producer Arthur Freed. Arthur Miller didn't own a dark suit, and Milton grudgingly bought him one.[57]

Lee Strasberg gave Marilyn away, and Hedda Rosten and Amy Greene were bridesmaids. Kitty Owens made the wedding cake. Marilyn recited the passage from the Old Testament in which Ruth states her loyalty to her mother-in-law, Naomi: "Wherever you go I will go; And wherever you lodge, I will lodge; your people shall by my people, and your God, my God." Marilyn addressed the sentiments to Arthur, but they certainly pleased his mother. Everyone shouted "mazel tov," and Arthur kissed Marilyn. The union was accomplished. Engraved on Marilyn's ring: TO MM FROM AM; NOW IS FOREVER. An ambiguous statement, it could mean eternal love or, ominously, momentary love that might not last. It was in line with Miller's existentialist convictions.

Then came the next step: the trip to London two weeks later so that Marilyn could make *The Prince and the Showgirl*. Amy, Milton, Arthur, and Paula would be traveling with her. Did she realize that she was in the process of creating a maelstrom that would come close to destroying her? In 1956 she was thirty years old. She had never been outside the United States. She had close friends around her, and she thought she had everything under control. But once again disaster loomed.

Chapter 10

Arthur, 1956–1959

Marilyn can't be understood without understanding Arthur Miller, with whom she lived for nearly five years. His autobiography, *Timebends*, reveals his thoughts and behaviors, hopes and dreams, and it often focuses on Marilyn. Understanding their relationship requires understanding the immense pressures that fame placed on them. A marriage between two famous people is never easy, and Marilyn and Arthur had to deal with the public's idolization of her. Fans stopped her on the streets; reporters and paparazzi followed her; she received anonymous phone calls. Life with her was like living in a goldfish bowl, as both DiMaggio and Miller separately declared. In addition to the pressures from the public and the press, both Arthur and Marilyn were already under the pressures that come from being deeply complex people, both of them idealists trying to discipline and refine their emotions as well as narcissists promoting careers that could easily go sour.

When Arthur and Marilyn reconnected in New York in the winter of 1955, he'd been married for fifteen years to Mary Grace Slattery, whom he'd met when they were undergraduates at the University of Michigan, involved in radical politics there. After their marriage, they'd settled in New York, where Mary worked as an editorial assistant in a publishing house, supporting them while Arthur worked on his writing. They had two children, Robert, born in 1941, and Jane, born in 1944. As early as 1951, when Arthur met Marilyn on the set of *As Young as You Feel*, the fire had left the marriage. Filled with guilt, however, he couldn't leave it. He would follow the same pattern in his marriage to Marilyn.

Mary Slattery Miller wasn't sophisticated or stylish. A small-town girl, she was ill at ease in the worldly circles that opened to Arthur once he became famous. Raised a Catholic, she never entirely rejected Catholicism's rigid morality. She didn't know about his first meeting with Marilyn in 1951, but when he had sex with a woman at a conference of intellectuals and told Mary about it, she became furious. Viewing his act as an ultimate betrayal, she became cold and sexually unresponsive. Then Marilyn appeared in Arthur's life in 1955, and Mary figured out what was going on. A friend advised her to wear sexy clothes and makeup, and to restyle her hair.[1] But she refused to compete with Marilyn.

Arthur was attracted to Marilyn because of her beauty, wit, gaiety, and identification with the working class, which he nurtured into a left liberal stance. She also met deep needs of his of which he was only partly aware. She resembled certain randy women in his extended family who had always attracted him. Both his mother, Gussie, and his uncle's wife, Stella, had "a lust for foul jokes, filthy punch lines, sex scandals, the whispered world of frank women and their scents." He was fascinated by his uncle Manny Newman, whose house seemed "dank with sexuality." Even as a child he competed with Manny's son, Abby. Abby failed in his career, but he became a sybarite who bested Arthur in sexual prowess: Arthur had once visited Abby in his apartment and encountered two prostitutes leaving Abby's bedroom after an obvious threesome. Now Arthur was involved with Marilyn Monroe, the world's major sex symbol. No man could top that.[2]

His memoir, *Timebends*, opens with a telling scene. Five years old, Arthur lies on the floor, looking up at his mother's clothed body. He sees "a pair of pointy black calf shoes . . . and just above them the plum-colored skirt rising from the ankles to the blouse." He admits to an incestuous desire for her. "As innocent as I was at five," he writes, "I was still aware of an exciting secret life among the women . . . And I knew that somewhere behind my sexual anxieties lay incestuous stains that spread toward sister and mother." He views his incestuous desires as metaphorical, not real, as an inevitable component of Freud's oedipal family drama, which is driven by repressed sexual desire.[3]

He'd initially bonded with Marilyn through Elia Kazan, his "blood brother," in a triangle driven by sexual tension, with Marilyn in the middle. But their friendship had broken apart in 1952 when Kazan named friends as communists before the House Un-American Activities Committee, an act that Miller found reprehensible. He criticized Kazan in *The Crucible*, which he wrote in 1953. It is an implicit attack on both the House committee and those who informed on friends as communists. By 1955, however, Arthur and Elia were slowly reconnecting. When Arthur testified before the committee in June 1956, he refused to name names, but he criticized communism as anti-American. Both Miller and Kazan had become left liberals.

When he first met Marilyn, Arthur overlooked her sexual past. In an interview in *Time* magazine he maintained that she may have had lovers, but she hadn't been promiscuous. "Any relation she ever had was meaningful to her, built on a thread of hope, however mistaken." He concluded with a flourish: "I've known social workers who have had a more checkered history than she has."[4]

Amy Greene was correct when she said that Marilyn parroted Arthur's political ideas, but he was deeply influenced by her beliefs, what he called her "revolutionary idealism." He had soured on Marxism and was exploring existentialism and Freudianism, but Marilyn offered another possibility. "Now that I know her somewhat better," he wrote, "I began to see the world as she did, and the view was new and dangerous." Marilyn was outraged by the sexual conservatism of the 1950s, which she found hypocritical. Arthur wrote, "America was still a virgin, still denying her illicit dreams." Marilyn was a central target of the nation's deep Puritanism. Salem in the 1690s had been deeply Puritan and thus sexually repressive, in his point of view. He interpreted the new Puritanism of the 1950s as a form of anticommunism taken into the moral realm.

"She had accepted the role of outcast years before, even flaunted it," he wrote in *Timebends*. She had constructed herself "first as a casualty of puritanical rejection but then with victorious disorder; from her refusal to wear bras to her laughing acknowledgment of the calendar photos." "Her bracing candor," he contended, "was health. It was the strength of one who has abandoned the illusions of a properly ordered life for herself." Arthur found her heroic, "the astonishing signal of liberation and its joys." She had accomplished a "healthy and generous confrontation with catastrophe. Out of the muck, the flower, and soon an amazing life."[5]

Moreover, her sexuality overwhelmed him. Arthur had married the first woman he dated seriously—Mary Grace Slattery—and he had remained faithful to her for fifteen years, except for the one-night stand at the conference. When he met Marilyn, he was a sexual naïf. Marilyn, on the other hand, was sexually experienced. In *Timebends* he described her sexuality as a whirling fire, accompanied by a magnetic spirituality, a combination he couldn't resist. In a screenplay he adapted from *After the Fall*, he called her a "naked spirit like something come out of the sea. The spirit of such love, such absolute selflessness that . . . there was almost a sense of holiness in it. When she was ill I was ill. I shared her skin, her blushes, her cold frights."[6] Marilyn had become a great actress, arguably more effective in her private life than on the screen. She told people what they wanted to hear, sensed the person they wanted her to be and became that person.

Given her manic-depressive tendencies and the anger she had brought to the surface of herself, Marilyn wasn't easy to live with. "She could say things that put a hook in my belly. Cruel, vicious insights," Arthur wrote. But she easily turned back into the women he loved. She knew how to use sex to woo him. "It's easy to mistake a wife for god," he wrote. "You make her happy some night and you begin to think you settled something global. A wife's contented smile gives purpose all day." Underlying their relationship was a euphoric sexuality that sustained the marriage.[7]

Arthur had his own power drives. On some level he relished the role of savior into which Marilyn had cast him. As she did with all her husbands, she called him Papa and Daddy in private. (She called him Arturo in public.) Like Lee Strasberg and Ralph Greenson, her last psychiatrist, Arthur thought that he could nurture her into mental stability. He knew he was her anchor against abandonment, but he didn't realize she might use her dependence to gain control over him by manipulating his own masochistic drives, of which he was hardly aware. At the beginning of their relationship, Marilyn idealized him. She realized he was frugal, impatient, and self-righteous; she wrote Berniece Miracle that these qualities in him made her nervous.[8] Before too long, they would make her impatient and angry.

Like Marilyn, he was focused on his career. Like hers, his ambition knew no bounds. When mired in an argument he became silent, which was guaranteed to frustrate an emotional antagonist like Marilyn and increase her rage. In some ways he resembled Joe DiMaggio, another man who fell silent for long periods of time. People said that from across a room he and DiMaggio looked alike. Norman Rosten reflected on the similarity. They were both stern authority figures, powerful public men. She gravitated toward power. This kind of figure, according to Rosten, gives a woman "security and absolution."[9] On the other hand, this kind of figure can be self-centered and controlling.

Even as a young writer, Arthur had been a workaholic. He put his emotions into his writing and hid them from others. His father had similarly retreated into himself in the face of his mother's anger over their sudden descent into poverty after the 1929 stock market crash. With his first financial rewards from his success, Arthur bought a farm in Connecticut, where he built himself a separate studio. Many successful New York artists and writers had second homes in Connecticut; to Arthur it was a place where he could write in solitude—and retreat from emotional confrontation.

There was another connection between Marilyn and Arthur. She had been raised in working-class and lower-middle-class families; he was also a man of the people. His father, Isidore Miller, had been born in a Polish shtetl. Sent as a young child to live with relatives in New York, Isidore followed a standard Jewish path to upward social mobility by establishing a clothing sweatshop in an apartment. By the 1920s he had turned it into one of the largest women's coat factories in the nation. Arthur had spent the 1920s as a child of wealth, living in an apartment off Central Park. But after his father lost his money in the 1929 crash, his family moved far out in Brooklyn, to a modest frame house in Flatbush. They now scrimped to get by.

Arthur got odd jobs to help support his family. He learned carpentry; played football in high school; did some singing on a local radio station and wanted to be a "crooner," like Bing Crosby. Working as a laborer in the Brooklyn shipyard, he was converted to Marxism. He decided to go to college, and he persuaded an admissions officer at the University of Michigan—then a center of student radicalism—to admit him. Once there, he watched his roommate write a play for a class. The process looked easy, so he wrote one himself. That episode launched him as a writer, leading to his great success with *All My Sons* (1943) and *Death of a Salesman* (1949), which won him a Pulitzer Prize.

On July 14, 1956, hardly six weeks after Marilyn had finished *Bus Stop* and two weeks after their marriage, Marilyn and Arthur flew from New York to London to film *The Prince and the Showgirl*. Once again, as she so often did, Marilyn was living her life at a breakneck pace. When they took off at Idlewild Airport, they were swamped by fans, while four hundred journalists, photographers, and fans were waiting at London's Heathrow. Several days later Milton Greene rented the ballroom at the Savoy Hotel in London for another press conference. This one drew seven hundred reporters and photographers. Laurence Olivier called it "the largest press conference in British history."[10]

At the conference, members of the British press were hard to handle, since cutting humor was their specialty and they disliked Olivier because he closed his sets to them. On the other hand, they considered Arthur Miller heroic because he'd stood up to the House Un-American Activities Committee; although he was so dull on this trip that they began calling him a "cold fish." Fleur Cowles thought Marilyn charmed the British press, but Maurice Zolotow, who was also there, thought they made fun of her. When they asked her what roles she hoped to play, she replied "Lady Macbeth." That reply seemed curious to the Brits, even though both Michael Chekhov and Lee Strasberg thought she could do it. Lee's concept of Lady Macbeth was as a sensitive, sexual, and compulsive woman who uses her sexuality to persuade her husband to commit murder.[11] That sounds like Marilyn.

The British public stalked Marilyn even more aggressively than the Americans. When she ate in a Regent Street restaurant, eight policemen had to be summoned to control the crowd. When she shopped in a department store, it was closed to the public. What she wore was described endlessly. The most photographed dress of the year was the one she wore at the Savoy press conference. Black in color and tight in fit, it was tailored decorously to the neckline, but an inset band made of see-through fabric bared her midriff. The international *New York Herald Tribune* reported that "you could see a strip of Miss Monroe's famous body, starting just above her hips to a position slightly south of her chest." The dress, designed by Norman Norell, was widely copied; it was even featured in home-sewing books.[12]

During the filming, Marilyn and Arthur were housed in an eleven-bedroom Georgian mansion just outside Windsor Great Park, where Queen Elizabeth's castle was located. The mansion was set on ten acres of land, with a small lake with swans near the house. It had a household staff. Paula Strasberg, Marilyn's coach, and Hedda Rosten, now her secretary, lived with them. Hedda had been close to Mary Slattery Miller, Arthur's first wife, but she had switched her loyalty to Marilyn. She had been a psychiatric social worker until she gave up her career to raise her daughter, Patricia. Long before feminism appeared, Arthur Miller later stated, Hedda regarded Marilyn as the quintessential victim of the male.[13]

Milton was the film's producer, but he and Amy lived elsewhere in London. Amy became close to Olivier's elegant wife, Vivien Leigh, and she and Marilyn grew distant. Vivien was determined to outclass Marilyn. Vivien had played the showgirl in *The Sleeping Prince* in London, and she made Marilyn feel insecure. Close to manic during the shooting, Vivien was both charming and intensely critical. Whitey Snyder and Sydney Guilaroff were there to do Marilyn's makeup and hair and give her emotional support, but they couldn't do much about the tension that was emerging among the stars making the film.[14]

Problems immediately erupted between Marilyn and Olivier. She found him patronizing, especially since he wanted her to copy Vivien in playing her role. He tried to control her, even though Joshua Logan, who had directed Marilyn in *Bus Stop*, told him that he should let her loose and keep the camera running, then edit her takes into a final cut, which would produce superb results. It took Olivier weeks of being overbearing before he followed Logan's advice. Even Arthur, who went out drinking with Olivier and commiserated with him about their difficult wives, found him quick to make cutting remarks, as when he told Marilyn to "be sexy," deeply offending her. Then Olivier told her that her teeth looked yellow and she should whiten them with lemon juice and baking soda. That advice infuriated her. She was the beauty expert, not Olivier. Marilyn began to call Olivier Mister Sir, not Larry, as everyone else did.[15]

Marilyn had never known anyone like him. A member of the English upper class, already knighted, he was a product of the elite English public school system. Rupert Allan, her publicist and friend, had gone to

Oxford, but he'd been raised in the United States. His Englishness was a patina, not deeply engrained, as was Olivier's. She decided that he was doing the film because he wanted the large box office returns that she would produce. She told W. J. Weatherby that he acted with her like someone who was slumming, so she asserted control by being late and calling in sick.[16]

She retreated to the safety of Paula Strasberg, using her as a go-between with Olivier. Olivier would rehearse a scene with Marilyn, showing her how he wanted her to do it. She would then consult with Paula. Olivier waited, humiliated, for her to begin filming. Sometimes she left him in midsentence and telephoned Lee Strasberg in New York for advice. Olivier tried to throw Paula off the set, but Marilyn got her back. After all, Marilyn's production company was in control of the filming and Marilyn was its producer, although Milton Greene did most of the production work. She took great pains with her appearance, on which she had built an empire. Asserting her prerogatives as producer, she would stop the filming to fix her hair, her makeup, or any other aspect of her look she felt was flawed.[17]

Arthur defended Olivier to her; he thought she was being too harsh on him. But Arthur soon realized that, like his first wife, Marilyn saw the world in black-and-white terms. People were either for her or against her; it was difficult for her to understand individuals in the middle. She berated Arthur for defending Olivier. To keep peace, he kept quiet.

As filming proceeded her insomnia became severe, and the pills that usually put her to sleep didn't work. Milton Greene got more from a doctor in the United States, since prescription drugs were carefully regulated in England (although Milton denied he had done so). He admitted he spiked her morning tea with vodka, as she requested, although he said he always watered it down. Marilyn defended the vodka drinking: "Here was the world's greatest actor, and I was supposed to match him scene for scene. Without the vodka, I couldn't have done it."[18]

According to a number of her friends, her major drug habit dated from the filming of *The Prince and the Showgirl*. She had been taking pills for years when making films, but the problems shooting this movie were especially severe. Arthur became the pill monitor, staying up late with her to restrict her intake, while Paula doled out amphetamines to her during the day to keep her going. Despite her physical issues, however, she looked brilliant in the evening rushes, with her glow intact and her fey personality dominating the film. Olivier, on the other hand, appeared wooden. Playing the ruler of a Balkan principality, he wore a heavy felt costume, adorned with cumbersome medals, to simulate royal clothing. He also wore thick makeup and a monocle. It's hard to believe that even a showgirl would be attracted to him. Sibyl Thorndike, a legendary British actress who played a dowager queen in the film, stated, "That little girl is the only one here who knows how to act before a camera."[19]

During the four months of filming, Marilyn's menstrual issues and her colitis acted up. She saw doctors and took to her bed. There were rumors that she had a miscarriage, plunging her into further depression. Several weeks after filming began, a disturbing incident occurred. Arthur jotted down ideas to use in his writing in a journal that he kept on a desk. Looking for her script, Marilyn chanced on it. The journal happened to be open, displaying the writing on one page. She read the open page.

What she read infuriated her. In the years ahead, she never forgot it. She showed it to Paula Strasberg. Arthur had written, "I've done it again. I thought I was marrying an angel, and find I've married a whore." He also wrote that she'd let him down badly and he didn't know how he could continue defending her to Olivier.[20] It's unclear why he used the term "whore." Had he learned about the purported affair with Milton Greene? Had she told him the truth about her Hollywood sex life?

Arthur left his journal open, where Marilyn might see it. Perhaps he was simply careless, but she took it as calculated behavior on his part. Arthur told Fred Guiles, the only Marilyn biographer to interview him, that the entry contained minor criticism, although Arthur often downplayed his negative actions. The incident was serious enough that Marilyn spent a week in therapy in London with Anna Freud, who later recommended New York psychiatrist Marianne Kris to her. She told Freud about her problems on the film and her deep urge to go naked. In addition, as I have noted, Freud thought she had bisexual tendencies, because of the way she tried to intercept the balls Anna rolled to her. Everyone on the set thought Freud's intervention helped Marilyn.

Paula Strasberg persuaded Marilyn to stay with Arthur. She argued that the journal entry reflected his sense of defeat, due to the failure of his plays in New York and the British adulation of Marilyn. He was jealous of her, and he lashed out. Paula wondered if she was wise to exonerate

Arthur, since she didn't like him. To finish the film, however, Marilyn had to stay with him. Paula didn't want to lose the large salary Marilyn was paying her for coaching.[21]

Arthur wasn't a saint. Olivier called him "self-satisfied" and "argumentative." He tried to interject his ideas into the script. Colin Clark, Olivier's assistant, thought that Arthur treated Marilyn as though she was his property. Amy Greene thought his presence was a huge distraction; she charged that he sat around in Marilyn's dressing room, drawing her into conversations, breaking her concentration.[22] Despite Marilyn's dependence on him, he sometimes left London, which angered her. A week after the episode with his journal, he went to New York for ten days to see his children.

Despite everything going on, Arthur and Marilyn were sometimes able to regain the lyricism of their courtship. During days off from filming they went bicycling in Windsor Great Park, and they drove to Brighton. They walked on the boardwalk and on the beach there. Relaxing on such trips, they discussed the house they wanted to build in Connecticut, and Marilyn spoke of going to school and studying history and literature. When they could put aside the intense pressures accompanying filming and were able to fantasize about their future, the marriage seemed on track.

Meantime, they were having problems with Milton Greene. Milton and Amy spent weekends at Olivier's country home, where Vivien ran what amounted to an ongoing house party for London's elite artists. Marilyn and Arthur were invited, but they never went. They gave no parties, and they attended almost none. Arthur began to suspect that Milton was using Marilyn for his own ends. That's not surprising. They had never really liked each other. Like Joe DiMaggio, Arthur may have been jealous of Milton. According to Sammy Davis Jr., Marilyn and a "photographer" borrowed his apartment in London to have an affair.[23] Milton, Arthur charged, was trying to take over MMP. Marilyn and Arthur suspected that Milton was using MMP money to buy antiques for himself, and they became angry when he negotiated an agreement with Jack Cardiff for a production company subsidiary to MMP. They hadn't known about it until they read an article about it in a newspaper.

In the fall Arthur began looking into Marilyn's finances. He cut out articles about her in British newspapers and pasted them into a scrapbook. He was getting too involved with her career. But he didn't become Marilyn's clone, as some biographers charge. He finished a longer version of *A View from the Bridge*, due to be produced that fall in London, and he wrote a story that became the basis for his screenplay for *The Misfits*. The story was about three Montana cowboys he had met in Reno while establishing residency for his divorce from Mary. Heroic figures from the American past, they now scrounged for money, making some of their income by rounding up mustangs from the decimated herds that had once roamed the Montana grasslands to sell them to a slaughterhouse for dog food.

Milton attempted to keep peace on the set by providing a distraction in the form of a presentation to Queen Elizabeth II. Marilyn, as usual, stole the show. She wore a décolleté, dazzling gown of gold lamé—"Her exuberant breasts defied Newton's law of gravity," remarked one British commentator. Arthur didn't mind when she showed off her body; he'd already decided it was part of her revolutionary idealism. He defended his position: "Why shouldn't she show off her god-given attributes; why should she have to dress like her maiden aunt?"[24] Even the queen didn't seem to mind the dress; she chatted with Marilyn for several minutes at the presentation.

When the film wrapped, Marilyn apologized to the cast and crew for any bad behavior on her part, stating that she had been ill during the filming—which was true, given her endometriosis, colitis, and a possible miscarriage. In a letter to a friend, Olivier implied that she referred to gynecological problems in her statement about being ill, even though some people on the set thought she was shamming.[25] Despite her absences from filming, Milton, acting as producer, brought the film in under budget and within the projected time frame.

Marilyn is superb in the film, outacting Olivier in every scene in which they are together. She plays Elsie, a showgirl performing in a London show whom Olivier, playing the ruler of a Balkan country visiting London, invites to his hotel suite, intending to seduce her. Much of the film involves their interactions in the suite: she resists him with her usual charm, then falls asleep from the effects of too much champagne before he can complete the seduction. In the film, she raises the redemptive elements of her Lorelei Lee figure to new heights, as she solves the political problems in Olivier's kingdom by tracing them to issues within his family. She is the ultimate wise woman, intuitively understanding how people and politics function. It's not surprising that she won both the French and Italian equivalent of the Oscar for Best Actress for *The Prince and the Showgirl*.

Nonetheless, Marilyn's insecurity was growing with every film she made, and so was her perfectionism. She demanded many retakes, even when her directors didn't think they were necessary. She was known as the hardest-working actress in Hollywood, although her sole concern was her own performance, which was, frankly, all she could concentrate on in doing a film. She often defined herself as a great film actress on the order of Garbo, whose idiosyncrasies were humored, as were those of Judy Garland, Elizabeth Taylor, and others. Yet despite a husband who seemed to support her and a drama coach who sustained her, she couldn't cope with her fears and insecurities, her lack of confidence in herself. She managed to hide her stuttering, her hearing difficulties, possibly caused by Meniere's disease, and her dyslexia, but they continued to hinder her.

The filming of *The Prince and the Showgirl* turned out to be a devastating experience for her, one from which she never completely recovered. It was supposed to prove her ability as a dramatic actress, but it ruined her relationship with Milton Greene and damaged her marriage to Arthur, when he became her pill monitor and go-between with Olivier. As she left London for New York, she intended to take a break from films, to improve her acting by studying at the Actors Studio, and to become a model wife and homemaker, so that she and Arthur could create the perfect marriage they had fantasized about. Now she would have the child she longed for. But with the filming over, she worried that Arthur might abandon her. Abandonment had always been one of her worst fears. It may be a truism that self-destructive individuals always court what they fear the most.

After Marilyn and Arthur arrived back in New York from London in November 1956, they went to Jamaica, in the Caribbean, for a two-week honeymoon, before setting up their new life in New York. They found a large apartment on East Fifty-third Street, on the thirteenth floor of a luxury building. Marilyn decorated the apartment in white and beige, with lots of mirrors and with silver and black accents. She adopted the art moderne look of 1930s movies, a look popular among film stars for their homes. She placed the white piano from her childhood in the living room, moving it from the Greenes' Connecticut home.

Patricia Rosten was often in the apartment with her parents as a child, and she remembered it vividly. It was large, although not huge, with a large foyer and a long hall opening into the living room, which had a fireplace flanked by bookshelves. There was a large bedroom, a study for Arthur, a kitchen, and a maid's room. She especially remembered the mirrored table in the dining alcove off the living room, in which "you could look at your reflection while you were eating." She also remembered the champagne-colored quilt on Marilyn's bed; when she flopped on it, she felt like "she was sinking in a pool."[26] Others remembered the bedroom as very dark. They also remembered dog stains on rugs throughout the apartment.

For the spring and summer of 1957, Marilyn and Arthur rented a weekend and summer home in Amagansett, Long Island, close to the beach and near the summer homes of the Rostens and Shaws. They now were living the life of well-to-do New Yorkers, with an apartment on the Upper East Side, easy access to theaters and boutiques, and a weekend and summer home on Long Island, only several hours by car from New York. It should have been idyllic—and it was for a time.

Marilyn described her life in New York to Georges Belmont of *Marie Claire* magazine. It revolved around Arthur, she said, although she continued studying at the Actors Studio and seeing her psychiatrist, now Marianne Kris. Arthur was up by seven, and she sometimes got up and fixed his breakfast. She said she didn't think a man should have to fix his own meals: "I'm very old-fashioned that way." After breakfast, Arthur retreated to his study, and he wrote for much of the day. Marilyn often returned home to have lunch with him, and they had dinner together. After dinner they went to the theater or a movie, or they saw friends. Often they stayed at home, listened to music, read books, or walked in Central Park. Marilyn sometimes had classmates from the Actors Studio over to practice scenes they were studying. She said nothing to Belmont about her up-and-down moods and her drug taking. She kept that behavior secret from journalists.

Marilyn and Arthur had many friends. She wasn't alone and lost to drugs during these years, as some biographers maintain. In New York she and Arthur socialized with people from the Actors Studio—Eli

Wallach, Anne Jackson, Kevin McCarthy, and Maureen Stapleton, in particular. She spent time with the Shaws and the Rostens. Sam photographed her; she and Norman wrote poetry to each other; Hedda answered fan mail and went shopping with her. Marilyn became friends with Lester Markel, a *New York Times* editor who lived in the same apartment building as the Strasbergs and Marianne Kris. She read Markel's columns, wrote him a letter about his political views, and happened to meet him in the building's elevator. She flirted with him, and he was smitten. After a session with Kris or Strasberg, she sometimes had dinner with Markel and his family. They talked politics, and Markel, a radical sympathetic to communism, influenced her to move farther to the left. She soon became more radical than Arthur.[27]

In Amagansett, Willem de Kooning, a leading abstract expressionist painter, was a next-door neighbor. Becoming acquainted with her, he painted her for his series titled *Women*. Totally abstract, his Marilyn looks like a cross between a grinning child and a screaming fury, not like the soft and gentle Marilyn. Yet he captured part of her essence— childlike, but angry when crossed. The portrait was hung in the Museum of Modern Art, and it produced a stir. Arthur detested it, but Marilyn didn't mind: she thought artists had the right to their own vision of the subject they painted. It led the way to the many pop art portraits of her.[28]

In interviews with journalists between 1957 and 1960, Marilyn praised Arthur and her marriage with such enthusiasm that it appears she was trying to convince herself as well as everyone else that it was working. She threw herself into the role of domestic goddess. She took up cooking. In her inimitable fashion, she consulted experts and became friendly with Mary Bass, editor of *Ladies' Home Journal*, who sent her recipes and cooking tips. Bass even asked Marilyn to do a cookbook under the imprimatur of the *Journal*, and Marilyn was interested. Arthur said she made the best leg of lamb he'd ever eaten and he liked her chicken with wine; Norman Rosten liked her bouillabaisse.[29]

She was a generous stepmother to Arthur's children. Marilyn loved children; she easily connected to them, probably because she sometimes seemed a child herself. Joe DiMaggio Jr. loved her, and so did Patricia Rosten and the Shaws' daughters, Meta and Edith. When the young Edie met Marilyn, she thought she was an angel, not a human being. Patricia Rosten's favorite memory of Marilyn was when, at the age of ten, she wandered into Marilyn's bedroom and began playing with her makeup. Marilyn discovered her, but rather than scolding her she made up her face.[30]

Marilyn became close to Arthur's father, Isidore Miller. A grumpy old man before Marilyn entered his family, he gained new vitality and pride under her attention. He remembered attending dinner parties that Marilyn and Arthur gave, with theater people present and talk about books and plays. Everyone sat on the floor. Marilyn talked about Marie Dressler, whom she remembered from her youth and who became a Hollywood star in her later years after a long career in vaudeville. Marilyn hoped to age into an actress like Dressler, cherished by her public. Norman Rosten remembered parties in Marilyn's apartment, with champagne and dancing. Designer Herbert Kahn went there to adjust a dress he had made for her. He observed great affection between Marilyn and Arthur. Many journalists made the same observation.[31]

Marilyn now indulged her love for animals. She and Arthur owned a basset hound named Hugo, which Arthur had given her. She also had parakeets, Butch and Bobo, a gift from Sidney Guilaroff, and a cat they named Sugar Finney. In his short story "Please Don't Kill Any Living Thing," Arthur wrote about her spiritual approach to the world of living things. In the story a woman walking with a man on a beach throws back into the sea the fish that fishermen have caught and left, still alive and flopping around. Like the woman in the story, Marilyn couldn't stand it if any living creature were hurt. She wasn't a vegetarian, but had she lived longer she might have become one.

In April 1957 Marilyn broke decisively with Milton Greene. She suspected he had embezzled funds from the company, and she was furious when he wanted to be listed as the producer in the credits of *The Prince and the Showgirl*. In a blistering telegram she stated the only money MMP had coming in was her salary, and she didn't want to pay it to someone else.[32] The MMP board of directors, now composed of friends and relatives of Arthur's, ousted Milton from the company. Marilyn had fifty-one percent of the company's stock; Milton couldn't stop the action. Despite the Millers' belief that he had embezzled funds, he asked only for repayment of his expenses during the year he had supported Marilyn, but not for any profit. He wanted Marilyn to realize that he hadn't exploited her.

Amy Greene was also out of Marilyn's life. They'd become estranged in London, and even before the break occurred they hadn't been seeing each other in New York. After Milton's dismissal, he didn't photograph Marilyn again, and they didn't see each other. Their brilliant collaboration as photographer and model was over. But Marilyn had been placed in an impossible position. She had to choose between her husband and her partner.

With Milton gone, Marilyn assumed the producer role. She fired off numerous telegrams to Jack Warner of Warner Brothers, the studio doing the film's final cut and its distribution. She argued with Warner and his assistants over who was responsible for paying her expenses on the film, especially for the many transatlantic phone calls she had made. She didn't like the final cut made under Olivier's direction, and she wanted a new cut made from the outtakes for the final distribution into theaters. When Warner Brothers destroyed all the outtakes by mistake, the issue was moot. But she was convinced that Olivier had used takes of her in the final cut in which she looked ill or as though she were under the influence of drugs.[33]

Marilyn was ecstatic that spring when Arthur dedicated the first edition of his collected plays to her. She played the loyal wife to the hilt when she went with him to Washington, D.C., for his hearing before a judge on the 1956 contempt-of-Congress charge. Trying to avoid fan mania, they stayed at the house of his lawyer, Joseph Rauh Jr., and his wife, Olie. Marilyn seemed deeply in love with Arthur; she was attentive to his every mood. One day they took a break and drove to Charlottesville, Virginia, to see Monticello, Jefferson's home. When Arthur went to the courthouse, Marilyn remained at the Rauh house. She picked books off their shelves to read, mostly about psychiatry. When she was scheduled to do a press conference one day, she looked in the mirror to see if her underpants were causing any ridges in the line of her dress. They were; and she took them off.[34]

That spring Marilyn also oversaw negotiations with lawyers from Twentieth Century–Fox over what film she would make for them. She still owed the studio three films under her 1955 contract, and Fox executives were pressing her to do one, since by her contract terms it had to be made by the end of 1957. (*Bus Stop* had been a Fox film; MMP had done *The Prince and the Showgirl*.) With Milton Greene out of MMP, she had replaced Milton's lawyer Frank Delaney with Robert Montgomery, Arthur's lawyer, as the lawyer both for herself and for MMP. Montgomery, like Delaney, proved to be a skilled negotiator on Marilyn's contract obligations, although it's not clear that Marilyn wanted to go back to screen acting. Her main interest was in having a child. So she stalled, rejecting the scripts Fox sent her. She finally expressed interest in playing the Marlene Dietrich role in a remake of the 1930 film *The Blue Angel*. Set in post–World War One Berlin, a center of postwar decadence, it's the story of a seductive dance hall performer who destroys the aging professor obsessed with her. Before the studio could sign Marilyn, they had to find a director and a costar. So the negotiations dragged.[35]

Once again Marilyn was living a complex life: she was operating as the president of MMP, as a producer, as a perfect wife, and—from time to time—as a movie star. She was also in therapy and studying at the Actors Studio, again doing brilliant work in scenes in Strasberg's classes. She played the prostitute in Eugène Brieux's *Damaged Goods*, first produced in Paris in 1901 as *Les Avariés*. She also recited Molly Bloom's soliloquoy, which ends James Joyce's *Ulysses*, in which Molly pours out her sexual longing and satisfaction in a burst of words. To highlight the eroticism of her performance Marilyn wore a black velvet dress that seemed painted on her body. Incredibly sensual, according to Susan Strasberg, the Molly Bloom she portrayed was an earthy, resilient woman. She was no waif when she played Molly Bloom. She was strong, "like a D. H. Lawrence heroine throbbing with life."[36]

Then she became pregnant in June, and her life once again seemed fulfilled. Arthur sent her a bouquet of three dozen Lady Bountiful red roses and a bunch of baby's breath as a token of congratulations and love. Their marriage once again seemed on track.[37]

One hopes that Marilyn was able to decrease her pill intake during this time of some stability in her life; Ralph Greenson, her last psychiatrist, thought she had a strong ability to kick addiction when she was determined. But drug addiction itself can produce insomnia, and Nembutal addicts experience an initial high before the calming effect of the drug kicks in. Withdrawing from it can be difficult, producing headaches, joint pains, and other symptoms. Marilyn had an addict's knowledge of drugs, so perhaps she also knew how to take them in ways that kept her functioning and allowed her to have respites from them. She became over-weight during the summer of 1957, on Amagansett, which suggests that she gave up amphetamines during that period; although she was also pregnant. Yet she still could be high one day and low the next, or cycle minute by minute. She seems to have had a chemical imbalance in her brain.

In July the judge for the contempt-of-Congress citation gave Arthur a suspended sentence and a five-hundred-dollar fine; at least he didn't have to go to jail.

In mid-August she miscarried, plunging her into deep depression. Arthur was beside himself; he didn't know what to do. Then Sam Shaw suggested that he turn his short story about Montana cowboys, which had been published in *Esquire* magazine, into a screenplay for Marilyn, a loving tribute that would give her the dramatic role she wanted. Arthur plunged into rewriting it, turning the story's peripheral female character into the central character of the screenplay. Marilyn seemed pleased about the endeavor. Sam Shaw took pictures of Arthur and her late that summer in Amagansett and in New York, looking radiantly happy. In September, in what amounted to another healing measure, they went to Roxbury to buy a house. They found an eighteenth-century farmhouse with two hundred acres of land near the first house he had owned. This was to be their bucolic retreat, where Arthur could write his books in solitude, close to nature, and Marilyn could cook and garden. They'd fulfilled the fantasy they had constructed on their walks in England. Roxbury was a close-knit community, and New York artists and writers had second homes there. Arthur already knew everyone, and Marilyn would quickly be accepted.

One night in early September Arthur noticed that Marilyn's breathing had become labored, which can indicate a Nembutal overdose, since a large dose of the drug relaxes the muscles of the upper body so much that it eventually shuts down lung function. He called the local emergency squad, and they revived her. When she awoke, she thanked Arthur repeatedly for having saved her; the overdose, if that's what it was, was probably accidental. She might flirt with suicide, but she wasn't ready to attempt it seriously.[38]

The negotiations with Fox over what film she would make continued. In October Lew Schreiber, now executive manager at Fox, went to New York to meet with her. Fox executives had had difficulty finding a costar to play the older professor in *The Blue Angel*, and they wanted her to agree to postpone the deadline for signing on the film until the end of 1958. Schreiber thought Marilyn agreed to the postponement if they secured Spencer Tracy for the role, but he made the mistake of not getting her agreement in writing.

In early January 1958, Robert Montgomery, now Marilyn's lawyer, wrote Fox a letter stating that because the studio had missed the contractual deadline Marilyn didn't have to do the film, but Fox still had to pay her $100,000 for it. Internal Fox memos reveal their anger at her. Schreiber contended that she had morally committed herself to the role in their October meeting, but he had no proof. According to Frank Ferguson, Fox's head lawyer, Montgomery was playing a game of poker with them, arguing over the specifics of her contract, again using her stardom as his major chip.[39] Neither Schreiber nor Buddy Adler, the new head of Fox, seems to have been as astute as Darryl Zanuck in dealing with Marilyn, although he had been outfoxed in negotiations over the 1955 contract. In this instance, Fox would eventually pay the $100,000 that Marilyn demanded.

Problems developed in the Millers' marriage. The specter of Marilyn's drug taking was always there, as well as her mood swings. She used her drug taking to manipulate Arthur, acting like a child, but in many ways Marilyn was still a child. She pouted; she had tantrums; she cried easily. Her childish ways could be delightful, as when she ran through the house, laughing and singing, or played hide and seek with children, entering deeply into the spirit of the game. But it could be annoying, inappropriate behavior to someone like Arthur, involved in his own world.

To get his writing done, Arthur sometimes went to Roxbury, leaving Marilyn alone with May Reis, her secretary, or Hazel Washington, Marilyn's housekeeper. But Arthur wasn't a paragon. He inserted himself into MMP and advised Marilyn on her career, which led to friction between them. He was also devoted to his own career, which could conflict with Marilyn's. He was setting himself up to be charged with betraying her, should he cross her. Fearful that he might abandon her, she had turned into a model loving wife, but that pose could change. She'd charged both Natasha Lytess and Milton Greene with betrayal, and not even a husband was immune from Marilyn's belief that, given her stardom, everyone wanted to get what they could from her.

Then money problems hit—at least Arthur thought they did. His plays weren't being produced widely, and his royalties were low. After he paid alimony and child support, his income was almost nil. Marilyn's settlement with Fox in 1955 had included back pay, and she was receiving a generous salary from MMP. She was supporting them, even paying Arthur's bills for therapy and for lawyers to fight the contempt-of-Congress charge. He didn't like her being the primary family earner, and neither did she. In the 1950s the male breadwinner ethic was strong. Husbands were supposed to support their wives. Moreover, Arthur was frugal, and Marilyn wasn't. She was going to the best designers for her clothes and spending a lot of money on cosmetics and facial treatments. The Roxbury farmhouse needed improvements. Marilyn approached famous architect Frank Lloyd Wright to build them a new house on the property, one appropriate to her stardom. The house he designed had a circular living room sixty feet in diameter with a domed ceiling, and a swimming pool seventy feet long jutting out from it. Arthur decided it would be prohibitively expensive to build. They decided on a much less expensive redesign of the original house, which still cost a lot.

The Misfits soon became an issue between them. Arthur began writing the script for the movie in August 1957, after Marilyn had the miscarriage. But Marilyn soon became ambivalent about the project, as Arthur turned the female character into a carbon copy of her, even naming his character Roslyn, which sounded similar to Marilyn. She surely knew that she had already been a model for the character Lorraine in "The Third Play," and for Abigail in *The Crucible*. She didn't like being taken over again. Arthur completed a draft by December 1957, but she agreed to do it only if John Huston directed it. He had been kind to her when he directed her in *The Asphalt Jungle*. He had a deeply aesthetic side, but he was a pugnacious Irishman who liked brawling and out-of-doors adventuring. Close to Ernest Hemingway, he resembled a Hemingway hero, quiet, courageous, introspective, a masculine man. Arthur was correct in thinking Huston would like the Nevada cowboy's world of horses, rodeos, and gambling and would see the pathos in the slow destruction of the open range and the cowboy's world by capitalist entrepreneurship and the advent of machines. When Arthur sent him the screenplay in the early summer of 1958, he accepted almost immediately.

In the spring and early summer of 1958 Marilyn still went to her psychiatrist, attended classes at the Actors Studio, and saw friends. Depression hit her from time to time; she could retreat to her bedroom, listening to Frank Sinatra records, not doing much of anything. Ralph Roberts called her the "bluest" person he had ever met. But the New York apartment easily became a hive of activity. When journalist Allan Seager interviewed Arthur there in the spring of 1958, it seemed to be "the home of an industry." Marilyn was in a dressing gown, her hair in curlers. "I've got to run; I've got an appointment for a *Life* sitting," she said. Arthur asked her, "Will you be home for dinner?" Marilyn replied, "I don't know."[41] To handle the many scripts sent to her and to do secretarial work, Marilyn hired May Reis, who had worked for both Kazan and Miller, and who now turned her devotion from Miller to Marilyn, as Hedda Rosten earlier had. That switch in loyalty is telling. May, known for her radical convictions, took over the small maid's room, and she sometimes spent the night there. Hedda Rosten still answered Marilyn's New York fan mail, and Marilyn had a housekeeper and a cook for the apartment.

The *Life* sitting that Marilyn mentioned when Allan Seager was in the apartment was the one she did with Richard Avedon that spring, in which she mimicked famous temptresses of recent history: Lillian Russell, Theda Bara, Clara Bow, Jean Harlow, and Marlene Dietrich. These photos showed her as encompassing the history of Hollywood actresses, as being a unique amalgam of them. Marilyn loved the Avedon photographs. When French actress Simone Signoret became close to her during the filming of *Let's Make Love*, in the spring of 1960, she couldn't stop talking about them. Signoret concluded that she didn't like her performances in film roles but she exulted in the photographs taken of her. That judgment was, unfortunately, probably correct.

By that spring the Roxbury house was becoming increasingly important to her. When the weather permitted it, she gardened. To her delight she seemed to have a green thumb with plants. She rode her bicycle and walked Hugo around the property; after all, she and Arthur owned two hundred acres. She went to the nearby farm owned by the Burchall family to watch the cows being milked and to the general store to gossip with the town's inhabitants. She became close to John Diebold, a business manager and a gentleman farmer who owned land near the Millers in Roxbury. He and his wife met Marilyn at a cocktail party. John was kind to Marilyn and she responded, treating the Diebolds as though they were her parents. They came to regard her as their daughter. She didn't wear any makeup; she seemed like a country girl to them. Robert Josephy, a communist sympathizer in the 1930s who was in the book publishing business, also met Marilyn at community cocktail parties. She confided in him about Arthur. They occasionally had dinner in New York. Josephy commented that Arthur had no understanding of women.[40]

Yet domesticity was starting to bore her, and she decided she should make a movie. Then Billy Wilder sent her the script for *Some Like It Hot*. Walter Mirisch's production company was to produce it, and Mirisch was connected to Fox, so the studio was willing to let her do it. She was reluctant to play the role of Sugar Kane (née Kowalczyk)—another ditzy blonde—but Arthur talked her into it. He recognized the strength of the screenplay and the excellent money she was being offered. In addition to her standard $100,000, she would be paid ten percent of the gross. Many stars worked under such percentage deals, which were often more lucrative than salaries.

Set in the 1920s, the film is a satire of the Al Capone mob and also of the day's standards of femininity and masculinity. Once again, as in *Gentlemen Prefer Blondes*, *How to Marry a Millionaire*, and *Bus Stop*, she would be called on to satirize herself. Two out-of-work musicians, played by Tony Curtis and Jack Lemmon, witness the Saint Valentine's Day massacre, a Capone mob killing of another mob in a public garage in Chicago. Spotted by the Capone mob, they flee. They dress in women's clothes and join an all-girl band, for which Sugar Kane is the vocalist. Curtis takes on the persona of Josephine, and Lemmon is Daphne. Much of the action of the film takes place at a Florida resort hotel, where the all-girl band has an engagement.

The film was shot from early August to mid-November 1958, mostly in Hollywood, with several weeks of shooting at the Hotel del Coronado in San Diego, a Victorian resort hotel on the beach that doubled for the one in Florida. Joe E. Brown, playing a much-married millionaire, chases Jack Lemmon (Daphne) as a potential wife. In a riotous scene, Tony Curtis plays the son of another millionaire. He is supposedly impotent, and

Marilyn seduces him back to potency. It's a variation on Marilyn's frequent stance in her films as a healer of impotent males; during a key scene she makes her usual plea for gentleness in men. At the end of the film the gangsters gun each other down; Lemmon finds that he prefers being a woman to being a man; and Brown wants to marry him no matter who he is. Thus the film upends notions about fixed gender roles and, through the ruthlessness of the gangsters, demonstrates the perils of the links between masculinity and violence. Lemmon and Brown—both of whom reject fixed gender roles—are the most sympathetic characters in the film, aside from Sugar Kane.

Relationships on the set during the making of *Some Like It Hot* were cordial at first. Billy Wilder was pleased to be directing Marilyn again after her success in *The Seven Year Itch*. He and Marilyn hadn't clashed much during its filming, and Natasha Lytess had been helpful. He expected Paula Strasberg, serving as Marilyn's coach, to do the same. Both Lemmon and Curtis praised Marilyn at the start of shooting. Curtis was especially solicitous, dropping by her dressing room daily to compliment her. He had briefly dated her in 1949, when they were both contract players, and he worried that she might be resentful because he hadn't called her after a few dates. But her only comment about it was to ask him if he still had the green convertible they had parked and necked in. According to Marilyn, they never had an affair. When he made his infamous remark that kissing her in the film was like kissing Hitler, she was surprised and then furious. He actually said that kissing her after fifty takes was like kissing Hitler. She noted that there was only one way he could comment on her sexuality, "and I'm afraid he has never had the opportunity."[42]

Jack Lemmon also appreciated her at first. When he first met her, he was amazed and flattered by her detailed knowledge of his film roles. He praised her for having left Hollywood to study at the Actors Studio; that action, he thought, had shown great courage. Like Joseph Cotten, her costar in *Niagara*, and Joshua Logan, her director in *Bus Stop*, Lemmon realized that whatever she did to create a character worked. He noticed that when her acting wasn't right, a built-in alarm would "go off" in her head. She would abruptly halt and stand with her eyes closed, sorting out the issue without consulting the director or the other actors. She would then figure out what she had done wrong and correct it. She frequently consulted with Paula, but Paula didn't direct her every movement, as Natasha had.[43]

Marilyn had problems with the script when she realized that Sugar Kane was mostly a foil for the two male characters. She didn't like it that Sugar was so dense that she didn't realize that the two new women in the band—Josephine and Daphne—were actually men. She fought with Wilder to allow her to make her character more distinctive. She persuaded him to reshoot her first two scenes in the film the way she wanted them. Having a blast of exhaust from the train hit Sugar's backside in her first scene in the film as she runs alongside the train gives the character a sexy panache from the outset and refers back to the subway grate scene in *The Seven Year Itch*. Wilder became stubborn after that, wanting his own way. In his defense, he had slipped a disk in his back and he was in terrible pain during the filming. But he was another director who wanted control, and dealing with Marilyn's stubborness made him furious.

Jack Cole was on the set, and he thought Wilder was exceptionally nasty to Marilyn; according to Cole, Wilder constantly made rude remarks to her. Barbara Diamond, whose husband worked on the script, was also present. She thought that Wilder, Lemmon, and Curtis were all hard on Marilyn, making her nervous and unable to perform. As Wilder ordered take after take, it was as though he was trying to show her who was boss. Marilyn wrote Norman Rosten in September that their "ship was sinking," but at least she didn't have "a phallic symbol" to lose, the way the men did. The reference was to their self-pride as men who were playing women in the film.[44]

As had become her habit, Marilyn dealt with the terror she felt at speaking lines in front of a movie camera by medicating herself. She drank coffee from a Thermos after each take, but most people on the set thought the Thermos contained vodka. She flubbed lines, required multiple retakes, and was late to the set either out of terror, as a result of being high, or to rattle Wilder to get her way. As a great star, she felt she had the right to appear when she wanted to, say what she wanted, and have her suggestions incorporated into the film. She made sure people on the set knew how she felt. During one day of filming she stayed in her dressing room reading Thomas Paine's *Rights of Man*, clearly indicating her feeling of being oppressed. Much was made of her saying "Fuck you" to an assistant director who was sent to bring her to the set.

Her behavior angered Lemmon and Curtis. They had to stand under the hot lights for hours wearing tight corsets, high heels, and heavy makeup to cover their facial hair. It was uncomfortable, and they wanted to get the shooting over. Neither Lemmon nor Curtis required many takes. By the time Wilder called "cut" they were exhausted, while Marilyn was just hitting her stride. They complained to Wilder, but he replied that he had to print Marilyn's best take, not theirs, because she brought in the audiences.

Arthur arrived on the set several weeks after shooting began. He mostly stood to one side and watched the filming. He'd become part of her entourage, the kept husband of the great star. Wilder wondered how he could be so subordinate. But Arthur felt loyal to Marilyn, as he had to his first wife. Deeply committed to *The Misfits*, he wanted to be certain that she would make it through this film. Many people who saw them together, even during the tumult of making *Some Like It Hot*, thought that their marriage was in good shape. The publicist on the film wrote that Marilyn seemed to lean on Arthur as though he was her father, while he basked in her "deep idolatry." Was it real? Or had it become a pose they put on at will?[45]

Despite their issues, Arthur was still devoted to Marilyn. Some commentators suggest that he had given up on her by the spring of 1958, but they are mistaken. In September he returned to New York to see his children, and he wrote three letters to her. In the first letter, he states he will love her forever. The bed seems a mile wide, he writes, empty as a field. Drawing from the original concept of their marriage, he envisions unity with her, that their wills are combined toward the same end. The second letter is similar. He calls her his dear baby girl and hopes that during the rest of the filming she will realize that her acting is superior to anything being done on the set. "I am your flesh, the air you breathe."[46]

In the third letter, he writes about his own faults in the marriage. He apologizes for the things he has done and those he has failed to do. He seems to refer to the upsetting journal entry in London and to his failure to support them financially. He states he is making important discoveries in his therapy, especially in understanding the blocks in his emotional life that so often make him distant. Their public face as a happy couple probably reflected at least some portion of their private life together.

During the filming of *Some Like It Hot*, Marilyn became pregnant;

her condition is apparent in the beach scenes. The movie wrapped in mid-November, and Marilyn miscarried a month later. Was the miscarriage caused by drinking and taking drugs? In an exchange of telegrams between Arthur and Billy Wilder after the miscarriage occurred, Arthur held Wilder responsible for it, accusing him of working Marilyn too hard.[47] Arthur had a point: in the closing scenes of the film, Marilyn, wearing spike heels, runs up and down stairs and around the hotel grounds, escaping from the mobsters. Such activity could hardly have been good for her pregnancy, especially in light of her endometriosis and the drinking and drug taking.

Leon "Red" Krohn, Marilyn's gynecologist at the time, told her to stop taking pills and drinking because it would hurt the baby. He wanted her to stay in bed during the pregnancy. Marilyn was unhappy with this advice, and she accused him of giving it to her because Walter Mirisch, the film's producer, was his friend.[48] Once the filming ended, she did cut back on her drinking and drug taking and stayed in bed. But it wasn't soon enough to do much good. A handwritten note from an unknown author contained in her file cabinets states that if she had gone to bed during the pregnancy and given up pills, she might have carried the baby to term. This wasn't an ectopic pregnancy; the fetus was in the uterus, indicating normality. Such confinement to bed is still used today in the case of pregnant women when miscarriage seems possible.

This miscarriage came after the possible one in 1956 during the filming of *The Prince and the Showgirl* and the one in August 1957 when she was in Amagansett. It fed her fears that she couldn't have a child, that "something was wrong inside her, a defect, an evil." According to Norman Rosten, "It was a dagger at her ego, the love goddess, the woman supreme, unable to have a child." She felt unloved, "cursed by the universe." She felt that it damaged her femininity, her status as the representative of all women. Internalizing 1950s domestic values, wanting to re-mother herself by mothering a child, she saw it as an ultimate blow. Yet she kept having gynecological operations, as though by going under the knife she could refashion her internal self into the perfect woman she wanted to be. Only by having a child could she prove her femininity and blot out her fear that she was really lesbian by nature.[49]

It's hard to determine what operations she underwent. During many of them she didn't stay in the hospital for long; thus her gynecologist probably didn't remove endometriosis, which, by requiring the opening of the scar over her pubic hair and then sewing it up again, would have been major surgery requiring a long hospital stay. In all probability she often had dilation and curettage done to clean out her fallopian tubes—a much less intrusive vaginal procedure. That procedure, which can cause scar tissue to form, isn't used by gynecologists much today, but it was commonly done then. Endometriosis, however, can't be removed vaginally.

Marilyn raged at Leon Krohn, who made her feel guilty, as though she had killed the baby. Given her capacity for guilt and self-punishment, she no doubt felt that way without Krohn reminding her. Yet the rage that she directed against him was so great that he refused to see her again. Still, as she often did in a traumatic situation, she managed to rally. She had her lawyer write a letter to Fox stating that she would do another movie for them as soon as they wanted her. *Life* published Avedon's photos, along with Arthur's encomium, in the December 1958 issue. "These pictures," Arthur wrote, "are a kind of history of our mass fantasy so far as seductresses are concerned . . . Marilyn has identified herself with what surely was naive in these women, what to them in their moment was genuine allure and sexual truth." Her spirit, he stated, is dominated by two qualities: "One is the spontaneous joy she takes in anything a child does; the other is her quick sympathy and respect for old people, for whatever has endured."

When Marilyn read the tribute, however, she didn't like it. She felt that Arthur's encomium was too simple, that it captured only a part of her. She wanted to be seen as mature and complex, not as a naive simpleton.[50] In her opinion, Arthur was avoiding the real Marilyn, just as he was avoiding who she was in his screenplay for *The Misfits*.

Still, *The Misfits* loomed ahead, with Marilyn still ambivalent about doing it. Huston had agreed to direct it. In December, just after Marilyn's miscarriage, he traveled to New York to talk to Miller about it. He demanded extensive revisions; it was too long, too talky, with too many speeches. Arthur accepted his criticisms and set to work on it again. Thus was put in motion a series of moves that would result in Marilyn's first dramatic role in a long time, the kind of role she'd said for years that she wanted to do, a role that might end her typecasting as a dumb blonde. Perhaps Arthur would be her savior, after all.

In the spring of 1958, several months before she left New York for Hollywood to film *Some Like It Hot*, Marilyn met Ralph Roberts at the Strasbergs' apartment. An actor and a masseur, he became a major figure in her life. Roberts had a modest career on Broadway, and he attended classes at the Actors Studio. To supplement his income, he worked as a massage therapist. Trained at the Swedish Massage Institute in New York, he was good at his job. A giant of a man, he had strong, soft hands. Many Broadway actors went to him to relax their bodies. They also liked talking to him: he was a good listener, quiet and gentle, a courtly gentleman from the South.

He was standing in the Strasbergs' kitchen when Marilyn walked in. She was one of the most radiantly beautiful creatures he'd ever seen. It wasn't so much her physical attributes as the inner glow "that penetrated every inch of that high-ceiling kitchen," he wrote in "Mimosa," his unpublished memoir. "And, when I say creature—that was it. An animal. The blue-whiteness one sees sometimes in the stars of a desert night. White-blonde hair, clear-white complexion framing violet-blue eyes."[51]

Ralph didn't become Marilyn's official masseur until she went to Hollywood to do *Let's Make Love* in November 1959. Feeling stressed, she called him to give her a massage. She arranged for a nightly one; massage can moderate the pain from endometriosis and shrink scar tissue. Marilyn and Ralph developed a bond. Both had speech issues—Ralph had suffered from a tied tongue as a child; both were spiritual; both were strong and shy at the same time. They didn't have an affair; Marilyn called him her "brother." Everyone I interviewed who knew Marilyn told me that Ralph (whom Marilyn nicknamed Rafe) was closer to her than anyone else. In "Mimosa," he reveals much of their relationship, which he characterized as emotional, spiritual, and intellectual. Marilyn revealed sides of herself to Ralph that she didn't show to others. During their first massage, Ralph mentioned a book he'd been reading, Willa Cather's *Professor's House*. She exclaimed that she'd just been reading it, that Willa Cather was her favorite author. Among her favorite books, Marilyn said, was Cather's *A Lost Lady*. What seemed like a telepathetic communication between them occurred.[52]

Marilyn told Ralph about the demons that populated her dreams. He would find images of them in Rossell Hope Robbins's *Encyclopedia of Witchcraft and Demonology*. To resist them, she said, she used the tools outlined in *Meditation*, by Friedrich Rittelmeyer. Rittelmeyer was a follower of Rudolph Steiner and a leader of Anthroposophy in Germany. His *Meditation* includes exercises to help one think about rest, purity, and peace in order to become like Jesus Christ. The Gospel of Saint John is his guide, and his goal is to overcome the darkness of depression with the light of the Gospel. Demons were as real to Rittelmeyer as they were to Marilyn.

Ralph was born and raised in the city of Salisbury, North Carolina, and he remained loyal to it and to the South throughout his life. During his nightly massages with Marilyn, he told her about the city, turning it into the site of a fairy tale. Like a parent putting a child to sleep, he told her his fairy story to soothe her.

Salisbury is impressive, having grown as a shipping entrepôt. Farm products were taken there before the Civil War to be sent north. Greek Revival mansions were built. After the war it went through the process of industrialization, generating small factories in the city and considerable wealth. Victorian mansions were built and they still stand, along with the antebellum Greek Revival counterparts. A large cemetery contains the graves of Confederate soldiers. In the center of the city is a statue of a woman—a reproduction of the Winged Victory of Samothrace that stands in the Louvre. She is dressed in a chiton, with her wings and her dress blowing backward as though ruffled by a strong wind. She is reminiscent of Marilyn in the *Seven Year Itch* photo.

As the massage progressed, Ralph took Marilyn through the Salisbury of his memory, as though she had arrived there for a visit and was walking through the city, looking at its buildings and meeting its residents. Arriving by train, she walks on West Council Street past the Yadkin Hotel, stopping at the Lash general store to buy a bag of roasted peanuts. Turning onto Main Street, she blows a kiss to the building where Ralph made his acting debut in a local production. Then past Al Berban's bookstore and a right turn at the square, to reach her favorite sight in

Salisbury, the Winged Victory statue in the center of the city. That was a Nike figure of the ancient world that recognized victory in poetry, in athletic contests, and in war. It was a symbol of a triumphant woman that she could think about in times of despair, to soothe her depression and encourage her to believe in herself.[53]

Chapter 11

The Misfits, 1959–1960

In *My Story* Marilyn described herself as a Hollywood misfit—someone who didn't follow the rules and was critical of the system. In Nevada horse culture a "misfit" was a horse too small to work in a rodeo, fit only to be sold for dog food. People who challenged conventional culture, who were heroic or foolish, had long been characters in Arthur's work. In *The Misfits* Roslyn, a former dance hall girl, and the cowboys, who are roustabouts, are aliens in a middle-class world. So are the various hangers-on in Reno, many of whom are waiting out the six-week period to get a Nevada divorce. Arthur had these images in his head as he wrote the screenplay for *The Misfits*.

Before Marilyn could do the film, to be produced by MMP, she had to do another film for Fox to fulfill her contract obligations. Under pressure from Arthur and the studio, she accepted *Let's Make Love* in the fall of 1959. That probably wasn't a smart decision, given its weak screenplay. Its filming turned into a disaster. It drove a wedge between Marilyn and Arthur that widened considerably during the filming of *The Misfits*, which finally went before the camera in July 1960.

Given her miscarriage in December 1958, Marilyn was depressed during the spring of 1959, but she didn't spend all her time in bed, as has been charged.[1] She was with Arthur when he was given the Gold Medal for Drama on January 27 by the National Institute of Arts and Letters, a considerable honor. She attended a dinner party given by Gloria Vanderbilt for visiting novelist Isak Dinesen. She had, she said, been deeply impressed by Dinesen's *Out of Africa*. She and Arthur went to several Metropolitan Opera productions: Verdi's *Macbeth* in February and Alban Berg's *Wozzeck* in March. But when Laurence Olivier visited the Actors Studio, she hid in a back room, afraid to meet with him after their conflicts in filming *The Prince and the Showgirl*. She was a vision in white at the premiere of *Some Like It Hot* in New York in March, but she stammered in interviews at the event. Several weeks later she went to the Italian Cultural Institute in New York to receive the David di Donatello Award, Italy's most prestigious acting award, given for her performance in *The Prince and the Showgirl*.[2]

That same month she went to Chicago to publicize *Some Like It Hot*. She was the sexy and witty Marilyn in interviews there, but she was also a dumb blonde. She tarted up her appearance and wore no underwear, playing Sugar Kane to the hilt. The height of her visit occurred, at least to the press, when a publicist accidentally spilled a drink on her thin dress at a reception and her pubic hair was revealed. Hairdresser Kenneth Battelle was there with her, and he chided her for not having bleached the hair with peroxide so that it wouldn't show. She had lunch with writer Saul Bellow, whom Arthur knew from Reno when both had been there seeking a divorce. In June she had another operation "cleaning out her fallopian tubes" to ensure that she could become pregnant. It appears that Arthur was willing to try for a baby again.

She did excellent work at the Actors Studio that spring. She played Blanche DuBois in the scene from *A Streetcar Named Desire* in which Blanche vamps a delivery boy who has come to the door. An aging Southern belle, Blanche is self-centered, manipulative, vulnerable, and sensual—and one of the great female roles in American theater. Marilyn also played a scene opposite Ralph Roberts adapted from John Steinbeck's *Of Mice and Men*. Roberts played Lennie; Marilyn was Curley's wife, a beautiful woman desperate to get the attention of men in a dull environment. She played Holly Golightly in scenes adapted from Truman Capote's *Breakfast at Tiffany's*. He loved her in them and wanted her for the film version, which Paramount was producing. But the studio didn't want to deal with her, and Audrey Hepburn got the part. Capote was outraged.[3]

Yet she still didn't have the nerve to take her success to the stage. She doubted that she could do a play night after night, which would require getting to the theater on time and remembering her lines. She didn't have enough self-confidence even to audition for Lee Strasberg to become a regular Studio member. Still, she was flourishing under Lee; his Method approach was working for her. Her acting was becoming richer, more complex.

During the first months of 1959, Marilyn's agent and lawyers negotiated with Twentieth Century–Fox for her next film. *Some Like It Hot* had been a major success, although it had been done under Walter Mirisch's production company. Technically Marilyn had done only *Bus Stop* for Fox. Buddy Adler, the studio head, assigned her to the female romantic lead in "Time and Tide," later renamed *Wild River*, and she accepted the role. Four days before Marilyn was to appear on the set in mid-April, Elia Kazan, the film's director, decided that he didn't want her. To all intents and purposes, she was fired. In his autobiography, Kazan refers to "an absurd casting conference with Buddy Adler," during which Adler pressured him to accept Marilyn.[4]

Somewhere on the way to making this film, communication had broken down. Lee Remick got the role. Marilyn's lawyers riposted to the insult by demanding immediate payment of the $100,000 for *The Blue Angel* and another $100,000 for the dismissal from *Wild River*, as well as counting them as two of her required movies for Fox. Fox executives agreed to their demands. Nonetheless, the rejection was hard on Marilyn. Even *The Brothers Karamazov* had passed her by. Breaking her connection with Milton had ended the possibility of MMP doing it. Sidney Guilaroff lobbied Richard Brooks, who directed the version finally made, to cast Marilyn in the role of Grushenka, but Brooks was another tough male who didn't want to deal with her. German actress Maria Schell played the role.[5]

At the same time, her marriage to Arthur was spiraling downward. He wasn't finishing his projects, and she was becoming increasingly resentful at having to support him. His Gold Medal for Drama from the National Institute of Arts and Letters was an ironic honor, given his lack of productivity. Although his plays were acclaimed in Europe, his last really successful Broadway play had been *Death of a Salesman* in 1949. Both *The Crucible* and *A View from the Bridge* received mixed reviews and attracted small audiences. Their popularity came later, when Miller's plays became standard productions nationwide for small theaters and high schools.

Arthur was putting most of his energy into writing the screen version of *The Misfits*, doing the revisions Huston wanted. He sent the play to Elia Kazan, perhaps hoping that Kazan might direct it. Elia's reply was cordial, but guarded. He thought that Huston was an excellent choice as director, but he also thought the screenplay needed rewriting. It was too wordy, with too much moralizing. It suffered from the lack of a real ending. The virtue of "the girl" was overdrawn: she was too pure, too spiritual. Kazan had identified real problems with the screenplay—and Marilyn independently saw those flaws. Despite continual rewrites, Arthur never really resolved them. But the fact that Kazan replied to Miller indicated the possibility of a rapprochement between them.[6]

Arthur continued writing "The Third Play"—in process since 1952—but he had yet to produce more than fragments. He began turning it into what would become *After the Fall*, another play about Marilyn, this one about her faults. He didn't like it that she was turning him into her lackey, the great star's husband who was part of her entourage. Maureen Stapleton saw him carrying her purse and her makeup case, "just doing too much for her. I had the feeling things had gone hopelessly wrong." Actor and director Martin Ritt had the same feeling when he had dinner at their home. "He was at her beck and call, running around after her all evening." At the same time Arthur was reaching a boil over Marilyn's behavior when they were in Hollywood doing *Some Like It Hot* and went to an occasional party at which men she'd slept with in her early Hollywood days would paw her cheaply in front of him. It's not surprising that Norman Rosten sensed that Miller was retreating from Marilyn emotionally, becoming an observer of his marriage rather than a participant.[7]

In the draft of a scene from a more complete version of *After the Fall*, Arthur describes a telling encounter between them in the Roxbury house. They've been arguing in the living room for a long time. Marilyn suddenly runs upstairs to the bedroom and locks the door from the inside. Arthur remains in the living room, sitting on the couch, exhausted from their fighting. He waits. Eight o'clock and then nine o'clock pass, and the house is quiet. Dinner is waiting on the table, cold. He doesn't know what to do. If he acts manfully, like a Hollywood hero, and breaks down the bedroom door, he might find her reading in bed. Or she might be dying from an overdose. He can't let her die. He has to do something. He knocks on the door. In a scene from the finished play, he manages to open the door and they fight over the pills she has in her hand.[8]

Yet he didn't leave her. They still had good sex. She could be the charming, lovable Marilyn, not taking pills, for stretches of time. He kept hoping that something would happen, some experience that would snap her out of anger and despair. He thought of the unhappy woman in a poem by Rilke who looks through the window of her room and sees an immense tree that she has seen a hundred times before and suddenly recovers from her depression and knows that life is good. That had been part of his motivation for writing *The Misfits* in the first place; it was why he agreed to a baby; it was an outgrowth of his existential philosophy. He saw life as a series of moment-by-moment events that a single experience could transform. That philosophy was central to *The Misfits* screenplay, especially to its ending, as Roslyn (Marilyn) is transformed when Gay and Perce (Clark Gable and Montgomery Clift) free the horses after they and Guido (Eli Wallach) have rounded them up to sell them to the slaughter house.[9]

At the same time, Marilyn was having career difficulties. After *Some Like It Hot* many reporters turned against her. Critics acknowledged her acting in the film as brilliant, but journalists excoriated her behavior on the set. Tony Curtis engaged in a one-man campaign of vituperation, winning over many critics by claiming she regularly held up shooting, paying no attention to his discomfort in his confining costumes. Billy Wilder, with cutting remarks, wasn't far behind. Dealing with Marilyn on this film brought out his latent misogyny. After the filming ended and his rage against Marilyn began to dissipate he told reporter Joe Hyams, "I can look at my wife without wanting to hit her because she is a woman."[10]

Marilyn alienated even Louella Parsons for a time. In contrast to her handling of the 1953 episode involving the sexy red dress she wore in *Niagara*, when she told Parsons her side of the story, she didn't defend her behavior on the set of *Some Like It Hot*. In October 1959, her publicist Joe Wolhandler begged her to tell him what to do to stanch the press criticism. "I have been stalling and fighting off, day after day, press that you have said you would see, going back to the release of *Some Like It Hot* [in March]. It is important that we mend fences with them."[11] Marilyn replied to him with a cursory note that didn't answer his concerns.

At some point that spring she took an overdose of pills, engaging in a serious suicide attempt. Arthur wasn't present in the apartment; he had probably gone to Roxbury to write. Her housekeeper found her and called a doctor, who went to the apartment to pump out her stomach, thus keeping her action from the press. The Rostens, called by the housekeeper, went to console Marilyn. Norman entered her bedroom, and he heard her softly crying. He leaned over the bed and asked her how she was. "Alive," she said. "Bad luck." Her voice was raspy and drugged. "Cruel, all of them, all those bastards," she said. "Oh Jesus . . ." This time she wanted to die. We don't know to what "bastards" she was referring. It could have been Arthur, Elia Kazan, or the Fox executives. She might have meant her father, her childhood abuser, or the men who had taken advantage of her in her career.[12]

In late spring David Lewin of the *London Daily Express* interviewed her about how she'd changed since she made *The Prince and the Showgirl*. She replied that she was more mature. I've been scared all my life, she said, but I'm getting over it at last. "It's getting used to happiness that is hard. What I'd like is a little more freedom in myself." She was hinting at the monsters in her dreams and the anger and despair she couldn't control. She was still in therapy with Marianne Kris, who did what she could to help her. Diana Trilling, a writer and a patient of Kris's, described Kris as "a most remarkable woman, warm-hearted, large-minded, sensitive, sensible, imaginative, a great unraveler of emotional knots. She looked wise and she was wise. Her very calm was therapeutic." Trilling wasn't surprised that Marilyn had chosen Kris as her therapist.[13]

During the spring and summer of 1959, Marilyn had happy times with Jane and Robert Miller, the Shaws and Rostens, Arthur's parents, and her friends in Roxbury. As always, she played with the animals, read, gardened, and supervised construction on the house. She expressed discontent to Susan Strasberg at being a housewife, but she told Dorothy Kilgallen that she loved gardening. (She made similar statements to journalists during the filming of *The Misfits*.) Lotte Goslar visited Marilyn in Roxbury and found her with a mangy looking plant in her hand, with

a flower growing out of it. She was ecstatic. She told Lotte she had re-
planted the dying plant, and it was now growing. She was excited by her
success at reviving a dying plant.[14] When in New York at the end of the
summer, she went to see Yves Montand in his smash-hit one-man cabaret
show, and she liked it so much that she took Arthur to see it the next
night. Thus, unwittingly, she set in motion the series of events that would
destroy her marriage.

Was Marilyn faithful to Arthur during their time of troubles? She stated
that she didn't stray when a marriage was working, but this one wasn't.
Dress manufacturer Henry Rosenfeld was still in her life, and Marlon
Brando occasionally appeared. Norman Rosten told both Anthony Summers and Donald Wolfe that she was seeing other men when the Miller
marriage went sour. "She had this terrible neediness," Rosten said.
"When she felt insecure she went with other men simply for something
to hold on to." Marilyn told W. J. Weatherby that when she was tired or
upset, she "ran for cover" and went out with "party people" who laughed
and joked and gave her a good time, chasing her worries away for a
while. Was she referring to the Kennedys? Lem Billings, who had been
close to Jack Kennedy since college, claimed that Marilyn and Jack saw
each other for years. "She visited on him a variety of moods and sexual
attitudes that excited his craving for variety," Billings stated. Earl Wilson
also stated that her relationship with Jack was long-term, as did James
Bacon and Arthur James. Marilyn's gynecologist Arthur Steinberg said
that she had fallen for Kennedy while she was still with Miller.[15]

Fascinated by Hollywood glamour and its beautiful women, Jack
had been visiting Hollywood since the mid-1940s, and he had bedded
both stars and starlets. He'd grown up around the movie industry, since
his father, Joe Kennedy, had owned studios, made movies, and had been
involved with Gloria Swanson, a major Hollywood star. When Jack went
to Hollywood, he stayed with the high-flying Charles Feldman, a member
of the Wolf Pack, who had provided Elia Kazan and Arthur Miller with
party girls in 1951. Grace Dobish, Feldman's longtime secretary, stated
that Jack and Marilyn met at Feldman's house in the early 1950s. In 1954
Jack's sister Patricia married film star Peter Lawford, whom Marilyn had
dated several times, strengthening the connection. That same year Jack
had serious back surgery; on a wall of his hospital room he had a pinup

poster of Marilyn turned upside down, with her legs in the air. By 1958 Peter and Pat were at the center of a trendy Hollywood group that met at their mansion on the Santa Monica beach, located on a private road, among a row of mansions called the Gold Coast. The other Kennedys, especially the three brothers, visited there. Dave Heiser, a surfing buddy of Lawford's, remembered trying to teach a teenage Teddy Kennedy how to surf.[16]

Jack Kennedy was charming and charismatic. Hollywood people who knew him said that he could have been a movie star. He also had a body riddled with pain—from a bad back, Addison's disease, and osteoporosis. Whether by nature or because of the steroids and testosterone he took for his ailments, he seemed driven to bed beautiful women he met, while singling out several for special attention. Marilyn was one of them, although her relationship with him was episodic, not frequent.

In New York the Kennedys had a penthouse suite at the Carlyle Hotel on East Seventy-sixth Street, eighteen blocks from Marilyn's apartment. Marilyn often wore disguises to mask her appearance. Even disguised, however, she could be recognized. Jane Shalam, the daughter of a New York family prominent in politics, who lived across from the hotel, saw Marilyn entering and exiting. Sheilah Graham heard Jack Kennedy make a date with Marilyn by phone on the set of *The Seven Year Itch* in New York in the fall of 1954. There was also her secret apartment on New York's East side. Senator George Smathers stated that she went on cruises on the Potomac River in Washington, D.C., with Jack and some of his close male friends. Jack took his friends along as "beards" to conceal that Marilyn was with him. Kennedy family friend Charles Spalding said she visited Hyannisport.[17]

Marilyn was as much a friend of the Kennedys as a lover. Norman Rosten referred to Marilyn's friendship with them, as did Pat Newcomb, who told journalist Seymour Hersh that they loved her sense of humor. Pete Summers, a Democratic political advisor, stated that he saw Jack and Marilyn together at the Lawford mansion during the spring of 1960, before the Democratic National Convention in July. Sidney Skolsky said that she participated in conclaves there that spring planning Kennedy's campaign. At that point she was in Hollywood making *Let's Make Love*. Marilyn was the world's major sex icon, but she also had a special gift for friendship—with men as well as with women.[18]

Marilyn lived her life in differing worlds and kept her relationships separate. She didn't want to destroy her marriage to Arthur. Like him, she continued hoping that something—perhaps a child—would revive it. But that hope doesn't mean that she didn't take breaks from it. She couldn't stand being controlled or being taken advantage of, and Arthur, it might be said, was doing both. He wasn't listening to her criticisms of *The Misfits*, although he was advising her on her career. He would continue to try to control her during her next two films, *Let's Make Love* and *The Misfits*, and she would fight back, both openly and subtly.

In September 1959 Twentieth Century–Fox assigned Marilyn to "The Billionaire," a fluffy romantic comedy about a wealthy man who falls in love with a showgirl and then disguises himself as a song-and-dance man to win her when she makes it clear that she doesn't like wealthy men. (It was renamed *Let's Make Love*.) Marilyn liked doing musicals, which allowed her to sing and dance. George Cukor was assigned to direct it. He was known as a women's director, able to deal with difficult female stars, but the designation was a code word for a homosexual. Renowned actor Gregory Peck was to play the billionaire. Marilyn successfully demanded that Jack Cole choreograph and provide instruction to her on her song-and-dance numbers.[19]

When Marilyn read the script carefully, she realized her role wasn't that large. Norman Krasna, the original screenwriter, refused to rewrite the script, so Marilyn persuaded the studio to hire Arthur to do it—a strange choice, since he had no experience writing romantic comedy. Nonetheless, he wanted the money, plus he wanted Marilyn to fulfill her responsibility to Fox so that they could get *The Misfits* into production. He rewrote *Let's Make Love* three times. But when Gregory Peck found that in the new script his role was reduced and Marilyn's increased, he pulled out of the project. Arthur came up with Yves Montand as the new leading man. Miller knew him because he and his wife, actress Simone Signoret, had starred in a production of *The Crucible* in Paris. It was a major career opportunity for Montand, since he wasn't known in Hollywood and Marilyn was a great star.

With Montand on board and a completed script that had Marilyn's approval, Marilyn and Arthur's problems seemed solved; but they were only beginning. The weak script continued to create difficulties during filming, even though Arthur kept rewriting it. Montand spoke little English, and his accent is thick throughout the movie. He wasn't a comedian; he was a sultry cabaret singer, and his attempts to do comedy seem absurd. When the screen tests for makeup and costume were done before the start of filming, Marilyn looked awful, and her appearance didn't improve during the filming. Her hair is limp, her skin mottled, and she's overweight. She was obviously taking too many drugs. In fact, the problem increased to the point that psychiatrist Ralph Greenson was called in to help her get off them. Still, Simone Signoret described her as "the most beautiful peasant girl imaginable."[20]

When the Millers and the Montands arrived in Hollywood in early November for preproduction work, they moved into adjoining bungalows in the Beverly Hills Hotel and quickly became friendly. Signoret, a sophisticated but down-to-earth French film actress, had just triumphed in *Room at the Top* as an older woman involved with a younger man. Maternal and caring, she was drawn to Marilyn. Both she and Yves were radicals; their politics were attractive to Arthur and Marilyn. The two men took long walks around Beverly Hills; the two women went shopping and sunned themselves by the pool; and the couples ate dinner together. The fan magazines loved to report their camaraderie, which continued for several months. Simone was fascinated when Marilyn found Pearl Porterfield living in Redondo Beach and had her travel to Hollywood each week to dye her hair. She was the hairdresser who had created the dye for Jean Harlow's hair—a combination of peroxide and bluing. Still obsessed with Harlow, Marilyn wanted her hair to be as white as possible, to create a halo around her head. Perhaps what Marilyn really wanted was to hear the many stories Porterfield told about Harlow.

Arthur and Marilyn could still act like a happily married couple. In late January 1960, soon after filming began on *Let's Make Love*, they were interviewed in their bungalow at the Beverly Hills Hotel by Henry Brandon of the *London Sunday Times*, who was writing a series of articles from conversations he held with important Americans. Marilyn and Arthur's topic was "Sex, Theatre, and the Intellectual." Brandon found Arthur intense, intellectual, and bitter about the charges made against him by the House Un-American Activities Committee. Marilyn sat by his side on the sofa, with her head against his shoulder. She seemed to Brandon "a little kitten." When she became apprehensive,

Miller took her hand, "affectionately and protectively." As her shyness dissipated, her common sense and happy outlook appeared. In the published interview Miller answered Brandon's questions, even the ones addressed to Marilyn. He was in control.[21]

The next day Brandon visited the set of *Let's Make Love*. Marilyn was bubbly and confident. Now she was in control and Miller was on the sidelines, looking shy and uneasy. Her puckish sense of fun was intoxicating to everyone. "That is her real gift—her ability to turn boredom into bliss, misery into joy," wrote Brandon.

Sidney Skolsky now reappeared in Marilyn's life. With Marilyn in Hollywood, they renewed their friendship. When Arthur wasn't there, Marilyn invited Sidney to dinner. Remaining loyal to Marilyn, he held Arthur responsible for their marital difficulties because he had become too involved in her career.[22] Between January 30 and February 4, Arthur returned to New York to work on *The Misfits*, since Marilyn's state of mind had improved and Simone and Yves were there to watch over her. On February 10 he went to Ireland for two weeks to consult with John Huston.

Despite support from Yves and Simone, Marilyn broke down. Even Yves, usually patient, became annoyed with her one day when she kept him waiting on the set all day and didn't appear. He knocked on her door that evening, but there was no answer. Then he slid a note under the door saying that she was behaving like a little girl and he didn't like it. Marilyn called Arthur in Ireland; Arthur called Yves and suggested that Simone join him at the door, since Marilyn felt especially close to her. Now sobbing, Marilyn opened the door and threw herself into Simone's arms and said she wouldn't do it again.

Of course, she did it again. Marianne Kris was finally contacted in New York, and she recommended bringing in psychiatrist Ralph Greenson to see Marilyn on a temporary basis. Greenson had a practice in Beverly Hills with many star patients. Between February 11 and March 12, he had fifteen sessions with Marilyn. He was appalled by the drugs she was taking, and he tried to get her off them. They included Phenobarbital, Amytal, and sodium pentathol. She was also taking Demerol—a narcotic similar to morphine which is highly addictive—and she was injecting it intravenously. Unlike the other three drugs, Demerol is a strong medication for pain; her endometriosis must have flared up. She justified her drug taking by citing her insomnia, and Greenson tried to get her to understand that she was making the insomnia worse by taking so many drugs.[23]

During their sessions, Marilyn poured out her resentments against Arthur. He was cool toward his father, she said, ineffective with his children, under the domination of his mother, attracted to other women, and insufficiently demonstrative with her. She was annoyed with him for going to Ireland. These complaints were legitimate, but they were exaggerated. Greenson didn't automatically take her side, especially after he talked to Arthur, who seemed concerned about her but nearly fed up. Greenson decided that her demands for total devotion were overwhelming Arthur, although once she obtained it she became manipulative. She had turned Arthur into a foster parent whom she then rejected. Greenson called her paranoid, but not schizophrenic.

During March the Writers' Guild called a strike, and production shut down on *Let's Make Love* for a number of weeks. Marilyn went to Roxbury with Arthur. Given her popularity in the community and her growing interest in politics, she was elected an alternate delegate to the state Democratic caucus, although she didn't attend it. She also signed up as a founding member of the Hollywood branch of the Committee for a Sane Nuclear Policy (SANE). Toward the end of the month, she wrote a letter to Lester Markel, urging him to include her ideas in his *New York Times* columns. Indicating her sharp turn toward the left, she informed Markel of her support for Fidel Castro in Cuba because he had thrown out the corrupt Batista regime. "I was brought up to believe in democracy," she declared. She told Markel that the *New York Times* coverage of Castro was biased against him. She suggested that Supreme Court justice William O. Douglas would be a good Democratic presidential candidate, with John Kennedy his running mate. Indicating the strength of her convictions, she attended meetings held that spring at Peter Lawford's house to plan a Kennedy candidacy.[24]

Then in April 1960 Simone Signoret won the Oscar for Best Actress for her performance in *Room at the Top*, and Shelley Winters won Best Supporting Actress for her performance as the mother in *The Diary of Anne Frank*. To her dismay, Marilyn wasn't even nominated for her role in *Some Like It Hot*, a critical and box office success. Hollywood seemed to be shunning her. Yet the overseas film communities and critics adored her. She won awards from Italy and France for *The Prince and the Show-girl*, while the Hollywood Foreign Press Association awarded her its Golden Globe for best comedy actress of the year for her portrayal of Sugar Kane in *Some Like It Hot*.

In sessions with Greenson, Arthur wasn't the only person Marilyn perceived to be her enemy. She identified both George Cukor and his cameraman on the film as homosexuals who wanted to take her over. Cukor, in fact, was the only major homosexual director in Hollywood—and he had a reputation as a gay queen. Billy Travilla charged that Cukor made a play for Yves Montand during the filming, contending with Marilyn over him. Unlike most directors Marilyn had worked with, Cukor didn't focus on the formal aspects of filming—lights, camera, sound. His interest was in the actors; he sometimes performed their roles along with them on the sidelines during filming. But Marilyn didn't understand his direction. Even though Jack Cole stated that she took a lot of drugs during the filming, he agreed with her criticisms of Cukor. He talked too much during filming, Cole said, and threw off her concentration. His verbal directions were sometimes incomprehensible, while Paula Strasberg seemed unable for once to translate them into language that Marilyn understood.[25]

In fact, relations between Paula and Marilyn became so frayed on this film that Marilyn began to regard Paula as akin to Gladys Eley, her disturbed mother. Paula, who had her own neuroses, decided that she had fallen into a folie à deux with Marilyn, in which she replicated Marilyn's neurotic symptoms. They managed to finish *Let's Make Love*, and they did better on *The Misfits*, Marilyn's next film. After that, however, their relationship broke down to the extent that Marilyn fired Paula during the filming of *Something's Got to Give* in 1961.

Despite problems with Paula, Marilyn still practiced Method acting, but Cukor detested it, calling it "pretentious maundering." Many evenings after a day's filming Marilyn attended the showing of the daily rushes, and she and Cukor often disagreed about them. Still a perfectionist, she demanded many retakes. As she had with other directors, she fought him for control. Cukor may have been gentle on the surface but he was tough underneath, even though he later claimed that Marilyn was in control during much of the filming. She did what she wanted in playing her role. All he could do was to foster a climate on the set that was agreeable for her because "every day was an agony of struggle for her, just to get to the set." He sympathized with Marilyn, although he also said that she was "as mad as her mother."[26]

Greenson pulled Marilyn together, although he wasn't able to do anything about her attraction to Yves Montand, who reminded her of Joe DiMaggio. Tall, dark, and handsome, Yves did resemble Joe—and Arthur. Unlike them, however, he exuded sexuality, had a Frenchman's charm, and openly admitted that he was insecure in playing his role. Both their childhoods had been difficult, and that was a connection between them. They began rehearsing together in their hotel rooms in the evening, going over their lines. Marilyn had never acted opposite such a sympathetic man. Meantime, Arthur kept leaving town, and in early April Simone went to Europe to do a film. Yves and Marilyn were left alone together.

The inevitable happened: they had an affair. In his autobiography, Montand defended Marilyn against charges that she was an unbalanced drug addict. She was "strong" and "full of good sense." On the other hand, others who were there at the time thought that Yves was ambitious to succeed in Hollywood and was using her.[27] Why Arthur and Simone left them alone together isn't clear, but Marilyn had never had an affair with a leading man, so perhaps they thought it was safe.

The final cut of *Let's Make Love* was still hampered by a weak script and a miscast leading man. Yves was known for his smoldering masculinity, which sometimes had a feminine edge. But male characters in the film mock him, and he looks self-conscious throughout it. In one scene he is embarrassed as Gene Kelly teaches him how to dance, and a man enters the room to find him twirling in Kelly's arms. Marilyn seems lost among a host of male characters, who tell jokes that aren't funny, while she sings the song "My Heart Belongs to Daddy," which draws from the 1950s fascination with women as girls. That fascination was taken to an extreme by Vladimir Nabokov, in his novel *Lolita*, a best seller about an aging pedophile who abducts an adolescent girl named Lolita and gains emotional control over her.

Marilyn repeats the name "Lolita" in the opening number of *Let's Make Love*, in which she sings "My Heart Belongs to Daddy." The best aspect of the film is Marilyn's role. Arthur wrote the real Marilyn into her character, Amanda Dell, who is charming, kooky, and wise. She is a dancer taking classes at night, isn't interested in money, and wants a gentle man. Much of the "real" Marilyn is in this film.

Marilyn's lateness to the set and repeated absences added a month to the filming, and the writers' strike in March delayed filming by another month. Thus it wasn't completed until the end of June. Shortly before it ended, Miller returned. He didn't seem to know about Marilyn's affair with Montand, although gossip columnists were hinting at it. Several days after he got back, he asked Rupert Allan why Yves hadn't gotten in touch with him, and Allan told him what was going on.

As a result, Arthur and Marilyn discussed divorce. He had come to represent betrayal to her, Arthur stated, because he didn't listen to her about the script of The Misfits; because he left her alone so often; because he seemed to be colluding with Hollywood rather than supporting her. Their sex life was nearly dead. The affair with Montand may have been the impetus for divorce discussions, but Arthur later said it didn't bother him. "Anyone who could make her smile came as a blessing to me."[28] That may be true, but surely he was angry at being cuckolded by a friend. The nation's press would soon focus on the affair, further humiliating him.

Another scenario was unfolding that Marilyn knew nothing about, and it might explain Arthur's seeming lack of concern about Montand. Arthur had begun meeting with Elia Kazan in New York. Funding had been raised for a national theater, with a resident company. It would become the Repertory Theatre at Lincoln Center. Kazan was to be its director, and he wanted to open it with a new Arthur Miller play. Arthur leapt at the chance.[29] The play would be After the Fall, Arthur's diatribe against Marilyn. Miller and Kazan were moving toward reconciliation. In the end, they would reconcile over what amounted to an attack on Marilyn for her promiscuous behavior with men, an attack on her body, even though they had both earlier loved that body. Perhaps Arthur needed to symbolically "kill" Marilyn before he could break his writing block and move on to other work.

Marilyn had almost no time off between Let's Make Love and The Misfits, even though she was exhausted from the long months she had spent

filming the former movie. The tension with Arthur and Yves was drain-
ing, especially since she kept pursuing Yves and he kept retreating. When
his airplane landed at Idlewild on June 26, on a trip from Paris to Hollywood, where he was scheduled to do another film, she was there in a
limousine with champagne and caviar waiting for him. She ran up to the
landing ramp as he exited from the plane and embraced him, making
their affair obvious to the journalists who were present. She'd reserved a
room in a nearby hotel, but he turned that down. Then there was a bomb
scare, and his plane was grounded from nine P.M. until one in the morning. They sat in the limousine; May Reis, Marilyn's secretary, was with
them. One wonders what they talked about. The next day journalists
reported what had happened. The newspapers were filled with it.[30]

How do these adventures fit in with the sightings of her with John F.
Kennedy at the Democratic convention, which was held in Los Angeles
from July 11 to July 15? It's possible that she was there; Marilyn was
skilled at concealing herself. She was reported to have had dinner with
him and to have attended a party at Peter Lawford's after Kennedy gave
his acceptance speech at the Los Angeles Coliseum. Marilyn seemed to
travel across the continent with aplomb, although it was a long flight in
those days, nearly eight hours in length. Still, Ralph Roberts claimed
that he was in Marilyn's New York apartment with her at the time of the
convention, watching it on television with her. And New York journalists observed her taking an airplane to Los Angeles on July 17, after the
convention had ended. They reported that she looked exhausted, with
pouches under her eyes and bloodstains on her skirt. Gloria Romanoff,
who was present throughout the convention, saw Jack Kennedy with a
blonde woman, but she wasn't Marilyn. Still, Marilyn, a master at deception, may have been there.[31]

The end of the Miller marriage played out in the Nevada desert, during
the filming of *The Misfits*. The filming began in early July; Marilyn arrived on the set on July 18. A stellar cast had been assembled, including
Eli Wallach, Montgomery Clift, and Clark Gable to play the three aging
cowboys. The technical personnel—cameramen, sound men, lighting
experts, set decorators—were the best in the industry. Everyone involved
with the film thought it would be a masterpiece. It turned out to be the
most expensive black-and-white movie in the history of Hollywood

films. Gable's compensation for the film, involving a salary and a percentage of the profits, was the highest yet paid to any actor in any film.[32]

The producer was Frank Taylor, an editor in New York publishing with experience in Hollywood who was a friend of the Millers. Tall and elegant, he spoke quietly and listened carefully, unlike most Hollywood producers, and he could soothe ruffled feathers. John Huston was the film's director. He'd already required many revisions to the script, and he would continue to do so during filming. He hadn't had a hit movie in some time and, with the script perfected, this might be the one.[33]

Marilyn liked the three male leads. She called Eli Wallach Teacake and thought of him as a brother. Clark Gable had been her fantasy father when she was a child. They had met at the 1954 party at Romanoff's restaurant celebrating her success in *The Seven Year Itch*. Monty Clift, who was homosexual, was her soul mate: Both were shy and sensitive, both were neurotic and hooked on drugs. Both were insomniacs who talked for hours on the phone during the night to friends. Each was the acting idol of the other. Monty had seen Marilyn in the scene from *Anna Christie* at the Actors Studio; he'd been offered the role of the cowboy in *Bus Stop*, and he now regretted having turned it down. They had formed a bond during the summer of 1958, when they were both making movies in Hollywood. After that, they saw each other frequently in New York.[34]

Frank Taylor had taken precautions to keep things running smoothly during the filming. He barred all reporters from the set without express permission from him to be there. He arranged for the prestigious Magnum cooperative of photographers to take all the still photos. Its photographers came in teams of two, each team for two weeks, eliminating any crush of photographers on the set. Inge Morath and Henri Cartier-Bresson were the first team to appear, and Eve Arnold was on one of the later teams. Taylor arranged for the cast and crew (some two hundred individuals) to stay at the Mapes Hotel in Reno and to be bused to the film's three major locations, each about fifty miles from Reno: a house near the cabin where Arthur had lived when he established residency for his 1954 divorce; a town with a rodeo stadium; and an alkaline lake bed. Limousines transported the major performers and technicians to those locations. It appeared that Taylor had thought of everything.[35]

Yet problems arose during the filming. The first was the terrible heat during the summer months in Reno and the region around it, as much as 110 degrees. Filming was supposed to start in March, in much cooler weather, but the delays on *Let's Make Love* had prevented it. In this heat, dehydraytion and sunstroke were threats. To provide some relief, the motors on the limousines were kept running, with the air-conditioning on high. Fortunate people assigned to those cars could take their breaks sitting in them. When scenes were filmed on the lake bed, there was hardly a breath of air; the only trees were those put up by the prop men. Any movement kicked up alkaline dust that got into eyes and lungs. One reporter called it "like one of Gustave Doré's paintings of hell for Dante's *Divine Comedy.*"

Controversies arose. Miller was determined that he and Huston would be in charge of the filming. After being with Paula Strasberg on the sets of *The Prince and the Showgirl*, *Some Like It Hot*, and *Let's Make Love*, Miller considered her a major problem. He met with John Huston and Frank Taylor about her before shooting began. They decided to freeze her out by not speaking to her during the filming except for pleasantries. According to Taylor, they carried out this decision, even though Marilyn became furious when she figured out what was going on.[36] She felt she needed Paula's support, and she didn't want the men ganging up on her.

The plan regarding Paula became the basis for two factions that emerged among the cast and crew, with Montgomery Clift on Marilyn's side and Eli Wallach siding with Miller and Huston, although Wallach later contended that he hadn't taken sides.[37] Marilyn had many assistants with her—Paula Strasberg, Whitey Snyder, May Reis, Hazel Washington, Rupert Allan, Ralph Roberts, and others—and they supported her. Each side drove in separate limousines from Reno to the film's locations; each had its own after-hours events. Marilyn stayed in her suite and didn't attend them.

Clark Gable stayed out of the dissension. He drove his own car to the set, rented his own house, and was there on time for every call. He left the set every day at five o'clock, no matter when filming had begun. That time was written into his contract. He knew about Marilyn's childhood fixation on him as her father and about her heavy use of prescription drugs. He was kind to her on the set, continually complimenting her on her work. His wife, Kay, was expecting their first child, and his emotions were focused on her pregnancy. But he felt the tensions on the set. He chain-smoked and drank whiskey throughout the day.

During the filming, Marilyn was alienated from Arthur. She was convinced he had betrayed her, even before her involvement with Montand. She didn't like the script; she thought Arthur had made the male roles more important than hers; and, in line with Elia Kazan's criticism, she thought her role wasn't nuanced. From the first day of shooting, as Marilyn spoke her lines, she realized she was speaking words she had spoken in real life, taken out of context. Doing so was even more difficult than she had anticipated. She was also in Reno, where Arthur had gotten his divorce—a grim forecast of where their marriage might end up.

Attempting to stop rumors of a breakup, she and Arthur occupied the same suite in the Mapes Hotel, which probably wasn't a good idea. At first Arthur felt obliged to get her to the set. So he stayed up at night with her, trying to calm her down so that she would go to sleep. But he kept rewriting the script, requiring her to memorize new lines every evening. That was always hard for her, and it was even more so now, because Huston required her to be word perfect in doing her scenes. No improvisations, no changing lines.

In his apologia for *The Misfits*, Arthur claims that not much rewriting was done and that Huston asked for most of it. Such claims don't match the recollections of others who were there. Rewriting on Hollywood scripts, even during filming, isn't unusual, although the rewriting on this script was extensive. After all, Arthur had been working on it for more than three years. Yet he could still be kind to Marilyn. To simplify doing the film, he persuaded Huston to shoot it in the sequence in the script, not broken up, which was the usual practice. As a result, however, actors interacted on the set in ways that suggested new motivations, which required additional rewriting.

Moreover, Huston and Miller often focused on Marilyn's body in the filming, as though they couldn't avoid sexualizing her. What seem to be polka dots on a dress she wears are actually red cherries, adding a disconcerting sexual crudeness to her character. In one scene, Marilyn bounces a small ball on a paddle. She'd been playing the game, at which she excelled, during a break in filming. Miller put it into the film, but he had a cowboy patting her behind at the same time, making her seem like a male possession.[38]

Marilyn was still taking drugs—Nembutal and Seconol to sleep, amphetamines for energy during filming—her usual combination. When the studio doctor on the set refused to give her more than a few pills, she went to a doctor in Reno to get them. In 1955 Delos Smith, a friend of the Strasbergs, said she was taking five to six Nembutal a day; John Huston said she was now taking twenty a day. She was also suffering from flatulence and a pain in her side: both were caused by gallstones. Her colitis, an old problem, flared up, and she had her usual menstrual pain, which caused some of her absences. Ralph Roberts massaged her body every evening and in between takes, helping to keep her going. Whitey Snyder got her up in the morning, sometimes throwing her under a cold shower to wake her. But she was still often late to the filming, sometimes by many hours. Huston set the filming call at eleven each morning, rather than the normal nine thirty, but it didn't help.

Marilyn's lateness made Huston furious, although he had his own behavior issues. Reno was a national center for gambling, and Huston was addicted. He gambled most nights, sometimes all night long, steadily consuming liquor. He'd sometimes fall asleep in the director's chair the next day. Once filming ended each day and the crew was back in Reno, many of them also went out drinking: they often welcomed Marilyn's lateness because they were hungover. Huston chided Marilyn for her lateness in his autobiography, although he grudgingly praised her acting. "She would go deep into herself to find an emotion and bring it up."[39]

Arthur and Marilyn began to argue so loudly in their suite that occupants of the rooms near them complained to the management. They quarreled over the filming, the script, and Miller's continued emotional withdrawal. Marilyn claimed that Montand was going to leave Simone Signoret for her. She brought up her litany of complaints: Arthur was cold to his father and his children and tied to his mother. She accused him of having excised Milton Greene, the only person who hadn't used her, from her life. Eli Wallach heard her yell at Arthur for interfering in Huston's directing and in her acting by telling both of them what to do. "You don't understand women," she screamed at Arthur. "I am a film actress and I know what I'm doing."

She thought he was eyeing other women, especially Angela Allan, the film's continuity supervisor. That wasn't the case, although Arthur wasn't entirely guiltless. Inge Morath, a Magnum photographer on the set for two weeks, married Arthur a year and a half later. Both she and Miller adamantly denied there had been anything between them on the set of *The Misfits*. Still, other people who were there thought that Arthur had a roving eye.[40] Arthur and Marilyn mostly didn't speak to each other on the set. Arthur's camp made much of an episode in which he was standing by the edge of the road hoping for a ride back to Reno and Paula and Marilyn drove by in a car without stopping. If Huston hadn't shown up, Miller would have been stranded in the desert.

According to Ralph Roberts and journalist Radie Harris, Arthur left a version of *After the Fall* on the desk in their suite. If that was true, it was an ultimate blow, given the dark depiction of Marilyn in the play. It would also have replicated the incident in London when Arthur left his journal open on a desk to a page criticizing her and she read it.[41] Neither Arthur nor Marilyn spoke of the incident, although Ralph was Marilyn's confidant and Radie Harris was close to the Strasbergs. Paula was still coaching Marilyn. If the incident happened, it contributed to Marilyn's anger at Miller.

She wasn't sleeping; her nerves were on edge; she was fighting with Arthur and upset about the continual rewrites. In mid-August Frank Sinatra invited the cast and crew to the Cal Neva Lodge on Lake Tahoe, an hour from Reno, to watch his evening show. Both Marilyn and Arthur went. Sinatra was in the process of buying the lodge. His invitation wasn't without an ulterior motive; he had heard rumors that there were problems in the filming and he wanted to see for himself how Marilyn was doing. He had taken a step toward becoming a presence in her life.

On August 27, Marilyn left Reno to go to Los Angeles. Once there, she consulted Hyman Engelberg, Ralph Greenson's associate and her internist, and he admitted her to the Westside Hospital for rest and to dry out from drugs. Stories circulated that she was wrapped in a wet sheet and rushed to Los Angeles by airplane, but the newspapers reported that she took a plane with Paula Strasberg by way of San Francisco and went to a Hollywood party the night before being admitted to the hospital.[42]

According to Rupert Allan, she ran out of sleeping pills several weeks before she flew to Los Angeles, and the doctor she consulted in Reno put her on a new, highly addictive medication. When she ran out of it she suffered withdrawal pains, and she went to Los Angeles to see her doctors and get new pills. Greenson and Engelberg put her in the hospital and on less potent drugs, including chloral hydrate, a sedative given to soldiers during World War Two. It is an opiate rather than a barbiturate; thus in a different class of drugs. Greenson was trying to wean her from Nembutal. She recovered in ten days and returned to Reno. If she hadn't completed the film her career would have been over, since no insurance company would have insured her on any future film.[43]

John Huston maintained that she reverted to heavy drug usage after her return from Los Angeles, but Ralph Roberts stated that Greenson gave the pills to him, with instructions on how to dole them out to her. Indeed, there were no overdoses during the last months of filming, from early September to early November. Ralph noted that Marilyn began sleeping in a hot room, with black curtains over the windows to shut out the light: she had created a womb—or a tomb—for herself. She seemed to him like a caged animal, afraid of both the day and the night. The bedroom arrangement somehow made her feel safe. Arthur Miller was obviously no longer sharing her suite.[44]

In the diary that journalist James Goode kept during the filming, Marilyn seems in good humor during the last several months. Paula was now central to keeping her going; even John Huston later said that they couldn't have finished the film without Paula. Yet Paula was suffering from the bone marrow cancer that would eventually kill her, and she was taking a lot of pain medication. Lee Strasberg went to the filming to chastise Huston and to give Marilyn energy, but Paula sent him back to New York after a brief stay.

The irony of *The Misfits* is that, as Arthur had intended from the beginning, the finished movie is a tribute to Marilyn. She is a pantheistic force of nature, never more radiant, never more wise. No matter her intake of drugs and alcohol, the sickly pallor of her face in *Let's Make Love* is gone. It's easy to believe that all three cowboys would desire her. Her acting is multifaceted, soaring over the script, as her emotions cycle from high to low and from one moment to the next.

The Misfits is a morality tale about the meaning of masculinity and femininity, set against a frontier being destroyed by suburbanization, technological progress, and a consumer culture. In the film masculine adventuring and pugnacity—flying airplanes, overcoming bulls in rodeos, roping wild mustangs—are contrasted to female generativity and domesticity, which Roslyn both embraces and rejects. She arrives in Reno to divorce a husband; there are hints that she had worked as a stripper. But she takes up housekeeping for Gay, the cowboy played by Clark Gable. The three cowboys aren't beyond redemption: all are critical of capitalist wage slavery. Riding the range represents freedom, an old theme in American life. The three men bond around drinking, going to rodeos, and chasing horses and women. Gay lives for the out-of-doors and on the money he makes from providing sex to wealthy women waiting for their divorces. Clift plays Perce, a sensitive rodeo contestant; Wallach plays Guido, a mechanic who pilots a Piper Cub and works only when he needs money. All three have been betrayed by wives or mothers. All are misfits in a middle-class culture. The cowboys, denizens of a dying world, are like the mustangs, once the proud inhabitants of a natural wilderness free from humans.[45]

Roslyn tries to stop them from rounding up the horses, thus playing the role of a civilizer of men that Marilyn often played in her films. Once again, as in so many of those films, Marilyn takes a stand against aggressive masculinity, although this time she screams at the men for their brutality against the horses.

> Killers! Murderers! You liars, all of you. Liars! You're only happy when you can see something die! Why don't you kill yourselves and be happy? You and your God's country. Freedom! I pity you. You're three dear, sweet dead men.

The roundup of the horses occurs, and Roslyn can't stop it. Then Perce and Gay let the horses go, but not before Guido attacks women as powerfully as Roslyn has attacked men.

> She's crazy. They're all crazy. You try not to believe it. Because you need them. She's crazy. You struggle, you build, you try, you turn yourself inside out for them, but it's never enough! So they put the spurs on you. I know—I got the marks!

In the end Roslyn goes off with Gay, the masculine man who frees the mustangs at her insistence, but not before he points out to her that she eats meat and feeds their dog canned dog food made from horse meat, perhaps from the mustangs. Thus she violates her beliefs against violence and killing animals every day. She needs to be more realistic about life.

The film's moral seems to be that men and women can live together successfully only if they compromise on a number of issues. Just as Gay cooks Roslyn breakfast, men must incorporate a measure of domesticity into their lives. At the same time women must recognize that male adventuring, even violence, is a necessary part of their natures. Even more important than this moral is the transformation produced from their experience with the mustang roundup, which is one of the lengthiest scenes in the film. The existential moment occurs when Gay and Perce free the horses. Gay and Roslyn realize their need for each other. Now they can have the child that will symbolize their love. Arthur described this existential moment in much greater detail in the novel he wrote from the film than in the film itself. Roslyn gives voice to that moment in the novel:

> For a minute, when those horses galloped away, it was almost like I gave them back their life. And all of a sudden I got a feeling—it's crazy!—I suddenly thought, "He must love me, or how would I dare do this?" Because I always just ran away when I couldn't stand it. Gay—for a minute you made me not afraid. And it was like my life flew into my body. For the first time.[46]

Before the filming was finished, a final breakdown in communication occurred between Arthur and Marilyn, due to another rewrite Arthur made on the script. According to Ralph Roberts, Arthur became so angry with Marilyn as the filming progressed that he rewrote scenes to make Roslyn into a prostitute and Gay into a bum, with Guido the man Roslyn chooses in the end. When Marilyn read the rewritten scenes, she became hysterical, and Gable intervened. He had contract approval over the script, and he refused to accept any ending other than the one he'd already approved, in which Roslyn and Gay go off together and Guido and Perce are left behind.

With Gable's intervention the film was over. Arthur's last rewriting was the final straw for Marilyn, and she ordered him out of her life. Indeed, Arthur may have engaged in a devious maneuver at the end of the filming. James Goode noted in his diary that "frantic" rewriting was going on, which Clark Gable stopped. Sidney Skolsky, who was present, agreed with Roberts that Arthur was rewriting the script to make Roslyn a prostitute and Guido the hero. Thus Arthur may have attempted to get at Marilyn with these last-minute rewrites.

During the last days of filming, the picture was wrapped up at Universal Studios in Hollywood. Rupert Allan informed Marilyn that he was resigning as her publicist to become the press attaché for Princess Grace of Monaco. The Jacobs agency assigned Patricia Newcomb to take over from him. Marilyn and Pat had fallen out during the filming of *Bus Stop*, but Marilyn was told that Pat had undergone analysis and was more stable. Marilyn accepted her, giving her the nickname Sib, for sibling rivalry. Rupert later stated that he had had nothing to do with Pat's taking over the publicity job and that he wouldn't have recommended her. She was a "pill pusher," he told Donald Spoto, and she couldn't be trusted.[47]

We do know that Pat Newcomb was close to the Kennedys. She knew Ethel Skakel Kennedy, Robert's wife, through her father, who had been West Coast representative of the Skakel family real estate holdings in Southern California. A Catholic, she knew the rest of the family through Ethel. Pat had become close to Pierre Salinger when she was a student of his at Mills College in Oakland. Later, as press secretary for John F. Kennedy, Salinger was close to the president and he continued to mentor Pat. Others have speculated that Frank Sinatra got Pat the position as Marilyn's publicist because the Kennedys wanted someone to watch over Marilyn for them.

On November 4, 1960, after nearly four months of filming and a month past the scheduled finish date, *The Misfits* was done. The next day Marilyn flew back to New York. Pat Newcomb, not Arthur, was with her. That same day Clark Gable had a heart attack at his home in the San Fernando Valley.

When Marilyn returned to New York, she reentered the world she'd left a year earlier when she had gone to Hollywood to make *Let's Make Love*. In the intervening year, she'd lost her husband and a lover (Montand)

Marilyn in a red sweater.
(Photographed by Bruno Bernard
© Renaissance Road, Inc. Bernard
of Hollywood is a trademark of
Renaissance Road, Inc.)

Marilyn in a yellow bikini.
(Photographed by Bruno Bernard
© Renaissance Road, Inc. Bernard
of Hollywood is a trademark of
Renaissance Road, Inc.)

Nude photo #1. Once Marilyn was identified as the model for these nude photographs, they were put on all sorts of commercial items, including playing cards from the 1950s.
(Golden Dreams and A Nude Wrinkle © Tom Kelley Studios)

Nude photo #2. (Golden Dreams and A Nude Wrinkle © Tom Kelley Studios)

Marilyn in a red dress at Niagara Falls. (Photographed by Bruno Bernard © Renaissance Road, Inc. Bernard of Hollywood is a trademark of Renaissance Road, Inc.)

Marilyn in a gold dress at the Photoplay Awards.
(© Michael Ochs/Getty Images)

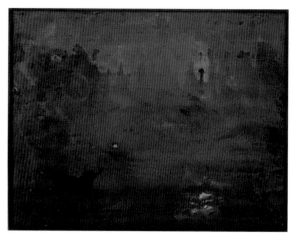

Le Taureau (*The Bull*), a painting by the French artist
Poucette that Marilyn bought in May 1962.

Marilyn with a balalaika. (Photographed by Milton H. Greene, © 2012 Joshua Greene)

Ballerina sitting. (Photographed by Milton H. Greene, © 2012 Joshua Greene)

Japanese photograph. (Courtesy of The Cecil Beaton Archives at Sotheby's)

Marilyn in the bulrushes in a leopard-skin bathing suit. (Eve Arnold/Magnum Photos)

and had struggled, physically and emotionally, during the making of two films. Her depression worsened as the year came to an end. On November 11, Pat Newcomb announced to the press that Arthur and Marilyn were separating. Then, a week later, Clark Gable died. He had been recovering from the first heart attack, but his intake of liquor and cigarettes, plus the grueling stunt work he had done in the scenes with the mustangs, had taken a toll.

Marilyn seemed all right at first, although she was too upset to attend Gable's funeral. She went with Ralph Roberts to the Strasbergs' apartment for a day of talking and listening to music. Pouring out her grief and love for Clark in a safe setting helped to assuage her deep mourning. Later that month she met with Arthur and they divided up their possessions: she kept the New York apartment, he the house in Connecticut. Marilyn wrote off the money she had spent repairing it. She didn't ask him to repay any of the other money she'd advanced him. They left Hugo at the Roxbury farm because he loved the open space there.

She spent Thanksgiving at the Strasbergs' and had drinks with Lester Markel that evening. Pat Newcomb claimed that Simone Signoret called Marilyn and begged her not to see Yves Montand when he went through New York on his way to Hollywood. The meeting didn't occur, but it seems that the romance with Montand didn't end so easily as is usually assumed. Joe DiMaggio now reappeared in her life. On Christmas Eve he took her masses of poinsettias, just as he had taken a Christmas tree to her on Christmas 1952, during the filming of *Gentlemen Prefer Blondes*. Several days later she excitedly told Ralph Roberts that Joe had agreed to the arrangement that she had long wanted: they would remain devoted to each other, while being free to date other people, in a classic free love arrangement. She even got Joe to attend a play with her in early January, a performance of Brendan Behan's *The Hostage*.[48]

She told Ralph of other changes in her life. Now that she had separated from Arthur, men were calling her for dates and sending her flowers, letters, and cards. In New York, she said, the availability of a desirable woman brought a rush of interest. Two men attracted her: Frank Sinatra and John Kennedy. Frank had a reputation for being attentive to friends in crisis, and he was being good to her. He wanted her to fly to Los Angeles and take the train with him to Florida, where he had a singing engagement. She was attracted to John Kennedy, but apprehensive. In early

January 1961 she told her friend Gordon Heaver, a story editor at Paramount, that she had recently had a date with him.[49]

The attention from Sinatra and Kennedy didn't lift her depression. When W. J. Weatherby interviewed her in December 1960 she seemed sad. "She gave me the impression of a child whistling in the dark. The more she tried to cheer herself up, the more she seemed aware of the dark around her." She told him that she was trying to control her temper, but she was also sitting in front of her mirror, looking at her face, worrying about aging. She spoke about suicide. "It's a person's privilege," she said. "I don't believe it's a sin or a crime." Then she added, "It doesn't get you anywhere."[50] She saw Marianne Kris forty-seven times in two months.

She was thirty-four years old, with neither a husband nor the child that she had thought would fulfill her. Given her drive for perfection, divorce was hard for her, since it was a major failure. She worried that the friends she had made through Arthur would drop her, but she didn't contact them. Losing Arthur's family hurt, for she considered Arthur's children as her children. But they didn't desert her, and she remained close to Arthur's father. She must have learned that Arthur was dating Inge Morath; some say he took Inge to the Kennedy inauguration on January 20, 1961, the day Marilyn went to Mexico for a divorce.

She decided she had caused Clark Gable's death because she had kept him waiting in the hot Nevada sun during filming *The Misfits*. She wondered if she had been late to the set so much because she had confused him with her father and had been punishing him for having abandoned her. The press had a field day, writing outrageous articles about her divorce, her romance with Montand, and her possible responsibility for Clark's death. Hedda Hopper led the pack when she alleged that Marilyn had killed the child she miscarried in December 1958 with her drinking and pill taking and had engaged in bad behavior throughout her career, from drinking vodka while filming, to having no discipline as an actress, to marrying Joe DiMaggio, with whom she had nothing in common. Stars have responsibilities, she exclaimed, and Marilyn had no sense of responsibility. She even attacked Marilyn for weight gain. As a star, she said, you must keep yourself thin. Underneath these complaints lay the fact that Marilyn had not given Hedda an interview for two years, and Hedda was smarting.[51]

Marilyn didn't see many old friends after she returned to New York from Reno. When Norman Rosten called, she often didn't pick up the phone, and when she did she sounded depressed, with her voice slurred by drugs. The Strasbergs were the only people she allowed to visit her. But she no longer went to their apartment in the middle of the night for solace, as she once had. She often talked about suicide. She contemplated jumping out of a window of her thirteenth-floor apartment. Pat Newcomb took her to ride the Staten Island ferry, and Marilyn stared into the water as though she were thinking of jumping.

On January 14, 1961, Aaron Frosch, her new lawyer, drew up a new will and rushed her to New Jersey to sign it, with Pat Newcomb accompanying them. Fearful that Marilyn might kill herself, they wanted to remove Arthur Miller as its beneficiary. In the new version Marilyn left most of her money to Lee Strasberg, with bequests to Marianne Kris, a small trust for her mother, and gifts of money to Xenia Chekhov and for Patricia Rosten for college. Frosch was Paula Strasberg's lawyer; Marilyn had found him through Paula. Inez Melson, among others, thought that undue pressure had been placed on Marilyn to sign this will. If so—and the charge has never been proven—the Strasbergs may have colluded with Frosch to obtain such a bequest.

On January 20, the day of the inauguration, Marilyn went to Juarez, Mexico, along with Pat Newcomb and Aaron Frosch, to secure a quick divorce. The idea was Pat's. With public attention on the inauguration, the hope was that Marilyn's divorce action might be overlooked. It also kept her away from the inauguration, where a lot of her friends, like Frank Sinatra, were performing, and where Kennedy would firm up his relationship with film star Angie Dickinson. After the divorce, she seemed fine for a while. She went to the preview of *The Misfits* with Montgomery Clift on January 31—it was rushed through production to qualify for the 1961 Oscars and to capitalize on Gable's death. The reception of *The Misfits* was mixed: critics found its perspective arcane, more European than American. Marilyn thought it had problems, although she told Ralph Roberts she thought that it would eventually become a classic.

But she kept spinning downward. She retreated into her bedroom, which she kept hot and dark, with blackout blinds over the windows, as she had during the last weeks in Reno. The Shaws and the Rostens had never seen her so depressed. Marianne Kris decided that something drastic had to be done. She persuaded Marilyn to enter a hospital for drug withdrawal. Marilyn had often been hospitalized—for gynecological surgery, for rest when she was worn out, for drug addiction—but this one was different. In what Kris later said was a mistake, she had Marilyn admitted to the Payne Whitney Clinic of New York–Presbyterian Hospital. It turned out to be a place for psychotic patients, with bars on windows, locks on doors, and windows in the doors so that patients could be observed at all times. Marilyn was now in an institution like the ones in which her mother had lived.

Once admitted, she wasn't treated well. At first she was simply abandoned, with no one visiting her. Yelling brought no results. "The furies came and went," she told Ralph Roberts. Remembering her neurotic behavior in *Don't Bother to Knock*, she smashed the window on the bathroom door and threatened to cut her wrists with a shard of glass. Nurses and attendants now appeared. She only wanted to attract someone's attention so that she could explain she was in the wrong hospital, but they wouldn't listen to her. Instead, she was restrained and threatened with a straitjacket. Four burly male attendants carried her, facedown, to the ward for violent cases, where she was placed in another cell. She managed to get hold of pencil and paper and to smuggle out a note to the Strasbergs, but they didn't appear. They said the hospital wouldn't let them see Marilyn because they weren't members of her family. Marianne Kris also didn't appear, although she had promised to go every day.[52]

In Marilyn's memory of the experience, it became even more horrible. She told Gloria Romanoff she had been sedated and constrained so that she couldn't move. She'd been forced to put on a hospital gown, and the doctors and nurses, fascinated by her body, had entered her room and checked it out. Some of them, she said, were lesbians. You can't imagine the horror, she said.[53]

Joe DiMaggio was her savior. She secured a dime and telephoned him in Florida, where he was with the Yankees in spring training. He immediately flew to New York and went to the hospital. He threatened to tear the building apart brick by brick if they didn't let Marilyn out. They released her, and he and Pat Newcomb took her to Columbia University Presbyterian Hospital Medical Center, where she was admitted for rest and drug-withdrawal treatment.

The Payne Whitney episode was a decisive experience in Marilyn's life. She didn't want to continue therapy with Marianne Kris, but she couldn't find another therapist in New York whom she liked. She'd maintained contact with Ralph Greenson after she'd seen him on an emergency basis during *Let's Make Love* and *The Misfits*, and she wrote him a long letter from Columbia Presbyterian about the terrible experience in Payne Whitney. In a postscript she told him that she'd had a "fling on the wing" with someone he'd always frowned upon. She was referring either to Jack Kennedy or to Frank Sinatra.

After a restorative two-week vacation with Joe DiMaggio in Florida, she decided to move to Los Angeles to undergo regular therapy with Ralph Greenson.[54] She would continue seeing Joe DiMaggio as a close friend and sometime lover. She was fascinated by Frank Sinatra, and she had already become close to Peter Lawford and Patricia Kennedy Lawford. Their house on the beach was a place that Jack Kennedy visited, using it as a "Western White House" once he became president in January 1961. The West Coast was beckoning to her. By midsummer 1961 she would establish her base of operations in Hollywood.

Part V

Return to Hollywood, 1961–1962

I wake and feel the fell of dark, not day.
What hours, O what black hours we have spent.
This night! . . .
I am gall, I am heartburn. God's most deep decree
Bitter would have me taste: my taste was me . . .

Gerard Manley Hopkins, "I Wake and Feel the Fell of Dark"
(a favorite poem of Marilyn's)

Chapter 12

Denouement, 1961–1962

In June 1961 British photographer Jack Cardiff, the cinematographer on *The Prince and the Showgirl*, visited Marilyn at her bungalow at the Beverly Hills Hotel, where she was staying. They had become friends during the London filming. He found her grief-stricken, upset over "an avalanche of problems," including her divorce from Arthur Miller and the death of Clark Gable. She told him what had happened at Payne Whitney, her voice rising hysterically. "Was I a nut, after all? There's my mother, paranoid schizophrenic, and her family, all destroyed by insanity." Then her mood shifted, and she seemed angry: "I've been used by so many people," she cried. "I was abandoned at the beginning, and I'm still being abandoned." She told him that she didn't want to play her "dumb-blonde" character anymore. She spoke about her many selves, but she seemed confused about who she wanted to be.

> A lot of people like to think of me as innocent, so that's the way I behave to them. If they saw the demon in me, they would hate me . . . I'm more than one person, and I act differently each time. Most of the time I'm not the person I'd like to be—certainly not a dumb blonde like they say I am; a sex freak with big boobs.

She began sobbing, and Cardiff took her in his arms and held her, as though she were a child.[1] By the time he left, Marilyn had calmed down, but the incident foreshadowed Marilyn's volatile state of mind in the ensuing months.

Marilyn was already deep into therapy with Ralph Greenson, seeing him as often as five times a week He thought she was improving, since she seemed more positive in her outlook and Hyman Engelberg told him she was taking almost no prescription drugs.[2] On June 1, her birthday, she sent Greenson a telegram: "In this world of people I'm glad there's you." According to friends, she called him Jesus. As she had with Arthur Miller and Lee Strasberg, she was developing a father-savior complex with him. During the next year their relationship would become a focal point in her life.

While coping with serious depression, she saw close friends, gave occasional interviews, and consulted her agent and lawyers, as they negotiated with Twentieth Century–Fox over what films she would make. On June 12, she went to the christening of Clark Gable's son, John Clark, who had been born four months after his father's death. Kay Gable greeted her warmly, inviting her to visit them and bring Joe DiMaggio along. At the end of June, she flew to New York and drove with Ralph Roberts to the Roxbury house to pick up possessions of hers that she had left there. She told Roberts of her love for the house and her sorrow at having to give it up. She reminisced: "It had been such heaven buying it, repairing it. Planting. Dreaming. Hoping."

She was upset to see signs of a woman living in the house and especially to find several volumes of Inge Morath's photos next to her gardening books. She must have known that Arthur was involved with Inge; Gussie Miller had died at the end of March, and Inge had been with Arthur at the funeral, which Marilyn attended. Yet the reality that Inge may have been living with Arthur in the Roxbury house bothered her. She was certain he'd placed the photography books on the shelf next to her gardening books on purpose; he knew she would retrieve those books when she went to the house to get her possessions. It was just like London, she said, when he had left his journal open to the entry about how she had disappointed him. Arthur knows how to hurt, she said. She threw Inge's books into the garbage.[3]

In late June she had an acute attack of pain in her side. In two hours of surgery at Polyclinic Hospital in New York, her diseased gallbladder was removed. The hospital took elaborate precautions to protect her privacy, hiring Pinkerton guards to patrol all corridors and building a special elevator in the rear of the building. When she left the hospital, so many people jammed the parking lot that it took an hour for her to get to her waiting limousine. Marilyn's magic was still there. Berniece Miracle stayed with her in her Manhattan apartment as she recuperated, and she became concerned about the number of prescription drug pills Marilyn was taking.[4] Joe DiMaggio was often at her apartment during her recuperation, frequently having dinner there, along with his friend George Solotaire. He had made his peace with Marilyn's behavior years earlier.

Marilyn still refused to marry him, despite his heroic rescue of her from Payne Whitney and their vacation together in Florida. They were spiritual friends—and occasional lovers. He telephoned her often and sent her roses. He was still traveling the world, visiting army bases with the Monette Company, but he was periodically in New York and Los Angeles and he saw her then. He remained deeply loyal to her, still obsessed with her. In early October 1961, when she was living in Los Angeles, he asked her to go to New York to attend the opening game of the World Series, where he was slated to throw the first pitch. It was a considerable honor; only U.S. presidents had previously thrown the first pitch. When she turned down the invitation, he wasn't upset. He told her to watch him on television as he threw the ball and he'd make a sign only she would understand.[5]

She was seeing Frank Sinatra, who pursued her after they had connected in New York in December 1960. He was jokey and playful, different from Joe and Arthur, both of whom could be stolid and withdrawn. He took a strong stand on civil rights, and she liked that. She'd listened to his songs for years—at home, in her dressing room, in her automobile—and that made her feel close to him. He was a balladeer and a crooner who sang in a melancholy, haunting manner about the difficulties of love and the loneliness of night. Billie Holiday and Ella Fitzgerald had been vocal models for him, as they had been for Marilyn. In a phrase that resonated with her, his singing was sometimes called "suicide music." He was intelligent; according to his daughter Nancy, he read all the time, history and biography mainly and everything published on Abraham Lincoln.[6]

She didn't travel by train with him across the country to Florida, as he'd proposed. Perhaps she saw him when she was in Florida with Joe DiMaggio; journalists speculated they were together there. Later that spring she visited him at his Palm Springs home, and she was his date for several of his Las Vegas openings. Louella Parsons declared that Marilyn had a "schoolgirl crush" on Frank. When I asked Jeanne Martin, Dean Martin's wife, why Marilyn and Frank were together, she told me they both loved sex and were highly skilled at it.[7]

Her relationship with Sinatra, like many of her friendships, wasn't simple. At times he seemed committed to her, as when he gave her expensive emerald earrings to go with a favorite green dress. But he often ordered her around and she obeyed him. Dating him, she met Hollywood social leaders like the Gary Coopers and William and Edie Goetz. (Edie was the daughter of Louis B. Mayer.)[8] They liked Frank because of his savoir-faire and his immense reputation as a singer and actor. He had vied with Clark Gable for the title "King of Hollywood," but after Gable died the throne was his. Very ambitious, he liked socializing with the Hollywood A-list.

Marilyn also joined other circles of his, including the Rat Pack, a male group composed of Peter Lawford, Sammy Davis Jr., Dean Martin, and Joey Bishop. Frank had brought the group together in January 1960 in Las Vegas to make the movie *Ocean's Eleven*, the story of five World War Two buddies who rob all the Las Vegas casinos. It presented men as pleasure-loving playboys in contrast to the heroes they had been in World War Two. Davis, Martin, and Bishop were well-known comedians and singers. Lawford was known for his elegant English style. That he was married to Jack Kennedy's sister Patricia mattered to Frank, who treasured his friendship with the Kennedys as a measure of success and had campaigned actively for Jack Kennedy during the 1960 presidential campaign. Marilyn was already friends with Lawford and Davis, and she knew the others from her years in Hollywood.[9]

The Rat Pack could be viewed as reflecting the disillusioned beat poets of the 1950s; as a forerunner to the youth rebellion of the '60s; or as a group of middle-aged men stuck in adolescence. It was an outgrowth of an earlier "rat pack," a nonconformist, heavy-drinking Hollywood clique led by Humphrey Bogart. Lauren Bacall, Bogart's wife, had given them their name when they arrived at the Bogart house disheveled after a night of partying. "You look like a pack of rats," she said to them.

Bogart and his group partied in private, while Sinatra's group clowned on stage during nightclub acts, using a language they invented that combined surfer talk, gangster patois, and Damon Runyon's Broadway vernacular. (Frank had starred in the film version of *Guys and Dolls*, which was based on two short stories by Runyon.) Their humor revolved around drinking liquor or making jokes about Davis's skin color and about women and their anatomy that drew from old strains of racism and sexism in American entertainment. Their acts also contained a lot of high school outhouse humor.[10]

Frank introduced Marilyn to Las Vegas night life, which centered around drinking, gambling, and fornicating. Mia Farrow, married to Frank for a time, described the women around Sinatra as appendages of the men: they sat quietly while the men talked, sipped white wine, and laughed at the men's jokes.[11] It's difficult to visualize Marilyn acting so subserviently, but she had the habit of turning herself into what her companion wanted her to be. In this case the male mythos of the Rat Pack drew from the James Bond mystique whereby highly masculine men casually bed beautiful women. In many ways she was retreating into the party-girl behavior of her early years in Hollywood.

Surely Sinatra realized that introducing Marilyn to Las Vegas nightlife wasn't helpful to her attempt to end her drug habit. He'd kicked alcohol and drugs, and perhaps he thought his example was enough to inspire her to change. Surely Marilyn knew that the compulsive, highly organized Sinatra looked askance at people who used drugs or drank too much in his presence. Sometimes she seemed to taunt him. She spent the month of August 1961 living in his house. One day he had a lunch date with Jack Kennedy at Peter Lawford's house. She suddenly disappeared, forcing him to spend the day looking for her. He missed the lunch.[12]

Later that month, she was supposed to go with him on his yacht to Catalina, along with a number of his close friends. Everyone met at the boat, which was moored in Newport Harbor, but Marilyn didn't appear. Jeanne Martin was deputized to get her from Frank's house, miles away in Beverly Hills. Jeanne found her sitting in front of a mirror, staring at herself. Jeanne got her dressed and to the boat, but Marilyn was so spacy from drugs that Frank was afraid she'd fall overboard if they put to sea.

The boat never left the harbor. They talked, drank, played cards, and slept on the moored boat. In the middle of the night, when everyone was asleep, Marilyn knocked on cabin doors, looking for pills. She couldn't seem to get enough.[13]

Frank must have forgiven her for that episode, because several weeks later he took her to an elite party at Romanoff's in honor of Billy Wilder and he gave her the emerald earrings. What happened there is quintessential Marilyn. She fascinated the guests with her wit and sparkling demeanor. By the end of the evening, the elite women stood in a row, as Marilyn taught them how to do her sexy walk. She was "roaring with laughter as she led them in the line."[14] Sinatra made it clear, however, that he didn't like her habits of going nude in his house and of telling stories about her childhood. When he chided her about the stories, she was furious, before deciding he was perhaps right. Did his criticisms further her self-awareness, or did she accept them because Sinatra represented a powerful male force in her life? Was Sinatra helping her or magnifying her already broken self-confidence? Some say that when Sinatra went to Hyannis Port, Massachusetts, at the end of the month to visit the Kennedy compound, she went with him, although the evidence isn't conclusive.

Tired of her behavior, Sinatra found her an apartment in September in the Doheny Drive apartment building where she'd once lived. Gloria Lovell, his secretary, had an apartment there, and he kept one there for himself. He didn't own the building, but he had such influence with its owner that, according to George Jacobs, his butler and confidant, it was called "the Sinatra Arms." Sinatra's close friends and assistants lived in some of its apartments.[15]

Although he had a habit of leaving relationships with women when they became serious, he remained friendly with his first wife, who had divorced him, and he never got over his fixation on Ava Gardner, who married and then divorced him. In the late fall of 1961 he became involved with the young dancer Juliet Prowse, even becoming engaged to her for a while before he suddenly broke up with her. Marilyn was upset by Prowse, especially because the dancer had beautiful legs and Marilyn didn't think much of hers. In a snit, she gave the emerald earrings Frank had given her to Pat Newcomb.[16]

Sinatra's involvement with Prowse was partly a way of freeing himself from Marilyn, even though he remained close to her. Like so many others, he felt paternal toward her, as he did toward Judy Garland; both were great stars who were neurotic and needy. Gloria Romanoff told me Frank was always concerned about Marilyn, always asking how she was, always worried about her pill taking. George Jacobs said Marilyn was a favorite of Frank's because she praised him extravagantly—his singing, his kindness, his sexual skill. When hairdresser George Masters did her hair, Sinatra's "invisible presence" was always there, "hovering over us like her guardian angel." He remembered that Frank had an apartment in the Doheny Drive apartment building on one side of Marilyn's, with Gloria Lovell, his secretary, in an apartment on the other side.[17]

But Frank was dangerous. He was tempestuous; he got into brawls. He consorted with gangsters, and he loved their casual, brutal, gentlemanly style. The mob kingpin killer Sam Giancana was a close friend: Sinatra traced his ancestry to Sicily, as did DiMaggio and Giancana. Sinatra said that if he hadn't become a singer he would have been a Mafia don. When Sinatra gave Marilyn a small white poodle to replace Hugo, she called it Maf, short for Mafia. Marilyn knew Mafia henchmen like Pat DiCicco and Johnny Roselli from her years as a Hollywood party girl. She'd met Giancana, Skinny D'Amato, and others when she was with DiMaggio. All Hollywood was fascinated with gangsters—both with the image and the reality. When W. J. Weatherby asked Marilyn to comment on *The Last Tycoon*, F. Scott Fitzgerald's novel about Hollywood, she replied that Fitzgerald had overlooked the violent and tough gangster element in the industry.[18]

The men in Sinatra's inner circle could be scary, and he wasn't often without them. He didn't like being alone; even as a young singer he had Italian toughs with him. In Mafia terms, he was the padrone; they were his acolytes. Like the power brokers in Hollywood and like the Mafia men, the Rat Pack passed women around. Cami Sebring, then married to Jay Sebring, Frank's hairdresser, told me she was pressured to have sex with Sinatra and the others, but she refused. The group, she said, passed women around like candy. They ruined Joi Lansing, a sensitive young actress, who fell in love with Sinatra, was passed around, and then got hooked on drugs. When I asked Cami why she was telling me this, instead of telling it herself, she replied, "You're the feminist. You tell it."[19]

George Jacobs maintained that Marilyn fell apart after Sinatra left her for Juliet Prowse in the fall of 1961: she didn't bathe or change her clothes for days on end, while she put on disguises at night and went to the bars on Santa Monica Boulevard to pick up men. These claims are impossible to substantiate, although Ralph Greenson told the story of a patient whose thinly disguised characteristics match those of Marilyn. She was so angry when he refused her sexual advances that she went to a bar, picked up a man, and had unprotected sex with him. The next day she told Greenson about it. Hildi Greenson, his wife, stated that she invited Marilyn to stay for dinner after her sessions with her husband and then drove her home because Marilyn had once invited a cab driver into her house, presumably for sex—which was dangerous. It's hard to accept that Marilyn, who was calculating about her career, would run the risk of blackmail posed by this, but her compulsions and her sense of failure in her marriage to Arthur Miller may have driven her to it.[20]

When Marilyn decided to remain in Hollywood, she persuaded Ralph Roberts to move from New York and join her as her driver and masseur. He did so. Once he arrived, her days followed a pattern: he would take her to Madame Renna's salon for a facial, then to a grocery store or a clothing store to shop, then to a session with Ralph Greenson. Marilyn and he would eat dinner together on her patio, often with Gloria Lovell and Pat Newcomb, often steaks that he barbecued on a grill. Betsy Duncan Hammes, a nightclub singer who knew Sinatra from performing with him in Las Vegas, lived in the Doheny Drive apartments. When she came back to her apartment after staying out late performing, she often heard Marilyn and Gloria Lovell talking and drinking on Marilyn's patio.[21]

In the late fall photographer Douglas Kirkland shot Marilyn for *Look* magazine. He was a neophyte, and Marilyn taught him a lot about camera angles and posing. He photographed her naked in bed, with a sheet covering her body—a classic Marilyn pose. He met her three times, and she was a different person each time. When he arrived at her apartment before the shoot to discuss it with her she was playful, easily making small talk. On the day of the shoot she was a superstar, seducing him by dropping her robe so he could gaze on her naked body. When he took her the proof sheet several days later, she seemed deeply depressed. She was wearing dark glasses, and she looked like she had been crying.[22]

Throughout the fall her lawyers and agents negotiated with Fox executives over casting her in a remake of the 1940 film *My Favorite Wife*, about a woman who returns to her children and her newly remarried husband after having been stranded on a South Seas island with another man for five years. It's not clear she wanted to do the film, but Ralph Greenson pressed her to finish her commitment to Fox. Marilyn was also offered the starring role in a television version of Somerset Maugham's *Rain*, with Lee Strasberg directing. Strasberg thought she would be superb as Sadie Thompson, the prostitute who seduces a missionary and ruins him by destroying his moral framework. Joan Crawford had done an acclaimed film version of *Rain* in 1932.

With this proposed television drama in mind, Marilyn wrote Strasberg, asking him to consider moving to Hollywood to set up a joint production company with her so she could get out of the "quicksand" she was in. She'd discussed the idea with Marlon Brando, she said, and he was interested.[23] Marilyn was looking for creative endeavors like MMP that would allow her to work with people she trusted. No record of Strasberg's reply exists.

Marilyn still had many friends, although she sometimes broke appointments that year or didn't show up. She was in touch with the Shaws and the Rostens, and she spoke on the phone with Xenia Chekhov, Anne Karger, Clifton Webb, Sidney Skolsky, and others. She saw Joe DiMaggio, Frank Sinatra, and Marlon Brando. Dorothy Parker and her husband lived around the corner from the Doheny Drive apartment, and they socialized with her. Dorothy wrote to a friend that she and her husband had written a darling, bawdy farce for Marilyn, but Fox, unfortunately, had turned it down. Marilyn was always "in terror," but that wasn't so bad because Dorothy also had that problem. All in all, she was "crazy" about Marilyn.

Marilyn had become close to poet Carl Sandburg, the populist biographer of *Abraham Lincoln*, after she met him when she was making *Let's Make Love* and he was using a former dressing room of hers as an office while working on the screenplay for *The Greatest Story Ever Told*. They joked and clowned around with each other like children and shared their poetry. Marilyn called him a poet "of the people, by the people, and for the people."[24]

* * *

Marilyn had been going to the Peter Lawford beach house by 1960, if not before. When she returned to Hollywood in 1961, she was already close friends with Patricia Kennedy Lawford. Pat's humor, her height (she was nearly six feet tall), and her horsey look complemented Marilyn's femininity, while Pat provided a link to the Kennedy brothers. Always drawn to Hollywood celebrities—part of the reason she married Peter Lawford—Pat liked Marilyn's emotional openness, which was not a Kennedy trait. According to Pat's son Christopher, the film star became like a little sister to her. Peter and Pat combined Hollywood's love of poker with the charades played at the Kennedy home in Hyannis Port, to hold casual parties featuring those games. Accompanied by Pat Newcomb, Marilyn often attended their parties. Peter still loved surfing and volleyball, and he played the game with friends at public courts laid out on the beach directly behind his house. Those games didn't appeal to Marilyn, who sat by the pool or went walking on the beach.[25]

When the Kennedy brothers were there, sex play was sometimes part of the activities. In an outline for an unpublished autobiography, Peter wrote that he suffered from sex addiction. The Kennedy brothers weren't far behind him. When the Kennedys went to the Lawford house, they sometimes acted like randy boys. Jeanne Martin said that Jack and Bobby Kennedy chased women and openly groped them. The Kennedy women didn't make a fuss; they'd been schooled in their family to find women for their brothers. As powerful men, they claimed the spoils of success, including women.

Patricia Tierney Cox, then the wife of Richard Livingston, a wealthy manufacturer and close friend of Peter Lawford, knew the Kennedy family. (She had dated Peter before she married Dick Livingston.) The Kennedy sisters pimped for the brothers, she told me. Peter and Pat Lawford tried to persuade her to have an affair first with Joe Sr., then with Jack, and then with Teddy. She refused. Tierney, who later married Wally Cox, had been a starlet in the MGM contract pool when Marilyn was at Fox. She was a great beauty, with many Hollywood lovers.[26]

The sources I have consulted validate that Jack Kennedy had sex with Marilyn at the Lawford house, especially individuals who listened to conversations on the electronic bugs and wiretapping devices that private detective Fred Otash and electronics expert Bernie Spindel had placed there. When I visited the house in December 2008, the servants joked with me about their trysts, showing me an elevator in which they said the two had had sex. The tiny elevator dated from the 1930s and had never been modernized; to me it looked like a very uncomfortable space. I suspected they were pulling my leg. I searched for the pink onyx bathtub that was, according to Peter Lawford's widow, Patricia Lawford Stewart, a favorite place for sex, but I couldn't find it, although the house is large and portions of it have been redone. The house resembles a Cape Cod mansion, with folk Mexican touches.

At some point during these years, when Pat was out of town with the children, at the Kennedy mansions in Hyannis Port or Palm Beach, Forida, Peter held what amounted to sex parties, with prostitutes present. According to screenwriter Mary Anita Loos, Anita Loos's niece who lived down the beach from Peter and Pat, "Peter Lawford would call Marilyn and say: 'Oh, Marilyn, so and so's going to be here. We're going to have a party. Some girls are here and you can join.' And Marilyn would say, 'That's what I am for him, a party girl with some girls at a beach house?' If prostitutes were there, Marilyn wouldn't stay long."[27]

Multiple sources maintain that the sex parties involved sadomasochism and the use of enemas. Some Hollywood people, I'm told, were jaded with conventional sex acts and turned to unconventional forms. George Jacobs said Frank's male entourage called the beach house "Hi-anus-port." Daniel Stewart, a member of the Beverly Hills Police Department, participated in police stakeouts of the house. When I asked him what kind of sex activities went on at the Lawford house he told me, "Anything you can imagine."[28]

John Miner, a Los Angeles assistant district attorney at the time, who participated in Marilyn's autopsy, became an authority on her death. I interviewed him on many occasions, and he told me about the parties. He had never been to them, but he had met a dominatrix who had regularly been there and she had told him about them. He said Peter had gone to the flea market in Paris and bought eighteenth-century piston syringes (a variant of the bag and water variety, with a large syringe, like a Fleet enema). They were used at the parties, according to Miner. In fact, enemas were a major form of medical treatment from the Greeks through the nineteenth century for almost any ailment. Daily use was supposed to aid the complexion. Eighteenth-century aristocrats used piston syringes as sex toys. When I asked Patricia Lawford Stewart, Peter's fourth wife, about this, she said Peter was uneducated, despite his elegant manner, and he was mostly interested in surfing and volleyball. He wouldn't have known about the Paris flea market.[29]

There were sightings of Marilyn at the Lawford house with Jack Kennedy and Bobby Kennedy during the fall of 1961. In October Bobby was at a party at the Lawfords'—as attorney general he traveled frequently, visiting local offices. Marilyn became intoxicated at the party, and Bobby, accompanied by his press secretary, Edwin Guthman, took her home and put her to bed. By then, if not before, Marilyn had been given Jack Kennedy's private number, a line that rang in the family quarters of the White House after hours. Jackie sometimes answered the phone when Marilyn called, but she was more concerned than jealous. She'd made her peace with Jack's philandering, and she chided both Jack and Bobby for playing with Marilyn, whom she saw as "a suicide waiting to happen."[30]

Shortly before Thanksgiving 1961 Jack Kennedy went to Los Angeles for a fund-raising dinner and spent time with Marilyn at the Lawford house. He was observed at an evening party talking to Marilyn. By November 1961 the house was bugged—by private investigators Fred Otash and Bernie Spindel. Some authors claim that Teamsters Union president Jimmy Hoffa commissioned the bugging, looking for evidence of Kennedy improprieties he might use to defend himself against Bobby Kennedy's vigorous attack on the ties between the Mafia and organized labor. Others say Joe DiMaggio hired Otash, and still others claim it was the Mafia, the FBI, or the CIA. Otash, a former police officer, was the major private detective in Los Angeles, and he often was hired by Hollywood stars to cover over or to discover untoward behavior. He had been present in 1954 at the "wrong-door raid." Otash assistants listening to the tapes heard the sounds of sexual encounters between Marilyn and Jack Kennedy, as did an anonymous associate of Otash's whom I interviewed.[31]

In early December Marilyn flew to New York to meet Jack Kennedy at a gathering at the apartment of socialite Fifi Fell. Wealthy New Yorkers were as eager as anyone else to meet her. But the insecurities of involvement with the Kennedys, added to Sinatra's inconstancy and Arthur Miller's new romance, were hard on her. Within three days of returning from the Fell party, she overdosed on drugs. The overdose seems related to these personal issues, but Greenson was convinced that it stemmed from her deep transference to him as a father figure and his exasperation at her constant complaints about Twentieth Century–Fox and about her friends.[32]

We don't know who found her after the overdose; it may have been Gloria Lovell or Pat Newcomb, both of whom were often with her, or someone else looking for her. (Gloria Romanoff stated that all Marilyn's close friends at one time or another had the experience of reviving her from an overdose.) In a stupor, Marilyn may have called Ralph Greenson, whose house in Santa Monica was about twenty minutes from the Doheny Drive apartment. In fact, the overdose may have been a cry for help, a way of getting special attention, which is not unusual among individuals suffering from severe depression.

Marilyn probably needed to be hospitalized for drug detoxification, but Ralph Greenson feared that another incarceration might remind her of Payne Whitney and cause her to engage in a serious attempt at suicide. So he had her treated in her apartment. He hired round-the-clock nurses and sent Engelberg to her apartment daily to give her injections of vitamins, especially B12, and decreasing doses of Nembutal. He probably put her on another class of drug. It was a standard detox method that minimized withdrawal symptoms, which can be lethal. Marilyn quickly recovered. But Greenson was just at the beginning of his problems with her.

Ralph Greenson was an important figure in Marilyn's life. His academic credentials were impressive. He had a BA from Columbia University and an M.D. from the University of Bern, in Switzerland, where he became interested in psychoanalysis and did a formal analysis with maverick psychoanalyst Wilhelm Stekel. He moved to Los Angeles to do his medical internship at Cedars of Lebanon Hospital, and he underwent a second formal analysis with Otto Fenichel, an orthodox Freudian. Psychoanalysis was then at the cutting edge of psychiatry, and Greenson was thought of as an innovative "young Turk." He gained a reputation during World War Two when he served as chief of neuropsychiatry at the Army Air Force Convalescent Hospital in Fort Logan, Colorado. He successfully treated servicemen suffering from post-traumatic stress disorder by giving them sodium pentathol injections to unlock their memories, and then doing individual and group therapy with them. His technique seemed successful, although follow-up studies showed that the traumas often returned later. He became a founding member of the Los Angeles Psychoanalytic Society and was appointed to the faculty of the UCLA medical school.[33]

A gifted raconteur, he became friendly with screenwriter Leo Rosten (no relation to Norman Rosten). Leo Rosten was a Jewish man from New York with a gift of gab, who was the brother-in-law of Margaret Mead. Rosten recommended Greenson as an analyst to his Hollywood friends. Psychoanalysis was then in vogue, and Greenson attracted many Hollywood clients. He was an amateur violinist, and he held a weekly salon in his house in Santa Monica, at which he played chamber music with several friends. To the individuals who attended the salons they seemed to be an outpost of sophisticated New York in provincial Hollywood.

Greenson was considered daring to take on Marilyn. Many psychiatrists wouldn't have treated her because of her suicide attempts. The suicide of a patient—particularly of so famous a patient—could destroy a psychiatrist's career. Greenson liked treating celebrities, and at one time or another he treated many famous performers, including Frank Sinatra and Vivien Leigh. He was well known among psychoanalyists for his theories about the relationship between therapist and patient. He published those theories in articles in academic journals and in his 1978 book *Explorations in Psychoanalysis,* which for a time was considered to be the definitive work on the subject.[34]

Sigmund Freud had described transference and counter-transference through his own psychoanalytic practice. These two states were considered to be the key elements in the patient-therapist connection. Transference refers to the emotional reaction of the patient to the therapist; counter-transference refers to the therapist's response to the patient's transference. By the 1950s, fifty years after Freud's initial formulation of these states, psychoanalysts were debating the analyst's proper stance. Should the analyst encourage a personal involvement with the patient or remain aloof? Greenson's answers to this question are relevant to his treatment of Marilyn, especially since he worked out much of his theory while she was his patient.

Greenson divided analytic categories into the "transference neurosis" and the "working alliance." The "transference neurosis" referred to the patient's emotional attachment to the therapist and the patient's comprehension of his own neurosis. Through the attachment, it was thought, the patient would come to terms with his neurosis, by projecting his fears and lusts onto the therapist and working them out through their converstation. The "working alliance" involved the rational connection between the patient and the therapist, their joint mental endeavor to understand the patient's neurosis and their own relationship.

Recent authors have charged that Greenson had sex with Marilyn. Yet both his theoretical stance and his reactions to her contradict that assertion. In analytic papers Greenson condemned sex between patient and therapist. In a paper on empathy, he criticized "uncontrolled" therapists who acted out their counter-transference. The therapist, he maintained, must be both detached and involved, oscillating between these two positions. In a paper about the "working alliance," he wrote that it was a "rationalized, desexualized, and de-aggressivized transfer phenomenon." He criticized what he called "corrective emotional experience" therapy and stated that the proper way to generate the necessary "transference neurosis" was by thwarting a client's desires. Marilyn may have attempted to seduce him, but he rejected her. That's what he stated in his paper on the use of drugs in psychotherapy.[35]

Marilyn's strong transference burdened him throughout 1961 and 1962. If he upset her, she obsessed about it—which meant threats of suicide and late-night telephone calls. And he easily upset her, especially when he focused on her neurotic reactions to others. She ranted not only against the people she claimed were persecuting her but also against anyone who acted in a way she considered to be against her interests. On the other hand, she idolized some individuals and wouldn't allow Greenson to criticize them. These individuals included Wayne Bolender, her first foster father, and Ana Lower, Grace Goddard's aunt, who had been a powerful force in her childhood.

Greenson decided at this point that Marilyn, who was sixteen years younger than he, was at base an adolescent waif who acted irresponsibly, sulking or throwing tantrums when crossed. In his paper on drugs he referred to his patient (obviously Marilyn) as having exposed herself to venereal disease, an act that was flagrantly self-destructive. In a radio lecture he gave on November 16, 1961, he criticized all his patients who suffered from insomnia. That blanket condemnation included Marilyn. Such patients, he said, were "infantile." "The more infantile people are," he said, "the more regressed, the more deadly, the more self-destructive they are."[36]

Greenson was overworked when he took on Marilyn as a patient. He'd already had a heart attack. He'd cut down on the number of his analytic patients, but he still taught classes at UCLA, supervised psychiatrists in training, and served on the board of directors of the American Civil Liberties Union (ACLU). Marilyn's insatiable needs threatened to overtake his life. His letters to Marianne Kris and others about Marilyn are filled with frustration. She called him at all hours, threatened suicide, and then improved, only to break down again. "I had become a prisoner now of a form of treatment which I thought was correct for her but almost impossible for me," he told Kris.[37]

Marilyn had brought the nation's most famous acting teachers to heel; she had done the same to the nation's most famous athlete and its most famous playwright. Now she was facing a famous psychoanalyst. He was brilliant, as was she. I suspect they enjoyed the intellectual fencing during their sessions, since Marilyn entered the "working alliance" while fighting against it, trying to maintain—perhaps unconsciously—a neurotic interdependence between the two of them that she could manipulate. Joshua Hoffs, a student of Greenson's and later his colleague, told me that they probably engaged in meta-conversations about their process, talking about literature and psychoanalytic theory during their long therapy sessions.[38]

In December 1961 Greenson called her a borderline paranoid schizophrenic in a letter to Anna Freud. Judging from his treatment for her, however, he had difficulty pinning her down under one category. Her nightmares and monsters could be viewed as symptoms of a number of psychic syndromes. In fact, the "borderline" designation still could mean someone whose symptoms swung between categories; it hadn't yet been fully distinguished as a separate category with its own dangerous effects, a special personality disorder replete with manipulative behavior. Besides, both Ralph Roberts and Rupert Allan, hostile to psychoanalysis, claimed that Marilyn told them she made up stories for Greenson.[39]

During her time with Greenson she had a recurring dream in which she was running through a cemetery in the early dawn frantically look-ing for a way to escape. She graphically described the tall headstones and the feel of the dewy grass on her feet, but she never got out of the ceme-tery. It sounds like an attempt to escape from the death she often re-garded as a welcome relief from a painful life, or a warning to Greenson that his therapy wasn't working. On one occasion when he was trying to persuade her to give up drugs, he told her that it was either "Mr. Nembu-tal or me." She replied to him that the drugs made her feel "womby and tomby."

In fact, Greenson contended that her ego was so weak that he couldn't analyze her and that he was only trying to help her attain a strong enough sense of self to undergo analysis, which would involve deep pen-etration into her past. Thus he had her sit up during their sessions; she didn't lie down on his analytic couch and free associate. He needed to have eye contact with her to keep her focused. But his discussions of his interactions with her in the papers he wrote indicate that he was, in fact, applying his analytic categories to her.[40]

Greenson was known as an innovator in psychoanalysis. On one level the personalized treatment he gave Marilyn attests to his creativity, as he held analytic sessions with her in his home, had her stay for dinner, encouraged her to become friends with his family, and invited her to his evening musicales. He has been severely criticized for overstepping the bounds of anonymity on the part of the therapist toward a patient, a credo in the field, but by 1962 the popularity of psychoanalysis was de-creasing with the appearance of new behaviorist therapies and new drugs. Greenson experimented with innovative psychoanalytic approaches in order to maintain the method's position as a primary treatment for men-tal disorders. In his paper "The Origin and Fate of New Ideas in Psycho-analysis," he saw himself as a strict Freudian, even as he tried out new approaches. "During my analytic sessions," he stated, "I had consciously to discipline my thinking and imagination or I would have forsaken the welfare of my patients for the allure of the new ideas." Anna Freud saw him as "a hard-living man of passionate enthusiasm and even flamboy-ance, a man for whom psychoanalysis was . . . a way of life."[41]

Yet in taking Marilyn into his home, he didn't seem to realize that he was repeating what others had done: the Kargers, Chekhovs, Rostens, and Strasbergs all had taken Marilyn into their families. His technique was not, in fact, unique. Becoming a member of families may have been part of her pathology, a way of endlessly re-creating the foster families of her childhood, trying to lessen their effect on her by finding better variations of them. And she did believe that everyone around her was manipulating her, just as drug addicts often perceive everyone around them to be part of a conspiracy against them. Realizing that she was a drug addict, Greenson may have tried to remove her from negative friendships, a common method of withdrawal therapy. He stated that she masochistically provoked people "to mistreat her and take advantage of her."

He tried to end her relationship with Sinatra, who had been his patient and whose neuroses he knew well. He also dismissed Ralph Roberts in November 1961, for he may have decided that Roberts, a vodka drinker, was enabling Marilyn. Greenson also wanted to get rid of the Strasbergs. That may not have been a bad idea; even the gentle Norman Rosten didn't trust them and thought they were trying to take over Greenson's role in her life.[42]

Marilyn's paranoia, however, was grounded in a certain reality. Many people were manipulating her. Her New York lawyer, Aaron Frosch, was embezzling funds from her, and Marjorie Stengel was so incompetent that she had to be fired. The FBI was still following her, and she knew it. Joe DiMaggio usually had detectives around, watching her. Greenson was aware that her complaints about being manipulated weren't all paranoid. He told film star Janice Rule, another patient of his, that "even if [a] star . . . is strongly motivated to change, the parasites and exploiters living off the mysteriously successful creature prefer the status quo." He was referring to Marilyn.[43]

Marilyn further believed that some of the homosexuals around her were trying to take her over. This belief had become evident in 1955, when she charged her hairdresser Peter Leonardi with trying to do so, in what may have been a projection of her own fears about her lesbian tendencies. Many individuals around her were gay: George Cukor, Rupert Allan, George Masters, Sidney Guilaroff, possibly Ralph Roberts. Marilyn had no animus against Allan, Guilaroff, or Roberts, but she was savage about Cukor. She also had problems with Patricia Newcomb, who she was constantly with and who controlled her so much on the set of *Something's Got to Give* that Fox executives wanted Marilyn to fire her.[44] In a therapy session, Marilyn accused Pat of trying to rob her of a valuable possession. By that "possession" Marilyn meant either her femininity or her sexuality. She worried that Pat was trying to take her over.

According to Greenson, Marilyn couldn't bear even the hint of anything homosexual, and yet she fell into situations that had homosexual coloring. She recognized her tendency in those situations, but she then projected it onto the other person involved, who became her enemy. Greenson did what he could: "Once I said to Marilyn deliberately, casually, of course, you know that all of us have both hetero and some homosexual components. Marilyn acted as though this was a catastrophe. I finally had to say that the relative percentage of those components varied in each individual and that she was more than 100 percent heterosexual." She was so paranoid about Pat Newcomb that she made Pat dye her blonde hair darker. She made hairdresser George Masters dye his hair a darker blonde after someone called them twins. Masters claimed that he dyed Marilyn's hair white blonde to stop her from complaining about the color of his hair, although she had already had Pearl Porterfield do this.[45]

In *My Story*, Marilyn stated she had thought she was a lesbian before she had an affair with Fred Karger. As the greatest sex symbol of her age, protecting her femininity was important to her. If anyone outed her, her career could be destroyed and she would be humiliated. With his statement about universal bisexuality, Greenson threw her into a homosexual panic. Before she left New York, an actress at the Actors Studio had kissed her lasciviously on the mouth in a restaurant, deeply upsetting her. Moreover, rumors were circulating that Natasha Lytess was planning to expose her affair with Marilyn in European tabloids.[46]

Greenson's position as Marilyn's therapist put him in a bind. In his letters he refers to individuals who were hurting Marilyn, but his professional ethics wouldn't allow him to identify them. In those letters Greenson identified Marilyn as being so alone that if he didn't see her she would have nothing to do. Either Marilyn falsely represented herself as living a lonely life—or she complained about having only a few friends to Greenson. Such claims to being friendless are typical of drug addicts, although in one of her guises she did regard herself as friendless, as an orphan who was always alone.

Throughout Marilyn's adult life the claim was made that she was sexually frigid. Now that she was in therapy with Greenson, some observers contended that he cured her. The cultural context is important in evaluating these claims. American society in the 1950s was fascinated by "nymphomania," while it was axiomatic that "nymphomaniacs" were frigid: they demanded ever more sex because they were in-orgasmic. By definition a sex queen like Marilyn, ever ready for a sexual encounter, had to be frigid. In an era deeply influenced by Freud, frigidity meant the lack of a vaginal orgasm, a point Greenson made in a 1955 paper. In 1972, influenced by second wave feminism, with its argument (based on the Kinsey studies) that all orgasms originate in the clitoris, he revised that stance somewhat, but he still held that "the inability to feel the vagina as a sexual organ indicates an inhibition of psychosexual development."[47]

My research on Marilyn suggests a more regular sexual response on her part, given the testimony of Hal Schaefer, Elia Kazan, Arthur Miller, and others I have cited, always taking into consideration the effects that the endometriosis and the scar tissue in her internal organs may have had on her sexual response. When I interviewed Hal Schaefer, he asked me rhetorically, "Why would Joe DiMaggio, known for his sexual drive and prowess, have kept coming back to Marilyn if she were in-orgasmic?" Marilyn called him "my slugger," said he could hit the ball out of the park, and stated that if sex were all there were to marriage, they would have been married forever.

According to Lucy Freeman, a writer on psychiatry who based her 1992 book on Marilyn on interviews with Ralph Greenson, Marilyn's issue with sex was not a lack of sexual response but that she usually lost sexual interest in a man after a period of time. I'm also not convinced by John Miner's transcript of a tape that Marilyn supposedly made for Ralph Greenson, in which she stated that she was frigid and that Greenson had cured her. Miner told me that Greenson did so through hypnotism and that he himself had used that technique to cure women of frigidity. Given my relationship with John Miner over the course of several years, that statement sounds dubious. In fact, I don't trust the validity of the Miner transcript. No record exists that Greenson played a tape for Miner, aside from Miner's claim. Still, rumors of Marilyn's frigidity—and her lesbianism—circulated in her own day. Alvah Bessie, one of the Hollywood Ten, wrote a 1967 novel based on Marilyn's life in which his female protagonist experiences orgasm only through sex with women.[48]

After the detox treatment in Marilyn's apartment in December 1961, Greenson brought Eunice Murray, a friend of his with some practical nursing experience, into Marilyn's life. He felt Marilyn needed a companion, both to keep her company and to watch over her for him. Many have suggested, on the basis of no evidence, that she was a Greenson toady, who spied on Marilyn for him. Eunice had served as a caretaker for some of Greenson's patients; she knew how to handle unstable personalities. She was a quiet, unflappable woman who had never seen a Marilyn movie when she met her and knew nothing of her fame. Marilyn had fought the nurses that Greenson brought in to care for her when she was undergoing the detoxification in December, and they all had quit. Marilyn was insulting to Eunice, but Eunice absorbed the abuse and remained calm no matter what Marilyn said.[49]

Soon after Eunice arrived in early January, Marilyn discovered Eunice was an excellent seamstress. Marilyn was delighted. She had lost a lot of weight after the gallbladder surgery, and her clothes needed to be taken in. Eunice did the alterations. Moreover, she was a Swedenborgian, a practitioner of the mystical religion based on the doctrines of the eighteenth-century mystic Emanuel Swedenborg. That involvement appealed to Marilyn, who was still exploring alternative spiritualities. She did so especially when she consulted skin specialist G. W. Campbell at Madame Renna's salon in Beverly Hills. Campbell (who was married to Renna) worked on the fat in Marilyn's chin with an electrical device his wife had invented. He was also versed in philosophy and religion, which he and Marilyn discussed. When she needed speedy expertise in them, she called him. He recommended books to her, which she read.[50]

By February 1962 Eunice was looking for a house for Marilyn to buy. The previous summer Marilyn had told Joe DiMaggio she wanted to own a home, and he'd encouraged her to look in Los Angeles, where homes were less expensive than in New York. Eunice found a house on Fifth Helena Drive in Brentwood, and Marilyn liked it. Medium-size, it was designed in a Mediterranean Spanish style similar to that of Ralph Greenson's home. The style had been characteristic of homes in Los Angeles since the city's early days, including those in the Whitley tract; it evoked the spirit of the city, and Marilyn also liked it for that reason.[51] Buying the house in Los Angeles, however, didn't mean that she was per-

manently leaving New York. She loved her apartment there, with its sophisticated art deco look. Her Brentwood house was folk Mexican,
warm and earthy. She had decided to become bicoastal, living alternately
in both cities. For years she had frequently flown across the country, apparently with little jet lag. With two places to live, she was joining the
sophisticated "jet set" that descended from the avant-garde society featured in *Flair* magazine.

On February 1, 1962, Marilyn again met Bobby Kennedy at a dinner
party at the Lawfords', which was held to honor him and his wife, Ethel,
as they set off on a goodwill tour of the Far East. Marilyn asked Bobby
a lot of intelligent questions about government policies concerning civil
rights, relations with Cuba, and the atom bomb. Danny Greenson, Ralph
Greenson's son and a radical student at Berkeley, had helped her construct
them. She wrote them down on a piece of paper she put in her purse, and
Kennedy was amused when he discovered her strategy. Kim Novak and
Natalie Wood were also at the party, but Bobby was interested in Marilyn. Some Marilyn biographers contend that this was her first meeting
with him, on the basis of letters she wrote that week to Isadore Miller
and Bobby Miller about him, but I'm not so certain. Marilyn kept her
relationships with the Kennedys secret, even from close friends.

Two weeks after the party, Marilyn went to Mexico with Eunice
Murray and Pat Newcomb to purchase furniture for her Brentwood
house. An adventurous Marilyn was evident during these weeks and so
was a tormented Marilyn. The latter persona took an upper hand after
Arthur married Inge Morath on February 17. According to FBI reports,
the marriage made Marilyn feel like "a negated sex symbol." She spent
several nights with dark-haired, handsome José Bolaños, variously described as a gigolo, a rising director of Mexican films, or an FBI plant.
She also spent time with Frederick Vanderbilt Field and his wife, Nieves.
Field was a scion of the Vanderbilt family whom the state department
tried in court and sent to prison because he had lied about his communist involvement. He spent nine months in prison before moving to
Mexico City, to join a group of expatriates. They were pariahs in the
United States because of convictions for communism. Mutual friends in
Roxbury had recommended Field and Monroe to each other, and they
clicked immediately.

Marilyn and he had long talks about politics in the evenings after they shopped for furniture during the day. Marilyn spoke about her strong support for civil rights and black equality, as well as her admiration for the revolution in China. If we add these sentiments to her praise for Fidel Castro in her letter to Lester Markel the previous year, it's clear that she had moved considerably to the left, far beyond the position she had espoused when married to Arthur Miller. J. Edgar Hoover, who had her under FBI surveillance for years, began to see a plot in her involvement with Field.[52]

FBI reports suggest that she may have had an affair with Field, although his wife was with them most of the time and Bolaños went to Hollywood at the same time she returned there. Just before she left Mexico City, she visited the National Institute for the Protection of Children and gave the director a check for one thousand dollars. She then tore up the check and made out another one for ten thousand dollars. She may have discussed adopting a child with the director. Once again, as often before, Marilyn combined professional and personal business with a charitable act, as though she were exonerating herself for any wrongs she had committed.

On March 5 she was awarded the Golden Globe as the 1961 Female World Film Favorite, at a ceremony at the Ambassador Hotel in Los Angeles. She was either drunk or drugged out at the event, since her acceptance speech was incoherent. She took José Bolaños with her to the ceremony, but he went back to Mexico the next day. Joe DiMaggio's biographer contends that DiMaggio went to Hollywood and forced Bolaños to leave. Two days later Joe helped Marilyn move into her house in Brentwood. Then, on March 24, two weeks later, she had another meeting with Jack Kennedy, this time at Bing Crosby's ranch in Palm Springs. She called Ralph Roberts in the middle of the night, asking him about issues concerning the spine, and she put Kennedy, who had a bad back, on the phone to consult with him.[53]

When in Hollywood in March and April, Marilyn met with Nunnally Johnson on the script he was writing for *Something's Got to Give*, the remake of *My Favorite Wife*, which she had agreed to do to fulfill her contractual obligations to Twentieth Century–Fox. As a result of those conversations Johnson revised the negative estimation of Marilyn he had formed in their earlier association on *How to Marry a Millionaire* and on *How to Be Very, Very Popular*, the film based on her that he'd written and that she'd refused to do. He no longer experienced her as "under water"; he now found her smart, funny, and highly intuitive. They agreed about the film. He described an evening they spent together drinking champagne as one of the "most enchanting three hours I'd ever spent." Marilyn had charmed him with her effervescence and intelligence.[54]

But there was a major problem with making the movie, and Marilyn should have realized it. Fox assigned George Cukor, her nemesis on *Let's Make Love*, to direct it. Cukor hadn't wanted to do *Something's Got to Give*, but he owed the studio a film. Perhaps Marilyn thought he wouldn't try to change the Nunnally Johnson script, which she liked. But her contract didn't include script approval; thus she couldn't protest to Fox executives if Cukor changed Johnson's script. Predictably, Cukor brought in a writer, Walter Bernstein, and had him make extensive revisions to the script. Even during filming, new pages of script were sent to Marilyn in the evening for her to memorize by the next day. It was *The Misfits* all over again.

To make matters worse, the studio itself was in disarray. Zanuck was gone; Buddy Adler had died; and Peter Levathes, whom Spyros Skouras brought in as head of production, was an advertising executive with little experience in running a film studio. According to veteran writer and filmmaker David Brown, Levathes was not used to "the demands and temperaments of talent." He had migraine headaches and fits of rage.[55] Profits were steadily dropping and *Cleopatra*, being filmed in Rome with Elizabeth Taylor, was going millions over budget. The back lot had already been sold off, and *Something's Got to Give* was the only film in production on the lot. Fox executives had gotten themselves into the position of pampering Taylor, even though she was even more difficult than Marilyn. In their panicked eyes, the future of the studio rested on Marilyn showing up at work. But ever since she became a star, she hadn't been good at that.

Levathes fired the experienced David Brown as producer on *Something's Got to Give* and brought in Henry Weinstein, a theatrical producer who had worked on only one previous film. Weinstein and Greenson had long been friends, and Greenson recommended him for the job through his brother-in-law Milton (Mickey) Rudin, who was now acting as Marilyn's agent. But Weinstein was a gentle man—not the tough sort of producer who easily stood up to the studio executives. Getting Marilyn to the set on time was the primary consideration for studio executives, and Greenson promised that he and Weinstein could do it. Another web of connections had been drawn around her, consisting of Greenson, Weinstein, and Rudin—with Sinatra, Pat Newcomb, and the Kennedys in the background.

Cukor wanted to undermine her in the film out of spite over her behavior on *Let's Make Love*. She was not going to control him this time, he decided. On April 23, as the film began production, Marilyn came down with a severe case of viral sinusitis and a high fever from a bug she had caught in Mexico. Doctors estimated that it might take several months for her to get over it if she took heavy doses of antibiotics and went on bed rest. They recommended that the start of filming be postponed. But studio executives refused to believe that she was really ill, despite the diagnosis of Lee Siegel, the official Fox doctor. Thus they placed reports in the newspapers that she was faking illness, and began filming. Siegel recommended that they begin filming at eleven or noon each day, so that Marilyn could sleep in, but they refused even to do that. They set the call to begin filming at seven and expected Marilyn to be on set. In order to make the seven o'clock deadline, Marilyn had to get up at five.

Marilyn did her best to arrive on time; she wanted to fulfill her commitment to Fox and to please Greenson. Biographers have claimed that Lee Siegel gave her "hot shots" of meta-amphetamines mixed with vitamins, but those allegations are debatable. He gave her shots of vitamin B12, a common practice then to provide energy, especially since she was often anemic. Marilyn could easily have gone to another doctor for such shots.[56]

Meanwhile, Greenson was planning to take a vacation in Europe. His wife had suffered a mild stroke in February; he wanted to see his in-laws in Austria; and he was scheduled to give a paper at an international conference in Israel. He was exhausted by Marilyn, and he needed a rest. There had been periods in February and March when she had improved, and he thought she could manage six weeks without him. One evening she held up a white knight from a chess set she had purchased in Mexico and examined it in the light. It reminded her that she had Greenson to protect her, and she carried it with her as an amulet when she sang at Jack Kennedy's birthday celebration and Democratic fund-raiser at Madison Square Garden on May 19.[57]

Despite Marilyn's illness, which resulted in her being absent from filming for the first two weeks of *Something's Got to Give*—from April 23 to May 11—Greenson flew to Europe on May 10. He left instructions that if she had a crisis she was to contact Milton Wexler, a psychiatrist and close friend. She seemed to rally after he left—like a dutiful daughter following her father's wishes. She was on the set from May 14 to May 16. Then on May 17 she flew to New York to sing for the Kennedy celebration. This performance would turn into a major tragedy for her.

The performers at the birthday celebration included Maria Callas, Harry Belafonte, Jimmy Durante, Peggy Lee, Ella Fitzgerald, and Diahann Carroll, with Milton Berle as master of ceremonies. Marilyn thought studio executives had given her permission to attend it, but they disputed that assumption and were furious when they found her carrying out what they considered to be a childish rebellion. They didn't understand how she could be well enough to attend the celebration, when she had missed filming for two weeks.

Whether or not she had permission to go to the celebration, Marilyn prepared carefully for it. Designer Jean Louis made her a special dress. She'd promised the event planners that she would dress discreetly, but she didn't. The dress was made of a transparent nude fabric, with rhinestones sewn in strategic patterns over her breasts and genitals. It wasn't entirely original: Jean Louis had designed such dresses for Marlene Dietrich to wear in her nightclub shows; and Marilyn had worn similar dresses in *Some Like It Hot*, when she performed at the hotel nightclub with the all-woman band.

The dress was deceptive. Under regular light it appeared to cover her. A member of the Women's Committee of the Democratic Party visited Marilyn backstage to check it out in terms of its respectability and was relieved to find that the dress covered her body. In the dressing room it seemed even modest. Under stage lights, however, the nude fabric melted away, making it seem that the flashing rhinestones were her only cover.[58]

Peter Lawford, drawing on his Rat Pack persona, introduced Marilyn at the celebration with a joke in bad taste, referring numerous times to her lateness, which was familiar to anyone who followed the movies. The joke was amplified since she didn't appear on stage after the first times he used it. Finally, after one last reference to "the late Marilyn Monroe," she came on stage, trotting to the microphone like a geisha girl because her dress was so tight. She wore a white mink wrap over her dress. Once again, as so often in the past at parties and premieres, she acted provocatively, throwing her wrap to Peter Lawford and slithering to the microphone. She flicked it, peered over the crowd, and then sang a slow and sensual unaccompanied version of "Happy Birthday to You," seemingly lost in her own eroticism, as she slowly drew her hands across her body, from her hips to her breast. She then sang another slow song to the melody of "Thanks for the Memory," with words specially written for the occasion, which thanked Jack Kennedy for what he had done as president. Then, in a sudden switch of tone, she led the audience in a rousing version of "Happy Birthday to You," with her arms pumping up and down. Now she seemed near manic in mood.

Why did she do it? The performance was tasteless, and Jack Kennedy broke with her because of it. Dorothy Kilgallen wrote in her column the next day that Marilyn had seemed to be making love to the president in front of four million viewers (the celebration was televised). Some writers maintain that she did it to show off to Arthur Miller, since his father, Isidore Miller, went with her to the event. Marilyn's intended target may have been Inge Morath, Arthur's new wife, who was dark and intense, a European intellectual with little sensuality. The week before, Arthur and Inge had been at a state dinner for André Malraux at the White House, seated next to Jackie Kennedy.

Jackie also may have inspired Marilyn's birthday party persona. In February, three months before the birthday celebration, Jackie had appeared in a televised tour of the White House, which she had redecorated. The contrasts between the well-groomed Jackie of the White House tour and the sensual Marilyn of the birthday celebration are striking. Jackie, dressed in a respectable linen sheath during the tour, has become in Marilyn a shimmering parody of respectability. Marilyn had Jackie's hairdresser, Kenneth Battelle, style her hair that morning. He did her hair in a bouffant style, with a flip on the left side. In the White House tour, Jackie's hair is arranged exactly the same way. Jackie's little-girl voice resembles Marilyn's, even sharing some of the same inflections.

Jackie doesn't look entirely self-confident in the White House tour; there is fear in her eyes. It seems that at the birthday celebration Marilyn intended to send up Jackie, and to showcase her own superior desirability to men. On the other hand, as Patricia Kennedy Lawford thought, Marilyn may have intended the performance as a joke, a caricature of "Marilyn Monroe." Suspecting what might happen, Jackie didn't attend the birthday celebration.[59]

Afterward, there was a party for the performers and major Democratic donors at the apartment of Mathilde and Arthur Krim, the head of United Artists. Secret Service agents, it is said, confiscated the negatives of all photos of Marilyn with the Kennedy brothers. One of the few remaining photos of them together shows a number of people in rapt attention as Diahann Carroll sings. Marilyn appears in the photo, as do Isidore Miller, Peter Lawford, Jack Kennedy, Maria Callas, Pat Kennedy Lawford, and Ethel Kennedy. Marilyn is still wearing the dress from her performance, which casts doubt on the allegation that her dress, into which she had presumably been sewn, had been cut off her after the performance to swath her in cold towels to break her high fever. In fact, if you look closely, there is a zipper on the back of the dress.

Marilyn took Isidore Miller home to Brooklyn in her limousine after the Krim party, which lasted until two in the morning, and Ralph Roberts gave her a massage in her apartment on Fifty-seventh Street at four A.M. Thus it seems unlikely that she spent time at the Carlyle Hotel with Jack Kennedy after the birthday party, as has been alleged.[60]

Arthur Schlesinger, special assistant to Jack Kennedy, and Adlai Stevenson, U.S. ambassador to the United Nations, were both at the Krim party. Both were attracted to Marilyn. Schlesinger was "enchanted by her manner and her wit, at once so masked, so ingenuous and so penetrating." "Bobby and I," he said, "engaged in mock competition for her; she was most agreeable to him and pleasant to me." Stevenson recalled getting to Marilyn "only after breaking through the strong defenses established by Robert Kennedy, who was dodging around her like a moth around the flame." Even Eunice Murray stated that at the after party it was difficult to tell which Kennedy she preferred.[61]

Larry Newman, a member of the Secret Service detail assigned to the Kennedys, told me that Bobby and Marilyn argued backstage before her appearance. Then, he said, they went into a dressing room and closed the door, remaining there for fifteen minutes. When they left the room, both were arranging their clothing. Newman believed that sex had occurred. I heard Mickey Song, who claimed to be the hairdresser for the Kennedys, tell the same story as Newman's on numerous occasions at Marilyn Remembered meetings. Song said Bobby brought him backstage to comb out Marilyn's hair. If that is the case, then by the spring of 1962 Marilyn was involved with both Kennedys. That was a heady position for a working-class girl, raised in foster homes and an orphanage. Whether she could hold that position while struggling with her studio, her demons, her drug addiction, and her various illnesses remained an issue as she returned to Hollywood and her regular life.[62]

Chapter 13

Defiance and Death

In May 1962 Marilyn visited an art gallery in Beverly Hills along with Norman Rosten, who was in Hollywood writing a screenplay. She bought an oil painting by the French artist Poucette and a sculpture by Auguste Rodin. The oil painting is called *Le Taureau* (*The Bull*). It is small, only ten inches by fourteen inches. Shades of bright red cover the canvas. Dark forms at its top rise out of a red mist, while a black bull dominates the bottom left corner. Anger seems the motif of the painting, with the bull blocking the way to an enchanted city or a group of macabre figures—both are suggested by the forms in the mist. The sculpture was a bronze original of Rodin's *Embrace*. Norman called the sculpture of a man and woman embracing lyrical, although menacing: "The man's posture was fierce, predatory, almost vicious; the woman innocent, responding, human." After buying the objects, Marilyn's mood shifted from cheerful to sullen. She insisted on stopping at Ralph Greenson's house to show him the sculpture. When they got there, she was belligerent. "What does it mean? Is he screwing her, or is it a fake?"[1]

Joe DiMaggio, Frank Sinatra, John and Robert Kennedy—some of the most famous men of her day—were her lovers. But what did she mean to them? Norman thought her questions about the sculpture concerned the dangers of love. "The tenderness of love, the brutality. If it existed, what was it, how to feel, recognize, be protected against it?" By the spring of 1962, if not before, despite her free-love inclinations, Marilyn felt bruised by men, felt she was sometimes nothing more than "a piece of meat" to them. She expressed her anger against men to Milton Ebbins, Peter Lawford's manager. Ebbins said to her, "Marilyn, everyone loves you." She replied, "The only guys that love me are the guys who jerk off in the balcony."[2]

The Poucette painting expressed her rage. The bull might be seen as representing the monster inside her created by her absent father and mother; by the man who molested her as a child and by the Hollywood men who used her. It symbolized major issues in her life. Could she find her way past the black bull of the painting to the enchanted city at its top? Or were the forms in the red mist dead people, ghosts from the cemetery in her dream? Did they represent the fetuses she had aborted, the miscarriages visited on her? Had she been damned by God because as a child she had committed an unpardonable sin?

Marilyn returned to Hollywood from the Kennedy birthday celebration on Sunday, May 20, in a triumphant mood. She had captured the nation's attention in a spectacular way. She was determined to finish *Something's Got to Give* and to counter the negative publicity she was receiving. She would show the world she was still desirable at the age of thirty-five. Three days later, on May 23, she did a swimming pool scene for the movie and slipped off her bathing suit to appear in the nude. It was a daring gesture, carrying her near-nudity at the Kennedy birthday celebration to an extreme. Elizabeth Taylor, who had become Marilyn's nemesis while making *Cleopatra* in Rome during these months, had done a titillating partly nude bath scene, photos of which had been featured in newspapers. But the line of the nude bodysuit she was wearing showed in the photographs. Marilyn's obvious nudity was more daring.

Marilyn had been on a high-protein, low-starch diet ever since her gallbladder surgery a year earlier, and she had lost a lot of weight. She was now thin and svelte. She dog-paddled in the nude swimming scene and then did a striptease flash while donning a robe. Newspapers went wild over her daring. Lawrence Schiller, a young photographer, took some of the photographs. According to him, they resulted from a conversation Pat Newcomb, Marilyn, and he had had about how to replace Elizabeth Taylor with Marilyn on magazine covers. They came up with the nudity in the swimming scene. Pat didn't want her to do it, but Marilyn insisted. Schiller then realized she was a shrewd businesswoman who knew how to market herself. The rest of the week she appeared on the set, ready for filming.[3]

The next Monday, May 28, her high fever returned, but she managed to rally and work through Friday. Yet by then, no matter what she did, Cukor and Levathes were furious with her. She had missed the first two weeks of filming and had gone to the Kennedy birthday celebration against their wishes. In addition, Cukor reported that Marilyn's acting was below par, although he may have concealed the truth. He and Levathes didn't notice that in the ten days she reported for shooting, most of her scenes for the film had been shot.

A new Marilyn was emerging in *Something's Got to Give*, but Cukor and the Fox executives were too angry at her to notice. She plays Ellen Arden in the film, in her thirties, the mother of two children. She does a brilliant comic turn as a woman returning to a newly remarried husband after five years on an island with another man, but she is also mature and dignified. She resembles Grace Kelly as much as the sexy Marilyn. The new persona is evident in takes from the film that were reedited into a final product years later by several filmmakers who found them in Fox storage vaults.[4] Shades of the mature Marilyn had been evident in Roslyn in *The Misfits*; both Roslyn and Ellen reflect the depth Marilyn brought to her acting in 1959 at the Actors Studio, when she played Blanche Du-Bois in *A Streetcar Named Desire*. She was becoming the dramatic actress she had wanted to be.

June 1 was her birthday. Studios gave major stars elaborate birthday parties if they were filming, but Fox paid no attention to Marilyn this year. *Cleopatra* was bankrupting the studio. They had put up with Elizabeth Taylor's bad behavior, and they feared that Marilyn would create similar financial overruns. In their minds Taylor was a golden girl, who had begun acting at MGM as a child, enchanting them all, while Marilyn was a studio slut who had fought them at every turn in her career. They detested Paula Strasberg, who was once again coaching Marilyn. Marilyn's stand-in bought a cake for the birthday and a bottle of champagne. Once filming ended that day, the cast and crew sang "Happy Birthday to you," and Marilyn cut the cake. Neither Cukor nor any of the Fox executives attended. It was a serious slight.

That evening Marilyn threw out the first pitch at the Los Angeles Angels baseball game, which was a benefit for the Muscular Dystrophy Association. The night was cold and misty. By the time she went home, her temperature was high and she had chills and a fever. The next day she broke down. She called Greenson's house, and his children went to her home. They found her huddling in her bed in her darkened bedroom, barely coherent as she poured out a list of woes: she was ugly and unloved; she had been badly used; her life wasn't worth living. They called Milton Wexler, Greenson's associate, and he went to see her. He threw away the many prescription bottles on her bedside table and left. Pat Newcomb then arrived with prescription drugs she had and drugged Marilyn for several days, sleeping at the foot of the bed. Eunice left food outside the bedroom door for them.[5]

What had happened? Why had Marilyn crashed on May 28 and on June 2? Negative turns in her relationships with the Kennedys played a major role. That spring, in her last interview with W. J. Weatherby, she stated that she was meeting a famous politician in secret because he had a wife and children, but she might marry him. The gossip among journalists was rife with stories about Marilyn and the Kennedys; Weatherby surmised it was one of them. He worried about her when they would invariably break with her; both were too dedicated to politics and to their families to stay with her.[6]

He was right to worry. On May 24, several days after her return to Hollywood from the birthday celebration, her access to the White House phone line was cut off. Peter Lawford informed her that the president would no longer see her. According to Patricia Lawford Stewart, Jack Kennedy wasn't kind in breaking with her. "There was no effort to let her down easily. She was told that she could never speak to the president again, that she wouldn't be first lady, that she wasn't even a serious affair to Jack. 'Look, Marilyn,' Peter said, 'You've just been another one of Jack's fucks.'"[7]

On one of those weekends she talked to Frank Sinatra, whom she had been trying to reach for days. He was bitter about the Kennedys, since they had cut off relations with him when J. Edgar Hoover told Bobby in February that the FBI had found out Sinatra was friendly with Sam Giancana. As attorney general, Bobby was crusading against the Mafia and Giancana, and no friend of his could be friends with a Mafia leader. Despite Sinatra's work for Jack Kennedy in the 1960 presidential campaign, he would no longer have access to the Kennedys. Given their rejection of Sinatra, Marilyn feared the Kennedys meant it when they cut her off. She had a terrible fear of abandonment, and this was a major one.

On top of the Kennedy issue, Marilyn had to deal with Fox, which was threatening to fire her. Moreover, Cukor remained impossible as a director. He and Walter Bernstein continued to rewrite the dialogue in *Something's Got to Give* and to send her corrections in the evenings, expecting her to have them memorized by the next morning, which was nearly impossible for her. Turning on her for demanding unnecessary retakes on *Let's Make Love*, Cukor now ordered unnecessary retakes on *Something's Got to Give*, which is apparent from the footage in the Fox archive.

Marilyn had Eunice Murray call Greenson in Europe. Since the previous winter he had negotiated with the studio on her behalf. Many stars were now using lawyers as their agents, in order to save money, and Mickey Rudin, Greenson's brother-in-law and a well-known Hollywood lawyer, had taken over this role for Marilyn from Lew Wasserman and MCA, which would end its talent agency that summer to focus on film production. Greenson and Rudin were working together. The studio's major concern was that Marilyn arrive at the set on time, and Greenson promised that Rudin, Weinstein, and he could get Marilyn to be prompt. Greenson arrived home from Europe on June 6, and he met with Mickey Rudin and Fox executives on Marilyn's behalf. Yet despite his assurances that he could get Marilyn to do anything, the studio fired her on June 9.

To cover their tracks, studio executives escalated their publicity campaign against her. She was irresponsible; she had been faking illness; she had caused the layoffs of more than one hundred workers when the picture was canceled. They even suggested that, like her mother, she was mentally imbalanced. According to Earl Wilson, she was taking thirty pills a day.[8] Was Wilson correct? Throughout the summer Greenson contended that Marilyn was cutting back on pill taking, and both Lee Siegel and Hyman Engelberg claimed the shots they gave Marilyn were vitamin B12, not amphetamines. A B12 shot does produce energy, although not an immediate high.

Marilyn retreated into her bedroom after the firing, but she quickly came back, displaying her characteristic pattern of retreating and then advancing in the face of disaster. Pat Newcomb and she orchestrated a campaign on her behalf. She appealed to the public; in fact, fan mail sent to the studio about the firing was in her favor. Toward the end of June she did photo sessions with Bert Stern and George Barris, and she dictated a brief autobiography to Barris. As the summer progressed, interviews with her appeared in *Redbook* and *Life*.

The Stern session was a turning point. It was commissioned by *Vogue*, the world's preeminent high-fashion magazine. *Vogue* had published scores of pictures of Audrey Hepburn over the years, but never any of Marilyn. Just the month before, Bert Stern had shot Elizabeth Taylor for *Vogue*, and Marilyn was following suit with something bolder. It was Stern's idea to photograph her nude, with transparent chiffon scarves over her body, concealing and revealing it. They shot all night. The next day Stern was contacted to do fashion photos of her. He photographed her in an elegant black dress demonstrating that, with her thin body, she could model high-fashion clothes.[9] *Vogue* followed the nude photo with the high-fashion photo.

Both her anger and her rationality are on display in her *Life* magazine interview, published the week before her death. She chided the studio for the way they treated her: "I'm not in a military school. I'm there to give a performance and not to be disciplined by a studio. An actor is a sensitive instrument, not a machine." She spoke of her shyness, her struggle with herself, her dislike of the "big American rush—you got to go fast for no good reason." She didn't want to be considered a commodity, a person selling a product. And on fame: "Fame will go by and, so long, I've had you, fame. If it goes by, I've always known it was fickle." She was angry at the studio for not preserving their history. "If you've noticed in Hollywood where millions and billions of dollars have been made, there aren't really any kind of monuments or museums . . . Nobody left anything behind, they took it, they grabbed it, and they ran—the ones who made the billions of dollars, never the workers." The Marilyn she portrayed in the *Life* interview was resilient and tough, although in the taped version of the interview, she has a nervous laugh that sounds as though something is bothering her.[10]

Then she had a lucky break. The studio, furious with Marilyn over past sins in addition to present ones, wanted to replace her with Lee Remick in the role of Ellen Arden. But Dean Martin refused to do the movie without Marilyn. She next called Darryl Zanuck in Paris, having heard that he was going to execute a power play and take over as corporate head of Fox. He knew that Peter Levathes, associated with Skouras, was running the studio into the ground. Zanuck hadn't liked Marilyn as an actress, but he was aware of her box office appeal, and money was his bottom line. It was her presence in the movie that would draw audiences. Zanuck, who had been her nemesis throughout much of her career, now became her savior. Within two weeks, she was negotiating with Fox to continue the film. They offered her one million dollars to complete *Something's Got to Give* and to do a second movie. The deal included firing Paula Strasberg, whom they detested, as well as Pat Newcomb. They would return to Nunnally Johnson's original script, which Marilyn had liked, and replace George Cukor with Jean Negulesco, Marilyn's friend.

Bobby Kennedy was in Los Angeles several times that spring and summer. He was visiting the local office of the Department of Justice and also was talking to producer Jerry Wald about making a movie out of his book *The Enemy Within*, the story of his investigation of Jimmy Hoffa, head of the Teamsters Union. Wald died in the middle of the summer, however, and the movie was never made.[11]

On June 26, 1962, Marilyn attended a party at the Lawford beach house at which Bobby was present. There had already been sightings of them together. Reporter James Bacon stated their relationship was long-lasting but she never talked about it. Rupert Allan said she had deluded herself into believing that Bobby would marry her. Jeanne Martin was aware of it, as were Anne Karger; Henry Weinstein; Natalie Trundy and Arthur Jacobs; George Chasin (Marilyn's agent at MCA); Phyllis McGuire, Sam Giancana's girlfriend; Janet Des Rosiers, a longtime lover of Joe Kennedy; and Lady May Lawford, Peter Lawford's mother. Lawford neighbors Peter Dye, Lynn Sherman, and Ward Wood knew about it, as did Peter Lawford's close friends Molly Dunne, George "Bullets" Durgom, and Milton Ebbins. At the time Marilyn died, Earl Wilson stated she was involved only with Jack Kennedy, but in 1976, in his biography of Sinatra, he wrote, "I couldn't expose Jack and Bobby's sharing of Marilyn Monroe and other girls in my previous work. Now I can expose it." By 1976 both Jack and Bobby had been assassinated.[12]

Harry Hall, a close friend of Joe DiMaggio's who was both a "wise guy" and an FBI informant, said Marilyn often broke dates with DiMaggio the year before she died to see Bobby Kennedy. (DiMaggio was still having her followed.) Michael Selsman, the third agent in the Arthur Jacobs firm, was assigned to persuade newspapers to pull stories on her meetings with Bobby. Joan Greenson said she was dating "the General"—a title Bobby's office staff had given him because he could be stern. On Friday, August 3, two days before Marilyn's death, Dorothy Kilgallen hinted at the relationship in her column. Even John Bates, the owner of the ranch near Santa Cruz where Bobby said he spent the weekend of Marilyn's death, stated that everyone knew they were close friends. Marilyn told some of her friends that Bobby was too puny for her, but Peter Lawford wrote in manuscript notes for his unpublished autobiography that she was mesmerized by Bobby's intellect. In 1992, when Ted Landreth of the BBC produced a documentary on Marilyn's death, he polled the members of the Washington Press Corps who had been reporters during the Kennedy administration asking them if they had known about Marilyn's involvement with both Kennedys. Most said they had.[13]

There was also the note Jean Kennedy Smith wrote to Marilyn: "Understand that you and Bobby are the new item! We all think you should come with him when he comes back East!" The Kennedys claimed the statement was a joke—an unconvincing explanation. Inez Melson, guardian for Marilyn's mother and executrix of Marilyn's Los Angeles estate, found the note when she was cleaning out the Brentwood house after Marilyn died. She kept it. She said she intended to use it if Bobby ever ran for president to prove he was immoral.[14] Inez had a strong sense of propriety. She knew about Marilyn and the Kennedys, and she didn't like it.

It was inevitable that Bobby would break with Marilyn. He was the most devoutly Catholic of the Kennedy brothers. He could be kind and loving, but he was ruthless at this point in his career. Considered the runt of the family because of his small size, he had kept up with the other brothers by sheer force of will. His wife, Ethel, bore many children and was a good Catholic girl. But she gave parties that defined Washington political society, was energetic and amusing, and was an excellent campaigner. She was valuable to Bobby, who loved her and their children.

The previous December Joe Kennedy had had a major stroke, which incapacitated him permanently and rendered him unable to talk. Since Jack Kennedy was absorbed by the presidency and his physical issues, by 1962 Bobby was the de facto head of the family, responsible for covering up sexual improprieties. As attorney general he went after the Mafia. He didn't seem to know—or he refused to admit—that his father had Mafia connections and that the mob had swung the 1960 presidential election to Kennedy through voter fraud. Robert Kennedy was a bundle of contradictions.

By mid-June, Marilyn seemed to have recovered from her virus. She spent time with Marlon Brando and his best friend, the intelligent and amusing Wally Cox, who played a supporting role in *Something's Got to Give*. She often saw the Lawfords. They went to her house for drinks and snacks, and she stayed overnight in their house when she wanted company. Peter never forgot the night Marilyn went into their bedroom, unable to sleep, and expressed the wish that she could have a marriage as wonderful as theirs. The truth was their marriage was falling apart, but they put up a good front. When Eunice Murray was Marilyn's assistant, she heard long, easygoing phone conversations between Marilyn and Pat Lawford.[15]

Marilyn also went to Ralph Greenson's musical evenings. She supervised revisions to her house and worked in her garden. Gloria Romanoff said she had never seen Marilyn so happy; she loved her house and loved to show it off. She liked having Eunice Murray around because she was never alone. She became close to Joan Greenson and gave her a surprise birthday party. She saw Ralph Greenson nearly every weekday for a therapy session.[16]

But the rage was still inside her. Michael Selsman, the third agent in the Jacobs office, was assigned to do publicity for her and function as a liaison to her, in addition to Pat Newcomb. Whenever Selsman saw her, she seemed in a rage. He found her duplicitous and demanding, a terrible diva. But he was married to Carol Lynley, a rising blonde star at Fox who had the dressing room suite next to Marilyn's. Lynley had everything Marilyn wanted—a loving husband, a reputation as a dramatic actress, and a baby—and she was challenging Marilyn's position as Hollywood's reigning blonde beauty. Lynley roused Marilyn's fear of being taken over, and Marilyn took it out on her husband Michael, who was young and vulnerable. Moreover, private detective Fred Otash had bugged her house, and now his operatives listened to her phone calls. She had a lot of angry exchanges with both Jack and Bobby, especially with Bobby, who made dates with her and didn't show up, citing career obligations. When she spoke with Jack Kennedy, he tried to calm her down, but Bobby was vituperative. Her anger against them was mounting; it showed in her exchanges with Selsman.[17]

On the weekend of July 19–21, Marilyn entered Cedars of Lebanon Hospital under an assumed name and had either a dilation and curettage or an abortion. In those days journalists bribed the staffs at hospitals for information when actors went in for treatment. Michael Selsman heard the story from reporter Joe Hyams.[18] Selsman and many others heard that one of the Kennedys was the father. Marilyn didn't see Bobby that weekend or the next week, although he was in Los Angeles at the end of the week to address the National Black Business Association. She did, however, spend the next weekend, the weekend of July 28 and 29, at Frank Sinatra's resort hotel, Cal Neva, on the shore of Lake Tahoe. Patricia and Peter Lawford took her there; Peter was a part owner of the lodge. It seems she expected to meet Bobby Kennedy there. Billed as a rest for Marilyn, the weekend turned into a disaster that set the scene for her death seven days later.

Joe Kennedy had been connected to Cal Neva since Prohibition, when he went there to meet his mobster friends. They liked the resort because of its isolation, its gambling, and its many hidden tunnels, which offered an escape route if law enforcement officers appeared. The main lodge was located on the California-Nevada border, which bisected its main gambling casino. Some writers contend that Joe Kennedy secretly owned Cal Neva, along with mob associates. In 1960 a consortium including Frank Sinatra and Peter Lawford bought a forty-nine-percent stake in the lodge, further obfuscating its mob connections. Sinatra's friend Skinny D'Amato was brought in from his 500 Club in Atlantic City to manage it. Hollywood entertainers performed in its dining room and lounge, and Hollywood people went there, along with the mobsters. When Marilyn was making *The Misfits* in August 1960, she went there to see Frank's show.[19]

Exactly what happened the weekend Pat and Peter took Marilyn there is murky. In fact, given the varying stories, two weekends may have been involved: that's what Peter Lawford implied to Anthony Summers when he stated that he and Pat had taken Marilyn to Cal Neva during an earlier weekend that summer. That may have been June 29, when Frank took a lot of his Hollywood friends to Cal Neva to see his new show and his expansion of the lodge. Marilyn seems to have been using drugs heavily. On one occasion she left her phone line open to the switchboard, with the receiver by her mouth, so that if the operator heard heavy breathing (the sign of a barbiturate overdose), she could summon the Lawfords. Patricia Lawford Stewart told me Peter and Pat were summoned. They revived her and took her to a local hospital.[20]

The weekend of July 28 was the important one, given its proximity in time to Marilyn's death. Sidney Skolsky contended that Marilyn went there that weekend to see Dean Martin, who was headlining, to talk about renewing filming on *Something's Got to Give*. Another claim is that Sam Giancana ordered Sinatra to take her there, because he had concocted a scheme to use Marilyn to bring down the Kennedys. Another claim is that Peter and Pat lured her there under the pretext of meeting Bobby Kennedy. They wanted to get her out of town and away from Bobby, who was in Los Angeles. Whether or not he was supposed to be at Cal Neva, he never showed up.

The lodge was crowded, with as many as five hundred people there. With Sinatra's bodyguard often near her, many people who saw Marilyn there thought she was a virtual prisoner. Sam Giancana and Johnny Roselli were there, but they often went to the lodge. Joe DiMaggio knew what was going on. Skinny D'Amato, his close friend from New Jersey, was the manager of Cal Neva. When Joe was in San Francisco he sometimes flew to Lake Tahoe and spent time at Cal Neva with Skinny. Through his private investigators and phone taps, he knew the Kennedys were breaking with Marilyn. He was worried about her, and she may have telephoned him in San Francisco to go to the lodge. He went there the weekend of July 28, but he and Frank weren't speaking and he was fearful that mayhem might ensue if he tried to enter the lodge, given Frank's tough henchmen. Thus he didn't try to rescue Marilyn, as he had when she was in the Payne Whitney Clinic in the spring of 1961.

He stayed at a nearby motel—or at another location on the lake. There's a touching story that Marilyn went outside early in the morning and, looking up the hill, saw Joe there. Marilyn told Ralph Roberts that Pat Kennedy Lawford had persuaded her to go to the lodge and she had spent much of the weekend avoiding both Joe and Frank.[21]

The story becomes more precise late Saturday night in the central dining room. Marilyn was sitting in the front of the room beside Frank and several burly men. She was drinking champagne and popping red pills, probably Seconal. Peter Lawford may have told her earlier that day that Bobby was ending their relationship. According to Betsy Hammes, who was there, she looked disheveled. At one point during the evening she slumped over, and the burly men beside her half carried and half walked her out of the room. The next day Betsy asked a Sinatra aide why Marilyn had been taken out of the dining room. He told her they had to "roll Marilyn over a barrel." In other words, they took her to her room and made her vomit, fearing that she had taken too many pills. In this version of what happened, Giancana, who went to her room, was a Good Samaritan trying to empty Marilyn's stomach of a possible overdose.[22]

In Marilyn's room someone took pictures of what went on. Frank Sinatra wasn't there, but his camera was used. When he got it back, he had photographer William Woodfield, who often took photographs for him, develop the roll. It turned out to have on it seven frames of Sam Giancana, fully clothed, on top of Marilyn's back, seeming to ride her like a horse. Was he raping her? Was he trying to help her? Woodfield saw the film before Sinatra destroyed it. It was blurry and imprecise. He couldn't tell exactly what was going on. Other men were in the room. Some say they were Giancana associates, and they gang-raped Marilyn; the story circulated in Hollywood that Giancana had visited "Sicilian sex" on her—in other words anal intercourse—as a punishment for her involvement with Bobby Kennedy. Such intercourse was used in Sicily as a means of birth control.[23]

Pat Kennedy Lawford, Peter Lawford, and Frank Sinatra were at the lodge that weekend. Why none of them helped Marilyn is perplexing, although Pat may have already gone to the Kennedy compound in Hyannis Port. For his part, Sinatra seems to have ordered his guards to take Marilyn out of the dining room because he didn't like her pill taking. Roberta Linn, a singer and friend of Sinatra's who was there, thought he was protective of Marilyn that weekend. Phyllis McGuire had a different version of events. No matter how angry Giancana was at the Kennedys, Phyllis told me, he wouldn't have harmed Marilyn, because of her involvement with his friends DiMaggio and Sinatra. Loyalty to friends was part of the Sicilian code of honor, and Giancana wouldn't violate it. (It's possible, of course, that Phyllis didn't tell me the truth.)

George Edwards contended that Sinatra even considered marrying

Marilyn as a way of protecting her against others and against herself. Edwards heard about the supposed orgy with Marilyn, but he was skeptical that it had happened. He drove Marilyn to the airport the next day, and she mostly talked about having upset Giancana because she hadn't acted like a lady and had taken so many drugs. Giancana disliked drugs as much as Sinatra did.[24]

Marilyn went back to Los Angeles in Sinatra's private plane, along with Peter Lawford—and perhaps Pat. (By one account the plane landed in San Francisco briefly, so that Pat could take a plane to Hyannis Port.) When they landed at the Los Angeles airport, a limousine picked up Marilyn and took her to her Brentwood home. The next morning she was up at eight, working in her garden. This early-morning activity suggests she wasn't upset by whatever had happened at Cal Neva. She made an eight-minute phone call to Bobby Kennedy at his office that morning; she may have been angry at him for not appearing at Cal Neva. Some say she had given up on him and wanted an apology in person for the way the Kennedys had treated her. She saw Ralph Greenson every day that week, but that was her usual practice. The only clear proof of untoward behavior at Cal Neva is that Joe resigned his job with the Monette Company and said he was moving to Los Angeles to take care of her. Yet no record exists that he called her that week; he didn't seem to think she was in any immediate danger.

After the weekend at Cal Neva, she may have considered remarrying Joe; that's what his friends and family thought. He had changed over the years. He had acceded to her demands that he accompany her to public events in which she played her sexy self and attend high-brow plays with her. He had followed her suggestion to undergo therapy, and it had taught him to control his anger. He no longer drank liquor or large amounts of coffee. He even came to like reading poetry with Marilyn. After he moved to Florida in his later years, he praised her intellectual achievements. He was impressed that she quoted from Chekhov and Dostoyevsky and listened to Beethoven.[25]

The Marilyn most people saw the last week of her life seemed contented, as she worked in her garden and went to a gardening nursery for an afternoon, choosing plants and bushes for her grounds. She and Eunice Murray oversaw the workers who were refurbishing the house, while they discussed plans for building a guest room over the garage where her

New York friends could stay when they visited. She spoke to Gloria Romanoff often that week, since Gloria had invited her to go to dinner with a friend from China on Sunday evening and Marilyn couldn't decide what to wear. Gloria told her to wear one of her brightly colored Pucci silk dresses.[26]

On Wednesday night, she called Red Krohn, the gynecologist during her 1958 pregnancy with whom she had become so angry. She hadn't spoken to him since. She sounded miserable, and she asked to see him. Are you still angry about the baby? she asked. He told her that he had put it behind him, and they agreed to have dinner the next week. Had her endometriosis flared up? Did she still hope to become pregnant? Was she considering adopting a child? Gloria Romanoff thought she wanted to talk to Krohn about breast implants, since her breasts had shrunk during her weight loss.[27]

Hairstylist Mickey Song maintained that Marilyn invited him to her house on Wednesday evening and questioned him about the Kennedys, since he was their hairdresser, although Lawford's friend producer William Asher didn't think that Song knew the Kennedys. On Thursday night Marilyn went to a party at Peter Lawford's house. According to Dick Livingston, Peter's friend, who was there that evening, she looked unkempt. "She had the damnest outfit on," Livingston said, "a pair of hip-huggers with a bare midriff and her gallbladder scar showing and a Mexican serape around her neck. She looked very white, and I told her she needed to get some sun. She said, I know, I need a tan and a man."[28] Natalie Wood, who was at the party, observed her in a corner dejectedly repeating the number thirty-six again and again. She had turned thirty-six on June 1. That was a rocky age in Hollywood: both Clara Bow and Greta Garbo had left the screen at thirty-six. That week was the fifth anniversary of Marilyn's 1957 miscarriage of a Miller baby, which must have depressed her. An hour after she left the Lawford party, however, she was at her home in Brentwood, drinking champagne with Whitey Snyder and Marjorie Plecher, Whitey's wife, who served as Marilyn's wardrobe girl and costumer. She was upbeat with them, happy about being reinstated at the studio.[29]

On Thursday and Friday she had a series of important phone calls. She spoke to Gene Kelly about doing a film and with Jule Styne about doing a musical version of *A Tree Grows in Brooklyn* on Broadway with

Frank Sinatra. She was supposed to meet with Kelly that Sunday in Hollywood and with Styne in New York the next week. On Friday she went to the Fox screening room to view several movies that J. Lee Thompson had directed. He was under consideration to direct her next film for Fox. That evening she went for dinner at a favorite restaurant with Pat Newcomb and Peter Lawford. Pat spent the night at Marilyn's house, supposedly because she had bronchitis and wanted to soak up the sun the next day on Marilyn's patio.

For twenty years after Marilyn's death, the official version of what happened on Saturday, August 4, didn't essentially vary. It was based largely on the initial testimony of Eunice Murray, Ralph Greenson, and Peter Lawford to journalists and investigators, although the police didn't interview Lawford until some years later. It begins with a description of Saturday as an uneventful day, with Marilyn and Pat Newcomb sitting by the pool. Ralph Roberts arrived at nine A.M. and gave Marilyn a massage; she took several phone calls, including one from Sidney Skolsky. (According to Steffi Skolsky, they talked about his biopic on Jean Harlow, not about the Kennedys, and Marilyn said she was going to remove the Strasbergs as beneficiaries in her will.) A series of claims have been built around Marilyn receiving a stuffed animal by mail that morning, but Pat Newcomb told me that no such animal arrived.[30] Pat and Marilyn began arguing, presumably because Pat had slept the night before and Marilyn hadn't. The argument became so heated that Ralph Greenson was called at four thirty that afternoon to calm her down. He stayed until seven.

He then left to go to a party with his wife. Marilyn was calmer, although Greenson asked Eunice Murray to stay at the Brentwood house that night, which she normally didn't do. At seven fifteen there was a phone call from Joe DiMaggio Jr. Marilyn talked to him for thirty minutes, expressing delight when he told her he wasn't going to marry his girlfriend, whom she didn't like. The time was seven forty-five. Marilyn called Greenson, telling him about Joe Jr. She seemed to be in excellent spirits. She called Peter Lawford to tell him that she wasn't going to the party he was holding that evening.

Then, according to the official version, she crashed. By eight fifteen she called Lawford, with a "good-bye" message. According to Lawford, she said, "Say good-bye to the president and say good-bye to yourself, because you're a good guy." It sounds like a suicidal plea for help, although we have only Lawford's word about it. He repeated it, however, for the rest of his life. Marilyn drifted off the phone. Lawford called her back, but the line was dead. He called the operator, who said the telephone was off the hook. He then called Milton Ebbins, his manager, to ask what to do, and Milt told him not to go to Marilyn's house. It would look bad if the president's brother-in-law was discovered there if anything was really wrong with Marilyn. For some reason he didn't try to call Marilyn on the second phone line she had or send any of the guests at the party to see what was going on. Ebbins called Mickey Rudin, who called Eunice Murray to check up on Marilyn. Eunice called back to say Marilyn was fine. Peter's party lasted until ten thirty. After that he went on a drinking binge, and passed out.

Meanwhile, in the official version, Marilyn retired early and Eunice Murray went to bed. Eunice woke up at three A.M., sensing that something was wrong. She looked in Marilyn's bedroom window to check on her, because the bedroom door was locked. Marilyn was in a strange position in her bed. Worried, Eunice called Greenson to come over, and he did. Because the door to Marilyn's bedroom was locked, he took a fireplace poker and smashed a window, so that he could open it and climb in. He found Marilyn dead, lying naked under a sheet. He called Engelberg to come over, and at four thirty he called the police, telling them that Marilyn had committed suicide. By the time the police arrived shortly after, rigor mortis was extreme, indicating that she had died six to eight hours earlier, which would be between eight thirty and ten thirty. (Rigor mortis sets in as soon as death occurs.)

Thomas Noguchi, an assistant coroner who did the autopsy on Marilyn's body, found no evidence of foul play, except for a bruise on her back, which could have been caused by bumping into furniture. He determined that she had taken huge doses of Nembutal and chloral hydrate, although she hadn't drunk any alcohol that day. Theodore Curphey, the coroner, hired the Suicide Prevention Team, a group of local psychiatrists who ran a suicide hotline, to determine if suicide was a possibility. They interviewed her psychiatrists and doctors, who testified to her many drug overdoses, some of which seemed to have been suicide attempts. The team discovered that Marilyn had obtained two prescriptions for twenty-five Nembutal pills each from a different doctor only days before she died. Thus she had as many as fifty Nembutal pills in her possession that Saturday. They concluded that suicide was probable. The district attorney closed the case after five days, ruling it a probable suicide. No inquest or grand jury investigation was held. It was assumed Marilyn had died as early as eight thirty, soon after the call to Lawford, from a massive overdose of Nembutal and a toxic dose of chloral hydrate.

What I have narrated was the official version of Marilyn's death, accepted by the police and the press, except for a few maverick journalists. It wasn't substantially challenged until 1985 with the publication of Anthony Summers's *Goddess: The Secret Life of Marilyn Monroe*. A well-known British journalist, Summers turned to investigating Marilyn's death after the editor of London's *Sunday Express* commissioned him to write an article about the Los Angeles district attorney's 1982 reinvestigation of Marilyn's death. Realizing that the reinvestigation hadn't been thorough, Summers decided to do his own investigation and write his own book. Indefatigable, intelligent, and bold, Summers interviewed some six hundred fifty people. He discovered an alternative scenario to the official one.

In the first place, Summers concluded that Bobby Kennedy had been at Marilyn's house the afternoon of her death and perhaps that evening. Fox publicist Frank Neill saw Bobby land by helicopter at the Fox lot that morning; neighbors of Lawford's saw Bobby at Lawford's beach house later that day; and neighbors of Marilyn saw him walking to her house in the early afternoon. The Los Angeles Police Department knew he was there that day. Summers discovered more. Greenson was called at four thirty that afternoon because Marilyn and Bobby had a major altercation, not because of her quarrel with Pat Newcomb. Greenson did stay until seven P.M. and Marilyn did talk with Joe DiMaggio Jr at seven fifteen, Ralph Greenson at seven forty-five, and Peter Lawford at about eight, telling him that she wasn't going to his party. By about eight fifteen he received the "say good-bye to the president" phone call, according to the official version.

But the official chronology for the calls Peter Lawford received during his party that evening was probably off by several hours, with implications for Marilyn's mood at the time of her death. The only people who attended Lawford's party were producers George "Bullets" Durgom and Joe Naar, along with his wife, Dolores. Dolores Naar (later Nemiro) told me that Marilyn didn't call Peter until nine o'clock. Dolores assumed this was the "say good-bye to the president" phone call. Lawford seemed concerned over the call, but not excessively so. He returned to the poker game they had been playing. There weren't any more phone calls before they left around ten thirty. Both Bullets Durgom and Irma Lee Reilly, Peter's housekeeper, stated that during the party no alarm was raised about Marilyn.[31]

It's possible that Marilyn's phone call to Peter at nine wasn't a suicidal plea for help; rather, she may have told him she was finished with the Kennedys. Fred Otash, the private investigator everyone in Hollywood used, revealed that Peter had come to his office at two A.M. to ask him to go to Marilyn's house to remove any incriminating Kennedy documents. According to Otash, Lawford stated that Marilyn told him that the Kennedys were treating her like a piece of meat and she didn't want to see them anymore. She had tried unsuccessfully to call the president. She wanted Peter to say good-bye to him for her. Lawford tried to persuade her to go to the beach house and talk to Bobby, but she responded that there was nothing more for her to say. She had served her purpose. Indeed, the Suicide Prevention Team discovered she had called the White House at nine P.M., West Coast time.[32]

In his interviews, Anthony Summers found that Marilyn spoke on the phone to several individuals between eight thirty and ten o'clock. She talked to Henry Rosenfeld, her New York dress manufacturer friend, and to hairdresser Sidney Guilaroff, her friend who was an intimate to many Hollywood stars. Guilaroff revealed the details of his phone conversation with Marilyn in his 1991 autobiography, *Crowning Glory*: Marilyn told him that Bobby Kennedy had been there that day and had threatened her.[33] At nine o'clock she called Jack Kennedy in the White House and didn't reach him. Next came a phone call to Peter Lawford, the "say good-bye to the president" phone call. She may have talked with José Bolaños; he said she dropped the phone in the middle of a conversation with him because she heard a noise in the house. At ten Ralph Roberts's answering service received a garbled message from a fuzzy-voiced woman whom Ralph was certain was Marilyn. (Some biographers place that phone call at eight thirty, which supports the official version of Marilyn's death, but overlooks the calls from Guilaroff and Rosenfeld. Roberts told Summers it occurred at ten.)

Joe and Dolores Naar left Peter's party about ten thirty. At eleven Peter called them, expressing concern about Marilyn and asking Joe to go over to her house and check on her. They lived four blocks away from Marilyn, and Joe agreed to do so. At about the same time Peter called his friend Bill Asher and his manager Milton Ebbins asking them to go with him to the house, but they refused.[34] As Joe was leaving his house, Peter called again, telling him not to bother because the doctor was with Marilyn. That's what Joe Naar told James Spada and that's what he told me. When I asked Naar why no one had come forward at the time of Marilyn's death with this information, he told me that Patricia Newcomb had asked them not to. It was the first indication I had of a cover-up.

In this revised version, at eight thirty Eunice Murray did check on Marilyn for Milton Ebbins and she was fine. By ten fifteen or thereabouts Eunice checked again and found Marilyn comatose. She called Greenson and Engelberg, both of whom rushed over. Marilyn was still alive, and Greenson called an ambulance, which took her to the hospital. She died on the way and was taken back to Brentwood and placed in her bed. This was the story Eunice Murray told Anthony Summers after she broke down in the middle of filming the BBC documentary *Say Goodbye to the President*. You can see it on the video.

If Peter called Ebbins at ten thirty alarmed about Marilyn, after the party was over, as well as at seven thirty, which was in the official version, and Ebbins then called Rudin, who called Murray, (replicating the pattern of the earlier calls) the time frames of everyone's stories would coincide, with the doctors arriving at Marilyn's house at about eleven. Someone would have called Peter at this point, telling him the doctor was there. Thus he called Joe Naar shortly after eleven to tell him not to go to Marilyn's house. In fact, Lawford probably didn't want Joe at Marilyn's house; what was going on was too dicey to involve anyone else.

When Eunice found Marilyn comatose, she also called Patricia Newcomb, who called Arthur Jacobs, the head of the firm. Jacobs was then at the Hollywood Bowl listening to a concert. His fiancée, Natalie Trundy, remembered that he received the phone call from Newcomb stating that Marilyn was comatose at about eleven o'clock at the Bowl, and he rushed over to Marilyn's house. An usher had tapped him on the shoulder during the performance and told him that he had an important phone call, and he went to the office to take it, returning to tell Trundy briefly about it before he left. Trundy didn't see him for several days, but he refused to tell her what had happened.

When Jacobs got to the house, Newcomb was already there, and Rudin arrived shortly after. Rudin said that Newcomb was hysterical when he arrived.

Peter Lawford may have gone to the house, although Patricia Lawford Stewart is adamant that he didn't go there but rather had Otash go in his place. In fact, all of Peter's friends interviewed by Summers and Spada—Rudin, Ebbins, Asher, Naar, Durgom—and his housekeeper, Irma Lee Reilly, stated that he was useless in a crisis like this and that he had been drinking so heavily that evening that he passed out. Thus he wasn't at Marilyn's. Besides, after Marilyn died, Bobby Kennedy had to be gotten out of town. In the revised version of Marilyn's death, Peter arranged for a helicopter to pick up Bobby on the beach in front of his house and to take him to the airport in Santa Monica or Los Angeles for a flight back to the Bates ranch in the Santa Cruz mountains.

Meanwhile, executives at Fox were contacted and they showed up at the Brentwood house to remove any incriminating evidence of their dealings with her. Everything that might be detrimental to the studio or might reveal her relationships with the Kennedys was taken out of her file cabinets. A cover-up story was put together. If the individuals involved in doing this arrived at Marilyn's house at eleven, they had more than five hours to concoct their story, since Greenson called the police at four thirty.

Some of the planning that night was brilliant, as the conspirators put together stories for Eunice Murray and the doctors in particular to use in talking to the police and the press. Yet some of it seems haphazard, as though the people involved were under great stress. Surely these friends of Marilyn knew that she never slept entirely in the nude: she wore a bra because she believed that it would keep her breast muscles firm. They were foolish to put her body nude in the bed. They must have known that the lock on her bedroom door didn't work and that after the Payne Whitney episode, Marilyn didn't lock her bedroom door, anyway. And, the glass from the broken window had fallen inside the bedroom, not outside it, indicating that it had been broken from outside the room. Thus the story that Greenson broke a window to get in was preposterous.

When the first policeman arrived at four thirty, he was disconcerted to find Eunice Murray doing laundry in the laundry room. She never gave much of an explanation for doing this. The conspirators placed a note in plain view that Marilyn had written to Joe DiMaggio. It stated that a life was justified if the individual was faithful to one person. It seems a plant to deny the relationships with the Kennedys and to suggest that she was going to reconcile with Di Maggio.[35]

Arthur Jacobs and Patricia Newcomb were publicists by profession, adept at concealing the truth and creating fictions. What better individuals to deal with Marilyn's death, making it seem like accidental suicide. They put the "official version" out on the wire. Patricia was devoted to Marilyn and was constantly with her, but she was close to the Kennedys, especially Bobby, whom she'd known for years. She didn't want him connected to Marilyn's death. Patricia was distraught; she had to get out of town. She attended Marilyn's funeral the next Wednesday, but she immediately flew to Hyannis Port, where she was seen with Pat and Peter Lawford and other Kennedys. The story was put out that Jacobs had fired her because she had screamed at the press, but Michael Selsman, her associate in the Jacobs firm, told me that he had never heard about the firing. She had just suddenly disappeared. (He also told me that she had shown no indication that she had bronchitis that weekend.) Arthur Jacobs called Selsman at five thirty Sunday morning and told him to go to Marilyn's house to deal with the press. When Selsman asked him what had happened, he replied, "You don't want to know."

In addition to the cover-up that night, the police conducted their own cover-up. It included Theodore Curphey's instructions to the Suicide Prevention Team not to investigate the possibility of foul play. Robert Litman, head of the team, told me he found these instructions strange; they ruled out murder as a possibility. Moreover, the day after the autopsy was done samples of Marilyn's blood and tissues that had been taken for further investigation disappeared, as did all records of any investigations the police conducted. Only someone with great authority could have ordered the disposal of the autopsy materials and the police files. Bobby Kennedy was close to both William Parker, head of the Los Angeles Police Department, and James Hamilton, head of the LAPD Organized Crime Intelligence Division. Kennedy often consulted with Parker and Hamilton about his investigative work as attorney general.

Joe DiMaggio allowed neither Kennedys nor the Hollywood crowd to attend Marilyn's funeral; he thought they were implicated in her death. Ralph Greenson told Robert Litman, when Litman interviewed him several days after Marilyn's death, that Marilyn was involved with men at the highest level of government. When reporter William Woodfield called Greenson and asked him what had happened the night of Marilyn's death, Greenson said, "Ask Robert Kennedy." This statement is well known among Marilyn researchers. What isn't known is that Greenson said he always thought Bobby should have admitted to having been there that day. He then clammed up and, ever after, denied that Marilyn had been involved with Bobby. Peter Lawford and his friends told variations on the official story, which ended with Marilyn committing suicide or taking an accidental overdose.

Still the question remains: Why did Bobby Kennedy go to Marilyn's house in the first place? Marilyn had been calling both Kennedys nonstop, and she was good at tracking them down. Department of Justice officials called her "out of control."[36] She was threatening to hold a press conference and make public a diary she had kept of her conversations with Bobby about politics, in which she had written down what he'd told her about such matters as Cuba, the nuclear bomb, and his crusade against the Mafia. Marilyn sometimes couldn't remember the details of politics, and she kept a record of her conversations about it. She also knew about the Kennedys' sexual involvements, which could destroy their political course if she revealed them. Reporters in that time rarely revealed what they knew about politicians' sex lives, and all Jack's conquests had kept quiet. Marilyn would be unique among them for speaking out.

Otash agents listening to Marilyn's conversations on Saturday, August 4, heard a fierce argument between her and Bobby. He could be heard rifling her house and asking her, "Where did you put it?" Turning belligerent, she refused to give "it" to him and began to hit him. He left after about an hour. Some say he took a doctor with him who gave her a shot. That sounds extreme to me; I can't imagine that such an attack wouldn't have terrified Marilyn to the extent that she would have left the house and gone into hiding. The best conclusion is that he was looking for the diary.

Some researchers believe Marilyn wouldn't have held the press conference, but I'm not so sure. When I interviewed photographer George Barris, he convinced me she would have held it. Barris is a gentle man, kind and soft-spoken; I can understand why Marilyn chose him to photograph her that summer and then dictated an autobiography to him. He told me I was the first Marilyn biographer since Gloria Steinem to have interviewed him. On Friday, August 3, Marilyn called Barris in New York and asked him to go to Los Angeles immediately because she needed to see him. Barris believed she wanted him to set up a press conference for her. He was a journalist as well as a photographer, and he could easily do it. She couldn't use the Jacobs agency because Pat Newcomb was close to the Kennedys. Barris told Marilyn that he couldn't get there until Monday, and they made a date to meet then. Rupert Allan stated that Marilyn had called him that Friday and left a message that she wanted him to set up a press conference for her, but he was ill and didn't respond.[37]

Bobby Kennedy had an alibi for the weekend. He maintained that he spent it with his family at the ranch of John Bates, an old friend, in the Santa Cruz Mountains, eighty miles south of San Francisco. John Bates's son recently sent pictures from that weekend to Susan Bernard, Bruno Bernard's daughter, who published them in her 2011 book about her father's photographs of Marilyn.[38] If they are accurate, the sightings of him in Los Angeles constituted a form of hysteria among a group of people who didn't know each other. But photos can be deceiving, and Mark Anderson, a photographer I consulted, stated that the position of the sun in them and the shadows on the faces of the individuals in them indicated that they weren't taken when John Bates said they were taken. Kennedy friends were loyal to the family; it's conceivable that, like so many people involved in Marilyn's death, they told only part of the truth.

Anthony Summers published his book in 1985. In the more than twenty-five years since then, new theories have periodically appeared about Marilyn's death, often based on new information provided by new witnesses. Primary among these witnesses are John Miner, the assistant district attorney who participated in the autopsy; James Hall, an ambulance attendant who claimed to have been at Marilyn's house with the ambulance the night she died; and Lynn Franklin, a Beverly Hills policeman who claimed he pulled over Peter Lawford on a speeding charge that night. Attention has also focused on Norman Jefferies, Eunice Murray's son-in-law, who worked as a handyman at Marilyn's house, and on writer C. David Heymann's claim that Peter Lawford told him that he, Greenson, and Bobby Kennedy were together that night. An allegation of murder runs throughout these testimonies.

John Miner was the first "authority" on Marilyn to maintain that she had been killed through the administration of a drug-laced enema. The theory makes sense as a way of explaining how such large amounts of Nembutal and chloral hydrate got into her blood quickly. Enemas were used by Hollywood actresses, including Marilyn, for quick weight loss. (She also suffered from constipation, caused by the drugs she was taking, another reason to use enemas.) Miner was the first individual to assert that Eunice Murray gave her the enema, although there is no proof for this charge. Eunice wasn't a nurse; she was a housekeeper and a companion. Marilyn gave herself enemas.

Miner also stated that he possessed a transcript of a tape that he claimed Ralph Greenson had played for him several days after she died. He first made this claim to Anthony Summers in 1982. Marilyn had presumably made this tape for her psychiatrist in the weeks before she died, and Greenson played it for Miner to prove that she hadn't killed herself when the district attorney sent Miner to question him. Greenson destroyed the tape, and Miner then went home and wrote it down from memory, producing thirteen pages in several hours. The tape has come to play a major role in Marilyn scholarship, given what appear to be its insights into Marilyn's sexual proclivities and her state of mind at the time she died.

I met Miner at a Marilyn Remembered event in 2005; we both taught at the University of Southern California, and we became friends. Over the next several years I interviewed him many times. He was a small man, eighty-five years old, with a booming voice. He gave me a copy of the transcript at our first meeting, and I was shocked by its claim that Marilyn was fixated on enemas. I became suspicious of him when he told me he had done interviews with Hollywood actresses about their sex lives for Alfred Kinsey's studies on sexuality. Checking him with the Kinsey Institute, I was told by the director they had never heard of him. My suspicions of him increased when he suggested that we write a study of the Marquis de Sade together, while extolling the virtues of enemas to me.

Miner told other Marilyn biographers he spent six hours interviewing

Greenson, but he told me he hadn't questioned him at all. He had too much respect for Greenson to question him; he simply listened to the tape and went home, he told me. Then I learned that Miner had gone bankrupt. Selling the transcript was an obvious way to make money. He first tried to sell it to *Vanity Fair*, but when they asked Anthony Summers to validate it, Miner had only a few handwritten notes on a yellow legal pad to give him. In other words, he hadn't written down a transcript of the tape until twenty years after he presumably heard it. On Summers's recommendation, *Vanity Fair* refused to buy it.

After this refusal, Miner constructed a transcript and sold the rights to it to Matthew Smith, who featured it in his 2003 book, *Marilyn's Last Words*.[39] Miner then sold it to *Playboy* in 2005, after the *Los Angeles Times* did a cover story on him. Then I found out more about Miner. Some years previously he had been convicted of suggesting to several women in the district attorney's office that he perform enemas on them, resulting in the revocation of his license to practice law for several years.

When I suggested to him that he should write an autobiography, he said he couldn't because of the "horrible things" he had done to women. He wouldn't tell me what those "things" were, although I suspect he was referring to his approaches to the women in the D.A.'s office. There were also his stories about being the featured speaker at a convention in Las Vegas on sadomasochists, discussing those who used enemas as well as whips and chains. After all he told me, I concluded that he had made up the transcript, which represented his sexual interests, not Marilyn's.

James Hall was the second new informant on Marilyn's death to appear. When the district attorney's office did a reinvestigation of Marilyn's death in 1982, Hall identified himself as an attendant with the ambulance that had arrived to take Marilyn to the hospital. He demanded to be paid for his testimony. When the district attorney's office refused, he sold his story to a tabloid. He said he was resuscitating Marilyn when a man entered the room carrying a doctor's bag, claiming to be Marilyn's doctor. The man brushed him aside and plunged a large needle into her heart. Hall later claimed the doctor was Greenson. Yet Hall wasn't able to explain why, if such a large needle entered her body, there wasn't a mark on it. Hall said the needle broke several ribs, but the autopsy found no bruised or broken ribs.

Lynn Franklin, a policeman in the Beverly Hills Police Department, was the third new informant to appear, after John Miner and James Hall. He claimed to have pulled Peter Lawford over for speeding shortly after midnight the night Marilyn died. Franklin said that Robert Kennedy was in the backseat along with another man that Franklin later identified from photos as Ralph Greenson. According to Franklin, Lawford told him he was going to the Beverly Hilton hotel, where Kennedy had checked in earlier that day, to pick up his luggage and then to take him to the airport.[40]

In his 1998 study of Marilyn's death, *The Assassination of Marilyn Monroe*, Donald Wolfe accepted the stories of James Hall and Lynn Franklin, while implying that Robert Kennedy had been directly involved in Marilyn's death. He reconstructed a new version of what happened from a long interview with Norman Jefferies. Jefferies told Wolfe he spent Saturday evening watching television with Eunice Murray in her room. Between nine thirty and ten o'clock, Robert Kennedy, along with two men, appeared at the door. Eunice let them in. Kennedy ordered Eunice and Norman to leave the house for a while. They did so, returning around ten thirty. The men were gone, but Marilyn was comatose in the guest cottage attached to the house. Eunice called Engelberg, Greenson, and an ambulance, in which Hall was an attendant. Wolfe now repeated Hall's story: He tried to resuscitate Marilyn, but Greenson plunged the needle into her heart, killing her. Marilyn was carried into her bedroom and placed on her bed. In this version of Marilyn's death, she died in her house, not in the ambulance.

Biographer C. David Heymann joined the theorists on Marilyn's death with his reported interview with Peter Lawford, which he used in his 1989 biography of Jackie Kennedy and his 1998 biography of Robert Kennedy. According to Heymann, Lawford told him that Ralph Greenson, Bobby Kennedy, and he were together the night Marilyn died. Lawford also stated that Marilyn had had an affair with Greenson. If that is true, which I doubt, Greenson had a motive to kill her. Yet Lawford told other biographers little about the evening of August 4. Intensely loyal to the Kennedys, on his deathbed he said he would never reveal what he knew. He consistently told his partner and then wife Patricia Lawford Stewart, who was with him for eleven years, that Marilyn had accidentally killed herself, while he blamed himself for her death because he hadn't gone to her house after she had called him. Whether drunk or sober, engaged in an ordinary conversation or sobbing with guilt, that's the story he repeated. He repeated that same story to everyone else he knew.[41]

Patricia Lawford Stewart became involved in litigation with David Heymann over misrepresentations of her in his biography of Robert Kennedy. She didn't trust any of the other allegations he made. Loyal to Lawford after his death, she had her lawyer demand that Heymann provide her with the tape of his Peter Lawford interview, but he never did so. When I went through Heymann's papers at the State University of New York at Stony Brook, I found a transcript of the tape, but not the tape itself. When I called Heymann and asked to listen to it, he told me that he was planning to use it in his next book and thus he couldn't honor my request. I challenge him to produce that tape because I question that it exists, even though authors are now using his transcript as proof that Ralph Greenson killed Marilyn.[42]

Greenson had no reason to kill her; she was his most famous patient, and her death devastated him. He hardly knew Peter Lawford. He was ambivalent about Bobby Kennedy; he had warned Marilyn many times that the Kennedys were only using her. In conversations with his family and in his letter to Marianne Kris of August 20, he put forth the "official version" of Marilyn's death, while suggesting a new scenario. He suggested she killed herself because she couldn't handle her lesbian urges. There may be some truth to the assertion. The European tabloids were soon to run Natasha Lytess's lurid story of their affair, which would be a considerable humiliation to Marilyn as well as a public exposure of her deepest secret: she was the world's heterosexual icon who preferred women as sexual partners. In fact, her long conversation that evening with Henry Rosenfeld, as reported by him to Anthony Summers, was mostly a diatribe against Patricia Newcomb, a woman who was very close to her. Her argument with Newcomb on Saturday is usually dismissed as a cover for her argument with Bobby Kennedy that afternoon, but it actually may have been more important than anyone has realized.

There are other possibilities to the Kennedy scenario. Even if Bobby was at Marilyn's house that night, it doesn't mean that his companions administered the fatal enema. Chuck Giancana, Sam Giancana's foster son, produced a best seller in which he argued that Giancana ordered the hit because he knew that Bobby Kennedy was there that day and he sent a Mafia hit man to deliver the enema to frame Kennedy as the killer. The plan didn't work because he didn't expect the extensive cover-up that happened that night and the one carried out by the Los Angeles Police Department, which drew attention away from Robert Kennedy.[43]

The role of the FBI in Marilyn's death is another avenue for exploration. Phyllis McGuire told me that the FBI had done what the Kennedys wanted in killing Marilyn. She even suggested that Hoover was in Los Angeles directing the operation: an FBI operative told Anthony Summers that a number of FBI agents were in town who normally wouldn't have been there, and they took Marilyn's telephone records from the Santa Monica phone company early on the morning of August 5. When Joe Hyams went there looking for them soon after Marilyn died, he was told that the FBI already had them.

Hoover himself was troubled by Marilyn Monroe. His agents had been following her ever since she had applied for a visa to go to the Soviet Union in 1955 and had become involved with Arthur Miller. He knew of her involvement with the Hollywood Twenty in Mexico City in February 1962; an informer had filed an accurate report on her conversations with Fred Vanderbilt Field as well as her conversations with Bobby Kennedy in the ensuing months. Field claimed that José Bolaños was the informant, but a report filed with Hoover identified Eunice Murray as the source of the report, making a complex situation even more complicated. Hoover's main concern for many years had been Communists, whom he believed were destroying the nation. Now the nation's most famous film star, close to the president, seemed to be involved with them. It's reasonable to assume, given Hoover's paranoia about Marilyn and the Kennedys and the willingness of Otash and his men to sell copies of the tapes from the bugs that Otash had placed in Marilyn's house initially for Joe DiMaggio or Jimmy Hoffa, that the FBI was also listening to those tapes.

The Kennedys' relationship with Hoover wasn't simple. Bobby Kennedy had to force him to turn his attention to the Mafia, not just internal Communists, which were his passion. They considered firing him, but he had too much information about Jack's womanizing for them to do that. Yet the FBI could help them.[44] If Kennedy went to Marilyn's house at ten o'clock the Saturday night Marilyn died with two men accompanying him, the men were in all probability FBI agents. Given that the FBI is experienced in putting devious scenarios into effect, it's also possible that FBI agents killed Marilyn. But no one has discovered Bobby Kennedy's movements that day, after he left Marilyn's house Saturday afternoon. He seems to have driven off with Peter Lawford, but none of the guests at the Lawford party, which began at seven thirty, saw him at the house that night. Lawford told Patricia Lawford Stewart that Bobby left before the party began.

Marilyn's many plans for the future—movies she was going to make, galas she was going to attend—seem to indicate that she didn't take her life. She even intended to go to the performance of Irving Berlin's new musical in Washington, D.C., the event of the season and a fund-raiser for the Kennedys. She was having Jean Louis make a special dress for it. Some individuals said the dress was for her wedding to DiMaggio, planned for the following Wednesday, but Jean Louis told Anthony Summers that it was definitely an evening dress.[45]

It's possible, however, that her improving mood was key to her death: that's what Robert Litman believed. It's characteristic of individuals who suffer from manic-depressive syndrome that entering the up cycle can give them enough energy to kill themselves. Marilyn was in deep transference with Greenson, according to Litman. When Greenson left her Saturday night to go to a party and told her he would see her the next day, it could have sent her over the edge, since such patients want total attention from their psychiatrists. What gives me pause in accepting this explanation is the amount of Nembutal and chloral hydrate that were in Marilyn's blood—enough to kill several men, more than the fifty tablets of Nembutal she had in her possession at the time she died. Some experts maintain that she had taken sixty Nembutal and large amounts of chloral hydrate, and the two do not interact well in an individual's blood. It speaks to the issue of the enema, the fast application of drugs in a piston syringe that would have quickly killed her.[46]

The *Los Angeles Times* of August 6, 1962, features an article titled "Film Capital Stunned By Blonde Star's Death." It contains statements by people who had seen Marilyn the week before she died, claiming she was happy when they talked to her. "I am deeply shocked," said Gene Kelly. "I was going to see her this afternoon [Sunday]. We had a project on file for next year." He had talked to her on the phone on Thursday.

"She was in excellent spirits—very happy and very excited about her future projects."

Dean Martin made a similar statement and confirmed that *Something's Got to Give* was going back into production in early 1963. Patricia Newcomb said Marilyn was planning to go to New York the next week to do a cover for *Esquire*. Lee Strasberg said she was finally going to audition for the Actors Studio. Joe DiMaggio expected to marry her on Wednesday. With so many projects, it seems unreasonable that she would take her own life. But that life is so filled with paradox, tricksterism, and passion achieved and thwarted that it is impossible to say what she would do. The geography of Marilyn's life remains wide and deep, filled with the magic and mystery that has made her into a transhistorical symbol of the American imagination.

Afterword

Marilyn's death garnered front-page headlines in every newspaper in the United States and most in Europe. *Life* gave her an eleven-page spread; *Paris Match* devoted thirty-six pages to a retrospective on her life. Every major European picture magazine gave her a feature and a cover. It's said that the suicide rate in Los Angeles doubled the month after she died; the circulation rate of most newspapers expanded that month.

Joe DiMaggio and Inez Melson planned Marilyn's funeral. They avoided the normal large Hollywood affair to bury her in a crypt in the Westwood Village Memorial Cemetery and Mortuary, a small cemetery and mortuary in Westwood, not far from Marilyn's house in Brentwood. It was one of the neighborhood cemeteries that had been built throughout the Los Angeles region in its early years. Many of Marilyn's family members are buried there, including Grace and Doc Goddard and Ana Lower. After Marilyn was interred there, many other Hollywood notables followed suit, including Natalie Wood, Darryl Zanuck, Truman Capote, Billy Wilder, Jack Lemmon, and Dean Martin.

The Westwood cemetery is a small place, a bucolic park in the midst of urban sprawl, a block away from the intersection of Wilshire and Westwood boulevards, one of the most heavily traveled intersections in the nation. Discreet gravestones are set in a sweep of green grass. Crypts have been built into walls at one side of the cemetery, with the walls open to the outdoors. An overhang protects the crypts and mourners from rain. After Ana Lower was buried there in 1948, Marilyn went there for spiritual regeneration. She would sit on a bench and read a book. It was a favorite place of hers. It's not surprising that she wanted to be buried there. DiMaggio and Melson invited only thirty-one individuals to the funeral, including family and close friends. Hollywood people and the Kennedys were kept out, and Pinkerton guards were hired to enforce the guest list. Joe was angry at Hollywood's treatment of Marilyn. He was also angry at Frank Sinatra and the Kennedys for their involvement in her death.

Marilyn's funeral, held in the mortuary chapel, was brief. A local minister read verses from the Bible; Lee Strasberg delivered a eulogy; and a record of Judy Garland singing "Over the Rainbow" was played. Flowers formed a huge array in front of the crypt. Joe had a large heart of red roses made, and Jane and Robert Miller, Arthur's children, sent a floral wreath with a card signed "Bobo" and "Butch." The wife of the Mexican president sent a wreath of gardenias and roses, with a card reading, "From the Children of Mexico." It honored the donation of ten thousand dollars that Marilyn had made to the National Institute for the Protection of Children when she visited Mexico City in March 1962.[1]

The funeral didn't end as discreetly as it began. Michael Selsman, who was in charge of monitoring the event for the Arthur Jacobs agency, told me that a crowd of thousands lined the streets in Westwood, hoping to get a glimpse. Several hundred people lined the walls of the cemetery, peering in. Once the invited guests and the Pinkerton guards left, that crowd couldn't be restrained. Many of them leapt over the walls and rushed into the cemetery. They descended "in one big wave" on the floral tributes and tore them apart. They grabbed every flower from the individual displays in a furious rush to take a souvenir. In death, as in life, Marilyn was an object of fan devotion and of the potentially out-of-control crowds those fans could turn into. Patricia Rosten called the possessiveness of Marilyn's normally adoring fans, the way they tried to take something from her—a lock of hair, a piece of her dress—the "dark side" of her fame. Now it was a flower from the floral tributes at her funeral that they were after.[2]

Marilyn has passed over into history, but the question I began this book with remains: Was Marilyn a feminist? Is she one of the women who changed the world's attitude toward women? She took actions that could be called feminist: she made herself into an actress and a star, she formed her own production company, she fought the moguls to a standstill, and she publicly named the sexual abuse visited on her as a child. But she never called herself a feminist. The term wasn't yet in widespread use, and the movement wouldn't appear until a number of years after her death. Hedda Rosten, her secretary and close friend, identified her as "the quintessential victim of the male." Norman Rosten, Hedda's husband, who was equally close to Marilyn, saw her relationship to feminism differently. He contended that Marilyn would have quarreled with her "sisters" on the issue of sexual liberation. She had achieved the financial and legal gains they sought. And she enjoyed her femininity, recognizing its power over men.[3]

Marilyn's stance as reported by Norman Rosten sounds like a post-feminist position, which privileges power over oppression and emphasizes the power women possess through their femininity and sexuality. On the other hand, one could argue that it was her fixation with her femininity—and her attitude toward it, sometimes regal and sometimes tormented—that caused her victimization in the end. No matter how hard she tried, Hollywood and its men refused to consider her as anything more than a party girl and in the end they treated her like a slut they could use with impunity. She commented to W. J. Weatherby, that "black men don't like to be called 'boys,' but women accept being called 'girls,'" as though she were offended by the latter term. And she didn't like male violence. That is apparent in the dispute she had with Weatherby over Ernest Hemingway. Weatherby liked Hemingway for his understanding of human nature. Marilyn didn't like his masculine heroes. "Those big tough guys are so sick. They aren't even all that tough! They're afraid of kindness and gentleness and beauty. They always want to kill something to prove themselves!" She praised the young people who were beginning to rebel against social conventions. In her best moments, she saw herself as part of that movement.

Yet Marilyn had no gender framework to support her stance, no way of conceptualizing her situation beyond her individual self, to encompass all women, whose rights were limited in the 1950s. Had she lived a few years longer, into the mid-1960s, the feminist movement could have offered the concept of sexism as a way to understand her oppression and the idea of sisterhood as a support.

The most important statement about Marilyn made after she died was Arthur Miller's play *After the Fall*. James Baldwin walked out of it and considered forming a group of celebrities to boycott it. Norman Rosten was deeply upset, and Hedda Rosten even more so. The critics didn't like it. The Marilyn of *After the Fall* is a monster—the opposite of Roslyn of *The Misfits*. She is addicted to drugs and to sex, bent on self-destruction and on destroying her marriage. The play takes place against a backdrop of the Jewish concentration camps in Germany after World War Two. They are now empty of people but filled with memories. Miller—Quentin, a lawyer, in the play—connects Marilyn—a singing star called Maggie in the play—to the camps. The central moment of the play occurs when Miller identifies her with a line of men she has serviced sexually and demands that she take responsibility for her outrageous sexual behavior. Marilyn refuses: the men did it to her; she doesn't feel that she needs to acknowledge any blame nor seek absolution through a confession of guilt.

The play is misogynist. Quentin's mother is flawed, and Louise, married to Quentin's friend Mickey, isn't much better. The only woman in the play that Quentin appreciates is Helga, a Jewish woman who escaped the concentration camps and came to the United States. She is strong and masculine in type. Inge Morath, Miller's third wife, was the model for her.

Marilyn reminds me of Barbara Loden, who played Maggie in the premiere production of *After the Fall* at Lincoln Center in 1964. She followed a life path appropriate for Marilyn, had she lived. Loden was Elia Kazan's second wife. She was cast as Maggie in the play: Miller and Kazan costumed her to look like Marilyn. The passages about Loden in Kazan's autobiography could be about Marilyn. A beautiful blonde, Loden tried to become both a Hollywood sex icon and a dramatic actress. Like many beautiful women Kazan had known in Hollywood, she felt she was worthless, given value only by a man's desire for her. She was ambitious; she could be tough and ruthless. She had no formal education, but she took many lessons: voice, speech, acting, dance.

Then Loden, inspired by the feminism of the 1970s, left mainstream Hollywood to join the independent film community. She wrote the screenplay for the film *Wanda* and made it in an improvisational manner. It was a success in Europe, and she was acclaimed a heroine of the feminist movement. She plunged into work, writing many screenplays. Giving up feminine clothing, she dressed in the clothes male directors wore in the field: trousers, leather jackets, and boots. She became devoted to an Indian master and meditated regularly. Then she was diagnosed with breast cancer. She died two years later, at the age of forty-eight, in 1980.[4] Kazan was proud of her transformation.

In the case of Marilyn, people believe what they want to believe. She lives in the fantasies of the national imagination, enshrined in a story with endless possibilities, plots, characters, and events. Marilyn's life and death have become flexible, plastic representations of a real person and a real event. As an icon of glamour and beauty, she remains celebrated around the world. Her image is endlessly reproduced on posters, photographs, and billboards, on playing cards, umbrellas, and handbags. The Sam Shaw photo of her with her skirt flying up became one of the most iconic images of the twentieth century and remains so in the twenty-first. No one can deny the power of her representation: she is the ur-blonde who has haunted the American imagination.

Marilyn was a genius at self-creation and at posing in front of the camera. That may be the ultimate act of self-presentation for women in the twenty-first century, driven by technology, visuality, and the homogenization of world cultures. The innocence and sorrow in Marilyn's eyes, transmitted in her photographs and in movies like *Bus Stop* and *The Misfits*, makes us, like the audiences in her own day, want to comfort and protect her. She is the child in all of us, the child we want to forget but can't dismiss. We want to know what would have happened to her if she had lived longer. To construct any approximation of that future, we need to know as fully as possible about her past—who she was when she was alive.

Acknowledgments

I began this biography nearly ten years ago, when I was a fellow of the Humanities Institute at the University of Canberra in Australia and found the newsletter of the Australian Marilyn Monroe fan club, Glamour Preferred, in the Australian National Library. That newsletter led me to Marilyn Remembered, the Los Angeles fan club. Its members welcomed me and provided me with invaluable information and support. I especially thank fan club members Greg Schreiner, Scott Fortner, Jill Adams, and Harrison Held. David Marshall exchanged much information and many e-mails with me. Roy Turner, a prince among human beings, talked about Marilyn with me and put his inestimable collection about Marilyn's childhood in my hands. Without Stacy Eubank and her extraordinary collection of Marilyn materials, this book could not have been written.

Mark Anderson provided me with access to the materials in the Marilyn Monroe file cabinets, then in the possession of Millington Conroy, in Conroy's home in Rowland Heights, California. My association with Mark resulted in *MM–Personal*, the book we did based on that material—which is now in the hands of Anna Strasberg and the Marilyn Monroe Estate.

My gratitude goes to the staffs of the libraries at which I did research on Marilyn, including those at the American Film Institute; Arizona State University; the Library of Congress; the New York Public Library for the Performing Arts at Lincoln Center in New York; the Newberry

Library in Chicago; the State University of New York, Stony Brook; the University of California, Los Angeles; the University of Southern California; the Harry Ransom Center at the University of Texas at Austin; and the Margaret Herrick Library of the Academy of Motion Picture Arts and Sciences. Among the many librarians who assisted me, special thanks goes to Barbara Hall of the Margaret Herrick Library and Ned Comstock of the University of Southern California. Most books written on the history of films acknowledge these two individuals, who are knowledgeable about the nooks and crannies of film history and always supportive of researchers.

My thanks goes to fellow Marilyn biographers who have given me support on this project: John Gilmore, Michelle Morgan, and Carl Rollyson. Above all, Anthony Summers gave me access to his many interviews of Marilyn friends and associates. This act of generosity on his part has inestimably strengthened my understandings in this book. I thank Hap Roberts of Salisbury, North Carolina, for giving me access to "Mimosa," Ralph Roberts's unpublished memoir, as well as other Roberts papers.

I am also grateful to Valerie Yaros, historian at the Screen Actors Guild, for providing me with addresses and other information, and to the doctors I consulted, all M.D.s, King Reilly, Robert Siegal, Carrie Rickard, Rebecca Kuhn, and Rosemary Rau-Levine. I also thank Robert Wood, Peter Loewenberg, Joshua Hoffs, and Elyn Saks, all practicing psychoanalysts, for leading me through the intricacies of psychiatric theory. I thank Amanda Gustin and Leslie Pitts of the Mary Baker Eddy Library at the First Christian Science Church in Boston for providing me information about Ana Lower and Norma Jeane Baker, Bob and Jenna Herre for their information about the Goddard family, and Twentieth Century–Fox for giving me access to the legal and production files on Marilyn Monroe. I thank David Wells and Susan Bernard for their many kindnesses to me.

During the years I have worked on this book, I have made many friends among the individuals I interviewed. Many led me to other friends and associates of Marilyn. I especially thank Meta Shaw Stevens and Edie Marcus Shaw, Patricia Rosten Filan, Patricia Lawford Stewart, Michael Selsman, and Noreen Nash. Arthur Verge, whom I knew as a scholar, turned out to be a lifeguard who knew Tommy Zahn and Dave Heiser—who were close to the Kennedys and knew Marilyn. Lary May of the University of Minnesota, a fine film scholar, helped me to understand the Hollywood film industry—as did my USC colleagues Steven Ross, Vanessa Schwartz, and Rick Jewell. Lynn Sacco of the University of Tennessee explained the history and multiple meanings of incest to me. Sioux Oliva and Jill Fields gave me support at many moments when my energy was flagging, as did Adele Wallace and Jean Melley, who read my manuscript with great sensitivity and flair. As always, Alice Echols and Elinor Accampo were scholarly cicerones to me, while the University of Southern California provided me with research funds and sabbaticals so that I could write this book.

My daughter, Olivia Banner, edited my manuscript at a crucial moment, improving it greatly. My son, Gideon Banner, taught me many truths about acting, as I watched him turn himself from an actor of modest talent to a star performer who has acted on Broadway and has long starred in the Blue Man Group at the Astor Theater in New York. I found out through him that one can learn the art of acting through dedication and the right teachers. That insight was crucial to my understanding of Marilyn.

I am grateful to my husband, John Laslett, for his loyalty, and to my agent, William Clark, for his nurturing support and hard bargaining. I thank Kathy Belden for her fine editing and encouragement and Bloomsbury USA for all they have done for me and my book. I thank the individuals who have served me as researchers and assistants: Karin Huebner, Lila Myers, Victoria Vantoch, and Lisa Raymond.

Manuscript Collections Consulted and List of Abbreviations

AFI

American Film Institute
  Charles Feldman Papers

AMPAS

Academy of Motion Picture Arts and Sciences,
Margaret Herrick Library
  David Benedit-Zeitlin, Lester Cowan, Katharine Hepburn, Hedda
    Hopper, John Huston, Guido Orlando, Louella Parsons, and
    Sidney Skolsky papers.
  Ronald Davis Oral Interviews, conducted for his book *The Glam-
    our Factory: Inside Hollywood's Big Studio System* (Dallas:
    Southern Methodist University Press, 1993).
  Donald Spoto, oral interviews for his Marilyn Monroe biography,
    Marilyn Monroe: The Biography (New York: HarperCollins,
    1993). (DS)
  Clipping files, Marilyn Monroe, Marie Wilson, Sheree North,
    George Arliss, Shelley Winters.

AS

Anthony Summers interviews (possession of Anthony Summers) for his book *Goddess: The Secret Lives of Marilyn Monroe* (New York: Macmillan, 1985).

ASU

Arizona State University
Peter Lawford, Ted Schwartz, Jimmy Starr collections; James Spada collection, interviews for his book, *Peter Lawford, The Man Who Kept the Secrets* (New York: Bantam, 1991).

BL

British Library
Laurence Olivier Papers

CUO

Columbia University Oral History Project: History of Hollywood Films
Howard Hawks, Henry Hathaway, Fritz Lang, Otto Preminger interviews

DFI

Danish Film Institute
Donald Spoto Collection

LC

Library of Congress, Washington, D.C.
Henry Brandon, Anna Freud, Marianne Kris, and Joseph Rauh papers

LMU

Loyola Marymount University
   Files from the Arthur Jacobs agency office

"MIMOSA"

Ralph Roberts's unpublished memoir of Marilyn Monroe,
unpaginated manuscript.

MM–PERSONAL

Book on Marilyn by Lois Banner and Mark Anderson, based on
the materials in Marilyn Monroe's file cabinets, in possession of
Anna Strasberg, Lee Strasberg's third wife.

NL

Newberry Library, Chicago
   Ben Hecht Papers; Marilyn Monroe files

NYPL

New York Public Library for the Performing Arts
   Clippings files: Marilyn Monroe, Paula Strasberg, Lee Strasberg
   Collections: Lotte Goslar and Gypsy Rose Lee

RR

   Ralph Roberts Papers, in possession of Hap Roberts, Salisbury,
      North Carolina

RT

   Roy Turner Papers—in possession of Lois Banner

SE

Stacy Eubank Collection; mss. for her book, "Holding a Good Thought for Marilyn," a collection of letters, press clippings, and other written memorabilia in possession of Eubank.

SU

Stanford University—Special Collections
Spyros Skouras Papers: files on Twentieth Century–Fox, Darryl Zanuck

SUNY-STONY BROOK

State University of New York, Stony Brook, Special Collections
C. David Heymann, oral interviews for his biography of Robert Kennedy, C. David Heymann Collection

UCLA

University of California at Los Angeles—Speciall Collections
Ralph Greenson Papers, Twentieth Century–Fox Legal Files, Twentieth Century–Fox Production Files

USC

University of Southern California
Constance McCormick Collection, clippings files
Warner Brothers Archives

UT

University of Texas at Austin, Harry Ransom Center
Norman Mailer, files for his books *Marilyn: A Biography* (New York: Grosset & Dunlap, 1973); *Of Women and Their Elegance* (New York: Simon & Schuster 1980).

Arthur Miller Collection
Maurice Zolotow, files for his book *Marilyn Monroe* (New York: Harcourt Brace, 1960).

VILLANI

Antonio Villani, unpublished interviews for his video, "Hold a Good Thought for Me," GS

PRIVATE COLLECTIONS

Lois Banner
Marilyn Monroe Estate—file cabinets
Scott Fortner
Patricia Rosten Filan
Greg Schreiner
Letters and documents sold at auction, information from catalogs or at auction houses. (Items are on view before they are sold.)

ABBREVIATIONS

AS Anthony Summers
AV Antonio Villani
DS Donald Spoto
GS Greg Schreiner
JK John Kobal
LB Lois Banner
MZ Maurice Zolotow
RT Roy Turner
SE Stacy Eubank

List of Interviewees

Allan Abbott, Jill Adams, Richard Baer, George Barris, Susan
Bernard, Sylvia Barnhart, Larry Billman, Malcolm Boyd,
William Carroll, George Chakiris, Millington Conroy, Patricia
Cox, Bennett Daubrey, Janet Desrosiers, Molly Dunne,
Felice Early Ingersoll, John Everson, Sondra Farrell, Audrey
Franklin, Kayley Gable, John Gilmore, Eric Goddard, Kirk
Goddard, Johnny Grant, Larry Grant, Cathy Griffin,
Joshua Greene, Betsy Hammes, Jenna and Robert Herre,
James Haspiel, Boze Hedleigh, Dave Heiser, Diana Herbert,
Joshua Hoffs, Cheryl Howell Williams (interviewed by Stacey
Eubank), Kathleen Hughes, Don Ingersoll (interviewed by
Victoria Vantoch), Arthur James, Nancy Bolender Jeffrey,
Jay Kanter, Douglas Kirkland, Bill Knoedelseder, Diane
Ladd, Jack Larson, Robert Litman, A. C. Lyles, Roberta
Linn, Alice Marshak, Marion Marshall, Phyllis McGuire,
Jeanne Martin, John Miner, Don Murray, Joe Naar, Noreen
Nash, Dolores Nemiro, Patricia Newcomb, Larry Newman,
Gloria Pall, Hap Roberts, Carl Rollyson, Gloria Romanoff,
Patricia Rosten Filan, Stanley Rubin, Barbara Rush, Gus
Russo, Lawrence Schiller, Cami Sebring, Michael Selsman,
Meta Shaw Stevens, Edith Shaw Marcus, Thomas Sobeck,
Mickey Song, Tanya Samura, Hal Schaefer, Steffi Skolsky

Slaver, James Spada, Anna Strasberg, David Strasberg, John Strasberg, Daniel Stewart, Patricia Lawford Stewart, Anthony Summers, Patricia Traviss, Arthur Verge, Terry Wasdyke, Gladys Wilson

Notes

PROLOGUE

1. I have borrowed the title of my prologue, "Let Us Now Praise Famous Women," from the title of James Agee's famed book *Let Us Now Praise Famous Men*, about the working class during the Great Depression. The term "famous woman" connects Marilyn to the working class, applauds her success, and hints at the underside of her fame in "infamous" behavior, her accommodating sexual self.

2. My description of the shoot is based on Lorie Karnath, *Sam Shaw: A Personal Point of View* (Osfildern, Germany: Hatje Cantz Verlag, 2010), 8; Sam Shaw and Norman Rosten, *Marilyn Monroe Among Friends* (New York: Henry Holt, 1987), 38–47; Bruno Bernard, *Bernard of Hollywood's Marilyn*, ed. Susan Bernard (New York: St. Martin's, 1993); Eve Arnold, *Marilyn Monroe: An Appreciation* (New York: Alfred A. Knopf, 1987); Earl Wilson, *Hot Times: True Tales of Hollywood and Broadway* (Chicago: Contemporary Books, 1984), 79–91; *Los Angeles Herald Examiner*, clipping fragment, Starr—ASU; "Marilyn and Joe," August 8, 1962, in *The Seven Year Itch* file, Billy Wilder—AMPAS: "The newspaper photographers and the fan magazines from everywhere were getting enough stills for years."

3. For pinups with the skirts of the models flying up, see Charles G. Martignette and Louis K. Meisel, *The Great American Pin-Up* (New York: Taschen, 1996).

4. Natalie Davis, "Women on Top," in *Society and Culture in Early Modern France* (Stanford: Stanford University Press, 1975) 124–51; Robert C. Allen, *Horrible Prettiness: Burlesque and American Culture* (Chapel Hill, N.C.: University of North Carolina Press, 1991); Henry Brandon, "Sex, Theatre and the Intellectual," in Brandon, ed., *Conversations with Henry Brandon* (London: Andre Deutsch, 1966), 196.

5. George Barris, *Marilyn: Her Life in Her Own Words* (New York: Citadel Press, 1995), 112–13.

6. Shaun Considine, *Mad as Hell: The Life and Work of Paddy Chayefsky* (New York: Random House, 1994), 120.

7. Earl Wilson, *Show Business Laid Bare* (New York: Putnam, 1974), 71; Susan Strasberg, *Marilyn and Me: Sisters, Rivals, Friends* (New York: Warner, 1992), 163.

8. W. J. Weatherby, *Conversations with Marilyn* (New York: Paragon, 1976), 112, 125.

9. Bernard ed., *Bernard of Hollywood's Marilyn*, 43.

10. See, for example, "Marilyn, Too Soon for Love," *Movieland*, April 1953; Jane Corwin, "Orphan in Ermine," *Photoplay*, March 1954; Rita Garrison Malloy, "Marilyn, Oh, Marilyn," *Motion Picture*, November 1954; "MM—Low-Brow to High-Brow," *National Police Gazette*, October 1957; "Too Hot Not to Cool Down?" *Movieland*, December 1954. The only other Hollywood personality to become as famed for witticisms was the independent producer Sam Goldwyn, who was known for malapropisms called "Goldwynisms."

11. Interview with Sam Shaw, *Runnin' Wild*, newsletter of All About Marilyn Fan Club, January 1993; David Zeitlin-Bevedit, interview with Jerry Wald, Zeitlin-Bevedit, AMPAS.

12. On Lembourn's visit to the United States, see Norman Norstrand, *New York Times*, June 3, 1979; on Lili St. Cyr, see Bruno Bernard, *Requiem for Marilyn* (Abbotsbrook, GB, 1986), 102–04, and Kelly DiNardo, *Gilded Lili: Lili St. Cyr and the Striptease Mystique* (New York: Back Stage, 2007). On Slatzer as a fabulist, see John Gilmore, *Inside Marilyn Monroe: A Memoir* (Los Angeles: Ferrine, 2007), 202–08. Slatzer initiated the fabulist tradition in 1974 with *The Life and Curious Death of Marilyn Monroe* (New York: Pinnacle, 1974).

13. In his Marilyn biography, Donald Spoto contended that Summers manufactured his interviews, Spoto, *Marilyn Monroe: The Biography* (New York: HarperCollins, 1993). I can testify to the validity of those interviews because I have listened to them. Summers won a judgment against Spoto in a London court for misrepresentation. On the other hand, Spoto was the first author to challenge the validity of Slatzer and Carmen. See Donald H. Wolfe, *The Assassination of Marilyn Monroe* (1998; New York: Time Warner, 2002), 122–23.

CHAPTER I

1. On Marilyn's childhood, I have used Gilmore, *Inside Marilyn Monroe*; Michelle Morgan, *Marilyn Monroe: Private and Undisclosed* (New York: Carroll & Graf, 2007); Spoto, *Marilyn Monroe*; Fred Lawrence Guiles, *Norma Jean: The Life of Marilyn Monroe* (New York: McGraw-Hill, 1969); and Guiles, *Legend: The Life and Death of Marilyn Monroe* (New York: Stein

and Day, 1984). I have consulted J. Randy Taraborrelli, *The Secret Life of Marilyn Monroe* (New York: Hachette, 2009); and Ted Schwartz, *Marilyn Revealed: The Ambitious Life of an American Icon* (New York: Rowman & Littlefield, 2009), although neither author uses footnotes, making it impossible to check their sources and evaluate their conclusions.

I have also used Marilyn's autobiography, published in 1974 as *My Story*; the many interviews she gave during her life; and the memoir of her half-sister, Berniece Baker Miracle (with Mona Rae Miracle), *My Sister Marilyn: A Memoir* (New York: Boulevard, 1994). I have drawn extensively from the primary materials collected by Roy Turner, which are in my possession.

2. For family backgrounds, I have used Marilyn biographies; on Ana, I have used her death certificate, March 14, 1948, in RT. On Los Angeles, see Carey McWilliams, *Southern California: An Island on the Land* (Layton, Utah: Gibbs Smith, 1946), and the works of Kevin Starr, especially *Golden Dreams: California in an Age of Abundance* (New York: Oxford University Press, 2009); *Embattled Dreams: California in War and Peace, 1940–1950* (New York: Oxford University Press, 2002); and *The Dream Endures: California Enters the 1940s* (New York: Oxford University Press, 1997).

3. Gladys misspelled Mortensen as Mortenson on Norma Jeane's birth certificate. On Gifford's background see Robert E. Brenneman, "New England in Hollywood, Part 3: The Possible Rhode Island Ancestry of Marilyn Monroe," in New England Historical and Genealogical Society, *Nexus*, 3, no. 2 (1990): 64–67, in RT. On Marilyn's father, see note 33, below.

4. Otis Monroe Death Record. 245–355, California State Board of Health, Bureau of Vital Statistics, in RT.

5. Lawrence O. Christensen and Gary R. Kremer, *A History of Missouri*, 4: *1875–1919* (Columbia, Mo.: University of Missouri Press, 1997). My thanks to Stephen Aron, Professor of History, UCLA, for advising me on Missouri culture in this period.

6. Lawrence Levine, *Highbrow/Lowbrow: The Emergence of Cultural Hierarchy in America* (Cambridge, Mass.: Harvard University Press, 1988).

7. Otis Monroe's death certificate lists Indiana as his birthplace. But the spaces for the names of his mother and father contain the word "unknown," suggesting that Della didn't have this information.

8. Documents in RT indicate home ownership. On the LA rail system, including time tables, important to understanding the geography of Marilyn's childhood, see Spencer Crump, *Ride the Big Red Cars: The Pacific Electric Story* (Glendale, Calif.: Trans-Anglo Books, 1983).

9. Susan Steinman Salter, "Toward Community Mental Health: A History of State Policy in California, 1939–1969," Ph.D. diss., University of California, Berkeley, 1978, 5. Venereal disease was epidemic in these decades, with no effective cure until penicillin was introduced in 1944. See Allan M. Brandt, *No Magic Bullet: A Social History of Venereal Disease in the United States Since 1880* (New York: Oxford University Press, 1985).

10. Miracle, *My Sister Marilyn*, 87.

11. Della Monroe Graves vs. Lyle A. Graves, Divorce Action, January 17, 1914, Superior Court, State of California, County of Los Angeles, in RT. See J. Herbie DiFonzo, *Beneath the Fault Line: The Popular and Legal Culture of Divorce in Twentieth-Century America* (Charlottesville, Va.: University of Virginia Press, 1997); and Glenda Riley, *Divorce: An American Tradition* (Lincoln, Neb.: University of Nebraska Press, 1997); LB, interview with Patricia Traviss, July 24, 2008. On Della and Gladys, I follow Miracle, *My Sister Marilyn*, 12–17, 86–89.

12. Tom Moran and Tom Sewell, *Fantasy by the Sea: A Visual History of American Venice* (Culver City, Calif.: Peace Press, 1980); Jeffrey Stanton, *Venice of America, 1905–1930: A History* (Venice, Calif.: ARS, 1980). In the late 1920s, developers filled in most of the canals to build houses and commercial buildings.

13. Elizabeth R. Rose, *A Mother's Job: The History of Day Care, 1890–1960* (New York: Oxford University Press, 1999), 167–68.

14. Barris, *Marilyn: Her Life in Her Own Words*, 5. Applications for passports filed with the U.S. State Department, Passport Division, by Charles Grainger in 1924 and Della Monroe in 1925, in RT. Della filed for divorce in 1926, but the action was nullified by her death two years later.

15. Lester Bolender, "Brother Lifts Lid on Past," newspaper clipping, courtesy of Stacy Eubank; MZ, interview with Emmeline Snively, in Zolotow—UT; Weatherby, *Conversations with Marilyn*, 186.

16. David Nelson to Inez Melson, August 14, 1962, in possession of AS. When I examined the file cabinets and their contents in 2006, the letter wasn't there. By then, some material in the file cabinets had been sold or given away. See Lois Banner and Mark Anderson, *MM—Personal* (New York: Harry Abrams, 2011).

17. Gilmore, *Inside Marilyn Monroe*, 35; Miracle, *My Sister Marilyn*, 22. Rickie Solinger, *Wake Up Little Susie: Single Pregnancy Before* Roe v. Wade (New York: Routledge, 2000), 61; Elaine Tyler May, *Great Expectations: Marriage and Divorce in the Post-Victorian Era* (New York: Basic, 1988), 92.

18. Marriage License, Gladys Monroe and Jasper Newton Baker, in RT. On Gladys and Jasper's marriage, see Miracle, *My Sister Marilyn*, 12–15.

19. In 1920 Della and Charles bought a second lot in Hawthorne, although they defaulted on the mortage in 1926 and forfeited it. See documents on second lot, in RT. See also Walt Dixon and Jerry Roberts, *Hawthorne* (Charleston, S.C.: Arcadia, 2005).

20. Divorce Petition, Baker vs. Baker: Superior Court of Los Angeles County, no. 8–8426, in RT.

21. When Gladys was in Kentucky, a friend in Los Angeles wrote her that Gifford was lonely for her. See "Coming Attractions," in *Runnin' Wild*, April 1994; Monroe, *My Story*, 19.

22. Matthew Sutton, *Aimee Semple McPherson and the Resurrection of Christian America* (Cambridge, Mass.: Harvard University Press, 2007).

23. Monroe, *My Story*, 32; Karen Ward Mahar, *Women Filmmakers in Early Hollywood* (Baltimore: Johns Hopkins University Press, 2006).
24. See Neal Gabler, *An Empire of Their Own: How the Jews Made Hollywood* (New York: Doubleday, 1989).
25. Rupert Hughes, *Souls for Sale* (1922; New York: Garland, 1978), 168–69. Hughes was the uncle of Howard Hughes, aviation mogul and owner of RKO.
26. Ibid., 168–69,184.
27. John Gilmore, interview with Ernest Neilson, in Gilmore, *Inside Marilyn Monroe*, 55.
28. Ibid., 38.
29. Anthony Summers, "How Marilyn Monroe Rejected Her Secret Dad in His Dying Days," *Star*, December 1, 1987. On Mortensen as Marilyn's father, see Ann Salisbury, "Marilyn Monroe's Father Dies with His Secret," *Los Angeles Herald Examiner*, February 12, 1981, in RT.
30. Divorce Petition, Gifford vs. Gifford, no. D-2488, Superior Court, State of California, in RT.
31. Divorce Petition, Mortensen vs. Baker, no. 053720, Superior Court, State of California, in RT.
32. In her 1960 interview with Georges Belmont, editor of *Marie Claire*, Marilyn denied that Mortensen was her father. See Belmont, "Interview with Marilyn Monroe," in *Marilyn Monroe and the Camera* (Boston: Little, Brown, 1989), 13. In a 1962 interview with photographer George Barris, Marilyn stated that Stanley Gifford was her father. See Barris, *Marilyn: Her Life,* 5. Arthur Miller, *Timebends* (1987; New York: Penguin, 1995), 371, 419, thought that Gladys actually wasn't sure. Miller detested Gladys, although he never met her.
33. In the Belmont interview (see note 32), 14, Marilyn stated that her mother was upset and confused after her birth and thus she filled out the birth certificate incorrectly.
34. Summers, "How Marilyn Monroe Rejected Her Secret Dad."
35. MZ, interview with Earl Theisen, in Zolotow—UT.
36. Rose, A *Mother's Job*, 167–68.
37. Ezra Goodman, *The Fifty Year Decline and Fall of Hollywood* (New York: Simon & Schuster, 1951), 225. Goodman interviewed the Bolenders at length, as did Fred Guiles. No recent Marilyn biographer refers to this material. My analysis of the Bolenders also draws from my interview with Nancy Bolender Jeffrey, December 1, 2005, and letters she sent me.
38. Marilyn Monroe, "I Was an Orphan," *Modern Screen*, February 1951; Richard Merryman, "Fame May Go By," *Life*, August 3, 1962; Margaret Parton, "A Revealing Last Interview with Marilyn Monroe," *Look*, February 19, 1979.
39. Barris, *Marilyn: Her Life*, 3; Merryman, "Fame May Go By."
40. LB, interview with Nancy Bolender Jeffrey, December 4, 2005; talk by

Nancy Bolender, recorded in "Some Like It Hot," German Marilyn Monroe fan club newsletter, December 2001; Nancy Bolender to LB, March 28, 2007.

41. On Dwight Moody, see *God's Man for the Gilded Age: D. L. Moody and the Rise of Modern Mass Evangelism* (New York: Oxford University Press, 2003).

42. G. Ted Martinez, *The Rise, Decline, and Renewal of a Mega Church: A Case Study of the Church of the Open Door* (Los Angeles: Biola University, 1997); William Edmondson, "Fundamentalist Sects of Los Angeles 1900–1930," Ph.D. diss., Claremont Graduate School, 1980.

43. Philip Goff, "Fighting Like the Devil in the City of Angels: The Rise of Fundamentalist Charles E. Fuller," in *Metropolis in the Making: Los Angeles in the 1920s*, ed. Tom Sitten and William Deverell (Berkeley: University of California Press, 2001) 220–51; George Mardsen, *Fundamentalism and American Culture: The Shaping of Twentieth Century Evangelicalism, 1870–1925* (New York: Oxford University Press, 1980); Gregory Singleton, *Religion in the City of Angels* (Ann Arbor, Mich.: UMI Research Press, 1978). R. A. Torrey, *Revival Addresses* (Chicago: Fleming H. Revell Company, 1903).

44. LB, interview with Nancy Bolender Jeffrey, December 4, 2005.

45. Miller, *Timebends*, 371.

46. Ibid.

47. On the history of masturbation, see Thomas Laqueur, *Solitary Sex: A History of Masturbation* (New York: Zone, 2003).

48. Marilyn Monroe, *Fragments: Poems, Intimate Notes, Letters*, ed. Stanley Buchthal and Bernard Comment (New York: Farrar, Straus and Giroux, 2010), 57, 101. The editors mistakenly identify Ida Martin as the "Ida" of these fragments.

49. Nancy Bolender Jeffrey to LB, March 28, 2007.

50. In the petition filed with the court on November 20, 1929, to declare Otis Monroe dead after he disappeared, as well as in the 1930 census, Gladys listed the Bolenders' address as her address. The claim that Gladys never visited Norma Jeane began when Donald Spoto misread an interview with Olin Stanley, a co-worker with Gladys and Grace, in RT, as stating that Grace took Norma Jeane to the editing studio and dressed her like Shirley Temple, although Stanley states that Gladys, not Grace, did this.

51. Maurice Zolotow, *Marilyn Monroe*, rev. ed. (1960; New York: Harper & Row, 1990), 17–18.

52. I have consulted general practitioner King Reilly M.D. and heart specialist Robert Siegel M.D. on myocarditis and heart disease as linked to manic-depressive syndrome.

53. Miracle, *My Sister Marilyn*, 53.

54. Barris, *Marilyn: Her Life*, 12.

55. *Los Angeles Times*, October 25, 1929.

56. Lisa Wilson, "The Truth About Me," *American Weekly*, November 16,

1952. In the Belmont interview, Marilyn stated that she lived with the English family after Gladys took her to Hollywood. Los Angeles city directories listing the Atkinsons do not include Nellie as living with them.

57. Gilmore, *Inside Marilyn Monroe*, 49.

58. On Grauman's theaters, see Charles Beardsley, *Hollywood's Master Showman: The Legendary Sid Grauman* (New York: Cornwall, 1983).

59. Jim Dougherty, *To Norma Jeane with Love, Jimmie*, as told to L. C. Savage (Chesterfield, Mo.: Beach House, 2000), 30.

60. Spoto, *Marilyn Monroe*, 46.

61. On Whitley Heights, see Gaelyn Whitley Keith, *The Father of Hollywood: The True Story* (Los Angeles: BookSurge, 2006). For a view of the location of Gladys's house before the city tore it down for a parking lot, see *Los Angeles Times*, July 16, 1956.

62. Arthur P. Noyes, *Modern Clinical Psychiatry* (Philadelphia: W.B. Saunders, 1934). Noyes's book was in its eighth edition in 1973. My discussion of the categories of mental illness draws especially from Emily Martin, *Bipolar Expeditions: Mania and Depression in American Culture* (Princeton, N.J.: Princeton University Press, 2007), and Elizabeth F. Howell, *The Dissociative Mind* (Hillsdale, N.J.: Analytic Press, 2005).

63. LB, interview with Patricia Traviss, February 27, 2010.

64. Gail A. Hornstein, *Agnes's Jacket: A Psychologist's Search for the Meaning of Madness* (New York: Rodale/Macmillan, 2009).

65. Joel Braslow, *Mental Ills and Bodily Cures: Psychiatric Treatment in the First Half of the Twentieth Century* (Berkeley: University of California Press, 1997). Braslow focuses on the California state mental hospitals. See also Salter, "Toward Community Mental Health."

66. Grace Goddard to Mrs. Van Hyming, August 15, 1935, Stacy Eubank Collection.

CHAPTER 2

1. Roger Newland, "The Lies They Tell About Marilyn," *Silver Screen*, June 1955.

2. A number of Hollywood stars were sexually abused as children, including Joan Crawford, Esther Williams, and Rita Hayworth, although they didn't reveal it publicly as Marilyn did. See Lawrence J. Quirk and William Schoell, *Joan Crawford: The Essential Biography* (Lexington, Ky.: University of Kentucky Press, 2002); Esther Williams, *The Million Dollar Mermaid* (New York: Simon & Schuster, 1999); and Barbara Leaming, *If This Was Happiness: A Biography of Rita Hayworth* (New York: Viking, 1989). See also "Marilyn Monroe's Secret Weapon," *Movieland*, February 1957.

3. Monroe, *My Story*, 14.

4. In 1935 the *Los Angeles Times* listed Grace as playing a role in *Up Pops*

the Devil at the Wilshire Ebell Theater, sponsored by the Columbia Drama League, composed of employees at Columbia Studios.

5.   Goodman, *Fifty Year Decline*, 226; Bolender, "Brother Lifts Lid on Past."

6.   "Report, Petition, and Account of Guardianship," Superior Court, Los Angeles, in RT; Roman Hryniszak, "We Wanna Know About . . . Guardianship Papers," *Runnin' Wild*, April 1994.

7.   George Atkinson listing on imdb.com. The 1935 Los Angeles census lists George and Maude, identifies them as movie actors, and gives their address as on Glencoe Way. Norma Jeane is not listed with them.

8.   Zolotow, *Marilyn Monroe*, 23; Strasberg, *Marilyn and Me*, 58. On the failed attempts to adopt Norma Jeane, see Guiles, *Legend*, 45–46. Guiles interviewed Goddard family members more fully than did any other Marilyn biographer.

9.   In chapter 6, I trace the book's provenance to prove its validity. Parts of the interview were published in a series of articles in *Empire News*, a tabloid in London and Manchester, England, in the spring and summer of 1954. Marilyn and Hecht's lawyers stopped publication before it appeared elsewhere. A manuscript draft of the autobiography is in Hecht—NL. A version of it was published as *My Story* in 1974.

10. LB, interview with George Barris, February 5, 2011. He also appeared on an early episode of the television show *Larry King Live* in which he discussed the interviews. In 1995 he published his interviews as a separate book, along with more photos he had taken of Marilyn.

11. In describing the sexual abuse episode, I follow Monroe, *My Story*, 17–19.

12. Belmont, *Marilyn Monroe*, 18.

13. Lynn Sacco, *Unspeakable: Father-Daughter Incest in American History* (Baltimore: Johns Hopkins University Press, 2009); Nancy Kellogg and the Committee on Child Abuse and Neglect, "The Evaluation of Sexual Abuse in Children," *Pediatrics* 116 (August 2005): 506–09; Jennifer J. Freyd, et. al, "The Science of Child Sexual Abuse," *Science* 308 (April 22, 2005): 501. Still definitive is David Finkelhor, "How Widespread Is Child Sexual Abuse?" *Children Today* 13 (July–August 1984).

14. RT, interview with Ida Mae Monroe, in RT.

15. In 1933 Murray Kinnell lived at 1264 Beverly Glen in Westwood. From 1934 to 1936 he lived at 279 Glenroy Avenue in Westwood. Screen Actors Guild, address files. John Gilmore, *Inside Marilyn*, claims that the abuser was a boarder in the Arbol Drive house, but he doesn't cite a source. Tracing analogues to "Kimmel" produces Atkinson as easily as Kinnell.

16. Marilyn identified the house as having four bedrooms in Barris, *Marilyn: Her Life*, 25.

17. George Arliss, *My Ten Years in the Studios* (Boston: Little Brown, 1940), 302. See also Robert M. Fells, *George Arliss, The Man Who Played God* (New York: Scarecrow Press, 2004). I expand here on Roy Turner's unpublished mss. "Saturday's Child."

18. Bette Davis, *The Lonely Life: An Autobiography* (New York: Putnam, 1962), 148.

19. *Hollywood Citizen News*, February 2, 1946, George Arliss file, in AMPAS. See also *Los Angeles Times*, February 6, 1946.

20. Jean Negulesco, *Things I Did and Things I Think I Did* (New York: Simon & Schuster, 1984), 216; Adele Whiteley Fletcher, "So That the Memory of Marilyn Will Linger On . . ." in Edward Wagenknecht, ed. *Marilyn Monroe: A Composite View* (Philadelphia: Chilton, 1969), 85; AS, interview with Peggy Fleury, in AS; Miracle, *My Sister Marilyn*, 31. Sidney Skolsky and Earl Wilson agreed that the abuse happened. *New York Post*, September 1962. Skolsky—AMPAS.

21. Guiles, *Legend*, 66.

22. *Los Angeles Times*, August 19, 1935.

23. *New York Times*, July 3, 1945.

24. Divorce Decree, State of Texas, County of Tarrant, case no. 85268, Eleanor Goddard vs. Ervin Goddard, March 5, 1931. Courtesy of Robert Herre.

25. Nona Goddard told Ezra Goodman that she didn't meet Marilyn until she was eleven. Goodman, *Fifty Year Decline*, 227–28. Her son, Robert Herre, gave me the same date. Bebe Goddard stated that she first met Marilyn in 1940. "Conversations with Bebe Goddard," *Runnin' Wild*, January 1994. Doc told Fred Guiles that his children visited him in the summer of 1935.

26. See Norma Jeane to Grace Goddard, September 12, 1942, courtesy of Charles Schwab.

27. Sacco, *Unspeakable: Father-Daughter Incest*; Rachel Devlin, *Relative Intimacy: Fathers, Daughters, and Postwar American Culture* (Chapel Hill, N.C.: University of North Carolina Press, 2005), 41.

28. Zolotow, *Marilyn Monroe*, 28; Marilyn Monroe, "Who'd Marry Me?" *Modern Screen*, September 1951.

29. Janet Leibman Jacobs, *Victimized Daughters: Incest and the Development of the Female Self* (New York: Routledge, 1994); Lenore Terr, *Too Scared to Cry: Psychic Trauma in Childhood* (New York: Harper & Row, 1990); Christine A. Courtois, *Healing the Incest Wound: Adult Survivors in Therapy* (New York: W.W. Norton, 1988); Diana E. H. Russell, *The Secret Trauma: Incest in the Lives of Girls and Women* (New York: Basic, 1986).

30. Howell, *Dissociative Mind*. See the controversies over the latest revision of the American Psychiatric Association's *Diagnostic and Statistical Manual of Mental Disorders* (DSMV), used by U.S. psychiatrists to diagnose mental disorders. See also R. Bentall, "Madness Explained: Why We Must Reject the Krapelian Paradigm and Replace It with a Complaint Oriented Approach to Understanding Mental Illness," *Medical Hypotheses* 66, 2006.

31. See Dana Becker, *Through the Looking Glass: Women and Borderline Personality Disorder* (Boulder, Colo.: Westview, 1997); and Jacob M. Virgil, David C. Geary, and Jennifer Byrd-Craven, "A Life History Assessment of Early Childhood Sexual Abuse in Women," *Developmental Psychology* 41 (2005): 553.

32. Strasberg, *Marilyn and Me*, 78.

33. Natasha Lytess, "My Years with Marilyn," 2, 4, in Zolotow—UT; MZ, interview with Lytess, in Zolotow—UT; Strasberg, *Marilyn and Me*, 66.

34. The "repressed memory" syndrome, identified in recent studies as a common result of sexual abuse, occurs mostly in very young children. By the age of eight, when the "elderly actor" attacked Norma Jeane, memory is fully functioning. Linda Meyer Williams, "Recall of Childhood Trauma: A Perspective Study of Women's Memories of Child Sexual Abuse," *Journal of Consulting and Clinical Psychology* 62 (1994): 1167–76; Christine M. Ogle et al., "Accuracy and Specificity of Autobiographical Memory in Childhood Trauma," in Mark L. Howe et al., *Stress, Trauma, and Children's Memory Development: Neurobiological, Cognitive, Clinical, and Legal Developments* (New York: Oxford University Press, 2008).

35. Sam Shaw, "Memories," in GiovanBattista Bambilla, Gianni Mercurio, and Stefano Petricca, eds., *Marilyn Monroe: The Life, the Myth* (New York: Rizzoli, 1995), 249; Sam Shaw and Norman Rosten, *Marilyn Among Friends* (New York: Henry Holt, 1987), 146. See also Milton Shulman, "Marilyn's Men: Stand-ins for Father," *London Daily Express*, 1955, in NYPL; David Connolly, "Marilyn's New Pitch," *National Police Gazette*, October 1957; Ralph Roberts, "Mimosa," unpublished memoir of Marilyn, unpaginated, Roberts Papers, in possession of Hap Roberts, Salisbury, N.C.

36. Wilson, *Hot Times*, 72; Strasberg, *Marilyn and Me*, 177; Buchthal and Comment, eds., *Fragments*, 111.

37. LB, interview with Robert Litman, January 28, 2009.

38. Louella Parsons, *Tell It to Louella* (New York: Putnam, 1961), 213. Natasha Lytess, Marilyn's first acting coach, stated in her memoir that she spent a good deal of time trying to help Marilyn get over her "bad-girl" syndrome. See Natasha Lytess, "My Years with Marilyn," in Zolotow–UT. Wilson, *Hot Times*, 72; Zolotow, *Marilyn Monroe*, 25.

39. Donald Kalshed, *The Inner World of Trauma: Archetypal Defenses of the Personal Spirit* (London: Routledge, 1996), 11. Monroe, *My story*, 17–19.

40. Some biographers maintain that Marilyn could see only the Paramount water tower from the window. They seem unaware that Paramount absorbed RKO in 1966 and removed the flashing part of the sign, observable from Marilyn's window. The globe on which the sign rested remains in place. See Eric Monroe Woodard, with David Marshall, *Hometown Girl* (HG Press, 2004), 19.

41. Miller, *Timebends*, 559; Edwin Hoyt, *Marilyn: The Tragic Venus* (New York: Duel, Sloan, and Pearce, 1965), vii; W. J. Weatherby, *Conversations with Marilyn*, 146. Hoyt's 1965 study draws from a series of interviews with Nunnally Johnson, a major Twentieth Century–Fox writer, one of Darryl Zanuck's major advisors.

42. Judith Sealander, *The Failed Century of the Child* (Cambridge, Eng.: Cambridge University Press, 2003), 99.

43. Ellen Herman, *Kinship by Design: A History of Adoption in the Modern United States* (Chicago: University of Chicago Press, 2008); Claudia Nelson, *Little Strangers: Portrayals of Adoption* (Bloomington, Ind.: Indiana Uni-

versity Press, 2003); Eileen B. Simpson, *Orphans: Real and Imaginary* (London: Weidenfeld & Nicolson, 1987).

44. Zolotow, *Marilyn Monroe*, 26–31.
45. Kirk Crivello, "Marilyn Monroe," in Crivello, *Fallen Angels: The Lives and Untimely Deaths of Fourteen Hollywood Beauties* (Secaucus, N.J.: Citadel, 238; LB, interview with Jay Kanter, October 3, 2007.
46. Barris, *Marilyn: Her Life*, 15.
47. Miller, *Timebends*, 489; "Questions and Answers to Ralph Roberts on Childhood," typewritten ms., in RR.
48. Monroe, *My Story*, 15.
49. Biographers dispute the date that Grace removed Norma Jeane from the orphanage. Financial records Grace filed with the court indicate that she ended paying the orphanage for Norma Jeane's care and began paying herself in October 1936. But Marilyn recalled staying in the orphanage for two years, which places her release in the summer of 1937. In *My Sister Marilyn*, Berniece Miracle gives the date as June 26, 1937. Zolotow, who gained access to orphanage records, gives the same date.
50. LB, interview with Ida Mae Monroe, October 2006. The editors of *Fragments* are in error in speculating that a "boarder" in the Martin-Monroe house molested Norma Jeane. With two adults and three children in their small house, there was no room for a boarder.
51. Marilyn's brief stay with the Mills family, unknown to previous biographers, is mentioned in Roy Turner, interview with Ida Mae Monroe, in RT.
52. On Marilyn's stay with the Atchinsons, see Bebe Goddard to Roy Turner, August 24, 1987, in RT.
53. Stacy Eubank, interview with Sheryl Williams, October 26, 2010. Howard Keel, *Only Make Believe: My Life in Show Business* (New York: Barricade, 2005), 47.
54. "Marilyn Monroe Tells the Truth to Hedda Hopper," *Photoplay*, January 1953, 85.
55. Goodman, *The Fifty Year Decline*, 227; Parsons, *Tell It to Louella*, 216, 224; Strasberg, *Marilyn and Me*, 104.
56. Monroe, *My Story*, 10.
57. Randy Taraborrelli incorrectly states that Grace put Norma Jeane in the orphanage because Norma Jeane and Nona Goddard, Doc's daughter who was living with Grace and Doc, didn't get along. I can find no evidence that Nona lived with them in 1935. Guiles, *Legend*, mentions a visit that summer.
58. Ben Hecht's notes for his autobiography of Marilyn are contained in his papers, NL.
59. James Gloege to Maurice Zolotow, February 20, 1953, in Zolotow—UT.
60. Transcript, Beverly Hills High School, Josephine Goddard (Jody Simmons) 1945–1946. I am grateful to Victoria Vantoch for gaining access to this document for me. See "Pert Miss, New Featured Player, Visits Hometown," undated, unsourced newspaper clipping, in Jody Lawrance file, possession of Robert Herre.
61. Nona Goddard to Grace Goddard, in GS.

62. Gary Grissman, a fifth-grade classmate of Norma Jeane, found her very unattractive. See AP wire service, February 5, 1953, in Stacy Eubank, "Holding a Good Thought"; Hedda Hopper, "They Call Her a Blowtorch Blonde," *Chicago Tribune*, May 4, 1952.

63. Kirk Crivello, interview with Bebe Goddard, Crivello, *Fallen Angels*, 239. Los Angeles City Schools, May 26, 1938, athletic awards to Norma Jeane Baker. Sotheby Parke Bernet Catalogue for Marilyn Monroe auction, New York, October 21, 1973.

64. Jane Corwin, "Orphan in Ermine," *Photoplay*, March 1954.

CHAPTER 3

1. "Conversations with Bebe Goddard," in *Runnin' Wild*, January 1994. DS, interview with Bebe Goddard, in Spoto—AMPAS.

2. I derived Ana Lower's addresses from the Membership Records, Mary Baker Eddy Library, First Christian Science Church, Boston. As a healer registered in the *Christian Science Journal*, Ana had to verify her address every year with the central church in Boston. My thanks to Amanda Gustin and Leslie Pitts of the Eddy Library for giving me this information. They also gave me the dates when Grace Goddard and Norma Jeane became members of the church.

3. Jack Fujimoto, *Sawtelle: West Los Angeles Japantown* (Charleston, S.C.: Arcadia, 2007); Christopher Rand, *Los Angeles: The Ultimate City* (New York: Oxford University Press, 1967), 121. Unlike Venice or Hollywood, Sawtelle was never an incorporated district or a separate city, although it was called "Sawtelle." That name is not used today. It is now part of West Los Angeles or the "West Side." *Los Angeles Times*, May 3, 1936; Monroe, *My Story*, 22. Lisa Wilson, "The Truth About Me," *American Weekly*, November 16, 1952.

4. Marilyn Monroe, "I Dress for Men," *Movieland*, July 1952. Some Marilyn biographers maintain that she attended Sawtelle Elementary School before entering Emerson. I can find no evidence for this claim, although she may have attended Sawtelle during the first months she lived with Ana Lower. She stated in some interviews that she failed mathematics in sixth grade and had to repeat it.

5. William Moynier to Roy Turner, October 26, 1986, in RT.

6. Dorothy Muir, "The Real Marilyn Monroe at Thirteen," *Tatler*, October 7, 1973, courtesy of Stacy Eubank.

7. DS, interview with Gladys Wilson, in Spoto—AMPAS; LB, interview with Gladys Wilson, October 27, 2008.

8. Spoto, *Marilyn Monroe*, 60–69, gives the fullest account of Norma Jeane's years at Emerson Junior High.

9. "What Is Your Favorite Type of Girl?" *The Emersonian* 5 (June 20, 1941).

10. Monroe, *My Story*, 22.

11. John Engstead, *Star Shots: Fifty Years of Pictures and Stories by One of Hollywood's Greatest Photographers* (New York: Dutton, 1978), 194; LB, interview with Edith Shaw Marcus and Meta Shaw Stevens, January 9, 2009; Jane Russell, "That Girl Marilyn," pamphlet, Affiliated Magazines, 1954.

12. Monroe, "I Was an Orphan," *Modern Screen*, February 1951; Eve Arnold, *Marilyn Monroe: An Appreciation* (New York: Alfred A. Knopf, 1987), 16–17.

13. My description of Crawford and Davis is based on Maria DiBattista, *Fast-Talking Dames* (New Haven, Conn.: Yale University Press, 2001).

14. Belmont, *Marilyn Monroe and the Camera*, 16.

15. On Christian Science, I have used Caroline Fraser, *God's Perfect Child: Living and Dying in the Christian Science Church* (New York: Metropolitan, 1999); Barbara Wilson, *Blue Windows: A Christian Science Childhood* (New York: St. Martin's/Picador, 1997); Gillian Gill, *Mary Baker Eddy* (New York: Perseus, 1998); Victoria Vantoch, interview with Christian Science practitioner Don Ingerson; and my reading of Mary Baker Eddy, *Science and Health*.

16. Miracle, *My Sister Marilyn* (Chapel Hill: Algonquin Books, 1994), 50.

17. Rolf Swensen, "Christian Scientists on the Pacific Coast, 1880–1915," *The Pacific Historical Review* 72 (May 2003), 229–63. Gregory H. Singleton, *Religion in the City of Angels* (Ann Arbor, Mich.: UMI Research, 1978), 169.

18. John Gilmore, interview with Ernest Neilson, Consolidated Film Industries, in Gilmore, *Inside Marilyn Monroe*, 55.

19. Zolotow, *Marilyn Monroe*, 34. Will Sykes to Marilyn, October 7, 1954, in Banner and Anderson, *MM—Personal*, 169.

20. Banner and Anderson, *MM—Personal*, 168–71; Mrs. E. Ana Lower to Dearie, October 22, 1949.

21. Monroe, *My Story*, 49–50.

22. I am grateful to Rebecca Kuhn M.D., who works with drug addicts, and to Carrie Rickard M.D., a specialist in gynecological surgery, for their discussions on medical matters concerning Marilyn's body with me, in September 2010 and August 2011.

23. Ibid.

24. AS, interview with Henry Rosenfeld, in AS; LB, interview with Noreen Nash, July 10, 2009. Robert Mitchum, "Introduction," Matthew Smith, *The Men Who Murdered Marilyn* (London: Bloomsbury, 1996), 1–2; Earl Wilson, *The Show Business Nobody Knows* (Chicago: Cowles, 1971), 282.

25. DS, interview with Ralph Roberts, in Spoto—AMPAS.

26. I have taken the quotes from "Marriage" in *Science and Health*.

27. Marilyn Monroe, "Who'd Marry Me?" *Modern Screen*, September 1951.

28. Elda Nelson, "Marilyn Monroe," *Modern Screen*, December 1952.

29. Amanda Littauer, "Unsanctioned Encounters: Women, Girls, and Nonmarital Sexuality in the United States, 1941–1963," Ph.D. diss., University

of California, Berkeley, 2006; Marilyn E. Hegarty, *Victory Girls, Khaki-Wackies, and Patriotutes: The Regulation of Female Sexuality During World War II* (New York: New York University Press, 2008.)

30. I derive the term "plain folk Americanism" from James Gregory, *American Exodus: The Dust Bowl Migration and Okie Culture in California* (New York: Oxford University Press, 1989). On the girl next door, see Jane Powell, *The Girl Next Door—and How She Grew* (New York: Morrow, 1988).

31. Ralph Greenson to Marianne Kris, August 1962, in Greenson—UCLA. Monroe, *My Story*.

32. Estelle B. Freedman, "'Uncontrolled Desires': The Response to the Sexual Psychopath, 1920–1960," *Journal of American History* 74 (January 1987), 83–106; Miriam R. Reumann, *American Sexual Character: Sex, Gender, and National Identity in the Kinsey Reports* (Berkeley: University of California Press, 2005), 165–98.

33. Monroe, *My Story*, 28, 93–4.

34. Zolotow, *Marilyn Monroe*, 35; Marilyn Monroe, "Who'd Marry Me?" *Modern Screen*, September 1951.

35. "Anthony Cordova's Memories of Marilyn," *Hollywood Studio Magazine*, clipping, n.d., in GS.

36. Arthur C. Verge, *Paradise Transformed: Los Angeles During the Second World War* (Dubuque, Iowa: Kendall Hunt, 1993); Starr, *Embattled Dreams*; Dougherty, *To Norma Jeane with Love*, 13.

37. "Wartime Health Problems Seen in Defense Drive," *Los Angeles Times*, February 6, 1941.

38. Marilyn Monroe, "Who'd Marry Me?" *Modern Screen*, September 1951.

39. Verge, *Paradise Transformed*, 12; Dougherty, *To Norma Jeane*, 13.

40. Buchthal and Comment, eds., *Fragments*, includes several typed pages the editors contend Norma Jeane wrote at the age of seventeen. Internal evidence in the document, however, proves they are mistaken. The document's writer refers to "being in a play." Norma Jeane wasn't in a play at the age of seventeen. Nor was she a "small, delicately built girl," as the writer of the document describes herself. She was 5 feet, 5½ inches tall, and she had a well-exercised body with observable muscles. She hadn't done any modeling or television work, unlike the writer of the document. The writer describes a man she is dating as an intellectual interested in classical music. Jim Dougherty had neither of those characteristics. In his memoirs about his relationship with Norma Jeane, he is a masculine man, not especially bright, who liked to hunt and fish.

    It's probable that Susan Strasberg wrote the document. She modeled at the age of sixteen and became a star of films and Broadway plays at the age of seventeen. She had a romance with an older man on Fire Island. See Strasberg, *Marilyn and Me*, 18; and Susan Strasberg, *Bittersweet* (New York: Signet, 1980), 34–36. The Strasbergs possessed Marilyn's New York papers for many years, but they were not well cataloged. A document written by Susan may have been mixed up with Marilyn's papers.

41. *Los Angeles Times*, June 2, 1942, and June 13, 1942.

42. Norma Jeane to Grace, September 14, 1942. My thanks to signature expert Charles Schwab for providing me with a photocopy of this letter. Norma Jeane ends the letter by asking Grace how she can get in touch with her mother's colleagues at Consolidated Industries so that she can find Stanley Gifford. She also tells Grace to "give daddy [Doc Goddard] a big hug."

43. Wilson, "The Truth About Me," *American Weekly*, November 16, 1952.

44. James Dougherty, "Marilyn Monroe Was My Wife," *Photoplay*, March 1953; Dougherty, "The Marilyn Nobody Knows," *McCall's*, February 1976.

45. Marilyn Monroe, "Love Is My Problem," *Silver Screen*, October 1951; Monroe, *My Story*, 29; Elia Kazan, *Elia Kazan: A Life* (New York: Da Capo, 1997), 404–05.

46. Jane Wilkie, *Confessions of an Ex-Fan Magazine Writer* (New York: Doubleday, 1981), 132; James Dougherty, *The Secret Happiness of Marilyn Monroe* (Chicago: Playboy, 1976), 46. Robert Mitchum, "Introduction," Smith, *Men Who Killed Marilyn Monroe*.

47. Spoto, *Marilyn Monroe*, 81.

48. Barris, *Marilyn: Her Life*, 43.

49. Dougherty, quoted in *London Sunday Express*, August 9, 1987.

50. Norman Rosten, *Marilyn: An Untold Story*, (New York: New American Library, 1973). 22.

51. Halsman's comments on Marilyn are in Ralph Hattersley, "Marilyn Monroe: The Image and Her Photographers," in Edward Wagenknecht, ed., *Marilyn Monroe*, 61–66.

52. Maria Elena Buszek's analysis of pinups as powerful in *Pin-Up Grrrls: Feminism, Sexuality, Popular Culture* (Durham, N.C.: Duke University Press, 2006) is persuasive, although she misses their conservative element. See also Kurt Vonnegut, "Foreword," *Varga: The Esquire Years: A Catalogue Raisonné* (New York: Alfred Van Der Marck, 1987), 6–7.

CHAPTER 4

1. Norma Jeane's employment record at Radioplane is reprinted in Woodard, *Hometown Girl*, 35.

2. Stacy Eubank Collection.

3. Miracle, *My Sister Marilyn*, 51. See also Membership Records, Mary Baker Eddy Library. First Christian Science Church, Boston.

4. David Conover, *Finding Marilyn: A Romance* (New York: Grosset & Dunlap, 1981), 6–7.

5. On genius, I have used Daniel Coyle, *The Talent Code* (New York: Bantam Dell, 2009); Michael J. A. Howe, *Genius Explained* (Cambridge, England: Cambridge University Press, 1999); and John Briggs, *Fire in the Crucible: The Self-Creation of Creativity and Genius* (Los Angeles: Jeremy P. Tarcher, 1990). On creativity and bipolarity, I have relied on Kay Redfield Jamison, *Touched with Fire: Manic Depressive Illness and the Artistic Temperament* (New York: Simon & Schuster, 1993). Most recent analysts reject the

still-popular nineteenth-century belief that genius is always evident in childhood and exists among only a few individuals.

6. Strasberg, *Marilyn and Me*, 104; Miller, *Timebends*, 436; Rosten, *Marilyn: An Untold Story*, 45.

7. Bruno Bernard (Bernard of Hollywood), *Requiem for Marilyn* (Buckinghamshire, Eng.: Kensal, 1986), 3–4. On fashion shows in 1930s and 1940s films, see Jeanine Basinger, *A Woman's View: How Hollywood Spoke to Women, 1930–1960* (New York: Alfred A. Knopf, 1993): 122–59. On models who became stars, see Shelley Winters, *Shelley, Also Known as Shirley* (New York: Ballantine, 1980); Lauren Bacall, *By Myself and Then Some* (New York: HarperEntertainment, 2005); Lee Server, *Ava Gardner: "Love is Nothing"* (New York: St. Martin's, 2006).

8. Dougherty expressed these concerns in his interview with Jane Wilkie. See Wilkie, *Confessions of an Ex-Fan Magazine Writer*, 129.

9. Both Summers and Spoto interviewed Conover, and neither trusted him. Spoto, *Marilyn Monroe*, 111; Summers, *Legend*, 17. I have used Conover's memoir with caution. Moreover, photographer William Carroll's account of his trip is similar to the one described by Andre de Dienes. Numerous sources verify the de Dienes trip, although there is little independent proof of the Conover trip. On the other hand, when I interviewed Carroll, a friend of Conover's, he told me that Conover gave him the negatives from the trip to develop. Thus he was certain the trip had happened. LB, interview with William Carroll, December 2, 2008.

10. On Snively, I have used Ted Thackrey, "Emmeline Snively," *Los Angeles Herald Examiner*, August 7, 1962; MZ, interview with Snively, in Zolotow—UT; Snively, "Marilyn's Life as a Model," *Photoplay*, July 1954; Snively, "The Real Marilyn Monroe Story: Hamburgers and Cheeseburgers," *Art Photography*, October 1954.

11. Goodman, *The Fifty Year Decline*, 228.

12. Lana Turner, *Lana: The Lady, the Legend, the Truth* (New York: Dutton, 1982), 99.

13. Joseph Jasgur and Jeanne Sokol, *The Birth of Marilyn: The Lost Photographs of Norma Jeane* (London: Sidgwick & Jackson, 1991), 3; MZ, interview with Earl Theissen, in Zolotow—UT; Bernard, ed., *Bernard of Hollywood's Marilyn*, 7.

14. Zolotow, *Marilyn Monroe*, 56. William Carroll, *Norma Jean/Marilyn Monroe, 1945: Photography by William Carroll* (Raton, N.M.: Coda, 2004); Barris, *Marilyn: Her Life*, 51.

15. Gilmore, interview with Bob Shannon, *Inside Marilyn Monroe*, 80–81.

16. On fashion modeling, I have used Harriet Quick, *Catwalking: A History of the Fashion Model* (London: Hamlyn, 1997); Charles Castle, *Model Girl* (Secaucus, N.J.: Chartwell, 1977); Martin Harrison, *Appearances: Fashion Photography Since 1945* (New York: Rizzoli, 1991); and my extensive reading in fashion, pinup, and general circulation magazines. On the illustrators, see Martignette and Meisel, *The Great American Pin-Up*.

17. Bernard, ed., *Bernard of Hollywood's Marilyn*, 8; Barris, *Marilyn: Her Life,* 54.

18. Earl Leaf, "The Marilyn Monroe I Used to Know," *Movie Time*, December 1954, 68.

19. Bernard, ed., *Bernard of Hollywood's Marilyn*, 7.

20. Andre de Dienes, *Marilyn, Mon Amour* (New York: St. Martin's, 1985). See also Louella O. Parsons, *Tell It to Louella* (New York: G.P. Putnam's Sons, 1961), 218; Monroe, *My Story*, 36; Goodman, *The Fifty Year Decline*, 229.

21. See sources on Snively in note 209.

22. Anthony Beauchamp, *Focus on Fame* (London: Oldhams, 1958), 234; Laszlo Willinger interview, *Beyond the Legend*, video produced by Gene Feldman and Suzette Winter.

23. On de Dienes and the trip with Marilyn, I have used Andre de Dienes, *Marilyn, Mon Amour,* and the longer bound typescript version, which is chapter 8, "Norma Jean," of "Hollywood: Photography: Andre de Dienes," 149–344. A facsimile of the typescript has appeared as Vol. 1 of Steve Christ and Andre de Dienes, *Marilyn* (Köln: Taschen, 2011).

24. Jorge Lewinski, *The Naked and the Nude: A History of the Nude in Photographs, 1839 to the Present* (New York: Harmony, 1987), 70–71.

25. Morgan, *Up Close and Personal,* 60.

26. De Dienes, *Marilyn, Mon Amour,* 83.

27. Gilmore, *Inside Marilyn Monroe,* 85; Norma Jeane to "Dearest Jean," October 27, 1946, "Rare Magazine," Autograph Collectors Website, courtesy of Stacy Eubank.

28. Andre de Dienes to Lawrence Schiller, January 3, 1954, in Mailer—UT.

29. On Marilyn's magazine covers, see Brambilla, Mercurio, and Petricca, eds., *Marilyn Monroe,* 30–36, and Clark Kidder, *Marilyn Monroe: Cover to Cover* (Iola, Wis.: Krause, 2003).

30. Earl Moran, "A Marilyn for All Seasons," *Life*, January 1983, 9–15; Martignette and Meisel, *Great American Pin-up,* 288–303.

31. United Press Wire Service, June 18, 1952: "Photographer Says Most Film Queens Could Never Pose for Nude Picture," Eubank, "Holding a Good Thought"; Dougherty, *To Norma Jeane,* 112.

32. I have constructed Jaik Rosenstein's biography from Rosenstein, *Hollywood Leg Man* (Los Angeles: Madison, 1950), and from the articles and columns in *Hollywood Close-Up,* in AMPAS. He wrote the newsletter himself.

33. On Colin Clark, see Clark, *My Week with Marilyn* (New York: HarperCollins, 2000), and Clark, *The Prince, the Showgirl, and Me: Six Months on the Set with Marilyn and Olivier* (New York: St. Martin's, 1996). On prostitution at the Ambassador Hotel, see DS, interview with Joseph Jasgur, in Spoto—AMPAS; LB, interview with William Carroll, December 7, 2008.

34. LB, interview with Malcolm Boyd, June 8, 2009; Charles F. Stocker, *Thicker 'n Thieves* (Santa Monica, Calif.: Sidereal, 1951), 253.

35. Wilson, *Show Business Laid Bare,* 68; AS, interview with Henry Rosenfeld, in AS.

36. Bruno Bernard, *Bernard of Hollywood: The Ultimate Pin-up Book* (New York: Taschen, 2002), 251. The classic free-love text for the twentieth century is Havelock Ellis, *The Art of Love,* Vol. 6 of his *Studies in the Psychology of Sex* (1910; New York: Random House, 1936). Ellis's work went through many editions and had a large readership. I can't find proof that Marilyn read Ellis, but his ideas run through her statements about friendship, love, and sex.

37. "Bourbon's Stage Review Puts Emphasis on Smut," *Los Angeles Times,* December 20, 1954; "Ray Bourbon Opens Review," *Los Angeles Times,* December 12, 1945. On Bill Pursel, see Morgan, *Up Close and Personal,* 62–64; on Ken DuMain, see Crivello, *Fallen Angels,* 242–43; for Miller's statement, see Miller file in Mailer—UT.

38. Columnist Sheilah Graham contended that Ben Lyon promoted Marilyn's career because he had an affair with her. I can find no proof for this allegation, except that Louella Parsons, who was friendly with Lyon and his wife, film star Bebe Daniels, stated that a rumor to that effect had circulated in Hollywood, but she didn't believe it. AS, interview with Sheilah Graham, in AS; Summers, *Goddess,* 40; Parsons, *Tell It to Louella,* 214.

39. Lawence Crown, interview with Whitey Snyder, in Crown, *Marilyn at Twentieth Century–Fox* (Los Angeles: Comet, 1987) 30–31; MZ, interview with Leon Shamroy, in Zolotow—UT; Parsons, *Tell It to Louella,* 213.

40. Typescript manuscript, "Marilyn Monroe's Childhood," in RR—Salisbury.

41. Richard Buskin, interview with Jean Peters, in Buskin, *Blonde Heat: The Sizzling Screen Career of Marilyn Monroe* (New York: Billboard, 2001), 14; Harry Evans, "What Caused Marilyn Monroe," *Family Circle,* June 1958.

42. Harry Lipton, "Marilyn's the Most!," *Motion Picture,* May 28, 1956.

43. LB, interview with Patricia Tiernan Cox, June 17, 2010. Cox's name as a starlet was Carol Eden.

44. Morgan, *Marilyn Monroe,* 54; Conover, *Finding Marilyn,* 13; Harry Lipton, "Marilyn's the Most!," *Motion Picture,* May 28, 1956.

45. Hortense Powdermaker, *Hollywood: The Dream Factory: An Anthropologist Looks at the Movie Makers* (Boston: Little, Brown, 1950), 29.

46. Douglas Gomery, *The Hollywood Studio System: A History* (London: BFI, 2005). Paul McDonald, *The Star System: Hollywood's Production of Popular Identities* (London: Wallflower, 2000). I have also used Neal Gabler, *How the Jews Invented Hollywood* (New York: Doubleday, 1989); Leo C. Rosten, *Hollywood: The Movie Colony, the Movie Makers* (New York: Harcourt, Brace, 1941); Shirley MacLaine, *You Can Get There from Here* (New York: W.W. Norton, 1975), 23–30; Kazan, *Elia Kazan,* 227. See also Robert Stack, *Straight Shooting* (New York: Macmillan, 1980), 184; and Shelley Winters, *Shelley II: The Middle of My Century* (New York: Simon & Schuster, 1989), 65.

47. Powdermaker, *Hollywood: The Dream Factory,* 22. Before studying the Hollywood film industry, Powdermaker had studied the antebellum South, including the plantation system.

48. Leonard Mosley, *Zanuck: The Rise and Fall of Hollywood's Last Tycoon* (Boston: Little Brown, 1984); Mervyn LeRoy, *Mervyn LeRoy, Take One* (New

York: Hawthorn Books, 1994), 210; Bob Thomas, *King Cohn : The Life and Times of a Hollywood Mogul* (Beverly Hills, Calif.: New Millennium, 2000).

49. LB, interview with Michael Selsman, October 9, 2008.

50. E. J. Fleming, *Carole Landis: A Tragic Life in Hollywood* (Jefferson, N.C.: McFarland, 2005).

51. Arthur Miller comment, in Mailer—UT.

CHAPTER 5

1. Ronald Davis, interview with Vanessa Brown, in Davis—AMPAS; Ronald Davis, *The Glamour Factory: Inside Hollywood's Big Studio System* (Dallas: Southern Methodist University Press, 1993), 6; Zolotow, *Marilyn Monroe* 59; Peter Harry Brown and Patte Barham, *Marilyn: The Last Take* (1992; Thorndike, Me.: Thorndike, 1993), 47.

2. For Fox activities, see the studio newsletter, Spring 1948, in LB; Shaw and Rosten, *Marilyn Among Friends*, 22; Amy Greene and Joshua Greene, *But That's Another Story: A Photographic Retrospective of Milton H. Greene* (Brooklyn: powerHouse, 2010), 174.

3. AS, interview with Ralph Casey Shawhan, in AS; Jill Allgood, *Bebe and Ben* (London: R. Hale, 1995), 145.

4. DS, interview with Rupert Allan, in Spoto—AMPAS; Clifton Webb, "You Really Don't Know Marilyn Monroe," an interview with Ernie Player, *Picturegoer*, 1955.

5. Delia Salvi, "The History of the Actors' Laboratory, Inc., 1941–1950," Ph.D. diss., UCLA, 1969; Cynthia Baron, "Actors' Lab in Hollywood," in Adrienne L. MacLean, ed., *Headline Hollywood: A Century of Film Scandal* (New Brunswick, N.J.: Rutgers University Press, 2001), 146–53.

6. Joseph R. Roach, *The Players' Passion: Studies in the Science of Acting* (Newark, Delaware: University of Delaware Press, 1985). Charles Marowitz, *The Other Chekhov: A Biography of Michael Chekhov, the Legendary Actor, Director, and Theorist* (New York: Applause Theatre & Cinema Books, 2004).

7. Spoto, *Marilyn Monroe*, 122, 125.

8. Weatherby, *Conversations with Marilyn*, 129.

9. Susan Strasberg, *Marilyn and Me*, 11.

10. On Phoebe Brand's reaction to Marilyn, see Zolotow, *Marilyn Monroe*, 72; on Lila Bliss Hayden see James Haspiel, *Young Marilyn: Becoming the Legend* (London: Hyperion, 1994), 34.

11. Strasberg, *Marilyn and Me*, 155–56.

12. Actress Janet Leigh describes the 1950s attitude toward divorced women and sex in *There Really Was a Hollywood* (Garden City, N.Y.: Doubleday, 1984), 15. See also Gene Tierney, *Self-Portrait* (New York: Simon & Schuster, 1979), 12; and Sammy Davis Jr., *Hollywood in a Suitcase* (New York: William Morrow, 1980), 231.

13. Richard Buskin, interview with Jean Peters, in *Blonde Heat: The Sizzling*

Screen Career of Marilyn Monroe (New York: Billboard, 2001), 24. Oleg Cassini, *In My Own Fashion: An Autobiography* (New York: Simon & Schuster, 1987), 110; Buskin, interview with Mary Anita Loos, in *Blonde Heat*, 16.

14. Sidney Skolsky, "Hollywood Harems," *Hollywood Citizen News*, in Skolsky—AMPAS; Cindy Adams, *Lee Strasberg: The Imperfect Genius of the Actors Studio* (Garden City, N.Y.: Doubleday, 1980), 253; Weatherby, *Conversations with Marilyn*, 144; Marilyn, *My Story*, 48; James Kotsibilis-Davis, ed. Joshua Greene, *Milton's Marilyn*, (Moss Runn, Schirmer/Mosel, 1994) 28; Robert Stein, "Do You Want to See Her?" *American Heritage*, November–December 2005, 144. According to Malcolm Boyd, the starlets slept with producers more for conversation than for sex. Rather than waiting in a producer's office all day and then not getting an interview, by sleeping with him they could sell their talents at breakfast the next morning. LB, interview with Malcolm Boyd, June 8, 2009.

   See also Powdermaker, *Hollywood: The Dream Factory*, 21; Ben Hecht, *A Child of the Century* (New York: Primus, 1985), 481; Arthur Miller, *Timebends*, 302; Ronald Davis, interview with Joan Fontaine, April 12, 1979, in Davis—AMPAS; Joan Fontaine, *No Bed of Roses* (New York: Morrow, 1978), 76.

15. Gloria Vanderbilt, *It Seemed Important at the Time* (New York: Simon & Schuster, 2004), 14–20; Vanderbilt, *White Knight, Black Knight* (New York: Alfred A. Knopf, 1987): Elia Kazan, *Elia Kazan*, 422; Cassini, *In My Fashion,* 147. Cubby Broccoli and Donald Zec: *When the Snow Melts: The Autobiography of Cubby Broccoli* (London: Boxtree, 1998).

16. Natasha Fraser-Caravansi, *Sam Spiegel* (New York: Simon & Schuster, 2003); Andrew Sinclair, *Spiegel: The Man Behind the Pictures* (Boston: Little Brown, 1987).

17. Fraser-Caravansi, interview with Budd Schulberg, in *Sam Spiegel*, 86. John Houseman, *Front and Center* (New York: Simon & Schuster, 1979), 121.

18. Evelyn Keyes, *Scarlett O'Hara's Younger Sister: My Lively Life In and Out of Hollywood* (New York: Lyle Stuart, 1977), 209; Keyes, *I'll Think About That Tomorrow* (New York: Dutton, 1991), 286; John Huston, *An Open Book* (New York: Ballantine, 1981), 43; LB, interview with Michael Selsman, November 11, 2009; W. J. Weatherby, *Conversations with Marilyn*, 144; Peter Bogdanovich, "Marilyn Monroe," in Bogdanovich, *Who the Hell's In It* (New York: Alfred A. Knopf, 2004), 484.

19. Powdermaker, *Hollywood: The Dream Factory*, 21; LB, interview with Malcolm Boyd, June 8, 2009; Monroe, *My Story*, 48; Mamie Van Doren, *Playing the Field: My Story* (New York: Berkeley, 1988), 7; Earl Wilson, *Hot Times: True Tales of Hollywood and Broadway* (Chicago: Contemporary, 1940), 70. The Kazan letter, which is undated, can be dated by internal evidence. It was sold at Butterfield's auction house in 1951. The original purchaser gave me a copy of it. It is reproduced in the catalog for the auction.

20. On Marilyn and fellatio, see Mickey Rooney, *Life Is Too Short* (New York: Villard, 1991), 233; DS, interview with Amy Greene, in Spoto—AMPAS; AS,

interview with Kendis Rochlin, in AS; Lawrence J. Quirk, *The Kennedys in Hollywood* (New York: Cooper Square, 2004), 221. On not using condoms, see Van Doren, *Playing the Field*, 115.

21. Powdermaker, *Hollywood: The Dream Factory*, 235.

22. Miller, *Timebends*, 359; ed. Greene, *Milton's Marilyn*, 28

23. On Marilyn and Alan Young, see Alan Young, *Mr. Ed and Me* (New York: St. Martin's, 1994). On Charles Chaplin, I have used AS, interview with Arthur James, in AS, and LB, interview with Arthur James, June 25, 2010. I asked James about charges that he spent time in jail and thus couldn't be trusted. He replied that he was a real estate developer living in Malibu, then a small town, when police buddies pulled him over on a DUI charge and he spent a night in jail. He became close to Charlie Chaplin Jr. when Charlie dated his sister, Janet. See also Malcolm Boyd, "Departures and Encounters," in Chris Freeman and James J. Berg, eds., *Love, West Hollywood: Reflections of Los Angeles* (New York: Alyson, 2008), 222; and Winters, *Shelley II*, 42.

24. LB, interview with Dave Heiser, November 24, 2008; LB, interview with Arthur Verge, September 29, 2009; AS, interview with Tommy Zahn, in AS. Kendis Rochlin, "Surfing Is One of Favorite Southland Beach Sports," *Los Angeles Times*, August 11, 1945. In creating tandem surfing, surfers copied Muscle Beach bodybuilders who lifted girls on the beach into acrobatic positions.

25. William Burnside, "My Life with the Young Monroe," *Observer*, May 11, 1975.

26. AP, interview with Edith Head, April 1960, in SE, "Holding a Good Thought." Eve Arnold, *Marilyn Monroe*, 21.

27. Summers, *Goddess*, 94–95; Graham, *Confessions of a Hollywood Gossip Columnist*, 141; Joan Greenson, "Memoir of Marilyn," 74, in Greenson—UCLA; Maureen Reilly, *Hollywood Costume Design by Travilla* (Atgen, Pa.: Schiller, 2003), 80.

28. See, for example, Sheilah Graham, "Sex Too Far," *Photoplay*, February 1953, and Robert L. Heilbroner, "Marilyn Monroe: The Fabulous Story of Hollywood's Biggest Buildup," *Cosmopolitan*, May 1953.

29. On Marilyn's relationship with Carroll and Ryman, I have used DS, interviews with Lucille Ryman and with Michael Korda, in Spoto—AMPAS; and Guiles, *Legend*, 122–24. Guiles is the only Marilyn biographer to have interviewed Harry Lipton. Ryman is incorrect in stating that Marilyn first met Carroll when she caddied for him at a charity golf tournament in late August 1947. See "Why Women Hate Marilyn Monroe," *Movieland*, October 1952, on the Marilyn-Ryman link.

30. LB, interview with Barbara Rush and Noreen Nash, November 30, 2010. See also Marjorie Hillis, "Your Hopes in Pictures," *Photoplay*, October 1938. A copy of the contract, dated December 7, 1947, was auctioned at Bonhams and Butterfields, June 14, 2009. See the catalog for the auction. It guaranteed Marilyn $100 a week; only John Carroll and Marilyn signed it. See also Lipton, "Marilyn's the Most!," *Motion Picture*, May 28, 1956.

31. Lipton, "Marilyn's the Most," *Motion Picture*, May 28, 1956. On October 8, 1947, Louella Parsons called Marilyn "John Carroll's new chick," in her column. On October 11, 1947, Patricia Clary referred to Marilyn's romance with John Carroll in a UP Wire Service story. On December 11, 1947, in his syndicated column Jimmy Fidler described an altercation between Lila Leeds and Marilyn in front of a nightclub. Leeds "straight armed Monroe," according to Fidler. These cites are from Eubank, "Holding a Good Thought."

32. Clarice Evans, "I Was Marilyn Monroe's Roommate," *Los Angeles Times, This Week Magazine*, November 21, 1954. Helen Hunt, chief hairdresser at Columbia, stated that Marilyn always read a Christian Science prayer book under the hairdryer. Antonio Villani, interview with Hunt, in Villani, ed., "'Hold A Good Thought for Me': The Screenplay That Never Was," 9, typescript, in GS.

33. "The Unwritten Words of Whitey Snyder," *Runnin' Wild,* January 1994; Maury Allen, interview with Angelo Delucco, manager of Westwood Memorial Cemetery and Mortuary, in *Where Have You Gone, Joe DiMaggio? The Story of America's Last Hero* (New York: Dutton, 1975), 160.

34. Gabler, *Empire of Their Own,* 258.

35. Graham, *Confessions,* 136; Monroe, *My Story,* 55; AS, interview with Marion Marshall, in AS, October 22, 2009; LB, interview with Noreen Nash, July 10, 2010; LB, interview with Gloria Romanoff, September 18, 2008; Louella Parsons, *Tell It to Louella,* 219; Rosten, *Marilyn: An Untold Story,* 16.

36. AS, interview with Marion Marshall, in AS; LB, interview with Marion Marshall; Monroe, *My Story,* 76; Ralph Roberts, "Mimosa."

37. Sidney Skolsky, *Marilyn* (New York: Dell, 1954), 54; Broccoli and Zec, *When the Snow Melts,* 39.

38. Monroe, *My Story,* 76; Roberts, "Mimosa."

39. Glenn Loney, *Unsung Genius: The Passion of Dancer-Choreographer Jack Cole* (New York: F. Watts, 1984), 211; Bernard, ed., *Bernard of Hollywood's Marilyn,* 10–11; Haspiel, *Young Marilyn,* 43–44; Kelly DiNardo, *Gilded Lili: Lili St. Cyr and the Striptease Mystique* (New York: Back Stage Books, 2007).

40. Buskin, interview with Rand Brooks, in *Blonde Heat,* 33.

41. MZ, interview with Fred Karger, in Zolotow—UT; LB, interview with Terry Wasdyke, August 16, 2009; LB, interview with Bennett Daubrey, November 20, 2009. Bennett was the son of Fred Karger's sister, Mary Short. He told me that he never saw Marilyn in bed with Fred, as has been reported, but he walked in on her once by mistake as she sat naked at the dressing table in Fred's bedroom.

42. Monroe, *My Story,* 90–93; Kazan, *Elia Kazan,* 405–06.

43. LB, interview with Terry Wasdyke, August 16, 2009.

44. Bernard, ed., *Bernard of Hollywood's Marilyn,* 11. Salka Viertel, a leader of the Hollywood German-Jewish refugee community, writes about Liesl Frank and her work with refugees in *The Kindness of Strangers* (New York: Holt, Rinehart, and Winston, 1969), 219, 229. Bruno Frank died in 1945. See also Cornelius Schnauber, *Hollywood Haven: Homes and Haunts of*

the European Emigrés and Exiles in Los Angeles (Riverside, Calif.: Ariadne, 1997). The address listed there for Liesl Frank is not the same as the addresses for Natasha Lytess.

According to Donald Wolfe, in *The Assassination of Marilyn Monroe*, 254, Lytess had a photo of Fritzi Massary on her wall. Agent Paul Kohner, who had ties to the European immigrant community, got Lytess her job at Columbia.

45. Beauchamp, *Focus on Fame*, 142; Armand Arburo, "The Power Behind Marilyn Is Her Talented Drama Coach," *Albuquerque Journal*, April 20, 1953 (syndicated column).

46. On Lytess's influence on Marilyn, see Jane Wilkie, interview with Natasha Lytess, in *Confessions of an Ex-Hollywood Fan Magazine Writer*, 172–87; Hank Fardell, "That Soul Doesn't Belong in That Body," *Movie Fan Magazine*, April 1953; Harry Evans, "What Caused Marilyn Monroe?" *Family Circle*, June 1953; Natasha Lytess, "The Private Life of Marilyn Monroe," *Screen World*, November 1953; Jack Wade, "The Two Worlds of Marilyn," November 1954; Natasha Lytess, "Marilyn Owes Me Everything," *Movie Mirror*, May 1957; Alex Joyce, "Marilyn at the Crossroads," *Photoplay*, July 1957.

47. Cassini, *In My Own Fashion*, 184–85.

48. Milton Berle, *Milton Berle: An Autobiography* (New York: Delacorte, 1975), 265–66. Journalist Joe Hyams verified the Berle affair in his interview with DS, in Spoto—AMPAS.

49. James Bacon, *Hollywood Is a Four Letter Town* (New York: Avon, 1977), 133. Hank Messick, *The Beauties and the Beasts: The Mob in Show Business* (New York: McCay, 1973); Norman Zierold, *The Moguls* (New York: Coward-McCann, 1969); Corinne Calvet, *Has Corinne Been a Good Girl?* (New York: St. Martin's, 1988–9) 8–9; LeRoy, *Take One*, 210; Harry Brown, *Kim Novak: Reluctant Goddess* (New York: St. Martin's, 1986), 44.

50. Lester Cowan to Brad Sears, November 5, 1948; Bill Chaikin to Lester Cowan, March 14, 1949, in Lester Cowan—AMPAS.

51. Gavin Lambert, *Natalie Wood: A Life* (New York: Alfred A. Knopf, 2004), 121; Doug McClelland, ed., *Starspeak: Hollywood on Everything* (Boston: Faber and Faber, 1987), 1957.

52. Roberts, "Mimosa."

53. Philippe Halsman, "Three Encounters with a Love Goddess: How A Shy Blonde with a Helpless Look Conquered a Whole World of Maledom," *Dreamgirl*, January 1955.

54. Beauchamp, *Focus on Fame*, 141.

55. Garson Kanin, *Hollywood: Stars and Starlets, Tycoons and Flesh-peddlers* (New York: Viking, 1974), 277; William Bruce, "Meet the New Marilyn Monroe," *Movieland*, November 1954. Graham, *Confessions of a Hollywood Columnist*, 132–33; MZ, interview with Whitey Snyder, in Zolotow—UT.

56. James Haspiel, *Young Marilyn* (London: Smith Gryphon, 1988), 41.

57. Russell Miller, *Bunny: The Real Story of Playboy* (London: Corgi, 1985), 48.

58. Adele Whiteley Fletcher, ". . . So That the Memory of Marilyn Will Linger on," Wagenknecht, ed. *Marilyn*, 81–82.
59. Earl Wilson, "M-m-m-my Marilyn," *Silver Screen*, April 1953.
60. Kanin, *Hollywood*, 319; Crivello, *Fallen Angels*, 248.
61. MZ, interview with Lytess, in Zolotow—UT. See also Michelangelo Capua, *Yul Brynner: A Biography* (Jefferson, N.C.: McFarland, 2006), 65.
62. I follow the account of Zanuck's intentions in Buskin, *Blonde Heat*.
63. Kazan, *Elia Kazan*, 405–06.
64. Devlin, *Relative Intimacy*.
65. Donna Hamilton to Diana McClellan, in McClellan, *The Girls: Sappho Goes to Hollywood* (New York: St. Martin's, 2000), 417; Skolsky, *Don't Get Me Wrong*, 231; AS, interview with Steffi Skolsky Sidney, in AS. LB, interview with Steffi Skolsky Slaver, October 2005. According to Robert LaGuardia, *Monty: A Biography of Montgomery Clift* (New York: Arbor House, 1977), 38, Kazan didn't like homosexuals, which might explain his dislike of Lytess.
66. See William J. Mann, *Behind the Screen: How Gays and Lesbians Shaped Hollywood, 1910–1969* (New York: Viking, 2001); McClellan, *The Girls*; Axel Madsen, *The Sewing Circle: Hollywood's Greatest Secret: Female Stars Who Loved Other Women* (Secaucus, N.J.: Carol, 1995); and Boze Hadleigh, *Hollywood Lesbians* (New York: Barricade, 1994).
67. Kevin Starr, *The Dream Endures: California Enters the 1940s* (New York: Oxford, 1997), 350; and John Baxter, *The Hollywood Exiles* (New York: Taplinger, 1976), 214–30.
68. Earl Wilson, "On Again, Off Again," *New York Post*, December 1954, in NYPL; Truman Capote, "A Beautiful Child," in Capote, *Music for Chameleons* (New York: Random House, 1975), 226.
69. Letters in the Guido Orlando Papers—AMPAS pertain to the Lytess interview, published in European tabloids. They include: Lytess to Orlando, November 23, 1961; Lytess to Rome "Gentlemen," December 16, 1961; David Skory to Orlando, May 23, 1962; Lytess to Orlando, May 30, 1962; Jean Neuncelle, *France-Soir*, to Orlando, May 30, 1962; Terence Feely, editorial director London International Press, to Orlando, July 30, 1962; and Bernard Valery to Orlando, December 26, 1961; January 8, 1962; July 15, 1962; August 20, 1962. A contract with *France-Soir* was signed by Lytess and Orlando as manager of Lytess. The Lytess interview in the Orlando Papers is the one published in *The People*, July 15, 1962. On Valery, see Obit., *New York Times*, June 13, 1984.
70. Orlando published his autobiography as *Confessions of a Scoundrel* (Philadelphia: Winston, 1954).
71. On the affair with Howard Hughes, see Wilson, *Show Business Laid Bare*, 58, and Patricia Lawford Stewart, with Ted Schwartz, *The Peter Lawford Story: Life with the Kennedys, Monroe, and the Rat Pack* (New York: Carroll & Graf, 1998), 153.
72. Skolsky, *Don't Get Me Wrong*, 49.

CHAPTER 6

1. I have reconstructed these events from Miller, *Timebends*, 303–07; Kazan, *Elia Kazan*, 409–12; and relevant biographies and memoirs.
2. The guests are listed in Feldman's date book in his papers at the American Film Institute. The men included Arthur Miller, Pat DiCicco, Elia Kazan, Raymond Hakim, and Jack Warner. The women, all starlets, included Mona Knox, Ruth Lewis, Cheryl Clark, and Diane Cassidy. Marilyn is referred to as "another girl." Marion Marshall turned down an invitation.
3. Miller, *Timebends*, 299.
4. Monroe, *My Story*, 138.
5. Miller, *Timebends*, 307.
6. Sam Shaw, *The Joy of Marilyn: In the Camera Eye* (New York: Exeter, 1979), 22; AV, interview with Shaw, in Villani, "Hold a Good Thought." DS, interview with Sam Shaw, in Spoto—DFI.
7. Karnath, *Sam Shaw*, passim.
8. Sam Shaw, "Memories," in Brambilla, Mercurio, and Petricca, *Marilyn Monroe*, 249–50.
9. LB, interview with Jack Larson, June 2, 2009; LB, interview with Diane Ladd, July 7, 2010; Shelley Winters, *Shelley II*, 68.
10. As Shelley herself admits, she was vague on dates. Thus it's doubtful that Laurence Olivier met Marilyn at her apartment. Olivier went to Hollywood for five months, from July to November 1950, to make *Sister Carrie*. Marilyn was then involved with Johnny Hyde, Natasha Lytess, and Joe Schenck 260–61. See Anthony Holden, *Laurence Olivier* (New York: Atheneum, 1988), 260–62. Dylan Thomas was also in Hollywood during the summer of 1950, not the spring of 1951. See John Malcolm Brinnen, *Dylan Thomas in America: An Intimate Journey* (Boston: Little, Brown, 1995).
11. Winters, *Shelley: Also Known as Shirley*, 295.
12. *Quick Magazine*, June 16, 1962; Winters, *Shelley: Also Known as Shirley*, 292–95; Lucy Freeman, *Why Norma Jean Killed Marilyn Monroe* (Mamaroneck, N.Y.: Hastings House, 1993), 31.
13. She wrote a check to the regents of California on October 5, 1951; *Movie Life* carried a picture of her studying for her UCLA classes on the cover of its November 1952 issue. See also Robert Cahn, "The 1951 Model Blonde," *Collier's*, September 8, 1951. "Notes from a Lecture on Renaissance Art" are in Buchthal and Comment, eds., *Fragments*, 42–43.
14. On Chekhov, I have used Marowitz, *The Other Chekhov*; Michael Chekhov, *On the Technique of Acting* (New York: HarperCollins, 1991), especially the introduction by Mel Gordon; and Richard Brestoff, *The Great Acting Teachers and Their Methods* (Lyme, N.H.: Smith and Kraus, 1995), 63–67. I have written about nineteenth- and early twentieth-century spiritualities in *Finding Fran: History and Memory in the Lives of Two Women* (New York: Columbia University Press, 1998).
15. Stark Young, *Glamour: Essays on the Art of the Theater* (1925; Freeport, N.Y.: Books for Libraries Press, 1971). See also Eva Le Gallienne, *The*

Mystic in the Theatre: Eleonora Duse (New York: Farrar, Straus, & Giroux, 1966).

16. Mabel E. Todd, *The Thinking Body* (1937; Princeton: Princeton Book Company, 1949).

17. Roberts, "Mimosa"; Greenson, "Memoir of Marilyn," 23–24. On Vesalius, see Jerome Tarshis, *Andreas Vesalius: Father of Modern Anatomy* (New York: Dial, 1969).

18. Margot Fonteyn, *Autobiography* (London: Star Books, 1976), 184.

19. Lotte Goslar, *What's So Funny? Sketches from My Life* (Amsterdam: Harwood, 1998), 97, 117–18; Marianna Vogt, "Lotte Goslar: A Clown Between Borders," Ph.D. diss., University of Missouri–Kansas City, 2007.

20. LB, interview with Jack Larson, June 2, 2009; Roberts, "Mimosa." Address book of Army Archerd, *Daily Variety*, March 29, 2010. Larson is best known for playing Jimmy Olsen in the original Superman movie and series. He was Montgomery Clift's last companion.

21. Monroe, *My Story*, 66–69. On Zsa Zsa Gabor, see "Why Women Hate Marilyn Monroe," *Movieland*, October 1952.

22. Philippe Halsman, "Three Encounters with a Love Goddess: How a Shy Blonde with a Helpless Look Conquered a Whole World of Maledom," *Dreamgirl Magazine*, January 1955; Monroe, *My Story*, 72–73.

23. AS, interview with Ralph Casey Shawhan, in AS; Goodman, *The Fifty Year Decline*, 234; Crown, interview with Walter Scott, in Crown, *Marilyn at Twentieth Century–Fox*, 68.

24. Paul Weeks, "Ex-Press Agent Recalls Monroe's Magic Appeal," *Los Angeles Times*, August 7, 1962; Peer J. Oppenheimer, "Body and Soul," *Screen Magazine*, May 1953. Aline Mosby, *Los Angeles Daily News*, August 23, 1952; Edward Halsey, "Strange Career of Marilyn Monroe," *Silver Screen*, August 1955; LB, interview with Michael Selsman, October 25, 2009.

25. Skolsky, *Marilyn*, 42. Merry Lewis, "The Row About Marilyn," *Movie Play*, March 1954. Sheilah Graham, *Hollywood Revisited: A Fiftieth Anniversary Celebration* (New York: St. Martin's, 1985), 114; Graham, *The Rest of the Story* (New York: Coward, McCann, 1964), 158.

26. Henaghan, "My Love Affair with Marilyn Monroe," *Motion Picture*, July 1955; Marilyn Monroe, "What I've Learned from Men," *Movieland*, January 1954; *Quick Magazine*, June 16, 1962; DS, interview with Joe Hyams, in Spoto—AMPAS.

27. Mike Connolly, "Farewell to Marilyn," *Screen Stories*, November 1962. See also Val Holley, *Mike Connolly and the Manly Art of Hollywood Gossip* (Jefferson, N.C.: McFarland, 2003), 6.

28. Steffi Skolsky Slaver granted me an interview to correct what she said were mistakes by earlier biographers in their use of interviews with her. Among those mistakes, she said, was the allegation that her father had given Marilyn barbiturates and amphetamines from Schwab's drugstore. He only recommended doctors to her and was concerned about her drug taking. LB, interview with Steffi Skolsky Slaver, September 14, 2006; Strasberg, *Marilyn and Me*, 11.

29. Alfred O'Malley, "They Cover Hollywood," no citation, 1938, in Skolsky—AMPAS.

30. See Cahn, "The 1951 Model Blonde," and Parsons, *Tell It to Louella*, 223–24; Bernard, *Requiem for Marilyn*, 50.

31. Imogene Collins, "I Want to Be Loved," *Modern Screen*, November 1952, has salary figures.

32. Fyodor Dostoyevsky, *The Brothers Karamazov* (New York: Wadsworth, 2010), 160; LB, interview with Joshua Greene, January 3, 2011.

33. See "Another Big Answer to TV," *People Today*, September 12, 1951.

34. Sam Shaw, "Memories," in Brambilla, Mercurio, and Petricca, *Marilyn Monroe*, 249; Jack Lait, "Broadway and Elsewhere," *Sunday Times Signal*, Zanesville, Ohio (syndicated column), September 2, 1951. Meta and Edie Shaw went on the visit to the Met, and they remember their father providing a running commentary on the art. LB, interview with Edith Shaw Marcus and Meta Shaw Stevens, April 15, 2010.

35. Arnold, *Marilyn Monroe*, 9.

36. Buchthal and Comment, eds., *Fragments*, 43; Marilyn Monroe, "I Live as I Please," *Motion Picture*, June 1953.

37. Rupert Allan, "A Serious Blonde Who Can Act," *Look*, October 23, 1951.

38. Guiles, *Legend*, 205.

39. Reilly, *Hollywood Costume Design by Travilla*, 84.

40. Hank Fardell, "That Soul Doesn't Belong in That Body," *Movie Fan Magazine,* April 1953; LB, interview with Hal Schaefer, June 29, 2008.

41. Winters, *Shelley II*, 47. For a photo of Marilyn with Nick Ray, see "Stuff of Hollywood," *Photoplay*, December 1952. On the brief affair with Brynner, see Strasberg, *Marilyn and Me*, 162–63, and Rock Brynner, *Yul: The Man Who Would Be King* (New York: Simon & Schuster, 1989) 89–90; LB, interview with Joe Naar, December 3, 2008.

42. Doug McClelland, ed., *Starspeak: Hollywood on Everything* (Boston: Faber and Faber, 1987), 202.

43. AS, interview with Nico Minardos, in AS. Patricia Cox confirmed the Minardos involvement to me, June 17, 2010.

44. *New York Mirror*, August 11, 1962.

45. Jane Wilkie, *Confessions of an Ex-Fan Magazine Writer*, 76–77. In 1934, according to Ezra Goodman, in *The Fifty Year Decline*, 77, the studios cut the number of writers on their approved list from three hundred to fifty, keeping on their "white list" only those whose writing what they considered "clean." Once *Confidential*, the first major Hollywood tabloid, appeared in 1952—and by 1955 had a circulation of three million—the "white list" began to break down. See Earl Wilson and Sidney Skolsky, "Marilyn Monroe: Tragedy's Child," *New York Post*, August 12, 1962, Skolsky—AMPAS.

46. "What's Wrong with Sex Appeal?" *Movieland*, January 1952; Ellis Whitfield, "Sex Symbolism and Marilyn Monroe," *Why? The Magazine of Popular Psychology*, June 1953; "Are Budgets Necessary?" *Movieland*, July 1951.

47. Tex Parks, "Lessons I've Learned in Hollywood," *Movieland,* May 1951.
48. Jack Wade, "Too Hot to Handle," *Modern Screen*, March 1952; Sidney Skolsky, "That's Hollywood for You," *Photoplay*, November 1953; Merry Lewis, "The Row About Monroe," *Movie Play*, March 1954; "What's Wrong with Marilyn?" *Movie Life* 1952–54, McCormick—USC; G. D. Sweeney, "MM: The Next Man She'll Marry," *Movie Stars Parade*, February 1956; Curtis Johns, "You've Gotta Stop Kicking This Kid Around," *Movie Fan,* December 1953; Celia Paul, "Marilyn's Hush Romance," *Movie Time,* June 1954; Ben Maddox, "Peeking In on Marilyn as a Housewife," *Screenland Plus TV-Land,* May 1954.
49. Goodman, *The Fifty Year Decline*, 236; John Crosby, "The Men Like Her Fine," *Washington Post*, November 4, 1952; Bob Ruark, syndicated column, August 30, 1952, in SE; Rita Garrison Malloy, "Marilyn, Oh Marilyn," *Motion Picture Magazine,* November 1954; "Who'd Marry Me?" *Modern Screen*, September 1951; "Home Life of a Hollywood Bachelor Girl," *Television and Screen Guide*, August 1951.
50. Daniel Boorstin, *The Image: Pseudo Events in America* (New York: Vintage, 1992), 25.
51. Bernard, *Requiem for Marilyn*, 33; Randall Riese and Neal Hitchens, *The Unabridged Marilyn: Her Life from A to Z* (1987; London: Corgi, 1988), 2; Zolotow, *Marilyn Monroe*, 167.
52. Jack Paar, *P.S. Jack Paar* (New York: Doubleday, 1983), 85; Macdonald Carey, *The Days of My Life* (New York: St. Martin's, 1991), 178.
53. Brown and Barham, *Marilyn: The Last Take*, 375; Riese and Hitchens, *The Unabridged Marilyn*, 229.
54. Edwin Hoyt, interview with June Haver, in Hoyt, *Marilyn: The Tragic Venus* (New York: Duell, Sloan, and Pearce, 1965), 84.
55. Monroe and Miller, "Sex, Theatre and the Intellectual," in Brandon, ed., *Conversations with Henry Brandon*, 186; Powdermaker, *Hollywood: The Dream Factory*, 219–21.
56. Zolotow, *Marilyn Monroe*, 190.
57. Gloria Steinem, "The Woman Who Died too Soon," *Ms.*, August 1972, 38.
58. Zolotow, *Marilyn Monroe*, 74.
59. "Interview with Henry Koster," in Ronald Davis, ed., *Just Making Movies: Company Directors on the Studio System* (Jackson, Miss.: University of Mississippi Press, 2005), 16–20.
60. Bacon, *Hollywood Is a Four Letter Town*, 142; Patrick McGilligan, *Fritz Lang: The Nature of the Beast* (New York: St. Martin's, 1997), 389–94.
61. Zolotow, *Marilyn Monroe*, 176; AV, interview with Rupert Allan, in Villani, "Hold a Good Thought for Me," 79.
62. Marilyn Monroe, "Love Is My Problem," *Silver Screen*, October 1951; Louella Parsons, "Joe and Marilyn Upset Gossips," clipping, in Wilder—AMPAS; Paul Benedict, "How to Solve the Riddle of Marilyn Monroe," *Silver Screen*, August 1957.
63. Lytess, "My Years With Marilyn," in Zolotow—UT; Todd McCarthy, *Howard Hawks: The Grey Fox of Hollywood* (New York: Grove Press,

1997), 494–99; John Kobal, "Howard Hawks," in Kobal, ed. *People Will Talk*, 483–86; Kazan, *Elia Kazan*, 255.

64. Tom Wood, *The Bright Side of Billy Wilder, Primarily* (New York: Doubleday, 1970), 3.

65. John Kobal, interview with Henry Hathaway, in Kobal, ed., *People Will Talk*, 615–17; Henry Hathaway interview, *Hollywood Studio Magazine*, August 1987; Ronald Davis, interview with Hathaway, in Davis, *Just Making Movies*, 149; interview with Henry Hathaway, in CUO; interview with Hathaway in Charles Hamblett, *Who Killed Marilyn Monroe? Or, a Cage to Catch Our Dreams* (London: Leslie Frewin, 1966), 142–44.

66. "Things They Never Told You About Marilyn," *Screen Stars*, November 1954.

67. Joseph Cotten, *Vanity Will Get You Somewhere* (San Francisco: Mercury, 1987), 111.

68. Jean Negulesco, *Things I Did . . . and Things I Think I Did* (New York: Simon & Schuster, 1984), 218, 223.

69. Crown, *Marilyn at Fox*, 142, 147. Mark Logue and Peter Conradi, *The King's Speech* (New York: Sterling, 2010), 42.

70. Holley, *Mike Connolly*, 6. LB, interview with Norman Brokaw, May 3, 2010. See also Morris Engelberg and Marv Schneider, *DiMaggio: Setting the Record Straight* (St. Paul, Minn.: MBI, 2003), 240–41.

71. Marilyn Monroe, "The Men Who Interest Me," *Pageant*, April 1954.

72. Roger Rosenblatt, "A Hero in Deep Center," *Time*, March 22, 1999; Pellegrino D'Acierno, "Italian American Musical Culture," in D'Acierno, ed., *The Italian American Heritage* (New York: Garland, 1999), 425.

73. On Joe DiMaggio, I have especially used Richard Ben Cramer, *Joe DiMaggio: The Hero's Life* (New York: Simon & Schuster, 2001), and Engelberg and Schneider, *DiMaggio*.

74. Gladys Eley to Inez Melson, May 4, 1965, and August 21, 1965; Gladys Eley to the Mother Church (First Church of Christ Scientist), undated, in LB. On journalist Erskine Johnson's discovery of Gladys in Los Angeles, see Erskine Johnson, "Marilyn Monroe's Mystery Mother," *Motion Picture*, September 1952. According to Randy Taraborrelli, Johnny Hyde removed John Eley from Gladys's life when he tried to blackmail Marilyn. But the Goddard family always called him Colonel, and Bebe Goddard contended that Gladys met him in a work program in Portland.

75. My information on John Eley comes from legal documents in RT.

76. Paul Weeks, "Ex-Press Agent Recalls Marilyn's Magic Appeal," *Los Angeles Times*, August 7, 1962.

77. Roberts, "Mimosa."

78. Mel Tormé, *It Wasn't All Velvet: An Autobiography* (New York: Viking, 1988), 162–65.

79. Earl Wilson, "M-m-m-my Marilyn," *Silver Screen*, April 1953.

CHAPTER 7

1. JK, interview with Howard Hawks, in Kobal, *People Will Talk*, 496.
2. Robert Stack, *Straight Shooting* (New York: Macmillan, 1980), 184.
3. Monroe, *My Story*, 134. Maureen Turim argues that Monroe and Russell are partnered in the film to appeal to the common male fantasy of lesbian sex. See Turim, "Gentlemen Consume Blondes," in *Issues in Feminist Film Criticism*, ed. Patricia Erens (Bloomington, Ind.: Indiana University Press, 1990), 101–11.
4. Glenn Loney, *Unsung Genius*; Adrienne L. McLean, "The Thousand Ways There Are to Move: Camp and Oriental Dance in the Hollywood Musicals of Jack Cole," in Matthew Bernstein and Gaylyn Studlar, eds., *Visions of the East: Orientalism in Film* (New Brunswick, N.J.: Rutgers University Press, 1997), 138–145.
5. Larry Billman, in a talk given to the Marilyn Remembered Fan Club, May 26, 2008; LB, interview with George Chakiris, November 26, 1998. Billman, who often danced in Cole's productions, was a dancer in *Let's Make Love*. Chakiris won an Academy Award for his dancing in *West Side Story*.
6. Adele Balkan oral interview, in AMPAS; Del Burnett, interview with Frank Radcliffe, in Burnett, "Marilyn: A Personal Reminiscence," *American Classic Screen*, 1986.
7. Sheilah Graham, *Hollywood Revisited*, 125. AS interview with Billy Wilder, in AS.
8. Sammy Davis Jr., *Hollywood in a Suitcase*, 231; Jane Russell, "Foreword," Belmont, *Marilyn Monroe and the Camera*, 9–10.
9. Jane Russell, *An Autobiography: My Paths and My Detours* (New York: Berkeley, 1986), 9–10.
10. MZ, interview with Jane Russell, in Zolotow—UT.
11. Spoto, *Marilyn Monroe*, 292.
12. Jane Russell, "That Girl Marilyn," pamphlet, Affiliated Magazines, 1954. AS, interview with Jane Russell, in AS.
13. LB, interview with Patricia Traviss, February 27, 2010. According to Pat Traviss, Randy Taraborrelli's tale that Marilyn took liquor to Rockhaven to drink with her mother is inaccurate. Gladys considered drinking a sin, and Marilyn never visited her. Taraborrelli also has Rockhaven mixed up with a nearby sanitarium, Kimball's, which was larger and had more Hollywood-connected patients. Marilyn wasn't present when Grace discussed placing Gladys at Rockhaven, and Gladys was taken to to Norwalk State Mental Hospital before Grace took her to Rockhaven some months later.
14. Bacon, *Hollywood Is a Four Letter Town*, 145.
15. Florabel Muir, *Los Angeles Mirror*, February 10, 1953; "Joan and Marilyn Talk to Louella Parsons," *Modern Screen*, May 1953.
16. Marilyn Monroe, "I Live as I Please," *Motion Picture*, June 1953.
17. Hildegard Johnson, "Hollywood vs. Marilyn Monroe," *Photoplay*, July 1953; Sheilah Graham, "Sex Too Far," *Photoplay*, February 1953; "Monroe and the Wild Life," *Modern Screen*, November 1953. See also *Time*,

November 17, 1952; Robert Heilbroner, "Marilyn Monroe: The Fabulous Story of Hollywood's Biggest Buildup," *Cosmopolitan*, May 1953.

18. Peter Bogdanovich, *Who the Hell's In It?*, 488; Guiles, *Legend*, 216, 222.

19. Nora Johnson, *Flashback: Nora Johnson on Nunnally Johnson* (Garden City, N.Y.: Doubleday, 1979), 81; Jean Negulesco, interview with MZ, in Zolotow—UT.

20. The shape, not the size, of a penis counts for women in interourse, since it relates to the ability to stimulate the clitoris and to reach the G-spot, located not far from the clitoris. LB, interview with Rebecca Kuhn, M.D.

21. Jonathan Van Meter, *The Last Good Time: Skinny D'Amato, the Notorious 500 Club, and the Rise and Fall of Atlantic City* (New York: Crown, 2003), 62–67.

22. Lee Server, *Robert Mitchum* (New York: St. Martin's, 2001), 249–51.

23. Shelley Winters, *Shelley: Also Known as Shirley*, 428–37; talk given by Stanley Rubin to the Marilyn Remembered Fan Club, August 5, 2010; Foster Hirsch, *Otto Preminger, The Man Who Would Be King* (New York: Alfred A. Knopf, 2007).

24. Sidney Skolsky, August 6, 1962, in Skolsky—AMPAS. LB, interview with Noreen Nash, November 10, 2010.

25. Andrea Tone, *The Age of Anxiety: A History of America's Turbulent Affair with Tranquilizers* (New York: Basic, 2009), 56–68.

26. *Los Angeles Herald Examiner*, September 25, 1980, Sheree North clipping file, in AMPAS; Kotsibilis-Davis ed. Greene, *Milton's Marilyn*, 72. On taking pills to parties as presents, see DS, interview with Milton Rudin, in Spoto—AMPAS. On pills as chips in poker games, see LB, interview with Patricia Newcomb, September 25, 2007. On pills being handed out at story conferences, see Kotsibilis-Davis ed. Greene, *Milton's Marilyn*, 72–73. When Maurice Zolotow looked in Marilyn's bathroom medicine cabinet in her studio suite, he found mostly medications for pain, as well as ergotrate to slow down bleeding.

27. Mailer interview with Amy Greene, in Mailer—UT; Strasberg, *Marilyn and Me*, 94.

28. Sammy Davis Jr., *Hollywood in a Suitcase*, 238.

29. Lipton, "Marilyn's the Most!," *Motion Picture*, May 28, 1956, 65. Interview with Roy Craft, in Crown, *Marilyn at Fox*, 35; Sammy Davis Jr., *Hollywood in a Suitcase*, 236–39. LB, interview with John Strasberg, June 11, 2007; Mailer, interview with Amy Greene, in Mailer—UT; AS, interview with Frank Neill, in AS; Neill was a Fox publicist on *Love Nest* and *Gentlemen Prefer Blondes*. According to John Huston, drinking wasn't Marilyn's problem; drugs were. AS, interview with Huston, in AS.

30. JK, interview with Jack Cole, in Kobal, ed., *People Will Talk*, 605.

31. LB, interview with Rosemary Rau-Levine M.D., a specialist in immune system disorders, October 3, 2011; LB, interview with Steffi Skolsky Slaver, Strasberg, *Marilyn and Me*, 113; Amy Greene, Mailer—UT.

32. For more details on Inez, see Anderson and Banner, *MM—Personal*, passim.

33. On Inez's relationship with Enid Knebelkamp, see Gladys Eley to Inez

Melson, August 8, 1965, in LB; see also "Transcript of Inez Melson Interview with Barry Norman, BBC," for *The Hollywood Greats*, in Banner and Anderson, *MM—Personal*, 54.

34. Rita Garrison Malloy, "Marilyn, Oh Marilyn," *Motion Picture Magazine*, November 1954; Mac Phillips, "A Very Pure Person in a Very Impure World," June 1, 1965, in Starr—ASU.

35. Mailer, interview with Amy Greene, in Mailer—UT; "Milton Greene," *B & W: Black and White Magazine*, Spring 1949.

36. "Milton Greene," in Mrs. Joe DiMaggio, "The Men Who Interest Me," *Pageant*, April 1954. Greene and Greene, *But That's Another Story*, 45.

37. Milton described the affair in his interview with Mailer, in Mailer—UT.

38. Negulesco, *Things I Did*, 222.

39. See William Barbour, "Why Joe Let Her Go," *Modern Screen*, January 1955.

40. Crivello, *Fallen Angels*, 258.

41. Aubrey Solomon, *Twentieth Century–Fox* (Metuchen, N.J.: Scarecrow Press, 1988), 64–88.

42. Elsie Lee, "Why Women Love Marilyn Monroe," *Screenland Plus TV-Land*, July 1954.

43. AP wire service, January 29, 1954, in SE.

44. United Press wire service, September 15, 1952, in SE.

45. "400 GIs Stampede at Sight of Marilyn Monroe," *Los Angeles Times*, February 18, 1954; C. Robert Jennings, "The Strange Case of Marilyn Monroe vs. the U.S. Army," *Los Angeles Magazine*, August 1966.

46. AS, interview with Henry Rosenfeld, in AS; AS, interview with Gladys Whitten, in AS.

47. Mrs. Joe DiMaggio, "The Men Who Interest Me," *Pageant*, April 1954; LB, interview with Hal Schaefer, June 29, 2008; AS, interview with Hal Schaefer, in AS; DS, interview with Hal Schaefer, in Spoto—AMPAS.

48. Negulesco, *Things I Did*, 224.

49. Amy Greene and Joshua Greene, eds., *But That's Another Story*, 174.

50. Shaw, *Joy of Marilyn*, 76; LB, interview with Gloria Romanoff, December 13, 2008; Vivien Brown, "What'll It Be: Curves or Straightaway?: A New U.S. Woman is Emerging," *Oakland Tribune*, January 3, 1954 (syndicated column).

51. Ralph Roberts, "Mimosa."

52. Mailer, interview with Milton Greene, in Mailer—UT.

53. For a photo of Joe and Marilyn boarding the airplane, see Joseph Bannon, Susan McKinney, and Joanna Wright, eds., *Joe DiMaggio: An American Icon* (New York: Daily News, 2000), 189.

54. Stacy Eubank Collection.

55. Skolsky, *Don't Get Me Wrong*, 22; reporters were aware that Marilyn was ambivalent about Joe. See William Barbour, "Why Joe Let Her Go," *Modern Screen*, January 1955; and Henaghan, "My Romance with Marilyn Monroe."

56. Richard Baer, *I Don't Drop Names Like Marilyn Monroe Just to Sell Books: A Memoir* (New York: iUniverse, 2005), 5–6; AS, interview with Amy Greene, in AS.

57. AS, interview with Sheila Stewart, in AS.

58. "*Life* Goes to a Party," *Life*, November 29, 1954.

59. Jerry Lewis (and James Kaplan), *Dean & Me: A Love Story* (New York: Doubleday, 2005), 224–26. Sammy Davis Jr., *Hollywood in a Suitcase*, 230.

60. Tormé, *It Wasn't All Velvet*, 165–66, 226.

61. Donald Bogle, *Dorothy Dandridge: A Biography* (New York: Amistad, 1997), 256; LB, interview with Audrey Franklin, November 5, 2008. Franklin was Ella Fitzgerald's business manager for twenty-seven years.

62. Mike Boehm, "North's Touches with Stardom," *Los Angeles Times*, January 3, 2000.

63. Samuel Bernstein, *Mr. Confidential: The Man, His Magazine, & the Movieland Massacre That Changed Hollywood Forever* (New York: Walford, 2006).

64. McClellan, *The Girls*, 366.

65. Talk given by Stanley Rubin to the Marilyn Remembered Fan Club, August 5, 2010; *Los Angeles Daily Mirror*, March 10, 1953; Louella Parsons, "Love Can Wait," *Sunday Pictorial Review*, *Boston Globe*, May 31, 1953.

66. In going through the Marilyn Monroe papers in the Hecht files at the Newberry Library in Chicago, I found many items overlooked by previous Marilyn biographers. The papers contain a draft manuscript of the autobiography and notes that Hecht took during the interviews with Marilyn in his own hand. The papers also include letters to publishers and lawyers about the projected memoir. Hecht's secretary, Nanette Herberveux, transcribed the interviews in stenographic notes as Hecht was doing them with Marilyn, but those notes have been lost.

67. See William MacAdams, *Ben Hecht: The Man Behind the Legend* (New York: Scribner, 1990); Doug Fetherling, *The Five Lives of Ben Hecht* (Toronto: Lester and Orpen, 1977): Florence Koven, *Ben Hecht Story & News* vol. 3, 2001.

68. Ben Hecht to Loyd Wright, May 19, 1954, in Hecht–NL.

69. DS, interview with Lucille Ryman, in Spoto—AMPAS; *People Today*, March 24, 1954.

70. Ben Hecht to Ken McCormack, late spring 1954; Rose Hecht to Loyd Wright, June 2; 1954, Rose Hecht to Greg Bautzer, September 23, 1962, in Hecht—NL; Hedda Hopper in *Los Angeles Times*, June 15, 1954.

71. *National Police Gazette*, autumn 1954; Erskine Johnson, "Overheard in Hollywood," *Motion Picture*, October 1954; "Too Hot to Handle," *Movieland*, December 1954.

72. Ben Hecht to Jacques Chambrun, April 14, 1954, in Hecht—NL.

73. Alice Finletter, "Don't Call Me a Dumb Blonde," *Modern Screen*, April 1955; Judith Martin, "A Tug-of-War Hitched to Marilyn Monroe's Star," *Washington Post*, May 8, 1954, clipping, in Mailer—UT.

CHAPTER 8

1. For the new use of the word "glamour" and the confusion over it among photographers, see "Round Table on Glamor," *Infinity*, October 1959.

2. On the stigma against bleached blonde hair, see Barnaby Conrad, *The Blonde: A Celebration of the Golden Era from Harlow to Monroe* (San Francisco: Chronicle, 1979).

3. Gore Vidal, *Palimpsest: A Memoir* (New York: Penguin, 1995), 284.

4. Thomas Hine, *Populuxe* (New York: Alfred A. Knopf, 1987), 11–12; Charles Phoenix, *Southern California in the 1950s* (Santa Monica: Angel City Press, 2001); Christopher Finch, *Highways to Heaven: The Auto Biography of America* (New York: HarperCollins, 1992), 212.

5. Martina Duttman and Friederike Schneider, eds., *Morris Lapidus: Architect of the American Dream* (Basel, Switzerland: Birkhäuser Verlag, 1992); Chris Nichols, *The Leisure Architecture of Wayne McAllister* (Salt Lake City: Gibbs Smith, 2007).

6. "To Aristophanes and Back," *Time*, May 14, 1956.

7. Marline Otte, *Jewish Identities in German Popular Entertainment, 1890–1933* (Cambridge, Eng.: Cambridge University Press, 2006), 236.

8. Rowland Barber, *The Night They Raided Minsky's: A Fanciful Expedition to the Lost Atlantis of Show Business* (New York: Avon, 1960), 199.

9. Gypsy Rose Lee, cited by Louella Parsons, *New York Examiner*, May 28, 1944, in Gypsy Rose Lee Papers, in NYPL.

10. Loney, *Unsung Genius*, 211.

11. On the history of the "dumb blonde," see Shirley Staples, *Male-Female Comedy Teams in American Vaudeville, 1865–1932* (Ann Arbor, Mich.: UMI Research Press, 1984); Nils T. Granlund, *Blondes, Brunettes, and Bullets* (New York: David McKay, 1957).

12. Gary Carey, *Anita Loos: A Biography* (New York: Alfred A. Knopf, 1988).

13. For comparisons to West, see Curtis Johns, "You've Gotta Stop Kicking This Kid Around," *Movie Fan*, December 1951; "Earl Wilson Reports on Conversation with Cary Grant," July 2, 1952; Hal Boyle, "Curves Still Paying Off," August 31, 1952, AP wire service, in SE; and Earl Wilson, "On and Off," 1954, unsourced clipping, in NYPL. Cary Grant was in several Mae West films and was a star of *Monkey Business*. Cecil Beaton, *The Face of the World: An International Scrapbook of People and Places* (New York: John Day, 1959), 183.

14. On Marie Wilson I have used the AMPAS clipping collection. Gary Carey, *Judy Holliday: An Intimate Life Story* (New York: Seaview, 1982), 62.

15. Philip Scheuer, "Billy Wilder Tells Plans for Marilyn," *Los Angeles Times*, February 10, 1958; Helen Lawrenson, "Inside Women," *Cavalier*, March 1960. "Beulah, Peel Me a Grape," *Show Magazine*, February 1955. Weatherby, *Conversations with Marilyn*, 148.

16. LB, interview with John Strasberg, June 11, 2007; Carroll Baker, *Baby Doll: An Autobiography* (New York: Arbor House, 1983), 145–47.

17. Goodman, *The Fifty Year Decline*, 235.

18. Jim Henaghan, "Marilyn Monroe, Loveable Fake," *Motion Picture*, November 1953: "Marilyn didn't think she was beautiful"; AV, interview with Billy Travilla, in Villani, "Hold a Good Thought for Me"; Strasberg, *Marilyn and Me*, 117; MZ, interview with Whitey Snyder, in Zolotow—UT; LB, interview with James Haspiel, May 2009.

19. MZ, interview with Whitey Snyder, in Zolotow—UT.

20. *Austin Daily Herald*, Austin, Minnesota, in SE; Crown, *Marilyn at Fox*, 69; Guilaroff, *Crowning Glory: Reflections on Hollywood's Major Confidant* (Los Angeles: General Publishing Group, 1996), 150–52; MZ, interview with Gladys Rasmussen, in Zolotow—UT.

21. MZ, interview with Gladys Rasmussen, in Zolotow—UT; Simone Signoret, *Nostalgia Isn't What It Used to Be* (New York: Harper & Row, 1978), 286.

22. Patty Fox, *Star Style: Hollywood Legends as Fashion Icons* (Santa Monica, Calif.: Angel City, 1995), 86–97.

23. *Movieland*, January 1954.

24. Edith Head, AP interview, 1950, in SE; Shelley Winters, *Shelley: Also Known as Shirley*, 117.

25. Adele Balkan, oral interview, oral interview collection AMPAS.

26. Marilyn Monroe, "Am I Too Daring?" *Modern Screen*, July 1952.

27. Riese and Hitchens, *The Unabridged Marilyn*, 255. As a graduate student in New York on a limited budget, I bought clothes at Jax. They weren't hugely expensive.

28. Andrew Tobias, *Fire and Ice: The Story of Charles Revlon—the Man Who Built the Revlon Empire* (New York: William Morrow, 1976), 119.

29. Elaine Rounds, "Thirty Years of Hollywood Lip Lines," *Motion Picture*, February 1954; Eve Arnold, *Marilyn: An Appreciation*, 17. Henry Brandon, ed., *Conversations with Henry Brandon*, 185; Lydia Lane, *Los Angeles Times*, October 9, 1960.

30. Brandon French, *On the Verge of Revolt: Women in American Films of the Fifties* (New York: Ungar, 1978).

31. Jessamyn Neuhaus, "The Importance of Being Orgasmic: Sexuality, Gender, and Marital Sex Manuals in the United States 1920–1963," *Journal of the History of Sexuality* 9 (October 2000): 447–73.

32. Norman Mailer, *Marilyn: A Biography* (New York: Putnam, 1973), 15. Mailer's comparison between sex technique and playing a violin is taken from Havelock Ellis, "The Art of Love" in Ellis, *Studies in the Psychology of Sex* (New York: Putnam, 1933).

33. Barris, *Marilyn in Her Own Words*, 32; Strasberg, *Marilyn and Me*, 217.

34. Richard Foster, *The Real Bettie Page: The Truth About the Queen of the Pinups* (New York: Kensington, 1997), 55; JK, interview with Jack Cole, in Kobal, *People Will Talk*, 593.

35. Wagenknecht, ed., *Marilyn Monroe*, 5; Pete Martin, *Will Acting Spoil Marilyn Monroe?* (Garden City, N.Y.: Doubleday, 1956), 32.

36. Richard Dyer first connected Marilyn to "whiteness" in *White* (New York: Routledge, 1997). For a fuller discussion of this issue, see my essay "The Creature from the Black Lagoon: Marilyn Monroe and Whiteness," *Cinema Journal* (Summer 2008): 4–29.

37. On the "parade of blondes" as an emblem of racism, see Steven Cohan, *Masked Men: Masculinity and Movies in the 1950s* (Bloomington, Ind.: Indiana University Press, 1997), 12–15.

38. Rosten, *Marilyn: An Untold Story*; Weatherby, *Conversations with Marilyn*. For the reporting on Marilyn in African-American newspapers, I read through such newspapers on www.proquest.com including the *Chicago Defender, Los Angeles Sentinel*, and *New York Amsterdam Times*. LB, interview with Larry Grant, October 15, 2009.

39. LB, interview with Jay Kanter, October 3, 2007; Weatherby, *Conversations with Marilyn*, 121.

40. Diane Negra, *Off-White Hollywood: American Culture and Ethnic Female Stardom* (London and New York: Routledge, 2001); Jonathan Freedman, "Miller, Monroe, and the Remaking of Jewish Masculinity," in Enoch Brater, ed., *Arthur Miller's America: Theater and Culture in a Time of Change* (Ann Arbor, Mich.: University of Michigan Press, 2005), 135–52.

41. Monroe, *My Story*, 118–21. See Hildegard Knef, *The Gift Horse: Report on a Life* (New York: McGraw-Hill, 1971), 254.

42. Norma Barzman, *The Red and the Blacklist: The Intimate Memoir of a Hollywood Expatriate* (New York: Nation Books, 2003), 96–99.

43. According to Frederick Vanderbilt Field, the Hollywood Twenty was a term derived from the original Hollywood Ten, who had moved to Mexico after serving jail terms, expanded to include ten others convicted of having ties to communism. Not all of the second group had worked in the film industry, but they had joined the initial group in Mexico.

44. Summers, *Goddess*, 30.

45. Bacon, *Hollywood Is a Four Letter Town*, 143–44.

46. *The Personal Property of Marilyn Monroe* (New York: Christie's, 1999), 346; Skolsky, *Don't Get Me Wrong*, 44; MZ, interview with Jane Russell, in Zolotow—UT; Shaw, *The Joy of Marilyn*, 66.

47. "Marilyn Monroe's Secret Tragedy," *Screen Stories*, February 1961. Edith Sitwell, *Taken Care Of: The Autobiography*, in Wagenknecht, ed., *Marilyn Monroe*, 56 (excerpt from original); Max Lerner, "What Marilyn Reads," *New York Post*, October 27, 1954. She told Lerner she was reading Steiner.

48. Strasberg, *Marilyn and Me*, 79; MZ, interview with Cameron Mitchell, in Zolotow—UT; AS, interview with Peggy Fleury, in AS.

49. Max Lerner, "What Marilyn Reads," *New York Post*, October 27, 1954. William Bruce, "Meet the New Marilyn," *Movieland*, December 1954; clippings from March 7, 1952, March 13, 1954, in SE; "Marilyn Doesn't Believe in Hiding Things," *Screenland*, August 1952. On Rilke's influence on Marilyn, see also Belmont, "Interview with Marilyn Monroe," in *Marilyn Monroe and the Camera*, 19; AV, interview with Rupert Allan, in Villani, "Hold a Good Thought," 25.

50. On Rilke, I have used Rainer Maria Rilke, *Letters to a Young Poet* (LaVerne, Tenn: BN Publishing, 2010); Volker Dürr, *Rainer Maria Rilke: The Poet's Trajectory* (New York: Peter Lang, 2006); Karen Leeder and Robert Vilain, eds., *The Cambridge Companion to Rilke* (Cambridge, Eng.: Cambridge University Press, 2010). On Wolfe, I have used Leo Gurko, *Thomas Wolfe: Beyond the Romantic Ego* (New York: Thomas Y. Crowell, 1973); and Robert Taylor Ensign, *Lean Down Your Ear Upon the Earth, and Lis-*

ten: Thomas Wolfe's Greener Modernism (Columbia, S.C.: University of South Carolina Press, 2003).

51. See Nathan G. Hale Jr., *The Rise and Crisis of Psychoanalysis in the United States: Freud and the Americans, 1917–1985* (New York: Oxford University Press, 1999); and Janet Walker, *Couching Resistance* (Minneapolis: University of Minnesota Press, 1993).

52. "The Explorer," *Time*, April 23, 1956.

53. See Sigmund Freud, *The Interpretation of Dreams*, trans. A. A. Brill (New York: Modern Library, 1938), 188–89.

54. On Marilyn's therapy with Anna Freud, see Detlef Berthelsen, *La Famille Freud au jour le jour: Souvenirs de Paula Fichtl* (Paris: Presses Universitaires de France, 1987), 154–60.

55. Eunice Murray and Rose Shade, *Marilyn: The Last Months* (New York: Pyramid Books, 1975), 39; Jack Wade, "Too Hot to Handle," *Modern Screen*, March 1952; James Goode, *The Story of the Misfits* (Indianapolis: Bobbs-Merrill, 1963), 180.

56. Negulesco, *Things I Did*, 220; Miller, *Timebends*, 366; Bernard, *Requiem for Marilyn*, 24; Van Meter, *The Last Good Time*, 134.

57. Marilyn Monroe, "What's Wrong with Sex Appeal?" *Movieland*, 1952; *Sir*, October 1956.

58. Bacon, *Hollywood Is a Four Letter Town*, 148.

59. Mailer, interview with Milton Greene, in Mailer—UT; AS, interview with Billy Travilla, in AS. Once, when she was in her apartment giving telephone interviews, she stripped in the presence of publicist Joe Wolhandler and asked him why he had never made a pass at her.

60. JK, interview with George Hurrell, in Kobal, *People Will Talk*, 266.

61. Strasberg, *Marilyn and Me*, 55–57; Roberts, in "Mimosa."

62. Gavin Lambert, ed. *On Cukor* (New York: Rizzoli, 2000), 275–80; AS, interview with Robert Mitchum, in AS.

63. Engelberg and Schneider, *DiMaggio*, 259; Shaw, *The Joy of Marilyn*; Wilson, *Show Business Laid Bare*, 67.

64. Arnold, *Marilyn Monroe*, 48.

65. Julia Paul, "Too Much Fire," *Motion Picture*, March 1953; Morton Miller, "My Moments with Marilyn: P.S. Arthur Was There, Too," *Esquire*, June 1959.

66. Dorothy Manning, "The Woman and the Legend," *Photoplay*, September 1957.

67. Patricia Vettel-Becker, *Shooting from the Hip: Photography, Masculinity, and Postwar America* (Minneapolis: University of Minnesota Press, 1994); Weatherby, *Conversations with Marilyn*, 168.

68. Richard Avedon, May 28, 1958, in SE.

69. Greene and Greene, *But That's Another Story*, 164.

70. Eve Arnold, *Marilyn Monroe*, 43.

71. Diana Vreeland, with Christopher Hemphill, *Allure* (Garden City, N.Y.: Doubleday, 1980), 142; Joe Hyams "Interview with Marilyn Monroe," *American Weekly*, December 11, 1960.

72. Samuel L. Leiter, "From Gay to Gei: The Onnagata and the Creation of Ka-
     buki's Female Characters," in Leiter, ed., *A Kabuki Reader: History and
     Performance* (London: M. E. Sharpe, 2002), 211–29. I am grateful to Jona-
     than Reynolds, a professor of art history at the University of Southern Cali-
     fornia and an expert in Japanese art and design, for identifying the wall
     hanging for me.
73. Peter Conrad, "Beaton in Brilliantia," in Terence Pepper, *Beaton Portraits*
     (New Haven, Conn.: Yale University Press, 2004) 58–75.
74. Cecil Beaton, *The Face of the World: An International Scrapbook of People
     and Places* (New York: John Day, 1957), 183–84.

CHAPTER 9

 1. *Screen Life*, March 1955.
 2. Fleur Cowles, "Marilyn Monroe: How She Took London," in Cowles, *Friends
     & Memories* (New York: Reynal and William Morrow, 1978), 188–90.
 3. AS, interview with Eli Wallach, in AS.
 4. Clifton Webb, "You Really Don't Know Marilyn Monroe," interview with
     Ernie Player, *Picturegoer*, 1955.
 5. Joshua Greene ed., *Milton's Marilyn*, 40.
 6. On Norell, I have used Sarah Tomlinson Lee, ed., *American Fashion* (New
     York: Quadrangle, 1975), 349–58. On Moore, see Virginia Pope, "Patterns
     of the Times: American Designer Series: John Moore," *New York Times*,
     April 8, 1954, 22.
 7. See also Dorothy Kilgallen, "Voice of Broadway," January 10, 1956, on
     Prince Rainier's approach to Marilyn.
 8. Louella Parsons, *Washington Post*, March 8, 1956, clipping, in NYPL; Earl
     Wilson, "This Is a New Marilyn," *Movie World*, June 1956; Joe Hymans,
     "This Is Hollywood," *New York Herald Tribune*, November 22, 1956. See
     also Alice Finletter, *Modern Screen*, April 1955; Edward Halsey, "Strange
     Case of Marilyn Monroe," *Silver Screen*, August 1955.
 9. Fragments of the play are in Arthur's notebooks, in Miller—UT.
10. Amy Greene's account of Marilyn and Arthur's affair is detailed and con-
     vincing, superceding previous accounts that date it to June 1955 and iden-
     tify either Sam Shaw or Paula Strasberg as the go-between in reintroducing
     them. They seem to have been in contact before Marilyn left Hollywood.
     The new dating of their meeting in New York doesn't negate the later
     meeting with Norman Rosten.
11. Kazan, *Elia Kazan*, 472.
12. Norman Mailer, interview with Amy Greene, in Mailer—UT; Reba and Bon-
     nie Churchill, "Marilyn Monroe—Pilgrim's Progress," *Motion Picture*, June
     1956; Barbara Leaming, *Marilyn Monroe* (New York: Crown, 1998), 163.
13. AS, interview with Amy Greene, in AS.
14. INS News Service, February 22, 1955, in SE; Betty Randolph, *Movie Show*,
     1955, clipping, in NYPL.

15. On the Actors Studio I have used Foster Hirsch, *A Method to Their Madness* (New York: Da Capo, 2002); John Strasberg, *Accidentally on Purpose* (New York: Applause, 1996); Brestoff, *The Great Acting Teachers and Their Methods*; Steve Vineberg, *Method Actors: Three Generations of American Acting Style* (New York: Schirmer, 1991); Cindy Adams, *Lee Strasberg: The Imperfect Genius of the Actors Studio* (New York: Doubleday, 1980); and Edward Dwight Easty, *On Method Acting* (New York: House of Collectibles, 1966).

16. Devlin, *Relative Intimacy*, 38–47.

17. Strasberg, *Bittersweet*, 20, 26; Adams, *Lee Strasberg*, 207.

18. Farley Granger, *Include Me Out: My Life from Goldwyn to Broadway* (New York: St. Martin's, 2007), 115; Kazan, *Elia Kazan*, 539; Marlon Brando, with Robert Lindsey, *Songs My Mother Taught Me* (New York: Random House, 1994), 85.

19. Louis Gossett Jr. and Phyllis Karas, *An Actor and a Gentleman* (Hoboken, N.J.: John Wiley & Sons, 2010), 76.

20. Strasberg, *Marilyn and Me*, 179.

21. Elaine Dundy, *Life Itself!* (London: Virago, 2001), 162–63.

22. "Who Will Be Her Next Husband?" *Movie Star Parade*, February 1956, in SE.

23. AS, interview with Eli Wallach, in AS.

24. Shaw, *Joy of Marilyn*, opposite page 174.

25. Gloria Vanderbilt, *It Seemed Important at the Time* (New York: Simon & Schuster, 2004), 93.

26. AV, interview with Norman Rosten, in Villani, "Hold a Good Thought for Me," 70, 146.

27. Rosten, *Marilyn: An Untold Story*, 23.

28. Ibid., 57.

29. LB, interview with Patricia Rosten, March 12, 2008.

30. "What Really Happened When They Were Filming *The Misfits*?" *Screen Stories*, May 1961.

31. LB, interview with John Strasberg, June 11, 2007.

32. Roberts, "Mimosa"; Buchthal and Comment, eds., *Fragments*, 79–81.

33. Ibid.

34. *Fire Island Press*, July 9, 1955, clipping, in Mailer—UT; Strasberg, *Marilyn and Me*, 49.

35. Strasberg, *Marilyn and Me*, 59.

36. *Waco Tribune-Herald*, Waco, Texas, August 7, 1955; Arnold, *Marilyn Monroe*, 49–62.

37. Arnold, *Marilyn Monroe*, 51.

38. Kazan, *Elia Kazan*, 539.

39. James Kaplan, "Miller's Crossing," *Vanity Fair*, November 1991; LB, interview with Lawrence Schiller, May 16, 2010. Miller, *Timebends*, 359.

40. Strasberg, *Marilyn and Me*, 73; Cowles, "Marilyn Monroe," 191.

41. Earl Wilson, "This Is a New Marilyn," *Movie World*, June 1953; Bob Willet, "Marilyn Monroe: Why I Love My Husband," *Liberty*, March 1959.

42. LB, interview with Joshua Greene, January 3, 2012.

43. Laurence Olivier, *Confessions of an Actor: An Autobiography* (New York: Simon & Schuster, 1982), 206.
44. Eugene O'Neill, *Anna Christie*, in *The Plays of Eugene O'Neill* (New York: Random House, 1954), 18. JK interview with Kim Stanley, Kobal, *People will Talk*.
45. Correspondence between Spyros Skouras and Darryl Zanuck, in Skouras Papers—SU.
46. *Look*, May 29, 1956.
47. Joshua Logan, *Movies, Real People, and Me* (New York: Delacorte, 1978), 38–42.
48. Mailer, interview with Amy and Milton Greene, in Mailer—UT.
49. Fred Guiles, interview with Joshua Logan, in Guiles, *Legend*, 287; Susan Strasberg, *Marilyn and Me*, 43–56; Carl Rollyson, interview with Fred Guiles, in Rollyson, *Marilyn Monroe*, 101–05.
50. LB, interview with Don Murray, June 26, 2010.
51. Strasberg, *Marilyn and Me*, 216.
52. Guiles, interview with Joshua Logan, in Guiles, *Legend*, 287; "Can Marilyn Really Act?" *New York Herald Tribune*, August 25, 1956.
53. DS, interview with Susan Strasberg, in Spoto—AMPAS.
54. Strasberg, *Marilyn and Me*, 102.
55. Simone Signoret, *Nostalgia Isn't What It Used to Be*, 290–91.
56. Interview, Mrs. Gittel Miller, July 9, 1956, *Jewish Daily Forward*, in Monroe file, NYPL. Martin Gottfried, interview with Merle Debuskey, Gottfried, *Arthur Miller: His Life and Words* (New York: Da Capo, 2003), 312. On Goldburg's unpublished memoir, see Joysa Winter, "Marilyn Monroe Was a Sincere Convert to Judaism," *Philadelphia Judaism Examiner*, March 6, 2010; on Marilyn's friendship with Goldburg, see Rabbi Robert E. Goldburg to Marilyn, September 29, 1961. Letter sold at auction, Bonhams and Butterfields, December 20, 2009.
57. Greene and Greene, eds., *But That's Another Story*, 178.

CHAPTER 10

1. Marjorie Peabody, "The Woman Arthur Miller Walked Out On When He Married Marilyn Monroe," *Photoplay*, February 1961.
2. Miller, *Timebends*, 128–9.
3. Ibid., 35, 3, 18.
4. Robert Ajemian, interview with Arthur Miller, *Time*, April 1956.
5. Miller, *Timebends*, 366, 381.
6. Screenplay for *After the Fall*, in Miller UT.
7. "Rejects for Second Typing of Act I, *Fall*," Miller UT.
8. Miracle, *My Sister Marilyn*, 138.
9. Maury Allen, interview with Norman Rosten, in Allen, *Where Have You Gone, Joe DiMaggio: The Story of America's Last Hero* (New York: Signet, 1975), 162.

10. Miller, *Timebends*, 413.
11. Zolotow, *Marilyn Monroe*, 306–08; Strasberg, *Marilyn and Me*, 171.
12. Fleur Cowles, "Marilyn Monroe: How She Took London," in Cowles, *Friends & Memories*, 192.
13. Miller, *Timebends*, 425.
14. On the filming of *The Prince and the Showgirl*, I have used Mailer, interview with Milton and Amy Greene, in Mailer—UT; Colin Clark, *The Prince, the Showgirl, and Me*; Kotsibilis-Davis, ed. Greene, *Milton's Marilyn*; Jack Cardiff, *Magic Hour* (London: Faber and Faber, 1996); and Fleur Cowles, "Marilyn Monroe: How She Took London," in Cowles *Friends & Memories*; and relevant Monroe biographies.
15. Miller, *Timebends*, 421.
16. Weatherby, *Conversations with Marilyn*, 84.
17. Jack Cardiff, *Magic Hour*, 207. I have also relied on Stephanie Morgan, "The Prince and the Showgirl: The Role That Turned Marilyn Upside Down," senior research paper, University of Southern California, Fall 2011. Morgan read the production files on the film in the Warner Brothers Archives at USC.
18. Gene Sheppard, *Hollywood Studio Magazine*, August 1987.
19. Cf. Bacon, *Hollywood Is a Four Letter Town*, 142.
20. I follow the version of the note in Roberts, "Mimosa."
21. Roberts, "Mimosa."
22. Clark, *The Prince, the Showgirl, and Me*, 114.
23. Sammy Davis Jr., *Hollywood in a Suitcase*, 238.
24. Ibid., 106; Robert J. Levin, "Marilyn Monroe's Marriage," *Redbook*, February 1958.
25. Laurence Olivier to Radie Harris, September 18, 1956, in Laurence Olivier Papers, in BL.
26. Patricia Rosten, statement, SE.
27. In *The Genius and the Goddess*, Jeffrey Meyers attacks Marilyn and glorifies Arthur. Among other problems, he is inaccurate on Marilyn's life in New York, partly because he relies on discredited sources, especially Lena Pepitone's memoir. Meyers, *The Genius and the Goddess* (London: Hutchinson, 2009). Interview with George Belmont, *Marilyn Monroe and the Camera*.
28. Roger G. Taylor, *Marilyn in Art* (Salem, N.H.: Salem House, 1954), n.p.
29. AP wire service story, May 28, 1958, in SE; Arthur Miller, ms. statement about Marilyn, in LB.
30. LB, interview with Patricia Rosten, March 12, 2008.
31. Flora Rheta Schreiber, "Remembrance of Marilyn," in Wagenknecht, ed., *Marilyn Monroe*, 48; Rosten, *Marilyn: An Untold Story*, 52; Herbert Kahn, "I Dressed Marilyn Monroe," *Hollywood Screen Parade*, January 1958.
32. Telegram, Warner Brothers to MMP, May 24, 1957; typed copy of statement to Warner Brothers in reply by Marilyn Monroe, in LB.
33. See Morgan, "The Prince and the Showgirl."
34. Olie and Joe Rauh, as told to Harriet Lyons, "The Time That Marilyn Monroe Hid Out at Our House," *Ms.*, August 1983.

35. The story of these negotiations is contained in letters and memos in the Marilyn Monroe file in the Fox Legal Papers at UCLA. See Lew Schreiber to Frank Ferguson, December 31, 1957; Frank Ferguson to Harry McIntyre, January 14, 1958; Robert Montgomery to Frank Ferguson, January 16, 1958; and Lew Schreiber to Frank Ferguson, January 21, 1958.
36. Strasberg, *Marilyn and Me*, 197.
37. See receipt for flowers, dated June 30, in Banner and Anderson, *MM— Personal*, 218.
38. Rosten, *Marilyn: An Untold Story*, 73.
39. See Chapter 11, note 39.
40. AS, interview with Robert Josephy, in AS; AS, interview with Olive Simpson, secretary for John Diebold, in AS.
41. Allan Seagar to Maurice Zolotow, Nov. 19, 1950, Zolotow—UT.
42. Banner and Anderson, *MM—Personal*, 63.
43. Carl Rollyson, interview with Rupert Allan, in Rollyson, *Marilyn Monroe*, 148; Walter Wagner, interview with Jack Lemmon, in Wagner, ed., *You Must Remember This* (New York: Putnam's, 1978), 303.
44. Jerome Delamater, interview with Jack Cole, in Delamater, *Dance in the Hollywood Musical* (Ann Arbor, Mich.: UMI, 1981), 197–200; talk delivered by Barbara Diamond to Marilyn Remembered Fan Club, February 18, 2001. Transcript contained in SLIH (Some Like It Hot) German Fan Club Newsletter, in GS.
45. MZ, interview with anonymous press agent on *Some Like It Hot*, in Zolotow—UT.
46. Copies of these letters are courtesy of Stacy Eubank.
47. The telegrams are in Wilder—AMPAS.
48. AS, interview with Leon Krohn, in AS; AS, interview with Henry Weinstein, in AS.
49. Rosten, *Marilyn: An Untold Story*, 43.
50. Arthur Miller, "My Wife Marilyn," in "Fabled Enchantresses," *Life*, December 22, 1958.
51. Roberts, in "Mimosa."
52. *A Lost Lady* is the story of a Nebraska woman coping with the new post–Civil War era. It foreshadows central themes in Thomas Wolfe's work.
53. Clipping, Salisbury, North Carolina, newspaper, Ralph Roberts Papers, n.d., in possession of Hap Roberts, Salisbury, N.C. To describe Salisbury's architecture, I have drawn on my tour of the city, conversations with Hap Roberts, and on David Ford Hood, *The Architecture of Rowan County* (Salisbury, N.C.: Historic Salisbury Foundation, 2000).

CHAPTER 11

1. For memos about Stengel's incompetence, see Banner and Anderson, *MM—Personal*, 290–91. Lena Pepitone, Marilyn's cook and maid in New York for several years, made similar allegations in her book, *Marilyn Mon-*

roe Confidential: An Intimate Personal Account (New York: Simon & Schuster, 1979), but even Stengel dismissed Pepitone's book as a fabrication. See AS, interview with Marjorie Stengel, in AS.

2. On their attendance at Metropolitan Opera productions in 1959, see newspaper clippings, SE. Patricia Rosten Filan possesses a program for *Wozzeck*, signed to Norman Rosten from Marilyn.

3. Carl Rollyson, interview with Ralph Roberts, in Rollyson, *Marilyn Monroe*, 162; Gerald Clarke, *Capote: A Biography* (New York: Carroll & Graf, 1988).

4. Kazan, *Elia Kazan*, 598.

5. Guilaroff, *Crowning Glory*, 154–55.

6. Undated letter, signed Gadge, in Banner and Anderson, *MM—Personal*, 100.

7. AS, interviews with Maureen Stapleton and Martin Ritt, in AS; Weatherby, *Conversations with Marilyn*, 144; Rosten, *Marilyn: An Untold Story*, 243.

8. Pamphlet catalog, "*After the Fall*: From Stage to Screen," Glenn Horowitz Bookseller, New York. My thanks to Nikki Smith for providing me with this pamphlet.

9. Miller, *Timebends*, 449.

10. Joe Hyams, "Marilyn Monroe—Upsetting," *New York Herald Tribune*, February 1959.

11. See the clippings for 1959 and 1960 in SE for a wide sampling of the press criticism. On Parsons, see Parsons, *Tell It to Louella*, 233. Joe Wolhandler to Marilyn Monroe, October 6, 1959, in SE.

12. Rosten, *Marilyn: An Untold Story*, 75.

13. Ibid., 145; David Lewin, "Marilyn Monroe," *London Daily Express*, May 6, 1959; Diana Trilling, *The Beginning of the Journey: The Marriage of Diana and Lionel Trilling* (New York: Harcourt, Brace, 1993) 246.

14. Goslar, *What's So Funny?*, 118.

15. Weatherby, *Conversations with Marilyn*, 188; Norman Rosten, interview with Donald Wolfe, in Wolfe, *Assassination of Marilyn Monroe*, 419; AS, interview with Norman Rosten, in AS; Quirk, *The Kennedys in Hollywood*, 213; Vanessa Steinberg, interview with Michelle Morgan, in Morgan, *Marilyn Monroe*, 274. See also Fred Otash, interview with James Spada, in Spada—ASU.

16. AS, interview with Grace Dobish, in AS; Joan and Clay Blair Jr., *The Search for J.F.K.* (N.Y.: G.P. Putnam's Sons, 1974), 549–50.

17. George Smathers described the Portomac boat trips to many authors. See, for example, Lawrence Leamer, *The Kennedy Men, 1901–1963: The Laws of the Father* (New York: William Morrow, 2001), 605; and Seymour Hersh, interview with Charles Spalding, in Hersh, *The Dark Side of Camelot* (Boston: Little, Brown, 1997), 103. Peter Lawford told Patricia Lawford Stewart that Marilyn was bothered by Jack's affair with Joan Lunberg, a former stewardess he met in a bar in Malibu, from the fall of 1956 to 1959, LB, interview with Patricia Lawford Stewart, May 10, 2011.

18. Norman Rosten stated that she was a friend of Jack and Bobby Kennedy in *New York Herald Examiner*, December 15, 1973.

19. Arthur Miller, interview with Guiles, in Guiles, *Legend*, 377; William J. Mann, *Behind the Scenes: How Gays and Lesbians Shaped Hollywood, 1910–1969* (New York: Viking, 2001), 168–69.

20. Signoret, *Nostalgia Isn't What It Used to Be*, 286.

21. Brandon, *Conversations with Henry Brandon*, 184–85.

22. Skolsky, *Don't Get Me Wrong*, 227–28.

23. Descriptions of his sessions with Marilyn are contained in letters to Marianne Kris, in Greenson—UCLA.

24. Marilyn to Lester Dear, March 29, 1960, in Banner and Anderson, *MM—Personal*, 182–83; Skolsky, *Don't Get Me Wrong*; 227–28: "Lawford was hosting, as he frequently did, a little group composed of his brothers-in-law President John F. Kennedy, Attorney General Robert Kennedy, Marilyn Monroe, and Frank Sinatra." Congressman Thomas Rees, a California Democrat, was at a series of meetings in 1959 and 1960 at the Lawford beach house with Frank Sinatra and a lot of studio people. Thomas Rees, oral transcript, John F. Kennedy Library, in James Spada Papers, ASU.

25. Billy Travilla, interview with Peter Harry Brown and Patte B. Barham, in Brown and Barham, *Marilyn: The Last Take*, 76; Patrick McGilligan, *George Cukor: A Double Life* (New York: St. Martin's, 1991), 119; Tom Stempel, *Screenwriter*, 172–5.

26. JK, interview with Jack Cole, in Kobal, *People Will Talk*; Delamater, interview with Jack Cole, in Delamater, *Dance in the Hollywood Musical*, 198; McGilligan, *George Cukor*, 273; "Notes from Cukor's Press Agent," in Zolotow—UT; Gavin Lambert, *On Cukor* (New York: G.P. Putnam's Sons, 1972), 174–75.

27. Yves Montand, with Herve Hamon and Patrick Rotman, *You See, I Haven't Forgotten* (New York: Alfred A. Knopf, 1992), 324.

28. Skolsky, *Don't Get Me Wrong*, 227; Guiles, *Legend*, 375; Christopher Bigsby, *Arthur Miller, 1915–1962* (Cambridge, Mass: Harvard University Press, 2009), 613.

29. Gottfried, *Arthur Miller*, 329–31.

30. Michael Selsman, who was there, reports on what happened in *All Is Vanity: Memoirs of a Hollywood Operative* (Los Angeles, Calif.: New World, 2009), 6–7.

31. James Haspiel, *Marilyn: The Ultimate Look at the Legend* (New York: Henry Holt, 1991), 175; LB, interview with Gloria Romanoff, September 19, 2008. For newspaper articles about Marilyn's activities in New York when the convention was taking place, see SE. See also Ralph Roberts, "Mimosa."

32. On the filming of *The Misfits*, I have used, in particular, Goode, *The Story of The Misfits*, and Arthur Miller and Serge Toubiana, *The Misfits: Story of a Shoot* (New York: Phaidon, 2000.)

33. Weatherby, *Conversations with Marilyn*, 33.

34. Patricia Bosworth, *Montgomery Clift: A Biography* (New York: Harcourt Brace, 1978); Robert LaGuardia, *A Biography of Montgomery Clift* (New York: Arbor House, 1977).

35. See Russell Miller, *Magnum: Fifty Years at the Front Line of History* (New York: Grove, 1997), 178–83.

36. Guiles, *Legend*, 383.

37. Eli Wallach, *The Good, the Bad, and Me* (Orlando, Fla.: Harcourt, 205), 220–24.

38. "Marilyn Monroe's Secret Tragedy," *Screen Stories*, February 1961.

39. John Huston, *An Open Book* (New York: Ballantine, 1961), 321ff.

40. Clark Gable thought that Arthur was eyeing other women on the set. Talk by Johnny Grant to Marilyn Remembered Fan Club, August 5, 2005. Both Jean Louis and Sidney Guilaroff were suspicious of Arthur's behavior on the set.

41. Roberts, "Mimosa"; Radie Harris, *Radie's World* (New York: W.H. Allen, 1975), 195.

42. See Stacy Eubank Collection.

43. AV, interview with Rupert Allan, in Villani, "Hold a Good Thought for Me."

44. Roberts, "Mimosa."

45. My analysis of *The Misfits* has been influenced by David Savran, *Communists, Cowboys, and Queers: The Politics of Masculinity in the Work of Arthur Miller and Tennessee Williams* (Minneapolis: University of Minnesota Press, 1992).

46. Ibid., 50.

47. DS, interview with Rupert Allan, in Spoto—AMPAS.

48. Henry Lee, "An Ex-Husband Can Be a Girl's Best Friend," January 21, 1961, in Bannon, McKinney, and Wright, eds., *Joe DiMaggio: An American Icon*, 198.

49. Seymour M. Hersh, *The Dark Side of Camelot* (Boston: Little, Brown, 1997), 106; Summers, *Goddess*, 236.

50. Weatherby, *Conversations with Marilyn*, 129.

51. "An Open Letter from Hedda Hopper to Marilyn Monroe: Don't Drink: It Won't Bring Back the Baby!" *Motion Picture*, July 1960.

52. Roberts, "Mimosa."

53. LB, interview with Gloria Romanoff, September 18, 2008.

54. The 1961 letter to Ralph Greenson is reprinted in Buchthal and Comment, eds., *Fragments*, 207–12.

CHAPTER 12

1. Cardiff, *Magic Hour*, 212–13.

2. Greenson to Marianne Kris, May 15, 1951, in Greenson—UCLA.

3. Roberts, "Mimosa"; Gottfried, *Arthur Miller*, 342.

4. Dr. Richard Cottrell, as told to C. Gervain Hayden, "I Was Marilyn Monroe's Doctor," *Ladies' Home Companion*, January 1965; Miracle, *My Sister Marilyn*, 153.

5. Roberts, "Mimosa."

6. Nancy Sinatra, *Frank Sinatra: My Father* (New York: Doubleday, 1985), 29.

7. LB, interview with Jeanne Martin, May 28, 2009.

8. Louella Parsons, "Marilyn's Life as a Divorcee," *Modern Screen*, October 1961.

9. On Sinatra, see Anthony Summers and Robbyn Swan, *Sinatra: The Life* (New York: Alfred A. Knopf, 2005), and Kitty Kelley, *His Way: The Unauthorized Biography of Frank Sinatra* (1986; New York: Bantam, 2010).

10. Arnold Shaw, *Sinatra: Twentieth-Century Romantic* (New York: Holt, Rinehart, and Winston, 1968), 272. On the Rat Pack, see Lawrence J. Quirk and William Schoell, *The Rat Pack: Neon Nights and the Kings of Cool* (New York: HarperCollins, 1999); Shawn Levy, *Rat Pack Confidential: Frank, Dean, Sammy, Peter, Joey, and the Last Great Showbiz Party* (New York: Doubleday, 1988); and Max Rudin, "Fly Me to the Moon: Reflections on the Rat Pack," *American Heritage*, December 1998.

11. Mia Farrow, *What Falls Away: A Memoir* (New York: Nan A. Talese, 1997), 102.

12. James Spada, interview with Milton Ebbins, in Spada—ASU.

13. LB, interview with Jeanne Martin, May 20, 2009.

14. Dominick Dunne, *The Way We Lived Then: Recollections of a Well-Known Name Dropper* (New York: Crown, 1999), 50. On Marilyn's trip to New York, see SE, clippings for September 2001.

15. George Jacobs and William Stadiem, *Mr. S: My Life with Frank Sinatra* (New York: HarperEntertainment, 2003), 154–55.

16. LB, interview with Patricia Newcomb, September 25, 2007.

17. LB, interview with Gloria Romanoff, George Masters and Norma Lee Browning, *The Masters Way to Beauty* (New York: Signet, 1979), 75.

18. Weatherby, *Conversations with Marilyn*, 169.

19. LB, interview with Cami Sebring, July 3, 2009.

20. Greenson, "Drugs in the Psychotherapeutic Situation," presented at a conference on "Psychotherapeutic Drugs: Indications and Complications," January 12, 1964, USLC Center for the Health Sciences.

21. Quirk, *The Kennedys in Hollywood*, 210; LB, interview with Jeanne Martin, May 28, 2009.

22. "Doug Kirkland," in Wagenknecht, ed., *Marilyn Monroe*, 71–75.

23. The auction of the letter and the letter itself were reported in the *London Sunday Times*, October 22, 2006, in AS, clippings.

24. Dorothy Parker, *The Portable Dorothy Parker Reader*, rev. and enl. ed. (New York: Viking, 1973), 613.

25. Christopher Lawford, *Symptoms of Withdrawal: A Memoir of Snapshots and Redemption* (New York: HarperCollins, 2005), 22.

26. LB, interview with Patricia Cox, June 17, 2010.

27. Ronald Davis, interview with Mary Anita Loos, in Davis—AMPAS.

28. See, for example, Laurinda S. Dixon, "Some Penetrating Insights: The Imagery of Enemas in Art," *Art Journal* 52 (Autumn 1983); Jacobs, *My Life with Frank Sinatra*, 162; LB, interview with Daniel Stewart. In *Marilyn's*

Men: The Private Life of Marilyn Monroe (New York: St. Martin's, 1993), 293, Jane Ellen Wayne interviewed a prostitute who went to the parties.

29. LB, interview with Patricia Lawford Stewart, November 19, 2007. AS, interview with Jeanne Martin, in AS. Jerry Oppenheimer, interview with Jeanne Martin, in Oppenheimer, *The Other Mrs. Kennedy: Ethel Skakel Kennedy: An American Drama of Power, Privilege, and Politics* (New York: St. Martin's, 1994), 241.

30. Taraborrelli, *Secret Life*, 179; Stewart, *Peter Lawford Story*, 157. LB, interview with Patricia Seaton Lawford Stewart, November 19, 2007.

31. Ralph Roberts discusses the invitation to Marilyn from Joe DiMaggio, asking her to come to New York, in "Mimosa."

32. I follow Stacy Eubank in dating the Fiffi Fell party.

33. On Greenson I have used the material in his papers at UCLA, including an obituary by Steve Zuckerman in the *Los Angeles Times*, November 27, 1979.

34. Stephen Farber and Marc Green, *Hollywood on the Couch* (New York: William Morrow, 1993), 85; Lloyd Shearer, "Marilyn Monroe—Why Won't They Leave Her in Peace," *Parade*, August 5, 1973; Ralph R. Greenson, *Explorations in Psychoanalysis* (New York: International Libraries, 1978).

35. Greenson, "Empathy and Its Vicissitudes," paper read at the Twenty-first Congress of the International Psychoanalytical Association, Copenhagen, July 1959; "The Working Alliance and the Transference Neurosis," presented before the Los Angeles Psychoanalytic Society, May 1963.

36. "Sleep, Dreams, and Death," a public lecture given November 16, 1961, on KPFK, in Greenson—UCLA.

37. Ralph Greenson to Marianne Kris, August 21, 1962, in Greenson—UCLA.

38. LB, interview with Joshua Hoffs, February 4, 2010.

39. Michael H. Stone, "The Borderline Syndrome: Evolution of the Term, Genetic Aspects, and Prognosis," in Michael H. Stone, ed., *Essential Papers on Borderline Disorders: One Hundred Years at the Border* (New York: New York University Press, 1986), 475–97.

40. LB, interview with Robert Litman; Murray and Shade, *Marilyn: The Last Months*, 40.

41. Greenson, "The Origin and Fate of New Ideas in Psychoanalysis," presented at the Fourth Freud Anniversary Lecture, the Psychoanalytic Association of New York, May 19, 1969, in Greenson, *Explorations in Psychoanalysis*, 333–57; Elisabeth Young-Bruehl, *Anna Freud: A Biography* (New York: Summit, 1988), 371. My interpretation of Greenson differs from that of Douglas Kirsner, who I think misreads the sources. See Douglas Kirsner, " 'Do as I Say, Not as I Do': Ralph Greenson, Anna Freud, and Superrich Patients," *Psychoanalytic Psychology* 24 (2007): 475–86.

42. Norman Rosten to Ralph Greenson, July 1962, AS collection.

43. Janice Rule, "The Actor's Identity Crises (Postanalytic Reflections of an Actress)," *International Journal of Psychoanalytic Psychotherapy* 2 (1975). My thanks to UCLA professor Peter Loewenberg for this source.

44. On Pat Newcomb and her closeness to Marilyn, see AS, interviews with George Jacobs, William Woodfield, and Kendis Rochlin, in AS; and DS, interview with Susan Strasberg, in Spoto—AMPAS. On Fox and firing Newcomb, see the legal documents for Marilyn, 1962 Fox–UCLA.

45. Freeman, *Why Norma Jeane Killed Marilyn Monroe*, 171; Masters and Browning, *The Masters Way to Beauty*, 74–75.

46. Haspiel, *Marilyn: The Ultimate Look*, 186–89.

47. Greenson, "An MCP Freudian Psychoanalyst Confronts Women's Lib," April 27, 1972, presented at a benefit for the Reiss Davis Child Study Center, Women's Division, Los Angeles. In 1955 Greenson had argued a strict Freudian position on the superiority of the vaginal orgasm in "Foreplea-sure: Its Use for Defensive Purposes," presented at the Annual Meeting of the American Psychoanalytic Association, Los Angeles, May 1955.

48. Carol Groneman, *Nymphomania: A History* (New York: W.W. Norton, 2000), 80–81; Alvah Bessie, *The Symbol* (New York: Random House, 1967).

49. On Marilyn's treatment of Eunice, see Joan Greenson, "Memoir of Marilyn," 31, in Greenson—UCLA.

50. Murray and Shade, *Marilyn: The Last Months*, 23.

51. Joe Hyams, *Mislaid in Hollywood* (New York: P. H. Wyden, 1973), 139.

52. Frederick Vanderbilt Field, *From Right to Left: An Autobiography* (Westport, Conn.: Lawrence Hill, 1983), 299–305.

53. FBI Dossier on Marilyn Monroe, Freedom of Information Act, Declassified.

54. Stempel, *Screenwriter*, 171.

55. Brown, *Let Me Entertain You*, 55.

56. LB, interview with Noreen Nash, June 15, 2010. A number of Marilyn writers have accused Siegel of giving Marilyn "hot shots." Noreen Nash, Siegel's wife, possesses a number of affidavits signed by Siegel's nurses, who assisted him during the years he treated Marilyn, stating that he had not given such a treatment to any patient. Once the studio fired Marilyn on June 9, Siegel was no longer her doctor, since he treated her through Twentieth Century–Fox.

57. Greenson describes this episode in "On Transitional Objects and Transference," 1974, in Greenson, *Explorations in Psychoanalysis*, 493–96.

58. Dale McConathy, with Diana Vreeland, *Hollywood Costume: Glamour! Glitter! Romance!* (New York: Harry N. Abrams, 1976), 247.

59. The hairstyling by Kenneth Battelle, including pictures of Marilyn with the flip, is described in Amy Fine Collins, "It Had to Be Kenneth," *Vanity Fair*, June 2003. Jackie's tour of the White House is available on YouTube.

60. For the photo, see Banner and Anderson, *MM—Personal*, 196–97; on Marilyn taking Isidore Miller home, see Flora Rheta Schreiber, "Remembrance of Marilyn: The Memories of Isidore Miller," in Wagenknecht, ed., *Marilyn Monroe*, 54.

61. Arthur Schlesinger Jr., *Robert Kennedy and His Times* (Boston: Houghton Mifflin, 1978), 590; AS, interview with Pete Summers, in AS.

62. LB, interview with Larry Newman, February 8, 2009. Mickey Song told the same story in interviews and in talks before the Marilyn Remembered Fan Club. He claimed that Bobby was angry because Marilyn's hairdo so closely resembled Jackie's. The best defense of Song against attacks that he wasn't the Kennedys' hairdresser is in Riese and Hitchens, *The Unabridged Marilyn*, 494.

CHAPTER 13

1. Rosten, *Marilyn: An Untold Story*, 102–15. A copy of the receipt for the painting and the sculpture, dated May 9, 1962, is in Banner and Anderson, *MM—Personal*, 266. The owner of the gallery stated that Rodin had made twelve castings of the statue and Marilyn had number five.

2. James Spada, interview with Milton Ebbins, in Spada—ASU.

3. LB, interview with Lawrence Schiller, May 16, 2010.

4. See Prometheus Films and Van Ness Entertainment, *Marilyn Monroe: The Final Days*.

5. Murray and Shade, *Marilyn: The Last Months*, 158.

6. Weatherby, *Conversations with Marilyn*, 199, 203–204.

7. Stewart, *The Peter Lawford Story*, 161.

8. Wilson, *Show Business*, 67.

9. See Bert Stern, *Marilyn Monroe, The Last Sitting: Bert Stern's Favorite Photos of an American Icon* (Paris: Musée Maillol, 2006).

10. Richard Meryman, "Fame May Go By . . ." in Wagenknecht, ed., *Marilyn Monroe*, 3–15.

11. LB, interview with Larry Newman, February 18, 2009; AS, interview with Earl Jaycox, in AS. Jaycox was a technician working with Fred Otash who listened to the tapes.

12. AS, interviews with Rupert Allan, Jeanne Martin, Anne Karger, Henry Weinstein, George Durgom, George Chasin, Peter Dye, Lynn Sherman, and Ward Wood, in AS; James Spada, interview with Molly Dunne, in Spada—ASU; LB, interview with Janet DesRosiers, April 30, 2010; Lady May Lawford and Buddy Galon, *Bitch! The Autobiography of Lady Lawford* (Brookline Village, Mass.: Branden, 1986), 79; Earl Wilson, *Sinatra: An Unauthorized Biography* (New York: Macmillan, 1976); Schlesinger Jr., *Robert Kennedy and His Times*, 590; AS, interview with Phyllis McGuire, in AS: McGuire maintained that Marilyn "was pressing Bob to make a decision about marrying her." Janet DesRosiers was Joe Kennedy's longtime mistress.

13. AS, interview with Harry Hall, in AS; LB, interview with Michael Selsman, November 13, 2009; Joan Greenson, "Memoir of Marilyn" in Greenson—UCLA; Peter Lawford, "Notes for an Autobiography," in Lawford—ASU. According to Skinny D'Amato, Bobby, not Jack, was her serious involvement. Since the inauguration Angie Dickinson had been Jack's major Hollywood girlfriend. Van Meter, *The Last Good Time*, 192. Ted Landreth, BBC

documentary, *Say Goodbye to the President*. Rupert Allan: "She said that the Kennedys passed her around like a piece of meat." Allan made a similar comment to Peter Evans, in Evans, *Nemesis: The True Story of Aristotle Onassis, Jackie O, and the Love Triangle that Brought Down the Kennedys* (New York: Regan, 2004), 80–81.

14. AS, interview with Inez Melson, in AS.

15. George Carpozi Jr., interview with Eunice Murray, in Mailer—UT; LB, interview with Patricia Lawford Stewart, November 19, 2007.

16. LB, interview with Gloria Romanoff; DS, interview with Ralph Roberts, in Spoto—AMPAS.

17. LB, interview with Michael Selsman, November 13, 2009.

18. Brown and Barham, interview with Rupert Allan, in Brown and Barham, *Marilyn: The Last Take*: "I heard that she was pregnant and that it was Bobby's child. She told Agnes Flanagan about it" (469–470). (Flanagan was Marilyn's personal hairdresser.) Arthur James claimed that Marilyn told him about it. LB, interview with Arthur James, June 25, 2010; LB, interview with Michael Selsman, November 13, 2009; AS, interview with Michael Selsman, in AS.

19. On the Kennedy connection to Cal Neva, see Van Meter, *Last Good Time*, 175–91; and Sally Denton, *The Money and the Power: The Making of Las Vegas and Its Hold on America, 1974–2000* (New York: Alfred A. Knopf, 2001).

20. LB, interview with Patricia Lawford Stewart, November 19, 2007.

21. Linda Leigh, testimony in BBC documentary *Say Goodbye to the President*; Roberts, "Mimosa." Leigh was a singer on the entertainment program that weekend.

22. Ibid; LB, interview with Roberta Linn, October 10, 2009; LB, interview with Cami Sebring, July 3, 2009; LB, interview with Betsy Hammes, September 4, 2009.

23. Jill Adams interviewed William Woodfield's wife, who saw the negatives. She said that Giancana was dressed and that Marilyn was in disarray. The negatives, however, were blurry, and the figures were hard to discern. LB, interview with Jill Adams, November 24, 2008. According to Donald Wolfe, Woodfield told him that the photos showed Giancana and Sinatra watching as several goons raped Marilyn; in Wolfe, *The Assassination of Marilyn Monroe*, 547. In his study of Marilyn's death, *The Final Years of Marilyn Monroe* (London: JR Books, 2010), Keith Badman argues that Mafia henchmen gang-raped Marilyn, forced her to crawl around on the floor, and made her participate in a lesbian sex act with prostitutes. Since Badman has no footnotes, it is impossible to check his sources. Indeed, Badman disagrees with most of the painstaking interviews done by Anthony Summers and others, who cite sources. Thus I can't consider him reliable.

24. LB, interview with Phyllis McGuire, March 18, 2009. The stories of sexual abuse come mostly from Mafia members. Vincent "Jimmy Blue Eyes" Alo, an associate of Meyer Lansky, told Gus Russo he was at Cal Neva that weekend and Peter and Frank kept her drugged every night. When the FBI

listened to a tap on Giancana's phone, they heard Johnny Roselli say to him, "You sure get your rocks off fucking the same broad as the brothers, don't you." Gus Russo, *The Outfit: The Role of Chicago's Underworld in the Shaping of Modern America* (New York: Bloomsbury USA, 2001), 432. Harry Hall made a similar statement to Joe DiMaggio. See also LB, interview with Thomas Sobeck, April 22, 2010. Sobeck was a "wise guy" who told me a similar story.

25. Engelberg and Schneider, *DiMaggio: Setting the Record Straight*, 248.

26. LB, interview with Gloria Romanoff, December 13, 2008.

27. AS, interview with Jeanne Martin, in AS, May 20, 2009. LB, interview with Gloria Romanoff, December 13, 2008.

28. DS, interview with Milton Ebbins, Spoto—AMPAS.

29. Suzanne Finstad, *Natasha: The Biography of Natalie Wood* (New York: Harmony Books, 2001), 245; "Interview with Whitey Snyder," *Runnin' Wild*, January 1992.

30. LB, interview with Steffi Skolsky Slaver, September 14, 2006. LB, interview with Patricia Newcomb, September 25, 2007. On the incidents surrounding Marilyn's death, I have often relied on David Marshall, *The DD Group: An Online Investigation into the Death of Marilyn Monroe* (New York: iUniverse, 2005), although I disagree with him about the time of death.

31. LB, interview with Dolores Nemiro, April 7, 2009. James Spada, *Peter Lawford: The Man Who Kept the Secrets* (New York: Bantam, 1991).

32. Matthew Smith, interview with Fred Otash, in Smith, *Marilyn's Last Words: Her Secret Tapes and Mysterious Death* (New York: Carroll & Graf, 2003), 179.

33. Guilaroff, *Crowning Glory*, 166.

34. James Spada, interview with Milton Ebbins, in Spada—ASU; James Spada interview with William Asher, in Spada—ASU.

35. The Ben Hecht Papers contain the same statement, written by Marilyn in 1954 and not addressed to anyone. Marilyn often jotted notes and sentiments down late at night on scraps of paper.

36. AS, interview with William Woodfield, in AS; James Spada, interview with Fred Otash, in Spada—ASU.

37. Brown and Barham, *Marilyn: The Last Take*, 479.

38. Susan Bernard, *Marilyn Monroe: Intimate Exposures* (New York: Sterling, 2011), 186–87.

39. Smith, *Marilyn's Last Words*, 273.

40. Lynn Franklin, *The Beverly Hills Murder File* (1999; Bloomington, Ind.: First Books, 2002), 108–09. Franklin didn't refer to this episode in his first book on his career, *Sawed Off Justice*, with Maury Allen (New York: Putnam, 1976).

41. AS, interview with Peter Lawford, in AS; C. David Heymann, interview with Peter Lawford, transcript, in Heymann, SUNY–Stony Brook. See also C. David Heymann, *RFK: A Candid Biography of Robert F. Kennedy* (New York: Dutton, 1998), 305–06, 320–22.

42. Patricia Lawford Stewart repeatedly asked Heymann for the tape through

her lawyer, but he never provided it. LB, interview with Patricia Seaton Lawford Stewart and Daniel Stewart, May 10, 2011. See also Daniel K. Stewart to Paul Mahon, September 21, 1998, requesting to listen to the tape. Mahon was Heymann's lawyer. The James Spada Papers at Arizona State University include a letter from Arthur Schlesinger Jr. to Spada, contesting many of the allegations about Bobby Kennedy in Heymann's biography. On the highly debatable charge that Greenson killed Marilyn, see Jay Margolis, *Marilyn Monroe: A Case for Murder* (Bloomington, Ind,: iUniverse, 2011).

43. Sam Giancana and Chuck Giancana, *Double Cross* (1993; New York: Skyhorse, 2010), 413–17. Antoinette Giancana, Sam Giancana's daughter, told Matthew Smith that *Double Cross* was a fabrication. Smith, *Marilyn's Last Words*, 273.

44. Anthony Summers, *Official and Confidential: The Secret Life of J. Edgar Hoover* (New York: Putnam, 1993), 301.

45. AS, interview with Henry Rosenfeld, in AS; AS, interview with Jean Louis, in AS.

46. Thomas Noguchi, *Coroner at Large* (New York: Simon & Schuster, 1985), 65–85.

AFTERWORD

1. Woodard and Marshall, *Hometown Girl*; interview with Angelo Deluco, in Allen, *Where Have You Gone, Joe DiMaggio*; Bob Considine, in *Herald Examiner*, clipping, n.p., n.d., in Starr—ASU; Dorothy Manners, filling in for Louella Parsons, August 13, 1962, in SE.

2. Descriptions of Marilyn's funeral were written by individuals who attended it. The term "in one big wave" comes from Lotte Goslar, *What's So Funny?*, 119. LB, interview with Patricia Rosten, March 12, 2008.

3. Rosten, *Marilyn: An Untold Story*, 21.

4. Kazan, *Elia Kazan*, 790–98.

Index

A Note on the Author

Lois Banner is a founder of the field of women's history and co-founder of the Berkshire Conference of Women Historians, the major academic event in the field. She was the first woman president of the American Studies Association and in 2006 she won the ASA's Bode-Pearson Prize for Outstanding Contributions to American Studies. She is the author of ten books, including her acclaimed *American Beauty* and most recently *MM–Personal*, which reproduces and discusses items from Marilyn Monroe's personal archive. In addition to her books on Monroe, Banner is a major collector of her artifacts. Lois Banner is a professor of history and gender studies at USC and lives in Southern California.